Iuzovka and Revolution

STUDIES OF THE HARRIMAN INSTITUTE

Columbia University

The Harriman Institute, Columbia University, sponsors the *Studies of the Harriman Institute* in the belief that their publication contributes to scholarly research and public understanding. In this way, the Institute, while not necessarily endorsing their conclusions, is pleased to make available the results of some of the research conducted under its auspices. A list of the *Studies* appears at the back of the book.

Iuzovka and Revolution

— VOLUME II —

Politics and Revolution in Russia's Donbass, 1869–1924

Theodore H. Friedgut

PRINCETON UNIVERSITY PRESS

PRINCETON, NEW JERSEY

Published by Princeton University Press, 41 William Street,
Princeton, New Jersey 08540
In the United Kingdom: Princeton University Press, Chichester,
West Sussex

Library of Congress Cataloging-in-Publication Data

Friedgut, Theodore H.
Iuzovka and revolution.
(Studies of the Harriman Institute)
Includes bibliographical references and index.
Contents: v. 1. Life and work in Russia's Donbass, 1869–1924 —
v. 2. Politics and revolution in Russia's Donbass, 1869–1924.
1. Donets'k (Ukraine)—Social conditions. 2. Working class—
Ukraine—Donets'k. 3. Donets Basin (Ukraine and Russia)—
Social conditions. 4. Working class—Donets Basin (Ukraine and
Russia). I. Title. II. Series.
HN530.D645F75 1989 306'.0947'71 88-36767
ISBN 0-691-05554-8 (v. 1 : alk. paper)
ISBN 0-691-08660-5 (v. 2 : cloth)

This book has been composed in Garamond

Princeton University Press books are printed on acid-free paper and
meet the guidelines for permanence and durability of the
Committee on Production Guidelines for Book Longevity of the
Council on Library Resources

Printed in the United States of America

1 3 5 7 9 10 8 6 4 2

This volume is affectionately dedicated to the "Iuzovka family" the world over and to the hardworking, long-suffering citizens of Donetsk.

CONTENTS

LIST OF ILLUSTRATIONS

LIST OF TABLES

PREFACE

The first volume of this work addressed the social and economic development of Iuzovka from its founding through the First World War. Its intention was to give an integrated description of the development of Donbass society. In the present volume, that knowledge will serve as a background to a discussion of the development of the political forces and outlooks in the Donbass and an analysis of the relations among the social and political groups active on the scene. The environment in which Iuzovka developed was riddled with contradictions and contentiousness. The political framework was that of the Russian autocracy in its latter days. Paternalistic and interventionist, the regime arrogated to itself a monopoly on judgment and policy regarding every aspect of society. It was, however, far too inefficient and corrupt, in the worst and most bureaucratic sense, to assume such a role at a level that would provide for the functioning of a modern society. Riven by interdepartmental rivalries, like the petty court cabals that are the curse of any autocratic system, the bureaucracy slowed, and often simply strangled, the adaptation that was necessary for a society attempting the transition from a manorial system of agricultural subsistence to market capitalism based on the industrial revolution. The regime itself was caught up in these contradictions. It sought to industrialize for a purely external reason: the maintenance of its empire in the face of Western European competitors. At the same time, it despised and feared capitalism, looking down on the industrialists, and actively working to prevent the emergence of a proletariat of urban, industrial workers with a sense of their own identity and a desire for autonomy. The Russian courtiers understood that the urban crowd would dig the grave of the autocracy. The concepts of rule of law, private property, and contract, on which civil society is based, were all weakly developed in the Russian Empire. The concept of the free citizen, the individual determining his or her economic and social status by achievement, was anathema to an autocracy that clung to the ascriptive structure of traditional society.

Despite these constraints, a modern society was inexorably coming into being. Physical and social mobility accelerated. The railroads that were the arteries of industrial development began to transport tens of thousands of peasants to the burgeoning cities and raw industrial settlements. The migrations of these peasants, and their persistent links with home, created a network of social communication that breached the insularity of the village. The educational system that grew up revealed new horizons to a multitude of young people. A thirst for knowledge began to develop and with it a curiosity about the world. New channels of communication were opened to other levels of society. Doctors, writers, journalists, artists of various sorts, students—the intelligentsia that was the yeast of Russia's social and political change—could now begin to spin the first strands of communication with the industrial workers; the two groups share a base of civilization, if not entirely the same norms. At the same time, industry's need for human muscle and technical skills offered the prospect of satisfying the peasant's thirst for property and for economic security. This became a plausible alternative to the fading dream of land ownership, which had been the peasant's sustaining hope for generations. The peasant turning worker thus could take one of two very different roads. One was that of political revolution, offering the workers, in its moderate version, the status of free and equal citizens, and in the version of its most violent proponents, sole power to rule society. These were dizzying prospects for persons whose past had been based on total subjection to authority. The other road led to the promised benefits of the industrial revolution: economic betterment, and perhaps even property ownership; brighter prospects for future generations; and the amenities of urban living—education, health, and culture. All these benefits depended on continued loyal obedience to the existing political and economic regime.

Two more groups of actors take their place on the stage of this drama: the industrialists and the revolutionaries. These, too, were subject to contradictory forces. Both were alienated from the values of their birth. The industrialists strove toward social and economic equality with the landowners (who were the pillars of grand society in Russia), but found themselves rejected as crass parvenus and competitors. The revolutionaries were drawn from the newly formed intelligentsia. The alienation of the intelligentsia from Russian society is its classic characteristic. Its opposition to autocracy developed as a universal and immanent feature of the group, but within the intelligentsia there were varied and changing prescriptions for the future of Russian society.

An additional factor must be considered here. Russia's late entry into the industrial world offered what Alexander Gerschenkron has called the economic advantages of backwardness. But this late entry also shortened the span of time within which the social and economic transformations took place, intensifying the pressures of transition. The rapidity of social change prevented the growth and rooting of new institutions. Neither regime nor subjects could cope with this problem. The regime was reluctant to adapt itself, and it blocked the innovative efforts of other social groups. The autocracy shared with later totalitarian societies the characteristic of politicization of all aspects of life. It therefore jealously guarded its prerogative of control and intervention, robing it in the excuse of a paternalistic duty to regulate the welfare of all the tsar's children. But the regime lacked the capacity to carry on such a level of activity. The result was a fragile and unstable society, vulnerable to crisis.

In the Donbass the developing society was unsettled. Raw and new in the sparsely populated Ukrainian steppe, it lacked the civilizing urban influences that existed in St. Petersburg and Moscow. The ethnic structure contained the seeds of conflict and social fragmentation. Foreign entrepreneurs hired Russian workers. The new settlements were served by Jewish artisans and merchants. These outsiders impinged on the lands and lives of the Ukrainian peasants, to whom they were foreign and unwelcome.

The development of these social forces in the period of industrialization, and the crossroads at which they contended over the path to be chosen for Iuzovka and the Donbass, are the subjects of this discussion. As J. N. Westwood pointed out in a review of the first volume of this work, Iuzovka was unique in Russia at this time, but then so was each such town and region. There existed no single pattern of development. It is my hope that an examination of both the uniqueness of Iuzovka and the characteristics it shared with other settlements will clarify the processes that brought on the disintegration of the tsarist regime and the transformation of Russian society. It may also shed light on the choices available to Russian society at the beginning of the twentieth century. This is not merely an exercise in the "ifs" of history, which, as Professor John L. H. Keep was wont to tell his students, are "as fruitless as they are fascinating." Rather, I hope that understanding the consequences of a regime that obstinately blocked change although the bases of its power had melted away, and the violence born of frustration generated by this blockage, may illuminate the implications of current political struggles in the former Soviet Union and elsewhere in the world.

ACKNOWLEDGMENTS

All the debts that I gratefully acknowledged in my first volume stand for this volume as well. Without the aid of so many librarians, archivists, and colleagues, whole areas of material would not have been available to me, and many of my ideas might not have emerged and matured into text. I am happy again to thank the individuals and institutions who have been my benefactors. But in the course of the three years since the first volume went to press, I have incurred new debts to acknowledge.

First and foremost I am grateful to the Hebrew University, which, through its Authority for Research and Development, provided generous financial assistance to the publication of this volume. Without this assistance, the constraints of a market economy would have meant my manuscript either would not have been published, or would have been published in eviscerated brevity.

With the onset of *glasnost'* in Donetsk, both Liudmilla Alexeievna Vassilieva, Senior Researcher of the Donetsk Oblast' Historical—Geographical Museum, and Nadezhda Borisovna Metalnikova, Director of the Donetsk Oblast' State Historical Archive, were able and happy to make available material that had previously been inaccessible to me. To them and to their staffs my thanks for their warm and courteous assistance. Sophia Aleksandrovna Gittis and Andrei Petrovich Bei of the museum staff were particularly helpful.

To the Glamorgan Archivist, Patricia Moore, and her associate, Susan Edwards, I owe a great debt for their professional skills and ingenuity, their energy, and their hospitality. They have built the Hughesovka Research Archive of the Glamorgan Record Office into a major historical source, mobilized the "Iuzovka family" from various continents, gathered the family's mementos and documents, and brought knowledge of John Hughes and his endeavors to a broad public, including to Donetsk itself. As important as the documents and information they made available to me were their moral support, their enthusiasm, and the professional rigor of their approach to history. I am proud to have been associated with them. I am also indebted to Colin Thomas and Professor Gwynn A. Williams of Teliesyn Productions in Cardiff for sharing with me the insights they gained during the production of their superb film "Hughesovka and the New Russia," and for their interest in my own research.

John and Kathleen Kay of Chevy Chase, Maryland, have been both generous and encouraging in sharing family photographs, memories, and documents they have discovered. It is a pleasure to have come to know them. Welcome to the Iuzovka family!

In addition to those colleagues whose help I noted in my first volume, many others in various countries have assisted me with comments, critiques, and ideas for this volume. Lewis H. Siegelbaum, Susan P. McCaffray, and Charters C. Wynn, in particular, deserve my thanks. Their written work, their lectures, and their informal comments have all been of great help to me. Professors Thomas C. Owen and Diane P. Koenker went above and beyond the call of duty in giving the manuscript a close reading and raising insightful questions, as well as in offering suggestions regarding terminology, orthography, and other matters both technical and substantive. Their efforts have added immensely to this volume, and I am most grateful.

Once again I express my appreciation to the editors of the *Slavic Review* and the *Canadian Slavonic Papers* for permitting me to use here materials first published in their journals.

The current work of a whole generation of scholars, Soviet and non-Soviet alike, is reflected here as both challenge and inspiration. There is hardly a volume or an article that I have read without being provoked or sensitized into examining my own theories and interpretations, sometimes revising them, sometimes clinging even more firmly to the way I understand this slice of modern Russian history. As contacts with the Russian and Ukrainian academic worlds become closer and more dynamic, this benevolent interaction can only grow. Even so, I must bear the ultimate responsibility for my conclusions and outlook, and prove their validity in open academic debate.

Jane Lincoln Taylor deserves my special thanks for her superb editing. She brought sensitivity and grace to her work, and displayed professional knowledge and thoroughness in working to produce an accurate and consistent book from an overgrown jungle of a manuscript.

The reader will find certain changes in terminology from the first volume. In the interest of using unified, or at least similar, terminology in academic discussions, I have accepted Thomas C. Owen's suggestion to adopt the name "Association of Southern Coal and Steel Producers" for the *S"ezd gornopromyshlennikov iuga Rossii*. Since Susan P. McCaffray has done the most extensive original research on this institution, I agree with Professor Owen that her terminology should be considered standard. I will also use English translations for many Russian terms—for example, province for *guberniia*, and district for *uezd*. Contemporary orthography has been used throughout in transliterating titles and terms from the Russian. I hope these changes will make it easier for the reader to follow my argument. They are the result of comments by readers and reviewers, whose help I acknowledge with thanks.

PART I

Political Forces in the Donbass

CHAPTER 1

Government and Capital in the Donbass

In the extended discussion of society, economics, and culture that occupied the first volume of this work, the government, both central and local, and the Association of Southern Coal and Steel Producers entered the scene, for long before the Bolshevik Revolution, Russia was already an administered society. The autocracy claimed the right to regulate all aspects of Russian life, and its bureaucracy, inefficient and conflict-riven though it was, intervened everywhere. The paternalist tradition of Russian society was strengthened, with employers reinforcing the totalitarian tendencies of government, although their interpretations of what was to be done for the workers often conflicted with the plans made in St. Petersburg. The long-running feud between the industrialists and the *zemstvos* (elected local councils), in which both sides appealed for central intervention, simply added to the fragmentation of authority.[1] In political terms it was this fragmentation, rather than an attempt at total intervention, that was decisive. The blocking of the emergence of any effective political community was as much a function of the weakness of the many contesting forces at the grass roots, and of interdepartmental jealousies in the central government, as it was a result of an intentional preservation of the autocrat's political monopoly.

This chapter will explore the various levels of state organizations, their interrelation with the Association of Southern Coal and Steel Producers as the recognized representative of the employers, and the common front of these bodies in their effort to deny legitimacy to the attempts of the workers to organize institutions capable of articulating their interests. Examination

[1] For a detailed and cogent analysis of the fragmentation of power in the Russian government, see Rieber, "Bureaucratic Politics."

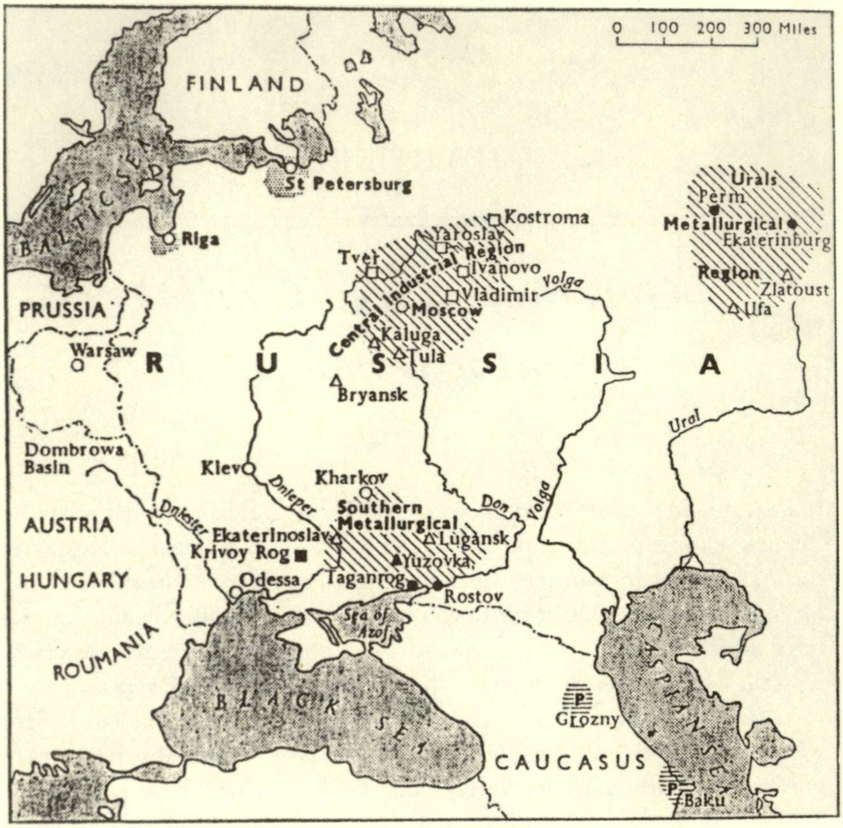

1.1 Major industrial areas of the Russian Empire before 1917.

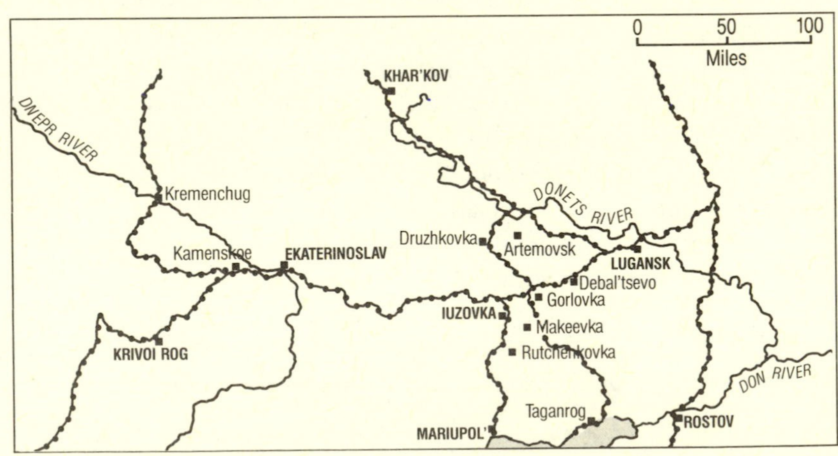

1.2 The Donbass industrial area.

of these relationships will be preceded by an analysis of the nature and development of these major institutions.

The Administrative Culture

There were clear ground rules of law and culture in the Donbass. Russia was a bureaucracy from top to bottom. If the actions of many of the people did not conform to bureaucratic prescription, it was not because the autocracy did not care. The tsar and his most powerful advisers were caught up in the struggle to maintain a system of social institutions threatened by the clash between Russia's aspirations as a great European power and its limited capacities for social mobilization and concentration of resources at a time of crisis.

The industrial revolution that had completed the modernization of Western Europe posed a political challenge to Russia. Iuzovka and the Donbass were an important part of Russia's response. The social philosophies that flourished along with the industrial revolution posed no less a political challenge. Though Russians debated this challenge fiercely, and proposed many possible responses, the Russian court was virtually unanimous in seeking to preserve and strengthen the autocracy. This involved control of all the institutions of society, and through this, of the lives of all the tsar's subjects. The instrument of control was the state bureaucracy, a hydra-headed creature of many minds and widely divergent capacities and outlooks. Rarely efficient, rendered sluggish by a cocoon of paper that encumbered its every initiative, it was still sufficiently effective to keep the empire functioning in normal times. In times of crisis, the regime's demand for total autocracy and the bureaucracy's ponderous inefficiency brought repeated failure, and ultimately, the downfall of the autocrat himself.

The political foundation of the regime was the preservation of the Romanov trinity of autocracy, the Orthodox church, and the Russian national spirit. In the growing population of the Donbass, the tsar and the Orthodox church were accorded reverent respect, and if, for economic reasons, the industrialists had some hidden reservations regarding the latter, these reservations were expressed obliquely and were more than balanced by a growing Russian nationalist fervor. For the people, the tsar was a far-off ideal, quite distinct from his local representatives, whose authority derived more from the knout than from the scepter. The same was true for the church. Orthodox principles and practices were followed willingly, but the local clergy enjoyed little prestige, and it lacked the authority to lead the public at crucial moments.

There was, however, another principle that guided the policies of both the government and the industrialists. This was the fear and mistrust of the "benighted folk"—the *temnyi narod* (literally, "the dark people"). The phrase is found repeatedly in writings of the time. It was used not only by government officials and industrialists, but by reformers as well. Rooted in the great peasant rebellions of Stenka Razin and Emelian Pugachev, this fear and distrust was only magnified when peasants began to leave the land and congregate in the cities. The specter of an urban proletariat resembling the sansculottes of Paris haunted the conservative Slavophiles of the Russian autocracy.[2] This mobile, unchecked mass, owing loyalty and obedience to no immediate master, was deemed to pose a threat to the entire political and social system. Traditional society had no place for an industrial working class, and Russia was reluctant to abandon its long-standing social structure.

Criticism of the social order, even implicit criticism of policies supported by the center, was rejected without investigation, even when raised by enlightened regime representatives. The governor of Ekaterinoslav province, Prince Peter Sviatopolk-Mirskii, wrote the following in his report for 1898: "From the time that the coal and iron industries first started here in the south, there has been almost continuous repetition of workers' unrest, often leading first to the smashing of industrialists' properties, and then frequently ending up with the properties of persons having nothing to do with the matters." The governor's suggested solution was completely orthodox—quick intervention of cossacks was the most efficient way to stop such unrest. He continued, however, by examining the causes for the unrest. It was not due, in his opinion, to the workers' penchant for drunkenness and absenteeism, as the conventional wisdom of the time had it. Sviatopolk-Mirskii put the blame on the industrialists' rejection of reasonable demands by the workers, noting that unrest arises from employers' attempts to get the most profit out of their workers, lengthening the workday, paying wages late, and ignoring regulations governing workers' housing and living conditions. In addition, he wrote that unrest came from the workers' relations with supervisory personnel, engineers, and adminis-

[2] Zelnik, *Labor and Society,* p. 24, notes the expression of this fear by the regime as early as the 1830s.

trators, who were often foreigners knowing no Russian, patronizing the Russian workers, and regarding workers' complaints as frivolous. Opposite the charges that the complaints were due to the employers' greed and malfeasance is a handwritten note: "Such comments are insufferable. We have the inspectorate to take care of this." Beside the remarks regarding foreigners is another such note: "Such an attitude to foreigners *is not to be permitted*."[3]

It is not hard to understand the difficulties created by such social instability. Even as a new population began to form in the Donbass, with improved living standards and education beginning to affect the self-image and aspirations of the workers in the mines and mills, the old social categories and institutions were maintained, despite the suggestions that had been made from time to time regarding creation of new village associations for mining settlements. The individual rights of workers to fair pay, decent conditions, and some measure of state protection were recognized in legislation, even if these laws, like many other state laws and regulations, were only erratically enforced.[4] No such recognition was given to any corporate rights of the workers. As noted in volume 1, even the attempt to organize mutual-aid funds, permitted in some other areas of the empire, was blocked in the Donbass. Any effort at organization was treated as illegitimate and punished as conspiracy. Strikes were a criminal offense.[5] Inefficient as the bureaucracy was, its police functions were largely effective.

Denial of corporate legitimacy did not extend to the industrialists. There was room in the traditional social structure for townspeople of property, merchants, and manufacturers. Their legitimacy did not, however, exempt them from control. The state regarded itself as above all the estates, and as arbiter of the relations among them. Just as the landowner had been theoretically responsible to the tsar and his government for the welfare of the serfs, so the employer was subject to state regulation of minimal standards for the employees. Yet the apparent basis of Russian society was held to be accommodation rather than compulsion or confrontation. The 1886 labor

[3] TsGIAL, F. 1263, op. 2, d. 5445, p. 87 (emphasis in the original).

[4] Glivits, *Zheleznaia promyshlennost' v Rossii*, p. 54, discusses the ineffective execution of state decrees, pointing out the issuing of a regulation banning the use of imported foreign materials in state enterprises six times in a twenty-year period, with no apparent effect.

[5] See article 3, paragraphs 2–4, of the June 3, 1886, regulations on employment of workers in factories and workshops. Zelnik, *Labor and Society*, chap. 4, discusses the awareness of the labor question in the 1860s, noting that the legislation outlawing autonomous workers' assemblies and strikes remained unchanged.

law assumed free agreement between employer and worker as to the terms of contract between them. The worker's pay book was to list these conditions, and acceptance of the book was taken to be acceptance of the contract.[6] Friendly persuasion was the first instrument of government policy in trying to bring the industrialists to treat their workers humanely. In December 1895, Count Witte sent a circular to officials of the Factory Inspectorate, suggesting that those manufacturers initiating measures to improve workers' living conditions should receive broad and favorable publicity. This, it was thought, would lend these leading figures prestige, and inspire their colleagues who were less forward-looking to emulate their example. At the same time, the inspectors were urged to observe closely and report promptly to the Ministry of Finance all unhealthy and improper conditions that might serve as sources of disorder.[7]

Persuasion alone, however, was quite clearly inadequate. As the factory inspector Sviatlovskii noted in his report for 1885, "Although there are not a few firms in the region headed by humane individuals with university educations, persons who in the press defend the 'deep and moral significance' of the new law [drafts of the 1886 labor law] . . . nevertheless it was surprising that until our inspection visits, everything in the enterprises of these manufacturers went on as of old, with children working the same twelve to fourteen hours a day as adults." Sviatlovskii added that even after inspection visits, the industrialists were slow to reform. Nevertheless, he did not altogether dismiss the possibility of improvement, noting that after his inspection of 658 out of 2,552 industrial premises in his district, he was able to list forty-four cases of improved safety measures and fifty-nine other cases of improvement of workers' living conditions.[8] The question was put on an entirely different footing in the memoirs of Emelian Kolodub, a miner who had advanced himself to the rank of foreman, and in no way a radical. He attacked the system of state paternalism, claiming that it was incapable of producing regulations appropriate to the life of the mines. "The workers themselves must receive the opportunity to discuss their needs and to take a living part in drafting legislation for the satisfaction of the workers' most urgent needs."[9] This was a claim that neither the authorities nor the industrialists were willing to face.

[6] Ivanov and Volin, *Istoriia rabochego klassa Rossii,* p. 153.

[7] Pankratova, *Rabochee dvizhenie,* vol. 4, pt. 1, p. 825.

[8] Sviatlovskii, *Kharkovskii fabrichnyi okrug,* pp. 5, 72.

[9] Kolodub, *Trud i zhizn' gornorabochikh*, p. 122.

In addition to creating new and problematic social relations, the Donbass industrialists, as a recently arrived interest group in Russian society, clashed with many other groups, and often with what the tsar's advisers saw as the state interest. In such cases, state control was merciless and unyielding, and the Association of Southern Coal and Steel Producers was helpless. The matter of the law on universal accident compensation (discussed in volume 1) is a case in point, and I shall have cause to discuss other such cases.

The advantage of the right to organize, granted to the industrialists while denied to the workers, was crucial. The employers, with the weight of their professional association behind them, could articulate their interests, had entrée into the court through "their" minister, and ultimately had their own representatives at court. N. S. Avdakov, and later N. F. von Ditmar, as chairmen of the Council of the Association of Southern Coal and Steel Producers, were given the rank of privy councillor (*tainyi sovetnik*) and became members of the tsar's state council.

Governmental Structure

At the beginning of their development, and for many years thereafter, the mines and factories of the Donbass came under the jurisdiction of the Ministry of State Domains.[10] If it seems strange that this great industrial development, financed by private investment, should have fallen under such anomalous supervision, it should be remembered that the early mining and smelting industries from the Urals iron works through the Lugansk and Lisichansk experiments described in volume 1, were largely state-initiated and state-owned.

The incongruity of supervising the welfare of hired workers in private enterprise did not escape the minister's notice, and when the law regulating the hiring and payment of workers was under discussion, P. A. Valuev attempted to avoid chairing the committee formulating the draft legislation, claiming that the subject fell within the competence of the chief of gendarmes, Count Shuvalov.[11]

[10] The ministry later became known as the Ministry of State Domains and Agriculture. Only after 1905 were the mines and factories of the Donbass put under the supervision of the Ministry of Trade and Industry.

[11] Valuev, *Politicheskii dnevnik*, vol. 2, p. 304. Valuev may well have anticipated the endless nature of the committee's work. For a chronicle of the long, slow deliberations and

Within the Ministry of State Domains was the Mines Administration, and with the rise of the Donbass this soon spawned a subordinate body, the Mines Administration for Southern Russia. It was as head of this office that V. Islavin had been sent by Valuev in 1874 to survey the development of the Donbass.[12] One of the duties of the head of the Mines Administration for Southern Russia was to sit ex officio as chairman of the annual meeting of the Association of Southern Coal and Steel Producers, thus symbolizing the subordination of the association to state authority.

The direct contact between the ministry and the enterprises was maintained by the district mining engineers, who were nominally responsible for enforcing the rules of mining and manufacturing. As the mines proliferated, the Donbass was subdivided into more and more districts, each with its own district engineer, and later, an assistant. Until 1871, the whole of the Donbass formed a single mining district. In that year it was divided in two, with the largely anthracite district of the Don Cossack territory as one region, and the predominantly bituminous area of the Bakhmut and Slavianoserbsk districts as the other.[13] In response to the growing economic activity in the Donbass, the governor of Ekaterinoslav province made his vice-governor responsible for the supervision of these two industrial districts.[14] As mining and metallurgy intensified, the mining districts were reorganized repeatedly, becoming smaller and more numerous. By 1899 a Bakhmut mining district had been formed, with the district engineer resident in Mariupol and his assistant in Iuzovka.[15] Eventually there was also a Iuzovka mining district with a full-fledged district engineer in the settlement.

The district engineers were personages of some importance, and their importance was not diminished with reorganization. The engineers were criticized as being flesh of the industrialists' flesh and leaning over backward

the numerous amendments to the labor laws, see vol. 2, pp. 507–8 n. 384. Pazhitnov, *Polozhenie,* p. 138, notes that amendments first proposed in 1863 were enacted into law only in May 1901.

[12] Gonimov, *Staraia Iuzovka*, p. 58.

[13] Keppen, *Istoriko-statisticheskii obzor* p. 32.

[14] Retivov, "Organizatsiia protivokholernykh meropriiatii," p. 75. The arrangement is similar to that used by the Communist party of the Soviet Union in its administrative practices.

[15] *Gorno-zavodskii listok*, no. 8 (1899), p. 3785; no. 21 (1899), pp. 4009–10. Engineer Abraam, who had been director of the Lisichansk foremen's school, was district engineer; his assistant was Alexander Rutchenko.

to please the employers, preparing the way for themselves to step later into lucrative careers as mine directors or metallurgy executives.[16] The source of most such criticism, however, was such that it carried little, if any, weight with the authorities, and most official communications gave a different impression. In a letter of May 1902, Count Keller, then governor of Ekaterinoslav province, assured the minister of the interior that the district engineers were most useful in solving misunderstandings between workers and management, and that, despite their inadequate numbers, they maintained satisfactory supervision of work safety and of the legality of all aspects of management activity.[17]

The district engineers were originally technical officials, intended to oversee the safe running of the mines. Their task had grown, however, as the mines themselves became the center of more complex social problems. I have already noted the suggestion that the district engineer oversee public readings and magic-lantern shows, guarding against the inclusion of immoral or subversive material. It was also suggested that they be entrusted with the quasi-judicial function of handling technical disputes regarding working procedures that might arise between workers and employers.[18] In the mining and metallurgy settlements, this function had hitherto been performed by the police chief, who was the leading local representative of the state. This proposal had a unique advantage for the workers, particularly passportless workers who had avoided any contact with the authorities for fear of deportation. They now had some defense against exploitation in that they had recourse to a technical authority empowered to rule on working conditions, but at least ostensibly taking no ex officio interest in their residential status.[19]

With the growth of social problems in the burgeoning mine and factory

[16] Gonimov, *Staraia Iuzovka*, p. 31. He cites the cases of Keppen, Fel'kner, and Letunovskii, the last having worked for several years in the Hughes factory after retiring as district engineer. Evgenii Nikolaevich Taskin, following an extensive civil-service career as a mining engineer, was hired by the New Russia Co. and represented it at annual meetings of the association. See *Trudy s"ezda gornopromyshlennikov iuga Rossii, Ekstrennyi s"ezd, 1902*, p. 6 (henceforth cited as *Trudy*, no. of session, year of session, page no.). For similar criticism of the factory inspectors, see *Rabochee dvizhenie v Ekaterinoslave*, p. 9.

[17] TsGAOR, F. DP, ed. khr. 4, ch. 18, L.G., 1898, p. 8. Letter of Count Keller to Minister of the Interior von Plehve, May 1902. From the tenor of his reports, Keller, like Sviatopolk-Mirskii, appears to have been one of the more enlightened and frank governors. He was killed at the front in the Russo-Japanese War.

[18] *Trudy, XVIII, 1893*, p. 356.

[19] Kolodub, *Trud i zhizn' gornorabochikh*, p. 41.

population, the authorities saw the need for a new institution, and as part of the labor legislation of 1892 the Mining Industry Inspectorate (*prisutstvie*) was created, parallel to the Factory Inspectorate.[20]

The new inspectorate was created both to free the district engineers for the technical work that was their professional field and to correct a situation that had not improved since Sviatlovskii managed to visit only one-quarter of the enterprises in his district in 1885.[21] By imperial rescript of June 7, 1899, the two inspectorates were unified and the number of mine inspectors increased from twenty-two to thirty-four, scarcely a sufficient number to meet the needs of the rapidly growing mine and metallurgy industries of the Russian Empire.[22] Prince Peter Sviatopolk-Mirskii noted that despite the unquestionably correct, firm, and timely use of armed force by the authorities, followed by arrests, trials, and heavy sentences, industrial unrest was not diminishing. Pointing out that prevention might be more efficient than such harsh curative measures, the governor suggested stricter supervision of the mines and factories by the appointment of more inspectors. This time, the note at the side of his proposal had a different tone. "This matter [industrial peace in the mines and mills of the Donbass] is highly important. Get more inspectors if there are not enough."[23]

The deficiency in the number of factory and mine inspectors persisted through the entire period of rapid development of the mine and metal industries of the Donbass, however, as it did throughout Russia. Twice in his reports to the minister of the interior, Count Keller had emphasized the inadequate numbers of engineers, inspectors, and even police. The result, he said, was that the smaller mines, already lacking in personnel to oversee the technical and social aspects of mining operations, were virtually unsupervised. He reported that a mass of passportless people camped at these mines, constituting a source of cheap and docile labor, and that these people were heartlessly exploited. Injustices, and often even crimes, were committed underground, and these went unpunished or even undetected. The

[20] Gonimov, *Staraia Iuzovka*, p. 94.

[21] Sliozberg, *Dela minuvshikh dnei*, vol. 2, p. 135, blames much of the poverty and unsanitary conditions prevailing in Iuzovka on the inadequacy of factory inspection and the consequent casual attitude of the industrialists to the inspectors' recommendations.

[22] *Rabochee delo*, nos. 4–5 (September-December 1899), p. 38. The inspectors also had sixteen assistants.

[23] TsGIAL, F. 1263, op. 2, d. 5445, p. 94.

conditions in which these miners lived and worked were said to be horrible.[24]

The addition of mining inspectors established an institution that not only gave some measure of ongoing supervision over a rapidly growing branch of industry, but also, as was noted by the members of the Association of Southern Coal and Steel Producers, provided the authorities with an independent audit of the living conditions of mine workers and of compliance with social legislation.[25] This agency, in keeping with the administrative culture of the empire, was not in essence confrontational, for each district had a mining inspectorate council on which representatives of the mining industry were seated. The council members could lobby in support of their positions on complaints or proposed programs of reform.[26] The creation of social norms that would spur positive action on the part of the industrialists was encouraged. When the Shtoffe Commission studied workers' living conditions in the Donbass in 1900, it noted that no law compelled the mine owners to construct churches and schools, yet they existed in almost every place; such activities were to be lauded.[27] Mine inspectors had the legal power to oblige the industrialists to meet state standards for the provision of decent living conditions for their workers.[28]

However, there does not appear to be any record of their having invoked legal sanctions to correct problems of housing and sanitation. Nothing resembling the prosecution of mine officials following fatal mine accidents appears to have taken place in the wake of the recurrent epidemics or the frequent doctors' reports of subhuman housing and sanitary conditions. Rather, the inspectors were seen as a sort of educative conscience, an extension of the presence of the *Batiushka tsar* (the "little father-emperor"), who would remind the powerful of their duty to obey the laws of the realm and deal justly with those entrusted to their supervision. The Shtoffe Commis-

[24] TsGAOR, F. DP, ed. khr. 4, ch. 18, L.G., 1898, pp. 8, 12. Letter of Count Keller to von Plehve, May 1902.

[25] *Trudy, Ekstrennyi s"ezd, 1900*, report of the Commission on Workers' Living Conditions, p. 3.

[26] See *Trudy, Ekstrennyi s"ezd, 1900*, p. 25, for the unanimous election of S. G. Zimovskii of the New Russia Co. to represent the association on the inspectorate council for Ekaterinoslav and Kherson provinces.

[27] TsGIAL F. 37, op. 58, d. 299, p. 2. Shtoffe Commission report, 1900.

[28] See the statements of Mines Administration official A. A. Sorokin to the annual meeting of the association in *Trudy, XX, 1895*, p. 563.

1.3 A zemlianka—a semidugout of earth and boards. Workers' housing up to the late 1890s.

1.4 The "Glass Houses." Built for executives of the New Russia Co. at the start of the twentieth century, the houses remain essentially the same today.

sion observed careless notation of hiring conditions in workers' pay books, failure to list workers' ages, inaccurate registration of fines—"all these are frequently to be found." Yet the commission's report assured the authorities that in this there was no trace of evil intent. Such oversights stemmed from inattention and lack of accurate knowledge of the law. The situation could be remedied through closer supervision by the mine inspectors.[29]

Yet the inspectors were to apply the law as well as interpret its subtle complexities. They were, after all, representatives of the state order. The inspectors took on the quasi-judicial tasks that had been devolving on the district engineers, and this was noted approvingly in the association's discussions. The news of a mining inspector punishing a miner for a breach of working procedure had spread among the miners, achieving some disciplinary effect.[30]

While the inspectors were part of the unified Inspectorate for Factory and Mining Affairs after 1899, the district mining engineers remained wholly under the supervision of the Ministry of State Domains and Agriculture until 1905, when the mines and factories of the Donbass were subordinated to the Ministry of Trade and Industry. The district mining engineers' reports, unlike those of the factory inspectors, were never published.[31] The engineers were, however, active and articulate in expressing opinions about the needs of the mining industry, and they provided the first generation of leaders for the Association of Southern Coal and Steel Producers.

While the district engineers and mine inspectors were local representatives of authority, the central government in St. Petersburg maintained a tight rein on all organizational activity in the Donbass. The annual meeting of the association had to receive approval from the ministry regarding time, place, and agenda. The annual volume of *Trudy s"ezda gornopromyshlennikov iuga Rossii*, a stenographic record of the meeting, with numerous statistical and documentary appendices, was presented to the minister as an official report.[32] The constraints on the meeting were multiple. The head of the Mines Administration for Southern Russia was chairman of the annual meeting. In addition, all materials presented to the annual meeting under-

[29] TsGIAL, F. 37, op. 58, d. 299, p. 2. Shtoffe Commission report, 1900.

[30] *Trudy, XXV, 1900*, pt. 2, stenographic reports, pp. 118–20. Taskin's comments appear in the often plaintive discussion of how to compel workers to respect their obligations to their employers.

[31] Pazhitnov, *Polozhenie*, p. 72.

[32] See, for instance, the dedication in *Trudy, VII, 1882* (or any of the other volumes).

went state censorship before presentation.[33] It can be assumed that the presence of such censorship and observation resulted in two levels of self-censorship: that of the speaker, and that of the stenographer.

The Association of Southern Coal and Steel Producers was not alone in suffering such stringent control. This was how Russia was ruled. When the Second Congress of Factory Doctors of Ekaterinoslav Province received permission for its meeting from the Ministry of Internal Affairs, the telegram read: "I grant permission for the congress." At the same time it noted that "in the case of digression from the program it will be closed immediately."[34]

Bureaucratic control of the tsar's subjects knew neither relaxation nor flexibility, even in times of crisis. When cholera entered the Donbass in July 1892, the mining industrialists belatedly decided to call a special meeting to determine measures to fight the epidemic. A proposed date and agenda were submitted to the chief of the Mines Administration for Southern Russia, Zelentsov, who had telegraphed them to St. Petersburg for approval. Only after a frantic second telegram from Avdakov, noting that cholera had already appeared in Lugansk, did permission arrive.[35] Even then the troubles were not over. The mining industrialists sat from July 11 to July 15 working out their program, and sent it to the capital by courier for special approval. Only on August 1 did the Mines Administration draft a twenty-two point reply recommending bright, dry housing, hot food, cleanliness, and disinfection of public places, as well as referring the employers to the standing instructions of the ministry. The bureaucrats were working in a model world that did not exist outside their kingdom of paper.[36] In the event, their advice was doubly irrelevant, for the day after it was written the commercial center of Iuzovka was burned to the ground in a two-day riot that cost close to a hundred lives and destroyed any possibility of controlling the cholera epidemic in the largest population center of the Donbass.

There were other occasions on which bureaucratic delays were not fatal, but simply frustrating. I have referred to the nine-year hiatus between suggestions of procedures for public readings and their approval by the authorities; such delays were the rule. The association waged a vain

[33] See *Trudy, XVII, 1892*, p. 507. Chairman: "Is the report ready?" A. F. Mevius: "The report is ready but we are awaiting the censor's permission."

[34] Vinokurov, "Vtoroi s"ezd fabrichnykh vrachei," p. 428.

[35] The telegram (undated) is printed in *Trudy, XVII, 1892*, p. 274.

[36] The text of the ministry's reply, signed by the director general, the chief of the Mines Administration, and the clerk responsible for transcribing the resolution, may be found in ibid., pp. 246–54.

eighteen-year war for reform of the zemstvo tax-assessment system. Much of this time passed simply because the various ministries involved never answered petitions forwarded to them through the Ekaterinoslav governor or the Ministry of State Domains.[37] Nor were inter- and intraministerial jealousies absent. As minister of the interior, von Plehve appointed A. V. Pogozhev senior editor of the ministry's statistical committee, and delegated him to prepare a comprehensive survey of the number of Russian factory workers and their living conditions. Pogozhev was unable to complete the project satisfactorily because he was denied access to the statistical materials and correspondence gathered in the archives of the industrial section of the police department.[38]

Within this bureaucratic environment, initiative was stifled and change came slowly and with great difficulty. Swift and flexible responses to crises were impossible, and despite a multitude of commissions and reports, adaptation to new challenges was partial at best. Despite the rich intellectual and technological ferment of Russia in the late nineteenth century, the regime insisted on clinging stubbornly to its archconservative values, and the tsar surrounded himself with like-minded people who confused immobility with stability and regarded a Witte or a Stolypin as a dangerous radical upstart. Perhaps even more important in terms of the functioning and survival of the regime was the preservation of an administrative system that had evolved over centuries of minimal government. Any reorganizations ended with the powerful but ill-informed central authority insisting on its prerogatives of decision making. And far too many of its decisions, whether appropriate or not, remained dead letters for lack of executive ability. Such an administration was a poor instrument for taking Russia through the vicissitudes of modernization.

Police Control

One administrative institution worked relatively effectively: the police department. In the spring of 1872, when rail and iron production was

[37] See *Trudy, VII, 1882*, p. 65, for a report of the Ekaterinoslav governor's letter of December 1881, stating that no reply had yet been received from the Ministry of the Interior regarding the association's petition of October 10, 1880. Similarly, see *Trudy, XXIV, 1899*, app. 2, p. 10, in which it is stated that no answer had yet been received from the Ministry of Finance to the tax reevaluation suggested in letters of June 5, 1896, October 12, 1896, and August 14, 1898. Numerous additional examples could be cited.

[38] Morskoi, *Zubatovshchina*, pp. 150–51.

getting under way, John Hughes requested the establishment of a police station in Iuzovka "to oversee order among the workers." In due time, an inspector and four constables arrived, to be housed, fed, and paid at the New Russia Co.'s expense.[39] This was two years before the earliest labor dispute in Iuzovka. Starting in the spring of 1888, this largely symbolic police force was reinforced by a cossack force, permanently stationed in Iuzovka despite the protests of the army against the use of soldiers for police duties.[40] It was explained to the French mining engineer Paul Chapuy, during his visit to the Donbass a year later, that "violence against the Jews of the area had brought on the presence of a detachment of Cossacks."[41] The cossacks remained and found frequent employment in Iuzovka and the surrounding region, despite E. M. Garshin's observation during his 1891 visit that "for Iuzovka itself these Cossacks are totally unnecessary. The population here is absolutely peaceful."[42]

Maintaining the police force or a cossack troop was one of the "special general costs" unique to the Russian coal mines. At Gorlovka, police maintenance cost twenty-five thousand rubles a year, in addition to an estimated eighteen hundred rubles for the goodwill of the cossack commander "so that he will not arrive too late when there is need of him."[43] The costs naturally increased as the populace grew. By the time Iuzovka's population reached twenty thousand at the beginning of the 1890s, there was a police force of sixteen and a night watch of twenty, all commanded by a single police chief (*ispravnik*).[44] The police chief was the local representative of the regime in a place like Iuzovka where no other state authority existed. He was not only an enforcer of law and order, but an arbiter of social norms. On March 12, 1887, when 140 workers at the Ivanov mine near Iuzovka blockaded the mine to prevent coal being removed until they had received their pay, the Iuzovka police chief, called to restore order, investigated the situation and then borrowed six hundred rubles in silver from Hughes to

[39] Potolov, *Rabochie Donbassa*, p. 180.

[40] Ibid., p. 205. Potolov notes (n. 106) that the presence of this force on holidays, paydays, and similar occasions was evidently effective in stopping disorders.

[41] Chapuy, "Journal de voyage," p. 131. The reference is to the disturbances during the strike at the Rutchenko mines in May 1887.

[42] Garshin, "Poezdka," p. 9. This was less than a year prior to the cholera riots.

[43] CL, 11582, n. 1607, *Special General Costs of a Colliery in Russia* (January 1903), p. 10. The cost of maintaining the police at Makeevka is given as three thousand rubles per month. The author remarks that in the circumstances this seems to be a bit high.

[44] TsGIAL, F. 1405, op. 93, ed. khr. 8555, p. 33.

advance to the workers for the food and clothing they needed, the sum to be repaid by the mine owner after the sale of his coal.[45] In another case in 1898, a group of workers appealed to the Iuzovka police chief for his intercession in a strike, and ended their letter with this appeal: "And if you cannot gain us our rights, then inform your superiors so that they will get us the rights we desire."[46]

Much thus depended on the ability and integrity of the police chief. A report of the district chief noted the type of problem that might crop up. On May 16, 1886, police employee Shulzhenko tried to suborn Chelikhova, the wife of a factory worker, to attack and loot the homes of Iuzovka Jews living in factory houses, promising that he would make sure she had time to escape and hide before the police intervened. Presumably there would then be a suitable division of the loot. When Chelikhova indignantly reported the incident to the police chief, Shemaev, he threw her out of his office: "Now Rubtsev is *ispravnik*. He is honest."[47] Low pay often led to police corruption. The unhappy lot of the local constabulary was forcefully presented by Count Keller. He noted the ever-growing responsibilities that lay on a Donbass policeman's shoulders as he faced the burdens of supervising the labor force and of maintaining public order. Count Keller pointed out that the number of police was inadequate, and their service conditions and pay miserable. "Their work is responsible—and for any error, let alone misdeed, they risk losing their positions. The many facets of their work demand a knowledge of legal testimony, tact, and a combination of intellect and physical health not easily found in any single person."[48] Perhaps the governor was exaggerating the talents demanded of the local constable, yet much did depend on his tact and social sensitivity.

Public order and protection of persons and property were the main concerns of the police. Political matters were handled by a separate agency, the Okhrana (internal security police). Until the last decade of the nineteenth century, political surveillance was a small part of police activity in

[45] TsGAOR, F. DP, deloproizvodstvo 3, d. 89, ch. 12, 1888, p. 7. This is somewhat different than the version found in Potolov, *Rozhdenie velikana*, pp. 143–44, based on documents from Pankratova. There, no mention is made of Hughes having provided the money to facilitate settlement of the dispute.

[46] TsGAOR, F. DP, deloproizvodstvo 3, ed. khr. 700, 1901g., p. 14.

[47] Ibid., F. 102, deloproizvodstvo 9, ch. 21, 1887, p. 60.

[48] Ibid., F. DP, ed. khr. 4, ch. 18, L.G., 1898, pp. 11–12. Letter of Count Keller to Minister of the Interior von Plehve, May 1902. For comments on police venality, see Wynn, *Workers, Strikes, and Pogroms*, pp. 71–72.

the Donbass. In 1890 there were only eighty-two permanent residents of Ekaterinoslav province under secret police scrutiny, and another twenty-five under open supervision. In addition, ten temporary residents of the region were being watched. All were suspected of hostile political activity.[49] Altogether the revolutionary movement represented a tiny segment of Russia's population and of its illegal activity. When in 1893 the Okhrana published a 623-page list of persons wanted by the police department, there were only four hundred revolutionary socialists among them.[50]

The need for greater police protection was felt sharply following the Iuzovka cholera riots. In addition, the industrialists' firm conviction that some revolutionary master plan had guided the rioters made the political element more salient in the policing of the Donbass. A commission chaired by the Ekaterinoslav governor, with Avdakov as a member, decided that in view of the growth and instability of the populace, police forces should be kept proportional to the size of the working population. In a discussion of this and other proposals for security by the Association of Southern Coal and Steel Producers, the mine owner Karpov suggested establishing a special police force for the mining settlements, free of any responsibility for the surrounding countryside. Engineer Wagner went a step further by saying that policemen, even if specially appointed to keep order in the mine labor force, would always be outsiders and therefore not completely privy to what was really going on among the workers. He proposed recruitment of what he called *desiatskie* (literally, "tenth men")—workers who would be paid to keep the police informed about the plans and actions of small groups of their fellow workers. Wagner's idea was rejected on the ground that it would be impossible to find a sufficient number of workers who could be relied on to fill such posts.[51]

Toward the end of the century, the authorities were becoming increasingly apprehensive about the labor movement. In a circular dated August 12, 1897, the Moscow police chief emphasized the dangers of industrial unrest and suggested strengthening police surveillance of factories, work-

[49] TsGAOR, F. DP, deloproizvodstvo 3, d. 44, ch. 7, 1891. The reasons given for surveillance revealed a general xenophobia that ranged from anti-Semitism to hatred of Poles, Germans, and Shtundists, "many of whom had portraits of Bismarck in their homes rather than portraits of the tsar."

[50] *Rabochee delo*, no. 1 (April 1899), p. 71. There is no indication of the total number of names on the list.

[51] *Trudy, XVIII, 1893*, pt. 2, p. 331. For Wagner's suggestion, see p. 331. For Karpov, see p. 333. Criticism of Wagner's proposal is on p. 334.

shops, and workers' neighborhoods. The surveillance was to regard all workers' demonstrations as political—and therefore illegitimate—but was also to report on justified complaints by the workers so that these might be corrected, avoiding disorders. The penalty for engaging in attempts to organize and propagandize to the workers was to be deportation to the miscreant's place of registration—evidence that the population of industrial workers was largely a migrant one.[52]

Deportation, though frequently used, was far from the only punishment. Indiscriminate public flogging with birch rods was used against persons thought to have taken part in illegal demonstrations, without resort to trial or any other legal procedure. It was this humiliating punishment, applied illegally to a student, that had brought Vera Zasulich to shoot General Trepov.

When the cholera epidemic reached the Donbass in 1892 and there was fear of an outbreak of disorder, Durnovo, the minister of the interior, sent coded telegrams to his representatives. "In the event of disorders, recommend on-the-spot flogging, and after that punishment of the leaders in jail."[53] So it was that flogging was meted out en masse after the riots, though most of those flogged were never subsequently charged in court. The tsar himself is said to have noted approvingly on the report of the minister of the interior that "corporal punishment is the only way to overcome this lawlessness."[54] During the August 1903 attempted general strike in Ekaterinoslav, a group of nonstrikers on their way to work in the railway shops encountered a patrol of cossacks who, thinking them strikers, laid into them with knouts, scattering them to the winds.[55] Brutality incorporated into law was standard behavior for the regime and its law-enforcement institutions. Corporal punishment had been part of serfdom, applied at the master's discretion, though formally limited by customary law. Despite the emancipation of the serfs, the state still applied this punishment, though the industrialists did not. Yet when strikes and demonstrations were punished by flogging, it is questionable whether the

[52] *Rabochee delo*, no. 1 (April 1899), pp. 29–30. Zelnik, *Labor and Society*, p. 173, has noted that the tsarist police and authorities acted for a paternalist autocracy, punishing both manufacturers and workers for their transgressions. In the Donbass, though the principle was formally the same, it is difficult to write of any such evenhandedness.

[53] TsGAOR, F. DP, deloproizvodstvo 3, d. 124, ch. 2, 1892, p. 32. Telegram dated July 6, 1892.

[54] Gonimov, *Staraia Iuzovka*, p. 109.

[55] Chugaev, *Vseobshchaia stachka v iuge Rossii*, pp. 175–76.

worker was able to distinguish which master was beating him, and for what. In addition, the flogged serf was still bound to his master's estate after the flogging. The industrial worker could, and evidently did, leave places where police brutality exceeded tolerable bounds.

The regime lived in deadly fear of the potential for violence that it was convinced lay just below the surface of the population. It clung rigidly to the most primitive forms of autocracy, excluding the vast majority of the people from even marginal participation in politics. The greater the social tension created, the more brutal the response of the authorities. With each passing year, the polarization of Russian society grew. The regime regarded as dangerous the reform-minded intelligentsia, which was moving into revolutionary opposition to the autocracy even though it was far from approving of the terror and violence that marked the populist tactics of the People's Will, and later, of the Socialist-Revolutionaries (S-Rs), or the concepts of proletarian dictatorship embraced by the Social-Democrats (S-Os).[56]

By 1899, the suggestions that had been debated by the Association of Southern Coal and Steel Producers six years earlier had ripened into general law. A special factory police force was established, made up of 60 police superintendents (*nadzirateli*) and 2,320 constables. Their salaries were to be paid by the state, but the industrialists, over whose property and workers they watched, were to provide housing as well as jail facilities. The calculation was that there should be one superintendent for each three thousand adult workers and one constable for each fifty workers.[57]

Repression was not, however, the only weapon in the police arsenal. Preventive measures through clandestine surveillance were found to be a more economical and effective way of identifying and eliminating agitators. A whole army of paid and volunteer agents worked for the Okhrana, ferreting out incipient revolutionary groups before they could take root. At the same time that the factory police were established, the employers were

[56] Zelnik, *Labor and Society*, p. 169, notes the extremity of punishment, including beating, that was meted out for even the most peaceful and justified of workers' demonstrations. Manning, *Crisis of the Old Order*, pp. 169–72, writes of beatings, killings, rape, and a multitude of harassments and humiliations initiated by ministers, governors, and their senior officials, and implemented by local commanders and their troops, in the wake of the 1905 revolution.

[57] *Rabochee delo*, nos. 2–3 (August 1899), p. 78. See also Johnson, *Peasant and Proletarian*, p. 87, who, drawing on a Soviet secondary source, writes that there were 160 new superintendents.

urged to pay for the upkeep of informers within their factories: one for a labor force of two hundred, two for between two hundred and five hundred workers, and so on.[58] On the whole these informers were quite effective, particularly in the Donbass settlements, in which, despite the great movements of population, the arrival of nonworkers (which the vast majority of the revolutionaries were) was easily spotted. A report of the Ekaterinoslav chief of gendarmes for the year 1890 notes the presence of "the Lipetsk *meshchanin* [townsman] Solomon Aronovich Rappoport, reading some sort of booklets to the peasants and workers, stories supposedly for the people's development, and for the raising of their literacy."[59] A later Donbass revolutionary noted in his memoirs that as soon as leaflets were distributed at any mine, the police would know of it and move to prevent any further activities.[60] In this way, the revolutionaries were kept on the move, and found it difficult to establish any lasting influence in wide circles of workers. Parizher was forced out of Baku in March 1905 and arrested in Ekaterinoslav in July; he went to Odessa after three months in jail and, pressured by the police there, emigrated at the end of the year.[61] Right up to the collapse of the tsarist regime, the Okhrana demonstrated its ability to control the contacts of revolutionary groups with the workers. Writing about the World War I period, David Mandel notes that police repression was so efficient that an underground revolutionary's career was, on the average, reduced to no more than three months.[62]

There were unintended consequences to the effectiveness of Okhrana control. Those who were organizing educational circles, strikes, and other activities involving contact with the public were relatively easily detected and eliminated. The terrorists, working alone or in small cells in completely isolated, conspiratorial conditions, and engaging in one-time assassination operations, were more often able to carry out their plans to the end.

[58] *Rabochee delo*, nos. 2–3 (August 1899), p. 78.

[59] TsGAOR, F. DP, deloproizvodstvo 3, d. 44, ch. 7, 1891, p. 1. Report of Ekaterinoslav chief of gendarmes for 1890. This was a *narodovolets* (a member of the People's Will) and future S-R, later author of the classical Yiddish drama *The Dybbuk*. His account of his year in the Donbass appears under his pen name, S. A. An——skii, in the first two issues of *Russkoe bogatstvo* for 1892.

[60] TsGAOR, F. 7592, op. 6, d. 120, p. 4. Memoirs of Shur.

[61] Shidlovskii, "Pamiati Semena Savel'evich Parizhera," p. 114. A similar career, that of Alexander Maslennikov, is described in "Rabochie organizatsii iuga v 1914 g.," p. 160. For a more detailed discussion of this problem, see Friedgut, "Professional Revolutionaries in the Donbass," pp. 284–300.

[62] Mandel, *Petrograd Workers*, p. 62, citing Shliapnikov's memoirs of the period.

Their successes, compared to the repeated breakup of more moderate educational activities, attracted young people who were already inclined to extremism in responding to the moral imperative of opposing tyranny. This only confirmed the fears and prejudices of the regime, justifying the use of violence against all who shared goals with the terrorists, irrespective of their attitude toward means. Once again the polarization of Russian society was reinforced.

Memoirs of the Donbass revolutionary underground are replete with stories of police agents. In 1913 there were said to be seventeen or eighteen Social-Democratic groups in the Donbass. Within these groups there were sixteen police agents, in addition to four others who had infiltrated Socialist-Revolutionary groups, two in the Bund (the Jewish Social-Democratic organization), and two among the anarcho-communists.[63] Some were coerced revolutionaries who became informers; some worked for money; some volunteered out of ideological conviction. A certain Potemkin volunteered his services to inform against the Iuzovka Social-Democrats because they were "blasphemers who believed in neither God nor Tsar."[64] At another time, the secretary of the Social-Democratic party group in Iuzovka was a police informer.[65]

So tightly woven was the network of police spies that, as will happen in such situations, one agent often ended up reporting on another.[66] As Avdakov once commented wryly, "So much material had been gathered by them [the police and Ministry of the Interior] regarding the history of the Hughes factory that they know the situation in the mines quite as well as we do."[67]

In self-defense the revolutionary movement publicized pictures and descriptions of agents who moved about the country betraying revolutionary groups. In Iuzovka, Karp Pavlovich, a revolutionary sympathizer who ran a coffee shop in the settlement's center, made it his business to know all the police spies and to warn the revolutionaries.[68] There were also professional

[63] Nesterov, "Rabochie organizatsii iuga v 1914 godu," p. 154. Wynn, *Workers, Strikes, and Pogroms*, p. 160, cites a police report stating that the Okhrana had failed to penetrate the ranks of Poalei Tsion, the Socialist-Zionists.

[64] Novopolin, "V mire predatel'stva," p. 39. For confirmation of workers volunteering to inform against the socialists, see Levus, "Iz istorii," p. 62.

[65] Elwood, *Russian Social Democracy*, p. 54.

[66] Pazhitnov, *Polozhenie*, pp. 183–84.

[67] *Trudy, XXIII, 1898*, pt. 2, p. 334.

[68] For example, see *Vpered*, no. 16 (1905), p. 6, warning of two agents, Vulf Satanovskii (also known as "Vulka"), who worked in the mine offices, and P. D. Brailovskii, a jack-of-all-

agent-hunters who tried to follow and expose police agents in areas where arrests were thought to be due to systematic betrayal. Often the informer's career lasted no longer than that of the professional revolutionary. Potemkin's lasted only three weeks. Frequently informers were executed by the revolutionaries when uncovered. Yet when the Okhrana archives were opened after February 1917, the lists of agents published showed many long careers.[69] Some informers were not discovered until years later.

A detailed examination of the effectiveness with which the police suppressed the revolutionaries leaves little room for doubt that the authorities faced only minimal political danger from that quarter. Yet suppression alone was no substitute for social policy and political reform. These were slow in coming throughout Russia, and doubly slow in the Donbass. The pose of evenhanded paternalism was little more than that. In its day-to-day decisions on social matters, the inner circle of the tsar's court showed little active concern for Russia's workers, and even less devotion to protecting them from abuse, so the laws protecting the workers went largely unenforced. At the same time, the principles of autocratic government were upheld with great vigor, blocking any broadening of the political stratum in the country. Unfortunately for Russia, this stand coincided with the interests and perceptions of the mining industrialists, who reinforced the authorities' policies against the workers.

The Association of Southern Coal and Steel Producers

The first suggestion that the coal and metal producers of South Russia should meet and coordinate their activities is said to have been made in 1870 by P. N. Gorlov, the engineer and director of Poliakov's South Russian Coal Co. mines at Gorlovka. A somewhat different version is put forward by A. A. Auerbakh, later a prominent coal producer, and one of the notables of the association, who claims to have taken the initiative for calling a meeting in Taganrog, attended by Gorlov along with mine owners A. V. Sheierman and I. G. Ilovaiskii, resulting in a petition to Valuev

trades, who were responsible for arrests in the Krivoi Rog iron mines for over a year. For the story of Karp Pavlovich, see Moiseenko, *Vospominaniia starogo revoliutsionera*, p. 184.

[69] See *Birzhevye vedomosti* (April 9, 1917) for the exposure of N. N. Veretskii, who served the Okhrana from 1902 through 1917 in Kharkov, Ekaterinoslav, and finally St. Petersburg.

1.5 The Association of Southern Coal and Steel Producers in session, May 1907.

during his 1874 visit to the Donbass requesting permission to hold a congress of mining industrialists.[70]

The central item on the proposed agenda was the labor problem that was to remain the focus of numerous association debates up to 1917. The opportunity to realize the plan for an industrialists' association came when Major General Gern, visiting Iuzovka in the spring of 1874, informed Hughes that the minister of state domains, Valuev, was scheduled to visit the Donbass in the summer. The consciousness of a need for such an association was sharpened by the onset of the first coal crisis, with production outrunning demand and coal prices collapsing. Evidently Hughes' price-cutting policies contributed to the crisis in no small measure, squeezing the less-efficient producers. The industrialists' reaction was to seek the formation of a professional organization to lobby the government on behalf of the new industries and to impose a restraining framework on the association's members.[71]

A fitting reception and banquet were arranged at Hughes' residence, with the participation of all the local notables. Professor Time lectured on the industrial potential of the Donbass, and at the conclusion of the evening A. A. Auerbakh, owner of coal, salt, and mercury mines, requested and received from the minister permission to hold at Taganrog a conference of mining industry owners to discuss railway tariffs and the problems of creating a labor force.[72]

This was the founding, in November 1874, of what was to become the Association of Southern Coal and Steel Producers. Despite his activity on behalf of the creation of the association, John Hughes is not listed among the thirty delegates attending the meeting.[73] P. I. Fomin remarks that the association regarded metallurgy simply as a customer for coal, and as a necessary instrument in the development of railways and shipping, both of

[70] Gonimov, *Staraia Iuzovka*, pp. 55–56; Auerbakh, "Vospominaniia o nachale," p. 460.

[71] Keppen, *Istoriko-statisticheskii obzor*, p. 33.

[72] Gonimov, *Staraia Iuzovka*, p. 61. Valuev, *Politicheskii dnevnik*, p. 311, contains an entry dated July 5, 1874, noting the minister's return from an extended trip to Poland, Silesia, and "the southern steppe." No details of the trip are given. The editors of the volume write that Valuev's itinerary and impressions were contained in letters written to his son. There is no indication whether these letters are still extant. TsGIAL, F. 37, op. 53, d. 746, pp. 215–16, letter of Hughes to Valuev dated October 15, 1874, thanks Valuev for having visited the New Russia factory in the summer.

[73] The description of the meeting and list of delegates appears in "Gornozavodskoe delo," pp. 3ff.

which were useful as consumers and transporters of coal.[74] Although there were representatives of the New Russia Co. at most of the meetings of the association through the years, and Hughes' sons sat in on the meetings even during their father's lifetime, he himself does not appear to have taken part in its activities.[75] Hughes, of course, did not speak Russian, but it is also possible that the long debates and inconclusive discussions were not to his taste. It is strange that though other, lesser personages were often eulogized at annual sessions of the association, the session following his death had no memorial to him by the chairman or any of the participants.[76] In fact, the only reference to Hughes as an individual in the many volumes of association proceedings is a sort of left-handed compliment: "Without detracting anything from the achievements of Hughes, it is Pastukhov who. . . ."[77] Quite clearly the businesslike, rough, and reticent Hughes was not popular among the Donbass coal merchants, with their aspirations to gentility. It is also significant that the Hughes family was foreign, in a time of rising Russian nationalism. Even more important was his individualism in business, in an environment that was partial to syndication of production and sales. As will be noted below, the refusal of the Hughes brothers to join a projected cartel helped delay its creation for close to seven years.

More important in establishing the character of the association than the personal relations within it was that throughout its existence the dominant influence over policy was set by the coal-mine owners of the second rank. It was the Avdakovs, Karpovs, and Alchevskiis who were the active factors here, rather than the giant foreign firms that had invested millions in the development of coal and metallurgy.[78] This remained true through the

[74] Fomin, *Gornaia i gornozavodskaia promyshlennost'*, vol. 1, p. 444.

[75] See the listing of John Hughes, Jr., as a delegate, together with a Mr. Hume, in *Trudy, VII, 1882*, pp. xxx–xxxi. Pastukhov, too, took no part in the deliberations of the association.

[76] The fourteenth meeting of the association took place from November 10 to 24, 1889, just five months after Hughes' death. Genrikh Osipovich Platz was the sole representative of the New Russia Co. at this meeting.

[77] See the remarks by engineer Wagner in *Trudy, XXI, 1896*, pt. 2, p. 289. Wagner praises Pastukhov both for introducing the technique of using anthracite in blast furnaces in Russia and for establishing his plant without subsidies like the ones Hughes received from the government.

[78] Kondufor, *Istoriia rabochikh Donbassa*, vol. 1, p. 33, blames the foreign capitalists for creating the recurring coal crises, but an examination of the debates and the control of the Council and Statistical Bureau of the Association that did the production planning for submission to the annual meeting shows clearly that the coal producers themselves ran the association and determined its policies.

entire history of the association, even though three distinct generations of leaders may be discerned during these years.

The first notables prominent in the association were the engineers. Men such as Taskin, Time, Wagner, Keppen, and Mevius had all been involved in the early prospecting and development of the Donbass from the technical side.[79] They created the vision of Donbass industry, and linked that vision to mining expertise and experience. Yet none of them possessed capital, nor did they themselves open commercial mines. They remained primarily academics (as Time did, for example), or entered the employ of mine and factory owners. These are the purest examples of the combined technological-managerial types noted by Rieber, and they serve as the chief models of "new work" and a new age in the analyses of Susan McCaffray.[80] Though they were honored in the association and continued to serve on its commissions and participate in its debates, they were soon retired from executive positions and replaced by the commercially minded mine owners and managers.

The most prominent of this generation was undoubtedly Nikolai Stepanovich Avdakov, who led the association from its founding in Kharkov in 1878 until World War I, although in his later years he concentrated his efforts in the St. Petersburg office of the association. There, through his role as member of the state council, he headed the association lobby in the capital. An engineer by training, Avdakov served as commercial director of the Rutchenko mines for the French owners. The Credit Lyonnais analysts wrote of him: "Mr. Avdakov, a Russian engineer of Armenian extraction, living in Kharkov, is the most prominent man in South Russia, and is rightly considered an excellent commercial director."[81] A thorough conser-

[79] Each meeting of the association elected the chief of the Mines Administration for Southern Russia as ex officio chairman of the annual meeting, but also elected a secretary from among the prominent members attending. The secretaries of the first three meetings were engineers: Ioss, Wagner, and Mevius. It should be noted that Time, for instance, also had managerial experience in metallurgy. For a somewhat different analysis of the nature and leadership of the Association of Southern Coal and Steel Producers, see Rieber, *Merchants and Entrepreneurs*, pp. 227–43. The definitive study of the association is McCaffray, "New Work and the Old Regime." More accessible to the general reader are her articles "Association of Southern Coal and Steel Producers" and "Origins of Labor Policy," and Fenin, *Coal and Politics*.

[80] Rieber, *Merchants and Entrepreneurs*, p. 232.

[81] CL, 11852, n. 1301, "Rutchenko Co." (May 1901), p. 2. Although Avdakov was an engineer, his duties at the Rutchenko mines were purely commercial, and a French engineer was in overall charge of the mines' technical operation.

vative and nationalist patriot, he personified the values of the Russian gentry and the tsarist regime, despite his representation of commercial and technical interests. It was he who in 1896 presented the association with the suggestion to limit, or even eliminate, the use of foreign engineers and technicians in the mines, salting his speech with references to national interest and native (*otechestvennyie*) technical forces.[82]

Local landowners such as Rykovskii, Rutchenko, and Ilovaiskii took part in the activities of the association, but had little influence, serving only on a few honorary bodies and taking little part in the debates. They had sold their properties to foreign firms, and though they performed some nominal activity, they played no entrepreneurial role. In this they were representative of that part of the gentry that saw its land only as a means to a leisurely urban life.

Other prominent association members were from different backgrounds. A. V. Sheierman had been a doctor in the short-lived Lisichansk foundry directed by Time. He formed a partnership with the mining director of the Lugansk factory, N. N. Letunovskii, and they took a ten-year lease on peasant lands near Shcherbinovka, establishing the Petrovskii mine. Within two years they were producing over a million *puds* of coal per year, and had a coking operation going as well. By 1874 they were installing steam engines and expecting to produce two and a half million puds of coal.[83] However, many other members of the association had no technical connections to the mining industry, nor did they necessarily live in the Donbass. Apart from a few owners of family mines in the Don Cossack territory, they were Russians (or Russified), and displayed no cultural or political connection to the Ukrainian national ferment.[84] Avdakov was from Kharkov. Others were residents of Rostov, Mariupol, or Voronezh, and their mines were run by hired managers (engineers or foremen). Thus, their connection with the industry was primarily commercial and financial.

This group, as reflected in the discussions at the meetings of the Association of Southern Coal and Steel Producers, apparently was dominant in setting the tone of the organization. Undoubtedly Alfred Rieber is correct

[82] *Trudy, XXI, 1896*, pp. 516–19, and pt. 2, pp. 273–83. Rieber, *Merchants and Entrepreneurs*, pp. 229–30, notes that after 1905 Avdakov became an Octobrist.

[83] Islavin, "Obzor," pp. 44–45. A pud equals 16.38 kilograms, or 36.06 pounds. Sheierman was one of the original group who met to suggest the founding of the association.

[84] See Rieber, *Merchants and Entrepreneurs*, p. 232, and Reshetar, *Ukrainian Revolution*, pp. 22–23.

in noting the ambivalence and contradictions within the organization, yet it is debatable whether the most important characteristics were technological innovation and economic risk taking, as he asserts.[85] Rather, these tone-setting people appear to have been first and foremost proprietary capitalists, more merchants than entrepreneurs, and only marginally industrial managers in the image of Pastukhov or Hughes.[86] In one of the early debates, a clarion call was sounded for a bold, decisive entrepreneurial spirit, but when it came to voting on resolutions and instructing the association's executive, the decisions were that the government should be petitioned for protective tariffs, and that with regard to the development of the industry, "private initiative in ore development explorations is inappropriate and even unthinkable here, since the time and scope of activity are too uncertain and undefined."[87] At the outset of the association, engineer Wagner emphasized the importance of investment in metallurgy, suggesting not only a government subsidy to metal producers, but also a guarantee of at least a 5 percent profit on invested capital.[88] In another instance, when the accident fund was nearly exhausted by the massive casualties of the Rykovskii gas explosion, Karpov moved that the association turn to the government to provide compensation.[89]

If the coal producers belied to a certain extent the thesis of a "missing middle class," they were nevertheless weak as entrepreneurs, weak as technical innovators, and totally lacking in autonomy of outlook and political resources in their relations with the Russian state.

The entrepreneurs consistently backed off from any comprehensive program of investment in housing and services, on the ground that their activities were not guaranteed over the long term due to land-leasing laws.[90] In addition, though there was a steady advance in the technical level

[85] Rieber, *Merchants and Entrepreneurs*, p. 422. Perhaps Rieber's judgment is made from the perspective of comparison with the other entrepreneurial groups studied in his book, of whose characteristics I am largely ignorant.

[86] As the most prominent examples of this group I would suggest P. A. Karpov, A. G. Aptekman, P. A. Shipilov, A. K. Alchevskii, and S. S. Mantsiarli.

[87] *Trudy, VII, 1882*, p. 173. So much for economic risk taking!

[88] "Gornozavodskoe delo," p. 10.

[89] *Trudy, XVI, 1891*, pt. 2, p. 87. He was rebuked by Alchevskii, who suggested that the association augment the depleted fund from its own resources before turning to others.

[90] For a late example of this, see *Trudy, XXXVII, 1912*, p. 35, discussion of a report of the Priadkin Commission on the labor shortage. After a comparatively fierce debate in which the split between liberals and conservatives, and the dominance of the latter in the association, emerges clearly, the problems are called "complex and difficult," and are referred to the

of much of the equipment in the mines, investment in the improvement of coal-cutting techniques through the use of electrical or compressed-air drills was virtually nonexistent. It is possible that failure to improve the professional skills of the work force, or to curb its migratory tendencies, made this strategy perhaps appear rational, but unwillingness to invest in technological improvement had been one of the four reasons cited by engineer Taskin for the lagging development of Donbass coal in a report to the Department of Mines in January 1877.[91] As one of the coal producers put it rather bluntly at the beginning of Donbass development, the South Russian coal industry could not enjoy full development until the mine owners "were convinced of the axiom that a commercial enterprise based on illusions can never bring positive results, and at the present time nothing can be achieved without expenditure of time and capital."[92] It is notable that although the metallurgical industry, established as a large-scale, capital-intensive undertaking, was thought to be as advanced in technology as, or even more advanced than European smelters, no such claims were made for the collieries of the Donbass.[93] It should also be noted that among the many administrative and technical bodies established by the association there was none that occupied itself with questions of technological innovation. Although the *Gornyi zhurnal* and the *Gorno-zavodskii listok* carried articles on technological problems, this can hardly be seen as a serious effort.

The final leader of the association, and the personification of its third generation, was a pure "organization man" and a product of the bureaucracy. N. F. von Ditmar first appeared at an association meeting in 1893, when he was listed simply as a mining engineer, without organizational affiliation. He was first listed as an office holder in 1898, when he was

---

Council of the Association for clarification. (The first debate on this subject was at the association's first meeting in 1874.)

[91] TsGIAL, F. 37, op. 5, d. 990, p. 7.

[92] Kavraiskii, "Rudnichnaia rel'sovaia otkatka," p. 188n.

[93] McKay, *Pioneers for Profit*, p. 135, writes: "In the first decade of the twentieth century, blast furnaces in South Russia were as large as in Europe, were newer, and used better ore. They therefore were competitive with European production." A caveat is sounded in CL, 11850, n. 214, "Briansk Aleksandrovsk Factory" (December 1898), p. 2, noting that "stoppages, accidents, and insufficient production materials" were the reasons that the blast furnaces, with a rated capacity of 780 tonnes per day, produced only 650–700 tonnes. In contrast, Arskii, *Donetskii Bassein*, p. 8, referring to the situation on the eve of World War I, claimed that Donbass mines were on a much lower technological level than German, English, or Belgian mines. For a comprehensive discussion of technological progress in the largest Donbass coal mines, see Brandt, *Inostrannye kapitaly*, vol. 2, chap. 3.

registered as head of the newly formed Statistical Bureau following the death of A. F. Mevius, who had until that year edited the statistics published by the association. Owner of a small machine-building factory in Kharkov, von Ditmar subsequently was elected as an association representative to the Council of the Mining Industry Inspectorate (1899), and from 1900 to 1906 was secretary of the annual meeting and held a series of other posts. In 1906 he joined Avdakov as a member of the tsar's state council, remaining active and influential through 1917.[94] Although his manner of speech marks him as a strong personality and an incisive analyst, von Ditmar cannot be said to have led the association in instituting new policies. He was the model chairman, maintaining consensus, capturing the sense of the meetings, and vigorously representing his constituents' points of view to the authorities.

The Association of Southern Coal and Steel Producers began as an ad hoc voluntary association. The budget for its first meeting in 1874 was 158 rubles, plus 97 rubles for the stenographer and petty cash. This was raised by voluntary subscription among the participants. It was not until the third meeting in Kharkov in 1878 that a decision was made to levy a tax on each wagonload of coal, salt, and iron shipped from the Donbass, to finance the association.[95] But the organization grew rapidly as it assimilated new areas of activity and institutionalized itself. By 1912 its expenditures had grown to three-quarters of a million rubles per year.[96]

The first institution established by the association (though it was formalized only in 1879) was the Freight Car Allotment Committee. It was born of the inadequate development of the railroads, and their reluctance to allot scarce freight cars to the haulage of low-value freight such as coal when there were higher-value cargoes to be had.[97] Despite the remarks of Islavin and others regarding speculation in scarce railway cars, the railways were the

[94] See the list of officers of the association, 1874–1906, in von Ditmar, *Kratkii ocherk*, pp. 2–10. This is evidently the same book listed by Rieber as P. I. Fomin, *Istoriia s"ezdov gornopromyshlennikov iuga Rossii*. In the edition I consulted in the Helsinki library, von Ditmar is listed as editor and Fomin as compiler (*sostavitel'*). Potolov also lists Fomin as author, but gives the title as I have given it.

[95] Von Ditmar, *Kratkii ocherk*, p. 17. The growth of the budget and the main items of expenditure to 1905, when it totaled 340,390.52 rubles, can be found on pp. 20–21.

[96] *Trudy, XXXVII, 1912*, chairman's report, p. xix. Income for the year was 942,014.80 rubles.

[97] Von Ditmar, *Kratkii ocherk*, p. 160, quotes an official of the Kursk-Kharkov-Azov Railway as saying that coal was something "to be hauled when there is nothing else to do."

main problem here; not only was coal low on their list of priorities, but when they did haul coal, they gave preference to their own needs, neglecting other Donbass customers.[98]

In October 1888 the committee took on an independent life when the association acceded to a government request to budget seven hundred rubles per month for office expenses.[99] This allocation was commuted in 1899 into a portion of the per-wagon tax levied by the association.[100] The establishment of a budget, important as it was to the bureaucratic life of the committee, gave it only internal vitality. From its inception, the committee had been classed as a temporary body, renewed periodically at the pleasure of the Council of Ministers. Only in 1905, when the need for such a committee was essentially a thing of the past, did a government decision extend sine die the existence of the Freight Car Allotment Committee.[101]

The second meeting of the association, in 1877, elected five plenipotentiaries (*upolnomochennye*), whose duty it was to present the association's decisions to the authorities and to the general public. Each of these three officials received an honorarium of one thousand rubles annually. At the following meeting, a second executive body was created in the form of an eight-member Committee of Delegates (*vybornye*). This group was to act as a full executive, preparing the agenda for the annual meetings, seeing to the implementation of association decisions, and coordinating with such bodies as the Freight Car Allotment Committee. The chairman of this committee was paid 4,500 rubles a year.[102]

This eventually led to the creation in 1892 of a permanent working executive, the Council of the Association, with a full-time office, and a

[98] See *Trudy, XIII, 1888*, p. 39, for the association resolution warning the railways against building up their own coal reserves at the expense of deliveries to other consumers. See also the discussion of an order by the Ministry of Railways to its representatives on the Freight-Car Allotment Committee, ordering them to consign 85 percent of all available coal cars to the haulage of coal for the railways, in von Ditmar, *Kratkii ocherk*, p. 165. See Rieber, *Merchants and Entrepreneurs*, pp. 238–39, for a discussion of the complex and petty interministerial and interentrepreneurial jealousies that beset the development of railway construction and operation in the 1870s and 1880s.

[99] Von Ditmar, *Kratkii ocherk*, pp. 165–66.

[100] CL, 11852, n. 1607, "Special General Costs of a Colliery in Russia" (January 1903), p. 8. See also von Ditmar, *Kratkii ocherk*, p. 170, where the maximum to be levied for the committee is set at .07 kopeks per pud.

[101] Von Ditmar, *Kratkii ocherk*, p. 169.

[102] For the amounts paid to the various officials, see *Trudy, XII, 1887*, chairman's report, p. xli.

budget of 1,500 rubles for furnishings and 5,600 rubles for salaries and costs for 1893. In addition to the chairman of the council, who was to be a full-time salaried official, all elected officeholders in the association were to be members of the council, which was to meet in plenary session at least once monthly.[103] The chairman of the council thus became, in effect, the leader of the association, commanding its economic and organizational resources. Avdakov, who until the formation of the council had been listed first among the plenipotentiaries, was chairman of the council until 1906, when he was succeeded by von Ditmar.[104]

Throughout its life, the association continued to create new bodies. In 1884, the Compensation Fund was formed, and though it covered a limited part of the work force, it commanded growing sums of money and was the focus of heated debate about administrative procedure and compensation policy.[105] A mutual-aid association that later gave rise to the Mining and Metallurgy Bank, a fire insurance program, mutual insurance against mass disasters, and a coal and metal bourse in Kharkov were among the more important institutions spawned by the association. The *Gorno-zavodskii listok*, which had existed independently (though enjoying some financial support from the association), was taken over by it in 1903, becoming the official publication of the council.[106] Though Prodameta and Produgol', the metal- and coal-marketing cartels, were not formally part of the association, it was their spiritual home. The contacts for their creation were first made at the annual congress of the association.

From the association's inception, planning of production capacities, marketing quotas, and transport possibilities were the focus of its activities. Although it had no authority to impose or enforce quotas on any producer,

[103] See the proposal of A. F. Mevius in *Trudy, XVII, 1892*, chairman's report, pp. lxiii–lxiv.

[104] In von Ditmar, *Kratkii ocherk*, pp. 3–10, the members of various committees are evidently listed by a ranking, perhaps the number of votes cast for them, rather than by alphabetical order. These tables offer clear evidence of the institutional growth of the association as new executive, honorary, and supervisory bodies were formed. True to bureaucratic organizational theory, none of these bodies ever seems to have been disbanded.

[105] In 1892, when the association wanted to borrow money from the Compensation Fund to meet emergency needs in fighting the cholera epidemic, doubtful practices in the holding of the fund by the association's own credit bank caused heated debate. In 1896, it was revealed that the association was holding and using funds paid by the railways and the industrialists for the Compensation Fund and for the Freight Car Allotment Committee, but was not paying interest on these funds. See *Trudy, XXI, 1896*, pt. 2, pp. 151–57.

[106] Von Ditmar, *Kratkii ocherk*, p. 12.

the association did attempt annually to anticipate the amount of coal or metal each enterprise would produce and ship, and the railway traffic that would be generated by that production. An examination of the planned and actual quantities for coal in 1880–98 shows clearly the gradual professionalization of these estimates. In the early years, the plan figures represent nothing more than wishful thinking, for the actual quantities of coal shipped amount to 43 to 63 percent of the plan. From 1885 to 1890, performance improved and the actual quantities ranged between 69 and 87 percent of the projections. From 1891 to 1898 the maximum error was 5 percent, as plan and actuality come close to meeting.[107] Nevertheless, the individual producers were reluctant to act in concert to restrain their growth, even in the face of impending recession, and the association did not appear to have any effective means of remedying this situation. Toward the end of 1900, when industrial activity was already slowing down, the representatives of the metallurgy industry informed the minister of state domains and agriculture that the planned increase in production would be "only" to 96 million puds and not 106 million as originally planned, a modest increase in the vicinity of 6 percent. At the same time, the planned increase in coal production was 25 percent over the previous year.[108]

The emergence of the Statistical Bureau under von Ditmar was of some importance. The association as a whole, and particularly A. F. Mevius, had previously published a great deal of statistical material, but under the leadership of von Ditmar the Statistical Bureau began to play a role similar to that played by zemstvo statisticians in rural Russia at the time. The questionnaires distributed by the bureau to mine and factory owners in the Donbass contained thirty pages of questions regarding all aspects of the life and work of the Donbass labor force, including food prices, housing conditions, work methods, and pay rates.[109] Much of the Statistical Bureau's

[107] Calculation of the percentages is from the tables in Taskin, "K voprosu o privlechenii i uderzhanii rabochikh," no. 9, p. 3778.

[108] *Trudy, XXV, 1900*, chairman's report, p. v; report of the Statistical Bureau, p. 2. Going into 1901, the New Russia Co. trimmed its sails, closing down two blast furnaces and planning for only two-thirds of capacity production. Ibid., report on the development of the iron industry, pp. 18–19. In *Trudy, XX, 1895*, p. 501, we find a similar phenomenon, with Avdakov complaining that overproduction was driving down prices, at the same time that an increase in production was planned.

[109] The questionnaire is discussed in *Trudy, XXIV, 1899*, pp. 156–86. The Statistical Bureau was subordinate to the Council of the Association. The records of the bureau, insofar as they have survived through the years, are in Fond 616 of the Kharkov Oblast' State Archive, where Potolov made some use of them.

research was published as individual booklets (with von Ditmar listed as author or editor), and each volume of the *Trudy* of the association contains masses of information, particularly on production and transport. The work of the bureau thus provided the raw material for supporters and critics alike for the lively polemics printed in the weighty journals of the time concerning the social and economic effects of industrialization.

Participation in the annual meetings of the association was not the same thing as membership. From the first meeting, interested bodies ranging from the steamship companies and railroads serving the area to representatives of various ministries, the zemstvo organizations, and the municipal administrations of the cities surrounding the Donbass participated. The annual meetings thus served as a forum for the coordination of various state and private interests under the watchful eye of a prominent government representative.

Useful as a forum for accommodation though the meetings might have been, the participation of what was essentially a marginal public did not meet the industrialists' needs. The association was intended to be the lobby for the coal and metal producers. In 1883, at the eighth meeting, a proposal was made that membership should be limited to dues-paying producers, that only members should have a vote in association elections or in matters of a financial and organizational nature, and that voting rights should be restricted to those shipping at least 250 carloads per year. This provoked "prolonged and heated discussions," and was not at first greeted favorably by the authorities, but after four years, government approval was given and the ruling was adopted. At the 1898 meeting the split between large and small producers opened once more, as voting rights were made proportional to the size of the enterprise. Those shipping over 4,000 carloads annually were to have three votes, those shipping from 1,000 to 3,999 would have two votes, and those shipping between 250 and 999 would enjoy only a single vote.[110] In his exposition of this development, von Ditmar emphasized that neither by personal vote nor by proxy could anyone command more than three votes. His somewhat self-righteous declaration reveals the unwilling compromise accepted by the large firms, who had demanded five votes, but had settled for only three.[111]

[110] Von Ditmar, *Kratkii ocherk*, p. 16.

[111] The same matter arose in connection with the executive council of the Compensation Fund in 1900, where once again the large firms demanded five votes, but were rebuffed. See *Trudy, XV, 1900*, pt. 2, pp. 264–69.

The data offered in the records of the association indicates that the above regulations had, over the years, a varying impact on participation in its policy-making decisions. In 1892, only 74 of the 237 listed coal shippers passed the minimum of 250 carloads.[112] Seventy percent of those involved in the coal business were excluded. In 1899, of 192 producers listed, only 94 were noted as having shipped less than the minimum of 250 carloads, another 48 were between 250 and 1,000, and the remaining 50 had multiple votes.[113] Thus half of the shippers were at this time voting members of the association. In 1906, despite five years of commercial and political crisis, and a trend toward concentration of production in the hands of the largest firms, there were 284 shippers listed. Of these, about forty shipped 4,000 carloads each, qualifying for three votes in the annual meetings, while another seventy or so shipped between 250 and 4,000 carloads, qualifying for one or two votes. The remaining shippers, 60 percent of the total, were excluded from membership and voting rights, though they were permitted to attend the annual meetings.[114]

As a result of the policy of restricting voting rights while encouraging a great variety of groups and individuals to participate in the meetings of the association, only 55 of the 313 persons attending the 1907 meeting are said to have enjoyed a voice in its decisions.[115] In 1914, there were 407 attending the association meeting, of whom 82 represented various government departments, zemstvos, railways, bourse committees, and so forth. Among the remaining participants, only 244 are listed as coal shippers or their representatives. Of the firms represented, only 103 had voting rights in the affairs of the association.[116] As the years passed, the weight of the larger

[112] *Trudy, XVII, 1892*, pp. 358–64. When the emergency meeting to fight cholera was called in July 1892, only eighteen of the largest coal and metal producers attended. The special meeting convened to vote the necessary funds for the program worked out by the eighteen magnates had only thirty members attending. In times of crisis the circle of power narrowed.

[113] In *Trudy, XXIV, 1899*, pp. 14 and 34–40, there are two different lists. I have attempted to combine and reconcile them to produce this analysis.

[114] The calculations are from *Gorno-zavodskii listok*, nos. 23–24 (1906), supp. These figures are in place of the usual publication in *Trudy*, since no annual meeting took place in 1905. It is significant that despite the unsettled economic and political conditions, the growth of the coal industry permitted a large number of peripheral entrepreneurs to enter the field.

[115] Rieber, *Merchants and Entrepreneurs*, p. 233. For the 1906 decision restricting the franchise and making the number of delegates of each enterprise proportional to dues paid (based on production), see von Ditmar, *Kratkii ocherk*, p. 16.

[116] *Trudy, XXXVIII, 1914*, vol. 1, pp. 42–46. Of those voting, seventy-five had three votes, four had two votes, and twenty-four had one vote.

companies in the voting became increasingly decisive. If in the early years the small shippers, with the help of only a few of the medium-sized firms, could control a majority of votes, by 1914 the 75 three-vote firms enjoyed overwhelming control of the 257 total votes in the association.

With the development of the Donbass, new elements were drawn into the discussions of the Association of Southern Coal and Steel Producers. By 1902 there were representatives of sixteen metal-working firms, half of which appear to have been family firms rather than large shareholding companies. Virtually all of them were local firms, only two having directors with Western European names.[117] This was a second wave of industry, working for the internal market that was then beginning to take on significant dimensions. As customers for metal and coal, they were welcomed by the association, winning its support for a resolution asking the government to grant tariff protection against the import of machines. The vote was thirty-three in favor, none against, with six abstentions. Only one of the machine-manufacturing representatives expressed reservations regarding the tariff, suggesting that his colleagues had made insufficient efforts to penetrate the market, and that entrepreneurs should be prepared to suffer some losses while the new branch of industry won its place.[118]

Only in 1904 did representatives of financial institutions begin to take their place in the association meetings, and it was not until 1910 that a more substantial representation of the central financial institutions of Russia was seen.[119] This change took place at the height of the trend to replace foreign capital by Russian capital in the enterprises of the Donbass.[120]

Though the Association of Southern Coal and Steel Producers met numerous needs, its most visible function was to lobby the authorities on behalf of its members. In this the association was tireless, and at times ingenious. Its spokesmen stood forth as pious ecologists, urging the government to ban the use of wood as fuel on the railroads, lest Russia's precious patrimony, her forests, be exhausted. At the same time, they preached economics, urging that oil be refined into high-value, exportable,

[117] See the list of names in *Trudy, XXIX, 1904*, p. 16. Fourteen have Russian or Jewish names, one is French, and one is Italian.

[118] *Trudy, Ekstrennyi s"ezd, 1902*, protocol of sixth session, pp. 35–41.

[119] *Trudy, XXIX, 1904*, p. 16, lists Lev Manuilovich Landsberg, from the Kharkov branch of the St. Petersburg International Commercial Bank, and Maksim I. Meier, director of the Kharkov branch of the Northern Bank, as participants.

[120] Kondufor, *Istoriia rabochikh Donbassa*, vol. 1, p. 73, also writes that the active involvement of the banks in Donbass industry dated from 1910.

finished products rather than being squandered as cheap fuel for the domestic market.[121] Their major achievement, as Rieber pointed out, was the tariff on foreign coal, and somewhat later, the tariff on imported pig iron.[122]

The government, however, was not always amenable to these pressures and exhortations. At times, the tariff could even be used as a two-edged sword. When I. S. Kannegisser, director of the Nikolaev machine-building factory, presented his report on the state of machine building as an infant industry, he noted the government's refusal to grant a request for tariffs.[123] The manufacturers were being pressured to reduce their prices. The supply of coal from abroad was remarkably sensitive to every change in tariffs. The tariffs of the 1880s had virtually eliminated the import of British coal through the southern ports. Yet when there was a shortage of coal at the beginning of 1900, the tariff was lifted and immediately coal imports rose to pre-tariff levels. Whenever the association seemed inclined to debate a real or artificially created coal crisis, the government's first response was the lifting of the protective tariff.[124] Count Witte, though protective of the Donbass industries, was forever urging them to modernize and to lower prices, and was willing to pressure them through his control of taxes and tariffs. In other matters, too, the government ignored the association's pressures, particularly when it was suspected of avoiding responsibilities or shifting expenses to the state. Such was the case of the hiring offices proposed by engineer Batalin. The authorities' approval of the project deftly shifted the full financial and organizational burden back to the industrialists, leaving only contact with the peasants under state control. The result was that although the hiring offices were to have opened in February 1897, von Ditmar could write in 1908 that "the mining industrialists did not, in fact, make use of these offices because of the inconvenience of hiring workers in their home village, as it entails disbursement of advances that were frequently not returned."[125]

[121] See the report by Vainer in *Trudy, XII, 1887*, p. 312. Naturally, Vainer suggested coal as an excellent substitute for both wood and oil.

[122] Rieber, *Merchants and Entrepreneurs*, pp. 236–37. See also Fomin, *Gornaia i gornozavodskaia promyshlennost'*, vol. 1, p. 440, and *Trudy, VII, 1882*, chairman's report, pp. xii–xiii, for the association's resolutions regarding the coal tariff.

[123] *Trudy, Ekstrennyi s"ezd, 1902*, protocol of sixth session, pp. 35–41.

[124] See *Trudy, XVIII, 1893*, pt. 2, pp. 73–76; Avdakov's report on the ability of the Donbass to supply coal to northwestern Russia in *Trudy, XXIX, 1904*, p. 64; and *Gornozavodskii listok*, no. 29 (1906), p. 8619.

[125] Von Ditmar, *Kratkii ocherk*, p. 31.

Indeed, there were times when the government used the association as an instrument of policy making, pushing it to prepare draft legislation, and if the industrialists proved reluctant, ramming through its own proposals. This was the case with the workers' accident compensation law, discussed in some detail in volume 1. Another, slightly different case came up when the minister of state domains and agriculture, in conjunction with the minister of finance, requested that the association discuss the granting of rebates on imported coal to metallurgy firms exporting their products. The question had been raised by the old Kerch smelter, revived in the boom of the 1890s, but suffering in the recession. Badly situated for using Donbass coal, it could profit from cheap English coal if the tariffs were removed, and was well placed for exporting its product to the Balkans and the Levant. The proposal sowed panic in the ranks of the coal producers. To refuse would be neither efficacious nor politic, yet to accede would be like breaching the tariff dike with their own hands. After considerable debate on how to approach the question, a two-point resolution was passed without discussion. It read: "(1) Recognizing the great importance of developing exports, the commission accepts as desirable all measures that the government wishes to inaugurate for support of metal exports, and which do not harm the coal industry. (2) The commission considers it necessary to petition the government to abolish the kopek port excise on exported iron." Avdakov commented: "Brief, and to the point!"[126]

The association also represented the industrialists as a group in their relations with other institutions. In most cases there was a measure of accommodation and cooperation, but with the railways and even more acutely with the zemstvo, association relations bore the stamp of protracted conflict.

The subject and acuity of the conflict with the railways varied over the years. In the beginning, the conflict was over rolling stock; this was succeeded by the question of priority for coal cargoes. Later there was also the problem of setting the price of coal sold to the railways, involving the railways' standards of grading the coal according to its mineral content, caloric value, and so forth. However, the most complex and long-lived dispute with the railways was over haulage rates. At the same time there was dissension within the ranks of the coal producers as the question of

[126] *Trudy, Ekstrennyi s"ezd, 1902*. For the government's request, see the letter of engineer Ioss, director of the Department of Mines in the Ministry of State Domains and Agriculture, p. 5. For the report of the discussion and resolution, see the chairman's report, pp. xxi–xxii. For another such case, see *Trudy, XVIII, 1893*, p. 34.

differences in the rates was debated for haulage from the western Donbass (bituminous coal) and the southeastern portion of the region (anthracite). Here the question of voting rights proportional to production came into play, since the mines in the anthracite region were generally much smaller than the bituminous mines. Virtually every annual meeting saw feverish debate over the strategy to be adopted regarding the most recent twist in the rate wars.[127]

Conflict with the Zemstvo

The most protracted, as well as the most intensely political, conflict involving the association was, however, its running battle with the zemstvo. This was also the one dispute in which the industrialists received virtually no satisfaction, either from their opponents or from the central authorities. Essentially this was a struggle between the traditional, entrenched, landed elite of Ekaterinoslav province, based in the northwestern, predominantly agricultural part of the region, and the new industrial elite growing up in the Donbass. This was only part of a similar struggle taking place within Russia as a whole.[128] The rivalry between the landed and the industrial gentry was, in turn, only one battle in the war between conservatism and reform that was being waged in Russian society.

The zemstvo in the Donbass encompassed a no less varied and contradictory group than did the association. It would be difficult to say that one was more reform-minded or more conservative than the other. The two institutions did, however, represent different ways of life and conflicting economic interests. The zemstvo elite derived its wealth and social position from land, which was held through inheritance and seen as the cornerstone of social and political stability. The parvenu industrialists were disturbing this tranquillity, introducing new social and economic values as well as the perceived dangers of a migrant industrial proletariat. Within this context,

[127] The entire question is treated in considerable detail in von Ditmar, *Kratkii ocherk*, pp. 97–124.

[128] For a broad discussion of this struggle for political and economic influence, see Manning, *Crisis of the Old Order*. Owen, *Capitalism and Politics in Russia*, pp. 95–101, discusses this conflict in Moscow. Despite the similarities, the zemstvo-industrial dispute in the Donbass was more focused on the economic aspects of power, with less of the conservative vs. liberal overtones that were prominent in the Moscow dispute and elsewhere.

and despite its devotion to education, health, and agricultural development, the zemstvo represented conservative tradition.

The district zemstvos in particular had a reputation for conservatism, and this reputation appears well deserved in the cases of the Bakhmut and Slavianoserbsk district officials.[129] In Slavianoserbsk district, the local zemstvo executive was accused of discriminating against the "village intelligentsia" after it denied representation to its paramedical employees (*fel'dshers*) in the county medical council. In another case, unfavorable newspaper comments about the speeches of local teachers attending a pedagogical conference in Moscow led to the pensioning off of eight teachers, and the resignation of eight others in protest.[130] In the wake of the 1905 revolution, the Bakhmut district zemstvo began discharging any of its employees who had joined a political party.[131]

The heart of the dispute between the zemstvo and the industrialists was taxation. Disputes over representation and services arose out of the failure to resolve this conflict. At the second meeting of the association, a governmental commission raised the question of the taxes to be paid by industry to the local zemstvo. The association agreed to consider the subject, but asked five years' grace for discussions and linked the resolution of the tax problem to the granting of import tariffs that would eliminate the threat of competition from foreign coal.[132] At the end of the five-year period, the association suggested that its plenipotentiaries meet with the zemstvo executive councils to determine a system of taxation, suggesting that one of three criteria be adopted as the basis for taxing industrial properties. Mines could be taxed in accordance with their rated capacities for bringing coal to the surface. Alternatively, industrial properties could be taxed with their value being determined on the same basis as real property in the rest of the district. A third idea was that the taxes be proportional to the royalties per pud paid by those mining rented land.[133] A different suggestion was offered by Hume of the New Russia Co., who, together with John Hughes, Jr., attended the meetings that year. Hume suggested that no universal crite-

[129] Manning, *Crisis of the Old Order*, p. 53, writes of the suspicion with which the *uezdniki* regarded the activities of their technical personnel. This sometimes led to the curtailment of medical and educational programs.

[130] *Revoliutsionnaia Rossiia*, no. 28 (1903), p. 18, and no. 32 (1903), p. 10. The paper comments on the conservative domination in the district executive.

[131] *Russkie vedomosti*, no. 253 (October 10, 1906), p. 4.

[132] Von Ditmar, *Kratkii ocherk*, p. 48.

[133] *Trudy, VII, 1882*, chairman's report, p. xxix.

rion of assessment be adopted, but that a zemstvo tax-assessment commission be formed, and with the participation of representatives of the industrialists, that the commission visit and assess each individual enterprise, weighing its profitability by taking into consideration such factors as the capital investment in the enterprise and its distance from the railroad or from water transport.[134]

Hume's proposal received no attention in the industrialists' deliberations. They appeared to rely on the advantages embodied in their preferred suggestions. If assessment by coal-raising capacity were to be adopted, the coal producers could rely on the assessment being considerably out of date, and with the rapid growth of the mines, a good part of their production would probably escape taxation. The same was true of assessing the properties in proportion to the royalties paid for rents. The rental agreements were revised only with lease renewals. Those coal producers who got in on the ground floor made more profit, for prices and royalties were rising steeply as the coal boom grew. If property should be the basis of tax, and the assessment of values made on the same basis as that for the rest of the property in the district, this would again result in an advantage for the industrialists, for the coal and metallurgy properties were far more productive than were agricultural properties. It is therefore not surprising that the zemstvo representatives did not agree to any of the three proposals. Instead, the Bakhmut executive board decided to tax the mines on the basis of an assessment of five kopeks per pud of production, while the Slavianoserbsk board put its assessment on the estimated value of the buildings and equipment of the mining industry, and not on the land alone.[135]

At this point the atmosphere was still friendly, but the problems were unresolved and dissatisfaction grew steadily. By 1896 Alchevskii openly stated that the district authorities were one-sidedly serving the interests of landowners and agriculture and that the industrialists were, in effect, shut out of the zemstvo decision-making process.[136] The dispute had been exacerbated because during the intervening years, the New Russia factory

[134] *Trudy, VII, 1882*, pp. 210–11.

[135] Von Ditmar, *Kratkii ocherk*, p. 49. With the development of metallurgy at the end of the 1880s, taxation of factories in the Bakhmut district was also based on an assessment of the value of buildings and equipment.

[136] *Trudy, XXI, 1896*, pp. 132–33. See a later development of this in *Zemstvo i gornaia promyshlennost'*, particularly p. 3.

had been assessed for tax purposes at a value of two million rubles, while the entire settlement of Iuzovka had been evaluated at only six hundred thousand rubles. The Hughes brothers had complained to the governor, who had ordered the assessment cut to one million rubles.[137] Despite general agreement among the industrialists that the zemstvo taxes were unfair, the majority of the association's members had opted for an attempt at conciliation, and sent P. A. Karpov at the head of a committee to attend the sessions of the district executive board and convince it to lower the assessment on coal production. At the same time the association noted that if, after the discussions, it still felt the assessment procedures were unfair, it could lodge an appeal with the authorities. When Karpov returned to the association to report, it turned out that for some unexplained reason he and his committee had not been included in the zemstvo assessment meetings. Karpov suggested that they try again the following year.[138]

By the end of the 1890s the zemstvo was feeling secure in its tax policies. Factories and coal mines in Bakhmut district were paying 56 percent of the district's taxes, and salt mines added another 14.5 percent. Each pud of the rapidly growing coal and iron production poured new money into the zemstvo coffers. The New Russia assessment, including both factory and mines, was now 11,765,000 rubles, one-fifth of the entire tax assessment value of Bakhmut district.[139]

The association as a corporate body, and its larger members as individual petitioners, appealed to the government, pointing out that high tax assessments on such assets as workers' housing discouraged entrepreneurs from providing their workers with the amenities demanded by government regulation. They also noted that land assessments of fifteen rubles per desiatina had been set in the early 1860s, and had not been changed since, though the

[137] See P. A. Karpov's comments in *Trudy, XIX, 1894*, pt. 2, p. 58. In *Trudy, XX, 1895*, p. 455, L. G. Rabinovich reports that the New Russia factory was assessed at 1.5 million rubles while the entire town of Bakhmut (population 16,000), with all its commercial, industrial, and residential properties, was assessed at only 900,000 rubles.

[138] See *Trudy, XXI, 1896*, pp. 132–33, for Alchevskii's remarks and the conciliatory approach of the association, and p. 501 for Karpov's failure to attend the assessment session. Apparently Ivan Alexandrovich Karpov, who at this time was chairman of the Bakhmut uezd zemstvo executive, was his brother. Similarly, N. V. Rutchenko, chairman of the Bakhmut district executive in 1912, and editor of the *Bakhmutskaia Narodnaia gazeta*, was the brother of A. V. Rutchenko of the Rutchenko Coal Co.

[139] *Trudy, XXIV, 1899*, pp. 52–53. The remaining 820,000 *desiatina* of land (approximately 2.7 acres) in the uezd was assessed at 14.25 million rubles.

coal boom had sent land values skyrocketing throughout the Donbass.[140] The New Russia Co. also had its chief legal consultant, Glazunov, prepare an eventually successful brief to the Imperial Senate, appealing against the high tax assessment of its properties.[141] The Donbass coal producers were thus relieved of what amounted to an income tax on their rapidly growing coal production.[142]

Meanwhile, the association had shifted the center of its attack on the zemstvo from the economic front to the political. Increasingly mistrustful of the integrity of the dominant landed elite, the association demanded representation in the district and province assemblies commensurate with industry's economic contribution, thinking to capture control of these bodies and thus of the tax assessments.[143] The response of the government was cool, though it stopped short of a total denial of the association's appeal. The government agreed that the importance of the mining and metallurgy industries justified an increase in the industrialists' representation within the second curia of the zemstvo, and suggested that they negotiate this with the minister of the interior. At the same time, it was pointed out that the existing law provided for representation of the industrialists in zemstvo institutions, and denied the need for any radical structural reforms to meet the association's demands.[144] In fact, nothing of any substance was achieved, and in 1904 the association was still grumbling about taxation without due representation, as von Ditmar explained to the session that the Bakhmut district zemstvo was then made up of twenty nobles, ten peasants, and only six representatives of the second curia, while in Slavianoserbsk the representation was seventeen, nine, and four, respectively.[145] Meanwhile, the share of taxes paid by mining, manufacturing, and com-

[140] Ibid., report on current state of evaluation for zemstvo tax purposes, pp. 6–8, 11. S. E. Zimovskii's appeal on behalf of the New Russia Co. against high assessments of the Krivoi Rog iron mines noted that the Slavianoserbsk district zemstvo, in contrast to the authorities in Verkhnodneprovsk, did not tax structures used for workers' housing.

[141] *Trudy, XXV, 1900*. See von Ditmar's report on zemstvo taxes, pp. 11–13.

[142] Rieber, *Merchants and Entrepreneurs*, p. 313, notes as general throughout Russia this tendency to shift the tax burden from land to industry by use of a graduated income tax. He also points out that it was part of an economic policy that struck at the vital interests of the entrepreneurs.

[143] See the letter to the minister of state domains and agriculture in *Trudy, XXIV, 1899*, p. 55.

[144] The government response is printed in ibid., p. 10.

[145] *Trudy, XXIX, 1904*, p. 23. The second curia was for representatives of municipalities; charitable, scientific, and other societies; and representatives of trade and industry.

merce in Bakhmut district had grown from 56 percent in 1896 to 83 percent in 1904, while the landowners' share had dropped from 25 percent to 9.84 percent.[146] Thirty years of pleading, protest, and politicking had produced no change in the power structure of imperial Russia.

While questions of taxation and representation were the central conflicts between the association and the zemstvo, there was a second dispute that was no less important to the development of society in the Donbass. This was the dispute over provision of services to the mining and factory settlements, particularly the provision of health and education services. The zemstvo was eager to exercise sovereignty over these areas of activity by setting of standards and conducting inspections, but was totally unwilling to fund the schools and hospitals. The industrialists on their part were unwilling to recognize the authority of the zemstvo unless it was ready to accept the financial responsibilities that went with the right of supervision.[147] At the same time, the industrialists consistently rejected the validity of the law that laid responsibility for workers' medical care on their shoulders.[148]

The pattern for industry-zemstvo relations had been set in the early 1880s when the association had petitioned the local authorities regarding the construction of access roads from coal mines to the existing rail stations. The negotiation of access agreements with a multiplicity of landowners and village associations was both time-consuming and expensive for the mine owners, and they suggested that the zemstvo exercise its right to expropriate lands for public use.[149] Five years of appeals produced virtually no results.

[146] Ibid., p. 20. The tax income of the district had meanwhile grown from 148,615 rubles in 1896 to 638,301 in 1904.

[147] See the lengthy report and argument of von Ditmar, replete with expert opinions, rejecting zemstvo regulation of medical and sanitary conditions in the mine and factory settlements in ibid., report on relations of mine industry enterprises of South Russia with the zemstvo, pp. 1–45.

[148] See the sharply emphasized statement by von Ditmar, "Neschastnye sluchai," p. 517. See also Liberman, *V ugol'nom tsarstve*, pp. 102–3, citing the association's appeal to the Ministry of Trade and Industry in 1915 to relieve the employers of responsibility for workers' medical care for the duration of the war, claiming that in fact it was the responsibiity of the zemstvo.

[149] *Trudy, XII, 1887*, pp. 117–18. Even at a considerably later date there is no reflection in the zemstvo publications of an interest in developing the mines and factories. In the gazetteer of the Ekaterinoslav provincial zemstvo between 1903 and 1905, virtually the only notice given to industry is the weekly listing of prices in the Kharkov coal and iron exchange. The *Bakhmutskaia Narodnaia gazeta* for 1914–15 is enthusiastic about agricultural develop-

In 1900, von Ditmar reported to the association that of twelve industrial and mining enterprises surveyed in Bakhmut district, only two had any zemstvo facilities near them: a hospital and school in the village of Grishino, and a zemstvo hospital in Grigorevka. For the use of the latter, the Annenskii mine paid the zemstvo sixteen hundred rubles yearly, in addition to paying substantial taxes on its property and production.[150] The Grigorevka subdistrict of Bakhmut included Iuzovka geographically, though not administratively. In 1908, the zemstvo maintained one doctor there, along with four paramedics and one midwife.[151] As noted in the discussion of Iuzovka's health services in volume 1, the medical staff maintained by the New Russia Co. was far larger. In 1898, factory workers were only .6 percent of all those who visited zemstvo doctors in Ekaterinoslav province, attesting to the virtually complete separation that existed between the independent industrial medical system and that of the local authorities.[152] The confrontation of interests and the consequent ill feelings were not limited to the industrialists and the zemstvo authorities. They penetrated the doctors' ranks as well. A reading of the proceedings of the two meetings of factory doctors that I have frequently cited reflects the tensions between the two sets of medical workers. Fialkovskii, a zemstvo doctor, accused the industrialists of ignoring the rightful demands voiced by the workers for better living conditions "four years ago" (i.e., in 1905), and rejecting all efforts toward accommodation and logical persuasion in solving the problems of personal and public health. At the same time, he implied that the factory doctors did not have the same social consciences as their zemstvo colleagues, and that therefore only state compulsion could bring about the changes so badly needed in the Donbass.[153]

Although universal primary education was adopted in 1899, and was to be applied immediately throughout the Bakhmut and Slavianoserbsk districts, it was reported that none of the new schools planned for construction

ment, but carries no news about mines and factories. The weekly question-and-answer column is mainly concerned with land rights.

[150] *Trudy, XXV, 1900*, pp. 20–23. Since there were certainly more than twelve industrial and mining settlements in the district at that time, it would appear that von Ditmar is making a somewhat selective presentation of the problem. Nevertheless, the general picture that he offers appears accurate.

[151] *Vrachebno-sanitarnaia khronika Ekaterinoslavskoi gubernii*, no. 3 (1909), app., p. 5.

[152] Kurkin, *Zemskaia sanitarnaia statistika*, p. 3.

[153] Fialkovskii, "Uchastie zemstva," pp. 511–12. Fialkovskii was at that time the chief public health officer of Bakhmut district.

by the zemstvo was to be located in a mine or factory settlement.[154] The relationship of the industrialists to the zemstvo was an open matter in all circles of Russian society. In the Social-Democratic newspaper, *Iskra*, a correspondent commented that "Iuzovka, standing on the land of the New Russia Co. stands also, as it were, outside the zemstvo."[155] This relationship persisted throughout the years, and the management of the New Russia Co. lost no opportunity to raise the question of zemstvo responsibilities. While fighting off a petition by part of the settlement's population for municipal self-government in 1913, the company brief made the point that since in that year Iuzovka would pay close to half a million rubles in zemstvo levies, it would only be fitting if the zemstvo were to take some measures for the welfare of Iuzovka—investment in the water-supply system that was such a chronic problem, for instance. In the opinion of the factory management this would do at least as much to improve the settlement as would any municipal self-government.[156]

The Bakhmut district zemstvo was only minimally forthcoming with assistance for Iuzovka. Its assembly was presented with a proposal for a program of control of infectious diseases in Iuzovka, but it deferred discussion. At the same session it refused to decide the question of recognizing the Iuzovka public health officer as an employee of the zemstvo.[157] An itemized review of Bakhmut zemstvo activities in mid-1904 made no mention of any educational or health expenditures in Iuzovka.[158] The isolation of the mine and factory settlements from zemstvo resources did not cease even in crisis conditions. In August 1907 the Bakhmut district zemstvo executive ordered that a sanitary commission be formed to work out anticholera measures. Of the twelve members of the commission, all were connected to the mines and factories, with the exception of a single representative of the local police. None represented the zemstvo. There was no unity for mobilizing the forces available in the district to fight the expected epidemic.[159]

[154] *Trudy, XXIV, 1899*, p. 53.

[155] *Iskra*, no. 79 (December 1, 1904), p. 10.

[156] DOGIA, F. 6, op. 1, d. 7, p. 1. Brief of the New Russia Co. against municipal self-government, 1913. In fact, the first zemstvo institution in Iuzovka, a typhus isolation barracks and hospital, dates from this time.

[157] *Vestnik Ekaterinoslavskogo zemstva*, nos. 10–11 (1903), p. 39. In 1913, the New Russia Co. was still paying the public health officer's salary of thirty-six hundred rubles per year. DOGIA, F. 6, op. 1, d. 7, p. 1.

[158] *Vestnik Ekaterinoslavskogo zemstva*, no. 17 (1904), pp. 514ff.

[159] Retivov, "Organizatsiia protivokholernykh meropriiatii," p. 68.

Even when some budgetary allotments were made, they were not always used. In 1914 the zemstvo had budgeted 3,750 rubles for upkeep and equipment of the vocational school in Iuzovka. None of this had been spent by the time the war broke out, and the zemstvo assembly voted that this money, along with other unspent funds totaling 86,643.18 rubles, be donated to the war effort.[160]

The mutual distrust and dislike of the industrialists and the zemstvo authorities at times harmed the interests of both. I have mentioned the growth of the iron-working industry and the growing presence of industry representatives in the association after the turn of the century. The zemstvo had a strong interest in the development of a good supply of low-priced, locally produced agricultural machines for the benefit of agriculture. For their part, the producers were desperately seeking to encourage the growth of local demand for their products. Yet when the discussion of development strategy went beyond the basics of tariff protection, it turned out that the manufacturers were not willing to use the zemstvo as a marketing agent. They were reluctant to extend to the zemstvo the necessary line of credit since they did not believe that they would receive full or timely payment for the goods they would supply.[161]

The landed elite was thus largely successful in keeping the industrialists from translating the wealth created by their mines and factories into institutionalized political power that might have worked for change in Russian society. The conflict between the association and the zemstvo meant that no local bloc of forces could be formed to apply general pressure from below on the central authorities. Rather, though the center and the zemstvo were far from seeing eye to eye, their common interest in maintaining the primary features of the existing social structure overcame whatever pressures for change might have been generated by New Russia's industrial revolution. At the same time, the central authorities and the industrialists, though at cross-purposes on many points, were united in their determination to prevent the emergence of any institutions of the Donbass working class, which was rapidly growing before their eyes.

[160] *Bakhmutskaia narodnaia gazeta*, nos. 49–50 (1914), p. 3.

[161] *Trudy, XXIX, 1904*, report on the condition of the iron industry, p. 23. See also Rieber, *Merchants and Entrepreneurs*, p. 240.

CHAPTER 2

Labor: Early Strikes and First Organizations

According to P. V. Volobuev, the hallmark of the 1885–94 decade was the appearance in New Russia's industrial areas of an organized workers' movement with mass strikes involving all, or at least the majority, of those employed in an enterprise.[1] In the Donbass this stage of development came much later, and the flood and ebb of consciousness was more marked than in Volobuev's scheme. Yet more important is that before this stage of mobilized activity was reached the workers went through a painful and slow development. In this process, the Donbass workers faced many problems common to newly forming working classes in other parts of the world, as well as others peculiar to the Russian political system that had appeared somewhat earlier in the central industrial districts of Russia. Other factors influencing the nature of the workers' movement were, however, products of the new and still unstable environment of the Donbass.

Social and Political Fragmentation

The organization of the labor movement in the mines and smelters of the Donbass was essentially a matter for outsiders, particularly if we have in mind the formation of an ongoing movement, rather than a sporadic joining together for specific short-range goals such as increases in pay, the firing of an obnoxious overseer, or a change in working conditions. Contact between these people and the workers, particularly the miners, was difficult. The differences in living conditions and outlook between mine

[1] Volobuev et. al., "O periodizatsii rabochego dvizheniia," p. 21.

workers and factory workers were also a problem, and this was compounded by the presence, particularly in Iuzovka, of a considerable group of Jewish merchants and artisans, and workers in small Jewish-owned light industries, tailoring, cobbling, and leather working, who constituted an entirely separate worker-public, responsive to needs and appeals rather different from those of the first two groups. The separateness of the "settlement workers" (Jews) from the factory workers (Russians) is a recurrent theme in the literature written by participants in the revolutionary movement in Iuzovka, though it finds virtually no expression in later Soviet historiography.[2] The Ukrainian peasants, with perceptions and interests different from those of any of the workers, and in many cases antagonistic to them, were a fourth group with whom would-be revolutionary organizers had to contend.

Those who sought to organize the Donbass workers were, from the beginning, revolutionaries. Their goal was the overthrow of the existing regime, rather than its reform or the delimitation within that regime of a broader sphere of participation for the working class. There was no "bread-and-butter unionism" in the Donbass. Even the *zubatovshchina*, the police-sponsored unionism that had a strong though short-lived influence in St. Petersburg, and an even shorter and much weaker history in a few cities of the south, never was tried in the Donbass. Neither the authorities nor the employers considered even this small measure of accommodation with the workers.

The fundamental fact informing the growth of the workers' movement in the Donbass was the complete lack of legitimacy accorded to any form of workers' organization. In Russia, as early as 1862, and more specifically in a law of March 1892, workers in privately owned mines were given the right to form a "mining industry association." The function of this body was to clarify disputes or misunderstandings with the employers and operate mutual-aid, sickness, and disability funds. Such associations were not general class organizations or corporate craft representatives; they were limited

[2] There is no mention of this aspect of the workers' movement in the works of Potolov, Gonimov, Ivanov, or Kondufor. Compare this with the much earlier discussions in *Rabochee delo*, no. 1 (April 1899), p. 85; Kharechko, "Sotsial-demokraticheskii soiuz," p. 19; Shestakov, "Na zare rabochego dvizheniia v Donbasse," pp. 157–58; and TsGAOR, F. 7952, op. 6, d. 120, pp. 78–79, Moshinskii's memoirs, all of which demonstrate clear cognizance of the complexities of this situation. This fragmentation of the workers, the social basis of which was examined in vol. 1, is strongly set forth throughout Wynn, *Workers, Strikes, and Pogroms*.

to the community of each mine. Nevertheless, they represent the beginning of a recognition of the right of collective bargaining and organization. No such associations were set up in the Donbass.[3] Strikes were regarded as rebellion and the labor laws stipulated jail terms for leaders and followers alike, no matter how disciplined and peaceful the strike.[4] Only in 1905 were there suggestions within the regime that the European example be followed and that there be criminal penalties only for the use of violence in a strike.[5] We have seen how the Association of Southern Coal and Steel Producers reacted when faced with the suggestion of workers' participation in the administration of the Compensation Fund. From its inception, Donbass society was polarized and its constituent groups remained in antagonistic isolation.

In their means, and frequently in their goals as well, the revolutionaries were no more united than were the workers. These intragroup splits on both sides were among the major obstacles to the success of the movement. Yet the greatest barriers were the lack of contact and understanding between the workers and the revolutionary intelligentsia, and an insufficient number of members of the worker-intelligentsia to bridge this gap. All of these problems affected the developmental dynamics of the labor movement in the Donbass.

The first attempt to make contact with the workers in the new mine and factory settlements in the Donbass came in the wake of the populist failure of the movement of revolutionary students known as the "going to the people" in 1874. Grigorii Goldenberg, an early revolutionary populist, tells of wandering with other like-minded youth through the Don Cossack territory and the Donbass that autumn, in the guise of traveling shoemakers, carpenters, or tinkers, to acquaint themselves with the peasants migrating in search of work. In the ensuing years, other populist propagandists followed in his footsteps. Among the places visited were a number of the coal mines in the south, and "the well-known Hughes factory."[6] In

[3] Pazhitnov, *Polozhenie*, p. 159.

[4] Ibid., p. 147. A natural corollary then suggested itself to even the most simpleminded worker. If this were the case, then why not have a *bunt* (violent riot)?

[5] See proposals of officials from the Ministry of Finance in *Materialy k izucheniiu rabochego voprosa*, pp. 18–25.

[6] "Svod pokazanii," pp. 105–6. Though this source does not specify that Goldenberg's Donbass visit was in 1874, Kondufor, *Istoriia rabochikh Donbassa*, vol. 1, p. 52, places it after the end of agricultural fieldwork in the year of the "going to the people." Kondufor telescopes the visits into one year, but the source is clear that Goldenberg's journey through

1884, some of the students in the Lisichansk mine foremen's school are said to have helped prepare and test several dynamite bombs for transfer to G. A. Lopatin of the People's Will in St. Petersburg.[7] The next report of agitation among Donbass workers came five years later, when young activists of the People's Will group visited the Golubovskii mine in Slavianoserbsk district in 1889, but left little or no trace of their activities.[8] In 1895, a group of young Jewish revolutionaries, harassed by the police in Vilna, Minsk, and Vitebsk, moved to the burgeoning southern industrial city of Ekaterinoslav, where there were no residence restrictions on Jews, and began attempting to organize the artisans and workers there for revolution.[9] By 1901, when the Social-Democratic party was already at least nominally in existence, one of its members, twenty-three-year-old A. V. Shestakov, finding himself in a group of party members without specific tasks, was urged to go to the Donbass to begin organizing. "You could not speak of an organization" he recalled, "but of individuals who passed you on one to the other."[10] By this time, there had been Social-Democratic organizations formed in Ekaterinoslav and in several of the Donbass centers.[11]

The police had already arrested several entire committees and their converts, but it was not only police surveillance that kept the revolutionary organizations weak. It was also the raw and dispersed nature of the mine and metallurgy settlements. Reminiscing about the revolutionary movement in 1905, K. G. Ershov wrote: "In the Donbass there were no large cities or

---

the region was earlier and his comrades' visit to the mines and the New Russia factory came two or three years later. The first publicized Iuzovka strike was in 1874.

[7] Kondufor, *Istoriia rabochikh Donbassa*, vol. 1, p. 53. The initiative for this was said to have come from the Ozhigov circle in Lugansk.

[8] Levus, "Iz istorii," p. 50. As noted, one of those who spent some months working in iron ore and salt mines, and reading to the peasants and workers in the evenings (under clandestine police observation) was the future author of the famous play *The Dybbuk*, S. A. An——skii.

[9] Babushkin, *Vospominaniia*, p. 89 n. 1. See also Wildman, *Making of a Workers' Revolution*, p. 44.

[10] Shestakov, "Na zare rabochego dvizheniia v Donbasse," p. 156. See also P. A. Moiseenko, *Vospominaniia starogo revoliutsionera*, p. 165. He recalls being driven from job to job by police pressure, and being helped to find a place by an engineer named Sokolov, whose brother, Sergei Sokolov, was one of the activists of the clandestine Donetsk Mine Workers' Union. Similarly, Rosenboim, *Zikhronotav*, pp. 116–17, recalls being able to get in contact with the populist Gershuni only through the latter's brother, a nonrevolutionary, and not through any movement channels.

[11] In addition to the account in Wildman, and the memoirs of Babushkin, see *Rabochee dvizhenie v Ekaterinoslave* for a full account of the activities and misfortunes of those who first attempted to organize revolutionary groups in Ekaterinoslav.

cultural centers. The local S-D organizations were small and weak. The conditions of work and life were extraordinarily difficult. A very significant portion of the mine workers and even in part some of the factory workers had not cut their ties with the land."[12] Ershov remarks here on two of the aspects of Donbass society that were important in forming the region's social and political character. First is the rootless nature of the Donbass. It was a newly founded series of small and isolated settlements without a natural and established large center to set a tone (as well as provide a source of indigenous intelligentsia forces). In addition, the population that did come was in considerable measure impermanent, oriented to returning to the village, and therefore little focused on improving the conditions of life and work in the mines and factories, let alone changing the political system of Russia.[13]

Perhaps when he wrote his impressions, time had smoothed some of Ershov's harsher memories, but in the "Report on the Donbass" sent by a certain "Petr" in 1908, the roughnesses are grating. "Living conditions among the miners are such that of ten party workers only one is willing to undertake such work, and of ten agreeing, only one can hold out for five or six months."[14] Here we have an indirect expression of the problem of the intelligentsia's relations with the workers, and the absence of a sufficient stratum of worker-intelligentsia. This was not a new problem for the revolutionaries. The thousands of young intellectuals who "went to the people" met with sometimes violent rejection by the peasants. The young rebels (*buntari*) who tried to turn the peasants' rage against the landowners and police during the famine and the cholera epidemic of 1892 were often beaten for their pains, as were the doctors who came to heal the sick.[15] As industry developed, the revolutionaries debated the problem of concentration of the young radicals in the larger cities, and the neglect of the new concentrations of workers in provincial areas.[16]

[12] Ershov, "Dekabr'skoe vooruzhennoe vosstanie v Donbasse," pt. 1, p. 12.

[13] Potolov, *Rabochie Donbassa*, p. 191, though referring specifically to the last half of the 1870s (when there was virtually no revolutionary movement present in the region), states that the constant migration of the mining population hindered the success of the revolutionaries.

[14] *Proletarii*, no. 52 (February 13, 1908), cited in Donii, Lavrov, and Shmorgun, *Bolsheviki Ukrainy*, p. 112. The voice here is identified only as "Petr," but the rough tone is consistent with that of Petr Moiseenko's memoirs.

[15] Wildman, *Making of a Workers' Revolution*, p. 14, notes that Kuskova, the future Social-Democrat, was one of the buntari.

[16] See the discussion in *Revoliutsionnaia Rossiia*, no. 26 (1903), p. 15.

This was exactly the case in the Donbass. In the mid-1880s, when the growth of the Donbass was already well under way, there was a southern network of populists belonging to the People's Will. They had circles in Kharkov, Ekaterinoslav, Rostov, Taganrog, and Novocherkassk. One of them, Shekhter-Minor, even spent time (under close police surveillance) in Bakhmut, but their memoirs make no mention of activity among the Donbass miners and metal workers.[17] The *narodovol'tsy* (members of the People's Will), and after them the members of the Socialist-Revolutionary party, had minimal political interest in the miners and factory workers as such. They saw contact with these concentrations of migrant peasants principally as a way of obtaining entrée into the villages.[18] When they did approach the factory workers, it was often to remind them that "Russia is a peasant country of 120 millions with only two million proletarians scattered across its vast expanse, and therefore it is unthinkable to attempt to overthrow the autocratic system by the efforts of the workers alone."[19]

One of the early revolutionaries in the Donbass recalls "the total absence of intelligentsia forces" as causing as many difficulties as did the police surveillance. The one exception he noted was in Shcherbinovka, where Moiseenko and G. I. Petrovskii enjoyed the broad cooperation of the mine intelligentsia.[20] When Iuzovka already had a population of close to forty thousand, it was said of it that "there is almost no receptive or even slightly original-thinking political intelligentsia here—no more than in any county hamlet." The particularity of the social environment of Iuzovka can be understood when compared to Saratov with its centuries-long history, an indigenous tradition of socialist political culture dating back to Radishchev, and in 1917, a cadre of professionals and students equal to half of Iuzovka's entire population.[21]

The young students or members of the intelligentsia who chose to provoke revolution among the workers thus had to come into an entirely foreign milieu. This was a test for them as they faced totally new physical

[17] See Shekhter-Minor, "Iuzhno-Russkaia narodovolcheskaia organizatsiia," and Kulakov, "'Narodnaia volia' na iuge v polovine 80-kh gg."

[18] See the explanation in *Revoliutsionnaia Rossiia*, no. 26 (1903), p. 15.

[19] Ibid., no. 27 (1903), p. 20.

[20] Moshinskii, "K voprosu," p. 235. The intelligentsia in this case included the radical doctor, Kavalerov, the mine's schoolteacher, and the engineer Priadkin, whom Moiseenko denigrates in his memoirs for not being a revolutionary.

[21] *Iskra*, no. 73 (September 1, 1904), p. 7. For Saratov, see Raleigh, *Revolution on the Volga*, pp.27–29, 45–46.

and cultural conditions, a test, as "Petr" noted with some bitterness, that few of the would-be revolutionaries passed. The cultural gap also made it difficult to earn the trust of the workers, who were not receptive to outsiders. Mendel Rosenboim, who had composed and smuggled numerous proclamations aimed at Russia's peasants and workers, who had been a founder of the league of Socialist-Revolutionaries abroad and an organizer of numerous circles, recalls his excitement when he was introduced at long last to a worker sympathetic to revolutionary ideas. "Until that day I had never come face-to-face with an actual Russian worker. I knew the Russian worker, and the Russian peasant as well, only from literature."[22] The meeting ended in disappointment, for the worker, despite his sympathies, evinced little interest in the political questions to which Rosenboim tried to turn the conversation, preferring general cultural topics. Rosenboim was, unfortunately for the revolutionaries, the norm and not the exception. With exquisite politeness, a worker from the Kamenskoe factory noted that, having heard "intelligent" people speak, he wondered that they knew so little about the working class.[23] At times the differences in culture simply made the revolutionary's work harder. P. G. Smidovich, the son of a minor nobleman, decided to become a worker, learning a trade so that he could share workers' lives and thus guide them toward revolution "from within." The workers among whom he tried to live confided that they found the leaflets in the Briansk factory "something strange and totally incomprehensible." When he tried to explain their contents, and they found that Smidovich did not believe in religion, they refused to sit with him at meals.[24]

Often the disparity in outlook went beyond misunderstanding and boiled up in resentment. Following the failure of the attempted general strike in Ekaterinoslav in August 1903, the workers raised accusatory voices against the committee of "socialists," "the educated." "If they hadn't

[22] Rosenboim, *Zikhronotav*, p. 54. Until that time his only contact with the proletariat had been with Jewish artisans in Vilna.

[23] P. T. [P. Timofeev], "Zavodnye budni," pt. 1, p. 30.

[24] Smidovich, "Rabochie massy," p. 165. See the discussion in Wildman, *Making of a Workers' Revolution* pp. 89–103. See also *Rabochee delo*, no. 1 (April 1899), p. 84. Writing of the arrest of the Ekaterinoslav S-D organization, the correspondent observes, "Based on this correspondent's inquiries, it was a rare person among the masses who understood what, exactly, was the object of the organization." See also Levus, "Iz istorii," p. 64. Regarding the most successful of the early revolutionary attempts to organize in the Donbass, the Social-Democratic Donbass Mine Workers' Union, he concludes, "It turned out that neither the peasants nor even the workers understood the union's leaflets."

attacked the government, hadn't demanded in their leaflets and speeches the overthrow of the autocracy, the workers undoubtedly would have won the strike."[25]

A major factor in the failure of the strike in this particular case was the interfactional bitterness between the various revolutionary groups, preventing coordination of the strike efforts—and this was no more comprehensible to the workers than was the socialists' theorizing. As even observers from within the revolutionary movement noted (not without a touch of schadenfreude), *Iuzhnyi rabochii* was busy engaging the terrorists in polemics, the Ekaterinoslav Committee of the Social-Democratic Workers' Party of Russia (RSDRP) was indignantly quarreling with the Social-Democratic Railway Workers' Group, and all the while workers were unemployed and strikes were failing.[26] The lesson of these failures was not easily learned in revolutionary circles. There was a strike in Iuzovka in September 1903, a month after the debacle in Ekaterinoslav. The small group of Social-Democrats in the settlement at that time joined in with a will, and produced a leaflet to encourage the strikers—adding the demand for a constituent assembly and the slogan "Down with the Autocracy" to the economic demands put forward by the workers.[27] This lack of understanding of what the workers wanted, of the limits to their culture and aspirations, and the attempt at doctrinaire imposition of the revolutionaries' worldview on tradition-minded workers, led directly to Iuzovka's bloody pogrom in 1905.

Because of the relative isolation of the factory and mine settlements, and the effectiveness of the police in interrupting revolutionary activities, it was not only the workers who had difficulty understanding the revolutionary message.[28] In her memoirs Bondareva recalls leading study circles in 1903, discussing the "driving forces of the revolution," the Erfurt program, and the program of the RSDRP, but confesses that she had no understanding of these, nor did she know anything of what had gone on at the second

[25] Posse, *Rabochie stachki*, pp. 81–88, discusses in some detail the enduring splits in the revolutionary movement and their disastrous influence on the August 1903 strikes. For the widely differing perceptions between masses and activists regarding the outcome of this strike, see Wynn, *Workers, Strikes, and Pogroms* pp. 165–74.

[26] *Revoliutsionnaia Rossiia*, no. 13 (1902), p. 14.

[27] TsGAOR, F. 7952, op. 6, d. 120, p. 4. Memoirs of Shur.

[28] For a discussion of these two factors in isolating the miners from each other as well as from revolutionaries, see Arskii, *Donetskii Bassein*, p. 11.

congress of the RSDRP until she was jailed in 1904 with party comrades from the big city.[29]

When Maxim Gorkii attempted to encourage proletarian writers, inviting them to submit their compositions to him, he was shocked to find that these works were characterized by a clear hatred of the intelligentsia. This was expressed in resentment, active hostility, and even an urge to murder, with the intelligentsia described as overbearing, ignorant of reality, and in the end, weak-willed.[30] Tim McDaniel discusses this in terms of a hostility that the workers themselves could neither understand nor explain, and blames the fragmentation of society on the autocracy.[31] The problem was even more acute when those workers who were inclined to be active on their own behalf expressed resentment of the intelligentsia organizers. A letter signed "Rabochii Pravdin" objected to a brochure authored by "Rabochii" and entitled "Workers and Intelligentsia in Our Organizations." "It sounds as though 'Rabochii' regarded the intelligentsia as some sort of harmful element. This comrade forgets that all of us who are conscious workers learned our consciousness from the intelligentsia. . . . This question is not important. It has been solved and is raised only by disorganizers from the minority."[32]

The Missing Link: The Worker-Intelligent

The question was apparently far from solved, however, for it cropped up repeatedly. The solution sought was the emergence of a "new identifiable social group, a worker-intelligentsia marked off from their fellows."[33] This was in no way easy, and Wildman characterizes the group as "a thin layer of worker-intelligentsia . . . almost as alienated from average workers as the intelligentsia."[34] He might have added that they were also almost as alienated from the intelligentsia as was the average worker. The gap was not to

[29] TsGAOR, F. 7952, op. 6, d. 120, p. 9. It may be edifying to note how jail or exile served to turn a dilettante into a trained professional revolutionary.

[30] Gor'kii, "O pisateliakh samouchkakh," p. 187.

[31] McDaniel, *Autocracy*, pp. 178–80.

[32] *Vpered*, no. 12 (1905), p. 5. Behind this polemic lies the split between Bolsheviks and Mensheviks regarding organizational tactics.

[33] Wildman, *Making of a Workers' Revolution*, p. 32.

[34] Ibid.

be easily bridged, except by the growth of a comparatively large contingent of such *poluintelligenty* (semi-intelligentsia) within the ranks of the workers among whom they were to become leaders.

In the south, the difficulty of creating this stratum was recognized. "As a phenomenon of the last two or three years, the workers' movement has not yet created a stratum of worker-intelligentsia that would take upon itself the organization of the workers' masses."[35]

In the Donbass there was Moiseenko, a genuine worker-intelligent. Babushkin came from the north to Ekaterinoslav, though not to the mines or smelters of the Donbass. Smidovich, an intelligent trying to turn worker, rather than a worker who cultivated his intelligence, also skirted the Donbass during his attempt to live among the workers. When Veniamin Ermoshenko produced the *Shakhterskii listok* (The miners' page), signing himself "Molodoi shakhter" (Young miner), it was a day of celebration for the Bolsheviks. Yet the worker-intelligentsia remained essentially a collection of scattered individuals right through 1917.[36] The sought-after stratum of indigenous leaders of the revolutionary movement never materialized and the movement had to be built around emissaries, outsiders who came and went with dizzying frequency, sometimes because of police activity, at other times because movement needs and the scarcity of people dictated a policy of moving Petr to replace Pavel. It is totally understandable that whatever the traveling revolutionaries' devotion and talents, the effectiveness of their work suffered from this instability of tenure. They could not get to know the peculiarities of the Donbass workers' lives, nor could the workers get to know and to trust these revolutionary birds of passage.[37]

In addition, if theoretically the function of the revolutionary worker-intelligent was to bridge the gap between thinking society and working society, bringing the two closer, his own perceptions were often different. I have already discussed the phenomenon discovered by Gorkii of workers'

[35] *Rabochee dvizhenie v Ekaterinoslave*, p. 2. This was written in 1900, thirty years after the founding of Iuzovka.

[36] In addition, it should be taken into account that not all the members of the worker-intelligentsia of whom we have record were inclined to revolution. Kolodub, whose memoir is quoted above, was a conservative, and Timofeev, though less is known of his beliefs, was not revolutionary in his expressed view of society.

[37] Johnson, *Peasant and Proletarian*, p. 119, writing about Moscow workers, states that even after decades of agitation and propaganda there was no sign of a mass revolutionary movement, and that the influence of the radical intelligentsia was indirect at best.

contempt for and mistrust of the intelligentsia. In Moiseenko's memoirs this emerges clearly, and if he is to serve as the archetypical worker-intelligent, one cannot ignore his opinions on the subject. Moiseenko's political world was sharply delineated. All contractors, *desiatniki* (foremen), and officials great and small were labeled "Black Hundreds." Bolshevism was a working-class theory, while Menshevism was for intellectuals. (This was written in hindsight, and he admits that "in those days there was little difference between Bolshevik and Menshevik.") The engineer Priadkin, who assisted Moiseenko in obtaining employment, and later also provided materials for a commune enterprise that Moiseenko and some other workers tried to organize, was treated with contempt because he was not a revolutionary. However vehemently Moiseenko claims that "I did not reject intelligentsia, but the opposite, I drew them into work insofar as they were useful to us," the weight of his account contradicts this. While his intelligence and agitational skills were of great value in reaching the workers, he could not bridge the abyss that divided intelligentsia and proletariat.[38]

Johnson characterizes the factory society as "closed," citing the difficulties that Babushkin, himself a worker, encountered in trying to win the confidence of textile workers.[39] It may be suggested, however, that the problem is not one of "openness" or "closure" per se, but of the degree of receptivity to a particular program or set of values. Smidovich, as an individual, was accepted by the workers, but when he began to expound the revolutionary creed, he was ostracized. In "Bez dorogi," an account of the 1892 cholera epidemic in the Donbass, Veresaev attempts to make the point that all the revolutionaries, including the populists, were essentially westerners, while the peasant-workers of the mines and factories were by instinct Slavophiles.[40] There was therefore both cognitive and affective dissonance between them.

In fact, the problem went even deeper. The Donbass was an extremely fragmented society with only the most fragile of bonds holding it together. The peasants were divided generationally, with the younger people willing to beat the landlords and have a revolution, while their elders still held onto

[38] While Moiseenko's attitudes find repeated expression throughout his memoir, and constitute one of its central themes, the most concentrated discussion can be found in Moiseenko, *Vospominaniia starogo revoliutsionera*, pp. 150–60. The one nonworker who is treated with respect and even admiration is Dr. Kavalerov, who collaborated with Moiseenko and Petrovskii in Shcherbinovka, and later treated Moiseenko's wife for cancer.

[39] Johnson, *Peasant and Proletarian*, p. 93.

[40] Veresaev, *Povesti i rasskazy*, p. 40.

the old loyalties.[41] A report from Kharkov bemoaned the fact that the students, the artisans, and the factory workers were not united in values, consciousness, or goals.[42] In Iuzovka a similar fragmentation frustrated the revolutionary movement.

> For active political work and protest, the difference between the conscious portion of the city workers [the Jewish artisans] and the factory workers on the one hand, and the grey mass of miners and blast furnace workers on the other, is too great. . . . There is absolutely no revolutionary intelligentsia. Neither is there any contact with liberal bourgeoisie. It is understandable why we feel a constant lack of propagandists for our circles, and orators for our gatherings. . . . The conscious proletariat reacts in lively fashion to every happening in our political life. In a lesser center they would be a force, but here they are swallowed up in the huge mass of miners eternally moving from village to mine and mine to village. In this we have the entire tragedy of our situation. In other places even with a smaller percentage of really conscious workers it would be easier for the conscious minority to lead the masses.[43]

The precise meaning of this lament is spelled out in the analysis of Iuzovka's economy, described by the *Iskra* correspondent as divided into three separate parts: the workshops and small factories of the town; the "12,000 workers of Hughes' factory" (in the prolonged recession the factory had, in fact, dwindled to 5,805 workers); and the mass of miners in Iuzovka and its vicinity. These last are described as the least conscious, least organized, and in the worst situation. So disorganized and isolated were they that in three mines, separated by no more than fifteen *verstas*, a coal cutter's wage varied from 90 kopeks to 2.5 rubles per day.[44] In short, not just the society but the working class within it was fragmented.

The isolation of the Jewish artisans from the Russian workers, and the Russian workers from the Ukrainian peasantry, is understandable against the background of the national and religious frictions that were rampant in the Russian Empire. Urban and industrial development not only dislocated

[41] *Revoliutsionnaia Rossiia*, no. 75 (1905), p. 17.

[42] Ibid., no. 6 (1902), p. 13.

[43] *Iskra*, no. 73 (September 1, 1904), p. 7.

[44] A versta equals 1.06 kilometers. The wage discrepancy was more likely due to differences in the richness of the coal-bearing stratum, and other factors unconnected to the workers' consciousness or knowledge.

the lives of uprooted peasants, but threw the peasants together with other national and religious groups alien to them.[45] Socioeconomic cleavages reinforced these basic antagonisms. The differences between miners and factory workers in the Donbass demand a different explanation, one in which the physical, social, and economic conditions were the primary factors in what became a fundamental political characteristic of the Donbass. Perhaps the most consistent social process explored in volume 1 was the differentiation between the factory workers and the miners of the Donbass. In terms of stability, professionalism, housing, and wages, there was continual progress, which gave the factory workers reason to feel that they had a personal interest in the continuation of the existing system. They had steady work, a rising standard of living, improving physical surroundings, a hope of realizing the dream of being property owners, and the promise that their children could be educated and rise in society. All of this was coming to pass for a substantial portion of the factory population. The miners did not share this experience, though they could see it taking place in the workers' lives. They worked in harsher, more dangerous conditions, had less stability and professionalism, and did not sense the same progress in their lives.

This was accepted as the conventional wisdom of the time. The factory workers were regarded as a settled and closed society. "The invalids leaving work here are being replaced by a younger generation that has grown up on the territory of the factory, and for outside newcomers it is almost impossible to enter the factory. In contrast, among the miners, as everywhere, the element of newcomers is predominant."[46] These distinctions were interpreted differently from various points of view. A 1902 memo on the labor problem presented to the governor of Ekaterinoslav, F. E. Keller, concluded that "in general the mine workers are less dangerous than the factory workers in terms of their propensity for disorder or their receptivity to different types of propaganda. From the point of view of intelligence and literacy the former are considerably lower than the latter. Mass movements among them [the miners] take place exclusively on a basis of unjust payment for work, or a lowering of wage rates."[47] The activists of the underground Donetsk Mine Workers' Union largely agreed with this assessment,

[45] For a discussion of the antagonism between the Orthodox and the Jews, and between Azeri Muslims and Armenian Christians in Baku, see Brower, "Urban Revolution," p. 349.

[46] Kir'ianov, *Rabochie iuga Rossii*, p. 33, citing a 1915 newspaper account. The reader may recall Professor Ivan Time's remarks when he visited Iuzovka in 1889.

[47] Quoted in Kharechko, "Sotsial-demokraticheskii soiuz," p. 13.

reporting that "it should, however, be recognized that many of the pamphlets were incomprehensible to the miners. They had much more success among the factory workers where on all sides one may find fully intelligent and conscious workers who openly call themselves Social-Democrats."[48]

The conservative newspaper *Novoe vremia*, noting that miners took a large part in the pogrom in Ekaterinoslav in October 1905, and were opposed by the organized factory workers, ascribed this to the miners' much lower cultural level.[49] Surozhskii characterized the miners' situation as total "abandonment and benightedness" (*zabroshennost' i temnota*), contrasting it with the relatively easier situation of the factory workers.[50] There was, in fact, a material difference in cultural level between the two groups of workers. The census of 1897 showed that the rate of literacy among workers in metallurgy and metal working was 60.2 percent, while that among coal miners was only 31 percent. There was also a generational difference, with 90 percent of the literacy found among workers under the age of forty (those born after 1857), and therefore coming of school age after the zemstvo reforms had given education considerable impetus.[51]

Yet the character of the miners was not one-sided. Avdakov noted that they were indeed a different breed, more traditional in outlook than were the factory workers, and he remarked particularly their respect for religion and their willingness to show disrespect for secular authority when it infringed on tradition or religion.[52] Indeed, the zeal of the miners and workers for tradition sometimes was a source of trouble to the local authorities. The 1887 report of the Ekaterinoslav chief of gendarmes notes that "the workers [in Iuzovka] are wild and ungovernable. They pay no respect to the police, and generally don't know how to conduct themselves. On the tsar's name day, a group of Hughes' factory workers gathered by the home of Police Chief Rubtsev and expressed dissatisfaction with the fact that no

[48] *Iskra*, no. 45 (August 1, 1903), p. 8. In 1903, the chief of gendarmes of the Don territory said virtually the same thing. "One must distinguish between the factory workers and the miners in the pits. The latter are generally an illiterate and undeveloped group. . . . The factory and railway shop workers are generally literate, well developed, and extraordinarily inclined to acceptance of Social-Democratic teachings." See Modestov, *Rabochee i professional'noe dvizhenie*, p. 21.

[49] *Novoe vremia* (October 31, 1905).

[50] Surozhskii, "Krai uglia i zheleza," p. 308.

[51] Potolov, *Rabochie Donbassa*, p. 133. At that time there were relatively few miners older than forty, and not many more metallurgy workers over that age. The age level of the literate thus loses some of its salience.

[52] *Trudy, XVIII, 1893*, pt. 2, p. 330.

flags were hung there, though all the residents, even the poorest, hung out flags as a sign of the general holiday, and they threatened to report him to the higher authorities."[53] To balance this, Garshin, praising the workers and miners with only a faint undertone of the damnation prevalent in Russia's higher society, wrote that they were "far from as bestial in appearance as is sometimes thought." As for the New Russia workers' participation in driving off the striking Rykovskii miners in 1887, he attributed that to a civic conscience generated among the workers by honest administration of local affairs, something Garshin claims could only be done by holders of large capital, who outlive passing crises and invest with a long-term view.[54] In essence, Garshin is claiming that the secular trend of improved living conditions within the urban industrial framework of Iuzovka's life was beginning to produce the civic consciousness that was lacking elsewhere in the Donbass, and generally throughout Russia. Though this statement, like much of Garshin's report, appears colored with excessive optimism—a pre-Webb Webbism, if you will—the observation of the basic social and political tendencies appears accurate.

The state was determinedly reactionary, grimly bent on preserving a paternalist autocracy, though its various arms might work at cross-purposes for lack of agreement about how this was best achieved. The rest of society, fragmented, weak, and politically inexperienced, was never able to maintain a united effort to achieve even modest liberalization. The Donbass industrialists both respected and feared the state, and in addition, saw themselves as dependent on the authorities' goodwill for the advancement of their own economic and political interests. Autonomous organization on the part of the workers was considered totally illegitimate, and it was desperately feared and punished by state and employers alike. Finally, those groups trying to unite, educate, and lead the workers were no less fragmented than were other parts of society, and the different fragments had divergent values and goals, both politically and socially. Nevertheless, there was a revolutionary movement. Repressed, fragmented, and confused

[53] TsGAOR, F. 102, arkh. 3, deloproizvodstvo 9a, ch. 21, 1887, p. 8. The reader has doubtless noted that the undisciplined excess of which the workers are blamed is, in fact, a zeal to be demonstratively patriotic.

[54] Garshin, "Poezdka," pp. 7, 9. An "official" view of the working class was voiced by the military governor of Moscow in 1848. He called the workers "homeless and immoral people, who readily attach themselves to every movement that is destructive of social and private tranquillity" (cited in Zelnik, *Labor and Society*, p. 26). The 1887 strike will be examined later in this chapter.

though it might have been, the revolutionary movement appeared in numerous forms, and like a phoenix rose from the ashes of each defeat, now following, now leading, always persisting in its search for influence among the Donbass miners and factory hands. But a coherent and cohesive movement was prevented from forming by the brevity of the organizers' experience and by the determined blockage imposed by regime and employers.

Early Protests and Strikes

It was the workers themselves, and not the liberal or radical intelligentsia, who carried out the first protests against the conditions of life and work in the Donbass. The first stage of class solidarity, as observed by Smidovich, was not to unite in a fight for better conditions, but simply to get back at the bosses by stealing from the factory, and to cover for and aid a fellow worker in trouble with higher-ups.[55] The latter point in particular became a factor around which repeated mass activity of the workers crystallized. Although it was difficult to get a large number of workers organized for industrial action, they responded willingly to calls to rescue fellow workers from the hands of the police, even when such action involved high personal risk.[56] Here were the first signs of an incipient class consciousness.

Another early form of workers' action was personal reprisal against oppressive officials. As part of the program to "indigenize" the supervisory staff of the New Russia plant, the friendly British foreman, Lowter, was replaced by "the Russian dictator Skachko, who permitted no politics and had one man doing the work of two."[57] The small Social-Democratic circle in the factory was undecided about how to deal with the new foreman. Should they ride him out of the factory on a wheelbarrow? Should they strike? Should they perhaps petition the management for his removal? Kadigrabov cut the discussions short by "accidentally" running into him with a fifty-pound rail, but Skachko survived the attempt, returning to work six months later, while Kadigrabov went to jail for six years.[58] In

[55] Smidovich, "Rabochie massy," p. 64.

[56] See two examples of workers rallying in an effort to free their arrested comrades in *Rabochee delo*, nos. 4–5, (September–December, 1899), pp. 100, 102.

[57] TsGAOR, F. 7952, op. 6, d. 120, p. 74. Memoirs of Kadigrabov.

[58] Ibid. See also Gonimov, *Staraia Iuzovka*, pp. 156–57. In 1906, Skachko was shot to death. See *Gorno-zavodskii listok*, no. 20 (1906), p. 8526.

Iuzovka, as all over Russia, the attempt to get the workers to organize for more abstract, long-term, and general goals, abandoning the immediate satisfactions of individual terror, was one of the early points of debate. Bondareva relates her fascination with the discussion at her first real RSDRP party meeting in 1903. Paperno (a Menshevik), the dominant personality in the circle, was locked in debate with Volgin, who was advocating the workers' use of terror.[59] The discussion had been going on since the earliest years of Marxist activity in the south, as Smirnov notes in his discussion of the workers' movement in Ekaterinoslav.[60] Terror, however, remained part of the Donbass political world, and following 1905 even foreigners, of whose safety the authorities were particularly solicitous, since they knew what xenophobia existed among the workers, were not immune.[61] As will be apparent in the discussion of 1905 in Iuzovka, however, the sole attack on a British employee of the New Russia Co. appears to have been unrelated to politics.

More prevalent than the use of personal terror was the use of mass violence as an expression of the workers' discontent when their needs were not met. In the Donbass, this problem was manifested in the intertwining of the bunt and the anti-Jewish pogrom. This element was absent from the central industrial areas of Russia, where Jews were not allowed to settle. In the Donbass, however, and in the adjacent cities such as Ekaterinoslav where a large Jewish population was concentrated, specifically anti-Jewish action was at times an integral part of labor unrest.[62]

Labor unrest was said to be frequent at the New Russia factory and mines, with "open disorder verging on rebellion" in the years 1869–83. The Ekaterinoslav chief of gendarmes noted in his political survey for 1892 that "disorders in the settlement of Iuzovka are repeated annually to a

[59] See Bondareva's memoirs, TsGAOR, F. 7952, op. 6, d. 120, p. 8. Later, when he was arrested, Volgin turned in the whole group. The continuing existence of the debate on "personal terror" in a Social-Democratic context in 1903, when such matters had supposedly been settled in Marxist circles much earlier, says much about the nature of ideological development in the Donbass.

[60] Smirnov, "O pervom kruzhke," p. 165. Tkachenko wanted to throw bombs, but he received this answer: "You won't go far with bombs. The workers have a cleaner way. When they smashed machines, beat, and even killed directors, that did nothing to help their condition."

[61] McKay, *Pioneers for Profit*, pp. 196–97, notes the assassination of Georges Raymond of the Donets Steel Co., and writes that numerous foreigners were killed.

[62] The problem of workers' participation in pogroms is the central theme of Wynn, *Workers, Strikes, and Pogroms*.

greater or lesser extent."[63] Nevertheless, in the first twenty-five years of Iuzovka's existence there were only five recorded work stoppages. The largest and most serious disorder, the 1892 cholera riot, involved fifteen thousand people and resulted in the burning of the commercial center of Iuzovka, and the deaths of nearly a hundred people. This riot appears to have been entirely devoid of industrial labor protest content, though it certainly may be seen as a rebellion against social structure and living conditions.[64] Apparently the annual unrest noted by the authorities was the unorganized discontent of a diffuse mass with only the most amorphous class or craft consciousness. Contemporary observers saw it as a ritual, played out by the miners even when they were clearly aware of its futility.[65] Its persistence over such a long period of time may be attributed to the nomadic nature of the coal miners and to the rapid growth of the factory, which swiftly added new and unseasoned workers, many straight from the village, to a relatively small core of stable veterans. These latter, as noted in volume 1, enjoyed a privileged position with regard to stability of employment, wages, and overtime earnings, and in many cases appeared inimical to violence, and particularly hostile to disruption of work where their closest personal interests were not directly at stake.

The disruptions recorded are one in the factory and one in the New Russia Co. mines in 1874, a joint strike of Iuzovka miners and workers in 1875, a strike in the nearby Rutchenko mines in 1887 that spilled over into Iuzovka, and the cholera riots of 1892. After that, only in January and October 1898 were there strikes in Iuzovka. Given the working and living conditions, and the numbers of workers employed in and around Iuzovka, this is a surprising record of labor peace.

The first strike in Iuzovka was a "guild action" by the steel puddlers Hughes had brought from the defunct Lugansk smelters. Hearing that a number of northern smelters had ceased working, Hughes had dispatched a hiring agent who signed a hundred of their experienced workers to three-year contracts on a piecework basis. The Lugansk workers, already ensconced in the New Russia plant, objected, "which resulted in a strike against working by the *pood*, although we pay them a very liberal price, six

[63] DOGIA, F. R-2069, op. 4, d. 4, p. 1. Preobrazhenskii church journal. Pankratova, *Rabochee dvizhenie*, vol. 3, pt. 2, p. 214.

[64] For a detailed discussion of the background, events, and results of these riots, see Friedgut, "Labor Violence and Regime Brutality." Here I will add only a few insights gained from the archival materials on the riots.

[65] See Fenin, *Coal and Politics*, p. 47.

kopeks per *pood*, which is double what they received at Moorom and even twenty per cent above the prices paid at Welsh Iron Works for a similar class of work."[66] Many of the Murom people were evidently intimidated by the strike and refused to work, and even the blandishments of the local authorities could not change their minds. There is, however, no account of disorder or violence connected to this strike, other than a hint from Islavin, who, following his visit to Iuzovka in the summer of 1874, reported that Hughes considered the former Lugansk workers "drinkers and brawlers," despite their "skill and boldness" in metallurgy. He adds that Hughes blamed the Luganis for instigating disorders at the factory.[67]

The other strike in 1874 developed in two stages. In February, some of the miners struck for two days, demanding higher pay. Potolov writes that they were fined, and that Hughes "simply tricked" them, promising to consider their demands favorably on his return from a business trip to St. Petersburg.[68] The report of the Bakhmut police chief, filed after the April strike turned violent, gives a somewhat different version. When a group of miners demanded a pay raise in February, the factory's chief engineer, Harris, agreed that all those who presented a valid passport and were willing to sign a three-year contract would be paid one ruble a day all year round, starting April 1, rather than having their pay rates lowered by 10 percent in the autumn, as was the general Donbass custom. The miners refused the conditions, but demanded the raise in pay as of April 1. Harris in turn refused their demand and stated that summer rates would be in effect from May 1 to the end of September.[69]

The next payday came on Saturday, April 13, and the miners who had demanded a raise found that the management had stood firm and no raise had been included in their pay packets. That Sunday, the miners' discontent

[66] TsGIAL, F. 37, op. 53, d. 746. Letter of Hughes to Valuev, October 15, 1874. This letter appears to be the only document relating to this strike, indicating that it was treated as an internal matter for the factory and not handed over to the police. I have reproduced Hughes' spelling of pud (*pood*) and Murom (Moorom).

[67] Islavin, "Obzor," p. 82. Hughes may have been referring to the fight between factory workers and miners that occurred during the 1874 strike. He was not alone in his low opinion of the former Lugansk workers. An Ekaterinoslav police official wrote years later that "from a political point of view they are the least promising of the entire population of Bakhmut and Slavianoserbsk districts and their outlook is one of hostility to the government." See TsGAOR, F. DP, deloproizvodstvo 3, d. 9, ch. 21, 1887, p. 47, report of assistant chief of gendarmes for Ekaterinoslav province.

[68] Potolov, *Rozhdenie velikana*, p. 98.

[69] TsGAOR, F. 7952, op. 6, d. 119, p. 7. Telegram of police chief Zagorianskii to the Ekaterinoslav governor, April 21, 1874.

found an outlet in even more drinking and fighting than was usual following a payday. On Monday morning, some of the miners decided not to work, and they made a halfhearted attempt to stop those who wished to go into the mines. Since the movement was neither organized nor determined, the mine shift was not disrupted. The factory management telegraphed news of the strike to Bakhmut, whence it was relayed to the governor in Ekaterinoslav.

At noon, a group of factory workers on their lunch break bought a bottle of vodka, but on the way back to the factory they ran into a group of the striking miners, who tried to steal the bottle. As the numbers were uneven, the four workers ran for the factory, chased by a crowd that grew to a hundred or more miners. Hughes and Gooch tried to get the miners to leave the factory but did not succeed. Missiles flew, and though the gendarme commander later claimed that nobody was injured, three workers claimed to have been beaten unconscious.[70] Hughes then organized a large squad of British and Russian factory workers and began to drive the strikers out of the factory, seizing and locking up those who resisted—a total of forty—and restoring a temporary calm. Warned that the miners were preparing for a nighttime raid to avenge themselves on the factory workers and free the prisoners, Hughes put forty of his men on horses, and prepared sixty more on foot, driving the miners away from the factory and taking thirty more prisoners. The next day, the Bakhmut police chief reported that work was normal except for sixty miners who had left the settlement.[71] The prisoners were taken by the police to Bakhmut and thence to Kharkov.[72]

This was clearly a strike. An organized group of miners presented a clearly defined demand, negotiating with management before stopping work. True, the stoppage was brief, and only about 150 of the 1,500 miners (by the Bakhmut police chief's account they were all from two shafts of one

[70] The telegram of the British consul (trying to maximize the seriousness of the events) claims that several people were seriously injured. The final report of the Bakhmut police chief says three were injured, one of whom needed hospitalization. See ibid., pp. 21, 26.

[71] The final report of the Ekaterinoslav governor to the minister of the interior on the strike, dated August 3, 1874, says that about half the Iuzovka miners quit after the strike. It should be noted that the strike was in the spring, and that it would be perfectly normal for miners to leave Iuzovka for agricultural work.

[72] The account of the strike is in TsGAOR, F. 7952, op. 6, d. 119, pp. 6–21, and includes the reports of the Bakhmut police chief, Hughes' telegram, and a report of the British consul at Berdiansk. Pankratova, *Rabochee dvizhenie*, vol. 2, pt. 1, p. 616, gives an account of the strike (together with an account of the 1875 strike) published in *Vpered*, no. 12 (1875), p. 373.

of the New Russia mines) in Iuzovka appear to have been involved. No violence was directed against the factory, the mines, or management. The violence that took place began due to drunkenness, and perhaps from resentment of the comparatively high wages and good conditions enjoyed by the settlement's three hundred factory workers. From this base, it grew (probably still fueled by alcohol, though none of the reports specifies this) to the question of a fight to free imprisoned comrades from the factory people, both workers and management, who were holding them. In this, the striking miners behaved much in the manner of George Rudé's "crowd."[73] They had a specific object, they appeared motivated by what they perceived as injustice and the inequities of the wage system, and they displayed a clear willingness to take out their resentment on the privileged. Yet the outburst was brief and gave rise to no new forms of organization or expressions of consciousness. Although this was the year of the populist movement's "going to the people," there is no sign of its influence on the events in Iuzovka. If a general zeitgeist touched the miners, that too has been veiled in the mists that cover any ideological motivation or political residue that may have remained with the participants.

There is no clear record of what happened to the prisoners taken by Hughes and turned over to the gendarmes. Presumably they were banished to their home villages—a standard punishment.[74] The authorities evidently expressed resentment at Hughes' usurpation of police functions in arresting Russian citizens, and at his having armed his men, though the Ekaterinoslav governor admitted that the inadequacy of the Iuzovka police force was a mitigating circumstance.[75] The British consul demanded an increase to twenty armed police to protect the estimated hundred British subjects and the British property in Iuzovka. In response, the police force was increased from four to twelve—at Hughes' expense, as was the custom.[76]

A year later there was another strike. This time the cause was nonpayment of wages. The wages due at the beginning of March had not been paid,

[73] See Rudé, *Crowd in History*, particularly pp. 224–29.

[74] Korol'chuk, *Rabochee dvizhenie*, p. 118, states that the people arrested were "beaten and exiled," drawing on the account a year later in *Vpered*. Potolov, *Rozhdenie velikana*, p. 99, writes of only four deportees, those arrested in Iuzovka by the police, and not those detained by Hughes' workers.

[75] TsGAOR, F. 7952, op. 6, d. 119, p. 30. Report of August 3, 1874, of the Ekaterinoslav governor to the minister of the interior.

[76] Ibid., p. 21; Potolov, *Rabochie Donbassa*, p. 181.

and the workers had evidently accepted this without protest.[77] It should be remembered that these were years of falling coal prices, and that Hughes had only begun the production of rails and was investing every penny in expansion. He was apparently undergoing a financial crisis and juggling funds desperately to make ends meet. Hughes later claimed that it was with the workers' best interests in mind that he had refrained from full payment of wages. He claimed that he did not want the workers to spend all their pay on drink on the eve of the Easter holiday, thus depriving their families of holiday fare.[78] However real the drinking problem was, Hughes' claim rings false against the background of the events.

On April 12, only a small advance was paid on the wages due. With the Easter holiday approaching the workers became increasingly restive. On Saturday, April 26, a large body of factory workers and miners came to demand their pay, but were told that no pay was scheduled. The next day, Sunday, they turned to Hughes personally, threatening to leave the settlement if they were not paid. Through a translator, Alexander Cameron,[79] Hughes asked the workers to wait one more week, promising full pay then. The workers refused to wait, claiming that they had no money to buy necessities, and that Iuzovka stores did not operate on credit. Hughes immediately offered to issue credit notes that the merchants would accept, but the workers rejected this as well. They were aware that they would lose a large percentage of their wages this way, since the merchants would discount the notes substantially; in addition, the workers very likely did not want to breach the Iuzovka custom of banning usurious credit. Hughes' own regulations and standards had evidently caught on among his workers.

What followed was predictable. By midafternoon Jewish stalls in the

[77] Except where otherwise noted, the account of this strike is drawn from TsGIAL, F. 37, op. 53, d. 746, pp. 239–40, report of Lebedev to head of the Mines Administration, and TsGAOR, F. 7952, op. 6, d. 119, pp. 33–38.

[78] TsGIAL, F. 37, op. 53, d. 746, p. 240. Report of Lebedev to the Department of Mines. The drinking would certainly have affected the supply of coal to the blast furnaces and the work time of the factory workers.

[79] Alexander Cameron was an early shareholder in the New Russia Co., and moved from Kharkov to Iuzovka in 1871 or 1872. He and his son are listed among those working in the factory in 1917, Cameron having remained in Russia and remained a shareholder even after the company was sold to a French-Russian syndicate in 1916. Steam-pump operators in the Donbass were known as *kameronshchiki*, but whether this relates to Alexander Cameron or to one of his ancestors is not known. See Companies' House, 4467 (lists of shareholders of the New Russia Co.). For the circumstances of the Cameron families' leaving Iuzovka, see the discussion of 1917 below.

bazaar were being smashed, and meat and drink looted. At Eisenberg's beer hall the crowd not only took all the drink, but burst into the family quarters, searching for money and throwing large stones to smash the furniture. Even when Baskin's tavern opened its doors and tried to pacify the rioters by handing out all the vodka that was there, both the tavern and the owner's home were looted. The riots spread to the Larinskii bazaar and to the Rutchenko mines, where the looting was indiscriminate, including Vepretskii's hotel, the Great Britain Hotel (run by an Englishman named Thompson), where several bottles of vodka were taken, and Batiste Deminanzhe's lemonade works.[80] A list of losses appended to the archive report totals 4,824 rubles at five different establishments, but does not include any of the bazaar stalls. No attempt was made to damage the factory offices or any of the New Russia Co.'s installations.

The following day there was a general refusal to work, and groups of workers roamed the bazaar, threatening the merchants and extorting money from them.[81] The Iuzovka police chief, Cherkasskii, and the highly respected Dr. Goldgardt, chief physician of the New Russia factory hospital, are said to have dissuaded the workers from continuing their rioting. When Dr. Goldgardt informed the workers that the money for their wages had been telegraphed from St. Petersburg and would be paid on May 1, tension subsided and work resumed.

In this incident, the strike was general, and so, evidently, was the rioting, in the sense that it was not only the miners who looted. At the same time, although the property damage and material loss was substantial for the size of the settlement, it would appear that far from all the workers and miners were involved in actual violence. It is also important to note that no attacks on persons were recorded. Even when houses were broken into, smashing and looting were the motives, and not beating, rape, or killing. Once again, as in the previous year, the rioters avoided attacking Hughes or the factory. The crowd had a clearly defined message. Gonimov writes that as the bazaar shops were looted the workers' cry was "Ni nam, ni im"—"If

[80] The police reports in TsGAOR specify that the looting began in the Jewish bazaar stalls and taverns. Lebedev's report says only that there was looting of stores, and in particular of those that had refused credit to the workers. Lebedev's report, however, also cites the workers as saying that they "have nothing to eat, and *nobody* gives goods on credit" (emphasis added).

[81] Pankratova, *Rabochee dvizhenie*, vol. 2, pt. 2, p. 645, citing the *Vpered* report, puts the number of strikers at fifteen hundred—virtually the entire working population of Iuzovka at that time.

we have not, neither shall they!"[82] The words may be the result of the author's literary license, but he has surely caught the strikers' spirit of outrage at the injustice of their families' going hungry while the bazaar stalls were full. The factory had only been in existence five years, and the ethos of money conferring right had not yet remolded their consciousness, formed in the community of village life.

The authorities appeared here in their dual role of guardians and arbiters. Of the rioting workers, twenty were arrested.[83] However, the Bakhmut chief of gendarmes investigated the workers' complaints, and determined that the uncertainty about when pay was due had been a central factor in causing the unrest. He then assembled all the workers and had Hughes clarify to them that henceforth they would be paid monthly.[84]

In evaluating this strike it is important to note the sequence of the workers' actions. In the beginning they were patient; then they petitioned; and only when these two failed did they protest, their violence calling attention to the violation of the social contract by their employer. They had worked honestly, yet did not receive their promised wages, and were going hungry though food was not scarce. In their protest they did not attack any of the authorities, factory or government, and were perfectly prepared to listen to them with respectful attention—though not necessarily to obey them with endless docility. The strike, in which the factory workers were the leading participants, did not attempt to impose new conditions on the employer or to change existing conditions. It was solely an attempt to gain the just implementation of the conditions to which both sides had agreed.

Over the years there was dissatisfaction whenever wage rates were changed. In the autumn the workers would try to prevent or minimize the lowering of rates. In the spring they would grumble and protest that the raises were insufficient, often giving this as the reason for leaving the mines. Yet after the two-day strike of 1875, it was more than twenty years before another strike was called. It was twelve years before any unrest in the Iuzovka district affected the settlement at all. These were years of slow growth, during which the factory established itself as a steady and reliable

[82] Gonimov, *Staraia Iuzovka*, p. 48.

[83] Potolov, *Rabochie Donbassa*, p. 183. Other sources relying on the reports in *Vpered* estimate the number of those arrested as thirty. See, for instance, Pazhitnov, *Polozhenie*, p. 151; Korol'chuk, *Rabochee dvizhenie*, p. 137.

[84] TsGAOR, F. 7952, op. 6, d. 119, p. 39. See also Potolov, *Rozhdenie velikana*, p. 103.

source of livelihood, and the factory work force became stabilized. From 1876 to 1887, the work force grew only from 2,135 to 2,580.[85]

At the beginning of May 1887, the French Co., which managed the former Rutchenko mines, near Iuzovka, instituted summer rates that were lower than the workers expected. This brought the fifteen hundred workers of the Rutchenko mines out on strike on May 5, demanding that the raise be as high as in the previous year, and evidently adding a string of demands for removal of a contractor who provided poor-quality meat, and for the firing of mine supervisory personnel who were particularly unpleasant.[86] Under pressure, the mine director, Vincennes, accepted the workers' demands, but sent a telegram to the authorities asking for the dispatch of troops to restore order, and when the troops were on the way, rescinded his agreement to raise wages.[87]

Outraged by what they regarded as a dishonorable trick, the miners who had returned to work left the pits, and "several hundred" of them rioted. Their first target was a tavern and brewery owned by Henry Church, chief accountant of the New Russia Co., and Goncharov's tavern, on the way to Iuzovka. This was on the night of May 5.[88]

Here a political legend was created. The march of the workers to the brewery and taverns took place at night, and many of the strikers carried mine lamps and torches. When this was reported a careless telegrapher changed miners with torches (*s fakelami*) to miners with flags (*s flagami*). The garbled version has persisted in support of the idea that this was a conscious and organized strike with political radicalism as its foundation.[89] The

[85] For 1876, see TsGIAL, F. 1284, op. 69, ed. khr. 194, 1877, p. 32. For 1887, see Rashin, *Formirovanie rabochego klassa v Rossii*, p. 30.

[86] See Ivanov and Volin, *Istoriia rabochego klassa Rossii*, p. 147; see also Potolov, *Rabochie Donbassa*, pp. 199–203. The reports of police and other officials who investigated the strike mention only the workers' demand for higher pay, but since the final report of the affair discusses company violations of hiring and pay conditions, such as fines and the giving of store credit coupons in lieu of wages, these issues were evidently raised. See TsGIAL, F. 1405, op. 88, ed. khr. 6183, p. 4.

[87] TsGIAL, F. 1405, op. 88, ed. khr. 6183, pp. 1–4; see also TsGAOR, F. DP, deloproizvodstvo 3, d. 89, ch. 12, 1888, p. 7. The manager's name is variously given as Vincent in these records; Vensage in Gonimov, *Staraia Iuzovka*, p. 93; and Vincennes in Potolov, *Rabochie Donbassa*, p. 199, and *Rozhdenie velikana*, p. 146.

[88] TsGIAL, F. 1405, op. 88, ed. khr. 6183, p. 1.

[89] The explanation of the garbled telegram is in ibid., p. 4. A photograph of the garbled version of the telegram of May 11, 1887, appears in Kondufor, *Istoriia rabochikh Donbassa*, vol. 1, p. 49, with the text "I have the honor to announce to your excellency that at the

drama of the night parade of torches and lamps has been used to emphasize the mass nature of the march.[90] This effect is further emphasized by intimating that the workers' indignation and their organized strike carried them directly to Iuzovka. This, however, is contradicted explicitly by the investigating prosecutor's report, where it is stated that it was only on the following morning, May 6, after the strikers once again smashed the locks on Church's brewery and pub, helping themselves freely to the stock, that they marched on Iuzovka.[91]

Their spirits inflamed by the drinking, the miners set out for Iuzovka, their purpose variously interpreted as "to cause disorder and beat Jews,"[92] or to recruit Hughes' workers in support of their strike.[93] What happened next is best told in the language of the Preobrazhenskii church journal.

> The years 1886 and 1887 were marked in public life by large-scale anti-Jewish disorders in many towns of South Russia. Iuzovka might have been the same since it had at this time a considerable Jewish popula tion. For some time there had been rumors in Iuzovka and around it that there would be a pogrom of the Jews. A date was even set, and finally, on the night of May 7, the workers of the mine of the French Co. and of other mines, several thousand in number, threw themselves noisily at Iuzovka, counting on the help of the factory workers. However, to Iuzovka's good fortune, Arthur Hughes, the director, was in the factory at the time and, because of their respect for him, was able to influence his workers. He suggested that they cease work and go out to meet the approaching mob. The workers agreed and there ensued a scuffle at the end of which the attackers were beaten and ran away. In this way, thanks to the good management of Mr.

French Mines near the New Russia Co. factory there was a strike of 1,500 workers, who, with flags in their hands, are brawling and destroying taverns." There is no explanation added to clarify that this is a garbled text.

[90] See, for instance, Potolov's accounts in *Rabochie Donbassa* and *Rozhdenie velikana*.

[91] TsGIAL, F. 1405, op. 88, ed. khr. 6183, p. 3.

[92] TsGAOR, F. DP, deloproizvodstvo 3, d. 89, ch. 12, 1888, p. 7. See also ibid., F. 7952, op. 6, d. 119, p. 46, extract from the journal of the Preobrazhenskii church in Iuzovka. Gonimov, *Staraia Iuzovka*, p. 93, disposes of the problem by writing that Hughes spread false rumors that the workers were coming from the Rutchenko mines to attack the Jews of Iuzovka.

[93] Ivanov and Volin, *Istoriia rabochego klassa Rossii*, p. 147. These authors lean heavily on Potolov, who presents this strike as the genesis of organized labor protest in the Donbass, and writes that the object of the march to Iuzovka was to "unite with the factory workers."

> Hughes, Iuzovka was spared bitter consequences. However, from that time, the destruction of Iuzovka became the standing desire of the workers in the surrounding mines.[94]

Five years later they were to gain this end.

The various official reports of the Rutchenko strike and riot are curiously different in their allocation of praise and blame for the affair. It was investigated personally by the vice-governor, V. P. Rokossovskii, who was responsible for supervision of industrial development in the region. He evidently found extenuating circumstances in the strike of the workers, for he decided not to flog all those who had been involved. Some sixty or so were deported to their home villages, and another sixty-two stood trial. The maximum sentence was a year and a half in prison, while thirty-five of the accused received only seven days, and six were evidently acquitted.[95] Credit for containing the riot until troops arrived was given to "the intelligent and energetic action of the factory administration, and particularly of engineer Serebriannikov."[96] In this report, the cause of the riot was given as "the unjust and absolute ignoring of the necessities of life for the workers by the mine owners, Mr. Uspenskii and the Jew, Umanskii." This apportioning of the blame ignores the detail that Uspenskii and Umanskii ran an entirely different mine and coal company than that at which the strike broke out. The Uspenskii mine later earned notoriety for a fire resulting in heavy loss of life caused by inadequate safety facilities, and, as one of the locally financed mines, it was likely below average Donbass standards in its provision of housing and other amenities. Though not mentioned specifically in any account, it may have been one of the mines that joined the unrest. Nevertheless, the strike and riot began in the French Co.'s Rutchenko mines.

The report of the investigating prosecutor, Zhezhero, gives credit to the Iuzovka police chief for organizing the factory workers against the invading strikers, thus maintaining the official version that it was not Arthur Hughes

[94] TsGAOR, F. 7952, op. 6, d. 119, p. 46, from the journal of the Preobrazhenskii church in Iuzovka. There is no indication of whether or not this entry was written at the time of the events. The number of invading miners is higher than in any other source, and this is the only source that indicates participation of miners from pits other than the Rutchenko mines. It should be noted that the journal gives the date of the invasion as May 7, and puts it at night. The prosecutor's report puts it at noon on May 6.

[95] Potolov, *Rabochie Donbassa*, p. 202. TsGIAL, op. 88, ed. khr. 6183, p. 4, states that sixty-one workers were tried.

[96] TsGAOR, F. DP, deloproizvodstvo 3, d. 89, ch. 12, 1888, p. 7. Report of Ekaterinoslav gendarme commander for 1887.

who rallied the factory against the miners.[97] The report stated that the miners' claims for higher pay were unjustified, and noted that they were ordered back to work on May 10 at the wages originally set by management. However, the French Co. was also blamed for violating laws governing conditions for hiring, for taking illegal deductions from the workers' pay, and for giving store credit coupons in lieu of cash wages.[98]

The pattern of protest seen in the early Iuzovka strikes was repeated here. The focus was immediate and economic. The workers had expected the usual spring raise in pay rates, but were offered less, which offended their sense of justice. The response was a riot, fueled by alcohol, and aimed not against the authorities or the employers, but against merchants and tavern owners. These were not necessarily Jews, as the example of the 1887 strike shows, yet Jews were the most vulnerable target, devoid of any of the powerful official connections that an Englishman like Church may have had, and without the ethnic and religious community that might have caused pangs of conscience over the looting of Goncharov's or Petrov's taverns. Even more important, the authorities consistently portrayed the Jews as illegitimate outsiders and merciless exploiters, and the pogroms that accompanied the riots were frequently seen as justified on these grounds, even when the disorder accompanying them was punished as criminal. In seeking the roots of the disturbances that marked 1887, the Bakhmut police superintendent followed the fashion for local officials of the time in making a blanket accusation against Jews as mine owners who were guilty of merciless exploitation that caused labor unrest in the mines.[99]

In each of the cases that I have examined, the turn to violence came after the failure of an attempt by the workers to appeal to the employers for redress of perceived wrongs. Violence was not the first resort; it was the last. Its function was to call in the authorities by sending an unmistakable message that traditional forms of negotiation had failed. The clearest possi-

[97] In his report on the 1892 cholera riots, Rodzianko, on the basis of conversations in Iuzovka (with, among others, Ivor Hughes), accepted the version that it was Arthur Hughes who in 1887 had organized the defense of the settlement by the New Russia factory workers.

[98] TsGIAL, F. 1405, op. 88, ed. khr. 6183, pp. 1–4. Report of investigating prosecutor Zhezhero.

[99] TsGAOR, F. 102, arkh. 3, deloproizvodstvo 9, ch. 21, 1887, p. 50. In fact, of the mines around Iuzovka in which disturbances occurred in 1887, none was owned by Jews. Those noted in the sources are: Rutchenko, Rykovskii, Karpov, Ilovaiskii, Drevnitskii, and others in the nearby area of the Don Cossack territory, where no Jews were allowed to reside. On the other hand, the Korsun mines at Gorlovka, cited by the inspector as ones in which the workers were treated honestly, were owned by S. S. Poliakov, who was Jewish.

ble expression of this was in the appeal written by the Rutchenko miners during their 1887 strike. "Not knowing where to seek aid and succor, the workers have decided to protest all as one, and not separately. . . . They assume that they will be punished for the disturbances, but at least there will be others who will understand their circumstances and alleviate them, if only by a little."[100]

Where the workers were more sophisticated, their appeal might be directed to the courts. This was evidently not an unusual phenomenon during the 1870s and 1880s.[101] As did the local police inspector, the regime's representatives often acted as mediators and arbitrators—authoritative judges over both parties to the dispute. In the resolution of the Rutchenko strike they played this role clearly, going beyond the immediate task of restoring order and punishing the rioters. This role was integral to the paternalist model of Russia's autocratic society, and worked as long as the people's faith in the tsar's justice could be sustained.

The authorities were quite naturally interested in the causes of workers' unrest, and explanations of such unrest became an integral part of the periodic reports of various officials. In the wake of the Rutchenko miners' strike the moral aspect of economic relations was emphasized. "Where the mine owners keep accounts with the workers honorably and accurately, as for instance at the Hughes factory, and at the Korsun mines near Gorlovka . . . the situation of the workers is more or less bearable."[102]

Late payment or short payment of wages loomed large in the early strikes around Iuzovka, with living conditions or interpersonal relations added almost as an afterthought, if at all.[103] Hughes, who eagerly offered advice to the authorities on questions of social and industrial management, had a somewhat simpler prescription. Some years before the earliest labor unrest in the New Russia mines or factory, he confided to the minister of state domains his father's secret for keeping workers happy. When the unrest of the Chartist movement had swept across Great Britain at the end of the

[100] Pankratova, *Rabochee dvizhenie*, vol. 3, pt. 1, p. 503. This traditional mode of petitioning the authorities persisted for many years in the strikes of the Donbass.

[101] See Ivanov, "Preemstvennost' fabrichno-zavodskogo truda," p. 84.

[102] TsGAOR, F. 102, arkh. 3, deloproizvodstvo 9, ch. 21, 1887, p. 50. Report of the Bakhmut police superintendent.

[103] Ibid., F. DP, deloproizvodstvo 3, d. 44, ch. 7, 1891, p. 10, the political report of the Ekaterinoslav gendarme commandant for 1890, notes five cases of miners striking or leaving the mines because wages had been withheld. He also notes the smashing of a tavern because its Greek owner was rude to the miners.

1830s, Hughes the elder had advised, "Give the men plenty of work." This was done, according to Hughes, and when there was an outbreak of violence nearby, not a single man from the Victoria works, where the elder Hughes was employed, took part in the disturbances. In view of the industrial unrest that was spreading in Russia, Hughes suggested the same strategy.[104] Despite the rapid growth of Donbass industry as metallurgy developed from the beginning of the 1890s, the cyclical nature of the Donbass economy, and the unstable social nature of the mine settlements surrounding each metallurgical center were to render this strategy largely ineffective.

The Rutchenko strike and the frustrated attempt to invade Iuzovka touched off echoes of unrest in the surrounding mines, though not on so large a scale. Workers in the Karpov and Rykovskii mines near Iuzovka, as well as those at smaller mines, struck briefly, though they achieved little or nothing. Evidently the diminished pay raise was general in the mines, as was the miners' dissatisfaction. In Iuzovka, the only signs of this were an anonymous letter to Hughes demanding equalization of Russian workers' pay with that of the British workers, and a leaflet threatening violence if prices in the bazaar were not lowered. Two workers thought to be behind the notes were fired, and a number of others were put under police surveillance.[105] The only lasting result of this wave of strikes was that a company of cossacks was thereafter permanently quartered in Iuzovka to reinforce law and order in the district.[106]

It has been claimed that the 1887 Rutchenko miners' strike "shook the entire Donbass."[107] This would appear exaggerated, for there were no attempts at fundamental institutional change in the wake of this strike. There were, however, a number of characteristics of the Rutchenko strike that mark it as a new stage in development of labor unrest in the Donbass. First, the entire labor force of the French Co. mines acted together in stopping work and making demands, and demonstrated its solidarity again when Vincennes' withdrawal of his agreement was revealed. Second, the work stoppage lasted five days, from May 5 to May 10. It would appear that

[104] TsGIAL, F. 37, op. 53, d. 746, pp. 305–8. Letter of Hughes to the minister of state domains, May 28, 1879.

[105] For all these events, see Pankratova, *Rabochee dvizhenie*, vol. 3, pt. 1, pp. 501–13; see also Potolov, *Rabochie Donbassa*, p. 204, and Potolov, *Rozhdenie velikana*, pp. 149–52.

[106] Chapuy, "Journal de voyage," p. 131.

[107] Ivanov and Volin, *Istoriia rabochego klassa Rossii*, p. 147.

not all the workers took part in the rioting, but none is recorded as having returned to work. Strikes, both before and after this period, rarely lasted more than a day or two. Five days of total work stoppage by fifteen hundred miners thus might well attract considerable attention.[108] Third, there was a clear "demonstration effect," for the strikes at the Rykovskii and Karpov mines began while the Rutchenko workers were still out. If the church journal is reliable, these workers may be assumed to have taken part in the Rutchenko miners' invasion of Iuzovka, and learning of their fellow miners' strike action, adopted it as a means of obtaining redress of their own similar grievances. While it would be exaggerated to read class-conscious solidarity into these actions, the first threads of community lie in this recognition of the similarity of problems and the use of similar action in solving these problems.

There was no other unrest recorded in Iuzovka during the next five years.[109] These were years in which the settlement's population grew to nearly 20,000, and the factory work force grew to over 6,000, with an additional 2,000 employed in the New Russia Co. mines. Between 1889 and 1890 the factory work force grew from 3,372 to 6,326, a one-year growth three times the total added manpower since 1876, when the work force had first passed the 2,000 mark. The Iuzovka mine labor force grew by 35 percent in 1891–92, and it may be assumed that all the mines around the settlement were also expanding as the boom of the 1890s began.[110] It was an unfortunate time for a wave of newcomers to swamp the stable, professionalized labor force that had been assembled over nearly a generation of Iuzovka's existence.

In 1891 famine ravaged Russia, driving before it thousands of hungry peasants searching for a bare living somewhere in their motherland. Surging toward the south, to the fertile Volga and trans-Volga agricultural regions that were rapidly developing, they were stopped and turned back by

[108] Pazhitnov, *Polozhenie*, p. 176, finds an average strike duration of 4.8 days for 1,765 strikes counted throughout the Russian Empire from 1895 to 1904, a period in which workers had already acquired experience in collective action.

[109] There was a riot at the Rutchenko mines in August 1888, for "no known cause." See TsGIAL, F. 1405, op. 93, ed. khr. 1855, p. 101.

[110] Rashin, *Formirovanie rabochego klassa v Rossii*, p. 30, gives the number of workers in the New Russia factory from 1874 to 1900. The number of miners comes from Kulibin, *Sbornik statisticheskikh svedenii*, (henceforth cited as Kulibin, by year and page); here, Kulibin, 1891, p. 251; 1892, p. 268). In the years 1890–1892, Donbass coal production grew by 19 percent. See Ziv, *Inostrannye kapitaly*, p. 55.

the appearance of cholera in May 1892. For many of those refugees, Iuzovka, with its promise of employment, appeared an attractive solution to their problems.

The details of the cholera riots that destroyed the center of Iuzovka, entailing the loss of eighty to one hundred lives, have been set forth elsewhere.[111] Here I offer a number of nuances brought out by examination of archival sources, and attempt to integrate the cholera riots as a social and political phenomenon with the earlier unrest. First, the cholera riots were in no way an industrial dispute. The unrest noted in the spring was that which always accompanied the change of wage rates in the mines. It passed without incident. The factory was working at full blast, presumably with plenty of overtime and high wages. In 1890 a third blast furnace went into operation and the three working furnaces were in operation 365 full days (*sutki*) each during that year. In 1891, two more furnaces were activated and the total blast furnace days rose to 1,103, though the average dropped to 221 full days each—allowing time for maintenance.[112] The company's coal mines had increased their production by 30 percent between 1890 and 1892, ending the year with increased production despite the disruption caused by the riots.[113] Just one week before the riots, the factory had signed a contract for fifteen hundred tons of rails for the Trans-Caucasus Railway, to be delivered by September 15.[114] In addition, the report of the prosecutor who investigated the riots notes that the defense of the factory against the rioting mob on the morning of August 3 was carried out by the workers, with the cooperation of Albert Hughes as director.[115] In this aspect, the factory's solidarity against invaders was exactly as it had been in 1874 and 1887.[116] In a summary of his investigation of the possibility that labor unrest lay behind the riots, Rodzianko wrote:

[111] See Friedgut, "Labor Violence and Regime Brutality."

[112] Kulibin, 1888, p. 231; 1890, p. 160; 1891, pp. 206–7.

[113] For the New Russia Co.'s production during these years, see Ragozin, *Zhelezo i ugol' na iuge Rossii*, p. 51.

[114] *Kontrakty*, p. 2.

[115] TsGIAL, F. 1405, op. 93, ed. khr. 8555, pp. 101–2. Report of prosecutor Rodzianko.

[116] The idea that a strike was imminent and that a strike committee's activity was interwoven with the riots was advanced first in Pazhitnov, *Polozhenie*, p. 176, published in 1908, and later was elaborated in Pasiuk, "Rabochee dvizhenie," p. 208. Potolov, *Rabochie Donbassa*, p. 213 n. 130, writes that no evidence exists to support Pasiuk's view. The extensive and detailed investigation of the riots by a special prosecutor from Kharkov completely negated the existence of any organization of the riots by local or outside people, whether for immediate redress of grievances or broader political aims.

> According to the testimony, both of employees who have served there since the day the factory was opened, and of newly arrived workers and miners, it is clear that the attitude of the workers to the factory is based on the most correct of foundations and is in order in all that concerns wages and labor (hours of work), and there never has been nor is there now any discontent, so that at the present time when the labor force is shrinking everywhere because of the riots and the cholera epidemic, and affecting the production of many mines, at the Hughes factory the work force is only 10 percent lower than in ordinary times.[117]

Industrial discontent as a significant factor in the cholera riots does not appear to be indicated.

The idea that the riots were the fruit of a revolutionary conspiracy, if not a concrete industrial dispute, was staunchly and unanimously defended by the mine owners and engineers who met with representatives of the authorities immediately after the riots.[118] Chief among their claims in this respect was the presence of the mysterious figure in a frock coat and velvet-topped beaver hat leading the crowd. Rodzianko's investigation revealed that there had, indeed, been such a figure leading the attack of the mob on the factory office. Repeated questioning failed, however, to reveal his identity.[119] The most probable identification reveals not an underground socialist agitator, but the former peasant turned mine labor contractor Aleksei Mosin, who went mad and died while awaiting trial.[120]

Nobody, apart from the mine owners and the district mining engineers, believed the conspiracy theory. In his report, Rodzianko was completely blunt about it, noting that "particular attention" had been paid to investigating this point. He strengthened his stand on this issue by arguing that had there been any organization behind the riots, someone out of the more than a hundred persons indicted for the riots would have testified as to the

[117] TsGIAL, F. 1405, op. 93, ed. khr. 8555, p. 100. Report of Valerian Pavlovich Rodzianko to the Kharkov prosecutor, September 22, 1892.

[118] The protocol of the meeting is given in TsGAOR, F. 7952, op. 6, d. 119, pp. 86–94.

[119] TsGIAL, F. 1405, op. 93, ed. khr. 8555, p. 32. See also pp. 100–107, in which Rodzianko returns repeatedly to the problem of the "leader's" identity.

[120] See Friedgut, "Labor Violence and Regime Brutality," pp. 257–58, and *Donskaia rech'* (November 26, 1892), p. 2. Potolov, *Rozhdenie velikana*, p. 163, names Mosin as one of several persons who went around to the Iuzovka houses on the morning of August 3, urging the inhabitants to renew the rioting.

ringleaders' identity, "as always happens in such cases." There had, however, been no such testimony.[121] Finally, Rodzianko stated openly that "were the mining industrialists frank with themselves they would admit that by these 'organizations' and 'unknown instigators' they seek to avoid the question that frightens them, of exploitation of the workers."[122] In light of these remarks it is perhaps surprising that his exhaustive series of reports touches little on this side of Iuzovka's life.

In one paragraph Rodzianko blames the riots on the poor living conditions of the Iuzovka workers, and on the "merchants' too exact demands for payment of debts."[123] In Iuzovka, a large proportion of the merchants was Jewish. One of the aspects of the riots on which both contemporary official sources and later Soviet historiography are virtually silent is that, both at their beginning and at their end, the cholera riots were a specifically anti-Jewish pogrom.

The first tense meeting had been at the home of the cholera-stricken Mrs. Pavlova, where a mob confronted the Ekaterinoslav officials who had come with the police inspector to try to convince her, or perhaps more accurately, her reluctant neighbors, that she should enter the cholera isolation barracks for treatment. A crowd of onlookers heard a drunken worker claim that Jewish doctors had been sent from Rostov to poison the workers.[124] This was not the first appearance of such feelings. Dr. Kazas later testified that the medical student Vegner, who had come to Iuzovka as part of the reinforced medical staff brought in to fight cholera, had already heard the workers in the settlement whispering as he passed the tavern, to the effect that the newly arrived stranger should be grabbed and dealt with. In addition, he noted that in the early afternoon of August 3 he had been advised to evacuate all the medical staff from the settlement, since only then could the riots be put down.[125]

[121] TsGIAL, F. 1405, op. 93, ed. khr. 8555, p. 104.

[122] Ibid., p. 103. This is only one of many official reports expressing sympathy regarding the workers' living conditions, and bitter criticism of the industrialists.

[123] Ibid., p. 34.

[124] Ibid., p. 41. See identical testimony by police inspector Ivanov in *Russkie vedomosti* (November 25, 1892), p. 4, reporting the trial of those accused in the riots.

[125] *Russkie vedomosti*, no. 329 (November 28, 1892). *The Times* (London) explained the anti-Jewish nature of the riots in a somewhat different manner, though with a common basis (August 30, 1892). "Hard drinkers having probably caught cholera, the cry was raised that the Jews had poisoned the vodka, so that the violence directed solely against doctors in the other recent riots was in this case turned entirely against the Jews, and those supposed to be Jews. When the mob left the Hughesofka [*sic*] mills alone to go and loot the town, this, in fact, was one of the cries heard."

The vice-governor arrived in Iuzovka on the night of August 3, 1892, after the riots had already subsided. The next morning, when he inspected the smoking ruins of the Iuzovka bazaar, he reported that he was "shocked by the terrible pogrom that had been reported as 'the smashing of a few Jewish stores.'"[126] As an elaboration of the vice-governor's report, Rodzianko wrote on August 21 that it had been established that at first the crowd attacked only Jewish shops. They would demand that the owner of a store display an ikon to prove that the premises were Russian-owned, and where the shopkeeper did so, all goods taken were paid for. Later, "drunk with vodka and violence," the mob began to smash, loot, and burn without differentiation.[127] At the outset, the crowd stoning the teahouse had begun to beat up the Jewish cobbler Itkin, who had come on the scene by chance, seeking the doctor. He was saved from possible death by the worker Koslosov, into whose home Itkin had run to escape. Koslosov barred the door to the mob, shouting that Itkin was a cobbler, not a doctor, and therefore should be treated as a Russian.[128] The Frenchman Gobier, who testified to Rodzianko that there was no sign of labor unrest or revolutionary conspiracy (he presented himself as an expert on such matters), dismissed the rioters as a rabble of thieves devoid of any national or patriotic conscience. During the riots, the mob had turned on him as a foreigner. Seeking safety, he ran into the local pharmacy, followed by a crowd bent on beating him and looting the pharmacy. The apothecary immediately displayed a portrait of the tsar, "at which the crowd's rage subsided, and all bared their heads."[129]

The following morning the mob had grown to fifteen thousand and had been reinforced by miners from surrounding settlements.[130] A number of persons were going through the workers' quarters, summoning them to the

[126] TsGIAL, d. 93, ed. khr. 8555, p. 105.

[127] Ibid., F. 1405, op. 93, ed. khr. 8555, p. 42. The indiscriminate looting included the burning of the town's consumer cooperative store. See *Russkie vedomosti*, no. 327 (November 26, 1892), p. 3. Six years later, in the Briansk factory riots in Ekaterinoslav, the cooperative store was also destroyed. See Balabanov, *Istoriia rabochei kooperatsii v Rossii*, p. 62. This would seem to strengthen the claim that, in the earlier years, the workers had little part in the direction of these institutions, and did not see the cooperatives as "their own."

[128] TsGIAL, F. 1405, op. 93, ed. khr. 8555, p. 42. The logic employed may appear curious to an outsider, but it was effective, and therefore evidently well grounded in the social imagery predominant in the situation. Doctors were outsiders, and therefore foreign. Cobblers worked with their hands, and were therefore acceptable.

[129] Ibid., pp. 46–47. Gobier notwithstanding, it would appear from this that the rioters possessed patriotic sensibilities.

[130] Potolov, *Rabochie Donbassa*, pp. 212–13, says that eleven neighboring mines were involved. Gonimov, *Staraia Iuzovka*, pp. 101–2, specifically mentions the Rutchenko mines as one place from which the invading mob came.

streets. One, Prokhor Shpigunov, was later accused in court of having shouted "Hey, folks, come out to riot!" (*Ei, narod, vykhodi na bunt!*).[131] The factory offices were the first target, while a small minority stormed the jail where the eighty to one hundred prisoners taken the previous evening were being held. When the factory was successfully defended, first by the factory workers and then by a squad of cossacks, the attack on Jewish property was renewed, as was the looting of whatever alcohol remained. By the end of the riots, only three shops in Iuzovka remained untouched.[132]

Nothing of the pattern seen in the previous labor disputes is evident here, yet throughout the development of the riots there was a consistent delineation between "ours" and "foreign." The Jews were the epitome of "foreign": socially, ethnically, religiously, economically. More important, they were powerless—regarded as alien and hostile by all the local and higher authorities.[133] As long as the mob retained any vestiges of sobriety, its hostility and looting ran along these lines. The doctors who reinforced the medical staff, and around whom the first tension arose, were seen as outsiders, and the officials who came from Ekaterinoslav were the first object of violence—escorted from the bazaar square, but stoned as they went. Itkin and Gobier were saved by the worker Koslosov and the pharmacist. There was no attack on the factory until the morning of August 3, when the greater part of the crowd was made up of miners from outside Iuzovka. At that point, the factory workers defended "their" property and livelihood against "outsiders," as they did in 1874 and 1887. To this extent, at least, there was consciousness and rationality in the activity of some of the workers.

Within this framework, the failure to accept the order to disperse, and the violent and prolonged attack on the cossacks, take on particular significance. The cossacks had been quartered in Iuzovka for five years, and were presumably not entirely a foreign or external group. Yet they were most certainly a group apart from the miners and workers, and were probably more feared than accepted.

[131] Potolov, *Rozhdenie velikana*, p. 163.

[132] *Donskaia rech'* (September 10, 1892), p. 3. The newspaper cites *Novoe vremia* as a source in reporting that ten merchants had been arrested for burning their stores themselves in an attempt to recoup from insurance money losses caused by the rioters.

[133] The powerlessness and docility of the Jewish population, even in the face of pogroms, was noted in various quarters. Sliozberg expands on this theme in his memoirs. *Russkie vedomosti*, no. 332 (December 1, 1892), p. 4, notes the accession of the court to the request of "most of those who lost property" to excuse them from testifying in court as witnesses, for fear of later retribution.

One factor in explaining the riot may well be found in the dynamics of the crowd's growth. The initial crowd around Pavlova's house was estimated at thirty to forty, but grew rapidly to an estimated two hundred.[134] At the beginning of the riot in the bazaar square, only eighty people were said to be involved, a few in stoning the teahouse, the others in egging them on. Within minutes the crowd had grown to an estimated seven hundred, again with the minority beginning to smash Jewish stores, while the majority encouraged them but took no part. These drove off the first cossack patrol that tried to intervene. By the time a larger force came, the crowd had grown to between two and three thousand and the fever of looting had taken hold.[135] The mob had moved only about a hundred yards from the teahouse to the bazaar shops, the first taverns sacked stood side by side in a row, and the growth of the mob had taken place in the space of perhaps an hour or so. Whether the fear of cholera was compounded by the appearance of outsiders, both doctors and officials, releasing the pent-up resentments of the worst-paid and worst-quartered of Iuzovka's population, remains speculative. What is certain is an outbreak of violence without any of its previous hallmarks. There was neither a clear object nor bargaining over any demands. From the beginning, the mob's violence was unrestrained and life-threatening. If in the end it was the authorities who were responsible for most of the deaths recorded, this was only because of better organization and equipment, not because of different intent.

In earlier years, John Hughes had exercised a personal and paternalistic control over events in Iuzovka. But he had died in 1889, and now his sons were carrying on the factory, maintaining many of the same policies, but doubtless lacking the charismatic authority of the factory's founder and longtime guiding spirit. And Iuzovka had changed radically as well. With a population of twenty thousand, a large percentage of them newly arrived during the previous two years, and with a large transient population, unemployed, impoverished, and fearful of cholera, Iuzovka in 1892 was clearly not amenable to any such personal and moderating influences as had operated in the settlement's earlier, more intimate days. Urban growth had brought with it anomie.

Retribution was swift and merciless. The birching of all 497 persons arrested in connection with the riots was decreed immediately by the

[134] See ibid., no. 326 (November 25, 1892), p. 4, inspector Ivanov's testimony, and TsGIAL, F. 1405, op. 93, ed. khr. 8555, p. 41, for the two estimates.

[135] *Russkie vedomosti*, no. 326 (November 25, 1892), p. 3, testimony of police inspector Ivanov.

governor upon his arrival on August 8. Rodzianko, as representative of the Kharkov prosecutor's office, objected successfully, both to the general application of this harsh punishment and to the conditions in which the arrestees were held, in "stifling, filthy, crowded sheds, stables, and cellars, from which cholera victims had been evacuated."[136] As a result, 176 men and 14 women were birched, but of these only 42 were among those subsequently charged for specific offenses and tried.[137]

The riots, the trial, and the sentences shocked Russia. The scope and ferocity of the events went beyond anything that had happened in those years. The attention of the Russian intelligentsia and of the authorities was suddenly focused on the Donbass, and particularly on Iuzovka—"the new California."[138] In protest against the irresponsible cruelty of both government and private individuals, Lev Tolstoi wrote: "They kill, hang, and lash women, the old, the innocent, as was done not long ago in Russia in the Iuzovka factory, and as is done everywhere in Europe and America in the struggle against anarchy and against all violators of the existing order."[139]

Yet little changed as a result. Neither in Iuzovka, nor in the Donbass, nor in Russia as a whole did the burning of the settlement center and the death of close to a hundred people trigger any innovative institutional reform. There were some gestures made to clean up the Donbass settlements, and there was some serious consideration of improving entertainment for the workers and controlling the sale of alcohol. Yet not even this modest program was implemented fully. Reginald Zelnik has written of a "functional threshhold" between the modest degree of unrest that reinforces traditional reactions in society, and a higher level of conflict that can stimulate innovative reform.[140] The lesson of the Iuzovka cholera riots was that the immobility of Russian officialdom and of the Donbass industrialists was so great that the threshhold for innovative change was placed dangerously high. The level of violence needed to bring out the forces for change was to prove destructive of the entire regime and society of Russia.

[136] TsGIAL, F. 1405, op. 93, ed. khr. 8555, p. 16. Report of Rodzianko dated August 10. Rodzianko credits Count Shuvalov with helping persuade the governor to exempt half of those arrested, including women and children, from flogging. Other accounts credit the military doctor who was present for the exemptions from punishment. In the revolutionary literature, Shuvalov, who was later assassinated by the S-Rs, is depicted as the malevolent soul behind the floggings.

[137] Potolov, *Rabochie Donbassa*, p. 215. "Many" of those beaten received 100 to 150 strokes with a birch rod. Potolov, *Rozhdenie velikana*, p. 165 n. 1.

[138] Sliozberg, *Dela minuvshikh dnei*, vol. 2, p. 135.

[139] Tolstoi, "Tsarstvo bozh'e vnutri nas."

[140] Zelnik, *Labor and Society*, p. 199.

What were the consequences of the riots? How did various elements in the Donbass react? The immediate effect of the riots was a mass flight of miners from the district. Here the effect of the cholera cannot be fully separated from the effect of the riots, but the impact of the exodus was clear.[141] From the New Russia mines, 50 percent of the workers had left within ten days, and production was down to 40 percent of its previous level. Comparing this to Rodzianko's observation that only 10 percent of the factory labor force had left underlines the differences between the miners and the factory workers. The Hughes brothers responded rapidly to this situation by signing up a thousand Tatar workers from Kazan province to replace all their other temporary workers.[142]

The effect of the riots was prolonged. During August, September, and October 1892, the New Russia Co. shipped no coal out of Iuzovo station, as against an average of 250 carloads per month before August, and 245 carloads per month in 1893. Other shipments from Iuzovo show a similar sharp decline.[143] Even with these setbacks, all categories of production of the New Russia factory were greater in 1892 than they had been in the previous year.[144] The mine owners and engineers who met with the Ekaterinoslav governor emphasized that the largest mines were the worst hit, and that overall the range of labor shortage was from a minimum of 30 percent to a peak of two-thirds. The effect on production was so serious that there was doubt regarding the sufficiency of supplies to the railways and to the metallurgical factories of the Donbass, the two largest and fastest-growing customers for Donbass coal. In the opinion of these authorities, the riots had precipitated the flight, for until the riots the exodus of workers had been moderate.[145] Some at the meeting claimed that fear of punishment after the riots had motivated the flight of many miners. All were

[141] The following discussion of the impact on the labor force and production, and the mine owners' suggestions to the governor, are drawn from the protocol of the meeting held August 13, 1892, in Iuzovka between the governor of Ekaterinoslav province and fifteen major coal producers, including Albert Hughes, N. S. Avdakov, P. A. Karpov, Ilovaiskii, and Umanskii. See TsGAOR, F. 7952, op. 6, d. 119, pp. 86–94.

[142] *Donskaia rech'* (September 10, 1892), p. 3. The presence of the Tatars was noted by various observers in 1909–12, and 334 were counted in Iuzovka in July 1917. See DOGIA, F. 10, op. 1, d. 5, p. 65.

[143] See *Trudy, XVII, 1892*, pp. 348–49, and *Trudy, XVIII, 1893*, p. 240.

[144] See table 3.1, p. 50, in vol. 1.

[145] One of Rodzianko's reports supports this, noting that as a result of the riots coal production had stopped entirely at some mines, and dropped by as much as two-thirds at others, and that "a mass" of workers had left the district. See TsGIAL, F. 1405, op. 93, ed. khr. 8555, p. 36.

agreed that the restoration of peace and order was the highest priority. None voiced any suggestion for how to restore the workers' confidence. The six-point program offered by the industrialists was predominantly coercive. All military forces were to be retained in the region. The whole of Ekaterinoslav province and the surrounding territories of the Donbass were to be put in a state of "enhanced security." All drinking establishments were to be closed for the duration of the epidemic. A new law on hiring was to be promulgated. (It was, in fact, in an advanced state of preparation.) Regulations banning mass resignation of workers were to be strictly enforced in an effort to stem the flight from the Donbass. The quarantine measures, instituted largely at the recommendation of the Association of Southern Coal and Steel Producers, to keep workers from cholera-stricken areas out of the Donbass were to be relaxed, so that new workers might enter the mines more freely.

Although the employers' view of the situation broadened over the following months, nothing significant was added to their program. In the beginning of September, Avdakov had submitted a memorandum to the minister of state domains and to the minister of the interior, proposing a supervisory board made up of representatives of the employers and of the ministries, to oversee and adjudicate problems of working and living conditions in the Donbass enterprises in connection with the new labor laws.[146] This legislation was so far advanced already that it was adopted almost simultaneously with Avdakov's submission. The mining board was not a new concept, but simply a redistribution of existing tasks to free the district engineer for his technical duties.

Iuzovka was returning to normality, but the trauma of the riots was not soon to be forgotten.[147] On October 16, 1892, the Ekaterinoslav governor visited Iuzovka once again. He met with Ivor Hughes and eleven of the district's mine owners, bringing the government's response to the demands voiced by the industrialists in the wake of the riots.[148] The Ministry of the Interior saw no justification for placing the entire region under enhanced security. Although the minister had initially sent the tsar a report expressing anxiety over the repercussions of the Iuzovka riots in other nearby

[146] *Donskaia rech'* (September 13, 1892), p. 3.

[147] Ibid. (October 8, 1892), p. 3, reports: "The Sixth Company of the Twelfth Regiment of Don Cossacks—commanded by M. A. Pavlov, officers Kutyrev and Khlebnikov—left Iuzovka accompanied by the good wishes and gratitude of the entire society of Iuzovka for their kind and good attitude to the local population. They took an active part in stopping the riots of August 2 and 3."

[148] The protocol of this meeting appears in TsGAOR, F. 7952, op. 6, d. 119, pp. 95ff.

centers, and reporting on the prophylactic dispatch of troops to a number of towns in Ekaterinoslav province, there had been no further serious disorders.[149] Hughes had refused to bear all the costs of the enlarged cossack force demanded by the employers, so the government was leaving the force as before—a single company. At this, the other mine owners announced that they would take up their own collection, and would pay for a company of cossacks to be stationed in Makeevka, and another at the Rutchenko mines.[150]

The governor urged the industrialists to take a long-range view of their labor problems. "You can't live forever under bayonets. . . . How will you soften the wild and coarse nature of the miners? It is created at least in part by their living conditions." The sole suggestion of the employers was that "orderly marketing of alcohol and the strengthening of police supervision will without doubt improve public order at the mines." It was at this point that Avdakov, elaborating on the need for improving the moral environment of the mines, made his oft-quoted statement that there was one church for every 5,094 people, one school for each 2,040, and a tavern for each 570 souls in the Donbass.[151] Gonimov claims that at this meeting the industrialists advanced the idea of workers' educational clubs to be set up under the supervision of the police, and with the participation of the local constables.[152] In the protocol of the meeting no hint of this Donbass zubatovshchina appears. The idea of adult-education courses in Iuzovka had been mentioned to Garshin during his 1891 trip to the Donbass, but no such plan was implemented until 1900. We find in the protocol of this meeting this statement: "There is no doubt that the mining industrialists wish to create a settled, family-centered working class."[153] Yet mention of housing, schools, and medical facilities came only in the vaguest terms, all familiar since the first debates on the "labor question" at the initial meeting of the Association of Southern Coal and Steel Producers in 1874. In the October 1892 meeting the only specific suggestion made was that of enforc-

[149] Potolov, *Rozhdenie velikana*, p. 164.

[150] Of this episode, *Rabochee delo*, nos. 2–3 (August 1899), p. 79, reports: "After the disorders in Iuzovka in 1892, a mine owner having influence in government spheres obtained a troop of cossacks through the well-known chemist Mendeleev. The mine owners later sent a picture of the troop to the professor for his services. The famous scholar showed this photo shamelessly to his friends."

[151] TsGAOR, F. 7952, op. 6, d. 119, p. 97.

[152] Gonimov, *Staraia Iuzovka*, p. 117.

[153] TsGAOR, F. 7952, op. 6, d. 119, p. 102.

ing the government monopoly over liquor sales, and the demand that no tavern should be allowed within two verstas of a mine—a demand that had been heard since the founding of the association.

There could have been other measures taken, both before and after the epidemic. In Taganrog, the municipality had acted in January 1892, seeking government funds for a program of public works to pave the streets and squares of the town to provide employment for the unemployed who had gathered. In Novocherkassk, a six-hundred-place barracks and an "almost-free" soup kitchen had been constructed to meet the needs of the flood of migrant peasants.[154] These are places in which some of the Donbass industrialists lived, and which they visited. There can hardly be one of them who did not read the *Donskaia rech'*, or have other opportunities to become familiar with similar relief projects taking place not far from them. Yet there was no hint of such initiatives in the Donbass, in Iuzovka or elsewhere. The district zemstvos sat silent, wrapped sullenly in their ongoing feud with the industrialists, and there were no municipalities or other institutions of local government in which such suggestions might be authoritatively advanced. The price that was paid was terrible for all. Most terrible was the fact that no lesson was learned, either by the authorities or by the employers.

[154] *Donskaia rech'* (January 12, 1892), p. 3.

CHAPTER 3

The Maturation of the Working Class

As the cholera riots showed, the absence of frequent labor stoppages does not indicate a lack of discontent and frustration. These existed in abundance. The relative rarity of strikes is probably an indication more of the efficacy of police surveillance and cossack control than of worker satisfaction. It is also a sign of the near-total lack of organization of the Donbass workers, and the almost complete absence of influence of the revolutionary movement. Both the church journal and the gendarmerie reports note annual unrest. Yet the culture and social structure of traditional Russia dictated the agenda of protest. Though often painfully aware of their economic grievances, the miners and workers did not engage in political protest at this time. They do not appear to have had any desire to restructure the power relations of Russia, which followed them intact in their migration from the village to the Donbass. It was the prerogative of the rulers to set the boundaries of what was permitted and what forbidden. Certainly it was a rare worker who would have thought that the world could be otherwise ordered, that tsar, church, and authority could be questioned.[1] The workers did, however, carry with them the consciousness of being subjects, of powerlessness, and in addition, the seed of a concept of justice, of certain natural rights and duties that belonged to the employer as well as to the workers. A worker might be discontented with the wage rate set by the employer, and exhibit discontent as a bargaining device, but the right of the decisive last word indisputably belonged to the master.

This culture was the despair of the revolutionaries. In a pamphlet circu-

[1] A fine conceptualization of the role of the powerful in defining the parameters of political and social discourse is found in Gaventa, *Power and Powerlessness*, chap. 1, particularly pp. 21–22. Gaventa's work is based on a study of mining communities in Appalachia, and rings particularly true when applied to the Donbass.

lated in the Briansk factory in Ekaterinoslav in 1899, the revolutionaries' frustration at the prevailing political culture comes through clearly.

> It is our misfortune that many of us, the workers, look upon the administration, and on the bosses as a whole, as though they were benevolent, doffing their caps in deference. . . . When the brick workers downed their tools, they went with tears in their eyes to their supervisor and asked for more pay as though for charity instead of demanding straight out what was rightfully theirs. Despite their pleadings they received no raise. The police chief arrived with police and gendarmes and shouted at them. "What's all this rioting about? I'll sling you in the hoosegow. I'll banish you to Siberia!" In the end the police chief and the rest of those crooks were invited by the factory administration to dinner.[2]

Mass protest came, as a rule, only when the workers felt that the existing contract had been ignored or broken, and riots were generally preceded by patient petitioning.

Perhaps the greatest barrier to the development of the forms of labor protest was the absence of stable organization. Despite the conviction of the employers that a hidden hand was guiding every outbreak of protest, there was little sign of revolutionary organization in the Donbass until the end of the 1890s. When it did appear, it was at first sporadic and tentative, lacking continuity and clarity of ideas. Even more important than the weakness of the revolutionary movement was that there was no workers' movement having an indigenous and autonomous organizational structure. The result was an absence of institutional memory among the miners and workers, an absence of learning and of development in organization and strike tactics. This was only augmented by the instability of the labor force, and inasmuch as this instability was greater among the miners, their adoption of the ideas and organizational forms of revolution was slower than that of the metallurgy workers. In the same fashion, the growth of organization among the metallurgists of the Donbass in the company-owned settlements came later and more slowly than that in the urban centers such as Ekaterinoslav and Lugansk, with their more varied economies, and more importantly, their established institutions of culture and administration.

The general pattern of strikes in the Donbass up to the late 1890s was similar to that in Iuzovka. Actual strikes were relatively infrequent in the

[2] *Rabochee delo*, nos. 4–5 (September-December 1899), p. 98.

mines and metallurgy plants. They were almost exclusively caused by late payment, nonpayment, or inaccurate calculation of wages. When the workers did strike, riot generally was part of their action, and was met by cossacks, the birch rod, and exile. This was the pattern at the Gubonin mine in 1884, at Gorlovka and Vetka in 1890, and Nikitovka in 1895, and an unprecedented two-week strike in September 1897 by more than a hundred workers employed by a contractor at the Petrovskii works at Enakievo.[3] The report of the gendarme commander of Ekaterinoslav province for 1890 notes five cases of workers' abandoning the mines or striking because their wages were withheld.[4] I have already mentioned the Ivanov mine strike of March 1887 as an exception, in that neither the workers nor the regime resorted to violence. Occasionally in this period there might be a work stoppage in which the resolution of complaints of maltreatment by foremen or contractors figures among the demands. This is, however, rare, and even in some cases where such developments are claimed, they are often unsubstantiated.[5] In listing demands for educational and cultural facilities in strikes, the editor of the *History of the Donbass Workers* offers examples only from later strikes in 1905, 1913, and 1916.[6]

A decade after the fact, the cholera riots were seen by the revolutionaries in the Donbass as the epitome of futility. In the attempt to wean the workers away from the tendency to riot, a pamphlet was written, entitled "How the Miners and Workers Have Hitherto Fought the Bosses, and How They Should Now Act."[7] Explaining the difference between a strike and a bunt, the authors point to the Iuzovka riots as an example of fruitless violence. Levus also characterizes the events as a fearful riot (*strashnyi bunt*) in which the simple workers did not understand what the socialists were talking about, but he nevertheless claims that they were the beginning of the revolutionary movement in the Donbass.[8] Kharechko carries the revision further, characterizing the riots as an expression of class consciousness and

[3] For details of these strikes, see Gonimov, *Staraia Iuzovka*, p. 94; Levus, "Iz istorii," p. 54; and Pankratova, *Rabochee dvizhenie*, vol. 4, pt. 1, p. 161; vol. 3, pt. 1, p. 674; vol. 4, pt. 2, p. 755.

[4] TsGAOR, F. DP, deloproizvodstvo 3, d. 44, ch. 7, 1891, p. 10.

[5] Both Gonimov, *Staraia Iuzovka*, p. 93, and Ivanov and Volin, *Istoriia rabochego klassa Rossii*, p. 147, claim that the demands in the 1887 Rutchenko strike included dismissal of rude personnel, but the archival documents do not support this, nor do Potolov's accounts of the strike.

[6] Kondufor, *Istoriia rabochikh Donbassa*, vol. 1, p. 129.

[7] The text of the pamphlet is printed in *Letopis' revoliutsii*, no. 3 (12) (1925), pp. 203–7.

[8] Levus, "Iz istorii," pp. 50–51.

power, and calling them a "notable event" (*zamechatel'noe sobitie*). There was, however, no follow-up to these riots, either in Iuzovka or in the Donbass as a whole. The return of cholera the following year caused no rioting. Nearly half the workers needed in the mines were missing. Though the employers congratulated themselves that "in the better-appointed mines where a settled population is beginning to form, the percentage of miners leaving for agricultural work in some cases does not exceed 25–30 percent," one-third of the thirty-four largest mines had lost from 35 percent to 80 percent of their labor force, and some mines had shut down altogether. Altogether in the Donbass that summer there were only 11,500 of the 20,470 miners expected and needed by the employers for the normal operation of the mines.[9] Although the mining industrialists, gathered in special session, blamed the attraction of agricultural work, the debate reveals that fear of cholera played a substantial role in the miners' exodus.[10]

Characterizing the strikes of 1893–95, Potolov writes that they were "rare, local, and short-lived, and all were put down by armed force."[11] Kondufor describes four outbursts in 1896, small in size and brief in duration, where the chief demands were raises in pay and timely payment. In 1897, he records six strikes that were "characterized by considerable spontaneity, not prolonged, and achieved small results."[12] Until the end of the century one cannot speak of strikes in the Donbass as a mass phenomenon, or as an organized movement in terms of disciplined and coordinated action. It would certainly be premature to claim great political content for the strikes of the nineteenth century. The change began to come on the eve of the twentieth century, when industrial development reached a peak, and when the revolutionaries began to create a continuous presence, as both an agitational and an educational movement.

The Maturation of the Strike Movement

The year 1898 marks the beginning of a long process of change in the strike movement. This is the zenith of the great "Witte decade" of development.

[9] *Trudy, ekstrennyi s"ezd, avgust 1893*, chairman's report, p. vii, and numbers of absentees in thirty-four largest mines, pp. 42–48.

[10] Ibid., stenographic record, speech of Mstsikhovskii, p. 78.

[11] Potolov, *Rabochie Donbassa*, p. 216.

[12] Kondufor, *Istoriia rabochikh Donbassa*, vol. 1, p. 63.

The New Russia plant in Iuzovka reached a peak of 11,000 workers, and in South Russia there were 37,654 metallurgy workers.[13] Where once only Hughes and Pastukhov smelted steel there were now twenty-one metallurgical plants with a total of sixty-four blast furnaces.[14] Both the metallurgy industry and the coal mines of the Donbass were concentrated in relatively large enterprises. The average metallurgy plant had 2,420 workers at the turn of the century, while 77.5 percent of the coal miners worked in mines employing over 500 workers.[15]

There remained, however, a fundamental difference between the metallurgy settlements and the coal mines. The metallurgy settlements grew like Iuzovka to populations of twenty and thirty thousand inhabitants, and attracted merchants and ancillary industrial enterprises. While they remained company settlements, and none of them was granted municipal status or any sort of self-government, they formed a relatively stable and heterogenous social unit. Though none of them appears to have overcome the raw and grimy character of the newly founded steel town, they were throbbing with a nascent urban character.[16] In the meeting of the different cultures that took place in these rapidly growing settlements, traditions and even prejudices began to be questioned, and community isolation to diminish. The mining settlements were smaller, less stable, and more homogenous, ethnically and socially. They too were fragmented, however, in that where a mine was very large, it tended to break into several settlements, each clustering close to a particular shaft or shafts. The parochialism of the work crews was thus less relieved than in the metallurgy settlements. The population of these mining settlements, moreover, remained dominated by young, unattached adult males. Iuzovka was developing into a full chain of human society, with relatively large numbers of school-age children, and a growing number of older workers and even pensioners. This was much less marked in the coal settlements, which were caught up in a vicious circle of poor housing and services, and in the instability of the labor force.

[13] Rashin, *Formirovanie rabochego klassa v Rossii*, p. 30.

[14] *Svod statisticheskikh dannykh*. See also AN, F 12, box 7175, report of Count de Montebello to the Foreign Ministry, July 11, 1900. He notes here the rapid growth of South Russian metallurgy and its production of over half the iron and steel of the Russian Empire.

[15] Kondufor, *Istoriia rabochikh Donbassa*, vol. 1, p. 38. The average metallurgy plant in the Urals employed 1,496 workers at this time, and only 48.7 percent of Russian factory workers were employed in enterprises with more than 500 workers.

[16] The most forceful description of this process is found in Surozhskii, "Krai uglia i zheleza."

Iuzovka started the year 1898 with a strike. It began on January 1, after the distribution of new pay books to the workers. The new books contained the text of the June 2, 1897, labor law, which, among other things, limited the working time in factories and mines to ten and a half hours, an hour less than was the custom at the New Russia factory, where the two shifts that worked around the clock overlapped, with each working eleven and a half hours and, in addition, taking two on-the-job meal breaks. Although the new regulations had been officially published in September 1897, this was the first time any of the workers had heard of the change.[17] The workers in the boiler shop decided that it was their right to shorten the workday by an hour, and decided that if management was ignoring the new law, they would implement it themselves. With no disorder, they stopped work at 6:00 P.M. The example spread rapidly through the factory, and by January 15 it was followed by the entire labor force.[18] The only hint of violence was a scrawled note hung in the plumbing shop saying that "for violating the work rules, Moldengauer should be beaten like a dog."[19] In the mine maintenance shops, the foreman threatened that the first worker to leave at 6:00 P.M. would be arrested. For two days the workers simply downed tools at 6:00, and sat doing nothing until 7:00. On the third day, the entire hundred-man crew left in a group at 6:00.[20]

On January 16, when the entire New Russia labor force was continuing to leave the factory after ten and a half hours' work, the company published regulations explaining that the former hours of work would be maintained within the framework of the new labor law. The announcement was ignored by the workers, who continued to disperse to their homes at 6:00 each day.

Only when the "seventh-hour strike" had been in effect for three weeks did management begin to exert external pressure. On January 21, Ivor Hughes brought in an official of the Mines Administration and the district

[17] The development of the strike is presented here according to the report submitted by the head of the Ekaterinoslav gendarme administration, as published in Pankratova, *Rabochee dvizhenie*, vol. 4, pt. 2, pp. 190–92. For publication of the new law, see ibid., p. 670 n. 46.

[18] Gonimov, *Staraia Iuzovka*, p. 127. Kondufor, *Istoriia rabochikh Donbassa*, vol. 1, p. 64, writes that sixteen hundred workers took part in the strike. The total labor force was eleven thousand. It would seem likely that only the permanent workers of some of the shops in the factory would have taken part in this strike. As noted in the discussion of working conditions, there were considerable differences in the hours of work between the different parts of the factory.

[19] Moldengauer was the shop foreman. (Moldengauer was also the family name of the architect of the New Russia Co.)

[20] Gonimov, *Staraia Iuzovka*, p. 130.

police superintendent, and explained to the workers that they were doing wrong, and that they should continue their work until 7:00 P.M. as always, and if they had any complaints or disagreements they should send eight men from each shop to negotiate on their behalf. The workers, for their part, noted that English supervisors finished work at 6:00, and claimed for themselves the same right. If they were to work an extra hour, they should be paid overtime for it. They also directed Hughes' attention to the fact that the shorter workday had been decreed by the tsar, and that other mines and factories were implementing the new law without dispute. The meeting broke up without agreement, and the workers continued their job action, preserving both complete solidarity and exemplary order.

Both officials agreed that the workers' actions were tantamount to a strike and that the instigators should be punished as the law provided, but discreetly, since the workers had been completely orderly. This was never done, nor were the workers' wages docked for the time they took off, as had also been suggested. On February 1, the management of the factory instituted a new work schedule that met the workers' demands. The workers had gained a complete victory.

Many factors contributed to the winning of this strike. Certainly the solidarity and order of the workers played a large part. The letter of the law and the authority of the tsar were also on their side. Indeed, it would appear that even a British foreman objected when the chief engineer ordered him to dock the workers' pay for unauthorized absence when they left at 6:00.[21] In addition, the management was enjoying unprecedented prosperity, profits and dividends were at a peak, and the board of directors in London had just allocated 150,000 rubles to be distributed as bonuses in celebration of twenty-five years of rail production.[22] To have a strike would have been most untimely, particularly since the other metallurgy factories in the Donbass would have been more than happy to fill whatever orders the New Russia Co. would find itself unable to complete.

The uneven pace at which the strike tactics of the Donbass workers matured can be judged by comparing the October strike at the New Russia plant to the spectacular success of the "seventh-hour strike" in January. In

[21] Ibid., pp. 127, 131–32. According to Gonimov, the British foreman, Pugh, who had served twenty-five years at the factory, was fired forthwith for violating the solidarity of the British colony.

[22] TsGAOR, F. DP, deloproizvodstvo 3, ed. khr. 700, 1901, p. 14. Report of Major General D. I. Boginskii, head of the Ekaterinoslav province gendarme administration, to the police department.

September 1898, the Don Committee of the RSDRP had made a concerted effort to spread leaflets in Mariupol, Lugansk, Taganrog, and Iuzovka, calling for a shorter workday and a coordinated struggle against the owners.[23] This leaflet, it is claimed, influenced the workers to strike. In fact, there was a strike in the factory three days later, of 150 blast furnace workers, seeking higher pay. The strike came to an immediate end when the local police corporal threatened the strikers with arrest.[24]

The next strike broke out October 11, when only 179 of 650 miners at one of the New Russia mines entered the shaft for work. The remainder, when asked by the police commander and the district mining engineer why they were not working, dispersed to their homes without presenting any demands. The root cause of the strike was the action, four years earlier, of the management in lowering the rates paid for extraction of coal from one ruble twenty-five kopeks per hundred pud to one ruble. The miners' daily pay remained the same, but the contractors now demanded that an *artel'* (a cooperative work gang) mine four wagons a day, instead of three.[25] Many complaints and demands were added when matters were finally negotiated. That evening only 110 out of 550 reported for the night shift. The next day about half the morning shift and a small part of the night shift worked.[26] An hour after the beginning of that shift, the 100 to 150 miners who had refused to enter the mine are said suddenly to have attacked the factory,

[23] Pankratova, *Rabochee dvizhenie*, vol. 4, pt. 2, p. 207. See also Ivanov, *Rabochee dvizhenie v Rossii*, p. 279.

[24] Pankratova, *Rabochee dvizhenie*, vol. 4, pt. 2, p. 203, report of the Kharkov prosecutor to the minister of justice, October 20, 1898. The report links the leaflets, distributed in Iuzovka on September 17, with the strike, noting that they called for a strike for higher pay. As noted above, Pankratova writes that a shorter workday was the demand put forth in the leaflets. The following account of the October strike is also based on this report.

[25] TsGAOR, F. DP, deloproizvodstvo 3, ed. khr. 700, 1901g., p. 15. Report of Governor Sviatopolk-Mirskii to the minister of the interior. It is unclear why a step taken in 1894 should have caused unrest four years later. The reader can easily calculate that the contractors, having had their rates cut by 20 percent, were raising the work norm by a third.

[26] TsGAOR, F. DP, deloproizvodstvo 3, ed. khr. 700, 1901g., has three different accounts of the evening shift on October 12, all in official reports. One claims that 416 miners worked; another says that 60 worked; the third says that no workers entered the mine. All are agreed that the crowd that remained at the mine and subsequently caused the disorders numbered between one and two hundred miners. Gonimov, *Staraia Iuzovka*, p. 145, offers a clue about the discrepancy in numbers reported working. He writes that the number of miners working was counted according to the number of lamps taken from the lamp house. During the strike, many miners who were afraid to strike, but also feared to enter the mine because of the sabotage rumors that had been spread, took their lamps, but then slipped away rather than entering the pit.

shouting, whistling, and throwing stones through the windows, driving out the two thousand factory workers, and then running through the settlement, coercing the residents to join their protest.

There was, however, an interim incident, omitted in the prosecutor's report as published by Pankratova.[27] As the crowd of striking miners stood around the pit head on the evening of October 12, the acting district mining engineer, Sutulov, appeared in a state of inebriation and asked why the miners were not starting their shift. A voice from the crowd shouted "We want a raise in pay!" Then one of the strikers stepped forward and, for the first time since the beginning of the strike, began to recite the miners' grievances. Sutulov then ordered the foreman to take the man's name and have him fired the next morning. At that point the entire crowd began to demand that they all be fired, and headed for the factory.

The riot brought the factory to a standstill, and the strikers began terrorizing Sobachevka, ("Dogpatch"—a slum neighborhood), trying to stir up a general uprising by threatening to loot the bazaar. The cossacks acted quickly, dispersing the crowd and arresting twenty-four strikers. Reinforcements were called in, and they cordoned off the settlement from surrounding mines, mindful of the miners' part in the 1892 riots.[28] These troops remained in town until the following Tuesday, October 20 (Saturday the 17th was payday, and Sunday was market day, when huge crowds were expected). All taverns were ordered closed for those two days, and the presence of the reinforcements was conspicuous.[29]

While the strikers were being dispersed, Ivor Hughes, Rotmistr Popov, the Iuzovka police chief, the cossack commander, and engineer Sutulov were monitoring the situation. Quiet had been restored by 9:00 P.M., and it would appear that the only actual damage inflicted had been to windowpanes and streetlights. An ultimatum was decided on, a notice was drawn up, and three hundred copies were pasted up throughout the settle-

[27] The additional material is in a report of Rotmistr (company commander) P. K. Popov, deputy commandant of the Ekaterinoslav province gendarmerie, dated October 16, 1898, in TsGAOR, F. DP, deloproizvodstvo 3, ed. khr. 700, 1901g., pp. 9a–10.

[28] Gonimov, *Staraia Iuzovka*, p. 142.

[29] TsGAOR, F. DP, deloproizvodstvo 3, ed. khr. 700, 1901g. This report credits engineer Sutulov with saving the factory boilers from explosion when the workers ran away. It would appear that Sutulov had sobered up quickly, and had taken the routine Donbass precaution of letting the steam out of the boilers and taking the release valve off the factory whistle. Some days later, two workers were arrested for searching for the hidden release valve.

ment. The notice read: "In view of the recent misunderstandings and upheavals in the factory of the New Russia Co., it is announced for the attention of all workers that the deadline for reporting to work has been set as 6:00 A.M. on October 13. Those workers not reporting for work may apply to the factory office to be paid off."[30]

The ultimatum was almost completely successful. On the morning of October 13, all the factory workers reported on time, and the factory was in full production again. At the Central mine, 150 men were missing, and at the Zavodskaia mine 250 men refused to enter the pit. As the miners reported for work they were questioned by Sutulov about their complaints. None asked directly for a pay raise, though some stated that other mines paid higher wages. The chief complaints were of improper levying of fines, nonpayment of compensation for disability (the workers cited twelve specific cases), and the sums that the *artel'shchiki* (leaders of the work groups) took from every pud of coal mined.[31]

Those miners who refused to enter the mines explained that they were afraid that the mine cables would be cut and the ventilators blocked. In the police investigation that followed, the New Russia Co.'s police superintendent testified that on the day before the outbreak of the strike, a foreman had been asked by one of the workers whether he had heard that the next day there was to be a strike and that the mine cables would be cut and there would be a riot.[32] Pankratova writes that this came from the misconstruction by the simpler workers of the message in the Social-Democratic leaflets. Distribution of the leaflets had started strike talk, and as this passed from person to person it became twisted so that when a strike date was set, the message was that there would be a sabotaging of the mine cables and that anyone breaking the strike would be in mortal danger.[33]

Here was the nub of the labor movement's problem. The attempt to wean the workers away from undirected violence was the central effort of the revolutionaries. If one takes the example of the factory workers during the January strike, it might appear that this lesson was well learned. The

[30] The list of those present at the consultation, and the text of the ultimatum, are presented in Gonimov, *Staraia Iuzovka*, pp. 141–42. The fact of the ultimatum and its posting in three hundred copies are from Popov's report, TsGAOR, F. DP, deloproizvodstvo 3, ed. khr. 700, 1901g., p. 10.

[31] Ibid., p. 10.

[32] Ibid., pp. 29–30.

[33] Pankratova, ed., *Rabochee dvizhenie*, vol. 4, pt. 2, doc. 50, p. 207.

October strike, however, was initiated and led by the miners. The workers left the factory to avoid violence, and perhaps from a feeling of solidarity with the miners, since they might otherwise have been expected to forestall the invasion of the factory as they had done in previous years. By all subsequent evidence, it was predominantly the miners who sought to create disorder and who began the attacks on Sobachevka and on the Larinskii bazaar that were nipped in the bud by effective cossack action.

Babushkin and Smidovich later reminisced sadly about this time regarding the volatility and violence of the workers. Listening to workers' conversations, Babushkin despaired of their understanding what a strike was. They only knew that repression from the employers' side should be answered by violent rioting from their own. "In the leaflets it was clearly stated that *bunt* was undesirable and brought only harm to the workers. A worker, having read the leaflet, immediately said 'They're ordering us to riot.'"[34] Smidovich wrote of the inability of the workers to organize and articulate their demands. "If the directors squeezed, the workers rioted, burned the office, beat the director, but did not know how to formulate their demands and stand behind them."[35] Yet the workers' reaction was, in reality, much more complex.

On the night of October 13, two battalions of infantry arrived in Iuzovka, accompanied by the governor, Prince Sviatopolk-Mirskii. In the morning the number of miners reporting for work at the Central and Zavodskaia mines was 65 more than usual.[36] The governor immediately ordered the banishment of 400 strikers, but only 276 who had refused to work on all three days of the strike were actually sent to their home villages.[37]

Ostensibly the strike was over, and the miners had failed to emulate the organized and disciplined determination that had won the factory workers their victory nine months earlier. There was, however, a postscript. The factory workers, some of whom had staged a brief strike in September, and who had been conspicuous in their passivity during the miners' strike, had the last word. On October 15, an ungrammatical letter addressed to the

[34] Babushkin, *Vospominaniia*, pp. 94–95. Babushkin was writing about the events in Ekaterinoslav's Briansk factory in 1898.

[35] Smidovich, "Rabochie massy," p. 164.

[36] TsGAOR, F. DP, deloproizvodstvo 3, ed. khr. 700, 1901g., p. 10.

[37] Pankratova, *Rabochee dvizhenie*, vol. 4, pt. 2, p. 207.

Iuzovka police chief was found in a postbox. This letter not only set forth demands in an orderly fashion, but revealed something of the workers' anxieties and perceptions.

> We don't want to murder, riot, or loot. Only our previous level of pay. Our master paid no attention when we entreated him, and now will not answer because we are rioting. Please tell him why we riot. We cannot answer when asked because we are such a mass of people that each shouts something different. Now we are being discharged, and we don't want to hear about discharge, so we ask you to stand up for us and present our letter, to restore the former price of our labor, and that we want to have three shifts each day, for we never see the light, for if we work by day, we sleep at night, and if we work at night we sleep by day and never see the light. And how the contractors squeeze us, so that we do not want to work for the contractors, but for the factory office. And if our masters agree to this then there is no need to call us to assemble at the office, but an announcement can be made calling us to work. And if he does not agree, let him distribute announcements saying with what points he agrees. And we would ask extra pay for the boiler shop, the turners' shop, the unskilled workers, and the stonemasons. In all hot work we want three shifts and we want to be paid as we were before, and we ask you that you achieve this as swiftly as possible, and that you make it clear to the soldiers that we are neither Turks nor English and that in no circumstances should they fire on people who are their own. And if you cannot gain us our rights then inform your commanders so that they will get us the rights we wish, and that we should not be called to the office and that we should not be discharged, for we do not wish to be discharged, for we have need to save money and we must pay for food and lodging and we have children at home, and among us a machine operator receives 60 kopeks a day when a machine operator should receive at least a ruble and 25 kopeks a day. And you should arrange all this, and demand that the money that was sent be given to us, ten rubles to each man, for they have taken thousands and our hearts boil to think of it.
>
> For all the workers of the factory, and for all the mines around the Hughes factory, we ask that as quickly as possible he publish an announcement as to what he agrees and asking us what we wish, and we will answer.

The letter was signed "Workers of the Factory of the New Russia Co."[38]

The workers' modest petititon is remarkable in several ways. First of all, it is addressed to the police chief, or to his superiors should he prove unable to give satisfaction. The police chief was accepted by the workers as a legitimate arbiter between them and their employer after direct appeal had failed. The miners had followed a different strike tactic, without petition or demands. The workers' fear that anyone personally associating himself with demands to management would suffer retribution was clear. As noted above, this was the policy followed by the drunken engineer Sutulov. It was a tactic of intimidation all too common in the Donbass.[39] For this reason they did not wish to be called to the factory office for negotiation. Most important is the opening statement of the letter—"We don't want to riot, murder, or loot. . . . Please tell him why we riot." For these workers the bunt was an instrument by which to signal—neither an end in itself nor a blind rage. It might sometimes turn to blind rage, particularly when alcohol was involved, but as in the miners' strike, it could also be used to bring out the workers and mobilize a crowd that would lend impressive mass to a street demonstration that had, in fact, only a relatively few activists in it. Last, but not least, is the appeal to justice—the plea for the restoration of what was formerly acknowledged as belonging to the workers, and the anger at what was seen as usurpation by the managers of the anniversary bonus in which the workers felt they should have a rightful share. Nowhere in this document is there a hint of class consciousness or political generalization. Organization is explicitly denied, whether out of knowledge of the regime's sensibilities or to protect those who, in fact, were the active leaders. Exactly as in previous strikes and petitions, there was an explicit recognition of the master and of the state, and a claim for justice under the social contract.

The workers' letter and other testimonies that gave an even fuller exposition of their demands were communicated to the governor, and he pressed for action on them with the director of the Mines Administration for Southern Russia, calling the relations between employers and workers "abnormal". The governor also observed that because of unjust treatment of

[38] TsGAOR, F. DP, deloproizvodstvo 3, ed. khr. 700, 1901g., pp. 12–14.

[39] See, for instance, the account of the strike of the workers of the Franco-Russian Railway Car Works in Ekaterinoslav in March 1898, in *Rabochee dvizhenie v Ekaterinoslave*, p. 4; another such incident is related in *Rabochee delo*, nos. 4–5 (September–December 1899), p. 102.

the workers, the secret leaflets calling for the workers to fight the capitalists were in keeping with the mood of the discontented workers.[40] When these matters were taken up with the New Russia Co. management, Hughes blandly claimed that he had never known that these were the workers' grievances, that many of them seemed eminently reasonable, and that he would take steps for a gradual reform of the wage system and the rectification of just grievances. One of the concessions made by management was the elimination of payments through contractors, a step long pursued by the company.[41]

Although the report of the Kharkov prosecutor, Davydov, states that Sviatopolk-Mirskii authorized the deportation of 400 strikers, and 276 were immediately banished from Iuzovka for having been on strike for the entire three-day crisis, later documents dealing with the investigation and trial of those arrested for rioting on the night of October 12 report only 11 deportees, all from among the 24 arrested.[42] Those arrested were all peasants. Six were miners, three were unemployed, five were of undefined occupation, one was a shoemaker, and the remaining nine were from the factory. Of those ultimately convicted and deported, eight were miners and three were factory workers. All were Great Russians by nationality and Orthodox by faith. Of those convicted, only one had any previous criminal record, a conviction for rioting. The deportees ranged in age from seventeen to twenty-six years, with five less than twenty years old, and five more aged twenty-three or twenty-four. Seven were bachelors; four were married, none with their families accompanying them. Eight were illiterate, with the remaining three having a home education, a church school education, and a popular primary school education. Of the eleven, only two consistently earned one ruble per day or more, while five were listed as receiving between sixty and eighty kopeks per day. Three of the eleven were convicted on the

[40] See Governor Sviatopolk-Mirskii's report to the minister of the interior setting forth grievance areas in TsGAOR, F. DP, deloproizvodstvo 3, ed. khr. 700, 1901g., p. 15. The governor lists six grievances of the workers: (1) the 1894 lowering of wage rates; (2) workers having to wait in the mines for hours, wet and hungry, while the lifts raised coal; (3) disabled workers receiving little or no compensation; (4) the twenty-fifth anniversary bonuses not having been shared with the workers; (5) workers fearing to complain lest they be fired; (6) seasonal lowering of wage rates.

[41] Pankratova, *Rabochee dvizhenie*, vol. 4, pt. 2, p. 207. On elimination of payments through contractors, see Kondufor, *Istoriia rabochikh Donbassa*, vol. 1, p. 265.

[42] Cf. Davydov's report as given in Pankratova, *Rabochee dvizhenie*, vol. 4, pt. 2, pp. 203–7, with the investigation and trial report in TsGAOR, F. DP, deloproizvodstvo 3, ed. khr. 700, pp. 39, 138–59.

basis of evidence from their peers, while in the remaining eight cases the evidence came from the police, from mine doctors and engineers, or from foremen and other supervisory personnel.

Although details of only the inner core of the hundred or two hundred who initiated the short-lived demonstration on the night of October 12 are available, some clear characteristics emerge. The demonstrators came from the ranks of the lowest paid, unskilled, and unlettered, for the better-paid, skilled workers of the factory ran home when a hail of stones came through the factory windows. The demonstrators were unattached young males, for the same higher-skilled, better-paid workers were those who could afford to keep a family in Iuzovka, married men with wives and children who had no desire to risk their domiciles and pay packets in defiance of authority. The core of the crowd was not made up of conscious and determined revolutionaries. Neither were they criminal elements bent on plunder. Once again, all the social characteristics of the deportees fit the analysis given by George Rudé for his "crowd."[43] In clear contradistinction to that in the cholera riots, the violence of this crowd was clearly directed and limited, though the potential for unlimited violence was perhaps present, and foiled only by the quick action of the cossacks who cut short the looting of the bazaar before it really got under way. Still, one cannot completely ignore the lack of response to the call to violence discernible here. Memories of the terror of the cholera riots, intertwined with the strong regime presence and with the consciousness of a steadily rising standard of living, served to leash the passions of a class war that was as yet no more than abstract words on a poorly understood leaflet. And in Iuzovka, the crowd that ran for home was much larger than that which took to the streets.

There were other instances of orderly and disciplined strikes. In March 1898 the Rutchenko miners, who had kept their violence directed to objects outside their own mine settlement in 1887, conducted an exemplary strike for eradication of the dugouts that had been outlawed four years earlier, but were still in common use at the mines. "The mine owners did everything to provoke a riot and end it with whips and cossacks. True the troops were called in, yes, the governor came, but the hovels of the mine workers were so frightful and the miners so orderly, that this time even the governor was on the miners' side."[44] Orderly strikes, however, appear to have been the exception. The riot at the Briansk works in Ekaterinoslav in

[43] See Rudé, *Crowd in History*, particularly pp. 254ff.
[44] Levus, "Iz istorii," pp. 55–56.

mid-May 1898 involved twelve hundred workers in looting, burning, and pogroms. Five hundred were subsequently deported.[45] This riot was not even within the context of labor demands or a strike; it began from the killing of a Russian worker by one of the Circassians employed as guards at the factory. A French observer blamed it on the low-quality work force, a result of the great expansion in metallurgy that had made skilled workers scarce in South Russia.[46] A strike of the workers of the Nikopol-Mariupol factory in July 1899 turned violent, with workers smashing the machines and a blast furnace when their delegates were arrested. After the rioters were arrested, an attempt by the remaining workers to free them resulted in the death or wounding of several dozen strikers at the hands of the soldiers convoying the arrested strikers to jail.[47] This strike took its place alongside the Iuzovka cholera riots as an example of how violence harmed the workers' cause.

How frequent was such labor violence during this period? It would appear that more often than not, violence was the workers' answer to a worsening of working conditions or a denial of demands they thought just.[48] Certainly outbreaks of destructive activity in the Donbass appear to have been far higher than in the figures presented by Pazhitnov for the whole of Russia. Dealing with the years 1895–1904, he lists only forty-four cases in 1,765 strikes.[49] The consensus of the revolutionary movement in the Donbass at that time was that in 1898 the workers were still smashing,

[45] *Rabochee delo*, no. 1 (April 1899), pp. 86–87. For a detailed analysis, see Wynn, *Workers, Strikes, and Pogroms*, pp. 117–27.

[46] CL, 11850, n. 214, du Marais, "Briansk Aleksandrovsk Factory" (December 1898), p. 5.

[47] The strike has been documented in Pankratova, *Rabochee dvizhenie*, vol. 4, pt. 2, pp. 348–55, 358; *Rabochee dvizhenie v Ekaterinoslave*, p. 17; and *Rabochee delo*, nos. 4–5 (September–December 1899), p. 102. Of the "several dozen" workers killed or wounded, two were killed, the rest injured. The manager of the factory was a twenty-eight-year-old American, Harry Laude, who had worked for Carnegie in Illinois, and was said to be intelligent and possessed of rare energy. See CL, 11850, n. 206, du Marais, "Nikopol-Mariupol" (December 1898), p. 2.

[48] For additional detailed descriptions of various incidents of labor violence, see *Revoliutsionnaia Rossiia*, no. 41 (1904), pp. 18–19; no. 49 (1904), p. 16, regarding an outburst triggered by the lowering of wages at the Kamenskoe factory; *Rabochee delo*, nos. 4–5 (September–December 1899), p. 100, on the violence of the workers at the Ekaterinoslav railway shops; Gonimov, *Staraia Iuzovka*, p. 152, and Pankratova, *Rabochee dvizhenie*, vol. 4, pt. 2, pp. 592–94, on three violent mine strikes near Iuzovka, resulting in the arrest of three hundred miners. *Iuzhnyi rabochii*, no. 3 (November 1900), p. 35, comments regarding this incident, "such strikes are becoming more frequent."

[49] Pazhitnov, *Polozhenie*, p. 176.

using arson, and resorting to random physical violence, though a move toward organized, conscious struggle for improvement was also said to be discernible.[50] Perhaps a more accurate assessment came from another revolutionary source. Commenting on the situation in Iuzovka, he wrote: "It is only a pity that most still believe in *bunt* and others in spite of the bloody clashes hope for succor and aid from the government. . . . People are saying: 'If the penalties laid on by those tyrants of the factory are not rescinded, we will have only one way. To take apart the factory as was done before, so that no stone is left upon another. To go on living this way is impossible."[51]

Was this an accurate view of what was happening in the Donbass as a whole? I will offer at least a tentative answer by assembling data on Donbass strikes from 1896 through 1899, classifying them not only as violent or peaceful, but breaking these categories into restrained and unrestrained violence, and provoked or unprovoked violence. There are said to have been forty-one strikes in the Donbass during these four years.[52] Of these, I have found accounts of thirty strikes in various sources. Although details are lacking for many of the strikes, ten for which data exist are said to have been marked by some measure of violence. Of these ten incidents, three involved provocations such as the arrest or discharge of strike delegates or attacks on strikers by cossacks. In three cases, the violence may be said to have been unrestrained, involving destruction of property and attacks on management personnel, and in two of the cases, loss of life. One of these three, the strike of July 1899 at the Nikopol-Mariupol metallurgical works, was provoked by the arrest of the workers' negotiators. In the other two, the riot at the Briansk works in mid-May 1898 and the February 1898 strike at the Petrovskii works in Enakievo, no action of management or of the authorities can be linked to the outbreak. In the remaining seven cases of violence, the workers' outburst was restricted to the tactics used in the October 1898 strike in Iuzovka, where workers smashed windows to get others out on the street with them, or to individual actions against management or the factory that were restrained or ignored by the main body of strikers.

In sum, the frequency of violence was much higher in the Donbass than it was for Russia as a whole. Where Pazhitnov found only 2.5 percent of labor

[50] *Rabochee dvizhenie v Ekaterinoslave*, p. 6.

[51] *Iuzhnyi rabochii*, no. 3 (November 1900), p. 34. The correspondence is probably from one of the activists of the Donetsk Mine Workers' Union.

[52] Kondufor, *Istoriia rabochikh Donbassa*, vol. 1, pp. 63–65.

disputes involving any destructive activity, I found 33.3 percent. While only 30 percent of these outbreaks developed into unrestrained bunt, the potential was almost always there, and sometimes, as in the Briansk riot, needed only some small spark of conflict to set it off. Avoidance of a full-fledged riot might often be a matter of timely and forceful intervention, as in Iuzovka in October 1898.[53]

This high potential for violence has several roots. One of them is almost certainly the nature of the labor force, and the mine labor force in particular. The predominance of low-paid, low-skilled labor in a highly migratory population of young, unattached males carries the clear potential for violence. There were too few family units in most of the settlements to create the stable society that might have damped down violence. The dominance of alcohol in the culture of the Donbass and the lack of other recreational resources reinforce this tendency. Conditions of work in the mines and smelters, with death and injury an everyday occurrence, further encouraged the acceptance of violence in all spheres of life. The newness and rapid growth of the region also contributed to instability through the weakness of social interdependence. There were few established norms other than those of the cossack knout and the police inspector. Though the church was generally present and revered by the workers, its authority in times of crisis proved weak. Last but not least, the total social fragmentation of the Donbass encouraged violence. As residents of the company towns or mine settlements, the workers had no part in their own governance. The social institutions of the village community had been left behind them, and there were no institutions of local urban self-government available for observation. Even the privileged classes of Iuzovka and Makeevka had no local government, and the zemstvo was totally inactive in the industrial life of the Donbass. The massive social and psychological dislocation caused by migration from a village to an industrial urban setting was an important contributor to the social instability of Russia.[54] Even such institutions as consumer cooperatives were not yet created or governed by the workers, so they had small influence as educational institutions for the developing of skills of self-government. The workers evidently regarded the cooperatives as foreign, for in both the cholera riots in Iuzovka and the Briansk riots, the

[53] In the trial resulting from the cholera riots of 1892, it was implied that had a stronger cossack force been present at the first moments of the outbreak, the results might have been quite different.

[54] Rosenberg, "Conclusion," p. 134.

cooperative stores were among those looted and burned. The workers were denied institutions of class organization, and as the revolutionaries noted, "Where the owner-capitalists are weak in defending themselves against the workers, the government intercedes, and at their first steps the workers encounter the full force of that government."[55]

Whatever its professed paternalist care for workers, and however much it developed its institutions of regulation and inspection of living and working conditions, the tsarist regime was not in favor of social and political pluralism. The growing conflicts and complexities of industrial society did not lead the regime to spin a flexible web of institutions to link its multiplying parts. Instead, each was to stand alone in subordination to the autocracy. The result was a weakly articulated system with a center less and less able to cope with the tasks posed by modernization and economic development. The workers' way of calling attention to this inadequacy was to resort to their one autonomous mode of action, violence. But this was a dangerous two-edged instrument. It was also one that the regime was not at all inclined to tolerate or understand. A circular of the Ministry of the Interior, written in 1897 noted: "False impressions are taking root among the workers as to the efficacy of all sorts of acts, including willfulness and violence, relating both to government authorities and to the manufacturers and their colleagues. This appears most dangerous to state order and social tranquillity." The circular recommended that violence be punished by discharge and deportation under convoy.[56]

Violence was thus a relatively frequent concomitant of labor disputes in the Donbass, and in significant measure can be linked to the weakness of social structure there. One of the earliest campaigns of the revolutionaries, when they came to the Donbass region to organize the workers, was the fight against violence. I now turn to examine the early activities and development of the revolutionary groups of the Donbass, to study their changing organization and aims, their internal dynamics, and the extent of their influence on the workers of the mining and metallurgy settlements of the Donbass.

[55] *Rabochee delo*, nos. 4–5, (September–December 1899), p. 97.

[56] Gonimov, *Staraia Iuzovka*, pp. 129–30.

CHAPTER 4

Organizing Revolution

The activities of the various populist groups in the Donbass were intermittent. Some, like those of Goldenberg or An——skii, appeared intended for general cultural awakening, while others, like those of the dynamite suppliers from Lisichansk, were used by populists in the region to further terrorist plots far from the Donbass. All of this was tentative and sporadic. In his political survey for the year 1886, the Ekaterinoslav governor noted that since 1882, "the intelligentsia" had been conducting itself circumspectly, and that undesirable political activity was negligible.[1] All the revolutionary movements were extremely limited in numbers and could not allot members to every potential group that came into being. It took many years until the Donbass proletariat was seen as embodying a political potential in its own right. Indeed, the minuscule size of the revolutionary movements, and their failure to generate a mass popular following, is one of the central political factors in the development of Russian society during this period. The persistence of this situation through to the Bolshevik Revolution has much to do with the ultimate fate of that revolution.

The first revolutionaries to settle in the Donbass and organize ongoing work there were the young Jews driven out of Minsk and Vilna by police vigilance in the early 1890s. They began their work in Ekaterinoslav among the artisans, working according to the familiar patterns they had followed earlier. By this time the coal industry was well developed and the large metallurgy factories were following the same path of rapid, large-scale development. Ekaterinoslav, though it was outside the Donbass proper, had a number of large metallurgical and metal-working enterprises, and underwent the same rapid growth of heavy industry. It was not long before a conflict sprang up between "a particular workers' group influenced by the

[1] TsGAOR, F. 102, arkh. 3, deloproizvodstvo 9, ch. 21, 1887.

success of work among Jewish artisans in the western regions, and the intelligentsia, which wanted to concentrate on the factory workers, regarding the artisans as secondary." The two groups also disagreed about whether to organize the workers as a mass movement or in a conspiratorial cell structure.[2] Along with their youthful fervor, the new revolutionaries brought with them all the divisions that split their groups in the western centers of the empire, and these divisions were reinforced by every new split that arose.

The beginnings of political organization in the New Russia factory and mines came in mid-1895, when the Ekaterinoslav group headed by Gavriel Leiteisen, which was trying to organize in the Briansk metallurgy works, borrowed money from the mutual-aid fund they had set up, to finance an expedition to Iuzovka by Mikhail Efimov, who was to carry with him propaganda material for distribution among Hughes' workers. This tentative contact was cut short when the entire Ekaterinoslav group was arrested in August 1895.[3] The arrest of the Ekaterinoslav group brought on a "general silence," which ended only when the renewed presence of the intelligentsia created the possibility of once again stimulating activity in workers' circles. The next mention of the existence of a revolutionary group in Iuzovka was in June 1898, when five workers were arrested, suspected of Social-Democratic activity. A soldier, Koshelenko, had been exposed to revolutionary agitation by two of his officers. He had returned to Iuzovka and given his brother, Mitrofan, the book *Labor and Capital*, published by Gustav List. Mitrofan Koshelenko and a group of his friends had read the book together, with the son of one of the workers serving as reader for the illiterate workers. They had thus become the first revolutionary circle in the blast-furnace shop of the New Russia factory.[4] Six months earlier, in

[2] The conflict is discussed in *Rabochee delo*, no. 1 (April 1899), p. 85. The multifaceted dispute was essentially among the Bund, the Economist tendency in the Marxist movement, and the outlook that was to characterize the Bolsheviks.

[3] See Pankratova, *Rabochee dvizhenie*, vol. 4, pt. 1, p. 167. For a brief history of the Ekaterinoslav group's founding, activity, and ultimate arrest, see Smirnov, "O pervom kruzhke," pp. 161–65. The arrest of one hundred participants and sympathizers of the group is noted in *Rabochee delo*, no. 1 (April 1899), p. 84.

[4] Gonimov, *Staraia Iuzovka*, pp. 132–34. Gonimov gives the names of the participants as Koshelenko, Chernov, Iashin, Klevtsov, Korogodin, and the brothers Moisei and Kirill Krizhanovskii. *Rabochee delo*, no. 1 (April 1899), p. 153, reports the arrest of five Iuzovka workers in June 1898, giving the names as Kashivenko, Chernov, and others. The newspaper also reports the arrest and subsequent release of a railway battalion soldier, Markian Kashivenko.

December 1897, the League of Struggle for the Emancipation of the Working Class had been formed in Ekaterinoslav and in Kharkov, and was beginning to disseminate leaflets. The new Ekaterinoslav group was arrested on the night of March 10–11, and the Kharkov group three months later, but nominally, the Don Committee of the RSDRP, set up at the beginning of 1898, still functioned, and this marked the beginning of a continuous organizing effort.[5] No matter how many times members of committees and organizations were arrested, new members reorganized the study circles and propaganda groups.

During this initial period, the focus of the revolutionaries' work was similar to that performed in other places. The Social-Democrats of Ekaterinoslav and Kharkov set up study circles, established mutual-aid funds, and began to collect library funds for the acquisition of both legal and illegal literature.[6] In February 1898 the Ekaterinoslav group began propaganda work, distributing leaflets to the workers in seven local factories. "The leaflets were economic in content. It was not yet time to make them political."[7] These apparently were the leaflets that were found in the New Russia factory at the time of the unsuccessful September 1898 strike of blast-furnace workers. The reasoning of the members of the Ekaterinoslav League of Struggle was that it was necessary to give the workers some experience in collective action for immediate and specific economic gains before it would be possible to motivate them in support of more abstract political action. In addition, the league members were under the impression that the police would intervene less in matters that were essentially between employers and workers than they would in political affairs.[8] While the first assumption was almost certainly correct, the second was totally wrong. The Ministry of the Interior saw any attempt to organize the workers as a political matter and responded vigorously to put an end to it.

As a new area of political opportunity, with a rapidly expanding population, the Donbass was a good place for returnees from political exile. Passports were not often demanded, and wanderers were a common phenomenon. In February 1898, on his return from exile, Petr Moiseenko came

[5] See *Rabochee dvizhenie v Ekaterinoslave*, p. 4, and Pankratova, *Rabochee dvizhenie*, vol. 4, pt. 2, pp. 761–62, 778.

[6] *Rabochee dvizhenie v Ekaterinoslave*, p. 13.

[7] *Rabochee delo*, no. 1 (April 1899), p. 85.

[8] *Rabochee dvizhenie v Ekaterinoslave*, p. 6. It would appear from these comments that the Economist viewpoint predominated.

to Mariupol. He was quickly able to make contact with an engineer in the Shcherbinovka mines, Sokolov, whose brother Sergei was later to be one of the activists in the Donetsk Union of Mine Workers. Sokolov and the mine director, Priadkin, introduced him to G. I. Petrovskii, who together with others of the "mine intelligentsia" carried on cultural and educational work among the miners.[9] When he left Shcherbinovka, Moiseenko wandered for almost a year and a half from mine to mine looking for work and trying to avoid the curiosity of foremen and police inspectors until he found a job as a pipe fitter at the Rykovskii mine near Iuzovka.[10] Though often forced to change jobs, he was to remain active in the Donbass until 1916, a rare example of continuity of political activity.[11]

In the spring of 1901, the twenty-three-year-old A. V. Shestakov was at a gathering of "unemployed" revolutionaries in Samara. It was suggested that he go south to the Donbass, where, though the work was difficult, there was an open field for organizers.[12] Organizational work demanded considerable independence and initiative, for despite the assiduous creation of local, district, and regional committees, there was no secure communication, and only an intermittent supply of direction, literature, and workers. Even years later, letters would be lost and remain unanswered on important points, addresses changed so frequently and secretly that contact with organizers would be broken, and codes would be garbled and undecipherable. Repeated complaints on this score make up a large part of the correspondence from the center to the local groups.[13]

News of workers' unrest, strikes, or arrests was slow in getting out of the small, isolated mine and factory settlements. Publication in the revolutionary press might come six months to a year after the fact, and no one could know how long after that it would be until a copy of the particular paper might make its way to some new group so that the incident might serve as an object lesson for other organizers. If there was no organizer on the spot to report situations and events, a false impression of quiescence might be

[9] Moiseenko, *Vospominaniia, 1873–1923*, p. 141.

[10] Ibid., p. 163.

[11] Regarding the length of Moiseenko's activities in the Donbass, see Mikhailik and Vysotskaia, "Nerushimaia druzhba," p. 129.

[12] Shestakov, "Na zare rabochego dvizheniia v Donbasse," p. 156.

[13] Such problems take up about three-quarters of Krupskaia's letter of June 23, 1905, to the Ekaterinoslav group. See Shklovskii, "Perepiska," p. 19, for a discussion of these problems as they appear in the correspondence.

created. The reverse was also true: an eager and active correspondent might create an impression of great activity on the basis of a modest reality.[14]

Revolutionary propaganda sometimes appeared from unexpected quarters, and brought unanticipated results. In mid-1899, district engineer Sutulov was visited by his son, a student, and two friends. The young people displayed a great interest in the mines and factory and visited a number of New Russia mine shafts and workshops before returning to the city. Almost immediately it was discovered that wherever they had been there were numerous RSDRP proclamations bearing the stamp of a "Donetsk Committee," as well as hectographed copies of one of the most popular socialist brochures, Wilhelm Liebknecht's *Spiders and Flies*. Sutulov, already under a cloud for having provoked the violence of the October 1898 strike by his drunken behavior, was implicated by association and forced to resign.[15]

The Donetsk Social-Democratic Union of Mine Industry Workers

The most effective and long-lived revolutionary organization of this period was the group that was known as the Donetsk Social-Democratic Union of Mine Industry Workers (*Donetskii Sotsial-Demokraticheskii soiuz gornozavodskikh rabochikh*). It began its activities in the beginning of 1902, pronounced itself a Social Democratic organization in March 1903 to participate in the congress of the RSDRP, and continued its work in a number of centers throughout the Donbass until the autumn of 1904. Up to 1901, almost all the organized activities of the various revolutionary groups had focused on the central cities. During 1901, with the economic recession deepening and causing discontent among miners and metallurgy workers, there was an attempt to set up "flying squads" that would distribute agita-

[14] A survey of *Iskra* for 1903 reveals the sudden prominence of reports from Iuzovka in the last quarter of the year, with virtually nothing preceding or following that time. The correspondent either was arrested or moved on to greener fields, but this brief view into the state of working-class organization remains most edifying. News of the September 1900 Prokhorov mine strike, which involved eight hundred men, with three hundred arrests and a chain of violent mine strikes in its wake, was not printed in *Iskra* until February 1901.

[15] Gonimov, *Staraia Iuzovka*, pp. 147–50.

tional literature in the mines and factories throughout the region. This proved to have little success.[16]

The idea of a secret union had first been thought of in 1899 by three young professional revolutionaries, A. V. Shestakov (alias Nikodim), I. N. Moshinskii (Hughes, Konarskii), and Dmitrii Takhchoglo (Emelian). They suggested a group that would be separate from any of the regime-sanctioned organizations in the south, and isolated from the various revolutionary committees, all of which were assumed to have been penetrated by police agents.[17] As Moshinskii later noted, working within the committees was like being in a goldfish bowl.[18] The Donetsk Mine Workers' Union was thus an independent creation at its inception, and maintained contact and exchanged literature with Socialist-Revolutionaries, the Ukrainian Spilka (Social-Democratic union), and other socialist groups in the region.[19] The center for the new union was set up in Rostov, a city chosen not only for its proximity to the Donbass but because its gendarme commander, Artemev, was said to be totally indifferent to revolutionary conspiracies, and because no Okhrana headquarters existed there.[20]

The union was to be totally independent, its activists recruited on the basis of long-standing personal acquaintance. These activists were to be trusted with all the stages of the union's activity: the writing and printing of pamphlets; their transport to the mine and factory settlements; and the work in these localities: preaching, teaching, and organizing strikes.[21] The union adopted only two ideological principles: (1) not to import literature from abroad, since the organizers thought that the reliance on leadership from abroad was demeaning, and (2) not to engage in intergroup polemics.

[16] Levus, "Iz istorii," p. 63.

[17] Moshinskii, "K voprosu," p. 230.

[18] TsGAOR, F. 7952, op. 6, d. 120, p. 75. Moshinskii's memoirs.

[19] Gonimov, *Staraia Iuzovka*, p. 158, claims that it was the Don Committee of the RSDRP that initiated the union, though he dates the union's first contacts with the Social-Democrats from March 1902, when organizational work had already been under way for several months. Moshinskii, TsGAOR, F. 7952, op. 6, d. 120, p. 75, notes specifically that it was not the Don Committee, and that the union was set up to be separate from the Don Committee. Kir'ianov, *Rabochie iuga Rossii*, p. 8, notes that early historiography, based on memoirs, left an exaggerated notion of the numbers of Bolsheviks and their leadership of strikes. "These testimonies have wandered from account to account for several decades."

[20] Moshinskii, "K voprosu," p. 231. Only after a wave of strikes in November 1902 did the Okhrana set up a Rostov office under Rotmistr Karpov, who assiduously planted agents throughout the region.

[21] Ibid., p. 232, has a list of eighteen union activists and the field of activity of each.

Moshinskii writes: "In setting up the operation we were under a great influence of the Bundists, and on the other hand we were under the influence of *Rabochee delo*. Beyond that, I as a *praktik* [a practical field organizer as opposed to a revolutionary theorist] didn't go too deeply into all the fine points of the party program."[22] The Bund influence referred to here should be understood as the attempt to organize the masses of workers by engaging their attention through agitation, the concentration of activity around specific, immediate problems. *Rabochee delo* was the organ of the Economist tendency, whose supporters believed in involving the workers themselves in leadership and activity, particularly in organizing to achieve economic gains. They believed that the experience gained in such activity would ultimately prepare the working class to act on more abstract political questions.[23]

The union's field activities began at the start of 1902. Shestakov established a legitimate presence in the Donbass by working as an assistant timekeeper in the Chulukov ore mines. He went to Iuzovka at the end of January or the beginning of February 1902, posing as a confidential clerk for a Rostov attorney, handling compensation cases for the families of crippled or killed workers. This gave him the chance to circulate widely among workers. Though he met numerous miners, he was totally unable to make contact in the factory during the year he spent in the settlement, and it took some time before he was able to meet with the small Social-Democratic groups there.[24] As Shestakov himself later recalled, the group he eventually organized was "predominantly small artisans, tailors, barbers, shoemakers, someone from the print shop, two or three of the intelligentsia, external students among the young people—among them the well-known worker Sonia Berlin. It was an almost solidly Jewish group. None of them had any contact with the surrounding mines, or even with the New Russia factory, and to get in touch with them by means of these comrades was difficult."[25] Moshinskii added: "You are surprised that we had no contacts in the Iuzovka factory. There was no link between the groups there. They were semicultural, and in the factory the circles of workers were independent. At

[22] TsGAOR, F. 7952, op. 6, d. 120, pp. 78–79. This portion of the manuscript of Moshinskii's memoirs was not printed in the 1927 article in *Proletarskaia revoliutsiia*.

[23] A complete discussion of the many doctrinal polemics that split the Russian Social-Democrats is available in Schapiro, *Communist Party*, chap. 2.

[24] Gonimov, *Staraia Iuzovka*, p. 159.

[25] Shestakov, "Na zare rabochego dvizheniia v Donbasse," pp. 157–58.

any rate, these were *kustarnye gruppy* [amateur circles] who had no connection to the broad party masses."[26] Attempts to proselytize were cautious, for there was a high price paid by those who were found out by the authorities. A curious Iuzovka worker who picked up a union leaflet when he went to get his tea water in the factory was brutally beaten by the police, and arrested along with eighteen others.[27] Leaflets were not passed personally, but stuffed into toolboxes and pockets, or pasted on fences and mine props.[28] This, of course, deprived the revolutionaries of much of the persuasiveness of their agitational work.

One of the successes of the Donetsk Mine Workers' Union was its ability to maintain continuity even when its activists were forced to move. Shestakov left Iuzovka in March 1903 under pressure of investigation. He was arrested only a year later. His replacement, a man named M. G. Gurskii, who had worked in revolutionary matters since 1894, and had been in the Donbass since the summer of 1902, was arrested quickly, only to be replaced by Otto Auss and Maria Barkova.[29] But the greatest success was in establishing a local leadership to carry on the work in various centers. In Iuzovka this consisted of Shur, Bondareva, Rozalia Paperno, Emma Ridnik, and Ekaterina Groman.[30] The quality and effectiveness of local leadership was often doubtful, but it did at least afford the prospect that the organization might eventually develop local roots.

By the end of 1903 the union had chalked up an impressive record of activities. It had issued a total of 63,000 copies of thirteen proclamations. Local bodies of the union had produced a total of 3,020 copies of seventeen proclamations. The union had also distributed 15,500 publications of other groups. A number of libraries had been founded, and thirty systematic study groups were meeting, with a total of five hundred members. The union had convened fifteen meetings drawing a total of a thousand listeners,

[26] TsGAOR, F. 7952, op. 6, d. 120, p. 77. Who, exactly, the "broad party masses" were at this point is not specified.

[27] *Iskra*, no. 45 (August 1, 1903), p. 8.

[28] Gonimov, *Staraia Iuzovka*, p. 156.

[29] Moshinskii, "K voprosu," p. 235. The first appearance of union leaflets set off a massive wave of searches that resulted in thirty arrests in Iuzovka, Lugansk, Taganrog, and Rostov. *Iskra*, no. 45 (August 1, 1903), p. 8. This source reports Shestakov among those arrested. Apparently *Iskra* is mistaken on this point. Despite the arrests, the union carried on.

[30] Moshinskii, "K voprosu," p. 233. The list published in this source is not complete, for we know that others were no less active, but that these were the people who later were active among the Bolsheviks. The prominence of women among the Iuzovka activists is striking.

and claimed to have organized ten strikes during the year, involving three thousand workers.[31] By Donbass standards of the time, this was activity on a massive scale. Among those who went through "a considerable course" of political training under the auspices of the Donetsk Mine Workers' Union were Mark Sheitlander (generally known as Zubarev or Kuznetsov) and Grigorii Petrenko-Tkachenko, both of whom were to earn their places in history in the December 1905 uprising on the Ekaterinin Railroad

Successful as the union was, it was not free of problems. With all the proclamations and leaflets of the union written in Rostov by a small group of conspirators, it was hard to move into agitational work and focus on a single immediate issue, which was thought to be necessary to move masses of people into action. "Naturally it was difficult for a group so detached from the Donbass to produce papers that would be understandable to the workers. For that, one either had to go to the workers, or come from them."[32] Here was the significance of the locally written leaflets. The leaders of the Donetsk union were too far away, both geographically and in a psychological and experiential sense. The ultimate failure of the union, however, came from its great success. As the operation grew, its human resources were strained beyond their capacity. Breaking its own rules, the union took two activists from the Don Committee to transport literature. Both Nikolai Sheparev (alias Vulkan) and Maximov (Cupid) turned out to be police agents, and in the spring of 1904 they betrayed the whole organization—over a hundred persons. An attempt was made to assassinate Maximov, but he was only wounded.[33]

During 1903 there were three independent party circles of about fifteen persons each in the New Russia factory. In addition, there was the town organization that Shestakov had met. No claim is made as to the existence of any revolutionary group among the miners. Shur relates how the town group would spread leaflets and attempt to give reports to workers in the mines and factories, all the while "looking for comrades, and they would be looking for us."[34] Shur also notes that his group followed up the attempted general strike in Ekaterinoslav with a September 1903 strike in Iuzovka. The strike leaflets giving the economic demands put forward by the workers

[31] *Iskra*, no. 52 (November 7, 1903), p. 8; Moshinskii, "K voprosu," p. 233.

[32] Levus, "Iz istorii," p. 64.

[33] Moshinskii, "K voprosu," p. 234. See also TsGAOR, F. 7952, op. 6, d. 120, p. 81.

[34] TsGAOR, F. 7952, op. 6, d. 120, p. 2. Memoirs of Shur. See also Gonimov, *Staraia Iuzovka*, p. 158.

contained the demand for a constituent assembly, and the slogan "Down with the Autocracy" was added.[35]

In the police report of the factory strike of September 1903, there is no mention of leaflets, though the spreading influence of Social-Democratic ideas is repeatedly emphasized. The strike was due to the seasonal lowering of rates that was to take effect in the factory on October 6. The workers requested an interview with the factory director, Anderson, but were told that he could not help them. They then turned to the police chief and requested that he bring the district engineer, Rutchenko. When these talks produced no results, the workers demanded to be fired with three months' severance pay as compensation for early termination of their contracts. This, too, was refused, though the management negotiators offered to lessen the pay cut. The workers then sent two of their negotiators to Ekaterinoslav to complain to the governor that the employers were violating the work contract.

The next evening, as the workers were going home, police officers reported seeing a crowd and hearing a voice shouting, "We should fight for our own rights and not rely on the governor or on management. Our wives and children are nearly dead in this dirt and poverty. These vampires suck our blood when all this [pointing to factory] should rightfully be ours." Seeing the police patrol, the speaker hid in the crowd, but the officers reported that his accent sounded Jewish. The police report emphasizes that these words were undoubtedly part of the Social-Democratic activity reported constantly by agents. The strike was quiet and there were no drunks among the workers; this was also attributed to revolutionary influence. The strike ended after six days with an ultimatum, obeyed by the workers, to return to work under the conditions offered by the employers.[36]

The workers, the police belief in revolutionary influence notwithstanding, still adhered to the idea of the social contract rather than that of class war urged on them by the revolutionaries. They sought to negotiate with

[35] TsGAOR, F. 7952, op. 6, d. 120, p. 4.

[36] Ibid., F. DP, ed. khr. 4, ch. 18, 1898–1904, p. 29. *Novoe vremia* (October 1, 1903) noted that all Donbass mines had cut wages by 10 percent, but that in Iuzovka the cut was 20 percent. There were two other strikes mentioned in Iuzovka in this period. One was a strike in the mines that was said to have won higher pay, a shortening of the workday, and the abolition of contractors. See *Iskra*, no. 50 (October 15, 1903), p. 6. The other was a strike of tailors that ended with the exiling of a number of the strikers. See ibid., no. 52 (November 7, 1903), p. 5. It is not difficult to imagine in which of these two strikes the political leaflets were used.

management, and when this was not efficacious, pursued their goals within the system, turning to the police chief as mediator, to the district mining engineer, and finally to the governor. The feeble and sporadic contact between revolutionaries searching for each other in the mass of conformist workers was too weak to have a noticeable influence in Iuzovka.

However, the disorganized nature of the Iuzovka organizations may have worked to their advantage, for repeated arrests failed to put an end to the activities of the union. When Volgin, who had argued in favor of terror tactics, was arrested on February 27, 1904, he turned in a whole group of fifteen activists and propagandists, including Paperno, whom Bondareva called the "dominant personality" of the group, and the pharmacist Markovich, who was secretary of the Iuzovka group, despite having been an unsuccessful organizer and propagandist. Markovich, too, told all to the police.[37]

Made anxious by the police successes against their activities, the union organizers moved their printing press out of Iuzovka to the Vosnesenskii mine, where a supervisor and a foreman were willing to turn a blind eye to the revolutionary circle. But there too, there were arrests through August, and finally, the whole organization—fifty-three people, and ten thousand pieces of literature—were taken in. These included Emma Ridnik, who had assumed leadership of the Iuzovka group after the arrest and confession of Markovich, and Bondareva. The decision to wipe out the union was evidently connected to the growth of protest against the Russo-Japanese War, for the final consignment of leaflets, brought from Rostov by a trusted activist, consisted of five thousand copies of "Lessons of the War," "To the Soldiers," "The War, the Crisis, and Unemployment," and the call to revolution "It is Time!"[38] Later, when the agent-hunter Petrenko managed to get taken on as a clerk in the Iuzovka police department, he found that the man who had transported the leaflets, Gavriel Evdokimov, a machinist in the New Russia factory, was registered with the police as secret agent no.

[37] See Gonimov, *Staraia Iuzovka*, pp. 170–75, for the events of this period, replete with Okhrana agents and an S-D counteragent. On Volgin's betrayal of the group, see Shur's memoirs, TsGAOR, F. 7952, op. 6, d. 21, p. 2. The police would have caught the group even without these confessions, since the authorities had infiltrated the union's center, and had an agent planted in the group in Iuzovka as well. See ibid., Moshinskii's memoirs, p. 81: "It is said that the whole thing was due to the provocations of Evdokimov and Markovich. In fact the Zubatovite provocation was right at the center. It was Sheparov. He turned in everyone with whom he had contact."

[38] Gonimov, *Staraia Iuzovka*, p. 183.

4. When this was discovered, the last four union activists remaining at liberty left immediately for Odessa, and it is said that Evdokimov "got what he deserved."[39] Moshinskii claims that the union continued to operate from Iuzovka and directed all the activity of the Donetsk proletariat throughout 1905, including the armed uprising in December.[40] This claim is apparently unsubstantiated and the activity of the Mine Workers' Union as an entity separate from the Social-Democrats appeared to end with the trial of the fifty-three.

Competition, Finance, and Culture in the Revolutionary Movement

There was good reason for the Donetsk Mine Workers' Union to join the RSDRP. This was the period of the growth of revolutionary parties out of the more amorphous movements that had characterized the preceding decades. In the party field, there was little competition for the Social-Democrats in the Donbass. The Bund and the Socialist-Zionists appealed only to a limited constituency of Jews. Because of its ideology of appealing to the Jewish workers in the Yiddish language, the Bund had almost no organized presence in the Donbass, where it appears that Yiddish was little used. Although a Bundist was one of the four members of the Jewish self-defense group killed in the 1905 Iuzovka pogrom, the Bund apparently never had an organized group in the settlement.

Neither were the Socialist-Revolutionaries active in the Donbass. When they began organizing in Kharkov they were dependent on the Mine Workers' Union for literature, since their party had no literature appropriate for factory workers, or even for the peasants of the region. It was concentrating on trying to woo the intelligentsia away from the Social-Democrats' "Marxist dogma."[41] Recounting his disagreements with the populists he had met in the Briansk works in Ekaterinoslav, Ivan Babushkin emphasized the need to teach the workers politics. The populists empha-

[39] See *Iskra*, no. 78, p. 8, no. 79 (December 1, 1904), p. 9, and Gonimov, *Staraia Iuzovka*, p. 184.

[40] Moshinskii, "K voprosu," p. 235 n. 2. Iuzovka took almost no part in the December 1905 uprising.

[41] See discussions in *Revoliutsionnaia Rossiia*, no. 31 (1903), p. 20, and no. 75 (1905), p. 14. The whole rationale of Levus, "Iz istorii," published in 1909, was to urge the Socialist-Revolutionaries to pay more attention to organizing among the Donbass workers.

sized natural sciences and Russian grammar, and told the workers that the study of Greek civilization was necessary for the understanding of Spartacus' slave revolt.[42] In terms of culture and society, this was an important difference between the two tendencies.

Though the Socialist-Revolutionaries took note of the favorable conditions created for propaganda work among the large concentrations of factory workers, the only place in the Donbass where significant activity was reported in their press during the summer of 1905 was in Grishino, where the Socialist-Revolutionary doctor, Deinig, who was to be killed leading the December uprising, had great influence.[43] Even here, the emphasis in the report was on literature that was "read avidly, and passed on to the village."[44]

In all the sources reporting on labor organization and revolutionary groups in the Donbass, there is no mention of the activity of any Ukrainian parties in the mines or factories. There were Ukrainian groups in Kharkov, and the Donetsk Union of Mine Workers maintained some contact with the Spilka. There was also some activity in a few villages in the region, where "Little Russian" literature was circulated and discussed.[45] Only in 1917 did the Ukrainian parties gain some representation in the elections to district zemstvos. Even then, they were to have no presence in the mine and mill soviets of the Donbass.

The greatest rivalry in the revolutionary movement of the Donbass was the internal split of the Social-Democrats. It was something that intruded on the youthful dedication of the revolutionaries from the outside. Indeed, it would seem that not only the rank and file but the district leaders had little sympathy for, or understanding of, the sectarian bickering that split their movement. Recalling the period of the most active work of the Mine Workers' Union, when the group had agreed to join the Social-Democrats, Moshinskii recalls, "One must say that at the time this split was incompre-

[42] Babushkin, *Vospominaniia*, p. 96. Evidently the populists were replying to a suggestion by Babushkin that *Spartacus* made excellent propaganda reading for the workers, for he mentions passing a copy to G. I. Petrovskii, along with some of Zola's works. See p. 86 n. 1.

[43] For the recognition of the opportunities in the Donbass, see *Revoliutsionnaia Rossiia*, no. 26 (1903), p. 15. For notice of the upsurge in activity in Grishino, see no. 70 (1905), p. 19.

[44] *Revoliutsionnaia Rossiia* in the years 1903–1905 has any number of such references, reflecting the S-R view that the workers were chiefly to be approached as a bridge to the village. See, for instance, no. 26 (1903), p. 15; no. 31 (1903), p. 20; no. 75 (1905), pp. 16–17.

[45] See *Revoliutsionnaia Rossiia*, no. 75 (1905), pp. 16–17, for one such account.

hensible not only to the working masses, but also to the higher-up groups (to the committees)."[46] Shur adds that in 1903, "Stepan" came to Iuzovka with literature. "I don't remember whether he was Bolshevik or Menshevik. We ourselves didn't differentiate very sharply in these matters."[47] Yet it did make a difference. In a protest to the Third Congress of the RSDRP, a group of Bolsheviks from Lugansk disputed the credentials of the (Menshevik) delegate claiming to represent the "Donetsk Committee" and the Donetsk Mine Workers' Union. Since the Don Committee of the RSDRP, the body that had supervised (or claimed to supervise) the union's activities had been arrested, and there existed no actual Donetsk Committee, a mandate to represent the committee and the union was fictitious.[48] Such disputes were generally avoided by the rank and file of Iuzovka, and the lack of factional discussion was noted as one of the features of the successful study groups that operated under the supervision of Paperno in Iuzovka during the last period of the union's activity there.[49]

Even Moiseenko, who found Bolshevism more appropriate for the working class, and appeared to have an instinctive antipathy to the intelligentsia, dismissed the operational significance of the split with the remark that in those days there was really very little difference between Bolshevik and Menshevik.[50] In Iuzovka (as in many, if not most, smaller centers of revolutionary activity), the practical approach predominated over the ideological in revolutionary work throughout the existence of the underground, and even into the 1917 revolution. It was only at the end of May 1917 that the Bolsheviks withdrew from the united Social-Democratic organization in Iuzovka and began an independent quest for power.

Two other obstacles hindered the movement's success: the problem of financing, and the frailty of the human organism and psyche. One of the problems of sending activists to the Donbass was that of finding employment for them, both as a cover, so that they should not be too obvious to the vigilant eyes of the authorities, and as a means of livelihood. Formally, the district committees were responsible for supporting committee agents. "Professional revolutionaries" were supposed to receive twenty-five rubles

[46] TsGAOR, F. 7952, op. 6, d. 120, p. 81. Moshinskii's memoirs.

[47] Ibid., p. 2. Shur's memoirs.

[48] Shklovskii, "Perepiska," pp. 38–40.

[49] Gonimov, *Staraia Iuzovka*, p. 173.

[50] Moiseenko, *Vospominaniia starogo revoliutsionera*, pp. 150–51.

4.1 An early Donbass revolutionary group, circa 1902. Left to right: P. A. Moiseenko, Dr. N. Kavalerov, the writer Khokhlov, G. I. Petrovskii.

4.2 Iuzovka Bolsheviks, 1912. Left to right: F. Zaitsev, S. Pevtseva, V. Ermoshenko, Samilyn, Ia. Zalmaev, Slavina.

per month, a minimal sum comparable to the wages of an unskilled miner or factory worker.[51] However, these committees were unstable bodies, liable to arrest at any time, with their assets open to seizure by the authorities. There were apparently times and places in which the workers themselves could provide a generous stipend to an organizer. Levus writes of workers asking for party propagandists, and willing to pay them as much as forty rubles per month.[52] Generally, the workers could contribute little from their wages. The Ekaterinoslav Committee of the RSDRP had a total income in 1899 amounting to 1,047.42 rubles. Of this, workers in the Lange factory contributed 2.65, and those in the pipe factory .62. Other "various enterprises" were listed at 76.20 rubles, and only from "one southern mine" was there the substantial sum of 242.50. The remainder came from "sympathizers," "various people," "other cities," and the sale of illegal literature in the amount of 10.50 to a workers' library fund set up by the party.[53] One of the sources of income was the setting up of a Red Cross group. How this was used is not clear, but in the report from Ekaterinoslav, such a group is credited with raising 110 rubles. One of the complaints against Markovich in Iuzovka was that, entrusted with the Red Cross group, he was able to raise only twenty rubles.[54]

One can see clearly from Moiseenko's memoirs how he went from mine to mine, pushed not only by the pressures of the police and the mine owners, but also by the need to find a place where he could obtain steady work. It is significant that the revolutionaries were generally members of the intelligentsia with no experience of physical labor. The example of Smidovich, who fell ill after two weeks of living in working-class conditions, and the complaint of "Petr" that few of those willing to work in the Donbass could stand up to the conditions for more than a few months, are evidence of this. The student Suglitskii, coming to carry on political work at the New Russia's Vetka mine and factory near Iuzovka, who was to play an important part among the Bolsheviks of the Donbass in 1917, first worked as a tutor to the manager's children, living with them in their home.[55] This circumstance must surely have constrained his activities, as well as straining his

[51] Elwood, *Russian Social Democracy*, p. 99.

[52] Levus, "Iz istorii," p. 82.

[53] *Rabochee dvizhenie v Ekaterinoslave*, p. 23. The statement of income and expenditure published here presents a balanced budget, but the income appears to have either a typographical error in presentation or an error in addition, showing a 50 kopek deficit.

[54] Gonimov, *Staraia Iuzovka*, p. 173.

[55] For details of Suglitskii, see *Perepiska sekretariata*, vol. 2, p. 334.

credibility among the workers. The deployment of revolutionary forces was thus often influenced by completely extraneous factors. Only occasionally does it appear that an agent in the Donbass was, in fact, fully supported, as was Shestakov. There were occasions when revolutionary emissaries were able to support themselves independently, as was the case with the Kaznitskii family, where the husband was a fel'dsher in private practice, and the wife ran a rag business from their home, as a cover for an underground press of the Donetsk Mine Workers' Union.[56]

In addition to support for field agents and transporters of literature, there were two other major claims on the funds of the movement. First, funds had to be provided for the support of the families of arrested revolutionaries. Moiseenko cites this as a first charge against the movement's meager resources.[57] In the bylaws of Nachalo, a Ekaterinoslav workers' library fund, 30 percent of the association's income was to be put away for this purpose. However, in the period from September to December 1899, only 5 rubles out of an income of 70 was actually spent for such needs. Aid to arrested and exiled comrades accounted for 62.20 of the 1,048.92 rubles expended by the Ekaterinoslav Committee of the RSDRP during 1899.[58] The second additional expense was for the acquisition or printing of illegal literature. Though this was meant to be sold to various study circles and workers' groups, and theoretically should have been self-financing, the reality appears otherwise. The financial statement of the Ekaterinoslav Committee noted an expenditure of 200.80 rubles for illegal literature, and an additional debt of 190 rubles that was not included in the statement of income and expenditure. On top of these items there were expenditures of 201 rubles for hectographed and printed leaflets (in 1899 the committee distributed six thousand pages of leaflets, including a May Day proclamation that included the first political slogans that they had put forward), and 330 rubles for the print shop and the publishing of *Iuzhnyi rabochii*.[59] The latter, started in 1899, was the Ekaterinoslav Committee's attempt at a regional newspaper, printed on the spot, and therefore able to bring local items to

[56] Gonimov, *Staraia Iuzovka*, p. 170.

[57] Moiseenko, *Vospominaniia starogo revoliutsionera*, p. 179. Elwood, *Russian Social Democracy*, p. 100, also notes this as a major expenditure.

[58] *Rabochee dvizhenie v Ekaterinoslave*, p. 23.

[59] Ibid. Printing of illegal literature thus accounted for about 70 percent of the committee's expenditures.

the attention of the workers without the many months of delay that attended the publication and circulation of the smuggled émigré papers.[60]

In addition to the financial problems of the revolutionary movement, there was a great human cost. Engaging in revolutionary politics in tsarist Russia was often literally a life-and-death affair. There was no knowing when a strike or demonstration might end in violence and death. Additionally, there was the ever-present threat of arrest.[61] Even a one-time engagement in a purely economic strike might result in banishment to one's home village. Faced with this, and with the threat that they might be barred from any future education or career, some young people hesitated to take any public role in revolutionary agitation, even at critical moments.[62]

Other young people, attracted by the romantic idealism of the revolutionary movement, simply grew out of it, returning to the families and values against which they had rebelled. Bondareva recalls that "Emma Ridnik, whose family were Zionists, played a great role [in early Iuzovka socialist activity]. She was a committee member, and was arrested in 1904. In jail she began to have doubts, perhaps of a nationalist character, perhaps other. In America she became a good housewife."[63]

The constant strain of underground life, the repeated changing of identities, and what must have appeared to be an unending succession of jail terms and periods of exile wrecked the psyches of many. On May 30, 1905, "Sergei" (Mikhail Moiseevich Leshchinskii) notified the party center that "Ivanich" (Professor Vladimir M. Makovskii) had worked himself out of his mind, and "by force we have made him leave work for a month since we would otherwise have to put him into a psychiatric clinic."[64] Sergei himself was "a marvelous Bolshevik" who came straight from the Butyrki prison to Ekaterinoslav, represented that city at the Third Party Congress, and then

[60] Ibid., p. 13. *Rabochee delo*, no. 7 (August 1900), p. 31, notes the publication of this paper, dating its circulation from January 1900. The eight-month gap between the paper's appearance and the notice in *Rabochee delo* neatly proves the point of the *praktiki* in the Donbass.

[61] *Poslednye izvestiia*, no. 57 (February 22, 1902) noted that the student Orekhov, beaten in a demonstration in January, had died of his wounds, while the student Kargin remained in critical condition.

[62] See Moiseenko's excoriation of Brodskii and Kravchenko for their wavering in 1905, in *Vospominaniia starogo revoliutsionera*, p. 154.

[63] TsGAOR, F. 7952, op. 6, d. 120, p. 9.

[64] Shklovskii, "Perepiska," p. 17.

served another jail term. In 1906 he was seen passing through Odessa showing extreme exhaustion, and soon left for America.[65]

These were evidently not isolated cases, but represented a major price paid for the single-mindedness of what was for many years a tiny band of professional revolutionaries. The same total devotion of life to the cause prevailed through the civil war and the famine, and into the reconstruction period. In 1925, 14 percent of all party members' deaths, and 11.9 percent of the deaths of candidate members, were suicides.[66] Even years later, when both the physical and the political conditions were easier, a Smolensk survey of one thousand Communist party members showed only 10 percent of them healthy, with one-third suffering from "shattered nervous systems," and one-third with active or incipient tuberculosis.[67]

There was a conscious attempt on the part of the socialists to alter the whole frame of reference of the workers. In changing where they lived and how they made a living, the workers themselves had started the process. In a political and social sense, however, little had changed. Throughout Russia they had only other transplanted peasants to compare themselves with, who like them were still largely subject to a rigid regime, and whose natural tendency was to accommodate themselves to their new circumstances while retaining the old set of values. Moshinskii appears to have understood the delicacy and complexity of this situation when he characterized the workers as "half-peasant, half-proletarian, and little developed."[68] One solution adopted by the revolutionary agitators was to try to broaden the workers' horizons by acquainting them with the activities of the international workers' movement. Along with Marx, Bellamy, Plekhanov, and Proudhon, the agitators read excerpts from *Russkiia vedomosti* about workers' representatives in the English or Belgian parliaments, as well as news of strikes.[69] By using a respectable publication (it was popularly known as "the professors' newspaper") the revolutionaries also

[65] Ibid., p. 8. See also p. 20, noting that Kir, a committee member from Ekaterinoslav, had to cease activities for a month due to exhaustion.

[66] Schapiro, *Communist Party*, p. 310n.

[67] From the Smolensk Archive, cited by Rigby, *Communist Party Membership*, p. 117.

[68] Moshinskii, "K voprosu," p. 235.

[69] Pankratova, *Rabochee dvizhenie*, vol. 4, pt. 1, p. 165. The activities of the Western European labor movement, and the claim that "despite arrests and persecution by spies and police some Russian workers have managed to band together and to start a great movement for the liberation and unification of the working class," were part of the May Day 1899 leaflet composed and distributed by the Ekaterinoslav Social-Democrats. For the full text, see Pankratova, *Rabochee dvizhenie*, vol. 4, pt. 2, p. 343.

gave their activity the semblance of legal status. This attempt to combat the parochialism and traditionalism of the workers, making the alternative of political freedom appear both feasible and proper, was a major theme throughout the Donbass revolutionary movement's early activities.[70] This was part of a process of exchanging superstition and belief in magic for abstractions that went far beyond the limits of daily experience. That, however, was a long process that could only be completed when daily experience itself had broadened tremendously.[71]

The workers of the Donbass were ready to begin this transition. The New Russia factory was already thirty years old. It had a stable labor force, and a second generation was beginning to grow into its ranks. Mines and factories had multiplied throughout the region. No less important, the same social stirrings that were to be seen in the rest of Russia were reaching the Donbass. The onset of political organization and the economic recession that came with the turn of the century set the stage for the first serious challenge to the Russian autocracy. I turn now to an examination of the years that led to the 1905 revolution.

[70] For additional examples, see, for instance, *Iuzhnyi rabochii*, no. 1 (January 1900), pp. 23–25.

[71] For an exhaustive discussion of this process in France, see Weber, *Peasants into Frenchmen*, chap. 2. My own development of this theme owes much to Weber.

PART II

Years of Contention: 1900–1917

CHAPTER 5

The Year 1905 in the Donbass

The first five years of the twentieth century had been a roller coaster ride in Iuzovka. The recession that struck the Russian Empire had reduced economic activity drastically, and the settlement had become a center of unemployment. All the lobbying of the Association of Southern Coal and Steel Producers for such projects as double-tracking the Trans-Siberian Railway, or creating a new fleet of large coal cars to carry Donbass coal to the northwest, fell short, and by 1903 only twenty-three of the thirty-five Donbass blast furnaces were in operation, ore and coal mines were closing, and employment had dropped by seven thousand in metallurgy and by nearly ten thousand in coal mining. Only in 1904 did a recovery begin, and then the onset of the Russo-Japanese War threatened the recovery, as government investments to which the industrialists looked as the basis of renewed growth were diverted to meet immediate military needs.

Economic recovery did not bring the Hughes factory work force back to its 1899 peak of eleven thousand workers. The new manager of the New Russia factory, John Anderson, a Russian-born Briton who had previously managed the Briansk factory, used the recession period to carry out a thorough modernization, and instituted a regime of intensified labor that touched off several small, and only partly successful, strikes. Iuzovka had weathered the crisis. Its population of forty thousand was based on a labor force described as "relatively stable, thanks to the town of Iuzovo [sic] where the company has constructed workers' housing. The company appears to be in a more favorable position from this point of view than other factories in the Donets Basin."[1]

There was boom and bust politically as well. The Donetsk Mine Workers' Union reached its peak in 1903, but was soon destroyed by the Okhrana. In

[1] CL, 13599, study 1255 bis, "New Russia Co.," January 1905.

the spring of 1903 the union had girded for a major effort. Twenty-five thousand pamphlets were prepared calling for a one-day work stoppage on May Day. Then came the Kishinev pogrom in mid-April. The Iuzovka police chief, Levitskii, was reported to have warned publicly that any attempt at a May Day demonstration would be met by an attack on the settlement's Jews. The revolutionaries took the threat seriously, and "because of the extreme lack of culture of the miners, the union decided to give up the demonstration."[2] Though propaganda work continued, the few strikes that marked the period had only partial economic success and showed the markedly limited influence of the revolutionary groups.

Although the political atmosphere in the Donbass was tense from the beginning of 1905, political activity was limited. The waves of arrests of leaders and members of the Donetsk Social-Democratic Union of Mine Industry Workers had crippled that body's organizing efforts. No less harmful was the split in the ranks of the RSDRP following the Second Party Congress. The factional infighting had destroyed the Donetsk Committee of the Social-Democrats, and when, in the first blaze of activity following Bloody Sunday, an attempt to reestablish a united committee had failed, competing committees were established, dividing the movement throughout the summer of 1905. It succeeded in reuniting only during the autumn crisis. Rather than working within the Menshevik-dominated Donetsk Mine Workers' Union, the Bolsheviks attempted to set up their own mine union, centered in Lugansk, where there was a strong Bolshevik group.[3]

The authorities had every reason to be confident that all organized agitation in Iuzovka had been stamped out. In the event of labor unrest, there were in Bakhmut district three companies of cossacks, a squadron of dragoons, and a battalion of infantry.[4] Yet the disorder that affected the rest of the country could not be kept out of Iuzovka. The Donbass, with its heavy industry and growing concentration of workers, was simply too great a

[2] For details of the Kishinev pogrom, see Baron, *Russian Jew*, p. 57. A report of the demonstration's cancellation is given in *Iskra*, no. 45 (August 1, 1903), p. 8.

[3] See Donii, Lavrov, and Shmorgun, *Bolsheviki Ukrainy*, p. 73, and Modestov, *Rabochee i professional'noe dvizhenie*, p. 28. Iakovlev, *Vooruzhennye vosstaniia*, pp. 318–19, gives a detailed description of the factional fights with which Bolsheviks and Mensheviks occupied themselves during much of 1905. Kondufor, *Istoriia rabochikh Donbassa*, vol. 1, p. 95, writes that the rival Bolshevik mine union was formed so that the Donbass Bolsheviks could claim the right to send delegates to the Third Party Congress.

[4] See the opinion of Rotmistr von Leus in Gonimov, *Staraia Iuzovka*, p. 188. For the military forces in Bakhmut, see Ershov, "Dekabr'skoe vooruzhennoe vosstanie v Donbasse" pt. 1, p. 24.

prize to be neglected for long. The educational institutions of St. Petersburg had closed, and radical students were spreading out through the empire. New faces appeared in Iuzovka, and they encouraged Moiseenko and the few remaining Donbass activists who had been quiescent during most of the previous year to prepare a strike in protest against the shootings on Bloody Sunday.[5] A new underground began to form. F. P. Prusakov, described as a "professional revolutionary," went to Iuzovka at the beginning of 1905.[6] Grigorii Mashchenko, suspected of revolutionary sympathies by police chief Levitskii, was fired from the factory, but then began to devote himself full time to conspiratorial work. He brought the Social-Democratic leaflet "To All Workers," telling of Bloody Sunday, and passed it to others in the Iuzovka mines and factory. In the well-organized February strike he would serve, along with "Comrade Methodius" (Ovchinnikov) from Rostov, as secretary of the underground strike committee formed as a safeguard against the breaking of the strike by arrest of its known leaders.[7]

Iuzovka on Strike

Eight days after Bloody Sunday, on January 17, the first Iuzovka strike of the year began. The previous night leaflets proclaiming "In Unity There Is Strength" had been spread through the settlement. The leaflet named eight demands of the workers, headed by the insistence on an eight-hour day and the demand that supervisory personnel address workers politely. A 20 percent raise in pay, an end to overtime, and various improvements in sanitary and working conditions filled out the list. At this stage, no demands of a purely political nature were raised. In a factory meeting the workers added five more economic demands, and an eight-person delegation representing the machine shop, the boiler shop, the press shop, and the casting shop brought the demands to Anderson. The director's response was

[5] Moiseenko, *Vospominaniia starogo revoliutsionera*, p. 153.

[6] Kondufor, *Istoriia rabochikh Donbassa*, vol. 1, p. 92.

[7] Gonimov, *Staraia Iuzovka*, p. 189. While Gonimov (p. 196n) and Kondufor, *Istoriia rabochikh Donbassa*, vol. 1, p. 92, say that Methodius came from Ekaterinoslav, Bondareva's memoir also names him as the organizer of the 1905 strikes, but says that he came to Iuzovka from Rostov, characterizing him as "a Bolshevik, active and authoritative." For the illegal strike committee, see Kondufor, *Istoriia rabochikh Donbassa*, vol. 1, p. 93. The forming of conspiratorial committees in parallel to public institutions became a formal principle of the Communist movement in the "21 conditions" of the Comintern.

that the eight-hour day was a political demand, and therefore outside his competence. He agreed that the workers should be addressed politely, and rejected out of hand seven substantive demands, leaving others open for consideration. At five o'clock the workers began leaving the factory, and though the night shift went in, Kharechko claims that it did not work. When, by noon on January 18, all the New Russia Co. workers gathered in the Larinskii bazaar for a strike meeting, three companies of soldiers, summoned by the district mining engineer to reinforce the 140 cossacks quartered in Iuzovka, moved in and dispersed the crowd. The workers then returned to the factory, having gained nothing. Later it was claimed that the strike was badly and hastily organized.[8] This was the first Donbass strike after Bloody Sunday, though none of the accounts places any emphasis on demands or speeches relating to that event. It was soon followed by a wave of Donbass strikes lasting until April. Significantly, though there were arrests by the soldiers, no violence on either side was claimed. The mature spirit that had been growing since the "seventh-hour strike" in 1898 was evident in the workers' activities.

If the January strike was only partial and bore the marks of hasty organization, Methodius and his comrades displayed an impressive ability to learn when, a month later, a second strike was launched.[9] In the January strike the workers had economic demands, and they are understandable, given the intensification of work in the factory and mines, and the stagnation of the workers' wages. Despite the recovery of business during 1904, the directors of the New Russia Co., in touch with international markets, foresaw a downturn. Arthur Hughes, now operating from St. Petersburg, warned of prospective losses if work should be interrupted. The management was considering a cutback in production, or even a total work stoppage.[10] Anderson, a tough manager by nature, was in no position to grant raises in pay. There were, however, whole categories of workers who were receiving

[8] TsGAOR, F. 7952, op. 6, d. 120, p. 18. Memoirs of Zakharkin. *Iskra*, no. 87 (February 10, 1905), p. 5, claims that the workers won higher pay, but no other source supports this claim. Kharechko, *1905 god v Donbasse*, p. 12, sets forth the eight original demands in the leaflet. These include free medical care, sick pay, and insurance against loss of the ability to work, items that were already standard in the New Russia factory and mines.

[9] The naming of Methodius as the guiding hand is the consequence of "the victors writing history." As is clear from all accounts, the Mensheviks were the dominant group throughout the factory and settlement, and the S-Rs had considerable influence, yet little mention is made of their names and actions, and these must be inferred indirectly in most cases.

[10] Gonimov, *Staraia Iuzovka*, p. 190.

wages as low as sixty kopeks a day. The assistant district engineer noted in a telegram to St. Petersburg that the cost of living was high, that sixty kopeks was an extremely low wage, and that as many as one thousand of the workers in the New Russia mines received this sum. He urged that a minimum wage for adults be set, pointing out that the law was not clear on the subject. The question, he wrote, should be considered urgent, as other companies had granted pay raises, and the New Russia workers intended to strike again in mid-February.[11]

The first step taken by the workers was to go to all the sections of the factory and all the mine shafts, urging each to elect two delegates who would form an Assembly of Workers' Delegates (*Sobranie rabochikh delegatov*) to draw up the strike demands.[12] This body formed and re-formed periodically during the year, ultimately emerging as the first Iuzovka soviet, and even published two issues of its own newspaper, the *Izvestiia Iuzovskogo soveta rabochikh deputatov*. The assembly drew up a general list of fifty-five grievances, and then each section—the blast furnaces, the rolling mills, the stables, the brick works, and all the rest—added specific demands. The list is a babel of general and specific demands, ranging from an option of free housing (or four rubles per month) for all workers, to the hiring of female supervisors in the brick works, where the bulk of the labor force was made up of women and children. Many of the items demanded already existed—provision of free work gloves and the opportunity for unlimited piecework, for example. The demands covered every conceivable facet of factory work and life. It was probably the first time in the history of the New Russia Co. that the workers had been given a universal opportunity to express an opinion, and they went to it with a will.[13]

The strike demands were handed to Anderson by Obishchenko, head of the assembly, on February 21. Anderson accepted them and promised an answer within twenty-four hours. In fact it took him a week, with the

[11] TsGAOR, F. 7952, op. 6, d. 119, p. 127. Telegram of February 8, 1905, from the assistant district engineer to the Mines Administration for Southern Russia.

[12] On the formation of the Assembly of Workers' Delegates, see the memoirs of Zakharkin, TsGAOR, F. 7952, op. 6, d. 120, pp. 18–19; see also Shmorgun, "Sovety rabochikh deputatov," pp. 24–25, who notes that numerous such commissions, assemblies, and councils were springing up all over Russia at this time, eventually bringing into being the concept of the soviet. The earliest use of the term *soviet* in the Donbass was in a telegram from Kadievka on July 11.

[13] The full list of demands and the response of management to each of them is given in TsGAOR, F. 7952, op. 6, d. 119, pp. 137–44.

assistance of his bookkeepers and shop foremen, to evaluate the demands and formulate a response.[14] However diffuse the workers' demands were, they were perceived as having been proffered in good faith, and were given serious consideration. In addition, taking into account the urgings of the assistant district mining engineer for a corrective policy regarding low wages, and his anxious warnings about the prospect of a strike, this was a rare occasion on which all three major actors, the central authorities, the employers, and the workers, met cooperatively to solve a common problem. There was to be no solution, however, for Anderson was bound by the business forecast of management, the workers were impatient, and the central authorities were painfully slow and reluctant when it came to implementing change.

When Anderson's response to the workers' demands did not come as promised after twenty-four hours, the workers began to leave the factory and mines. Despite the efforts of the foremen, Skachko and Sobolev, and the factory police constable, Gladchenko, to dissuade or prevent workers from leaving, more and more of New Russia's workers joined the strike. By noon on February 22, four factory sections had closed, and the workers at the Vetka mine, emulating their Iuzovka comrades, had chosen a twenty-four member strike committee.[15] The impatience of the workers can be explained not only by the economic pressures they felt, but also by the nearby example of the Petrovskii factory. There, after a well-organized and disciplined two-week strike, the workers had won fifteen of twenty points presented, including a 10 percent increase in wages, although they had demanded 50 percent.[16]

As Modestov points out, each successful strike became a model to be copied, spurring the workers on to new demands, and the Iuzovka strike was soon followed by others. The Petrovskii strike had been purely economic in character since "the masses here are rather benighted, mostly newcomers only lately plucked from behind the plowshare." However, after winning most of their demands in their first strike, "they are ready to strike whenever a new leaflet appears."[17] Success whetted appetite.

When Anderson's reply to the assembly's demands was finally presented,

[14] Gonimov, *Staraia Iuzovka*, p. 194. The list of demands and management responses in the Moscow archives is, in fact, dated February 25. It may, however, have been held over the weekend by Anderson before presentation to the strike committee.

[15] Ibid., p. 195.

[16] See *Iskra*, no. 89 (February 24, 1905), p. 4, and Modestov, *Rabochee i professional'noe dvizhenie*, pp. 26–27.

[17] *Iskra*, no. 92 (March 10, 1905).

the workers were deeply disappointed. Twenty-eight of the workers' demands were flatly rejected. These included all demands for higher pay or benefits; the rejection was accompanied by an explanation that the demands would result in 3,250,000 rubles in additional expense to the company, "a sum unwarranted in present market conditions." The rejections also covered all demands related to staffing and to work procedures. The company was not about to establish any precedent for having the workers participate in setting factory rules. Only five demands were unconditionally accepted, six more partially accepted, and six more taken under consideration. These were generally in the realm of living conditions and welfare: the coal allotments for workers' families, the construction of a second teahouse, and the building of more housing at the outlying mines. Thirteen demands were dismissed as covering conditions already existing and not in need of change, while five others were said to be regulated by law, and therefore outside the purview of the factory management.[18] In particular, Anderson was said to have emphasized that as of February 20, a government order had forbidden all changes in the length of the workday, charging a legislative commission with regulating this question.[19] He thus rejected the demand for the eight-hour day as being beyond management competence. In the January strike he had rejected the demand as "political," which, indeed, it was in the context of the workers' demands in 1905.

The tone of the employers' response is clear. Mild and conciliatory on marginal points, it is unambiguously blunt and unyielding in everything economic and organizational, the heart of the workers' substantive demands. On some points the tone is contemptuously patronizing ("since the points raised here are unspecified and vague, no answer can be offered"; "in any case where there is a complaint . . . the company is always willing, as noted in point eleven, to give every possible cooperation"). When the Assembly of Workers' Delegates had digested the meaning of Anderson's reply, there were those who wanted "to deal with him, and with Skachko as well." The assembly included a number of members of revolutionary parties as well as rank-and-file workers, and along with the few Social-Democrats there were anarchists and Socialist-Revolutionaries, though many of the latter were said to have already "left off the S-R methods."[20]

[18] TsGAOR, F. 7952, op. 6, d. 119, pp. 137–44. Many of the demands covered several items, so that the total number of answers is more than the fifty-five principal points under which the demands were presented.

[19] Gonimov, *Staraia Iuzovka*, p. 202.

[20] Ibid., p. 203. Skachko was, indeed, shot to death later in the year. The Socialist-Revolutionary party, heirs to the People's Will, used individual terror extensively.

On the evening of February 28, with the strike deadlocked but spreading to neighboring mines, the vice-governor (in his capacity as the official responsible for industrial development and relations), the prosecutor of the circuit court, and the commander of the provincial gendarmerie all arrived in Iuzovka. To emphasize their neutral position between management and the strikers, they quartered themselves in the home of the merchant Nikolaev, rather than staying in the Hughes mansion, as was the general custom of visiting officials.[21] The scale of the occasion emphasizes the gravity of the crisis. Nothing like this had happened since the cholera riots. Most earlier strikes had been relatively brief and partial, but by this time the factory had been closed for a week and the strike was growing, rather than dying out. At a reception attended by two hundred local merchants and personalities, the vice-governor heard police chief Levitskii and district mining engineer Zhelkovskii explain that if it were not for the revolutionary intimidation of Ivan Obishchenko and Grigorii Mashchenko, the workers never would have gone on strike.[22]

In private conversations with the vice-governor, Anderson emphasized that acceding to the workers' demands might force the closing of the factory, and that this would be a scandal throughout Europe, where Russia's diplomats were at that very moment seeking loans. In addition, he warned that any harm to the Hughes factory might totally destroy Russia's shaky financial structure. This was part of a well-orchestrated campaign by the Hughes brothers, who had already persuaded the British Embassy to press the Russian government for assurances as to the safety of British citizens and property in case of labor unrest. The request had been submitted to Russia's Foreign Ministry, which had communicated it to the Ministry of Internal Affairs.[23] From the tone of these conversations one can infer that the New Russia Co.'s owners were genuinely worried that the government might take the workers' side and press for pay raises. Perhaps the assistant district engineer's memo had had some effect. These conversations are also testimony to the status enjoyed by the New Russia Co., and its importance to the Russian economy even at this late date.

[21] Ibid. To judge by the description of the facilities and the habitués given in Paustovskii's autobiography, Thompson's Hotel Grande Bretagne was not a fit accommodation for such grand personages.

[22] Gonimov, *Staraia Iuzovka*, p. 204. How secret Mashchenko's underground strike committee could have been is open to question at this point. His role as a strike leader was known to the authorities, and to the public at large as well.

[23] TsGAOR, F. 7952, op. 6, d. 119, p. 134. See also Gonimov, *Staraia Iuzovka*, p. 204.

The next morning, the vice-governor met with the strikers and, apparently influenced by the reports of the local officials, attempted to persuade the workers to elect new delegates in place of the revolutionary agitators. He was greeted with whistles and jeers. At the Rutchenko mines he was more successful. The vice-governor dismissed peremptorily all demands deemed political, but insisted categorically that the workers' economic demands be negotiated with them by management. He also promised that none of the striking workers would be arrested, a demand that the Iuzovka workers had also made, and one to which Anderson had agreed.

That night the vice-governor returned to Iuzovka in a second unsuccessful attempt to convince the workers to end their strike. The sources do not indicate whether he proposed the same compromise that had proved successful at the Rutchenko mines, or whether Anderson's pressures had closed that avenue. The talks having failed, notices were pasted up saying that if work was not resumed, the factory would close for an indefinite period at 6:00 A.M. on March 3. When only a few workers appeared, the factory was closed, but this step boomeranged. The following day, all the other workers and artisans of Iuzovka joined the New Russia strikers.[24] For the first time in its history, the settlement faced a general and coordinated labor action. This was the fruit of three years' organizing by the Donetsk Mine Workers' Union, and in particular attested to the work of Methodius in coordinating the factory groups with the settlement circles.

There was another innovation. For the first time, the strike organization went beyond the immediate needs of the strikers and became a vehicle for social mobilization. The greatest accomplishment of the strike committee was an agreement with the small merchants of the settlement that they would provide the strikers with food through the strike, though it is said that they knew they would probably never be paid back for this. This support gave the strikers the strength they needed to hold out for a long time. Eventually the secret of the source of the workers' strength leaked out, and a number of the storekeepers were arrested by the police.[25] The workers also took public order into their hands. Two years earlier, the union had already displayed its sensitivity to the volatility of Iuzovka's society by

[24] Posse, *Rabochie stachki*, p. 111.

[25] TsGAOR, F. 7952, op. 6, d. 120, p. 20. No hint of how the workers convinced the storekeepers to support them is provided. It is possible that a fear of pogrom violence and the participation of the largely Jewish artisan force in the strike combined to provide both the stick of compulsion and the carrot of persuasion.

canceling its May Day demonstration. In 1905, the idea of pogroms was very much in the air again. The assembly called for the workers to stop drinking. A workers' militia was created to patrol the settlement and maintain quiet in the streets. The local police were not trusted; they were suspected not only of inciting pogroms, but also of hiring local hooligans to murder activist workers. With the workers' militia in the settlement "throughout the fifteen-day strike not only were there no pogroms, but there were no fights or scandals."[26] There was a need for such patrols, for with all its impressive solidarity the strike still had its doubters and scoffers. The blacksmith Ivan Kovalev is quoted by Gonimov as asking scornfully, "Who's running this? . . . Mashchenko, Obishchenko, Stepanenko—a bunch of Ukes and Yids!"[27]

Throughout the strike, though, the broad and inclusive organization that had given the strike its first impetus was maintained. Each workshop had a workers' meeting every morning, and there were general meetings held each afternoon. When the police attempted to disperse one such meeting that was discussing the threat of lockout, five thousand workers retreated to the church, carrying on their discussion in the sanctuary.[28] Another such meeting had decided on a total cessation of maintenance work in the mines, shutting down the pumps and ventilation system. Suddenly it was remembered that the mine ponies in one shaft had been forgotten, and a whole rescue operation had to be mounted to get them out. In the end, the rescuers themselves were in danger, and the disaster emergency team maintained at each New Russia mine had to go into action to bring the workers out safely.[29]

After several additional vain attempts to persuade the strikers to accept the employers' terms, the vice-governor announced that the factory would remain closed indefinitely, and declared the entire province to be in a state of enhanced security. All meetings and gatherings were forbidden. The painful process of paying off all the New Russia Co. workers began on

[26] Ibid., pp. 23–24, Zakharkin's memoirs. See also Gonimov, *Staraia Iuzovka*, p. 199. The strikers' militias also enforced abstemiousness in the July 1989 Donbass mine strike.

[27] Gonimov, *Staraia Iuzovka*, p. 200. The words attributed to Kovalev are *Khokholy* and *Zhidy*, derogatory terms for Ukrainians and Jews.

[28] Ibid., p. 209.

[29] TsGAOR, F. 7952, op. 6, d. 120, pp. 21–22. Zakharkin's memoirs. The first report of mine flooding because the pumps were stopped is dated February 24. See the report of the vice-governor to the Ministry of the Interior in *Donbass v revoliutsii 1905–1907 godov*, p. 242.

March 7, and continued for three days. At the same time, blacklists of the strike leaders were drawn up and deportations began. District engineer Zhelkovskii notified the Mines Administration that out of a total of 13,700 workers fired, 651 would not be accepted back to work when and if the factory reopened. Fifty-one of these were said to be local property owners. In addition he reported that there were 132 persons deemed to be a pernicious influence in the settlement, and recommended that they be deported forthwith.[30] Since Zhelkovskii's report deals only with those fired from the New Russia factory and mines, the property owners referred to would appear to be longtime, settled workers who had actively taken up the strike cause.

The paying off of the workers and the factory's shutdown, at first announced as indefinite, and then scheduled to last three months, put an end to the effective organization of the strike. Thousands of workers were left standing idly at the factory gates. Two thousand or more workers found no alternative employment in the district but remained in Iuzovka. Deprived of any hope of winning the strike, their allegiance to its organizers waned. Rumors circulated, reportedly originating with Anderson and the factory management, that Obishchenko had been bought off by the authorities.[31] The strike had been organized on a purely economic basis, and reputed attempts by the Bolsheviks to raise political issues had been rejected. The blame, in recent Soviet historiography, has been laid on the nonfactory workers of the settlement, who, acting under the influence of Mensheviks, are said to have prevented the formation of a general strike committee.[32] This accusation does not stand up in the light of the evidence. It would appear that the strike was a remarkable demonstration of organized solidarity, but that it had its limitations, both in its local nature and in the vast asymmetry of political resources once the company and the central authorities were acting in concert.

Revolutionary politics in Iuzovka retreated once more underground, with Methodius still active. Through March and into April, leaflets appeared and were distributed, with the police hot on the trail. At the end of April, fifteen thousand pieces of literature, type, printing ink, and the rubber stamp of the Iuzovka RSDRP were seized in a raid. May Day was celebrated, but in secret, with only one hundred men and women attending

[30] Gonimov, *Staraia Iuzovka*, pp. 214–17. See also TsGAOR, F. 7952, op. 6, d. 120, p. 25, Zakharkin's memoirs, regarding the blacklists and the declaration of enhanced security.

[31] Gonimov, *Staraia Iuzovka*, p. 225.

[32] Kondufor, *Istoriia rabochikh Donbassa*, vol. 1, p. 93.

the five-hour meeting. Compared with previous years, this may have seemed like a success, but against the background of the upsurge of organized activity that had accompanied the February strike, it is much less impressive. The meeting went according to the union's plans. Bondareva delivered a rousing speech, and presented the meeting with a political resolution, provided to her by "Maxim," who had organized the entire meeting, designating the speakers and their topics. The one new development at this meeting was that here, for the first time, a collection of money was taken up to buy weapons for armed insurrection.[33]

The failure of the two strikes against the New Russia Co. took the keen edge off the Iuzovka workers' enthusiasm, but the rest of the Donbass was rapidly coming to a boil. From mid-January through March, fifty-nine strikes were recorded, involving nearly two-thirds of the miners and metal workers of the Donbass. While the strikes were mainly economic in their demands, and varied greatly as to their level of organization, over 40 percent lasted more than one week, and only 10 percent were one- or two-day affairs.[34] The most prominent characteristic of these strikes is the broad participation of the workers in discussing the issues of the day under the tutelage of elected strike committees. At the mines and metal smelters, this sudden immersion in participatory politics bred radicalism. A letter of April 1905 from Ekaterinoslav to the Bolshevik center abroad announced "more and more contacts in the mining union. Lugansk is ours, we have our own man there. Only Iuzovka remains in the hands of the Mensheviks. If we had more people we could win Mariupol and Krivoi Rog by sending one person to each."[35] Even such concentrations of workers as the seven-thousand-worker Druzhkovka metallurgy complex had only two Social-Democrats to take part in organizing a strike in emulation of Iuzovka. When they appealed to Ekaterinoslav and Gorlovka for assistance, they were told to make do with their own forces.[36]

The growing activism of the Donbass workers was only the last link in a

[33] See TsGAOR, F. 7952, op. 6, d. 120, p. 11, Bondareva's memoirs, on the organization of the meeting, and Kharechko, *1905 god v Donbasse*, p. 48, on the collection. See also *Iskra*, no. 101, for a record of the meeting.

[34] For a discussion and statistical analysis, see Kondufor, *Istoriia rabochikh Donbassa*, vol. 1, pp. 91–95.

[35] Shklovskii, "Perepiska," p. 15.

[36] Smirnov, "Pervaia zabastovka na Druzhkovskom zavode," pp. 90, 93. Smirnov notes the horror with which the workers reacted to news of Bloody Sunday, as well as their resistance to introducing demands for a universal franchise and a constituent assembly.

chain that was being formed throughout the Russian Empire in 1905. Roberta Manning has emphasized the heightened political consciousness and the greater capacity for political organization that manifested themselves during that year.[37] Society was mobilizing in every possible way. In Ekaterinoslav in July, five hundred children, aged nine to thirteen, who were workers in trade and industry went on strike. Each day they gathered for discussions and for lectures from their leader, a twelve-year-old. "We are the unfortunate children of the oppressed proletariat," he told them. "We must first of all fight to achieve those working conditions which will allow us the possibility of also getting an education, of having time for our own development, of growing up as human beings. The first demand we must make of our bosses is for free time for study." Only on the third day did the young agitator launch into an explanation of labor and capital, put so simply that the observer exclaimed that no adult could have improved upon it. Then the twelve-year-old stated that the ultimate goal of the entire working class must be socialism, carefully defining the term and going into the problems of the constituent assembly, the "four-tailed" voting system (universal, direct, and equal voting, by secret ballot), and other intricacies of current politics. The assembled children then formed a committee together with local store clerks, preparing to return to work, but maintaining their organizational structure to facilitate a new strike should the employers not meet their demands.[38] The Christian Brotherhood of Struggle was formed to press the government for change, and it issued an appeal calling for the church to play an honorable role in solving Russia's social problems.[39]

These groups grew through the summer of 1905, and with the October Manifesto they began to come together in various ways in an attempt to give society a new political structure. In Ekaterinoslav on the third day of the October general strike, representatives of forty-five organizations got together in a single general meeting. A peasant union activist, Anatolii Kulichenko, recorded in his diary: "October 12, 1905, the revolution can be felt. There are continuous meetings in Ekaterinoslav. Ukrainian Democratic circles, Progressive (K-D) groups, Zionists, S-D, S-R, and Bundists attend. There are also Russian S-Ds and S-Rs. All these have joined in a common platform and have formed a central election coalition commit-

[37] Manning, *Crisis of the Old Order*, pp. 148, 166.

[38] *Proletarii*, no. 13 (August 9 [22], 1905), p. 6.

[39] *Vpered*, no. 11 (1905), p. 3; no. 14 (1905), p. 4.

tee."[40] A different description of what is evidently the same meeting remarks on the participation of groups representing lawyers, engineers, women's rights activists, office workers, shop clerks, and doctors, as well as various political organizations.[41] These were the first signs of a nascent civil society. Without such autonomous groups no pluralist society can exist. They are the foundation of citizenship defended from state coercion.[42] The contrast with what had been before made the wave of revolutionary fervor stand out in even brighter colors. "The south is so attractive in its revolutionary work that there is no desire to escape. Whoever has the soul of a revolutionary and loves revolutionary work must come to the south. . . . The whole proletariat lives only for the revolution. . . . In every corner of the cities, almost openly, study circles, meetings, and mass demonstrations gather. Everywhere the workers speak of political strikes. Even for the least conscious workers, the question of arms stands to the fore."[43]

Something of this atmosphere certainly had penetrated Iuzovka and the surrounding areas. In the summer, four hundred peasants from Aleksandrovka declared their support of the Iuzovka workers.[44] Strikes broke out sporadically at surrounding mines. Yet neither the industrial nor the agrarian unrest was as intense in this region as in others. A police report given to Count Witte lists nine provinces with what is described as "a serious situation." Ekaterinoslav is not listed. During 1905 only six violent incidents were noted in the villages of the province, and only one of these, the burning of a landowner's sheds and barn in July, took place in Bakhmut district.[45] In comparison to the fifty-nine strikes listed in the Donbass between January 15 and March 31, there were only forty strikes between April 1 and the end of August 1905.[46] The first wave was ebbing.

The Bolsheviks of Iuzovka maintained their activities. Following the Third Congress of the Bolsheviks of the RSDRP, a meeting with a group from the Vosnesenskii mine, attended by thirty people, adopted resolutions for arming the workers and preparing a general strike, as well as in favor of

[40] Cited in Novopolin, "Iz istorii tsarskikh rasprav," p. 107.

[41] Iakovlev, *Vooruzhennye vosstaniia*, p. 292, citing *Pridneprovskii krai*, no. 2650 (November 17 [30], 1905).

[42] For a cogent discussion of the function and importance of such groups, see Bradley, "Voluntary Associations."

[43] Quoted in Levus, "Iz istorii," p. 65.

[44] Modestov, *Rabochee i professional'noe dvizhenie*, p. 31.

[45] Dubrovskii, "Krestianskoe dvizhenie 1905ogo goda," pp. 70, 87.

[46] Kondufor, *Istoriia rabochikh Donbassa*, vol. 1, p. 96.

removing the administrations of the mines and factories, replacing them with workers.[47] But such thoughts were still far from the mass of workers, and there were few Bolsheviks to share and propagate this line. "Comrade Sonia" wrote bitterly that the Mensheviks had twenty-five propagandists, while the Bolsheviks had only eight or nine, and in addition, few ties with society, and therefore little money.[48] In addition, the workers wanted to boycott the Bolsheviks, the Mensheviks, and their factionalized committees, uniting in a purely workers' party without the intelligentsia.[49]

In addition to the urge of the workers to organize independently, there was a powerful undertow of patriotic conservatism among the workers, and this made itself felt strongly in Iuzovka. The organizational center of the Social-Democrats, so full of optimism during the February strike, moved from the factory to the settlement group because of antirevolutionary organizing among the workers in the factory. The authorities were active as well, searching for illegal literature among those who entered the factory.[50] Most of the engineers in the factory were categorized as belonging either to the right wing of what was to become the Octobrist party or to the extreme radical right, the Union of the Russian People. The Black Hundred, a fighting group of this ultranationalist movement, also existed. It consisted mostly of Russian householders, small businesspeople, and artisans, precisely those who stood in direct commercial competition with the settlement's Jewish population.[51] During the summer, antitsarist leaflets, signed "from the Jews," were reported to have been found in Iuzovka, but they were denounced as police forgeries, created to incite a pogrom.[52] To counter such tendencies, there were active calls from members of polite society warning against any pogrom.[53] As in other communities throughout South Russia, a self-defense unit of 150 persons was formed. Funds were

[47] TsGAOR, F. 7952, op. 6, d. 119, p. 135. Report of the Bakhmut police superintendent to the Ekaterinoslav governor. See also Gonimov, *Staraia Iuzovka*, p. 219.

[48] Iakovlev, *Vooruzhennye vosstaniia*, p. 287. See also Shklovskii, "Perepiska," p. 35, for the letter from Alexandrov complaining that there are no good agitators, that there is nobody in charge of propaganda, and that local activists must service Lugansk, Taganrog, Nikopol, and an "as yet unformed mine union." This stands in considerable contrast to the euphoria evinced a few months earlier.

[49] Letter of Essen from Ekaterinoslav, June 15, 1905, in Shklovskii, "Perepiska," pp. 20–21.

[50] Gonimov, *Staraia Iuzovka*, p. 222.

[51] Linden, ed., *Die Judenpogrome in Russland*, vol. 2, pp. 211–12.

[52] Ibid., p. 212.

[53] Ibid., p. 353n. Linden notes such calls in six communities in Russia.

gathered to buy arms, and an agreement was made with the non-Jewish revolutionary groups that there would be cooperation in stopping any pogrom attempts in the settlement. This added a potential of seventy more armed men to the self-defense forces.[54] The existence of the self-defense group gave confidence to at least part of the Jewish community, and during the summer a visiting journalist was told: "If they try a pogrom, we will show them in an organized way."[55] Conservative Russian society saw this organizing effort quite differently. Under the headline "Mania of Revolt," *Novoe vremia* wrote that the Jewish population throughout the Pale of Settlement was agitating for full revolt, preparing bombs, learning how to shoot, and threatening to kill.[56] The fragmentation of Russian society was rapidly turning to polarization; communication was blocked and violence spiraled. Iuzovka was part of this pattern, and the tragic development of events was to be shaped by just such distorted perceptions.

The October Manifesto: Freedom and Pogrom

In the first half of October a new wave of strikes began. At the Rutchenko mines and the Lydia mine near Iuzovka, four thousand miners walked out. The strike committee was re-formed in the New Russia factory as well, but the workers and miners did not strike for fear of another lockout.[57] Revolutionary agitation was carried on in the manner of guerilla warfare. On the night of October 8, the lights at the exit of the Iuzovka theater were suddenly extinguished, leaflets were scattered, and shots were fired at a policeman, wounding him. This was reported by the authorities as part of the general tendency to unrest and street demonstrations.[58] Such was the atmosphere in Iuzovka when the tsar granted the October Manifesto.

[54] Ibid., vol. 1, p. 391; vol. 2, pp. 213–14. For other discussions of joint self-defense groups, see Lawrynenko, *Revolutionary Ukrainian Party*; see also Kazdan, *Mein Dor*, pp. 56–57. Kazdan dates these efforts from 1903 or 1904. In the wake of the pogroms that followed the October Manifesto the complaint was heard that all the interparty quarrels were carried over into the self-defense effort, weakening it. See Sukenikov, "Evreiskaia samooborona."

[55] *Voskhod*, nos. 47–48 (December 1, 1905), p. 19.

[56] *Novoe vremia* (September 2, 1905).

[57] See Modestov, *Rabochee i professional'noe dvizhenie*, pp. 31, 36, for strikes and strike committees; Gonimov, *Staraia Iuzovka*, p. 233, for the fear of a lockout.

[58] TsGAOR, F. 7952, op. 6, d. 19, p. 135. Report of the Bakhmut police chief to Ekaterinoslav governor A. B. Neidgardt.

In the cities, the fever of organization for the all-Russian October strike had boiled over into open revolt. In Kharkov, three thousand people had barricaded themselves in the university. Ten were killed trying to break into the armory in the city.[59] In Ekaterinoslav, total paralysis was reported. "The city is in darkness, the shops are closed, the streets are empty. Patrols of soldiers pass occasionally. The railway station is closed. Some of the telegraph wires are damaged."[60] Throughout the Donbass, speakers and emissaries of the various parties were drumming up support for the strike. L. I. Lutugin, a geologist who had organized the Union of Mining Engineers and Technicians, and who had been a delegate to meetings of the Association of Southern Coal and Steel Producers, was one. V. G. Bogoraz (alias Tan), the distinguished ethnographer, was another, speaking as a representative of the Trudovik party.[61] Krupskaia wrote to the Ekaterinoslav Bolsheviks, telling them that they could get some literature in Iuzovka, and that they would also find there "a comrade who can be very useful to the organization, and who wants to come to Ekaterinoslav. In addition, he also wants to set up a discussion with local workers. Only hurry, for he may have to leave the place."[62]

In the midst of this turmoil, the October Manifesto was granted. The tsar's advisers hoped to pour oil on Russia's troubled waters, but in the south it was fuel for the already-raging flames. The day after the manifesto was issued, pogroms began.[63] The news of the manifesto reached Iuzovka only on the morning of October 19. A spontaneous parade began, attracting some three hundred people. Three socialist speeches were made, and flags of the anarchists, the Social-Democrats, and the Socialist-Zionist Poalei Tsion were unfurled. It was decided that a formal rally for the entire settlement would be organized for the following day. On October 20, the shops and small factories closed down and a crowd of one thousand paraded through Iuzovka's streets. This time the participants included supporters of the Constitutional-Democrats as well as of the revolutionary groups. Even

[59] *Proletarii* (October 11, 1905).

[60] Quoted in Mavor, *Economic History of Russia*, vol. 2, p. 483.

[61] Moiseenko, *Vospominaniia starogo revoliutsionera*, pp. 177, 271 n. 23. For Lutugin's call for an autonomous union of mining engineers of South Russia, see *Gorno-zavodskii listok*, no. 2 (1899), pp. 3642–43. For Lutugin's political outlook, see Fenin, *Coal and Politics*, p. 24. The Trudovik party was an urban affiliate of the peasant-oriented S-Rs.

[62] Shklovskii, "Perepiska," p. 35. The probability that a hasty departure from Iuzovka might be necessary hints strongly at the political situation in the settlement.

[63] Modestov, *Rabochee i professional'noe dvizhenie*, p. 32.

so, the crowd was distinctly Jewish. Prominently absent were the New Russia Co. workers and miners, who had been urged by the Union of the Russian People to boycott the celebration and hold a church service instead.[64] In fact, the steel mill and mines were working as though it were any ordinary day. Feeling somehow cheated because the Russian people, whose tsar had just granted them civic freedoms, did not appear to appreciate this great gift, several hundred young enthusiasts, carrying their parties' flags, marched to the factory. The remaining participants of the celebratory meeting, more soberly skeptical, ran home to bar their shutters.[65]

At the factory, the crowd of three to five hundred, led by the rolling-mill worker Panarin, waving a red flag, pushed open the factory gates, shouting "Let the workers out." The workers responded with "Traitors! You sold us out!" and followed this with a hail of stones, coal, and, spurred on by cries of "Bei zhidov!" (Beat the Jews!), a frontal assault with iron bars.[66] At this point, Persin, a member of the self-defense group from the Socialist-Zionists, pulled out his revolver and fired at the onrushing workers. This act only further enraged them. Demonstrators were seized and thrown alive into the hot slag and the blast furnaces.[67] The fight then spilled into the streets of Iuzovka, where it turned into a pogrom that lasted three days and resulted in an almost total destruction of Jewish property in the settlement. The pogrom attracted peasants from Vetka and Grigorevka, who, as in 1892, came to loot; in addition, a unit of cossacks came from Kadievka to protect the factory and the non-Jewish commercial premises in town. On October 22, the police and soldiers were reported to be "energetically" at work restoring order. The police had been summoned by a telegram from Anderson to Associate Minister of the Interior Trepov, "in view of the armed uprising of the Jewish population which began yesterday."[68] Even after the

[64] Linden, *Die Judenpogrome in Russland*, vol. 2, p. 214. Gonimov, *Staraia Iuzovka*, p. 224, writes of the priest Matveevskii holding a special church service on October 20.

[65] *Voskhod*, nos. 47–48 (December 1, 1905), p. 19. See similar accounts in Linden, *Die Judenpogrome in Russland*, vol. 2, p. 214, and Gonimov, *Staraia Iuzovka*, p. 224.

[66] Gonimov, *Staraia Iuzovka*, p. 225, and Linden, *Die Judenpogrome in Russland*, vol. 2, p. 214. Gonimov suggests that the workers' resentment was carried over from the failure of the February–March strike, and the rumors that Obishchenko had been bribed.

[67] Gonimov, *Staraia Iuzovka*, p. 227; *Voskhod*, nos. 47–48 (December 1, 1905), p. 19; Surozhskii, "Krai uglia i zheleza," p. 304. Wynn, *Workers, Strikes, and Pogroms*, p. 207, notes that "the actions of self-defense units more often enraged than deterred crowds of rioters." Wynn does not discuss the Iuzovka pogrom, though it fits his model perfectly.

[68] Kharechko, *1905 god v Donbasse*, p. 67. Gonimov, *Staraia Iuzovka*, p. 229, cites an additional telegram sent by Anderson to the governor on October 29, characterizing funerals and memorial services for the pogrom victims as "Jewish disturbances."

settlement was quiet, miners in the district were reported to be hunting down Jews who had sought refuge in neighboring villages. Twelve dead and one hundred wounded were counted in the factory hospital. Four of the dead, one Bundist, one Social-Democrat, and two Socialist-Zionists, were members of the self-defense group. Some of the victims had died when the synagogue was burned. It was said that the police had secretly buried others to keep the published death toll low. Two hundred seventy-three families were left destitute by the pogrom, and the losses in property were estimated at 930,000 rubles.[69]

The story was by no means the same in all places. In Debaltsevo, Lugansk, and Shcherbinovka, miners and workers stopped attempted pogroms.[70] In Kamenskoe and in Ekaterinoslav, workers' groups fought pitched battles with the peasants, miners, and soldiers who were attacking the Jews, confiscating loot from pogromists and driving away those who attempted to incite the workers to pogrom, though they were unsuccessful in completely preventing the pogroms.[71] After a series of pogroms around the iron mines of Krivoi Rog, Annovka, and Terny, soldiers fired on the rioters, leaving nineteen dead and many others wounded.[72]

Pogroms could be prevented wherever there were officials who conscientiously maintained law and order, or where there was some social core that could arouse in the workers and miners a sense of dignity and decency. Debaltsevo and Shcherbinovka were settlements no better than any others in the Donbass, yet the workers and miners there could be organized to prevent murder and looting. There was some measure of organization among the workers there, for Debaltsevo and Gorlovka (near Shcherbinovka) are mentioned as two settlements that formed soviets during

[69] *Novoe vremia* (October 25, 1905); Gonimov, *Staraia Iuzovka*, p. 226; Linden, *Die Judenpogrome in Russland*, vol. 2, p. 214; and *Voskhod*, nos. 47–48 (December 1, 1905), p. 19. The various accounts are similar, differing only in apportionment of blame for the onset of the violence. One eyewitness to the pogrom was young Nikita Khrushchev, then a boy of eleven. See Khrushchev, *Khrushchev Remembers*, pp. 266–67. The material losses are mentioned in *Novoe vremia* (November 28, 1905), and *Khronika evreiskoi zhizni*, no. 47 (December 2, 1905), p. 34. For comparison's sake, the total damage from rural disturbances in Ekaterinoslav province during 1905 was estimated at 750,000 rubles.

[70] See *Novoe vremia* (October 28, 1905); Modestov, *Rabochee i professional'noe dvizhenie*, p. 32.

[71] *Novoe vremia* (October 31, 1905); Osherovich, *Shtet un Shtetlekh in Ukraine*, vol. 1, p. 106; Heilprin, *Sefer Hagvura*, vol. 3, p. 163.

[72] *Gorno-zavodskii listok*, nos. 50–52, (1905), p. 8268. Both *Gorno-zavodskii listok* and *Vestnik Ekaterinoslavskago zemstva* skipped publication during the three weeks of strikes and rioting in mid-October, resuming only at the end of the month.

October 1905.[73] At times, the same isolated nature of a small mining settlement that made it so materially and culturally backward created a community in which human solidarity overcame the isolation that was so prevalent in a larger and ostensibly more developed settlement such as Iuzovka. What stands out in Iuzovka's 1905 pogrom is the total estrangement among the different sectors of society. It is estimated that of the fifteen thousand workers in and close to Iuzovka, no more than five hundred at most had any connection with revolutionary groups, and therefore might have had some cooperative political and social contact with local Jews.[74] As was ruefully realized in the aftermath of the pogrom, the ten thousand Jews of Iuzovka were tailors, traders, and artisans, who were totally isolated from the great rail-producing works that was the heart and soul of Iuzovka. They remained foreigners in the eyes of the factory's workers, and hated competitors in the eyes of the small middle class of Russian merchants and property owners that was slowly growing in the settlement. Whatever momentary community had been achieved in the days of the March general strike, and whatever tenuous cooperation had developed between Jewish shop clerks and Russian steel workers, were devastatingly absent in October. The total lack of understanding displayed by the revolutionaries who forced their way into the New Russia factory is staggering. Their euphoria at the brave new world they saw dawning was dirctly opposite to the bitter disorientation of the factory workers, who saw the traditional national foundations of their Russian world crumbling under their feet. Neither had had the opportunity to see into the world of the other.

The factory's management had seized on this. In their fight against the strike movement they had fanned the hate and suspicion with which the Jews were regarded.[75] This approach was accepted as reasonable in the British diplomatic community as well. Reporting on the pogroms to the Foreign Office, the British chargé d'affaires in St. Petersburg wrote: "I am bound to add that the Jews themselves by their open revolutionary propaganda, especially among the workmen, cannot be held altogether guiltless. They are regarded by the workmen as responsible for the intimidation

[73] Shmorgun, "Sovety rabochikh deputatov," p. 26. In 1917, Gorlovka and Shcherbinovka acted together.

[74] Linden, *Die Judenpogrome in Russland*, vol. 2, p. 213. The estimate seems on the high side. Also, as noted above, while participation in a revolutionary group might expose a person to universalist and humane ideas, there was, for most of the period, separation (if not active hostility) between the factory and the settlement S-D groups.

[75] Linden, *Die Judenpogrome in Russland*, vol. 2, p. 218.

exercised in the factories with a view of forcing the men to strike, with the result that very great suffering now exists in consequence of closing of the mills."[76]

The educated diplomat from enlightened Western Europe apparently could not ask himself whether the Iuzovka synagogue was really a bastion of revolutionary conspiracy, or whether the Jewish would-be bourgeoisie, small manufacturers and retailers who had fervently demonstrated in support of the tsar and his war at the beginning of 1904, should indeed be beaten and butchered for supporting the tsar's manifesto. If this was the atmosphere in the high circles of society, what could be expected of the workers and miners, torn between tradition and modernity, or of the peasants, clinging to their land and their customs? Hatred of the Jews was for them a handy and easily understandable metaphor for the frustrations of their insecure lives. It provided them with the enemy they so desperately needed if they were to understand their woes. Drowning in a whirlpool of change, they clutched at any straw of stability. In Bakhmut, where on November 5 the tsar's decree on easing of terms for land redemption was read out in the local bazaar, speakers of the Union of the Russian People explained to the peasants that this was the tsar's way of expressing his pleasure that the peasants had beaten the Jews and the intelligentsia.[77] The tsarist authorities were both unwilling to confront and constitutionally incapable of dealing with the pogrom movement. Soviet historiography proved equally incapable, either omitting any reference to pogroms, or making do with superficial explanations. Upon reviewing Gonimov's manuscript of *Staraia Iuzovka* in 1937, G. I. Petrovskii, one of the leading veteran Donbass Bolsheviks, commented to the editors: "That's the way it all was. Only there appears little about the pogrom against the Jews. It was much fiercer in Iuzovka" (*On byl v Iuzovke sil'nee*).[78]

The strike movement had swelled through October. Seven Donbass strikes in the first half of the month grew to twenty strikes in the second half, including factory, mine, and railway strikes that ended by October 25.[79] But emboldened by the backlash of conservative and nationalist violence that was turned against the liberals and revolutionaries—the intelligentsia—as much as against the Jews, the employers stiffened their

[76] FO, 371/124–12813, p. 360, Cecil Spring-Rice to Sir Edward Grey, April 11, 1906.

[77] *Khronika evreiskoi zhizni*, no. 47 (December 2, 1905), p. 30.

[78] TsGAOR, F. 7952, op. 6, d. 120, p. 84.

[79] Kondufor, *Istoriia rabochikh Donbassa*, vol. 1, p. 98.

resistance. The lockout movement that had started in March reemerged with even greater vigor. The General Co. in Makeevka locked out its three thousand workers. The Russian-Donetsk Co. closed its doors on eight thousand, and seven thousand more were left idle in Ekaterinoslav. In Iuzovka, the workers were in no mood for strikes, and the active revolutionaries, sobered and shaken by the violence of the pogrom, walked on tiptoe.[80] The strikes and pogroms of mid-October had evoked a flood of telegrams from foreign entrepreneurs to the authorities in St. Petersburg. On October 25, Trepov notified the Ekaterinoslav governor, Neidgardt, "In view of the request of the Association of Southern Coal and Steel Producers, informing us of the dangerous situation of the coal mines and metallurgical factories due to the ubiquitous workers' upheavals in the province and the anti-Jewish pogroms accompanied by arson, I once more request you to take the most decisive measures to safeguard the aforementioned enterprises. . . . Pay particular attention to the centers: Gorlovka, Almaznyi, Iuzovka."[81] It was, however, difficult to please all at once, for in the circumstances, the tsar's forces were spread dangerously thin. In addition, the year 1905 was far from over. Though the pressures for change slackened in many circles once the manifesto was granted, frustration and extremism grew among the revolutionaries.

The idea of armed struggle did not arise from the violence and repression of the October strike. Moiseenko wrote of making bombs in the winter of 1904, and the Iuzovka May Day of 1905 was made an occasion for collecting money for the purchase of weapons. But armed struggle became the main objective of Donbass revolution after the failures of October.[82] By the start of December, collections were being taken up for weapons almost everywhere in the Donbass. In Enakievo it was a ruble and a half per person; in Gorlovka and Avdeevka, a tax of 5 to 10 percent was levied on wages. In Popasnyi, skilled workers, administrators, merchants, and even landowners were assessed for the arms fund. Thousands of rubles were collected.[83] With such funds the Avdeevka railway station fighting group purchased fifty American Berdan rifles for three and a half rubles each from

[80] For the plant closings, see *Novoe vremia* (November 2, 1905). For the change of mood in Iuzovka, see *Voskhod*, nos. 47–48 (December 1, 1905), p. 19.

[81] Quoted in Ershov, "Dekabr'skoe vooruzhennoe vosstanie v Donbasse," pt. 1, p. 23.

[82] See Iakovlev, *Vooruzhennye vosstaniia*, p. 289, for police reports of open solicitation of money for arms. See also Levus, "Iz istorii," p. 71.

[83] Ershov, "Dekabr'skoe vooruzhennoe vosstanie v Donbasse," pt. 1, p. 17.

the military stores in Pavlograd.[84] The Donbass revolutionaries were girding for a last, explosive effort.

The Seizure of the Ekaterinin Railroad

The 1905 revolution appeared to be ebbing. At the beginning of December the St. Petersburg soviet was dispersed and its leaders arrested. In Moscow, however, an armed uprising began on December 7, in an effort to fan the embers into new flame. That same day a telegram arrived in Ekaterinoslav, announcing a general political strike called by a conference of delegates of the Moscow and St. Petersburg soviets (though the latter no longer existed), and of twenty-nine railways. The following day a conference of delegates in Ekaterinoslav voted fifty-one to three to join the strike. Half a dozen stations of the Ekaterinin line, including Iuzovo, struck immediately, and the next day, the entire line was on strike. The Fighting Strike Committee was formed, with representatives of all the socialist parties joined by representatives of the postal-telegraph union and of the Ekaterinin Railway Strike Committee.[85]

All along the line, in the railway yards and the mine and factory settlements, fighting groups began to form, some new, some based on self-defense units that had been in existence since the summer. A group from the Ekaterinoslav Fighting Strike Committee toured the area, urging preparations for an armed uprising. On December 9, a meeting of five thousand workers, miners, and curious peasants in Gorlovka heard the strike declared.[86] As a large mining center and the site of a substantial factory, Gorlovka was one of the central points on the Ekaterinin line. Unlike the March and October strikes, this uprising was a clearly political affair. Orators cast doubt on the government's sincerity and on the prospect that the October Manifesto and the Duma would ever become reality. They called for a constituent assembly. Similar meetings were held in Debaltsevo, Grishino, and the Petrovskii factory in Enakievo.[87]

Yet the December events of the Donbass were far from a mass popular uprising. The Ekaterinin railway line struck, but the Donetsk line and the

[84] Ibid., p. 19.

[85] Ibid., pp. 7–9. See also Gonimov, *Staraia Iuzovka*, p. 232.

[86] Levus, "Iz istorii," p. 79.

[87] Ershov, "Dekabr'skoe vooruzhennoe vosstanie v Donbasse," pt. 1, p. 11.

Kursk-Kharkov-Sebastopol line worked through December. In addition, none of the factories along these lines stopped work, including the New Russia factory in Iuzovka, the Druzhkovka factory, and the Konstantinovka factory.[88] All these factories had been on strike in the spring. Ershov explains this as a result of the poor economic conditions of 1905, with factories working short time or at reduced capacity due to lack of materials and transport. Where factories did join the general strike, it was only for a day or two, though their meetings abounded with resolutions of proletarian solidarity. Levus writes of fears that miners were preparing attacks against the factory workers, though such fears eventually proved unfounded.[89] Most astonishing of all Ershov's examples is that of the Gorlovka machine works. There, where the decisive battle of the December uprising was fought and lost, and the spark that touched off the battle was the factory manager's decision to reduce the hours that the plant would work, the strike lasted only from December 9 to December 11. On December 17, when four thousand armed miners battled infantry and dragoons, the factory hands were at work as though nothing were happening. At the same time, the factory's chief engineer and doctor, the Kadets Danchich and Shoshnikov, were members of the strike committee.[90]

There existed other anomalies that bring home the political complexities of the Donbass and of Russia as a whole. A strike meeting at the Donetsk-Iureev factory began with prayers. At Debaltsevo, on December 14, a large crowd with a red flag marched to the church to hold a special mass for the strike, singing a hymn and revolutionary songs, followed by a speech denouncing the autocracy given by Mark Sheitlander, an organizer from Gorlovka.[91] Sheitlander, a fel'dsher by profession, had been an active member of a study circle in the Donetsk Mine Workers' Union. He appears to have been a wandering revolutionary who participated in Donbass Social-

[88] *Gorno-zavodskii listok*, no. 2 (1906), p. 8300.

[89] Levus, "Iz istorii," p. 74.

[90] Ershov, "Dekabr'skoe vooruzhennoe vosstanie v Donbasse," pt. 1, p. 8. See also *Gorno-zavodskii listok*, no. 1 (1906), p. 8286, for confirmation that the Gorlovka factory was at work through the two days of battle. The roles of Danchich and Shoshnikov are in the report of the Ekaterinoslav gendarmerie commander; see Nevskii, *Revoliutsiia 1905 goda*, p. 136. *Novoe vremia*, (December 14, 1905) reported that the white-collar workers at Gorlovka had joined the railway workers in their strike. No mention was made of the factory workers.

[91] Sheitlander was generally known as Zubarev or Kuznetsov, his underground names. See, for instance, Iakovlev, *Vooruzhennye vosstaniia*, p. 329. For his Menshevik affiliation, see the report of the Ekaterinoslav gendarmerie commander in Nevskii, *Revoliutsiia 1905 goda*, p. 136.

Democratic circles.[92] Moiseenko names him as having been particularly active in the first wave of Donbass strikes following Bloody Sunday, and Levus calls him a marvelous orator, at home with both intelligentsia and workers, convincing them that since the workers had poured no small amount of blood and sweat into the building of the factories, the factories should belong to the workers rather than to the capitalists.[93] The police report on Sheitlander, identifying him only by his underground names of Kuznetsov and Zubarev, following his capture, accused him of being the central figure in the preparation of the Gorlovka armed uprising. "By type and accent he is Caucasian-born. Tall and energetic, he speaks with ardor and conviction. Does not deny belonging to Social-Democratic Mensheviks. *Poluintelligent*. Arrived in Gorlovka November 1905 to organize trade union."[94]

At the same time, the Donetsk Committee of the RSDRP held its fourth conference in Mariupol during the height of the December strikes, but was said to have omitted any discussion of the armed uprising that was then taking place.[95] There was evidently good reason for the omission.

Kharechko points out several cases of peasants declaring their support for striking workers in both October and December, and writes of a "worker-peasant uprising."[96] This is doubtful, for though some peasants from two villages were later noted as joining the Debaltsevo fighting group, these are the only cases cited. In addition, the evidence Ershov offers in discussing proletarian leanings in these two villages is from 1893, and these two particular villages are drawn from a list of twenty-two villages whose inhabitants combined mine work with agriculture, either working their own coal holdings or hiring on in commercial mines during the winter.[97] There were

[92] Ershov, "Dekabr'skoe vooruzhennoe vosstanie v Donbasse," pt. 2, p. 50.

[93] Levus, "Iz istorii," p. 78. For Sheitlander's part in the 1905 strikes, and other details, see Moiseenko, *Vospominaniia starogo revoliutsionera*, pp. 179, 271 n. 30.

[94] Nevskii, *Revoliutsiia 1905 goda*, p. 136: "From the report of the commander of the Ekaterinoslav province gendarme administration on the progress of the case of the seizure in 1905 of the Ekaterinin railroad line."

[95] Ershov, "Dekabr'skoe vooruzhennoe vosstanie v Donbasse," pt. 1, pp. 12, 15. Ershov's criticism of the Donetsk conference of the RSDRP is aimed at the Mensheviks, who, though evidently part of the Ekaterinoslav Committee, were soberly reluctant to get involved in schemes of armed uprising after the experiences of October.

[96] Kharechko, *1905 god v Donbasse*, p. 122.

[97] See Ershov, "Dekabr'skoe vooruzhennoe vosstanie v Donbasse," pt. 1, pp. 20–21, and cf. the report of Avdakov in *Trudy, XVIII, 1893*, pt. 1, p. 334. Note that the villages of Vasilevka and Georgievka are both mentioned in Avdakov's list.

many degrees of support or hostility shown by the peasants during these months. Some provided the strikers with food; some villages were willing to conclude pacts of mutual defense. In other cases, they listened to hostile agitators urging them to beat the striking miners and railway workers, "who deserved to be fought."[98] The decisive point was that the peasants were relatively few, independent, and weak in the mining country, and therefore tended to stay away from the revolution. The Peasant Union was active in Ekaterinoslav province, but had no district committee in Bakhmut or Slavianoserbsk.[99] Though the peasants were demanding that their rents be cut in half, and often were the tenants of the big coal and metallurgy companies on lands that had been bought for future development, these discontents found little expression in actual disturbances. From November 1905 to March 1906, Ekaterinoslav province had 84 cases of rural disturbance, none of them in the Bakhmut or Slavianoserbsk districts. In comparison, there were 700 cases in the Saratov region, 149 in Tambov, and 156 in Kursk.[100] The official statistics of the Ministry of the Interior put Ekaterinoslav ninth in a list of twenty provinces regarding losses through agrarian disturbance during 1905, with 774,000 rubles' worth of damage.[101]

During the second week of December there were incidents at Iasinovata, Avdeevka, Grishino, Alexandrovsk, and Debaltsevo in which soldiers and police were disarmed. At Iasinovata, the Socialist-Revolutionary leader Deineg, who had brought a group of armed strikers to the station, shot and killed the cossack commander, Karamyshev. Elsewhere, only in Alexandrovsk were an officer and a cossack wounded. The strikers now had larger quantities of arms than they had ever before possessed, and having also expropriated almost two and a half tons of dynamite, they were able to prepare a large number of bombs, which were distributed to the various stations. They began to gain confidence in their strength, and in the continuation of the easy victories they had so far gained.

Meanwhile, the strikers were organizing their society in a variety of ways. The most basic measures were those taken to assure financial re-

[98] Ershov, "Dekabr'skoe vooruzhennoe vosstanie v Donbasse," pt. 1, pp. 19–22.

[99] Novopolin, "Iz istorii tsarskikh rasprav," p. 103.

[100] FO, 371/120–9773, p. 231, report of Vice-Consul Bosanquet in Nikolaev, March 16, 1906, using unspecified official Russian sources. See also *Vpered*, no. 16 (1905), p. 3.

[101] Nevskii, *Revoliutsiia 1905 goda*, p. 230, citing Obninskii, *Polgoda russkoi revoliutsii* (Moscow, 1906), p. 53. The table given in this source differs only slightly from that in Manning, *Crisis of the Old Order*, p. 143.

sources. Contributions for arms had been levied on workers and nonworkers alike. This system continued as strike committees and soviets were set up. Tolls were extracted from railway passengers by the various station committees, and the funds of the railways and telegraph offices were expropriated to provide workers' wages and assistance for the families of those arrested or serving in the fighting groups. In Debaltsevo, the settlement constable complained to the government that the strike committee had taken twenty thousand rubles from a contractor to cover strike expenses.[102] The disarming of police and soldiers was one of the first orders of business of the strike committees. The Grishino Strike Committee, among the best organized and most militant, sent out a telegram to all stations on December 11, calling for the disarming of all soldiers and military officials. The next day a train passing through the station was stopped and thirteen soldiers were disarmed.[103] The following day, the Enakievo soviet, formed in November and headed by the former Iuzovka worker G. F. Tkachenko-Petrenko, took over the railway settlement, disarming the police there. This was the general pattern followed along the Ekaterinin line.[104]

Not all the stations were equally well organized. In contrast to the militant efficiency of Grishino, nothing went right in Avdeevka. They had a fighting group of sixty members, decked out in red armbands and carrying several Berdans and revolvers. Their attempts to confiscate the funds of the local wine shop and post office were termed "vacillating" and ended unsuccessfully. When they attempted to disarm a squadron of twenty-five dragoons, a scuffle ensued and one horse was slightly wounded, but the soldiers retained their arms.[105]

For two weeks the strikers controlled the rail line and the stations, regulating and taxing traffic and running society. They set up their own system of revolutionary justice and passed all manner of political resolutions. Though they held political power by force of arms, Ershov empha-

[102] Ershov, "Dekabr'skoe vooruzhennoe vosstanie v Donbasse," pt. 1, p. 17. For tolls on passengers, see the complaint of the Alexandrovsk police chief in Iakovlev, *Vooruzhennye vosstaniia*, p. 320.

[103] Ershov, "Dekabr'skoe vooruzhennoe vosstanie v Donbasse," pt. 1, p. 15.

[104] Iakovlev, *Vooruzhennye vosstaniia*, p. 320.

[105] For the numbers and armament of the Avdeevka group, see ibid., p. 321. For their ineffectiveness, see Ershov, "Dekabr'skoe vooruzhennoe vosstanie v Donbasse," pt. 1, p. 17, and pt. 2, p. 43. Ershov criticizes Kharechko, *1905 god v Donbasse*, for promoting the legend that there were 150 cossacks and 75 dragoons in Avdeevka, and that an officer was wounded and four dragoons disarmed by the workers.

sizes that there was no thought of expropriating the factories and mines.[106] This idea would be realized only far in the future. The Donbass workers awaited decisive actions and instructions from Moscow or St. Petersburg, and these were not forthcoming.

The denouement of the December uprising came in Gorlovka. The factory workers had ended their strike after two days. On December 12 the strike committee had sent a desperate telegram to all stations. "We are totally without arms and demand immediate aid from all sides."[107] The other strike committees, still in the first stages of their own organization, apparently did not respond at this point. On December 15, the factory director, a Belgian named Loest, notified the workers that the factory would operate only six hours a day instead of ten and a half, with a proportionate reduction in pay. The workers' delegates, headed by Sheitlander, countered with a proposal that they would continue working as before, but take pay in cash for only six hours' work, with the remainder to be paid when times were better. The director refused.[108]

The following day, December 16, the strike committee returned in strength and imprisoned Loest in his office, threatening to hold him until he agreed to their offer. Someone had telephoned the local police, and soon Nemirovskii, a constable, and Captain Ugrinovich, at the head of a band of soldiers, came to the factory and freed Loest. They then demanded the surrender of Sheitlander, and were opposed by fifteen or twenty "bodyguards" who accompanied him. The soldiers opened fire, killing between eight and fifteen workers and wounding many others, including Sheitlander. He was taken to the hospital, where his arm was amputated, and from there he was taken to prison. After this incident, Snezhko and Grechnev, in the name of the strike committee, sent out telegraphic calls to all points for fighting units to come to Gorlovka.[109]

Armed miners and workers began to converge on Gorlovka. The Grishino people, more than a hundred strong, were led by Deineg and his daughter-in-law, Dobrova, who was a nurse. Of all the armed units this was

[106] Ershov, "Dekabr'skoe vooruzhennoe vosstanie v Donbasse," pt. 1, p. 16. Iakovlev, *Vooruzhennye vosstaniia*, p. 320, claims that the Bolshevik leader in Enakievo, Tkachenko-Petrenko, had taken over management of the Petrovskii factory. I have found no corroboration of this unique claim.

[107] Los', "Dekabr'skoe vooruzhennoe vosstanie," p. 80.

[108] *Gorno-zavodskii listok*, no. 1 (1906), p. 8285. See also Levus, "Iz istorii," pp. 77–78.

[109] Ershov, "Dekabr'skoe vooruzhennoe vosstanie v Donbasse," pt. 2, pp. 51–52. Moiseenko, *Vospominaniia starogo revoliutsionera*, p. 271 n. 30, writes that it was Sheitlander who opened fire on the police.

the only one that had had any training or target practice.[110] A group came from Lugansk. The Debaltsevo *boevaia druzhina* (battle group), though poorly armed, turned out, as did the Enakievo group headed by Tkachenko-Petrenko, and the hapless Avdeevka fighters.[111]

The Iuzovka druzhina had been formed early in the strike, when news had came through that the entire Social-Democratic group at the Rutchenko mines had been arrested.[112] Forty of them had gone to Avdeevka to help in the unsuccessful attempt to disarm the dragoons, and, enlightened by their experience there, had returned home to arm themselves with thirty-seven iron-tipped pikes.[113] An unknown number are said to have joined the Gorlovka fight, and the Bolshevik Iashin died there.[114] The sending of the Iuzovka group was not supported by the majority of the settlement committee members. A police archive quotes one Iuzovka leader as writing: "The day we received the telegram from Gorlovka [calling for help in the armed uprising] was for us a sad one, since our [fighting] organization was little more than a fiction, and an attack on the soldiers and police was a nonsensical plan."[115] This was not the view of Iuzovka alone. The Popasnyi machine workers refused "to go to their deaths," and the Kadievka druzhina set out belatedly and missed the battle.[116]

By the morning of December 17, between three and four thousand of the thirty thousand armed workers then organized in the Donbass had gathered in Gorlovka. They had among them a total of 100 rifles, 150 Berdans, 200 shotguns, 200 other weapons (bombs and incendiary bottles), and 3,000 pikes.[117] At first light, the workers converged on the army barracks, and at

[110] Ershov, "Dekabr'skoe vooruzhennoe vosstanie v Donbasse," pt. 1, p. 18.

[111] See Beligura, *Bol'shevistskaia gazeta*, p. 10; Ershov, "Dekabr'skoe vooruzhennoe vosstanie," pt. 1, p. 19; pt. 2, p. 57.

[112] Gonimov, *Staraia Iuzovka*, p. 238. This was evidently in addition to an armed unit of railway workers at Iuzovo station.

[113] Ibid., p. 239.

[114] Zaitsev, "Bolsheviki Iuzovki v 1917 godu," p. 77. Eight people from Iuzovka were among the 132 who eventually stood trial for the seizure of the railway. See Volskii, "Grigorii Fedorovich Tkachenko-Petrenko," p. 208.

[115] Quoted in Shmorgun, "Sovety rabochikh deputatov," p. 45. The same author, pp. 42–43, states that the Iuzovka soviet took a formal resolution against armed uprising. I have found no corroborative evidence for that. The two editions of *Izvestiia* issued by the soviet seem to be the only documentary evidence extant regarding the soviet's deliberations. They are presented as appendixes to Kharechko, *1905 god v Donbasse*, and contain no such resolution.

[116] Ershov, "Dekabr'skoe vooruzhennoe vosstanie v Donbasse," pt. 2, pp. 53–55.

[117] Ibid., p. 56, brings a range of estimates of the workers' strength, from one thousand up to the police estimate of four thousand.

the sight of this mob the 90 dragoons and 104 infantrymen fled into the steppe. The workers, victorious once more, deployed their forces around the settlement, set up a command post at the railway station, and began to think about what to do next. But the soldiers' move had been a withdrawal, not a flight. Reinforced by sixty cossacks, and under cover of fog and snow, they mounted an organized counterattack. The command post was captured, and Deineg and Dobrova were killed.[118] The small band of disciplined troops overran the untrained workers, and by three o'clock in the afternoon the battle was over. Official figures speak of three hundred killed and a thousand captured, with the rest fleeing to their home stations. The soldiers' losses were put at three dead and twelve wounded.[119]

Retribution came swiftly. Twenty-two people accused of being members of the Gorlovka Strike Committee were arrested, while eight others succeeded in fleeing. Those arrested included Sheitlander, Shoshnikov, Danchich, Dr. Klingenberg from the smelter, three foremen, three telegraphers, five workers, five peasants, one fel'dsher, and one office clerk. The strike appears to have attracted a broad spectrum of supporters, even though most of the factory workers had abandoned it and returned to work on the terms dictated by Loest. At their trial, Danchich, Shoshnikov, and Klingenberg, labeled by the prosecutor "not just liberals, but Liberationists," that is, supporters of the Constitutional-Democrats, the Party of National Liberation, claimed that they had joined the committee only to supply the authorities with information about the rebels, but this claim was rejected by the court.[120]

[118] Here Kondufor, *Istoriia rabochikh Donbassa*, vol. 1, p. 141, introduces "The Ballad of Deineg": "'My comrades, though I die here,' was Deineg's final cry / 'Fight on, fight on untiring, fight on 'til freedom's born / Until at last from Caesar's brow, his crown our hands have torn.'" *Sotsialisticheskii Donbass* (December 13, 1990) claims that the "Internationale," translated into Russian by a young mine foreman, A. Ia. Kots, was first sung at the Gorlovka battle. As Professor T. Lehrer has commented, "They won all of the battles, but we had all the best songs."

[119] Nevskii, *Revoliutsiia 1905 goda*, p. 138, report of Ekaterinoslav gendarme commander. See also Ershov, "Dekabr'skoe vooruzhennoe vosstanie v Donbasse," pt. 2, p. 61. Ershov disputes the official casualty figure. He claims that the zemstvo first-aid unit that arrived later found only twenty-one bodies, and that this is indicative of the level of casualties. Kondufor, *Istoriia rabochikh Donbassa*, vol. 1, p. 104, cites the *Gorno-zavodskii listok* to the effect that only thirty-three workers were killed. All other sources use the official figure of three hundred.

[120] Nevskii, *Revoliutsiia 1905 goda*, report of the Ekaterinoslav gendarme commander, p. 136. Valerian Danchich had been an early sports enthusiast in Iuzovka, and was instrumental in building a bicycle track for racing there. He had been exiled from the settlement by the

After the repression of the Gorlovka uprising, troops swept through Avdeevka and Grishino, capturing large quantities of arms and arresting every worker and member of the intelligentsia who might have had a hand in the uprising. At Debaltsevo, engineer Erichovich, head of a section of the Ekaterinin line, and two station nurses were among those arrested.[121] The fifty-eight jails of Ekaterinoslav province were soon filled to overflowing. When there was no more room for prisoners in the police buildings of Lugansk, the authorities rented a private house, barred its doors and windows, and put fifty or sixty people into each room.[122] Yet such mass arrests interfered with the operation of the railways, and that, after all, was the key to the restoration of normality. A special committee was formed to make a preliminary determination of the degree of involvement of each arrested person, and as a result about three hundred were released and returned to their previous posts.[123]

Martial law had been declared throughout Ekaterinoslav province on December 20. Governor Neidgardt, hampered by a lack of troops throughout the strike, finally received additional regiments, and by December 24 the Ekaterinin line was back in operation, with soldiers posted in large numbers at all stations.[124] After the crushing of the Gorlovka uprising there was no effective resistance. An attempted rebellion in Kharkov was quickly snuffed out, and the Bolshevik-inspired "Liubotin Republic" existed for only four days.[125]

police for his support of a strike in 1903. Danchich received a four-year prison sentence for his role in the seizure of the Ekaterinin line. After the October 1917 revolution, he played a prominent role in developing a coal field in Abkhazia, only to be accused of "wrecking" (sabotage) in 1937. He was formally rehabilitated in 1956. See Razanov, "Takim bylo nachalo," p. 4.

[121] *Gorno-zavodskii listok*, no. 2 (1906), p. 8300.

[122] Modestov, *Rabochee i professional'noe dvizhenie*, p. 41; Ershov, "Dekabr'skoe vooruzhennoe vosstanie v Donbasse," pt. 2, p. 66.

[123] Anisimov, *Kak eto bylo*, p. 102. Anisimov was one of the defense lawyers in the trial of those arrested for the Ekaterinin railway seizure, and he gives us a detailed view of the trial and the social and political events around it, based on archives, minutes of the trial, and correspondence.

[124] On the scarcity of forces, see Iakovlev, *Vooruzhennye vosstaniia*, p. 325. See also Ershov, "Dekabr'skoe vooruzhennoe vosstaniia v Donbasse," pt. 2, p. 65.

[125] Shmorgun, "Sovety rabochikh deputatov," pp. 146–47. Liubotin was a village twenty-five kilometers from Kharkov, where coal had been mined commercially since 1899 by a small entrepreneur named Bogdanovich. In mid-1906, several high-school students, tried for their part in armed resistance at the Liubotin station, had their sentences confirmed. See *Byloe*, no. 8 (1908), p. 304.

The wave of disorder was sufficient to arouse British apprehensions regarding the safety of Iuzovka. Ambassador Cecil Spring-Rice reported to the British Foreign Office, "Desperate encounters between workmen and troops have taken place in many parts of the South. At Bakhmut it is stated that three hundred workmen were killed in one such conflict."[126] The Gorlovka uprising and its bloody outcome became a symbol of proletarian determination and of the implacable cruelty of the old regime in modern Soviet historiography. At the time, though, it aroused dissension, recriminations about irresponsibility and putschist tendencies, and above all, demoralization. All attempts to re-form and rearm the fighting groups failed as the Donbass workers awaited the inevitable government reprisals.[127]

It took much longer until the Ekaterinin railway trial could be put aside within Russia. It remained a festering sore in the flesh of Russian society for nearly four years. In the indictment, 184 people were named, and the investigation dragged on until the autumn of 1908. The trial itself took place from November 7 to December 19, 1908, ending almost three years to the day after the Gorlovka uprising. Only 131 people eventually stood trial. Of these, 32 were condemned to death, and another 60 to hard labor for life. Of those indicted and not tried, some had escaped, some died in prison, and a number were shot in an abortive attempt to escape involving the dynamiting of the walls of the Ekaterinoslav prison.[128] The case was accompanied by great tensions as the authorities attempted to counter terrorist threats against all concerned with the trial. Just before it started, leaflets signed by the Iuzovka-Petrovskii Committee of the RSDRP urged people to "wipe out completely" all witnesses in the trial. There were also fears that the convoy bringing the accused from jail to court and back would be ambushed to free the prisoners.[129] Even after the trial had ended, the tragedy and furor continued. Two of the 32 condemned swallowed cyanide. Prominent citizens, including the Kadet Duma deputy Valerii V. Kamenskii, petitioned Stolypin to commute the death sentences.[130] On September 4, 1909, eight of the condemned who had refused to write requests for pardons were hanged, including Sheitlander and Tkachenko-

[126] FO, 371/119–757 (January 3, 1906), p. 222, Cecil Spring-Rice to Sir Edward Grey. The reference is evidently to the Gorlovka battle.

[127] Ershov, "Dekabr'skoe vooruzhennoe vosstanie v Donbasse," pt. 2, p. 63.

[128] Anisimov, *Kak eto bylo*, p. 101.

[129] Ibid., p. 111.

[130] On the suicides, see *Obshchestvennyi vrach'*, no. 2 (1909), p. 77. On petitions for clemency, see Anisimov, *Kak eto bylo*, p. 148. Kamenskii's daughter was married to Montagu Balfour of the New Russia Co.

Petrenko.[131] Recommendations for clemency that had been forwarded to the Ekaterinoslav governor lay unexamined as the eight were executed.[132]

What was happening in Iuzovka during the period up to and after the December strike? When the Ekaterinin line went on strike, the railway workers at Iuzovo, Iuzovka's principal connection to the main lines, struck immediately. Two days later, on December 11, following the example of other settlements along the railway, Iuzovka formed a soviet that began to organize the affairs of the settlement. This was a district council, with representatives from sixteen different mines and enterprises in and around Iuzovka. Except for one delegate from "the print shop" (and this probably refers to the print shop of the New Russia Co.), there appear to have been no delegates representing the artisan shops and smaller factories of the settlement. The pogrom had scattered and demoralized the previously active Jewish groups.[133] At the first session, on December 11, there were fifty voting delegates and thirty alternates. By the second session of the soviet, on December 14, there were 146 deputies, led by a 27-member delegation from the New Russia Co., 20 representatives of the Ivan mine of the Russian Donetsk Co., 20 from the Rykovskii mines, and 22 from the Markov mines. Among the deputies were Zelkovich, a mine owner; Bykov, manager of the Ivan mine; and Ditman, an engineer at the Sophia mine.[134]

The first item of business on the agenda of the soviet was its attitude to the all-Russian political strike. The declaration of the executive committee to the soviet read:

> The workers of Iuzovka, for various reasons, could not take part in the all-Russian strike. Nevertheless they are threatened by hunger. Facto-

[131] Anisimov, *Kak eto bylo*, p. 147, and Kondufor, *Istoriia rabochikh Donbassa*, vol. 1, p. 112, list the others hanged as Il'ia Matusov, Vasilii Grigorashchenko, Andrei Shcherbakov, Andrei Vashchaev, Vladimir Shmuelevich, and Petr Babich. This list is also given in *Sotsialisticheskii Donbass* (December 12 1990), p. 3. Iakovlev, *Vooruzhennye vosstaniia*, p. 321, writes that Novikov, who (together with Matusov) led the unsuccessful Avdeevka druzhina, was also hanged, but this appears to be untrue.

[132] Anisimov, *Kak eto bylo*, p. 148.

[133] For a graphic description of the change of mood, see *Voskhod*, nos. 47–48 (December 1, 1905), p. 19. The headline of the article, "Temnye o chernye?"—implying uncertainty about whether the pogrom had its roots in the general benightedness of the *temnyi narod* or in political fanaticism of the *chernye sotniia*, the Black Hundreds—expresses the dilemma of the Jewish community.

[134] The list of enterprises and their delegations is in Kharechko, *1905 god v Donbasse*, pp. 138–39. Gonimov, *Staraia Iuzovka*, pp. 233–34, names the nonworker delegates and states that though the executive committee was formed in the New Russia factory, the seat of the soviet was in the school at the Rykovskii mines. The date of formation of the soviet is in Shmorgun, "Sovety rabochikh deputatov," p. 29 n. 36.

> ries and mines are closing. Thousands of workers are thrown on the streets. Citizens! We still remember the terrors of the October pogrom. The soviet is taking measures to stem the pogrom movement. While it is the defender of the workers' interests, the Soviet of Workers' Deputies is at the same time the defender of the interests of all the citizens of the district.[135]

The views of the executive were accepted by the soviet. The fifty delegates adopted a three-part resolution. Noting that the state was grinding to a halt, and that industry was paralyzed, the soviet agreed that hunger was creating a pogrom atmosphere, and the soviet must alleviate hunger in order to thwart the incipient pogrom. To this end, the soviet would: (1) tax the district; (2) prevent food prices from rising; and (3) negotiate with the striking railroad employees about returning workers to their home villages, as well as allowing flour and foodstuffs to enter Iuzovka. This final point indicates that it was the railway workers at Iuzovo who were the militant strikers, using their strategic position to control the mine and factory settlements, as indeed was the case in many places.[136]

At the initiative of the railway workers, a "strike fund tax" had been levied on all passengers traveling through the Iuzovo station. In addition, the Iuzovka soviet appealed to the local merchants' committee to set its own rate for taxes to be turned over to the soviet. After some heated discussions, the merchants agreed, stipulating only that the soviet must promise to prevent riots. In the end, large merchants paid one hundred rubles, medium-sized merchants paid fifty rubles, and artisans, twenty-five rubles. Government clerks, professionals, and the intelligentsia went untaxed.[137] When the Grishino telegram ordering the disarming of police was received, the soviet's executive committee explained to the local police that orders had been received to disarm them, and this was done, with committee members visiting the policemen's homes to pick up the weapons of those who were not on duty.[138]

[135] Kharechko, *1905 god v Donbasse*, p. 137.

[136] Moiseenko, *Vospominaniia starogo revoliutsionera*, p. 184, does not differentiate between the two and writes as though the Iuzovka soviet controlled the rail movements.

[137] Gonimov, *Staraia Iuzovka*, pp. 232, 237. Wynn, *Workers, Strikes, and Pogroms*, p. 240, notes that in Ekaterinoslav the merchants offered a substantial "tax" to the strike committee in return for the right to keep their businesses open during the strike, but were turned down.

[138] See Ershov, "Dekabr'skoe vooruzhennoe vosstanie v Donbasse," pt. 1, p. 16. Ershov, whose article is strewn with bitter anti-Menshevik barbs, comments on the delicacy with which the police were disarmed: "This peaceful tableau is typical."

At the second session of the soviet, four additional members were added to the five New Russia Co. workers who had formed the original executive committee. The negotiations with the railway workers had ended successfully, and the railway delegate who addressed the soviet announced that the railways would transport all workers desiring to leave Iuzovka, and that those who held a certificate from the executive committee testifying to their poverty could travel free. Food would be allowed into the settlement for all those remaining. The soviet gave a vote of confidence to the railway workers and their strike, recognizing it as a "mighty tool" serving all workers.[139]

But the Iuzovka soviet did not raise the political slogan "Down with the Autocracy!" that was so popular in the militant stations. Instead, its resolution read: "The bureaucracy wants to renege on the freedom achieved in the bloody October strike. Workers and other salaried persons bearing on their shoulders the struggle for liberation, have plunged into the decisive battle for freedom."[140]

Though the Iuzovka soviet reportedly continued to function until December 28, when a punitive expedition worked its way down the railroad to the settlement, and martial law was imposed, only these two first sessions were documented by publication of the *Izvestiia*. There were other things happening at the same time. During November there had been a large workers' demonstration in Iuzovka, in the course of which it seems the prison was attacked, and prisoners freed.[141]

At the end of the month, anticipating renewed unrest, Anderson had written to Neidgardt that "as a result of a chronic shortage of railway cars (4 months) we have piled up such a reserve of various materials that continued full production is not financially possible. From the third of the coming month (December) we will gradually reduce production. I consider it my

[139] Kharechko, *1905 god v Donbasse*, p. 139.

[140] Gonimov, *Staraia Iuzovka*, p. 235. See Ershov, "Dekabr'skoe vooruzhennoe vosstanie v Donbasse," pt. 1, p. 13, for a sardonic discussion of this moderation.

[141] Zaitsev, "Bolsheviki Iuzovki v 1917 godu," p. 76, mentions the demonstration without details. For the attack on the prison, see the report of consul Medhurst, FO, 371/123–10524 (March 19, 1906), p. 395. Medhurst mentions this in connection with the freeing of a British subject, one W. Clark of Iuzovka, age twenty, born in Russia, who spoke no English, and whose mother was a widow. He had been jailed for antigovernment activity, and was released for lack of proof that he had participated in the attack on the prison. At his mother's request, he was being sent to England. The ignoring of this demonstration and of the attack on the prison in Bolshevik historiography raises the thought that this was probably an action to free those imprisoned in connection with the October pogrom. This would also explain the anxiety of the Iuzovka soviet regarding a renewal of pogrom activity.

duty to inform you of this and to request the posting of troops in Iuzovka in accordance with the norms set with your office by the meeting of representatives of surrounding factories." On December 3, Anderson closed a Bessemer furnace, a rolling mill, and a number of mine shafts, laying off three thousand workers.[142] These, then, were the circumstances that stopped the Iuzovka workers from joining the general strike. The mass of workers still employed by the New Russia Co. feared a total lockout as there had been in the spring, and threatened a renewed pogrom if attempts were made to pull them out of work. In the spring they had struck more in hope than in belief. That they were then for the first time being consulted about their desires, and that it had appeared that management was willing to listen to these demands, had been a heady combination. But when the strike had been crushed, they turned in their disappointment against their leaders and not against their masters. This time they would engage in no such utopian dreams. The power relations were clear. Though Ershov writes of this quiescence as an exception for the period, Modestov writes that "a significant part of the factories and mines took no part in the December strikes and in the uprising," which, as noted above, was limited to a single railway line.[143]

Revolutionary activity became sporadic and underground once more. The Iuzovka-Makeevka-Petrovskii Social-Democratic Committee was dispersed, and would be re-formed only in 1910.[144] The printers at the Zozula typography plant refused to set the type for the declaration of martial law.[145] A police agent, Samuel Chertok (code name "fabrichnyi," which means "factory man"), who had revealed information regarding the arms and printing facilities of the Social-Democrats in the Donbass, was shot dead.[146]

On December 23, when martial law was already in force in the province, but even before the soviet was dispersed, Anderson shut down the New Russia plant completely for a seasonal overhaul. The lockout movement

[142] Gonimov, *Staraia Iuzovka*, p. 230.

[143] Compare Ershov, "Dekabr'skoe vooruzhennoe vosstanie v Donbasse," pt. 1, p. 14, and Modestov, *Rabochee i professional'noe dvizhenie*, p. 40. Both sources blame the Mensheviks for the nonmilitance and hesitancy of the Iuzovka soviet, as does Shmorgun, "Sovety rabochikh deputatov," p. 25. Kazimirchuk, "Revoliutsionnoe dvizhenie," p. 69, contrasts Iuzovka's Menshevik "tradition" of quiescence with the militance of Gorlovka and Shcherbinovka.

[144] Zaitsev, "Bolsheviki Iuzovki v 1917 godu," p. 77.

[145] Moiseenko, *Vospominaniia starogo revoliutsionera*, p. 184.

[146] Novopolin, "V mire predatel'stva," p. 38.

that had proved so effective in the spring became a general and systematic phenomenon in the Donbass at the end of December. Iuzovka was quiet. In a dispatch dated February 23, 1906, consul Medhurst from Rostov reported to Sir Edward Grey:

> The greater part of the small Cossack garrison quartered at Hughesovka has been sent to Makeevka where French capital is represented by metallurgical works, with, however, few resident Frenchmen. The French Consul from Kharkov is said to have established his residence there, and on learning this, I ran down to Hughesovka to ascertain the real state of things. I returned convinced that there appeared to be no cause for apprehension and can only regret that men have been taken away from the care of British interests to watch those of Frenchmen who are in no special danger. The strike leaders and most of the suspects are either in prison or have disappeared and the men generally appear only anxious to earn their wages in peace. Should trouble occur in the spring it will be agrarian in nature and be of a far more serious kind.[147]

To sum up the year 1905 in the Donbass: perhaps the most reliable sign of the true state of affairs was that in January 1906, when the mine labor force should have been growing, consul Medhurst reported that "miners are leaving the district in large numbers, moving towards the central provinces."[148] Although there were no mass shootings of strikers in the Donbass as was the case on the Kazan railway line and the Siberian railway line, miners and workers feared retribution and disorder. A. A. Auerbach reported to the Association of Southern Coal and Steel Producers that up to 50 percent of the miners had left.[149] All seventy-five hundred iron miners of Krivoi Rog had been at work throughout December, but when the railway shut down on December 9, the strikers told everyone that their stoppage would go on until the spring. Five thousand iron miners then left for their home villages, leaving the mines effectively closed, though there were large stockpiles of ore.[150]

In five countries, Jews had contributed to a relief fund for pogrom victims in Russia, and 70,223 rubles had been earmarked for Iuzovka.

[147] FO, 371/120–7214 (February 23, 1906), Medhurst to Sir Edward Grey.

[148] Ibid., 371/119–1540 (January 6, 1906), p. 351, Medhurst to Sir Edward Grey.

[149] Ershov, "Dekabr'skoe vooruzhennoe vosstanie v Donbasse," pt. 2, p. 66.

[150] *Gorno-zavodskii listok*, no. 1 (1906), p. 8286.

When the money was transferred to the relief committee in the settlement it was confiscated by the police, who claimed that the funds would be used for revolution.[151] Their shops ruined, and lacking capital to make a fresh start, the Jewish merchants and artisans were in sad straits. The United Organization of Zionist-Socialists of Iuzovka published an anguished appeal for aid: "Many of our comrades have been deprived of their last crust, losing their place of work since most of the local stores and workshops have been looted and they have no one to whom to sell their labor. The local organization has also suffered in that we used up all the funds of the library and other property for our killed and wounded comrades."[152]

The New Russia Co. fared rather better, though its production year was somewhat mixed. A production graph giving details of the various products of the factory rises steadily throughout 1905 for all those items shaped or forged in the factory from its own iron and steel billets. Production of steel rails, profile iron, and iron sheeting are in this category. Where the factory was dependent on the railways to bring supplies (iron ore, limestone, flux), production dropped. This was particularly evident in the production of pig iron from the blast furnaces. That dropped from 5.5 million puds in January 1905 to 3 million in December.[153] Nonetheless the factory produced a profit, albeit less than in the preceding period.

In the first five years of the century, the number of deaths per year in Ekaterinoslav province had fluctuated from a low of 63,713 in the comparatively peaceful and prosperous year 1900, to 72,000 in the recession and cholera-plagued year 1902. In 1905 there were 84,528 deaths, without the help of cholera.[154] The bloody year drew to its close, its battles as yet undecided. But Russia had placed change on its agenda, and now the question had to be faced. How this was done in the Donbass will be the subject of the next chapter.

[151] For the relief fund and the allotment to Iuzovka, see Linden, *Die Judenpogrome in Russland*, vol. 1, pp. 401–2. FO, 371/121–350 (January 4, 1906), p. 315, Cecil Spring-Rice to Sir Edward Grey, says: "The Czar has been informed by someone in his entourage that 600,000 pounds sterling had been raised in London for the relief of Russian Jews and that part of it was being spent on revolutionary aims." For confiscation of the money in Iuzovka, see FO, 371/124–12096 (April 3, 1906), letter from Cecil Spring-Rice to Sir Edward Grey.

[152] *Khronika evreiskoi zhizni*, nos. 48–49 (December 23, 1905), p. 62.

[153] See the chart in TsGIAL, F. 23, op. 19, ed. khr. 319.

[154] *Materialy dlia izucheniia narodonaseleniia Ukrainy*, table 1, p. 2.

CHAPTER 6

Years of Uncertainty: 1906–1914

Suppression of the wave of strikes and the armed uprising in December 1905 did not put an end to revolutionary unrest in the Donbass. Instead, the frustration and the feeling of having been betrayed that took root among socialist groups in the rest of the Russian Empire found fertile soil in the coal mines and steel mills of the Donbass as well. Donbass society had been shaken by the lockouts, the armed violence, and the regime retribution of the preceding year, and it had emerged more fragmented than ever. The year 1905 had ended with large numbers of miners fleeing the Donbass, and this exodus proved to be more than a seasonal affair; the following summer an analysis of the labor force showed that while there was no overall shortage of mine workers, the workers coming down from the north were mainly young and inexperienced, while the older, more practiced coal cutters stayed in their home villages, apparently "awaiting land and freedom" from the Duma.[1] The landowners and mine owners had been horrified by the seizure of the Ekaterinin railroad and the armed battles that had followed. The Bakhmut district zemstvo had denounced the December strikes and uprising, calling them "inhuman acts, harming innocent third parties, and terrorizing all who disagreed with them."[2] The pogroms had frightened and shaken the Jewish communities, where a steady *embourgeoisement* had until then fostered an increasing sense of belonging and well-being. The small intelligentsia was accused of betrayal by both sides, the revolutionaries regarding it as vacillating and having turned back in the middle of the fight, and the conservatives denouncing it for having had any part in bringing on the revolution and supporting demands for radical democratization. The violence of the regime's repression of all revolutionary gains, and

[1] *Gorno-zavodskii listok*, no. 21 (1906), p. 8537.

[2] Ershov, "Dekabr'skoe vooruzhennoe vosstanie v Donbasse," pt. 1, p. 24.

the increasing turn toward revolutionary violence, left the small Donbass liberal intelligentsia in a state of frustrated paralysis.

The politics of the region were certainly at the heart of this situation, but the lack of progress in building a decent society also contributed to it. Observing the living conditions of Donbass workers, Pazhitnov commented that for over forty years there had been hopes for a simple solution of the social question in Russia, through commercial share companies undertaking the construction of low-cost, hygienic housing for workers. But not even a start had been made.[3] In the autumn of 1906, Viscount Cranley reported the ensuing polarization in one of his fortnightly reports to London.

> Altogether the Centre parties seem to be in a very difficult situation and seem to be losing ground either to the reactionaries or the revolutionaries. As an example of this, the results of the elections for the Alexandrovsk division of Ekaterinoslav Zemstvo may be mentioned. All the liberal members were defeated here and none but adherents of the League of Russian People were returned. This is striking in view of the fact that hitherto the Zemstvo elections have nearly always resulted in the return of Octobrists.[4]

What was to have been the birth of an integrated civil society in Russia had been distorted into polarized, mutually hostile solitudes.

Industrial, Civil, and Rural Unrest

The violence that had been unleashed throughout Russia was particularly intense in the Donbass. Political and economic unrest were intertwined with criminal outbursts, and at times the three were indistinguishable, especially as there were always those among the observers and reporters who were anxious to interpret every breach of order as a sign of revolutionary conspiracy, and to equate all political dissent with crime. The summer of 1906 was particularly active, and British consular reports abound in such phrases as "the bulk of disturbance and unrest is, as usual, in this district," or "the further south you go, the worse is the situation." In 1906, rural

[3] Pazhitnov, *Polozhenie*, p. 216.

[4] FO, 371/122–32932 (September 25, 1906), p. 265.

unrest in the Donbass also flared up much more strongly than it had in the previous year.

The general number of strikers in the Donbass was reported as one hundred thousand in 1906, and it dwindled each year until it reached ten thousand in 1909 before rising to twelve thousand the following year. The Lena goldfields massacre in 1912 gave rise to a wave of protest strikes that boosted the year's total to twenty-nine strikes involving 25,800 people. Of these, twelve were classified as economic strikes involving 8,200 strikers, and seventeen as political strikes with 17,600 participants. In prewar Russia and in 1917 (as in later years), the political strikes tended to be larger than the economic ones.[5] In 1913 Modestov records 15,000 miners and metal workers as striking in the Donbass, growing to a total of forty strikes and 44,625 strikers in the first seven months of 1914, when a flood of labor unrest was sweeping the country.[6]

The year 1906 began quietly in Iuzovka. The factory had been closed down at the end of December for an overhaul, but it reopened on January 24.[7] It was only in May that a strike wave began; it revealed the tensions in the region. May Day had passed without any public recognition of the date by the workers. "On the eve of May Day, Zaks and several committee members, as well as a few factory workers, were arrested. All night the police patrolled the factory, and in the morning there was a police detail at every gate, and with it a group from the Union of the Russian People. In such circumstances we couldn't convince the workers to down tools, and for a single shop to strike alone was meaningless."[8] It was not only the workers who were reluctant to take action in such circumstances. Moiseenko expressed disgust with engineers who claimed to be Social-Democrats but

[5] See the discussion in Koenker and Rosenberg, *Strikes and Revolution in Russia*, pp. 73–76.

[6] *Ukrains'kaia radians'kaia entsiklopediia*, vol. 17, p. 107, gives overall figures of strikers in the Donbass for 1906–10. Kondufor, *Istoriia rabochikh Donbassa*, vol. 1, pp. 108–17, specifies strikes of miners and metallurgy workers, and arrives at much more modest figures; e.g., p. 116, a total of 10,300 strikers, as against 60,000 in the encyclopedia, and only a few individual strikes for 1909–10, as compared with 22,300 strikers in the encyclopedia. The figures and classification for 1912 are from p. 117. Modestov, *Rabochee i professional'noe dvizhenie*, p. 86, gives the figures for 1913 and the first seven months of 1914.

[7] FO, 371/120–2716 and 3548 (January 22 and 23, 1906), reporting the scheduled reopening, and the safety of Mr. Evan Evans of Iuzovka, whose wife and children had reached England safely after being evacuated during the December troubles.

[8] Gur'ev's description of the New Russia factory is in Moiseenko, *Vospominaniia, 1873–1923*, p. 167.

refused to take action by organizing a May Day strike. He dismissed contemptuously their reasoning that only a widespread strike would have an effect, and that if only two or three shafts struck, the owners would prefer to close them rather than give in.[9] The engineers were shown to be correct, for after a quiet May Day, one shaft of the mines at Makeevka struck for higher pay. The miners were given three days' grace to return or be fired, and, unsupported by other mines, they returned to work without satisfaction of their demands.[10]

Moiseenko followed his principles, though it nearly cost him his life. He was working then in the Kalachev mines. He attempted to organize a May Day strike, which was broken up by miners who beat up his fellow leader and tried to lynch him, while a squadron of dragoons watched the proceedings.[11] There nevertheless must have been some support for May Day demonstrations, for strikes by workers lowered coal loadings by 25 percent in the first two days of May at the Rutchenko, Shcheglovka, Russian-Donetsk, and Golubovskii mines, while a backlog of loaded cars in Iuzovka caused the interruption of iron-ore transport by the Ekaterinin railroad.[12]

The wave of strikes that swept the Donbass mines from May to August generated almost purely economic and social demands, yet a political background can be discerned clearly in the events that took place at the same time as the strikes. The pattern of the strikes was consistent. A total of 44,800 miners at thirty-six mines went on strike.[13] The average of over 1,200 miners per strike would appear to indicate that the strikes were not cases of one shift at a single mine shaft, but were organized industrial actions taking in entire mine settlements. Of these strikes, the demands, duration, and outcomes of sixteen are known. The workers wanted more money; they added social conditions, improvement of housing, baths, and similar issues, often as an afterthought resulting from general meetings of the strikers. In none of these did any political demands find expression. Except for miners at the Zheleznaia mine, and the case of two hundred youths (*maloletnye*) on strike at the Shcherbinovka mines, who were offered half the raise they demanded, the economic demands were refused in every case, though many of the social improvements were granted. Military and

[9] Ibid., p. 166.

[10] *Gorno-zavodskii listok*, no. 21 (1906), p. 8536.

[11] Moiseenko, *Vospominaniia starogo revoliutsionera*, p. 191.

[12] *Gorno-zavodskii listok*, no. 18 (1906), p. 8506.

[13] Ivanov, "Pod"em," p. 369.

police forces were present in strength, but the level of violence was low. Workers requested permission to hold strike meetings, and where they held them without permission, or in spite of refusal, they were dispersed with force, but not by firearms. In Gorlovka, the 1,700 miners of shaft no. 5, on strike for seven days, threatened to destroy the mine if their demands were not met, but no such action took place, though all their demands were refused. In July, the six thousand striking miners at the French Co.'s Rutchenko mines and the Karpov and Lydia mines brought the horses up and stopped the pumps, flooding the mines. In four cases, the workers quit or were laid off, but without the three-month severance pay that they demanded.[14] Although this last strike was the largest of the wave, and took place close to Iuzovka, there were no strikes at any of the New Russia mines or in its factory during this period.[15]

Perhaps the most significant development was the discipline and organization shown by the workers. There was no sign of mass drunkenness or of a bunt. The largest of all the strikes, that of six mines just outside Iuzovka, had begun with thousands of strikers pledging "no vodka."[16] Meetings were held frequently during the various strikes, and there exist a number of references to changes in strike demands due to workers' suggestions, indicating broad participation in the leadership of strikes.

The Elections to the First Duma

These changes are perhaps best understood against the background of a separate but clearly relevant political campaign that was going on: the fight for the Duma. While the economic strikes and the political meetings associated with the election of the Duma were kept separate, there was a clear connection. For the first time the Donbass workers and miners were involved both in bettering their own lives and in projecting their experience onto a wider screen of national affairs, where they could legitimately influence the gaining of benefits and the redress of grievances. At last, a start had

[14] The most detailed accounts of these strikes, including lists of demands, and of management's response, are given in *Gorno-zavodskii listok*, nos. 21–28 (1906) and supp. to no. 28. The journal *Pravo* also has an informative section on civic events throughout this period. The improvement in information carried by these publications is clearly a gain to be attributed to the 1905 revolution.

[15] Ivanov, "Pod"em," p. 369.

[16] *Gorno-zavodskii listok*, supp. to no. 28 (1906), p. 3.

been made at breaching the parochial walls that hitherto had circumscribed the workers' existence. Yet the mass of the workers responded reluctantly and suspiciously, uncertain about the deeper meaning of the changes that were taking place.

The campaign for Duma electors was a novel experience for all the various strata of Donbass society. It was also confusing, for the law was complex, and there were few, even among the educated, who had experience with such matters.[17] Moiseenko recalls reading to the workers of the Rutchenko mines from the Poltava *Sotsial-Demokrat*, to explain to them their right to choose three electors to the Duma. The workers had never before heard such ideas openly expressed.[18] At the annual meeting of the Association of Southern Coal and Steel Producers it was difficult to arrange a schedule since elections were held in different districts on different days, and no delegate to the association meetings was willing to forgo participation in the election activities. Almost immediately after the October Manifesto, a group of ninety-one individuals and companies, members of the association, along with five groups of mining-industry employees, had sent a telegram of confidence and support to Count Witte, calling for an election law and for a prompt convocation of the proposed Duma.[19]

The excitement with which the association members were filled came through clearly in their debate, as they spoke of feelings of duty, and of fateful days, enunciating proudly their different factional allegiances.[20] Here, too, we see a professional group breaking out of its parochial concerns and seeking a place for itself within the mosaic of national affairs. On the eve of the October Manifesto, the Council of the Association had sent a supportive telegram to Count Witte calling for radical reform, but the weight of opinion in this group was the Octobrist view that the manifesto had been sufficient, and should be implemented as proclaimed rather than expanded. There were also urgent factional interests that the coal producers sought to guard. When the Duma had convened, and there was talk of land reform, the Council of the Association sent the Duma chairman a memorandum noting that before any steps were taken that might impinge on private,

[17] The law governing the elections to the Duma is given in *Pravo*, no. 1 (1906), special addendum, pp. 1–15.

[18] Moiseenko, *Vospominaniia starogo revoliutsionera*, p. 185.

[19] *Gorno-zavodskii listok*, nos. 48–49, (1905). Anderson and engineer Zimovskii had signed for the New Russia Co.

[20] *Trudy, XXX, 1906*, stenogram of seventh session, pp. 105–8. Octobrists predominated, with a smaller number of Kadets.

church, or government landholdings, the question of mineral rights clearly had to be legislated.[21]

Among the miners and factory workers, both the participation in the election proceedings and the results varied from place to place. There can be little doubt, however, that the mass of the Donbass proletariat found this a fascinating process—strange and fraught with potential dangers, yet at the same time one to which they would have liked to become accustomed. The workers were being granted dignity and self-esteem in that their opinion was being asked, and they were able to voice legitimately their concerns, despite all the restraints imposed by representatives of power. At the Golubovka mines, there was considerable interest in the elections, with politically active miners making an effort to see that their names were included on the election rolls. The pre-election meeting was conducted by two cochairmen, miners, who consulted with the mine management about the proper procedures for conducting such an assembly. When few voters turned up at seven o'clock in the morning on March 7 for the voting, an additional voting period was scheduled for the afternoon, and sixty additional voters appeared. Two delegates were elected, neither of whom was one of the cochairmen.[22] Such independence of choice was not always evident. At Krivoi Rog, Grushevsk, and Gorlovka, the elected delegates were office personnel and foremen, elected by an open show of hands, with participation of about one-third of the electorate. The pre-election discussions were either truncated or entirely done away with, as a state of enhanced security was in effect in these areas.[23]

Moiseenko describes a miners' meeting to elect delegates to the electoral college of the Duma. The police constable addressed the assembly, enjoining his audience to elect worthy people who had long and unblemished records of service in the mines. Moiseenko interrupted, arguing that the police should not be intervening in the people's election meetings. There should be a proper hall provided, and the meeting should choose a chairman who would conduct the elections for the delegates. The policeman had a different view: the assembled miners should choose a worthy chairman, and the chairman would instruct them about who should be elected. In the end,

[21] For the attitudes of the industrialists in October 1905, see Ershov, "Dekabr'skoe vooruzhennoe vosstanie v Donbasse," pt. 1, p. 22. For the memorandum on mineral rights, see *Gorno-zavodskii listok*, no. 28 (1906), p. 8609.

[22] *Gorno-zavodskii listok*, no. 13 (1906), p. 8453.

[23] Ibid., no. 12 (1906), pp. 8436–37.

Moiseenko prevailed. There was a hall and an independently elected chairman, and the police constable was excluded.[24] Where there was an active and bold group, or even a single individual, to demand the workers' rights, they could be upheld. Such cases, however, were in the minority. One might ask what a loyal Bolshevik such as Moiseenko was doing campaigning in the Duma elections. It would seem that Lenin's anathema on this representative assembly was ignored in Iuzovka, for Moiseenko makes a point of the unity with which Bolsheviks and Mensheviks worked to register voters and get them to meetings.[25] This was evidently not the case throughout the south; in Kharkov, twenty-two out of thirty-one industrial enterprises sent telegrams refusing to elect delegates for the Duma elections.[26] Moiseenko, however, notes that in this election campaign the prevailing outlook in the Donbass was that of joint work with no Bolshevik-Menshevik split.[27] Much later, too, at the time of the Fourth Duma, Moiseenko noted that the "Liquidator" controversy that rocked the Social-Democrats was not understood at the local level.[28] Nevertheless, Okhrana materials indicated that the Iuzovka Bolsheviks had decided after three discussion meetings that they would set up an independent organization, and even two years later, though the decision does not appear to have been implemented, Zalmaev is said to have been almost frantic at rumors that Petrovskii was attempting to heal the split with the Liquidators.[29]

Electoral registration and the procedures of election meetings and reporting were often cumbersome and not always scrupulously fair, as might well have been foreseen. Consul Medhurst reported, "At Hughesovka little interest was taken in the elections by the small traders who refused to leave their business to travel to Bachmout, where the registration took place, and undoubtedly the same cause prevented many men from the pits and the

[24] Moiseenko, *Vospominaniia starogo revoliutsionera*, pp. 153–62.

[25] Ibid., p. 163.

[26] *Gorno-zavodskii listok*, no. 10 (1906), p. 8409. There is no indication in this report of whether the boycott came from the left or the right.

[27] Moiseenko, *Vospominaniia starogo revoliutsionera*, p. 185. The editors append an explanatory note: "The author in this case expresses the desire of the workers and rank-and-file members of the RSDRP for unity of the class forces of the proletariat, characterizing the situation existing in the lower party organizations at that time."

[28] Ibid., p. 204. The Mensheviks suggested abandoning underground conspiracy and focusing on legal, public political activity, which aroused violent condemnation from the Bolsheviks.

[29] See Modestov, *Rabochee i professional'noe dvizhenie*, p. 74; Kondufor, *Istoriia rabochikh Donbassa*, vol. 1, p. 119; and Rubach, *Rabochee dvizhenie*, pp. 495–500.

works from attending."[30] At the Konstantinovka bottle factory, only 1,100 of the 2,000 workers were listed on the electoral rolls, and due to various "restrictions and clarifications," only 180 of these were actually enfranchised. In addition, other, cruder methods of exclusion were noted, including a simple refusal to register left-wing candidates, and frequent stuffing of the ballot box.[31] Then the whipping-up of pogroms became part of the radical right's campaign against the elections. A printing press in the prefecture of police, run by a Captain Komissarov, a protégé of Interior Minister Durnovo, was turning out pamphlets bearing the imprimatur of the Union of the Russian People and the seal of the censor, reading in part: "The Jews of the whole world, who hate Russia, [together with] the Armenians, and Germany and England, have made an alliance and decided to destroy Russia from top to bottom, to partition her into petty kingdoms and abandon her to the enemies of the Russian people. . . . As soon as these sellers of Christ appear among you, worry them and thrash them, so that they may wish never to come near you any more."[32] The combination of dangerous disruption of internal life and opprobrium in the international community brought Stolypin to have his reluctant minister of the interior issue urgent instructions to governors in the south that disorders were to be prevented. From Rostov, Medhurst reported: "The Governor of Rostov has again warned the public that he will not tolerate the slightest attempt to cause disorder, and that any Jew-baiting will be severely repressed by the troops—the first time I have seen any special warning given to the people to refrain from ill-treating their Hebrew fellow-citizens."[33] A similar policy was evidently being followed in the Donbass area, for when a Black Hundreds plot to smash an ikon and blame the Jews was discovered in Bakhmut,

[30] FO, 371/124–12744. Report of A.F.H. Medhurst, April 7, 1906. *Gorno-zavodskii listok*, no. 9 (1906), p. 8392, also notes that the Donbass workers were generally apathetic about the Duma elections. It evidently took some time before the workers began to believe and participate with a will, after their recent disappointments.

[31] Beligura, *Bol'shevistskaia gazeta*, pp. 86–87.

[32] The existence of the pamphlet, its form, and its provenance were confirmed by Cecil Spring-Rice in answer to a Foreign Office inquiry from London about the truth of a report in *The Times* (London). See FO, 371/124–9369 (March 17, 1906). The quotation from the pamphlet's text is from a note written by Spring-Rice to the Russian foreign minister, Count Lamsdorff, expressing concern over the pamphlet. See FO, 371/124–9502 (March 19, 1906).

[33] The existence of governmental instructions against pogroms was reported to Spring-Rice by the "President of the Jewish Committee (Gunsburg)" and passed on to London in FO, 371/124–12078 (April 9, 1906), p. 340. Medhurst's report is in FO, 371/124–12744 (April 7, 1906), p. 357.

the police there published a report stating that the ikon had not been damaged by Jews, and threatening prompt and stern repression of any outbreaks.[34]

The preparations for the Duma thus aroused some anticipation among the people of the Donbass. They had in many instances rioted over what they regarded as "foreign" rebellion against the tsar and Russia, which demeaned traditional authority by forcing the limitation of the ruler's power. But now in quieter times, the tsar, through his own appointed ministers, was proceeding to grant the people a voice. These same conservative mine and factory workers gave every indication that most of them accepted the establishment of the Duma as a way in which their petitions might reach the sovereign, bringing him closer to them. Other currents of opinion had also changed. Among many of the revolutionaries who had campaigned mightily against the autocracy, this Duma was seen essentially as a tainted and vastly imperfect institution, useful only as a stepping-stone to further political concessions. This is reflected in a report regarding the Donbass, contrasting economic recovery with the growing political tensions. Trapped among manipulation, skepticism, and passivity, the majority of Donbass workers stood aloof from the tentative beginnings of democratization. "The temper of the workmen is sullen, and they refused to celebrate the opening of the Duma, to which they attach little importance."[35] Nevertheless, when the elections were complete, the Donbass workers had one of their own sitting in this august assembly. Mikhailichenko, elected as a representative of the Trudovik list, had worked in Karpov's Uspenskii mines and had been a prominent figure in 1905.[36] Thirty-five years of age, he was described as "a peasant workman. More of a dreamer, and less intelligent [than Saveyeff] and very much in love with himself, but honest and simple."[37]

Those who had faith and interest in the Duma were quickly disappointed, for Stolypin soon clipped that institution's wings, and in mid-July 1906 he dispersed it. There was a rapid and large-scale reaction in the Donbass. On July 30, a meeting of ten thousand people took place in Iuzovka. They listened to reports on the dispersal of the Duma, and passed a

[34] FO, 371/122–23119 (July 4, 1906), p. 134. Cranley's fortnightly political report.

[35] FO, 371/125–18150 (May 23, 1906), p. 188. Cecil Spring-Rice to Sir Edward Grey.

[36] TsGAOR, F. 7952, op. 6, d. 120, p. 28. Zakharkin's memoirs.

[37] FO, 371/126–21427 (June 12, 1906), p. 35. Ambassador Nicolson to Sir Edward Grey.

resolution calling for a stoppage of work in all mines in the district.[38] Dragoons were called in to disperse the assembly. The call for a strike was particularly worrisome, for the second round of strikes at the Rutchenko, Karpov, and Lydia mines, involving some six thousand miners, had ended on July 18, but as the fortnightly British political report noted, "the dispute is not definitely settled, and the lull is only due to a truce between employers and employed."[39] Two days later, the military governor had arrived with troops and arrested the strike leaders. Now, although the formal demands posed by the workers were the same economic questions that had been raised in June and mid-July, the focus of the strike was the militant political agenda of the Iuzovka meeting, and the miners stopped the mine pumps.[40] The governor immediately published a statement saying that the flooding of the mines was a matter of state concern, laid a prohibition on any meetings, and ordered a wave of arrests. The strike continued for ten days, and the damage to the mines through flooding was said to have amounted to one million rubles.[41]

The British report of the strike accused Mikhailichenko of being the leader of those who were agitating the workers to strike. This, however, contradicts earlier reports of his activities. Mikhailichenko was twice noted as urging restraint on striking workers, telling them that disorder made it harder to solve the agrarian and labor problems besetting the south.[42] On August 9, just as the massive strike in the mines was ending, Mikhailichenko arrived in Druzhkovka to speak to his constituents. A crowd of four thousand gathered to hear him report on the work of the Duma and the plans for future activities. The police had offered no objection to the beginning of the meeting, but toward the end, the police chief appeared and ordered the dispersal of the crowd. It would appear that the reason for the chief's change of heart was the interruption of the meeting by hostile

[38] *Pravo*, no. 30 (1906), p. 2494, and no. 32 (1906), p. 2600. Ivanov, "Pod"em," p. 369, states that Mikhailichenko was the principal orator at this meeting, but identifies him as a Menshevik and states that only five thousand persons attended. His source, however, is referring to the August 9 meeting at the Druzhkovka mine, though the news item is datelined Iuzovka.

[39] FO, 371/122–24900 (July 18, 1906), p. 145. Cranley to the Foreign Office.

[40] *Pravo*, no. 30 (1906), p. 2494.

[41] FO, 371/122–28272 (August 16, 1906), p. 193. Fortnightly report written by Mr. Norman. *Russkie vedomosti*, no. 202 (August 13, 1906), p. 3, reports that all mines were again working normally, including some of those that had been flooded.

[42] See the accusation in FO, 371/122–28272 (August 16, 1906), p. 193, and the reports in *Gorno-zavodskii listok*, no. 25 (1906), p. 8574, and nos. 26–27 (1906), p. 8591.

revolutionary slogans shouted in the midst of Mikhailichenko's speech. Mikhailichenko left the scene hastily; after he was gone, a shot was fired from an unknown quarter. The police chief ordered the cossacks to fire, and they did so, killing and wounding members of the audience. The next day their funeral was turned into a political demonstration attended by ten thousand workers with black flags, singing revolutionary anthems, while work in all the neighboring mines and factories stopped for a day.[43]

The politicization of the Donbass public had spread even earlier. Society was polarized, with both extremes tending to violence. The Ekaterinoslav governor had been shot and killed in early May. The enhanced security during the Duma pre-election campaign had only thrown the tensions into bolder relief. As the wave of strikes grew through the end of May and the beginning of June, the military units stationed in the Donbass had been reinforced. When, on June 6, a large contingent of soldiers arrived at Iuzovo station on their way to Iuzovka, they were greeted with cheering and a tossing of caps in the air by a crowd of eight thousand miners from all over the district. The soldiers responded in kind, and joined a meeting, waving flags and singing.[44] A week later, ten cossacks refused to turn out for target practice and were arrested. Hearing of this, five hundred workers came to free them, but were fired upon by other cossacks, and two workers were wounded. Then a mob of three thousand miners from the New Russia Vetka mines attempted to stop the train on which the arrested cossacks were being transported to prison, but failed. The following day a crowd of five thousand from the Rykovskii and Vetka mines wanted to protest by holding a march through Iuzovka, but were dissuaded by their fellow workers. All enterprises in and around Iuzovka worked as usual that day.[45] The workers and miners were still far from being of one mind.

Other gatherings followed through the summer of 1906. On June 22, a mass political meeting was held at the Rutchenko mines, attracting

[43] *Pravo*, no. 33 (1906), p. 2656, writes that the meeting was "interspersed with revolutionary calls from the crowd" and that eight were killed and thirty-two wounded. A similar figure is used by *Russkie vedomosti*, no. 202 (August 13, 1906), p. 3. A later report in *Pravo*, no. 35 (1906), citing testimony of a local constable, claims that forty-four shots were fired, but that only two were killed and two wounded. Kondufor, *Istoriia rabochikh Donbassa*, vol. 1, p. 138, claims that twenty-five thousand attended the funeral.

[44] *Gorno-zavodskii listok*, nos. 23–24 (1906), p. 8561. Ivanov, "Pod"em," p. 364, adds that the authorities later announced that should such gatherings be repeated they would be put down by force of arms.

[45] *Gorno-zavodskii listok*, supp. to no. 28 (1906).

workers from the Karpov mine and from the Bosst Gennefeld factory in Iuzovka. The first strike at the mine had ended just four days earlier, and though it had involved only four hundred workers, and they had received some satisfaction of their social demands, the atmosphere was understandably tense. The subject of the meeting was the rallying of support for the fourteen workers' deputies who had been elected to the Duma. The chief orator came from outside the district, and his name has not been preserved in any of the sources, but he drew what was called a "particularly large meeting." Troops were sent from Iuzovka, and though the cossacks assured the workers that they would not interfere with the meeting, the orator was arrested by a squadron of dragoons. When the dragoons were surrounded by a thousand angry workers, and warning shots had already been fired, a cossack officer intervened, freeing the orator, and calm was restored. During the melee, ten cossacks refused to take part in arresting workers, and others refused to fire. Altogether, thirty cossacks of the Third Company (*sotnia*) of the Twenty-third Battalion of the Don Cossacks were arrested. Then the scene of ten days earlier repeated itself, with workers surrounding the barracks where their benefactors were detained. The cossack guards fired on the demonstrators, wounding some and dispersing the others. To prevent the transport of the arrested cossacks, the workers seized Iuzovo station, stopping all traffic from Iuzovka, and taking over the telegraph office. This aroused painful memories for the authorities, who moved swiftly. With reliable troops, they recaptured the station, wounding twenty workers. Even then, the trouble was not over. On June 27, another workers' protest meeting took place near Iuzovka. The entire sotnia sent to disperse it refused to fire on the workers, and was promptly transferred from the district.[46]

Two central points emerge here. One is the link that formed between the cossacks and the miners. Although incidents of this nature were few, and the evidence indicates that the entire phenomenon may have been restricted to one or two units, the incidents become significant when put in context. I noted above that where strike meetings were dispersed, firearms had not been used. Now, where peaceful political meetings were being held, discussing lawful institutions sanctioned by royal decree, some of the cossacks,

[46] The events are chronicled in ibid. See also no. 25 (1906), p. 8574, and Ivanov, "Pod"em," p. 365, who is the only source mentioning the attack on the railway station. FO, 371/122–24900 (July 18, 1906), p. 145, states that the thirty cossacks arrested were stationed in Bakhmut, but gives the other details as related here.

at least, were reluctant to intervene. This is a postrevolutionary novelty, for neither before nor during 1905 had any such thing taken place. The cossack units posted in Iuzovka had returned from the Far East in March, and their war experience had no doubt influenced them. A British diplomat, observing the behavior of the troops in the Donbass, commented, "Two striking points with regard to all the present series of mutinies are the cruelty of the men, and the savage hatred they seem to bear their officers, and the suddenness with which the movement collapses in a few days or even hours."[47]

Second, the New Russia factory workers do not appear to have taken part in this wave of unrest, nor did any significant meetings take place in Iuzovka. Rather, it was in the surrounding mine settlements that the strikes, meetings, and consequent clashes occurred, and when there was a suggestion by miners in the district that thousands of workers should demonstrate in the streets of Iuzovka itself, "their fellow workers" dissuaded them. It would seem that the same differences of outlook that in 1887 generated enmity between Iuzovka and the miners of Rutchenkovo and the other neighboring mine settlements still persisted. In all the news items dealing with protests and arrests, there appears only one regarding a meeting in Iuzovka, on June 23, the day that the attempt to free the thirty cossacks failed. Two workers were arrested at a workers' meeting, and when other workers tried to free them, one was slashed with a saber.[48]

Affected by these tensions, the miners of the district began to react as they so often had before. They began leaving the district in large numbers, warning that "a great storm would soon come" (*Bol'shoi budet skoro shturm*). The natural assumption was that the armed uprising of the previous year was about to repeat itself. In the *Gorno-zavodskii listok*, a news item reported "frequent" meetings around Ekaterinoslav supporting the Duma and calling for armed uprising.[49] When the "Vyborg Appeal," calling for a tax strike and for support of the Duma, was distributed around the Donbass, those passing it out were arrested.[50] Mass meetings at various mines created a vicious circle of arrests of orators, followed by attempts to free them, followed by more arrests.[51] In the Council of the Association of Southern

[47] FO, 371/122–2872 (August 16, 1906) p. 193. Fortnightly report of Mr. Norman.

[48] *Gorno-zavodskii listok*, no. 25 (1906), p. 8574.

[49] Ibid., nos. 23–24 (1906), p. 8562.

[50] See reports in *Pravo*, no. 31 (1906), p. 2553, and no. 36 (1906), p. 2904.

[51] For such a process at the Prokhorov mine, see ibid., no. 30 (1906), p. 2489. For Shcherbinovka, where seventy were arrested, including two engineers, see ibid., no. 35 (1906), p. 2779. For Iuzovka, see FO, 371/122–28272 (August 16, 1906), p. 191, fort-

Coal and Steel Producers, S. F. Ianchevskii warned that the population of the mine and factory settlements had completely lost faith in the administration, the courts, and the police.[52] The situation that had been created appeared to be a classic case of rising expectations running far ahead of reality and eventually leading to bitter, frustrated violence.

Nor was all the popular violence revolutionary by any means, though it sometimes became difficult to separate the political from the criminal. There were rising numbers of attacks on individuals and shops for the sake of robbery. In Iuzovka and elsewhere, serious fires, believed to be the result of arson, were reported. A police constable, Trubinikov, was wounded near the main offices of the New Russia Co. in Iuzovka, and his three assailants escaped. In mid-October, twelve "militant anarchists" were arrested in the settlement and tried by "drum-head court" (a field court-martial). Six were shot on the spot, and six were handed over to the civil authorities for a second trial. They were accused of having held up a number of shopkeepers, one of whom they murdered.[53] This sentence was handed down after the creation of field courts-martial throughout the Donbass, a step that caused alarm and opposition in the more liberal press. *Russkie vedomosti* reported the summary execution of a number of persons who had carried out an armed attack on a store, noting: "In addition to sentences passed by court-martial, five death sentences have been passed this week, but editors have been forbidden to print the news."[54] So tense was the atmosphere that a religious procession on the streets of Iuzovka broke up in panic when a large crowd of workers appeared. The town constable fired a shot and was seized by the crowd, but was freed by the police chief, aided by dragoons who dispersed the panic-stricken people. Evan Evans, a Welsh employee of the New Russia Co., who had taken home leave to visit his wife and children, was advised by the Foreign Office that in view of the recent and continuing disturbances, it would not be advisable to bring them back to Iuzovka at the

nightly political report, noting that five of eight people arrested were freed by the crowd. The eight were described as "several agitators surprised at night."

[52] *Gorno-zavodskii listok*, no. 31 (1906), p. 8645.

[53] FO, 371/129–35606 (October 16, 1906), p. 112. Report of consul Medhurst. See *Russkie vedomosti*, no. 204 (August 17, 1906), p. 4; FO, 371/122–26851 (July 31, 1906), p. 170; and FO, 371/122–29746 (August 29, 1906), p. 234, for various reports of criminal and political violence through the summer of 1906. See also *Gorno-zavodskii listok*, nos. 23–24 (1906), p. 8562; *Russkie vedomosti* (August 10, 1906), p. 2; and Levus, "Iz istorii," p. 82.

[54] *Russkie vedomosti*, no. 253 (October 15, 1906), p. 4. For other reports of restrictions on the press and on open speech, see ibid., no. 225 (September 12, 1906), p. 4.

moment.[55] Taganrog district and the settlement of Makeevka were placed under martial law in the second half of July, and the situation was sufficiently tense that an imperial decree of August 10 created a temporary governor-generalship for Bakhmut and Mariupol districts, though the new governor-general, Bogaevskii, took up residence in Iuzovka only toward the end of October.[56]

The only attack on a British employee of the New Russia Co. took place during this time. On August 18, Medhurst reported that two days earlier, William Chambers, later identified as the assistant chief engineer of the New Russia plant, was wounded by gunshots. Two men had approached him and asked for work, then fired four revolver shots, wounding him slightly, and threw a bomb that fell short. This led to a flurry of British diplomatic pressure and police activity that resulted in a multitude of searches and arrests, though it appeared in the end that the entire episode was on personal, rather than ideological, grounds.

The principal political difference in 1906 was not the diminution of following for the revolutionary parties in the mines and factories, but the unrest that swept the Donbass and Ekaterinoslav rural areas in contrast to the relative quiet of 1905. Beginning in the early summer, there were reports of peasant seizures of grain and the burning of farm buildings. Near Iuzovka a local landowner named Almazov led three hundred peasants in forcing other landowners to sign over their lands to the peasantry. The owners were then banished from their farms. Cossack intervention—the arrest of Almazov and some of his followers—put an end to this movement.[57] At Peski, the New Russia Co. farm, peasants burned the farmhouse and a quantity of hay, and took grain. Agricultural workers near Bakhmut were on strike. In Bakhmut itself, unknown persons broke into Grillikher's print shop at night and printed an estimated two thousand copies of a leaflet entitled "A Call to the Russian Peasants." The perpetrators escaped, and the authorities sealed the print shop.[58] Throughout the summer there were repeated clashes between peasants and cossacks, following

[55] For the panic, see *Pravo*, no. 28 (1906), p. 2387. The advice to Mr. Evans is in FO, 371/128–31488 (September 26, 1906), p. 373.

[56] Modestov, *Rabochee i professional'noe dvizhenie*, p. 43. British consul Medhurst reported this step as proof of the good faith of the Russian authorities regarding protection of British interests. See FO, 371/129–38044 (November 12, 1906), p. 349, Medhurst to Grey.

[57] *Gorno-zavodskii listok*, nos. 26–27 (1906), p. 8591.

[58] Ibid., p. 8592; *Pravo*, no. 31 (1906), p. 2554. It does not seem to have occurred to the nocturnal printers that the peasants of the region were Ukrainian, not Russian.

the same cycle as occurred in the mines: arrests, attempts to free the arrested, and the killing or wounding of persons along with new arrests.[59] At the end of the year, reporting on the burning of farm buildings belonging to the British owner of fifteen thousand acres near Taganrog, the British ambassador noted that the young peasants of the region in particular were disaffected, had lost faith in the tsar, and believed that soon they would be able to take all the land.[60]

These events reveal a complex mixture of attitudes. The Iuzovka workers took no part in strikes and demonstrations, yet they would not testify against a man accused of killing a police spy, and they attacked the police to free arrested persons. They might still cling to tsar and church, but they had contempt for the police, who were reportedly terrorized and ineffective. In September the British consul reported that the men actually at work were peacefully disposed, despite the chain of violent events of the previous month that brought the assignment of extra detectives and the presence of an armored train to the settlement. The autumn of 1906 was threatening, and the *Gorno-zavodskii listok* nervously commented that it was all very reminiscent of November and December 1905.[61] Yet even the limited organization of mass uprising that characterized the autumn and winter of the previous year was no longer in evidence. The city and railway workers who led the strikes and uprising of 1905 were quiescent, and whatever the violent turmoil in the mine settlements, and whatever the disaffection of the peasantry, these were easily contained by the determination and ruthlessness of Stolypin's government.

Revolutionary Organization and Propaganda

In such conditions, with the government militantly repressive and the authorities ferreting out revolutionaries after every real or supposed action, revolutionary organization was difficult. After the debacle of 1905, the experienced leaders of the Donetsk Social-Democratic Union of Mine Industry Workers had left the Donbass for other areas.[62] Moiseenko was

[59] See *Russkie vedomosti*, no. 193 (August 3, 1906), for such an incident. See also *Gorno-zavodskii listok*, no. 31 (1906), pp. 8649–50, and *Pravo*, no. 32 (1906), p. 2602, and no. 34 (1906), p. 2744.

[60] FO, 371/129–4293 (December 7, 1906), p. 579, Nicolson to Grey.

[61] *Gorno-zavodskii listok*, supp. to no. 28 (1906), p. 2.

[62] Moshinskii, "K voprosu," p. 237.

driven from one workplace to the other by police surveillance and "Black Hundreds influence," ending up in a manganese mine near Nikopol in the spring of 1907, where he started anew to get to know the workers.[63] The old problem of instability of leadership had reemerged.

Clearly the government was on the offensive and the socialist parties were in decline; this process continued until World War I changed the entire constellation, creating the crisis that was to bring the downfall of the Romanov dynasty. The Iuzovka-Petrovskii Committee of Social-Democrats claimed two thousand members at the end of 1905, and even as late as June 1907. Then on July 21, 1907, all those who had been delegates to a joint conference of the two branches were arrested, and membership fell to 450 that autumn, and 100 at the beginning of 1909.[64] There were similar figures for the Social-Democratic membership at other Donbass centers and for other revolutionary parties in the Donbass. Despite such extreme measures as a complete review of membership credentials, the Iuzovka group remained riddled by police agents. In such a situation, the organization had to start anew each year in its agitational and organizational program. According to one correspondent, at the beginning of 1908, the Iuzovka-Petrovskii group had no leading party organs, no committee, and no periodic conferences. Only here and there was an active circle to be found at some mine, or a chance gathering of a few party members and sympathizers.[65] When an attempt was made to organize a district conference it was found that only four of twenty-six former Social-Democratic groups still existed. That the organizing committee only discovered this in the course of its efforts to set up the conference is eloquent testimony to the disorganized state of party affairs.

As this situation continued, those who were attempting to organize were close to despair. Even though P. G. Smidovich went to the Donbass in the autumn of 1908 to inform party groups there of the RSDRP congress that was scheduled to be held in Paris in December, he evidently did not get in contact with the Iuzovka-Petrovskii Committee. They felt cut off from party life, perhaps not realizing that a similar situation prevailed throughout Russia. They only knew that they received no help and no answers to

[63] Moiseenko, *Vospominaniia starogo revoliutsionera*, pp. 173–75, 183.

[64] See *Istoriia mist i sil*, p. 372, for arrests. Kondufor, *Istoriia rabochikh Donbassa*, vol. 1, p. 112, claims five hundred members in 1907. Elwood, *Russian Social Democracy*, p. 47, writes of three thousand members in 1905.

[65] Donii, Lavrov, and Shmorgun, *Bolsheviki Ukrainy*, doc. 52, p. 111.

their letters. "The center seems to have forgotten a region with over 200,000 workers."[66] Veniamin Ermoshenko, a Iuzovka Bolshevik miner who used the pen name "Molodoi shakhter" ("Young miner") wrote at the end of 1913: "Silence. Not a sound of public activity is to be heard from this giant factory with its 12,000 workers." He wrote of himself and his comrades as surrounded by spies and repression, blundering in the darkness.[67] When M. Derman visited Iuzovka in July 1911, he wrote of the factory working at full capacity and of electricity replacing steam, but he found no such progress among the Social-Democrats. Mass arrests had meant that for the past year nothing had been done in the settlement, and when a new comrade arrived, he was able to gather only seven people for a meeting. What Derman did not know was that the police received a full report of his efforts to get a group of workers together to discuss organizational techniques and the prospects of setting up a printing press, including the information that no practical decisions were taken.[68]

In preparation for the elections to the Fourth Duma in 1912, the Social-Democrats of the Iuzovka district had prepared several small groups to call for a general strike. Iuzovka was to lead the way with a walkout in the New Russia Co's. factory and mines. Other mines and steel mills would then follow. But Colonel Bashinskii's eyes and ears were on the job, and on September 16, the police scooped up the entire leadership, including Iakov Zalmaev, who was to emerge as the leader of the Iuzovka Bolsheviks in 1917. The police reports of 1913–1914 state, "In general in the Iuzovka mining district and in Konstantinovka there is at present no effort at party activity among the workers and this is in part to be explained by a dearth of experienced ideologists as well as by a mistrust engendered among the workers in connection with the recent liquidations [of S-D organizations]."[69]

Despite the regime's success in frustrating the organizational efforts of the revolutionaries, there was still a steady, ongoing propaganda effort. In the interval of comparative freedom that followed the October 1905 manifesto, the Lugansk Social-Democrats succeeded in setting up the *Donetskii*

[66] Ibid., doc. 123, pp. 241–43.

[67] *Za pravdu* (November 30, 1913), quoted in Rubach, *Rabochee dvizhenie*, p. 465.

[68] For Derman's report in *Sotsial-Demokrat*, no. 29 (October 18, 1911), see Rubach, *Rabochee dvizhenie*, pp. 96–97. For the police report of his visit, see p. 107. The significance of the detailed report is that a police agent was among the few activists who met with Derman.

[69] "Rabochie organizatsii iuga v 1914 g.," p. 160.

kolokol, publishing the first issue on October 17, 1906. The second number was delayed until November 19, while Bolsheviks and Mensheviks wrestled for control of the editorial board. Despite these factional frictions, twenty issues of the paper came out between October 1906 and January 21, 1907, when it was closed down by order of General Bogaevskii, the governor-general of the southern mining district.[70] The principal agitational weapon of the Social-Democrats remained, however, the leaflets that were produced by their underground presses. Occasionally "mystification" was used. After the July 1907 arrest of the Iuzovka-Petrovskii Committee, fifteen thousand copies were printed of a leaflet bearing the committee's name, urging workers to protest the dispersal of the Second Duma and to nominate their own candidate for the coming elections.[71] When that press was found hidden in the village of Semenovka, near Iuzovka, its seizure was announced in twelve thousand copies of a new leaflet from an alternate press, promising to continue the revolutionary battle.[72] In the Aleksandrovsk-Grushevsk area, the police reported that the Social-Democrats had "neither meetings, nor literature, nor funds. Their print shop is not functioning and has been buried. It is therefore difficult to locate."[73] The head of the Don Cossack territory security department of the police wrote in 1912 that for four years no criminal literature had been received in the Makeevka district (only a few kilometers from Iuzovka), and that none was presently being received.[74]

With local production of literature sharply restricted, and no local Social-Democratic newspapers, the aspiring revolutionaries were forced to rely on legal literature from the capital, or smuggled illegal papers. It was considered a great day for the movement when Ermoshenko and Zalmaev could report having distributed a hundred copies of *Pravda* in a single day, and ask for an additional fifty.[75] Seeking to make the central party papers more attractive to the Donbass public, Zalmaev urged the inclusion of a Donbass-focused miners' page (*Shakhterskii listok*) in the Social-Democratic newspapers dispatched to the south. Here Ermoshenko made his party reputation, becoming the source of many of the militant articles and news reports from the Donbass, printed under his nom de plume.[76]

[70] Beligura, *Bol'shevistskaia gazeta*, pp. 13, 25.
[71] Donii, Lavrov, and Shmorgun, *Bolsheviki Ukrainy*, doc. 16, pp. 37–40.
[72] Ibid., doc. 104, p. 202.
[73] Modestov, *Rabochee i professional'noe dvizhenie*, p. 66.
[74] Rubach, *Rabochee dvizhenie*, p. 249, report of Bashinskii to the Ekaterinoslav governor.
[75] Ibid., p. 464, letter of November 23, 1913, to the St. Petersburg Committee.
[76] Ibid., pp. 499–500.

Yet the response was minimal. The close to thirty thousand miners and factory workers in Iuzovka district contributed a total of 104 rubles to an appeal for funds to establish a miners' page in the *Proletarskaia pravda*.[77] Certainly the regime's coercion had much to do with keeping the revolutionaries from open or easy contact with the workers, but the failure of the revolutionaries to create any broad area of common understanding and sympathy between themselves and the Russian workers is also a prominent factor in the lack of support shown for what was an attempt to create a Donbass voice for workers' aspirations.

The Donbass authorities were well aware that though they had achieved complete penetration of the Social-Democratic circles around Iuzovka, much literature was still entering the region in the guise of a legality proclaimed in the capital, but only grudgingly acknowledged on this wild frontier. Colonel Bashinskii and Iuzovka police chief Iavorskii only looked for the slightest pretext to cut off the import of such subversive journals as *Voprosy strakhovaniia* or *Prosveshchenie*, which came from St. Petersburg. An opportunity offered itself when the Social-Democrats put out a leaflet calling for a strike in the settlement on October 4, 1913, to protest the "accusations of cannibalism against the Jewish people" in the Beilis trial.[78] The call for a strike was answered in the Iuzovka population by calls for a pogrom.

In the event, there was neither strike nor pogrom. The deputy commander of the Ekaterinoslav gendarmerie arrived in Iuzovka, and from October 3 to October 7, under his personal supervision, a series of eighty searches took place. The library of the Shop Clerks' Mutual-Benefit Society was closed down, its subscribers' homes were subjected to search, and two members of the library committee, along with the bookkeeper, were among twenty-five people arrested. As an additional warning, several workers were dismissed from the factory. When there was protest against the confiscation of legally published material, the answer was, "Its sale is prohibited here; therefore it is illegal." The postmaster had turned over to Iavorskii lists of all those receiving publications regarded as objectionable by the local authorities. They were then subjected to house searches and warned to stop subscribing to such scummy scribbling (*svolochnaia literatura*). In describ-

[77] See the report of the fund drive in ibid., pp. 501, 507–8, 524–25, 528.

[78] The date of the strike was also chosen to mark the anniversary of the October Manifesto. Mendel Beilis was arrested in Kiev in 1911, accused of the ritual murder of a Christian child. His trial in 1913, resulting in acquittal, was a cause célèbre in Russia and throughout Europe. He subsequently emigrated to Palestine. For a brief description of the case, see Baron, *Russian Jew*, p. 62.

ing these events, G. I. Petrovskii described the settlement as one particularly closely watched by local and provincial authorities, and permeated by fear.[79] Petrovskii, then a Bolshevik deputy to the Fourth Duma, had been invited to visit the region by Andrei Batov, so that Petrovskii might "get the full picture of the coarseness and administrative arbitrariness prevailing, as well as to learn about the miners' world."[80] Since Petrovskii had been among the early Social-Democratic activists in the Donbass, working at the Shcherbinovka mines with Moiseenko at the turn of the century, the phrasing of Batov's invitation simply strengthens the impression of isolation and neglect among party workers that was noted so prominently above.

Despite the repeatedly effective dousings of the flame of revolution, the embers remained glowing. In addition to leaflets and contributions to the central press, it was a point of honor for the revolutionaries to attempt a demonstration on May Day, the anniversary of Bloody Sunday, and, as in the case of the Beilis trial, whatever other special event offered itself. The death of Lev Tolstoi, who, as I have noted, had eloquently memorialized the victims of the Iuzovka cholera riots, served as an occasion for memorial strikes in several Donbass centers.[81] The object of these activities was both to demonstrate a presence and to engage in what today would be described as consciousness raising: the attempt to bring the Donbass workers once more to that realization of common problems and interests that had moved them in the February and March strikes of 1905, and in the first elections to the Duma. In Iuzovka itself, in the years after the 1905 revolution, there is no record of a successful May Day demonstration until 1911. On May Day 1907, the workers at one shaft of the Lydia mine struck, and a brief May Day meeting was held. The night shifts of the Pesterov mines and of a shaft of the Karpov mine stayed out as well. Those strikes resulted in the authorities' disbanding the Mine Workers' Union that had been formed there. At the New Russia Co.'s Vetka mine, four thousand workers observed the holiday, and large numbers of socialist proclamations were distributed.

In Iuzovka itself, the day shift worked, but when the night shift reported, some workers attempted to stop them from entering the factory, and a fight ensued. The political situation in the factory at this time

[79] See Rubach, *Rabochee dvizhenie*, p. 249, for a list of objectionable newspapers and periodicals by Bashinskii; p. 457 for a *Za pravdu* report of searches and arrests; and pp. 455–57 for Petrovskii's article in *Za pravdu* (November 9, 1913), describing the harsh political atmosphere and physical conditions of Iuzovka.

[80] *Istorik Marksist* 61 (1937), p. 129.

[81] Modestov, *Rabochee i professional'noe dvizhenie*, p. 72.

indicates that this was a conflict between miners from outside Iuzovka and the New Russia factory workers. When the police intervened, they were first stoned and then shot at. One constable was wounded and another killed. Cossacks came, were in their turn pelted with stones, and opened fire, killing two strikers and wounding several others. Order was then restored and work in the factory resumed.[82] In 1908, all the miners around the settlement observed the holiday. By some estimates fifty thousand miners stayed away, but there is no mention of the New Russia workers joining them.[83] On May Day 1913, a worker dutifully turned in to the police two folded leaflets that he had found in the factory. Handwritten in poor Russian and hectographed, the leaflets were said to be crumpled and dirty, as though they had been in someone's pocket a long time. The text called for the international proletariat to celebrate May Day. It did not include a call for a work stoppage, but it denounced the Balkan War. A policeman commented that the war was causing some anxiety among the workers, who were afraid of being drafted. The same day, a red flag was hoisted over the Bosset plant, and it flew for an hour before being hauled down. One worker was arrested for calling for a work stoppage. The main event, though, in this great proletarian center, with its ten thousand steel workers and coal miners, was the strike and demonstration of six hundred tailors. This strike was supported by a portion of the cobblers, though not all, as "both administrative and economic pressures had been applied." The governor had threatened three months' imprisonment for anyone not working on May Day.[84]

The reaction of the workers to the Lena goldfields massacre stands in stark contrast to their reserve regarding May Day demonstrations. Here, as in their early strikes, the outraged sense of justice is evident. On April 4, 1912, over a hundred workers were killed and wounded by soldiers in the Lena goldfields. In the next month, according to Victoria Bonnell, there

[82] TsGAOR, F. 7952, op. 6, d. 112, p. 127. Report of the district engineer to the Mines Administration for Southern Russia, May 4, 1907.

[83] For the mines that struck, see Modestov, *Rabochee i professional'noe dvizhenie*, p. 67. For the estimate of the numbers, see Elwood, *Russian Social Democracy*, p. 47. *Istoriia mist i sil*, p. 87, claims that the Bosset plant workers in Iuzovka took part in the 1908 May Day strike.

[84] Rubach, *Rabochee dvizhenie*, pp. 379–80. For the Bosset incident and the tailors' strike, see *Pravda* (May 11 and May 15, 1913). Kondufor, *Istoriia rabochikh Donbassa*, vol. 1, p. 120, claims that six hundred workers from the Marten ovens in the Iuzovka factory struck that day, but there is no other source supporting this. Perhaps he has confused the tailors and the steel workers. Kondufor also notes (ibid., p. 150) that in 1910 the tailors had struck successfully to cut down the length of their work day.

were twice as many participants in protest strikes in Russia as there had been in the entire four preceding years.[85] In the Donbass, the outburst was perhaps somewhat less dramatic, yet it is still significant in contrast to the quiescence of the preceding years. In the months of April and May, there were between ten and fifteen strikes, with about thirteen thousand participants.[86] The only report of a strike in Iuzovka at this time is at the Bosset plant, where, in the course of a one-day memorial strike, a collection was taken up for the families of the victims. A report of demonstrations near Iuzovka claims that the workers protesting the deaths of the gold miners also demanded civil rights, and abolition of the death penalty and the June 3 laws.[87] Even these strikes were quickly broken up, and the same fate befell attempted demonstrations against three hundred years of the Romanov dynasty, and attempts to celebrate May Day and the anniversary of Bloody Sunday in 1914.[88]

Under unceasing attack by the regime, the revolutionary movement was forced, against some leaders' instincts, to seek open and legal forms of association. The public atmosphere after the October Manifesto appeared more favorable for this. Led by the trade and service groups that began changing their "friendly societies" into trade unions, a movement for unions for mine and metal workers, and later for widespread health and insurance societies, grew up in the Donbass.[89] The history of the trade unions in particular was to be brief, as another opportunity to create participatory institutions among the workers was snuffed out by a fearful and shortsighted regime, aided and abetted by the industrialists.

In its movement to set up trade unions, the Donbass was considerably behind the rest of Russia, and it was only in the summer of 1906 that the mines and the metallurgy factories began choosing provisional committees to work out bylaws for local unions, permitted under the "provisional laws" of March 4, 1906.[90] But when the movement began, it spread rapidly, and

[85] Bonnell, *Roots of Rebellion*, p. 353.

[86] Modestov, *Rabochee i professional'noe dvizhenie*, p. 74. Maksimov, "Revoliutsionnaia volna," p. 137, gives the higher number of strikes and claims "several tens of thousands" of participants.

[87] Rubach, *Rabochee dvizhenie*, pp. 184, 173.

[88] See Modestov, *Rabochee i professional'noe dvizhenie*, p. 84; Rubach, *Rabochee dvizhenie*, pp. 468–69, 497–98.

[89] Mavor, *Economic History of Russia*, vol. 2, pp. 424–25. For a list of thirty-seven "professional associations" formed in Ekaterinoslav province in 1906 and 1907, see McCaffray, "New Work and the Old Regime," app. F, p. 284. Of the associations listed, three were metal workers' unions, one covering the entire province and two in individual plants.

[90] Modestov, *Rabochee i professional'noe dvizhenie*, p. 44.

the *Gorno-zavodskii listok* commented in June 1906 that unions were being formed "daily and hourly."[91]

The first Donbass miners' union to be approved was in the Lydia mine, where two hundred members were signed up and a charter was granted in September 1906. An additional ten coal miners' unions received approval by the end of 1906. They were, however, short-lived. Following attempts to hold May Day demonstrations in 1907, the unions were dissolved. By 1910 there remained only an illegal union group at the Zhilov mine, and no new miners' unions were permitted in the period up to the outbreak of World War I.[92]

The unions of the metallurgists and metal workers were larger, and appear to have had a somewhat more auspicious beginning, but their history is tragically similar to that of the coal miners' unions. On June 4, 1906, a meeting of fifteen hundred workers at the Briansk factory in Ekaterinoslav gathered to hear a draft charter for a trade union read and discussed. The meeting was interrupted by a group of about thirty hecklers who vociferously opposed any union, and succeeded in preventing a vote.[93] A week later, a second meeting of one thousand workers approved the charter establishing the union.[94] The Donetsk-Iureev factory in Kamenskoe also had a thousand members in its metallurgical union, and in December a union was formed and approved in the Petrovskii factory in Enakievo, growing from an initial two hundred members to seven hundred two months later.[95] The workers of the New Russia factory in Iuzovka decided in favor of having a union in the autumn of 1906, but it was refused registration by the authorities, though eight other unions of metallurgists and metal workers had been approved, and only two others refused.[96]

The pressures for denying the workers the right to unionize were said by the Ekaterinoslav governor to have come from "the English directors of the works, through their consul in Ekaterinoslav," a phenomenon seen by the governor as displaying "the greedy instincts of people entirely indifferent to

[91] *Gorno-zavodskii listok*, nos. 23–24 (1906), p. 8563.

[92] For the creation of the miners' unions, see Modestov, *Rabochee i professional'noe dvizhenie*, p. 48, and Kondufor, *Istoriia rabochikh Donbassa*, vol. 1, p. 112. For the breakup of the unions, see *Istoriia mist i sil*, p. 87; Kondufor, *Istoriia rabochikh Donbassa*, vol. 1, p. 112; and Modestov, *Rabochee i professional'noe dvizhenie*, p. 76.

[93] *Gorno-zavodskii listok*, nos. 23–24 (1906), p. 8563. The political orientation of the objectors was not recorded.

[94] *Iuzhnaia zaria* (June 13, 1906).

[95] *Vestnik finansov, promyshlennosti i torgovli*, no. 7 (1908), p. 241; Modestov, *Rabochee i professional'noe dvizhenie*, p. 48.

[96] Sviatlovskii, *Professional'noe dvizhenie v Rossii*, pp. 184–85.

Russia. Neither Belgian nor French workers would live even one day in the barracks and dugouts that foreign entrepreneurs have built for Russian workers, where entirely justified protests, even when expressed in the most moderate form, give their foreign employers an excuse to scream of rebellion and of the need for drastic repression, etc."[97] In December 1906, the first Conference of Trade Unions of the Donbass was held illegally in Druzhkovka to attempt some coordination of policy and activity, breaking the local restraints placed on the unions by the authorities. Twenty-eight representatives of "large enterprises" attended the conference, but little appears to have come of it.[98] The union of metal workers set up in the Hartmann factory in Lugansk was particularly active and successful, offering medical and legal assistance to its members, as well as the services of a savings fund. Its primary distinction, though, was that it was the only Donbass union of metal workers to enjoy an uninterrupted existence from its formation to the middle of 1916, when it was disbanded in the wake of a wartime strike attempt.[99]

Amazingly enough, these few brief paragraphs cover the entire trade-union history of the coal miners and metal workers of the Donbass in these crucial years when much of Russia, having gained a precarious toehold on freedom, was searching for ways to grasp that freedom more firmly and ease the transition to a modern social and political structure. The discussion about the development of workers' rights and the role of trade unions was carried on within the Association of Southern Coal and Steel Producers, an organization heavily, but not wholly, influenced by Octobrist views. A lecturer, A. V. Ososov, was brought to speak to the industrialists and merchants on how strikes were really harmful to workers as well as to employers, not only in Russia, where strikes were "undefined, uncultured, and disorganized," but also in other countries. His arguments were opposed by Professor Isaev and by V. E. Varzar, who was later to publish the definitive statistical study of the 1905 strike movement. They were supported by V. D. Belov, whose views I have previously noted. Belov summarized the defense of strikes by saying, "Here in Russia, the best means of

[97] Modestov, *Rabochee i professional'noe dvizhenie*, p. 49. There was no British consul in Ekaterinoslav. As noted above, the consul in Rostov, Medhurst, supervised British interests in Iuzovka. The governor's opinion is from *Krasnyi arkhiv*, no. 25 (1927), p. 197.

[98] For mention of the conference, see *Vestnik finansov, promyshlennosti i torgovli*, no. 7 (1908), p. 241, and Kondufor, *Istoriia rabochikh Donbassa*, vol. 1, p. 108.

[99] Kharechko, "Nakanune," p. 176; Modestov, *Rabochee i professional'noe dvizhenie*, p. 69.

making strikes purely economic—keeping the revolutionary element out of them—is to introduce trade unions as quickly as possible."[100]

The attempts to organize health insurance and mutual-aid societies among the workers, though they ultimately bore little fruit in the Donbass, suffered relatively less interference than did the trade-union movement. The workers' insurance law promulgated by the tsarist authorities on June 23, 1912, opened the way for workers to organize insurance and mutual-aid funds on their own initiative. These were to supplement, and not to duplicate, the pension, compensation, and disability funds established by law at the turn of the century. The law also made possible the publication of journals that, under the cover of discussing the insurance of workers, were able to advance much more general questions of the organization of workers and the conditions of labor. In the Social-Democratic movement, irrevocably split by this time (though many local organizations still worked together), two such journals appeared. The Menshevik-sponsored *Strakhovanie rabochikh* was published from December 1912 to June 1918, and the Bolshevik *Voprosy strakhovaniia* came out from October 1913 to February 1918, with some interruptions.

The setting up of a health-insurance fund was hedged about with limitations, yet it did provide the workers with a legitimate forum for the management of their own affairs. The model charter allowed for up to one hundred workers' delegates to sit on the council of a health-insurance fund, with representatives of management numbering only 40 percent of the number of workers, but it reserved for the manager or entrepreneur the right to be chairman or nominate the chairman of the council; it let him keep and manage the fund's money, and in some cases it granted him a veto over decisions of the fund's executive or assembly.[101] A minimum of two hundred members had to enroll for an insurance fund to be registered, but this was no obstacle in the Donbass, where both mines and metallurgy factories concentrated thousands of workers.

While the urban centers enjoyed considerable success in setting up workers' insurance funds, the mines and the mills of the Donbass made much less progress. In Kharkov ninety-four factories with a total of 10,000 workers organized health-insurance funds, while only twenty smaller enterprises totaling 1,500 workers failed to do so.[102] In contrast, the Donbass

[100] *Gorno-zavodskii listok*, no. 2 (1906), p. 8300.
[101] Korbut, "Strakhovaia kampaniia," p. 93.
[102] Ibid., p. 111.

proper had only two independent funds, with a total of 4,800 members up to the eve of World War I.[103] There were two major difficulties. The workers were reluctant to accept the burden of the costs that came with the establishment of independent funds, and apparently did not feel sharply the inadequacies of the existing health and disability funds. This is quite understandable regarding that part of the mine labor force that was as yet highly migrant, but is less clear regarding the substantial number of metallurgy workers. Nevertheless, a strong recommendation was made by a senior factory inspector in mid-1913, suggesting that there be a campaign of meetings initiated by the Factory Inspectorate to acquaint the metallurgy workers with the benefits of the program.[104]

Probably much more important in this respect was the reluctance of those in authority—from the tsar's senior advisers, through the various levels of police, down to individual factory and mine managers—to entrust the workers with any say in the affairs of such a fund. They saw such funds as just another stratagem of the revolutionaries to organize the workers, substituting for the unions that had been disbanded. This was not completely wrong. The Bolsheviks in particular regarded the health-insurance funds in this way, and put little faith in them. A leaflet found in the Makeevka plant, where a Iuzovka Bolshevik known only as "Bekovets" was enjoying success organizing the workers into a fund, urged them to join as a symbol and measure of the organized strength of the working class.[105] The leaflet encouraged the workers to take part in the insurance campaign as a way gradually to better their lot, winning small concessions from the employers. It warned that the owners wanted nothing better than to keep the workers passive and apathetic, and called on them to "acquaint yourselves with the law, and prepare to be firm and unwavering defenders of the working proletariat. . . . Enough sleeping, comrades! Organize workers' circles without which it is not easy for a worker to live."[106] Without a doubt the aim expressed in this call goes far beyond the achievement of insurance benefits for the workers.

The Bosset workers in Iuzovka, who exhibited considerable militance

[103] Kondufor, *Istoriia rabochikh Donbassa*, vol. 1, p. 118.

[104] Rubach, *Rabochee dvizhenie*, p. 402.

[105] On Bekovets, see ibid., pp. 498–99. For the Makeevka leaflet, one in a series distributed in the autumn of 1913, see Korbut, "Strakhovaia kampaniia," pp. 109–10. Korbut also expresses the opinion that the insurance campaign was useful only as a means of facilitating the organization of political strikes in 1914. See p. 117.

[106] Quoted in Korbut, "Strakhovaia kampaniia," pp. 109–10.

during these years, were one of the workers' groups setting up a health-insurance fund under the 1912 law. When the managers of the plant offered free secretarial help and the use of offices in the plant, the workers refused, and hired a reliable secretary through the help of the Office Workers' Union in St. Petersburg.[107] This was fairly typical of the difficulties the authorities experienced in maintaining the domination of government and employers in the administration of those insurance funds that were set up. The workers often boycotted elections in which they had not had a sufficient hand in the arrangements, or alternatively, boycotted the delegates elected in such proceedings. Altogether, senior factory inspector Dmitrash reported, an atmosphere of general discontent prevailed.[108] In the events of 1905 and after, in the course of well-organized strikes in which workers' elected representatives conducted the affairs of their constituents, and with the example of election campaigns for the Duma, at least some of the workers were beginning to develop a sense of politics. Their ideas of fairness and of rights were transcending personal benefit and beginning to focus on the common good.

The development of the workers' consciousness met with a mixture of responses. At the beginning of 1914, N. S. Avdakov, chairing a meeting of representatives of trade and industry, explained to the minister of the interior, N. S. Maklakov, that the workers quite naturally chose the most articulate, active, and popular of their fellows to head the insurance funds. The nature of these people brought them under the surveillance of the authorities, and they were often arrested, which interfered with the functioning of the funds. The minister is said to have listened attentively, if noncommittally.[109] In a similar discussion, a state councillor criticized the efforts of the Factory Inspectorate to spread the idea of workers' insurance and advised against establishing health-insurance funds, as workers' organizations of any sort were seen as "extremely undesirable from a state point of view." The minister of trade and industry, participating in the discussion, pointed out that the councillor's position contradicted the concepts under which the 1912 insurance law had been passed, and added that the law did, after all, restrict the workers to discussing fund charters that had been drafted by the employers.[110] This was another of the frequent cases in

[107] Rubach, *Rabochee dvizhenie*, p. 475.
[108] Ibid., p. 402.
[109] *Strakhovanie rabochikh*, no. 5 (March 1914), p. 29.
[110] Rubach, *Rabochee dvizhenie*, pp. 469–71.

which people at various levels of authority in the regime worked at cross-purposes because their interests and outlooks were quite different, despite the umbrella of autocracy under which all of them sheltered. Ultimately, the harassment and limitations within which the workers' health-insurance funds operated, and the brief span of time during which they were active, kept their impact on the socialization of the workers to a minimum.

Coal and Steel Cartels: Economic Vicissitudes

The social upheavals of 1905 to 1907 were accompanied by economic difficulties for the Donbass producers. They had felt themselves on the way to recovery from the recession of the first three years of the century, when the Russo-Japanese War had drained off resources that otherwise might have gone for transport development and government orders for metal and fuel. The paralysis of the railways at the end of 1905 was an economic disaster for the coal and metal producers. At the New Russia factory, the lack of limestone made it necessary to extinguish two blast furnaces in December 1905, and it was not thought possible to rekindle them during January. A million puds of pig iron and two million of coal were piled up in the factory yards, awaiting transport.[111] Eight hundred men of the factory's work force of five thousand were laid off.[112]

The Russian economy continued in a depressed state until 1911, and the Donbass industrialists sought a remedy in re-forming and strengthening the coal and iron cartels that first arose in the recession of 1902. The metallurgy industry began to press for a syndicate once more because of the instability and dependency of its market and because of the disorganized manner in which production had grown in the 1890s, protected by the government, without regard for economic efficiency. The French ambassador reported from St. Petersburg: "The consumption of iron in all of Russia is two-thirds that of the city of Berlin. Orders for rails have fallen to nothing. One of Russia's factories could meet the entire demand." Another diplomat explained that the object of the cartel was the intelligent sharing of the market, since the government was almost the sole customer. "The peasant has always used wood. Houses are constructed without the use of a

[111] *Gorno-zavodskii listok*, no. 1 (1906), p. 8287.

[112] Ibid., no. 2 (1906), p. 8300.

nail, and in some parts wagons are built without a gram of iron." As for the cartel, it would, in his opinion, be formed if the Dneprovienne Co., the Russo-Belgian Corporation, and Hughes agreed.[113] The cartel, Prodameta, was formed at the end of February 1908 as a joint-stock company in which the holders could neither sell nor transfer their shares without the agreement of the company's directorate. It included 60 percent of Russian metallurgy at its inception, and though it was conceived and formed in the Donbass, it grew to include twenty-eight enterprises from all parts of the Russian Empire.[114] The New Russia Co. was assigned 12.62 percent of the market in steel rails, 12.48 percent in iron beams, and smaller shares of other forms of iron and steel production.[115] Pig iron, which together with steel rails was the mainstay of the New Russia's profits, does not appear to have been included in the cartel's authority.[116]

The talk of establishing cartels aroused mixed feelings. Prodameta had as one of its bases the restriction of production to raise prices. The French consul in Moscow reported violent public hostility to the idea that the metal trust would cause unemployment among Russian workers.[117] This anger found a political outlet as well. A French observer reported that within the Duma, "M. Gonchakoff" headed a group opposing the cartel and its aim of raising prices.[118]

The revival of Prodameta had local repercussions as well.

> The settlement of Iuzovka is, for instance, influenced by rumors of the Trust's buying the factory and cutting its production until the crisis passes. Large numbers of stores and lumber yards have ceased purchas-

[113] AN, F 12, 7274. M. Bompard to the Foreign Ministry, December 24, 1907; see also M. Destries to Foreign Minister Pichon, May 2, 1908.

[114] AN, F 12, 7273. Report of M. Destries to Foreign Minister Pichon, May 2, 1908, includes the report from Kharkov on the formation of Prodameta. Destries claimed that the cartel controlled only 34 percent of metal production, though other manufacturers would surely join. See Glivits, *Potreblenie zheleza v Rossii*, pp. 36–37, who discusses the forming of the cartel. Glivits, *Zheleznaia promyshlennost' v Rossii*, pp. 127ff., contains a detailed description of the cartel, its origins, and its operation.

[115] Glivits, *Potreblenie zheleza v Rossii*, p. 38.

[116] In 1910 the New Russia Co. was fifth in the empire in pig iron, producing only 7.19 percent of the total. See Glivits, *Zheleznaia promyshlennost' v Rossii*, p. 123.

[117] AN, F 12, no. 7273. Consular report of July 27, 1908.

[118] Ibid., letter of July 22, 1908, from Destries to Clemenceau. It is probable that Destries was referring to Guchkov, the Octobrist leader, but that the letter was mistranscribed.

6.1 Executives of the New Russia Co. Department of Mines, May 1908. Center: S. A. Negrebitskii, chief engineer. Other featured figures (in rectangular frames), clockwise from upper left: V. K. Zaparozhets, P. V. Fenin, A. L. Horsefields, A. A. Shimikin, K. I. Iancharskii.

6.2 Iuzovka in 1912.

ing. The sawmill has cut back its activity. The numbers of workers and clerks have been reduced. And all around it turns out as though the Trust had been thought up and implemented by the Jews to the detriment of the Russian people and state. This idea is put forward by the Union of Truly Russian Workers and was given expression by the heads of the Union in Ekaterinoslav on the second day of Passover. And this thought now spreads back into the benighted mass.[119]

The predictions that, despite opposition, Prodameta would be formed in the end proved true. The recession was particularly tenacious in metallurgy. An engineer of the Ministry of Railways visited the New Russia factory toward the end of 1908, and complimented the director, Anderson, on the quality of the technical personnel, the organization, and the high production standards. "The only thing lacking is a sufficiency of orders."[120] By the end of 1909 the French were reporting the cartel's success in fixing prices, and though blast furnaces were still working at only 68.8 percent of capacity, the production of the Donbass had grown, and the prospects through 1910 were for continued improvement.[121] Glivits shows iron-industry profits recovering from a low point in 1906 to more than double by 1908, and doubling again by 1909. Yet all this spectacular growth merely brought the industry back to the profit level that it had reached in 1904.[122]

In June 1910, a fierce cholera epidemic set in, with 3,000 falling ill in Ekaterinoslav province. In July 13,878 cases were recorded, over half the total for the previous three years.[123] Then came the great flight, causing the population of the Donbass to drop by 40,000.[124] Production fell to half or less, and a number of mines closed. Loading stopped, and the great reserves of coal that had piled up at the pitheads became immovable burdens, while at the stations, and along the main lines, reserves dwindled. A French diplomat, watching this tragedy unfold, could only remark, "The cholera, which has reappeared, and seems to visit South Russia each year, has seriously harmed industry by causing the flight of many workers in a

[119] Larskii, "Protsent levy i protsent pravy," p. 90, quoted from an Ekaterinoslav Jewish newspaper.

[120] TsGIAL, F. 266, op. 1, ed. khr. 394, pp. 26, ob-27. John Hughes had spoken the same sentence in 1874.

[121] AN, F 12, 7274. Consular report of December 10, 1909.

[122] Glivits, *Zheleznaia promyshlennost' v Rossii*, p. 122.

[123] Smidovich, "K voprosu," pp. 8, 12.

[124] Liashchenko, "Usloviia truda," pt. 1, p. 271.

country that complains unceasingly of a shortage of skilled work hands."[125] His unspoken question was why so little had been done to prevent the annual epidemics.

The huge wave of fleeing miners only served to spread the disease, despite the health inspection stations and quarantines that were set up along all the rail lines. Like a brush fire, the cases of cholera burst out in new localities: 80 in May, 176 in June, and 245 in July, when the epidemic reached its peak.[126] This only intensified the terror caused by the illness. By the autumn, the coal glut had turned to famine, hindering movement on the Ekaterinin line, and the dissatisfaction of the producers led to the resignation of engineer Priadkin, the director of Produgol, at a special meeting attended by Avdakov, the state councillor. The failure of Donbass coal to establish itself firmly in the Moscow market was seen as an additional factor in his resignation.[127] Rampant as the dissatisfaction evidently was, the newspaper reported a categorical denial that the question of dissolving the coal syndicate had even come up. Indeed, Produgol became more active.

Given extra emphasis by the flight of the labor force, the rapid swings of the coal industry from feast to famine emphasize the fragility of the entire industrial structure that had been created. The producers saw the almost unlimited richness of the Donbass coal mines, easily capable of doubling and redoubling their output every decade. Development of the market and the transport system was much more gradual. Despite syndication and the planning of production by von Ditmar's Statistical Bureau, it would appear that members of the association had little inclination to restrain themselves in developing their productive capacities. It was coal, mined and delivered, that yielded them profit, and immediate profit was the dominant goal.

As it had before, the crisis passed. The cholera ended in December 1910, and the new year began a cycle of economic expansion. By 1913, coal production in the Donbass reached 1,543,790,000 puds, a hundred times what the Donbass had produced in 1870 when John Hughes had first arrived. On the eve of World War I, the Donbass not only had a concentration of 262,000 workers in the coal and metal industries, but it was producing 67 percent of the Russian Empire's iron, and 70 percent of its coal. In the climate of growing revolutionary tension, and of the growing tension in Europe that developed after 1910, it was clear that, both domes-

125 AN, F 12, 7273. Report of the consul in Odessa, October 14, 1910.

126 Smidovich, "K voprosu," p. 12.

127 *Russkoe slovo* (September 24, 1910), p. 4; ibid. (September 26, 1910).

tically and internationally, control of the Donbass might well be the key to the fate of the empire.

Social Relations in Iuzovka, 1905–1914

What of Iuzovka in these years? Three of the Hughes sons, Albert, Ivor, and John Jr., though still active in the administration of the New Russia Co., appear to have returned to England after 1905, and only Arthur maintained a Iuzovka address. Montagu Balfour remained in Iuzovka as business manager of the factory and overseer of the general managers, first Anderson and then Adam Aleksandrovich Svitsyn, who took over the plant in 1911.[128] The company was embarking on a cycle of increased production and rising profits.

But what of the society of Iuzovka? What was the appearance and culture of this Donbass metropolis of fifty thousand souls? The same dualities of coarseness and vitality that marked it from its beginning persisted. The *pervaia liniia* (first street) was paved, and boasted electric lights. On the other muddy streets there were flickering kerosene lamps, if anything. The houses were crowded together on the small lots of 86 to 150 square *sazhen'* (390 to 680 square meters) that Hughes had originally laid out, with little or no greenery, although the Ekaterinoslav governor had decreed a minimum of 200 square sazhen' in 1903. On the one hand, Iuzovka was described as "rich and industrial"; on the other, it was "the sore point of the Donbass . . . today they don't know what to do with it or what to make of it." The persistent epidemics, the dirt and crowding, the motley population of passers-through and hangers-on, were counterbalanced by the presence of banks, notaries, hotels, good stores, "and life bubbling everywhere." Above all, the growing number of educational institutions was noticeable.

The countryside was progressing as well, and Iuzovka was playing its part in this growth. The chemical plant at New Russia's Novosmolianinov mine produced ammonium sulfate fertilizer that was advertised for use by the peasants of Bakhmut district. The district newspaper also advertised

[128] Companies' House, 4467, report of June 5, 1906, gives the addresses. See also CL, 13599, study 1255 bis, M. Gibeil, p. 2, and *Trudy, XXXVII, 1912*, p. 10, for Svitsyn's appearance at the meeting of the association as director of the New Russia factory. *Rabochaia gazeta*, nos. 4–5 (April 15, 1911), refers to "the new director of the factory."

imported American varieties of berry bushes, and improved breeds of Malboro [*sic*] and Yorkshire piglets. There appears to have been some prosperity among the peasants, permitting them to invest in these improvements, for the local peasantry had celebrated the fiftieth anniversary of emancipation by subscribing 6,650 rubles to erect a statue of Alexander II. The unveiling was celebrated on May 6, 1915, to the music of the bands of the Bakhmut men's technical high school. The zemstvo teachers in the countryside were advised to subscribe to *Uchitel' i shkola* (Teacher and school) for the improvement of their pedagogical techniques.[129] A sense of progress was in the air of the Donbass.

Central as it was to the economy and development of the Donbass, Iuzovka was physically isolated. Company rules stipulated that no passengers be allowed on the coal and ore trains that moved ceaselessly from the settlement to the main line links at Iuzovo and Mushketovo. For travelers, a horse-drawn cab was the link to the railway, but the dirt roads were often cut off for weeks at a time in spring and fall, stranding the population. This company-imposed isolation was actually a metaphor for the settlement's political situation. Education and culture had spread, and the economy had diversified, bringing banks and other commercial and industrial interests. These, however, had no part in the management of the settlement. The New Russia Co. was the landowner, and the sole arbiter of Iuzovka's destiny. As noted in volume 1, the company successfully staved off any challenge to its total control of the settlement, turning back all petitions and pressures for municipalization. Whatever diversification might have been taking place in its economy and society, Iuzovka remained "the kingdom of coal and iron," repressing all legitimation of other local interests in a replication of the central authorities' repression of trade unions, and their attempt to emasculate those political institutions that did come into existence after 1905.[130]

Within Iuzovka's society, the associations that were permitted remained

[129] *Bakhmutskaia Narodnaia gazeta*, no. 18 (1915), p. 11; no. 21 (1915), p. 12.

[130] For the description of Iuzovka's physical and social condition, see Surozhskii, "Krai uglia i zheleza," pp. 296–302. Surozhskii's description, published in April 1913, may be assumed to apply to the end of 1912, or early 1913. The New Russia Co. report and brief against municipalization, DOGIA, F. 6, op. 1, d. 7, p. 1, although undated, is also from 1913, and refers to ten "lines" with electric light, and 25 verstas of pavement. It is significant that 1912–13 was an exceptionally favorable business year, and it may be assumed that after the years of epidemic and depressed economic conditions, the settlement was more than ripe for a burst of municipal improvement.

parochial. The large consumer cooperative, "Rabochii trud," was within the New Russia Co. The church maintained its educational activities and religious presence. Sports and culture were also company projects. A separate Jewish drama group and choir existed in the settlement's Jewish community. The Association for Assistance to Poor Jews was, naturally, a purely Jewish organization, but so, apparently, was the Association for Assistance to Poor Students, for the heads of these two charitable organizations were Khokhlovkin and Khokhlovkina, evidently man and wife. The Iuzovka Mutual Credit Association and the Donetsk Commercial Labor Artel', as well as the Shop Clerks' Mutual-Benefit Society, appear to have been solely Jewish as well.[131] The integration of Jews and non-Jews in the private secondary schools of Iuzovka does not appear to have been preceded by social or economic integration. Jewish workers were not in evidence in the New Russia Co., and the lists of senior administrators and supervisory personnel do not contain Jewish names. The only exceptions to this appear to be the veterinarian, Feireizen, and the head of the printing shop, Papernyi.[132]

Labor and Management on the Eve of the War

The political activity of the Donbass recovered in parallel to the economy. When Svitsyn had taken over as director of the New Russia factory, one of his first acts had been to discharge all workers who were under police surveillance, causing the Social-Democratic party group in the factory to fall apart once again.[133] In October 1913, the organization re-formed, with the Iuzovka-Petrovskii Committee becoming the Iuzovka-Makeevka Committee, and taking in the Rykovskii, Vosnesenskii, and Berest-Bogodukhov mines, as well as the New Russia and Petrovskii factories and mines. At the start of 1914, these enterprises had over thirty thousand workers. The Social-Democrats claimed four hundred members among them.[134]

Three months after the formation of the new committee, the pay system

[131] For lists of the various Iuzovka associations and their officers, see *Adres-kalendar*, pp. 97–98.

[132] See DOGIA, F. 6, op. 1, d. 30, p. 101, and op. 9, d. 241, p. 5.

[133] *Rabochaia gazeta*, nos. 4–5 (April 15, 1911).

[134] Kondufor, *Istoriia rabochikh Donbassa*, vol. 1, p. 120. While this number may seem a small proportion of the workers, it is large compared with the membership of the revolutionary groups up to that time.

at the Rykovskii mines was changed, without the workers having been consulted fourteen days in advance, as was required under the work contract. The miners in two of the Rykovskii shafts, twenty-five hundred in number, struck in protest on December 16, 1913, and were joined by workers from the mines' workshops. The management warned them that if they did not report for work within three days, they would all be fired. The workers, at a general meeting, drew up twenty-seven demands and asked that the district engineer come to discuss them.

It may be useful to examine these demands as an expression of the growth of the workers' sophistication and organization over the years. The first demand reflected the custom, begun in 1905, that there be no punishment of any of the strikers for taking part in the strike. The next demands concerned pay. There followed demands for an improvement in the technical conditions of work (payment for hauling and placing pit props, no arbitrary changing of work teams), free coal and housing, improved bath conditions, a new school, polite address to the workers, and the firing of a certain Gorshkolepov. These are typical of the demands made in almost every strike since 1874. In twenty-fourth place on the list was the demand for an eight-hour day, yet this was the subject that the workers are said to have discussed most while waiting for the district engineer; he addressed himself to it when he arrived two hours later, accompanied by a troop of cossacks. "I believe that these contain a demand for the eight-hour day," he said, holding up his copy of the strike demands. "That is a political demand and cannot be considered. Moreover, nowhere do they work an eight-hour day—not even in Germany where 'your kind' are so strong."

When the strikers, whose numbers had grown to thirty-two hundred, decided to uphold the demand for an eight-hour day, the cossack commander took the place of the engineer. "Go and work gentlemen, a strike will bring you nothing. You can't make *borshch* from strikes." He ended by announcing that any workers not back on the job by December 20 would be summarily evicted from their housing. In view of the cold, and the approaching holidays, the miners decided to end their strike. They were aided in this by the management's announcement that some of the demands would be met fully, and others partially, though a number of the twenty-seven demands were rejected summarily. Like the inclusion of some traditional demands, this is a pattern that was repeated in many strikes.[135]

[135] The account of the strike and its developments comes from Rubach, *Rabochee dvizhenie*, pp. 476–79.

The strike was orderly and participatory, with the rank-and-file workers encouraged to voice their specific demands in the strike meetings. Though it was on a large scale, it did not spread, nor were there demonstrations of solidarity at other mines. The police report of the strike notes that the workers of the New Russia factory remained on the job and were quiet, with no demonstrations at all, and that their mood was under observation. The observation was, in all likelihood, the result of a leaflet that had been found at the mines in Iuzovka, calling for support of the Rykovskii strikers and inveighing against "the bloodsucking capitalist vampires" who were accused of piling up "mountains of corpses" and spilling "rivers of workers' blood." It ended with "Long live the miners' strike and the eight-hour day! Long live the kingdom of socialism! Long live the RSDRP!" The signature was "The Iuzovka-Makeevka Committee of the RSDRP."[136] The available documents do not specify whether the change in the pay system that had provoked the strike was rescinded. The workers' leader followed the participatory pattern of formulating demands, drawing the rank and file into active identification with the strike. But this resulted always in a diffuse and sometimes contradictory list of demands. The workers thus paid the price of allowing themselves to be distracted from what should have been the immediate central issue, making it possible for management to evade response. If the main point of the strike was to build the workers' movement through the practice of cooperative action, the outcome may have been worthwhile. The price that had to be paid was the frustration of the workers and their heightened feeling of powerlessness when they saw their strike dispersed under threat without satisfaction of their central demands.

The final Donbass strike of the prewar years was even less successful. On April 15, 1914, sixty workers at the Petrovskii factory in Enakievo struck for higher pay. This was simply a "leading edge" for bringing about a general strike of all the plant's workers. An experienced Bolshevik party worker, Aleksandr Maslennikov, had been sent from St. Petersburg to prepare the strike. The first day, the strike was a success, and between nine and ten thousand workers left the plant. A list of twelve demands was submitted orally to the managers, including demands for free housing, coal, and water (traditional privileges that had recently been abolished, causing considerable discontent). Other demands were for the firing of three people, improvement of the bath and hospital, polite address to the

[136] Ibid., p. 466.

workers, and of course a raise in pay and a no-retribution guarantee. At five o'clock in the afternoon on April 16, a crowd of five thousand workers went to the factory to hear management's response. When no answer was given, they tried to force their way into the factory yard, in the face of eighteen mounted guards. Stones were thrown, and three shots were fired from a revolver, wounding a guard and an engineer. Kirst, the governor's special representative observing the strike, promptly called in the gendarmerie and strengthened the guard around the factory. Several strike leaders were arrested, with arrests continuing whenever militance was shown. In the end, thirty-three people were arrested, and the strike lost energy. Management's response to the strike demands was that the hospital and bath would quickly be improved, and that the demand for politeness was legitimate and would be enforced, but that there must be mutuality, with the workers polite to supervisory personnel and to each other. Finally, it was promised that no worker who had not broken the law would be discharged for striking. The rest of the demands were dismissed as "not meriting satisfaction."

Following the shooting incident and the arrest of the leaders, the strike had been quiet. A call had been sent out to surrounding mines and factories asking for a sympathy strike. This did not take place at first, but on April 24 it was reported that strikes were starting in Makeevka and Gorlovka. These do not appear to have developed. Police and management, aware of the approach of May Day, began increasing pressure for an end to the strike. The socialists spread leaflets, attempting to boost morale and make May Day a large-scale demonstration. By April 30, 820 workers had returned to their jobs. On May 1, 1,000 worked, and the next day, 4,500 workers were back. The strike ended on May 3, and was termed a failure, with the blame placed on a lack of organization. Those arrested included Maslennikov, as well as Zalmaev and two other members of the Bolshevik faction in the committee. Most of those arrested were sentenced to only two or three months' imprisonment, but Maslennikov and Zalmaev, well known to the police, received long terms of exile.[137] Following this defeat, the Petrovskii workers were quiescent, conforming to what was the general pattern of Donbass workers, who were less militant in these years than were workers elsewhere in Russia.[138]

[137] Details of the strike are given in ibid., pp. 542–47, 551–55, 561–62.

[138] Elwood, *Russian Social Democracy*, p. 244.

During the decade following the 1905 revolution there were clear indications of the direction in which the Donbass should be moving so as to develop stability in social and political life. More energy appears to have been spent in internal friction and repression, however, than in the building of a network of community institutions that could serve as the foundation of society. The economic problems that had hindered the region's development were overcome. New records were achieved in production, and the Donbass was becoming steadily more important to the empire's economy. Yet coal and steel, vital as they were, were insufficient to carry Russia through the new crisis that was about to break, as Russia entered World War I.

CHAPTER 7

The World War in the Donbass

As the clouds of war thickened on the horizons of the Russian Empire, the Donbass became a particular focus of concern. Fuel and metal, the sinews of war, originated there, and if the Russian juggernaut was to roll westward, the Donbass would have to provide both the energy and the weapons for that advance. Seventy percent of Russia's coal was mined in the Donbass in 1913, the remainder coming from seven scattered sources, none of them so well placed as the Donbass.[1]

Not only was the Donbass supplying the South Russian metallurgy industry, producing more than 70 percent of the Russian Empire's iron and steel, but by 1916, the Donbass coal merchants had achieved a good many of their ambitions, and Donbass coal was over half of the fuel used by the metal-working industry of the Moscow region.[2] Even the far northwest had been penetrated—one of the fondest dreams of the Donbass coal producers. In 1914, Petrograd had consumed 31.58 million puds of Donbass coal, but in 1915, with the restriction of foreign imports and the loss of the Polish coal fields, consumption of Donbass coal in the capital grew to 98.18 million puds.[3] The riches of the Donbass, in close proximity to the agricultural wealth of the Ukraine, made this region one of the strategic centers of the empire, and a prime target for invasion by the armies of the Central Powers.

The Outbreak of War

The war came as an unpleasant shock to the Donbass workers. Their industries were flourishing, employment was steady after years of recurring

[1] Arskii, *Donetskii Bassein*, p. 5. The Dombrowa coal basin in Poland fell quickly under German control, making the Donbass all the more important for Russia.

[2] *Metallist*, no. 5 (1918), p. 11.

[3] *Gorno-zavodskoe delo*, no. 1 (1917), table 2.

depression and instability, and wages were rising. The prospect of being drafted was one that never found much support among the miners and factory workers, and it is no great surprise that despite the patriotic fervor promoted throughout the country at the outbreak of war, there were anti-conscription riots in many Donbass centers. In Lugansk, these riots left three dead and twenty injured, and the number of deaths rose when the governor arrested eighty-five rioters and ordered several of them shot to enhance the patriotism of the survivors. In Bakhmut, seven rioting draftees were wounded and another seventy began their military service before a court-martial. A later riot there left a police officer, a local storekeeper, and thirteen rioters dead, and the railway station in a shambles.[4] In Makeevka, riots against conscription also left over a dozen dead and seventeen wounded.[5]

In Iuzovka the drafting of workers did not evoke protests. The reason offered by Zaitsev is that the mobilized workers were given severance pay by their employers. It would appear, however, that patriotic sentiment had strong roots in Iuzovka's populace. When Zaitsev and his fellow Bolshevik Grigorii Zinukov, together with the Menshevik Dolgopol, attempted to demonstrate against a patriotic parade of "a few hundred" organized by Zuzula, a reactionary foreman at the factory, they were chased off by both the police and the townspeople of Iuzovka, who supported the parade.[6]

The Labor Force and Production

The first important question raised in the Donbass by the mobilization of the Russian army was the fate of the labor force. As soon as mobilization was announced, the Council of the Association of Southern Coal and Steel Producers sent telegrams to all those ministers who might have influence in the matter, asking exemption from military service for all miners in Bakhmut and Slavianoserbsk districts, and in the Don Cossack territory. Despite the clear strategic importance of the work of the coal miners, this request was satisfied only with regard to the white-collar employees (*sluzhashchie*) of the mines. The initial mobilization took nearly half the number of mine workers usually found in the Donbass at that season.[7] In the metal industry

[4] Koshik, *Rabochee dvizhenie na Ukraine*, pp. 69–70.

[5] Modestov, *Rabochee i professional'noe dvizhenie*, p. 88.

[6] Zaitsev, "Kak my tvorili oktiabr'," p. 132.

[7] *Gorno-zavodskoe delo*, no. 34 (1914), p. 9467.

as a whole, the effect of the mobilization was more moderate, but nevertheless considerable. Over 17 percent of the workers in the smelters and metalworking factories of the south were mobilized.[8] Only on April 23, 1915, nine months after the initial mobilization, did the government get around to deferring the military service of production workers in the mining and metallurgy industries. Following this first wave of mobilization, miners were registered as mobilized and under army discipline, but were left working in the mines. They were forbidden to change jobs or to leave the mines for their home villages under penalty of being called for active service. L. A. Liberman claims that this caused a psychological and physical degeneration of the labor force, resulting in lower productivity.[9]

Immediately following the disastrous mobilization, no fewer than 1,030 agents were sent out to the villages of central Russia to recruit laborers for the mines.[10] It was not a simple matter, for the military mobilization had been thorough and had hit the villages hard. In the course of the war, 50 percent of Russian men between the ages of sixteen and sixty were to be mobilized.[11] Many of those recruited into the mines were underage, and their percentage in the mine labor force grew sharply during the war. These were generally illiterate, backward young men, who swelled the percentage of Donbass miners with village ties to nearly 40 percent.[12] The miners were thus not only less rooted than before, but younger and less well educated than one might have had reason to expect after fifty years of development of the coal industry. In my analysis of the miners' behavior during and immediately after the 1917 revolutions, these factors will take on some significance. In addition, the sons of local peasants began paying bribes to be taken on as defense workers, and they became part of the mine labor force. Of these new proletarians, Trofim Kharechko comments: "This was the most conservative and cowardly element, always ready to break strikes and workers' demands."[13] Though it would appear that this group was small, the various contradictory processes of recruitment and dispersion in the mine labor force were making its political structure more complex.

The Donbass mine labor force, which had numbered 182,000 on the eve of the war, dropped by one-third through the first month of mobilization,

[8] Ibid., no. 36 (1914), p. 9528.

[9] Liberman, *V ugol'nom tsarstve*, pp. 110–11.

[10] *Trudy, XXXIX, 1914*, p. 5.

[11] Rodzianko, "Ekonomicheskoe polozhenie Rossii pered revoliutsii," p. 79.

[12] Atsarkin, *Zhizn' i bor'ba rabochei molodezhi*, p. 272.

[13] Kharechko, "Nakanune," p. 166.

TABLE 7.1
Structure of Donbass Metallurgy Labor Force, 1914–1916

	1914 (%)	1915 (%)	1916 (%)
SKILLED			
Men	64.8	49.2	43.0
Women	0.1	0.3	0.5
POWs	___	0.3	0.3
Total (skilled)	64.9	49.8	43.8
UNSKILLED			
Men	32.8	31.4	29.6
Women	1.8	3.2	5.1
Children	0.5	7.4	7.3
POWs	___	8.2	14.2
Total (unskilled)	35.1	50.2	56.2

Source: Kir'ianov, *Rabochie iuga Rossii,* p. 44. Based on the five largest Donbass metallurgy plants.

and then started to climb steadily to a peak of 286,000 in February 1917, as women, children, and rural youth took up mine work.[14] A similar though more moderate change occurred in the metallurgy labor force. Yet more significant is the degradation of the skill structure of the labor force, illustrated for metallurgy in table 7.1.

Of the ninety-five thousand workers in the largest metallurgy plants in June 1916, thirteen thousand were women and children, accounting for the entire increase in the labor force in these plants since mid-1913. In addition, there were sixteen thousand prisoners of war.[15] Where indigenous adult males had made up 97.6 percent of the labor force in the month before the outbreak of hostilities, by mid-1916 they constituted only 72.6 percent. The percentage of unskilled workers had increased from just over one-third at the beginning of the war to over half in 1916. This means that although there had been fifty-seven thousand skilled adult men working in

[14] For 1914, see *Trudy, XXXIX, 1914*, p. 4. For 1917, see *Narodnoe khoziaistvo*, no. 2 (1918), p. 31.

[15] *Vestnik finansov, promyshlennosti i torgovli*, no. 31 (1916), p. 175.

1914, their numbers actually decreased to under forty-one thousand by 1916, despite the growth in the labor force. The sixteen thousand men taken in the first mobilization were never really replaced.

The situation in the mines was little better. There the impact of the Russian government's ill-advised mobilization policy had been much harder, and the eventual growth of the labor force had been much larger. As a result, the degradation of the skill structure was greater. There had been a stable division of about 78 percent underground workers and 22 percent

TABLE 7.2
Structure of Donbass Bituminous Mine Labor Force, 1916–1918

	1916		1917		1918	
	Number	%	Number	%	Number	%
BY AGE, SEX, ORIGIN						
Draft-eligible men	78,603	44	93,713	46	95,731	77
POWs	31,361	18	48,528	24	12,605	10
Women	5,649	3	7,484	4	6,074	5
Children	12,601	7	16,060	8	10,198	8
Chinese or Koreans	540	0.3	1,323	0.6	—	—
Refugees	1,695	0.9	—	—	—	—
Others[a]	47,926	27	36,505	18	—	—
BY WORK						
Coal cutters	38,235	21	38,696	19	20,864	17
Other underground workers	74,560	42	79,805	39	45,847	37
Surface workers	65,580	37	85,112	42	55,605	45
Total	178,375		203,613		122,316	

Source: Adapted from *Narodnoe khoziaistvo*, no. 5 (1919), p. 75.

Note: Percentage discrepancies are due to the rounding of decimals.

[a] The category of "others" was created to reconcile differing totals between the two sections as presented in the source. In 1918 this took the form of a *negative* quantity of 2,292, and was therefore not entered in the table. It may be hypothesized that in the 1918 figures, the category "draft-eligible" includes those who were in 1916 included under "others." Gritsenko, *Robitnichii klas Ukraini,* p. 30, using archival sources, gives a total bituminous mine labor force in 1917 of 206,104, with the division into categories very close to that presented here. The category of "others" thus appears legitimate, and may be assumed to represent male, adult mine workers of various categories who were not eligible for the draft. *Istoriia mist i sil,* pp. 88–89, notes that in mid-1916, a quarter of the mine workers in the Iuzovka mining district were "overage."

surface workers in the Donbass coal mines from 1884 until the first decade of the twentieth century.[16] Even with the doubling of the percentage of surface workers, an acute shortage was felt at the mines during the summer of 1916. There was at the time a large influx of refugees from the areas taken by the Central Powers. Over half the refugees arriving in Mariupol in June 1916 were redirected to Iuzovka to alleviate the mine labor shortage there.[17] In addition, women and children made up only a little over 8 percent of the mine labor force for the greater part of this period, growing to 9.4 percent in 1916.[18] Their work was almost entirely confined to tasks on the surface, though in September 1917, two women were listed as underground workers in the New Russia mines.[19] Table 7.2 gives figures for the participation of various nonprofessional categories in the mine labor force and the changing division of that labor force into the various und erground and surface categories.

Both industrially and politically, the war weakened the Donbass working class. It grew in numbers, but it was less skilled, less mature, and less stable. Women, children, and raw peasant youth could hardly be considered the stuff from which a workers' movement might be molded, or an efficient industry built.

Wartime Politics in the Donbass

The first effects of the war on Donbass politics were an increase in police repression of the revolutionaries and a wave of preventive arrests in the various underground groups. Throughout the south—Odessa, Kiev, Kharkov, Ekaterinoslav, Lugansk—revolutionary activists were arrested at the very beginning of the war. Unions and health funds that had served as organizing centers for workers' activities were closed down as well.[20] This is instructive in regard to the regime's perception of these institutions. Other party members and sympathizers were taken to the front. The Iuzovka-Makeevka Bolshevik Committee had been arrested in May 1914, and con-

[16] See tables 8.8, p. 246, and 8.9, p. 252, in vol. 1.

[17] *Vestnik trudovoi pomoshchi*, no. 6 (1916), p. 31.

[18] Kir'ianov, *Rabochie iuga Rossii*, p. 42.

[19] DOGIA, F. 6, op. 1, d. 9, p. 10. At the time there were 349 adult women employed by the mines.

[20] Modestov, *Rabochee i professional'noe dvizhenie*, p. 87.

tacts with the Petrograd center, as well as the distribution of revolutionary literature, ceased until the end of 1915.[21]

However, the police were not the only problem with which the socialist movement had to contend. The workers' mood was little inclined to revolution at the start of the war. Perhaps the miners and factory workers had no great enthusiasm for risking their lives at the front, but neither were they yet angry and disillusioned with their rulers. As long as they had work at a living wage, and affordable food for their tables, the Donbass workers remained essentially loyal to their rulers. Petr Moiseenko recalls the atmosphere in his memoirs.

> We made contact with the Iuzovka district. Thanks to Priadkin, the police weren't on to us. But Glinka [a conservatively inclined foreman] then quietly went about his dirty work. All the workers under his supervision were inclined to pogroms, and we could in no way influence them. We got to a few of the sorters, but the coke workers absolutely would not listen to socialists. From the plumbing shop they had been mobilized for the war. Disaffection with the war was growing. The newspapers carried stories of misappropriation of contributions, goods, and supplies. In Bialystok, Warsaw, and Lodz—everywhere there were antiwar protests. The Donets Basin was as yet silent.[22]

One of the reasons for the silence was that the Bolsheviks, and very likely other socialist groups as well, fearing the total destruction of their organizations, held the workers back from "anarchistic and spontaneous outbreaks."[23]

Fear of being drafted into the army as punishment for either political or economic protest was also a factor in the quiescence of the workers.[24] This punishment was used against Donbass strikers at Gorlovka and at the Vera mine. When the mobilized miners refused to believe a junior officer who informed them of their being conscripted, the district military commander

[21] Koshik, *Rabochee dvizhenie na Ukraine*, pp. 53–55. See also Kharechko, "Otvet kritikam," p. 344.

[22] Moiseenko, *Vospominaniia starogo revoliutsionera*, p. 149.

[23] For the sending of Veniamin Ermoshenko to Gorlovka on such a mission, see Batov and Ostrogorskii, "Pis'mo," p. 340.

[24] Kir'ianov, *Rabochie iuga Rossii*, pp. 224, 227, offers documentary reports attesting to this.

himself came to enforce the order.[25] There were limits to the use of this tactic, however, and when thirty thousand striking Donbass miners were threatened with conscription in April 1916, thousands of them are said to have reported at the railway stations with knapsacks on their backs, knowing full well that coal production was far too important for the war effort to be sacrificed once again by indiscriminate mass mobilization.[26]

Police surveillance of the mines and factories of the Donbass was ubiquitous and apparently effective. Contact with the central bodies of the revolutionary parties was weak and intermittent at best. Vishniakov, one of the more successful Bolshevik organizers in the Donbass, lists seven Bolsheviks sent from the north and arrested during 1916.[27] Nevertheless, the revolutionaries persisted in sending cadres to the Donbass; they realized the political potential of this huge and unstable mass of workers. Pavel Alferov, who was to be one of the central figures among Iuzovka's Bolsheviks in 1917, arrived from Petrograd in the spring of 1915.

Other activists went to the Donbass as part of an ongoing attempt to avoid arrest. A young Kiev Bolshevik was forced to leave his home city for spreading antiwar propaganda. Under the name Stomakhin he organized Ekaterinoslav shoemakers for a strike and had to flee. For a short time he lived as Goldberg in Melitopol, and then as Kosherovich in Iuzovka. He was in Iuzovka when the February Revolution made it possible for him to emerge from the underground and use his real name, Lazar Moiseevich Kaganovich. For a short time he was active among the Iuzovka Bolsheviks and in the soviets of the district. His oratory and energy greatly impressed a young future Bolshevik, Nikita Khrushchev, who became first his protégé and ultimately his political nemesis.[28]

The recently escaped Bolshevik Veniamin Ermoshenko ("Molodoi shakhter") tried to circulate copies of the Zimmerwald Manifesto and was promptly rearrested, together with another Bolshevik. Emmanuil Kviring, who had established himself in Ekaterinoslav, had his home and office raided by the Okhrana, with the result that four other Bolshevik activists

[25] Shcherbina, *Rabochee dvizhenie*, p. 193, doc. 158.

[26] Kharechko, "Nakanune," p. 172.

[27] Vishniakov, "K bor'be," p. 220.

[28] For Alferov, see Zaitsev, "Kak my tvorili oktiabr'," p. 132. Kaganovich's wanderings are recorded in Osherovich, *Shtet un Shtetlekh in Ukraine*, vol. 2, p. 107. The Mensheviks and to a lesser extent the S-Rs were also sending emissaries to the region, but few of these are mentioned in the multitude of Bolshevik memoirs.

were incriminated and exiled to Irkutsk.[29] Party activists were kept on an endless treadmill of flight, jail, and exile. In addition to police harassment, the other source of instability was the shortage of professional revolutionaries and local leadership. Relative to the development of Russia's industrial working class, the skilled revolutionaries were few indeed, and the Bolsheviks formed only a small part of the general movement. Thus, even when the Bolsheviks were able to send skilled organizers to particular places, the organizers were often quickly called away to meet some new need that had suddenly appeared. Dedicated though they were, few had the opportunity to become true local leaders of the workers. Instead, police pressures and party exigencies transformed them into traveling salesmen of the revolution.

In mid-1916, with galloping inflation and food shortages stimulating workers' discontent, a half-dozen Bolsheviks from the Donbass mines and factories met in Makeevka under the auspices of what was designated the Makeevka District Committee. It was the first such conference since the outbreak of the war. Though they decided that the economic situation left a wide-open field for Bolshevik propaganda, there appears to have been no organized activity as a result.[30] On a clandestine press at the Vosnesenskii mine, Kharechko, with two fellow Bolsheviks, printed two issues of a newspaper, *Pravda truda*. From Kharechko's own account, the newspaper carried antiwar slogans and articles, most of them copied from other Social-Democratic papers. No mention is made of its discussing the economic issues that were uppermost in the workers' minds at the time.[31] One of the reasons for this seems to be the isolation of the Donbass Bolsheviks from the party centers.

Only at the end of 1916 did "Comrade Borisova" from Bakhmut manage to get to Petrograd, to arrange direct contact with the Bolshevik Central Committee Secretariat, and most important of all, to bring back Iurii Lutovinov (under the code name Ivan) as a "permanent" professional organizer. Lutovinov, however, stayed in Makeevka only long enough to prepare

[29] For the arrest of Ermoshenko, see Zaitsev, "Kak my tvorili oktiabr'," p. 133. For the raid on Kviring's quarters, see Bachinskii, Kviring, and Perel'man, *Kviring*, p. 30.

[30] Kharechko, "Nakanune," p. 181.

[31] Ibid., pp. 178–79. Batov and Ostrogorskii, "Pis'mo," p. 342, attack Kharechko for having represented the paper as having been produced by the "Donetsk Collective of the RSDRP," a formulation, they claim, that intimates Menshevik participation. They have, however, no criticism of its contents.

a leaflet for the anniversary of Bloody Sunday before leaving for Lugansk to organize in the cartridge factory of the Hartmann works, which had no Bolshevik organization whatsoever. In January 1917, he was traveling through Ekaterinoslav, Odessa, and Nikolaev, trying to organize a conference of Bolsheviks of all South Russia.[32] In such conditions it was difficult to gain the confidence and loyalty of any large number of workers, or to gain a deep knowledge of their problems and outlook. The schematic, sloganeering nature of the Bolshevik publications, composed far from where the workers lived, and copied from publication to publication, may be attributed in some part to this instability.

There were only about ten Bolsheviks in Iuzovka during the war years, and they were scattered as usual among different groups, refraining from forming a single committee for fear of police agents. The latter were, of course, present and watchful, as the repeated arrests of political organizers showed.[33] The Donbass Mensheviks focused their efforts in the workers' cooperatives and in the health-insurance funds, and campaigned with vigor, and with some success, for participation in the military-industrial committees.[34] Such programs gave them a degree of legality, and more important, experience in public activity that was to prove sorely lacking in the Bolshevik movement after February 1917.

As the war ground on, and conditions of work and life deteriorated, the strike movement in the Donbass grew. However, it did not regain the intensity that had marked the immediate prewar period. The combination of police surveillance, the dilution of the professional core of the labor force, and the basic belief of the populace in the country and its government were sufficient to prevent any massive outbursts. From July 1914 to February 1917, only seventy-one strikes were registered in the Donbass, and they involved only 73,083 workers, compared with seventy-nine strikes involving 86,900 workers from January 1912 to mid-1914.[35] There was, however, a gradual intensification of the strikes. As time passed, they grew longer and involved more workers. In 1914, the average strike length was

[32] For the sending of Lutovinov to the Donbass as a "resident professional," see Kharechko, "Otvet kritikam," p. 346. The brevity of his stay in the Donbass is mentioned in Batov and Ostrogorskii, "Pis'mo," p. 339. The travels around South Russia are noted in Vishniakov, "K bor'be," p. 220. Lutovinov is a perfect example of the traveling salesman of revolution.

[33] Kharechko, "Nakanune," p. 177, gives this as the main cause of Bolshevik inactivity.

[34] Ibid., pp. 177, 179.

[35] Kondufor, *Istoriia rabochikh Donbassa*, vol. 1, pp. 121, 124.

only 1.2 days. In 1915, it had grown to 4.8 days, and by 1916, to 5.5 days.[36] Political demands were injected into the strikes by the revolutionaries whenever this was possible. After the arrest of the Bolshevik faction of the Duma in November 1914, the Vera and Sofia mines near Iuzovka held protest strikes.[37] Despite such sporadic phenomena, Kir'ianov has concluded that even the comparatively intense strike wave in the Donbass in the latter part of 1915 and through 1916 was primarily economic, that the workers were still patriotic, and that there is no basis for classifying the strikes primarily as antiwar protests.[38]

In mid-March 1915, a wave of strikes began that was to last until the end of August. The demands were primarily for pay raises on the order of 30 percent, as compensation for the wartime inflation. In Enakievo, a planned strike at the Petrovskii works was avoided by preemptive arrest of the organizing committee, and in other places the drafting of some strikers into the army, the firing of others, and the granting of pay increases of 10 to 15 percent broke the strikes after one or two days.[39] Although the Rykovskii mines and the Rutchenko mines were both early participants in the strike wave, it was only in September 1915 that the wave reached the New Russia workers in Iuzovka. They struck when they learned that sugar and tobacco workers were earning more than those in metallurgy.[40]

As the economy of the Russian Empire deteriorated, and the unrest among the workers grew, the government sought to keep the lid on with new regulations for the prevention and suppression of strikes. In new regulations issued by the Ministry of the Interior at the beginning of 1916, the workers were warned that "any person interfering with legitimate activities will be subject to immediate arrest and exile."[41] Nevertheless, the strike wave intensified. Records of the Department of Mines show a wave of unrest beginning in the spring of 1916, against a background of increasing inflation and a lack of food. Wage demands were generally for an increase

[36] Ibid., p. 123.

[37] Modestov, *Rabochee i professional'noe dvizhenie*, p. 87.

[38] Kir'ianov, *Rabochie iuga Rossii*, p. 14.

[39] Koshik, *Rabochee dvizhenie na Ukraine*, pp. 84–85, 97; Kharechko, "Nakanune," p. 169. The former claims 26,935 strikers in forty-eight strikes during this period; the latter, thirty strikes and 40,000 strikers. Austrian prisoners of war in one striking plant, many of whom were no doubt good Social-Democrats and union members in peacetime, resolved their uncomfortable situation during the strike by claiming mass illness.

[40] Koshik, *Rabochee dvizhenie na Ukraine*, p. 92.

[41] Kharechko, "Nakanune," p. 171, citing *Birzhevye vedomosti* (February 11, 1916).

of 50 percent, with the employers willing to pay only 25 to 30 percent more.[42] The crest of the 1916 strike wave came in April and May, and was centered in the Gorlovka-Shcherbinovka area, where some thirty thousand miners struck. The Ekaterinoslav governor, Kolobov, brought a force of a thousand cossacks, police, and soldiers, dispersed the strike committee, arrested three hundred workers, and ordered that a thousand miners be mobilized into the army and sent to the front. The miners frustrated this action by reporting en masse for service. Four miners were killed and two others wounded in an armed clash with cossacks when they attempted to free their arrested comrades.[43]

The strike was a partial success. The workers were granted a pay rise of 25 percent—half of what they had demanded, but more than double what the employers had originally offered. The strike was accompanied by a number of events that should have caused anxiety to the employers and the government. First, workers' militias were formed to protect strike meetings from police attacks. This was a renewal of the tradition of the boevaia druzhina that had been largely dormant since the fiasco of December 1905. Second, soldiers, called in to intervene in the Gorlovka strike, refused to act against the workers, expressing sympathy with them. Third, the April strike (and the Easter holiday in the earlier part of April) cut Donbass coal production nearly in half, from 131.23 million puds in March to only 76 million puds in April.[44] At the same time, it is notable that a new pattern had entered the strikes. No longer did the employers avoid the workers' central demands. The basic justice of the workers' needs was acknowledged and the negotiations focused on to what extent and in what way they should be satisfied.

The April strikes did not bypass Iuzovka. Earlier in the year, the New Russia Co. management had granted a raise in pay of 15 percent to all miners who fulfilled twenty-two norms a month. On April 18, three hundred miners of the Central mine in Iuzovka, finishing their shift in the early

[42] TsGIAL, F. 37, op. 58, ed. khr. 870, pp. 1–6, 11.

[43] Modestov, *Rabochee i professional'noe dvizhenie*, p. 95.

[44] For the results of the strike, see Kazimirchuk, "Revoliutsionnoe dvizhenie," p. 41. The reappearance of workers' militias is mentioned in Modestov, *Rabochee i professional'noe dvizhenie*, p. 94, and the reluctance of soldiers to intervene is discussed in Moiseenko, *Vospominaniia, 1873–1923*, p. 184. *Gorno-zavodskoe delo*, no. 3 (1917), p. 15099, blames the strike movement for the fall in coal production, without mentioning the effect of the Easter recess.

evening, presented the mine director with a demand that this raise be applied to all miners, and that an additional cost-of-living allowance of 50 percent be granted to all the company's coal miners. Under the supervision of the settlement constable they elected three delegates to negotiate the matter with the employers. The response of management was mixed. Svitsyn, the company director, refused to grant a general pay raise on the grounds that there had recently been such a raise. He was, however, willing to give additional pay linked to increased productivity, and offered to increase the amounts of subsidized food sold in the cooperative, adding a subsidized clothing store and outlets for other goods. This satisfied enough of the workers that there was no further work stoppage.[45]

Three days later, 398 workers at the Bosset-Gennefeld mine equipment works also demanded a raise, but were informed by Pavel Bosset that no decision could be taken in the absence of his father, who was scheduled to return from a business trip to Kharkov in a week. The workers expressed a willingness to wait, and work in the factory proceeded normally. In reporting this incident, the Bakhmut district police inspector noted that he was pressing the employers to grant the "justified demands" of the workers so that there would be no additional strikes in the district. At that time at the Uspenskii, Olga, and Sergei mines 957 miners were on strike, part of ten thousand who had rejected an initial offer of a wage increase of 30 percent, demanding 50 percent.[46] Despite the efforts of the authorities to preserve industrial peace, at least eight other mines, including the Rykovskii and Berest-Bogodukhov mines near Iuzovka, struck briefly at the beginning of May, winning wage increases of 10 to 15 percent, as against the 40 to 50 percent that had been demanded. All these strikes, including the Gorlovka-Shcherbinovka strike, were brief, lasting only three or four days.

It would appear from the above examples that labor relations in the factories of Iuzovka were less strained than in other parts of the Donbass. To what extent this was due to the greater stability of the work force, a somewhat better food supply, or more tactful and intelligent management is hard to say. Nevertheless, as the year 1917 approached, this was a fact of some political significance. Iuzovka, after all, had grown to be the de facto

[45] Shcherbina, *Rabochee dvizhenie*, doc. 158, p. 191.

[46] Ibid., pp. 192–93. For an additional report of the phenomenon of police officials supporting workers' demands, see Kharechko, "Nakanune," p. 173, citing police archive reports.

capital of the Donbass, housing its greatest industrial enterprise, and serving as a center for a heavily populated and economically important mining district.

Not all industrial plants had reached the same level of accommodation between workers and management. The Petrovskii works in Enakievo and the Union Co. pipe factory in Makeevka were the scenes of repeated, and sometimes violent, strikes through 1916 and into 1917. In the Petrovskii factory there was a clear generation gap between the radical younger workers, who were more inclined to strikes and violence, and the older workers, who ignored strike calls.[47]

Growing tension and hardship were evident in the mines and factories of the Donbass. In the mines, in particular, the intensification of labor and the deteriorating food situation were clearly leading to a crisis in productivity. In late February 1917, the chief engineer of the Iuzovka mining district wrote: "All the enterprises report a general shortage of flour, barley, oil, and other food products. A shortage of fodder for horses is felt, and there is insufficient lubricating and illuminating oil."[48] Nevertheless, there was not yet evidence here of a mass revolutionary alienation between employers and workers. Although the Makeevka police reported seeing a Social-Democratic antigovernment leaflet pasted on a factory wall during the January strike, there was less reflection of political demands, and less claim of influence by the Social-Democrats, than was the case in the strikes at the turn of the century. Corrupt and incompetent as the tsarist government was in administering its society and economy, it was still effective as a ruling agency, and its organs of repression were well in control of the political situation. This, however, should not have been a cause for complacency, for the war and economic hardship were rapidly eroding the patience and faith of the people. A report by the director of police to the Ministry of the Interior noted that the revolutionary movements were well watched and largely ineffective, but warned:

> In the interior of Russia, the irregularity of food supply and the rising cost of living are explained as either lack of ability or lack of will of the central government to deal with these problems, and for this reason the attitude toward [the government] is extremely negative. There is

[47] See the description of the August 1916 strike in Shcherbina, *Rabochee dvizhenie*, doc. 240, p. 301.

[48] Korolivskii, Rubach, and Suprunenko, *Pobeda Sovetskoi vlasti na Ukraine*, p. 25.

> little faith in representatives of local administration either. . . . Everywhere, and in all strata of the population, there is war-weariness and hunger for the most rapid peace, no matter on what terms it may be concluded.[49]

With the sale of the New Russia Co. to a Russian-French consortium in April 1916, an era ended for Iuzovka. A new era was dawning, but it was far from anything that either the founders or the new owners had anticipated. On January 31, 1917, a month before the collapse of the tsarist regime, a Petrograd journalist brought an English industrialist to see the new Iuzovka. Mr. Brown, the Englishman, was not much impressed with what he saw, but the Russian journalist was ecstatic. To his eyes, "anyone who has visited such areas before sees clearly the improvement, and the local people themselves speak of it." Sobriety, prosperity, and above all industrial and social development stood out boldly before him, despite the bureaucratic sloth that was strangling Iuzovka's economy. The journalist had contempt for his English companion, who could not discern "the forging of the sword of victory." "But I am content," he wrote. "I see the hammer of labor beating, strongly and soberly, assuring our lives, and our radiant future."[50]

[49] Grave, *Burzhuaziia nakanune fevral'skoi revoliutsii*, p. 137.

[50] Volin', "V tsarstve chernoi zolota." (Yes, dear reader, he actually does use the phrase *nashe svetloe budushchee*!)

PART III

Revolution, Civil War, and Reconstruction

CHAPTER 8

Iuzovka and Revolution, 1917

The revolution came to Iuzovka by telegraph. The first news of the tsar's abdication was greeted by a demonstration led by the settlement's teachers, cheering Rodzianko, the chairman of the provisional committee of the Duma.[1] At Iasinovata station on the evening of March 2, a large, handwritten notice of the abdication was posted. A mine owner who expressed regret and anxiety was threatened with a beating by a crowd of miners. But when the Bolsheviks Vishniakov and Semin tried to exploit the opportunity for propaganda by saying that the tsar's abdication was unimportant, that the real enemy was the capitalist class, and that the war should be stopped immediately and replaced by class war, they were denounced as provocateurs, there were calls for their arrest, and they barely escaped from the station.[2] The next day, in Iuzovka, the workers entered the picture when a meeting, attended by two thousand workers of the New Russia factory, heard a report on the war and on the revolution, and elected a committee to organize elections for a soviet of workers' deputies.[3]

These two events were only the beginning of a dizzying round of meetings, processions, demonstrations, and harangues that tried to satisfy in one enormous gulp the hunger for legitimate political participation that had been growing unappeased among the Donbass workers for half a century. In the settlement, the Bolsheviks, the Mensheviks, the Socialist-Revolutionaries, the Kadets, and the Anarchists all held meetings.

[1] Zaitsev, "Kak my tvorili oktiabr'," p. 133.

[2] Vishniakov, "K bor'be," p. 222.

[3] *Velikaia oktiabr'skaia sotsialisticheskaia revoliutsiia (khronika sobytii)* (henceforth cited as *VOSR {khronika sobytii}*), vol. 1, pp. 62–63. The March 3 date given in the document is said to be approximate. The meeting was probably held a day or two earlier. Gorlovka heard of the tsar's abdication on the evening of February 28, and it is unlikely that Iuzovka heard much later, since such messages on the telegraph were usually directed "to all stations."

The workers did not know how to sort out such a babel, and applauded everyone.[4]

A group of Donbass workers paraded with banners and slogans to a nearby village. The peasants met them, led by the priest and his acolytes. The priest called for redoubled efforts to capture the Dardanelles, "without which Russia cannot live." The workers vehemently denounced the policy of taking the Dardanelles, while the peasants listened eagerly, if in confusion, to this strange debate.[5]

There were those who from the beginning applied themselves seriously to understanding the events around them, and to choosing a new political structure to replace the fallen autocracy. In mid-March, the committee of workers and employees of the Seleznev mines of the Iureevsk metallurgy factory in Slavianoserbsk district wrote to the Petrograd soviet, requesting large shipments of political literature. The 4,000 workers and 150 employees complained of their provincial isolation, and having come across the *Izvestiia* of the Petrograd soviet, were prompted to seek direct, continuous contact with Petrograd, and emphasized that they were interested in receiving literature from all parties and tendencies.[6]

It took some time for a new regime and a new program to emerge. In the mines and factories of Gorlovka on the morning of February 28, the mine administration, trailing a retinue of officials, congratulated the workers of each shaft on the tsar's downfall, and called on them to redouble their efforts for the defense of the country and for their newfound freedom.[7] The provisional revolutionary committee set up in Borisovka consisted of the police constable, the garrison commander, a priest, the mine managers, and some teachers.[8] Patriotism was strong. When the Bolshevik Ostrogorskii spoke against the war at a demonstration in Shcherbinovka on March 2, he was called a German spy, arrested, and sent for trial to Ekaterinoslav.[9] Immediately upon hearing of the tsar's abdication, Vishniakov set out from Ekaterinoslav to the Donbass, equipped with leaflets calling for the immediate cessation of the war and for an armed rising to overthrow capitalism. At Khartsisk station he came upon a meeting decorated with religious

[4] Zaitsev, "Bolsheviki Iuzovki v 1917 godu," p. 75.

[5] Kuranov, "Sovety na Artemovshchine," p. 165.

[6] *Velikaia oktiabr'skaia sotsialisticheskaia revoliutsiia (dokumenty i materialy)* (henceforth cited as *VOSR {dokumenty i materialy}*), vol. 1, p. 506.

[7] Kuranov, "Sovety na Artemovshchine," p. 163.

[8] Vishniakov, "K bor'be," p. 224.

[9] Kazimirchuk, "Revoliutsionnoe dvizhenie," p. 43.

banners and a red flag bearing a Menshevik slogan. A soldier harangued the crowd on the theme that a strong rear meant a strong front and victory, followed by a priest who spoke of God blessing the people with freedom. Vishniakov introduced the theme of "down with the government—long live civil war," and appeared to draw little attention. However, at the next station he was arrested and transferred to Borisovka jail, "the central headquarters for physical methods of determining the political opinions of persons under investigation for German espionage." He was freed only the next morning thanks to the personal intervention of a fellow Bolshevik from Makeevka.[10] Such disputes were to affect relations within the workers' movement throughout 1917, and were frequently colored with both class and professional feelings. When supporters of the Petrograd soviet demonstrated against Miliukov's declaration of support for the war aims of the allies, the Society of Mine Engineers sent a telegram of support to Prime Minister Lvov, referring to themselves as "representatives of the Russian intelligentsia, and as representatives of cultured labor . . . against the machinations of the less conscious forces who do not take into account the dangers of the moment, and thus play into the enemy's hands."[11]

Building a New Polity: The Emergence of the Soviets

In the Donbass, two main trends of organization appeared in the first days of the February Revolution. In many places, committees of public safety were set up, generally headed by merchants or engineers at the mines, dedicated to a minimum of change in the status quo, and marked by a common anxiety lest public order break down in the face of a wave of strikes, demonstrations, and destructive disorder. These later generally gave way to executive committees or commissars appointed by the provisional government, sometimes involving continuity of the leading personnel and only a change of name.[12] In other instances, generally in the smaller and more isolated localities, the self-appointed public committees gave way to elec-

[10] Vishniakov, "K bor'be," pp. 223–24.

[11] *Birzhevye vedomosti* (April 23, 1917). The declaration uses the term *culture* four times in three sentences, referring to the social groups supporting the provisional government.

[12] See, for instance, Borshchevskii, *Rabochii klass i sovety*, vol. 1, p. 26. The director of the Ekaterinoslav Land Commission, von Gesberg, who was part of the Provisional Executive Committee of Public and Workers' Organizations, was appointed Ekaterinoslav province commissar by the provisional government on March 6, 1917.

ted workers' soviets.[13] This appears to have been the case in Iuzovka, where it is said that at the beginning of the February Revolution, the Provisional Civic Committee was formed, made up almost exclusively of engineers and executives of the factory.[14] One may surmise that the blocking by the New Russia Co. of all previous attempts at civic organization, and the greater part of the commercial class of the settlement being Jewish and having no authority in the predominantly Russian population of Iuzovka, contributed to the transitional nature of this body. Its only recorded act is the setting of norms for the election of the first Iuzovka Soviet of Workers' Deputies. The large industrial enterprises were to elect one deputy for each one thousand workers, while the smaller factories and workshops elected a representative for each hundred, fifty, or even twenty-five workers.[15] There was to be no institution competing with the soviet for authority in Iuzovka until the election of a town duma in August after the granting of municipal status to the settlement by the provisional government. Despite its Menshevik leadership, the Iuzovka soviet declared that "power in the settlement of Iuzovka has been transferred to the Soviet of Workers' Deputies." This was perhaps less from ideological persuasion than from the simple absence of any other effective ruling body.[16] The soviet exercised this power sparingly, and the various committees set up in the New Russia factory did the actual planning and implementation of policies affecting daily life, while the soviet served mainly as an arena of debate, reflecting the interparty struggle taking place in Russia as a whole.

The second trend in organization was the creation of revolutionary committees, headed by members of the various socialist parties. These committees quickly formed soviets, following the example of Petrograd and the traditions of 1905. Almost immediately the soviets began forming networks, resulting in an eventual hierarchy that linked the local soviets of the mine and factory settlements to district soviets. These were united into provincial soviets and then into regional soviets that were connected to Petrograd. Thus, within a few months of the tsar's downfall, a five-tier system of soviets covered the whole of Russia.[17]

[13] Borshchevskii, *Rabochii klass i sovety*, vol. 1, p. 28.

[14] Zaitsev, "Bolsheviki Iuzovki v 1917 godu," p. 79.

[15] Korolivskii, Rubach, and Suprunenko, *Pobeda Sovetskoi vlasti na Ukraine*, p. 83.

[16] See the declaration of the Iuzovka soviet in the latter half of March in *VOSR* (*dokumenty i materialy*), vol. 1, doc. 199, p. 260.

[17] A description of the five-tier system may be found in ibid.

The first action of both types of organization was generally the disarming of the police. In Iuzovka the police were disarmed, those police constables who were of military age were delivered to the district military commander to be drafted into the army, and an elected militia was formed, commanded first by the Mensheviks Zhelondek and Lekhkii, and later, as the political balance changed, by the Socialist-Revolutionary Kliuev, who remained as militia commander until the capture of Iuzovka by the Germans in late April 1918.[18] The previous police chief, Sinkovskii, whose removal from his post was one of the first changes made when the revolution came to Iuzovka, was said to have requested the protection of the soviet even before it was officially formed.

In Iuzovka the soviet was elected on March 4; it was one of the first places in the Donbass to set up a soviet of workers' deputies. It had four hundred deputies and an executive committee of fifty members.[19] The elections were organized by persons largely from the factory administration, who were also given some representation on the first executive committee. The voting precincts were organized around small businesses and workshops, factory sections, public organizations, and parties, with each identifiable group represented by at least one deputy. The election was, in the first instance, for a period of three months, the standard term of office for a soviet at the time.[20] The result of the election system was that the great majority of the deputies to the soviets were nonparty representatives, active public figures picked by their fellow workers because they were more literate, more articulate, or considered more knowledgeable about the great world and its affairs. This was the basis on which the workers of the Rutchenko mines near Iuzovka chose Nikita Khrushchev to represent them in their soviet and

[18] Ibid. For the commanders of the Iuzovka militia, see Zaitsev, "Kak my tvorili oktiabr'," p. 134. *Birzhevye vedomosti* (March 22, 1917) reports a similar delivery of police to the army in Rostov.

[19] Kondufor, *Istoriia rabochikh Donbassa*, vol. 1, p. 125. Anweiler, *Soviets*, p. 116, writes that the Iuzovka soviet was established on March 5, and had three hundred deputies. Mints, "Obrazovanie sovetov," p. 14, dates the Iuzovka soviet from March 5, together with the soviets in Makeevka and Lugansk. For the size of the soviet and its executive committee, see *VOSR (dokumenty i materialy)*, vol. 1, doc. 199, p. 260, the declaration of the Iuzovka soviet.

[20] Zaitsev, "Bolsheviki Iuzovki v 1917 godu," p. 79, and "Kak my tvorili oktiabr'," p. 134. Kuranov, "Sovety na Artemovshchine," p. 169, states that three months was the standard term of election for the early soviets, though there were numerous exceptions made, both lengthening and shortening this term. See also Kazimirchuk, "Revoliutsionnoe dvizhenie," p. 46. He states that the Bolsheviks generally preferred shorter terms of office.

at the regional conference of soviets held in Bakhmut in mid-March.[21] These representatives, like their constituents, were the same workers who attended all the meetings of the various parties, and cheered them all, frequently supporting contradictory resolutions with impartial enthusiasm. "Today they accept one resolution, tomorrow another. It's a jumble."[22] The instability engendered by this phenomenon was a direct result of the persistent denial of civic experience to the great mass of the population by the tsarist regime.

The executive committee of the Iuzovka soviet was of a different complexion. The fifty members were largely representatives of political parties. The cooperative, and the few representatives of professional groups such as the shop clerks' association, also had representatives, though many of these were also identified with one party or another. This multiplied the presence of the parties in the executive committees. Elsewhere the trade unions and other workers' organizations were given representation in the executive committees of the soviets, but in Iuzovka no trade union had ever been allowed among the miners or metal workers of the New Russia Co., and other civic and professional organizations had been forcefully discouraged.

The Mensheviks had twenty representatives on the Iuzovka Executive Committee, the largest representation of any group, and their representative, M. G. Nosenko, who had stood trial as a participant in the 1905 seizure of the Ekaterinin railroad, and who was later to be killed by one of Makhno's detachments, was the first chairman of the soviet. In the new environment of freedom and open activity, the Mensheviks had a clear advantage. As Zaitsev remarked many years later, the Bolsheviks were fully at home in the conditions of underground conspiracy, but had not taken great part in public, legal activities.[23] The Bolsheviks were young, inexperienced, and few in number—only a dozen local members emerged in March from the underground. Nevertheless, they had four delegates on the executive committee.[24] Similarly, when they were only one-quarter of the

[21] Khrushchev Archive, Columbia University, American transcript, pt. 1, pp. 34, 58. Khrushchev joined the Bolsheviks only in February 1918. The phrase "active public figure" (*obshchestvennyi deiatel'*) is his own.

[22] See McDaniel, *Autocracy*, p. 350; pp. 373–77 contain instances of this phenomenon and a discussion of its place in the February Revolution. See also Rabinowitch, *Prelude to Revolution*, p. 104, for workers' undefined outlooks.

[23] Cited in Borshchevskii, *Rabochii klass i sovety*, vol. 1, p. 16. Bonnell, *Roots of Rebellion*, pp. 342–43, notes this as well, and on p. 440 generalizes about the effect of limited civic experience in producing frustration and political extremism among Russia's workers.

[24] Kondufor, *Istoriia rabochikh Donbassa*, vol. 1, p. 125. See also Anweiler, *Soviets*, p. 116. The Socialist-Revolutionaries and the various Zionist and Jewish socialist parties also had

Lugansk soviet the Bolsheviks received one-third of the places on the executive.[25] The executive committees, which by their nature were the power centers of the soviets, were thus from the beginning weighted more toward the parties and their various contradictory platforms than toward the public mood. They came to lead and instruct the public rather than to serve it.

The organization and standardization of the more or less spontaneous development of soviets in the Donbass began with the calling in mid-March of a district conference of soviets in Bakhmut. On March 15, 138 delegates from forty-eight soviets, representing 187,000 workers, met in Bakhmut.[26] Among them were 3 delegates from the Iuzovka soviet. This was part of the organizational activity directed toward an all-Russian meeting of soviets, scheduled for the end of March, which was to prepare the ground for the First All-Russian Congress of Soviets that was eventually held in June. Gradually, a new political structure was emerging.

In its organizational work the Bakhmut district conference set standards for the composition and structure of the soviets. Bakhmut district was divided into six subdistricts: Iuzovka-Enakievo, Makeevka, Lisichansk, Bakhmut, Gorlovka, and Konstantinovka-Shcherbinovka, each of which was to have a district soviet. All the local soviets were to have one deputy for each twenty-five workers voting, with elections held in places of employment. This unified standard replaced a hodgepodge of electoral standards in which an entire soviet might be elected by a show of hands at a general meeting of a settlement, or by ratios that varied, as noted above, from one deputy for twenty-five voters to one for one thousand. Reacting to the prominence of management personnel in the first soviets the Bakhmut conference resolved that factory directors and other senior administrators who had assumed decision-making powers from the owners of mines and

representation in Iuzovka. Zaitsev, "Kak my tvorili oktiabr'," p. 134, claims that the Bolsheviks were denied a place on the executive committee and lost out to the Mensheviks because of their youth and political inexperience. Zaitsev's memory would appear to be faulty here, though the categorization of the Bolsheviks as young and inexperienced is important for an understanding of the development of Iuzovka's politics through the revolution, as it is for other places as well. Koenker, *Moscow Workers*, pp. 199–200, notes that in the Moscow city duma the Bolsheviks were younger and less experienced in public activities than were the Mensheviks. Lane, *Roots of Russian Communism*, offers extensive evidence to support his conclusion that the Bolsheviks generally attracted younger and less-educated persons than did the Mensheviks or other socialist parties.

[25] Goncharenko, *Sovety Donbassa v 1917 g.*, p. 21.

[26] Borshchevskii, *Rabochii klass i sovety*, vol. 1, p. 36. The numbers of delegates in various sources vary from 132 to 138. See, for instance, Modestov, *Rabochee i professional'noe dvizhenie*, p. 100.

factories should neither vote nor have the right to be elected to the soviets.[27]

Social polarization had not been a ubiquitous feature of the first phase of revolutionary organization in the Donbass, though the gulf between educated society and the people was apparent at every step. Polarization was introduced, however, at this early stage, and grew steadily. The resolutions also confirmed the practice that whole factories might be represented in the executive committees of soviets, along with parties, cooperatives, and workers' health-insurance funds or cultural groups. To assist the fledgling soviets, the conference established a five-person information bureau in Bakhmut, headed by "the Bundist, Lipshits." The task of the bureau was to gather and disseminate news of how various soviets were organized, how they solved the problems facing them, and what innovative activities they were undertaking. The information bureau was dissolved in May, "lacking a broad proletarian base in Bakhmut."[28]

Organization was only one facet of the work of the conference. I would venture, however, that from the point of view of preparing a system of administration for an area that had no tradition or experience of self-rule, the determining of organizational principles was the most important long-term problem facing the gathering. In addition, the conference considered the gamut of issues debated in Russia at the time. The Menshevik predominance was evident in the resolutions. On the question of the war, the Bakhmut conference adopted a resolution in favor of a peace without annexations or indemnities, to be decided by an international conference, at which either the provisional government or the proposed constituent assembly would represent Russia.[29] At the same time, there was explicit recognition of the Petrograd soviet as the ultimate authority in matters of policy regarding classes in society, as well as the model and arbiter of questions of organization, alongside a recognition of the provisional gov-

[27] For the documents and resolutions of the Bakhmut conference, see Vilisova et al., *Bor'ba za vlast' sovetov v Donbasse*, pp. 12–17.

[28] Kuranov, "Sovety na Artemovshchine," p. 167. To the best of my knowledge, the Bund had no organization in Bakhmut. However, in the turbulent conditions of March 1917, the Bund might have sent organizers to take part in the political activity of Bakhmut, an artisan center with a substantial Jewish population.

[29] The expressions of support for the provisional government, the generally peaceful nature of the change of regime in the Donbass, and the rejection of slogans for establishing a dictatorship of the proletariat were noted with relief in *Birzhevye vedomosti* (March 19 and March 23, 1917).

ernment as the legitimate ruling power of the Russian Empire. The leaders at the Bakhmut conference apparently understood the volcanic pressures that existed among the workers of the Donbass, and the weakness of organizational discipline, for they warned against the danger of "individual initiatives," particularly regarding the demand for an eight-hour day, and emphasized the importance of an orderly collective appeal to the provisional government.[30]

Among the resolutions adopted by the conference was one calling on the government to institute the eight-hour day immediately, and another in favor of the equality of women. Naturally, the food situation was one of the questions debated at the conference, but it was one to which the delegates could not give a practical answer at this stage. The resolutions urged the formation of workers' cooperatives at each factory, and condemned the practice by which factory and mine owners provided their workers with subsidized food at factory stores, claiming that this practice "blurred the wage question."[31] The subsidizing of food by the New Russia Co., and by other employers in the Donbass, was a major factor in helping the workers maintain a bearable standard of living given the inflation of wartime Russia, and this was an essential element in maintaining social peace. The conference called for the printing of a newspaper by the district soviet, and instructed the soviets to take control of all funds levied from the workers as fines by the industrial and mining enterprises.[32]

The question of funds was important, for if the soviets were to become active and gain influence, they would need a steady source of income. This was not only a problem of the local bodies, but of the central bodies of the soviet movement as well. Their constituents, the workers, gave financial support, but reluctantly. A meeting of the rail-casting shop of the New Russia factory was asked to donate a day's pay for the Central Executive Committee of the Soviets, but voted to limit their contribution to 1 percent of one month's pay. The "Bazaar Office," meeting to elect new delegates to the food committee, and a new elder as chairman, voted a day's pay to help

[30] Vilisova et al., *Bor'ba za vlast' sovetov v Donbasse*, p. 16. The explanation of these resolutions in this source, and generally in Soviet historiography, is that the "proletarian core" was absent, serving at the front, and thus the petit bourgeois defensist elements were able to dominate the conference. See also Borshchevskii, *Rabochii klass i sovety*, vol. 1, p. 16, for a variant on this.

[31] Vilisova et al., *Bor'ba za vlast' sovetov v Donbasse*, p. 17.

[32] Ibid., pp. 14–16.

meet the needs of both the local and the central executive committees.[33] In mid-October the chairman of the Iuzovka soviet complained that only 10 percent of the funds promised by the workers had been paid.[34]

The network of soviets in the Donbass grew swiftly, and within a month there were over 150 soviets, many of them combining soldiers' and workers' deputies as the local garrisons organized and joined the settlement soviets, following the example of Petrograd. This at times led to tension within the soviets. In Makeevka, for instance, the representative of the cossack unit in the local soviet was the junior officer Chernetsov, who had been since the end of February a member of the Committee for the Salvation of the Homeland and the Revolution, and who was arrested at the end of August on the orders of engineer Bazhanov for declaring his loyalty to Kornilov when the latter attempted a coup. Chernetsov was later to lead the first Kaledin forces in attacking the soviets of the Donbass.[35]

At the same time that the Bakhmut conference was held, representatives from the Kharkov soviet were touring a broad area to set up a regional conference of soviets that would include the whole of South Russia—Kharkov, Kherson, Tauride, and Ekaterinoslav provinces.[36] The organization of self-government was not confined to the Russian workers of the mines and factories. The villages of the area set up peasant soviets as well, and at the end of March a Peasant Executive Committee was formed in Bakhmut district and opened negotiations with the workers' soviets to formalize relations between them.[37] In the central cities, Rada committees

[33] *Izvestiia Iuzovskogo soveta*, no. 28 (September 16, 1917), pp. 3, 4. There was no end to the good causes that needed financing. At the same time as the above levies were approved, the boiler shop collected 308 rubles (one ruble from each worker except women and children) for Comrade Mamre, "a poor soldier who escaped from a prisoner-of-war camp and is very needy." At the urging of the Iuzovka Soldiers' Benefit Council, workers at the Vetka mine gave 2 percent of their July salary for the benefit of Iuzovka's soldiers serving at the front—a total of 1,466 rubles. Similar notices appear repeatedly in the Iuzovka *Izvestiia*. The impression created is of a strong response by the population to the idea of mutual aid, particularly for those serving in the army.

[34] *Izvestiia Iuzovskogo soveta*, no. 42 (October 24, 1917).

[35] Troshin, "Fevral' i oktiabr' v Makeevke," p. 150.

[36] Borshchevskii, *Rabochii klass i sovety*, vol. 1, p. 38. See also *VOSR* (*khronika sobytii*), vol. 1, p. 208. *Birzhevye vedomosti* (April 30, 1917) reports the opening of this meeting in Kharkov on April 28.

[37] Kuranov, "Sovety na Artemovshchine," p. 165. Kuranov credits the mine and factory workers with "generally" initiating the organization of peasant soviets. While there were such cases, there is ample evidence that the rural areas undertook their own organizing, particularly on the basis of their Ukrainian national identity.

were set up, supporting the Central Ukrainian Rada (council or soviet—the provisional Ukrainian government, formed in 1917), and the Bakhmut conference recognized their authority along with that of the various local Hromada committees formed in Bakhmut district.[38] (Hromada means "the Society"—a movement for Ukrainian national independence.) At the same time, there was a clear split in Donbass society. The factory and mine settlements, overwhelmingly Russian and Jewish in ethnic composition, paid little attention to the Ukrainian question at this stage, and offered no support at all to the Rada, while the rural areas, organized primarily under the influence of a nationally inclined leadership, took little part in the soviets.[39] In every part of Donbass society there were efforts to replace the former powerlessness of the people with institutions that would give expression to more groups and interests in the structure of the state. The rapidity and energy with which this took place testified not only to the intensity of repression that had been applied by the autocratic regime, and was now removed, but also to the political energies and outlooks that had been developing below the surface.

Nor was all the initiative to be found at the grass-roots level. The provisional government was active as well, appointing replacements for the deposed governors and their staffs who had ruled the various provinces on behalf of the tsarist government. These new commissars and their assistants were subordinate to the minister of the interior, as their predecessors had been. Eventually this provoked a discussion of whether it would not be more in keeping with the spirit of the times to have the provincial authorities elected by the local populace rather than appointed from the center.[40] The provisional government's commissars in the south were drawn from society, as was only natural to that regime. The former head of the Ekaterinoslav Land Commission, von Gesberg, became commissar for the province, while Duma member Tuliakov was appointed to Kharkov.[41]

[38] See *Istoriia mist i sil*, p. 28, and Kazimirchuk, "Revoliutsionnoe dvizhenie," pp. 56, 60. *Birzhevye vedomosti* (April 16, 22, and 23, 1917) reports on the Kharkov Ukrainian Congress. The report notes the appearance of speakers from the Social-Democrats and Socialist-Revolutionaries, as well as an internal quarrel centered on an attempt to bar Archbishop Anthony from office in the Ukrainian church because of accusations regarding his activities on behalf of the Black Hundreds.

[39] Kuranov, "Sovety na Artemovshchine," p. 185.

[40] See *Russkie vedomosti* (July 2, 1917) for this discussion.

[41] The seamy side of the revolutionary uproar in the south was quickly made clear to Commissar Tuliakov. Arriving in Kharkov, he energetically convened a series of meetings,

The establishment of authoritative state institutions was urgent, for within the Donbass, law and order, always somewhat tenuous, were tottering. In Staro-Mikhailovsk county, in Bakhmut district, the peasants had invaded V. I. Karpov's estate, taking away ninety-six prisoners of war who had been working there. Prince Lvov, as head of the provisional government, wrote to the Ekaterinoslav commissar, urging that he put an end to land seizures by the peasants, and to arbitrary searches and arrests by parties of workers and miners.[42] At the end of March the Provisional Committee of the Donetsk Basin was established, with its seat in Kharkov. It was chaired by the head of the Central Fuel Administration of the region, and its members were three representatives of the defense establishment, four representatives of the Association of Southern Coal and Steel Producers, and four representatives to be named by the soviets of the Donbass, Ekaterinoslav province, and Kharkov province. The goal of this committee was "to coordinate and unite the actions of delegates and representatives of special assemblies . . . and to take immediate steps toward the implementation of the tasks laid upon these delegates."[43] Here at last was an initiative of the central authorities to establish an institution that would integrate all sectors of society to achieve a common interest, rather than perceiving each other as antagonists. There were to be other, more serious, initiatives of this nature, to which I will give detailed attention below.

Up from the Underground: The Iuzovka Bolsheviks

During 1915 there were said to be only six or seven "real" Bolsheviks in Iuzovka.[44] However, from two different lists given by Zaitsev one can derive the names of fourteen Bolsheviks who emerged from the underground in Iuzovka, including Kosherovich (L. M. Kaganovich) and his wife who soon moved on to Saratov.[45] These Bolsheviks acted as part of a united

---

and at a late hour retired to his hotel. Upon awakening the next morning he found that he had been robbed of his credentials, two hundred rubles, and his revolver. See *Birzhevye vedomosti* (March 29, 1917). For other references to criminal terror in Kharkov, and riots of criminal prisoners demanding to be released as political prisoners were, see ibid. (March 14 and May 7, 1917).

[42] Vilisova et al., *Bor'ba za vlast' sovetov v Donbasse*, p. 24.

[43] Borshchevskii, *Rabochii klass i sovety*, vol. 1, p. 36.

[44] Zaitsev, "Kak my tvorili oktiabr'," p. 132.

[45] See ibid., p. 133, and "Bolsheviki Iuzovki v 1917 godu," p. 78. Zalmaev, who is mentioned in the latter list, was in exile and returned to Iuzovka only in May. Borshchevskii,

Social-Democratic organization, together with the Mensheviks. This was one of fourteen such joint organizations in the Donbass.[46] Unlike other southern industrial centers such as Ekaterinoslav and Kharkov, or even such relatively small Donbass centers as Makeevka and Gorlovka, in which independent Bolshevik groups were organized immediately at the beginning of March, Iuzovka was to remain in the joint Bolshevik-Menshevik framework until the end of May.[47] Nor did the Bolsheviks have any separate factory committee or organization such as existed in other Donbass settlements, though there are records of such Bolshevik groups existing in the Donbass in places with as few as thirty party members.[48]

Ideologically, the joint Menshevik-Bolshevik organizations were not alien to the understanding of most Donbass Bolsheviks. When a conference of thirty-six existing Bolshevik groups, claiming 334 members, was called in Ekaterinoslav on March 5, the decisions defined the revolution as "purely bourgeois," and the soviets as "one of the most active revolutionary organizations, capable of leading the movement, and of constituting representative organs of working-class self-government." At this point, more than a month before Lenin's return from exile, there was no thought among the Bolsheviks of the soviets' acting as organs of overall state power, though the Menshevik-dominated Iuzovka soviet saw itself as such a body within the settlement. The meeting called on the Bolsheviks to participate energetically in fortifying the new system and to support the new government in extending and strengthening civic freedoms.[49] These positions were similar to the ideas then prevalent in the Petrograd soviet and accepted by its leading Bolsheviks, newly returned from Siberian exile. They were, however, far more moderate than the Leninist slogans of uncompromising

Rabochii klass i sovety, vol. 1, p. 18, claims that during March and April 1917, there were eighteen Bolsheviks in Iuzovka.

46 Kondufor, *Istoriia rabochikh Donbassa*, vol. 1, p. 145. The last of these, the Mariupol Bolshevik organization, went out on its own only in July 1917.

47 Although Kharkov had an independent Bolshevik group beginning in early March 1917, *Birzhevye vedomosti* (March 17, 1917) reports a conference of the Kharkov Social-Democrats in which a majority called for a united party organization, and was supported in this by representatives of the Bund and the Ukrainian Social-Democratic party.

48 Anikeev, "Svedeniia o bol'shevistskikh organizatsiiakh," pt. 2, pp. 108, 127–29.

49 Borshchevskii, *Rabochii klass i sovety*, vol. 1, p. 12, gives the numbers of organizations and members. Institut istorii, *Bol'shevistskie organizatsii Ukrainy*, p. 3, claims that there were more than five hundred Bolsheviks represented at the conference. The editor (p. 911 n. 1) criticizes the Donbass Bolsheviks for not regarding the soviets as potential organs of state power. See also *VOSR (khronika sobytii)*, vol. 1, p. 59, for the portion of the resolutions supporting the provisional government.

opposition to the provisional government, and of the soviets as the core of a socialist government.

The first meeting of the United Social-Democrats of Iuzovka had twenty to thirty former underground activists attending, and the Bolsheviks were given "two or three" places on the seven-member party committee.[50] While it would appear that the Iuzovka Bolsheviks had trouble attracting new members during the initial period of the revolution, the Mensheviks are said to have soon numbered 150.[51] Of the six delegates from the Donets–Krivoi Rog region attending the Seventh (April) Conference of the Bolsheviks in Petrograd, none came from the mines or factories in or near Iuzovka. All of them represented the urban concentrations around the periphery of the Donbass: Lugansk, Kharkov, and Ekaterinoslav. Only one of them, Klement Voroshilov from Lugansk, was a locally raised activist. All the others were emissaries of the Central Committee who had been sent to work in the Donbass.[52] The Bolsheviks of the Donbass began their legal existence as a small, uninfluential, and unpopular group.

It is clear from both the personal and the political context that relations between Bolsheviks and Mensheviks in Iuzovka were strained from the beginning. One meeting broke up in chaos when Zaitsev refused to obey the chairman's demand that he either apologize for insulting the Menshevik Gerbanenko or leave the hall.[53]

The 1917 May Day celebration in Iuzovka provided an illustration of the prevailing relations between the factions, and the culture in which those relations found expression. In Lugansk that day, there was a celebratory parade from early morning until midafternoon. Waves of people marched through the town with banners, and there were numerous revolutionary speeches. Socialist democracy celebrated, and the town was closed down.[54] In Gorlovka-Shcherbinovka the Bolshevik organizer, Gruzman, led a mass rally with banners reading "Long Live the Third International," "Long Live the Eight-Hour Working Day," and (evidently his only deviation from pure

[50] Zaitsev, "Kak my tvorili oktiabr'," p. 134. The Menshevik activists thus were not much more numerous than were the Bolsheviks.

[51] Borshchevskii, *Rabochii klass i sovety*, vol. 1, p. 15. Zaitsev, "Bolsheviki Iuzovki v 1917 godu," p. 82, gives the S-D membership at the end of April 1917 as 150 Mensheviks and 50 Bolsheviks.

[52] See the list of delegates in Borshchevskii, *Rabochii klass i sovety*, vol. 1, p. 47.

[53] Zaitsev, "Kak my tvorili oktiabr'," p. 135.

[54] Institut istorii, *Bol'shevistskie organizatsii Ukrainy*, pp. 161–62, citing a report in *Zvezda*.

Leninism) "Immediate Peace without Annexations or Indemnities." The celebration had the Bolsheviks, the Bund, and other small socialist groups on one side, with the Mensheviks and Socialist-Revolutionaries cooperating on the other, but with both camps attending a single, united demonstration. Gruzman's oratorical abilities were said to have swayed the meeting to the Bolshevik side.[55]

In Iuzovka, the holiday developed differently. The May Day celebration was held in the settlement's park, by the shore of the artificial lake. The procession was led by garlanded children bearing a large portrait of Kerenskii. The banners read "War to Victory" and "Long Live the Coalition Government." The Menshevik leader Myshkin marched at the head of a large column of workers from the factory, along with what Vishniakov describes as "all the philistines of Iuzovka, with Black Hundreds mixed in." The Bolshevik committee arrived, led by Zalmaev, and was immediately surrounded in a near-riot, evidently because of the placards and banners they carried. They were defended by some of the miners, a few factory workers, and the small contingent of local Bolsheviks. Just at this tense moment, a group of Bolsheviks arrived from the Berest-Bogodukhov mine, a center of Bolshevik strength. They came with banners reading "Down with the Capitalist Ministers," "Down with Kerensky's War," "Land to the Peasants," "Workers' Control in the Factories," and "All Power to the Soviets." As they drew near, the Berest-Bogodukhov miners saw Bolshevik banners ripped down and some of their party comrades being hustled toward jail by the militia.

At this point, acting from instinctive emotion, they committed a grievous tactical error and split their forces, half joining the fray by the lake, where they were quickly beaten up and thrown into the water, and half running to the militia headquarters to rescue the arrested Zalmaev, where they found themselves surrounded by mounted militia and threatened with arrest. The crowd then reinforced the militia and, joyous at the prospect of meting out justice to Bolsheviks who were also outsiders, closed in. It was an opportunity for sweet revenge, since a month or so earlier the Iuzovka Mensheviks had organized a meeting of a thousand miners at the Berest-Bogodukhov mines "at a time when all the Bolsheviks were busy." In that meeting army officers and metal workers called the miners simpletons for

[55] Ostrogorskii, "Stranichki iz istorii," p. 12; Kazimirchuk, "Revoliutsionnoe dvizhenie," p. 45.

following the Bolsheviks, "a gang of idlers and German spies." The miners had beaten the Iuzovka orators half to death.[56] Now the out-of-town Bolsheviks took refuge in the jail, "and so as to keep themselves out of the hands of the Iuzovka hangmen, were compelled to resort to the use of firearms." A momentary standoff ensued and negotiations began, with Myshkin as intercessor. He suggested that since the mob was indeed intent on lynching the Bolsheviks, they would be better off surrendering their arms and themselves to the militia. The beleaguered Bolsheviks found this logic convincing, and they surrendered. The May Day ceremonies then went on without them, and they were released to return to their mine in the evening.[57]

These events did nothing to enhance proletarian solidarity in the settlement. The ultimate split between the two factions came about, however, on political rather than personal grounds. There are three reasons given for the split, all of which undoubtedly contributed to it. One reason was the defensist stand of the Mensheviks, following the line of the provisional government and the Petrograd soviet.[58] The activists among the Iuzovka Bolsheviks had been Leninist in their opposition to the war since 1914, and they maintained that position through most of 1917. Only later, with the threat that the Brest Litovsk negotiations would cut them off from Russia, did the Donbass Bolsheviks swing over to supporting a continuation of the war.

The second reason offered was the influence of Lenin's April Theses, brought to Iuzovka by Iacov Zalmaev at the end of May, with his release from exile and reassignment to political organizing in the Donbass by the Bolshevik secretariat in Petrograd.[59] These theses demanded a sharpening of conflict not only in relation to the war, but regarding the provisional government as well. This version emphasizes the isolated nature of the Iuzovka Bolsheviks. Lenin's April Theses were pronounced upon his return to Russia in the first week of April, and were hotly debated in the Bolshevik press and in the entire Russian revolutionary camp immediately thereafter. However, only with Zalmaev's return to Iuzovka seven weeks later did this debate reach the Bolsheviks in the settlement.[60]

[56] Vishniakov, "K bor'be," p. 225.

[57] The entire account is based on the memoirs of Vishniakov (ibid.).

[58] Vilisova et al., *Bor'ba za vlast' sovetov v Donbasse*, p. 41.

[59] Zaitsev, "Bolsheviki Iuzovki v 1917 godu," p. 82.

[60] Vishniakov, "K bor'be," p. 227, writes of the reading of Lenin's April Theses in the Donbass immediately after the April conference of the Bolsheviks, and dates the prepara-

8.1 The Rykovskii mine workers' militia, 1917.

8.2 "Neither Separate Peace with Wilhelm Nor Secret Agreements with English and French Capitalists." A demonstration in the New Russian factory, 1917.

The third reason offered was tactical rather than a matter of revolutionary principle. Zaitsev explains that the Bolsheviks had hoped to gain a majority in the local Social-Democratic organization, and to expel the Mensheviks. When the balance tilted more and more in favor of the Mensheviks (due to the joining of new members described by Zaitsev as petit bourgeois—*meshchanstvo*), the Bolsheviks saw no alternative but to form their own independent group.[61] On May 26, 1917, a meeting attended by eighteen of the Iuzovka Bolsheviks picked a nine-member committee (called the *kollektiv*) and declared the existence of the Iuzovka Committee of the RSDRP, alongside the existing Menshevik-dominated Iuzovka Organization of the RSDRP. The Bolshevik group was chaired by Pavel Alferov, who had been sent from Petrograd in 1915, and Zaitsev was elected secretary. At the time of the split, three months after the revolution, the Bolshevik membership had grown from the dozen undergrounders to approximately fifty.[62] On May 31, after five members of the committee had drawn up a list of theses to guide the new group, the Bolsheviks of Iuzovka held their first meeting. The main problem considered by the thirty members attending the meeting was the refusal of owners of buildings in Iuzovka to rent office space to the Bolsheviks. The meeting resolved to lodge a complaint with the local soviet against the arbitrary behavior of the landlords.[63] The problem was resolved when the union of needle workers agreed to sublet to the Bolsheviks a room above the storefront that served as their union offices.[64] The Bolshevik organization was not yet stabilized, for a week after the nine-member kollektiv was formed one member resigned, and at the end of July two other members had to be replaced.[65]

---

tions for an armed uprising from then. As I have noted, no representatives of the Donbass mine and factory settlements were delegates to the conference. In comparison, the Saratov Bolsheviks heard Lenin's theses on April 12, six weeks earlier. See Raleigh, *Revolution on the Volga*, p. 137.

[61] Zaitsev, "Kak my tvorili oktiabr'," p. 135.

[62] Zaitsev, "Bolsheviki Iuzovki v 1917 godu," p. 82. Zaitsev gives a list of the members of the committee, as well as naming a total of thirty-two out of the fifty members claimed for the Bolsheviks. The committee included two of the five women Bolsheviks included in Zaitsev's lists. Bolshevik membership in Iuzovka had reached fifty by the end of March. The organization thus appears to have been stagnant during the two months preceding the split.

[63] Institut istorii, *Bol'shevistskie organizatsii Ukrainy*, p. 167.

[64] Zaitsev, "Kak my tvorili oktiabr'," p. 135.

[65] Institut istorii, *Bol'shevistskie organizatsii Ukrainy*, pp. 169, 565. Although the language of the source is that these members "left" the kollektiv, the circumstances are not set forth. Of the original dozen 1917 Bolsheviks it is recorded that one went over to the Mensheviks and three others joined the anarchists.

The way to increasing Bolshevik influence in the vicinity of Iuzovka lay in organizing the outlying mines under the auspices of a broad district committee. On June 3, 1917, the Iuzovka Committee hosted a meeting that reestablished the Iuzovka-Makeevka-Petrovskii District Committee with seventeen full members and five nonvoting alternates. The committee held its first session the following day and initiated a large-scale organizational and propaganda effort based on the combined resources of the three committees. Speakers were sent out to the mine villages of the Grishino district and to meetings of miners anxious to understand the great changes that were taking place around them.[66] Connections with the party's central authorities were also established, for at the meeting of the Iuzovka Bolsheviks on June 3, 1917, a resolution was passed obligating each member to subscribe to *Pravda*, and fifty copies of the Kronstadt *Golos pravdy* were ordered for distribution within Iuzovka.[67] Nonetheless, the growth of the Iuzovka Bolsheviks, both in numbers and in influence, was slow. Though Iuzovka had by far the greatest concentration of industrial workers in the region, as well as a considerable population of artisans and workers in light industries, Makeevka had a much larger and better-organized Bolshevik group. A general meeting of the Makeevka Bolsheviks on July 8 was attended by three hundred members and passed resolutions calling for nationalization of industry and for workers' control in the factories and mines. In Iuzovka on the same date, twenty members turned out.[68]

The first Makeevka soviet, elected in March 1917, had included only seven Bolsheviks among its ninety deputies. Visits by Zalmaev, Lutovinov, and Vishniakov, who read reports and made speeches, bolstered Bolshevik morale but helped little with the basic organizational problems. It was only when three Bolshevik engineers, Bazhanov, Garikol, and Passov, arrived to work in the Makeevka factory before the second round of elections to the soviet that the party's situation improved "both quantitatively and qualitatively."[69]

The ability of the Bolsheviks to maximize their resources was further strengthened by uniting the various district committees into a regional

[66] For details of these activities, see Zaitsev, "Kak my tvorili oktiabr'," p. 135, and the protocols of the Iuzovka Bolsheviks' meeting in Institut istorii, *Bol'shevistskie organizatsii Ukrainy*, p. 556.

[67] Institut istorii, *Bol'shevistskie organizatsii Ukrainy*,, pp. 168–69.

[68] Ibid., p. 924 n. 126. At that time Makeevka had approximately one third the population of Iuzovka.

[69] Troshin, "Fevral' i oktiabr' v Makeevke," p. 149.

(oblast') committee. This was organized by a plenipotentiary of the Bolshevik Central Committee, who arrived from Petrograd to set up a local *buro* (bureau or office) to prepare the conference. Rivalry between the Bolsheviks of Kharkov and those of Ekaterinoslav evidently made this intervention necessary after a previous attempt in April had produced no concrete organizational steps.[70] The new *obkom* (regional committee), elected during the conference that took place in Ekaterinoslav from July 13 to 16, 1917, was to sit in Kharkov, and its newspaper, *Donetsk proletari*, was to be distributed from there to Ekaterinoslav, Rostov, Lugansk, all the towns and settlements of the Donbass, and as far west as the Krivoi Rog iron mines. Altogether thirteen district and city committees, claiming 13,648 Bolsheviks, were to be supervised within the region. The obkom was headed by F. A. Sergeev (Artem), who had just returned to Russia after seven years in Australia, and its members included Kviring, Zalmaev (as head of the Iuzovka-Makeevka-Petrovskii Committee), and Ostrogorskii (representing the Shcherbinovka-Gorlovka district).[71]

In the early summer of 1917 the Bolsheviks of Iuzovka still had little influence in the New Russia factory. The protocols of a party meeting on June 6 include a discussion of an agreement that had been reached in the factory regarding overtime pay, supported by the Mensheviks and the Socialist-Revolutionaries, but criticized by the Bolsheviks. The speaker expressed a fear of "undesirable excesses in the form of strikes and violence by the workers," and called on the Bolsheviks to try to explain their criticism of the agreement without having their followers take any action.[72] The reluctance to attempt to organize any action was clarified by another speaker at the same meeting. In discussing the party's situation in the New Russia factory, he reported: "Bolsheviks in a number of shops undergo repressions from nonconscious workers (who are a majority). They accuse you of all sorts of nonexisting sins and heap filth on you. You can neither convince nor clarify; they just hiss you down."[73]

[70] Donii, "Obrazovanie Kommunisticheskoi Partii Ukrainy," p. 36. Regarding the unsuccessful earlier conference, see Borshchevskii, *Rabochii klass i sovety*, vol. 1, p. 39. Comments on the Kharkov-Ekaterinoslav rivalry are in Ostrogorskii, "Stranichki iz istorii," p. 25.

[71] Institut istorii, *Bol'shevistskie organizatsii Ukrainy*, pp. 394–95. Akhankina et al., "Pis'ma Artema," pp. 55–56, 74, claims that Sergeev remained in Australia until after the October Revolution and that in May 1917 he organized Australia's first May Day parade in Port Darwin.

[72] Vilisova et al.,, *Bor'ba za vlast' sovetov v Donbasse*, p. 48.

[73] Institut istorii, *Bol'shevistskie organizatsii Ukrainy*, p. 174. In a note on p. 917, the editor explains that 40 percent of the "core" workers had been drafted into the army and their

Despite these difficulties in the largest of the industrial centers within the Donbass, the Bolshevik cause was growing. In the excited climate of revolutionary debate that prevailed everywhere in Russia in 1917, there was ample opportunity for any group that had an articulate organizer. In the first months in particular, success was built around individuals who commanded the respect of the inexperienced and confused workers and peasants. This laid a new and heavy burden on the party centers, which were called on endlessly to supply orators and organizers to exploit the myriad of opportunities that suddenly presented themselves throughout Russia. Such persons were in short supply, and there was thus a constant shuffling as the best organizers were sent from one place to another to meet new needs. I have already mentioned this phenomenon, and its effect in retarding the development of relations between workers and intelligentsia. This constant shifting of central organizers also destabilized many groups. When the organizer was moved, the group collapsed, having no authoritative and effective personality to sustain it. Lutovinov made a brief stay in the Donbass and was dispatched to Lugansk to organize a Bolshevik group in the cartridge factory at the end of 1916. As soon as he moved from there, the group collapsed and was reorganized only in June 1917.[74] The shortage of high-quality activists also allowed a certain number of doubtful characters to slip into positions of power. The Bolshevik worker Krasnikov, who had become chairman of the executive committee of the Kramatorsk soviet, was revealed to have served as a paid Okhrana agent between 1913 and 1916.[75] Tulupov was active and influential in the Konstantinovka soviet before he seized his chance and stole the New Russia payroll.

This scarcity of authoritative talent would appear to have been the prob-

places taken by numerous "draft-dodging clerks, small property owners, and artisans, to whom proletarian psychology was foreign." The note adds that there were also honorable workers honestly confused by the defensists; they provided an attentive constituency for those parties that carried on the defamation of the Bolsheviks. There is an element of truth in the claim regarding the changed composition of the labor force in the factory. However, to judge by the relative success of the Bolsheviks in recruiting among the coal miners, the lowering of the skill and education levels of the factory workers does not explain the Bolsheviks' lack of success in the factory.

[74] Anikeev, "Svedeniia o bol'shevistskikh organizatsiiakh," pt. 2, p. 105. For a chronology of Lutovinov's wanderings in and out of various Donbass settlements, chased by the police, see Nikolaenko, "Pamiati tovarishcha," pp. 182–83.

[75] *Birzhevye vedomosti* (April 12, 1917). Kondufor, *Istoriia rabochikh Donbassa*, vol. 1, p. 125, notes a Bolshevik majority in the executive committee of the Kramatorsk soviet in March 1917, but names no local leader as he does for the few other soviets named. *Istoriia mist i sil*, p. 28, names the Kramatorsk soviet as one of three Donbass soviets that had Bolshevik majorities in March 1917.

lem with the Iuzovka Bolsheviks. Pavel Alferov, first chairman of the independent Bolshevik group in the settlement, was spread thin over the entire Makeevka-Iuzovka-Petrovskii area, running from mine to mine, organizing and speaking.[76] Zalmaev, who took over leadership of the group, and who was briefly chairman of the soviet, proved weak, and fled town under a cloud of criminal suspicion. Neither Zaitsev nor Kharechko, who later enjoyed some prominence as a member of the Central Committee of the Communist Party of the Ukraine between 1918 and 1920, appears to have been a leader of any stature. Kaganovich, later described as "a storm, who might break or chop down good trees, but who would get things done," was quickly sent elsewhere at the start of the revolution.[77] Neither in contemporary press sources and documents nor in the memoir literature does one find descriptions of Iuzovka Bolsheviks who involve themselves in the problems of daily life of the settlement as do Myshkin and Dr. Kantorovich, the leaders of the Menshevik factions. In the accounts of activities of the New Russia Factory Workers' Committee, the Iuzovka Food Committee, the cooperative, and the town's duma, the Bolsheviks do not appear to have had any appreciable role.

Two Bolsheviks, active in the Donbass, illustrate the importance of talented individuals in influencing party fortunes. A student named Suglitskii went to the Vetka factory settlement just outside Iuzovka, evidently during the war, when Putilov opened an arms factory there. His first job was that of tutor to the factory manager's children, and he lived in the manager's home, a circumstance that must have limited his influence among the workers. Only after the February Revolution did he shift his residence to the Bolshevik committee offices.[78] Nevertheless, Suglitskii led a twenty-member self-education group at the factory, and later led the group into the Bolshevik party, maintaining and expanding its influence despite all hostile pressures.[79] Judging from the reports from Vetka, it

[76] Chernomaz, *Bor'ba rabochego klassa Ukrainy*, p. 7, credits Alferov with organizing the first Bolsheviks at the Rykovskii mines. Institut istorii, *Bol'shevistskie organizatsii Ukrainy*, p. 556, notes his speech in July at the Prokhorov mine.

[77] On Kharechko's career, see Boris, *Sovietization of the Ukraine*, pp. 76 n. 41, 144–51. Zaitsev's record is found mainly in his own writings. On Kaganovich, see Khrushchev Archive, Columbia University, American transcript, pt. 1, p. 64.

[78] *Perepiska sekretariata*, vol. 2, p. 334.

[79] See Zaitsev, "Bolsheviki Iuzovki v 1917 godu," p. 81. A number of Suglitskii's reports, with details of achievements and difficulties, are printed in the first two volumes of *Perepiska sekretariata*.

would appear that Suglitskii's energy and personality were the crucial factors in winning the factory over to the Bolshevik side.

Shulem Gruzman appeared at a mass meeting of miners and workers of the Shcherbinovka-Gorlovka district early in 1917, and won his place among them with a blazing Leninist oration. Gruzman was a member of the intelligentsia who had been in Siberian exile, where, "not yet a fully-defined Bolshevik," he had met and been influenced by Lomov, Kosior, and Antonov-Ovseenko, all of them later active Bolsheviks who were to rise to considerable prominence in the party, including work in the Donbass.[80] Returning to Petrograd after the February Revolution, he asked to be sent to the Donbass. Although he was totally unknown to the Donbass workers, even to the Bolsheviks among them, he was accepted on the strength of his personality and his Petrograd credentials. The dozen Bolsheviks of the region had been trying unsuccessfully to set up a district organization, and as Ostrogorskii later recalled, they were happy to have Gruzman, for "there were few who could express themselves freely and sensibly." Gruzman was installed as chairman of the local Bolshevik group and within two weeks had created a large district organization and set up elections for a committee. In mid-May a public meeting elected Gruzman as a delegate to the First All-Russian Congress of Soviets in preference to a Menshevik who was also an emissary from Petrograd. Ostrogorskii credits Gruzman personally with engineering the passage of a resolution condemning socialist participation in the provisional government, and demanding for the first time in the Donbass that state power be transferred to the soviets. By October the Gorlovka-Shcherbinovka organization embraced nine large mines, the Gorlovka artillery factory, and a number of small peasant mines, while other mines, as yet unorganized, were inquiring about the possibility of joining. Yet the whole project rested on Gruzman's shoulders, for on October 13, 1917, he wrote to the Central Committee: "During the whole time I was in Piter [St. Petersburg] they didn't meet once. The masses started leaving our party by whole organizations."[81]

[80] However, it should be noted that Antonov-Ovseenko, for instance, was close to Trotsky, and joined the Bolsheviks only in mid-1917.

[81] For details of Gruzman's activity, see Ostrogorskii, "Sh. A. Gruzman" and "Stranichki iz istorii." Gruzman's reports appear in *Perepiska sekretariata*, vol. 1, pp. 356–57. He was elected to the Central Committee of the Communist Party of the Ukraine in July 1918, and was killed by Petliura's army in Ekaterinoslav in 1919, when he tried to lead a group of Bolsheviks into the occupied city to set up underground activity.

Many of the rank-and-file workers who threw themselves into political and public work were simply worn down by the effort. They earned their living as miners or factory workers, and after hours were torn among party affairs, the soviet, cooperatives, health-insurance funds, and all the other luxuriantly growing institutions springing up on what had been the arid social landscape of autocratic Russia. Suglitskii was able to earn his living as chairman of the Vetka workers' health-insurance fund, relieving the party of the necessity of paying him, but adding new responsibilities on top of his party duties as organizer. In Iuzovka the session of the soviet accepted the resignation of two deputies because of exhaustion.[82] Although the political parties grew rapidly in membership throughout 1917, relatively few of the new members appear to have taken on active roles in their various organizations. While the Bolsheviks of Iuzovka were growing from the dozen who emerged from the underground to an eventual claim of two thousand members in October, the attendance at their weekly meetings never passed thirty-five to forty members until late September, when it rose as high as one hundred.[83] As a result, there were relatively few persons who could be relied on to shoulder all the new responsibilities, and expansion of activities depended even more on the professional politicians who were supported in whole or in part by their parties.

The finances of the party were a matter of some importance. If the center enjoyed some generous contributions to sustain its institutions and personnel, the outlying areas had little such support. Traditionally, local sympathizers had been canvassed to support the various newspapers and journals circulated by the revolutionaries. In 1917 the need grew astronomically as political opportunity beckoned from every direction. When the Bolsheviks of the Ukraine decided in June 1917 that they would publish their own newspaper, and the *Donetsk proletarii* was about to appear in Kharkov, the workers of the forging shop of the New Russia plant sent greetings, but their monetary contribution amounted to only seventeen rubles and fifty kopeks.[84] A month after its inauguration the newspaper had to be temporarily suspended for lack of funds—this at the center of one of the great concentrations of the proletariat in the Russian Empire. It was different

[82] *Izvestiia Iuzovskogo soveta*, no. 28 (September 16, 1917), p. 3.

[83] The protocols of these weekly meetings, singularly devoid of principled discussions, appear in Institut istorii, *Bol'shevistskie organizatsii Ukrainy.* See, for instance, p. 570 for the meeting of August 5, 1917, attended by thirty members.

[84] Vilisova et al., *Bor'ba za vlast' sovetov v Donbasse*, p. 50.

when an energetic organizer like Suglitskii set up a large branch. In November 1917, the Vetka Bolsheviks gathered 1,054.92 rubles, of which 40 percent went to the Central Committee, 10 percent went to the regional committee in Ekaterinoslav, 25 percent supported the activities of the Iuzovka-Makeevka-Petrovskii Committee, and the remainder was kept in Vetka.[85]

The first real political test of the year came at the beginning of June, when reelection of the local soviets of the Donbass coincided with the selection of delegates to the First All-Russian Congress of Soviets, held in Petrograd. Although the results of the elections to the Iuzovka soviet do not appear to be available, a meeting of the Iuzovka Bolsheviks named only two delegates, Shishkin and Petrunin, to the soviet's executive committee, with Efanov as a candidate.[86] They were among twenty representatives of parties in the executive committee. This is about the same representation that the Bolsheviks had in the first executive of the Iuzovka soviet, but unlike in March, when they were accepted, in June the Bolshevik nominees were challenged by the Menshevik leadership of the soviet.[87] Zaitsev claims only ten Bolshevik deputies in the Iuzovka soviet after the June elections.[88] Clearly there was as yet no appreciable growth of Bolshevik influence within Iuzovka.

This was reflected in the outcome of the Iuzovka celebration of the Congress of Soviets. Essentially it was a replay of the May Day events. Although the Bolsheviks were conscious of the disfavor in which they were held, and complained vociferously among themselves of the defamations to which they were subject, they proceeded to organize for the June 25 demonstration that was to be held in Iuzovka to celebrate the Petrograd Congress of Soviets.[89] The night before the demonstration, the Bolsheviks of Iuzovka had twenty-five people attending their weekly meeting to hear the arrangements for the next day. Pavel Alferov was the organizer, and he persuaded a

[85] Pavliuk et al., *Bol'shevistskie organizatsii Ukrainy*, p. 335.

[86] *VOSR (khronika sobytii)*, vol. 1, p. 239.

[87] Vilisova et al., *Bor'ba za vlast' sovetov v Donbasse*, p. 372 n. 13. The grounds for the challenge are not specified. In addition to the Mensheviks and S-Rs this source names the Bund, Poalei Tsion, and the SERP (United Jewish Workers' Party) as represented in the Iuzovka Executive Committee.

[88] Zaitsev, "Kak my tvorili oktiabr'," p. 136. The total number of deputies appears to have remained at four hundred.

[89] For Iuzovka Bolshevik laments about "defamation," and the Bolsheviks' decision to complain to the district party committee, see the protocols of the meeting of June 17 in Institut istorii, *Bol'shevistskie organizatsii Ukrainy*, pp. 178–79.

dozen volunteers to distribute newspapers and leaflets at the demonstration. Five Bolshevik speakers were named, and the fear that the party's representation might be a bit on the thin side was assuaged by the reported promise of the Berest-Bogodukhov miners to turn up en masse, despite their earlier experience in Iuzovka.[90]

The next day, June 25, about a hundred Bolshevik supporters turned out, and, "not wanting our slogans to be mixed in with those of the Mensheviks and S-Rs, formed a separate column."[91] The main body of the demonstration was led by a banner reading "Forward with the Attack on the Germans." The relatively small group of Bolsheviks proclaimed "Down with the Ten Capitalist Ministers" and "All Power to the Soviets." Allegedly led by the Socialist-Revolutionary militia commissar, Kliuev, a large group of demonstrators demanded that the Bolshevik banners be taken down. Zalmaev protested, only to be pushed aside by the commissar's horse. The crowd then tore down the Bolshevik slogans and banners, beating and arresting their bearers. Meanwhile, the commander of the Iuzovka militia, Lehkii, was raiding the Bolshevik offices, searching for "literature and weapons," while a crowd outside threw stones at the windows.[92] At the railway station, only a handful of the Berest-Bogodukhov Bolshevik leaders showed up, accompanied by a few comrades from Ekaterinoslav. They inquired of the militia commissar on duty about the rumors that Bolsheviks were being beaten and arrested, but were refused any information. When they protested, they were arrested and one was searched. They were then informed that an order had been received from Kerenskii to shoot all of them, and that if they did not submit quietly, it would be carried out. Only the intervention of one of the members of the soviet's executive committee achieved their release. During their period of arrest, the visiting Bolsheviks were able to engage in ideological debate with their captors. On the question of the war, one militia officer explained: "You are demanding peace without annexations or indemnities. We think that if our government gets some reparations then we here might receive some part of them."[93]

[90] Ibid., p. 181. See also Zaitsev, "Bolsheviki Iuzovki v 1917 godu," p. 88.

[91] Zaitsev, "Bolsheviki Iuzovki v 1917 godu," p. 89.

[92] Institut istorii, *Bol'shevistskie organizatsii Ukrainy*, pp. 186–87, report given at a meeting of Iuzovka Bolsheviks, June 29, 1917; Zaitsev, "Kak my tvorili oktiabr'," p. 136.

[93] Institut istorii, *Bol'shevistskie organizatsii Ukrainy*, pp. 188–89.

Four days later the Bolsheviks of Iuzovka gathered to assess their position. Despite the sound and fury, nobody had been injured, nor was any of the Bolsheviks charged or held in jail. Politically, however, Zalmaev categorized the demonstration as a debacle. A poll had been taken of the attitudes of the workers about what had happened. In the shoe factory and a few other shops, there was some indignation over the disruption of the demonstration. In the electrical shop of the New Russia factory, one worker said, "previously they had a bad attitude toward our party. Now it is worse." In the Rykovskii mines, where the commissar had confiscated the party library and newspapers, there was sympathy for the Bolsheviks in the mechanical section, but feelings in the mines themselves were "undefined." Iuzovka was said to be the only place in the Ukraine in which the Bolsheviks suffered defeat in the June demonstrations.[94] Later Zaitsev was to claim that the Menshevik and Socialist-Revolutionary repressions against Bolshevik freedom had boomeranged, kindling sympathy for the Bolsheviks among the workers.[95]

Elsewhere in the Donbass there was an entirely different outcome. In Lugansk an enthusiastic crowd listened to five hours of speeches and demanded more, "unanimously" supporting the Bolshevik resolutions offered by Voroshilov.[96] In "merchant Bakhmut" there was an orderly debate in the Petrograd congress. The Bakhmut soviet, with only the two Bolshevik deputies dissenting, voted to support the resolutions of the Congress of Soviets, as well as the call of the provisional government for a "Liberty Loan." A public demonstration was organized, during which three hundred thousand rubles' worth of bonds were sold, "which for Bakhmut must be considered a large sum."[97]

The clearest Bolshevik achievement in the Donbass came at the Nikitovka District Congress of Soviets, held on May 23 to pick delegates to the Petrograd meeting. One hundred seventy-six delegates, representing 36,000 workers in 10 large factories and mines, including those of

[94] Ibid., pp. 186–87; Korolivskii, Rubach, and Suprunenko, *Pobeda Sovetskoi vlasti na Ukraine*, p. 157.

[95] Zaitsev, "Kak my tvorili oktiabr'," p. 137.

[96] Institut istorii, *Bol'shevistskie organizatsii Ukrainy*, pp. 184–85. A report from the Bolshevik *Donetsk proletarii* is cited. The meeting was not quite unanimous, for one of the placards read: "Neither separate peace with Wilhelm nor secret agreements with English and French capitalists." Note the same slogan in Iuzovka in fig. 8.2.

[97] Kuranov, "Sovety na Artemovshchine," p. 176.

Gorlovka and Shcherbinovka, and in 150 smaller mines, gathered for the discussion and voting. The contest for influence involved Gruzman and Trubitsyn, a Menshevik-defensist emissary from Petrograd who had been active in the Shcherbinovka area since mid-March. Gruzman had done his work thoroughly, and the delegates were clearly pro-Bolshevik. A first ballot was disputed by the Mensheviks on the ground of disproportionate representation, and there were threats to telegraph Petrograd for intervention. In the end a secret ballot was taken with all the representatives voting. Gruzman received 102 votes, and his fellow Bolshevik, Sementsev, got 86 votes. Trubitsyn received only 62, and other candidates fewer.[98]

The July Days and the subsequent wave of opposition to the Bolsheviks throughout Russia did nothing to enhance the status of the party in Iuzovka. Along with the first news of the disorders in Petrograd came a rumor that the Bolsheviks had murdered Kerenskii. The needle workers refused to continue the rental of their quarters to the Bolsheviks, forcing them to move out.[99] A special session of the Iuzovka soviet was called to discuss the Petrograd events and to hear a report of a visit to the front by a member of the soviet in the wake of the failure of Kerenskii's June offensive. Two hundred deputies gathered on July 8 for the special session. Only five or six of these were Bolsheviks, approximately half of the ten Bolsheviks who were members of the soviet at the time. Of the leaders of the group, only Zaitsev was present, for Zalmaev was in Ekaterinoslav, and Alferov was busy trying to organize at the Rykovskii mines.[100]

The evening started badly. The Socialist-Revolutionary deputy who reported on the conditions at the front told tale after tale of how "Bolshevik units" had fled in panic from the battle, throwing the wounded off railway cars to make room for themselves. Twenty deputies, none of them Bolsheviks, spoke that evening, adding fuel to the flames. Zaitsev found the atmosphere so threatening that he casually sat on a windowsill, prepared to jump out if violence erupted. Nonetheless, he screwed up his courage and proposed a resolution "greeting the avant-garde of the Petrograd workers

[98] Borshchevskii, *Rabochii klass i sovety*, vol. 1, pp. 53–54; Institut istorii, *Bol'shevistskie organizatsii Ukrainy*, p. 165; Ostrogorskii, "Stranichki iz istorii," pp. 14–15. Ostrogorskii claims that another fourteen thousand workers in the district lacked representation. This testifies to the shortage of political organizers in the Donbass at that time.

[99] Zaitsev, "Kak my tvorili oktiabr'," p. 136; Institut istorii, *Bol'shevistskie organizatsii Ukrainy*, p. 924.

[100] Zaitsev, "Kak my tvorili oktiabr'," p. 136.

who took up arms to struggle for the power of the soviets." Only a few scattered votes were given in support of Zaitsev, while "a whole forest of hands went up for [the Socialist-Revolutionary] resolution, condemning the uprising of the Petrograd workers."[101]

The hostility to the Bolsheviks went beyond the single meeting of the soviet. In mid-July the weekly meeting of the Bolsheviks, attended by twenty members, was informed of a decision to move the seat of the Iuzovka-Makeevka-Petrovskii Committee out of the settlement since committee members arriving for meetings were being systematically arrested by the local militia, making the committee's existence insupportable.[102] Suglitskii reported from Vetka that the formerly flourishing Bolshevik organization there was now half underground, and that there were threats to beat, or even murder, Bolshevik activists. A member of the local soviet's executive committee had formally forbidden Suglitskii to speak or appear at public meetings, though he refused to put the order in writing. One of the Bolshevik activists had been arrested in Iuzovka for reading a letter from Lenin to the workers. On the positive side, Suglitskii wrote that the district Bolshevik committee had resumed its work, with Zalmaev as chairman.[103] The Mensheviks and the Socialist-Revolutionaries sometimes went to dramatic lengths to press their point against the Bolsheviks. At one Donbass mine two thousand Donbass miners kneeled with bared heads in front of a crowd of five thousand, and repeated the words of a leader. "We swear, by our children, by God, by the heaven and earth, and by all things that we hold sacred in the world, that we will never relinquish the freedom bought with blood on the 28th of February, 1917; believing in the Social Revolutionaries and the Mensheviks, we swear we will never listen to the Leninists for they, the Bolshevik-Leninists are leading Russia to ruin with their agitation."[104]

A report by a representative of the Donbass–Krivoi Rog Oblast' Committee of Bolsheviks to the Sixth Party Congress, convened in Petrograd on

[101] Ibid.

[102] Institut istorii, *Bol'shevistskie organizatsii Ukrainy*, pp. 557–58.

[103] Ibid., pp. 566–68. The reference is evidently to the Iuzovka-Makeevka-Petrovskii Committee. One of the achievements claimed by Suglitskii was success in fighting tendencies within the party rank and file toward joining in an alliance with the Menshevik Internationalists. Similar reports of threatened violence against Bolsheviks at this time are given in Kuranov, "Sovety na Artemovshchine," p. 179.

[104] Trotsky, *History of the Russian Revolution*, p. 792.

July 26, claimed sixteen thousand members as of July 1, but this must have declined sharply even before the congress.[105] Here and there in the Donbass, there were pockets of Bolshevik influence. Shcherbinovka was a hotbed of radicalism. At the end of July, a Bolshevik was elected chairman of the local soviet, though, as he himself testified later, the majority in the soviet were nonparty people sympathizing with the Bolsheviks.[106] The Bolshevik group in Gorlovka and Shcherbinovka was at that time in favor of an immediate local seizure of power by force of arms, declaring the soviet to be the sole authority. The group had to be restrained by Gruzman from "uncoordinated moves that would harm the party."[107] The district, with its thirty-six thousand miners, had in mid-May adopted Bolshevik-sponsored resolutions against the war, and called for "All Power to the Soviets," along with nationalization of banks, industry, and landlords' lands. In June the mine committees had begun to implement workers' control, and mine and factory executives had started leaving the area.[108]

Alerted by the July Days in Petrograd, the Ekaterinoslav soviet decided on dissolution of the Red Guard.[109] Part of the June raid on the Bolshevik offices in Iuzovka involved a search for arms. The specter of armed uprising was real throughout Russia, and had been an integral part of Bolshevik planning since 1905, but nowhere was this more so than in the Donbass, where explosives were used in everyday work, and firearms had been a "normal" part of social and political discourse from the earliest days of the revolutionary movement. From the beginning of June, the Lugansk Bolsheviks were setting up armed units, obtaining weapons from garrison stores or taking them out of the places in which they had been hidden after the defeat of the December uprising in 1905.[110] The July Days gave

[105] "Mestnye organizatsii RSDRP(b)," pp. 115–16. As noted, the founding conference of the regional committee in mid-July claimed only 13,648 members.

[106] Kazimirchuk, "Revoliutsionnoe dvizhenie," p. 52.

[107] Ostrogorskii, "Stranichki iz istorii," pp. 16–17; "Sh. A. Gruzman," p. 372.

[108] For the number of workers in the district in 1917, see Kazimirchuk, "Revoliutsionnoe dvizhenie," p. 40. The adoption of the resolutions is noted in Institut istorii, *Bol'shevistskie organizatsii Ukrainy*, pp. 162–63. Kuranov, "Sovety na Artemovshchine," p. 177, credits a Bolshevik named Kizhniakov with piloting the resolution through a joint mass meeting of miners of the Shcherbinovka, Nelepovka, and Nikitovka mines. This is evidently the same meeting at which Gruzman was delegated to the First All-Russian Congress of Soviets, and at which he is said to have proposed "All Power to the Soviets." The early institution of workers' control in the area is discussed in Modestov, *Rabochee i professional'noe dvizhenie*, p. 108.

[109] *Russkie vedomosti* (July 7, 1917).

[110] Voroshilov, "Iz nedavno," p. 262.

impetus to anti-Bolshevik sentiment in both the public and the political establishment. What is more, the interpretation placed on the events in Petrograd lent legitimacy to putting the Bolsheviks beyond the pale of the united democratic camp. In the Donbass, even more than in most of Russia, it appeared that the Bolsheviks were on their way from unpopularity to total ignominy.

Labor and Production in the Summer of 1917

There were, however, other winds blowing in the summer of 1917, and these were ultimately to help revive the Bolshevik fortunes. Starting in March, enterprises began to cut back or to close altogether, and the closures gained momentum as the months passed. By the start of May, the acid factory that had been set up to supply saltpeter and nitric acid for the artillery shells produced in Iuzovka had cut its staff in half compared with December 1916.[111] In mid-June Voroshilov wrote from Lugansk that the flight of industrialists from the region was leaving workers without money or food.[112] The first expulsions of factory directors by the workers were reported in March. By June, unpopular engineers and mine managers had been chased out of the Rykovskii, Tikhonov, and Bogodukhov mines, and from the New Russia factory, and pay raises were extracted from directors at the threat of violence, though at this point there was as yet no attempt by the workers to take over the management of the enterprises.[113] The *Torgovo-promyshlennaia gazeta* commented that "one may note a significant weakening of interest of the factory owners in their affairs, such as providing the enterprises with materials, fuel, and other necessities. All this creates a basis for additional closing of enterprises."[114]

By August the closure of mines and factories had become a mass phenomenon, though it was primarily the smaller enterprises that succumbed at this stage. In an attempt to maintain supplies to high-priority users, the government had imposed price controls on coal, raised wages, and blocked

[111] Gaponenko, "K voprosu o chislennosti," p. 161.

[112] Institut istorii, *Bol'shevistskie organizatsii Ukrainy*, p. 177.

[113] See Chernomaz, *Bor'ba rabochego klassa Ukrainy*, p. 33, for expulsion of managers in Kiev and Kharkov. For extraction of pay raises by threats and expulsion of mine management, see Gudzenko, *Robitnichii kontrol' i natsionalizatsiia*, doc. 38, p. 102.

[114] *Torgovo-promyshlennaia gazeta*, no. 101 (1917), cited in Lozinski, "Vremennoe pravitel'stvo," pt. 1, p. 164.

the sale of coal to small local coal merchants by imposing a ban on the haulage of coal by horse and cart.[115] The smaller mines, serving local needs, were driven out of business by these decrees. The subsequent unemployment brought the Metal Workers' Union to publish an appeal addressed to the councils of elders in all Donbass factories to employ only union members, and to refrain from hiring nonlocal workers.[116] Sergeev notified the Bolshevik Central Committee that *Proletarii*, the newspaper inaugurated in July, had to be closed temporarily in August. The workers' funds had been exhausted due to lockouts of the metal workers and a dragging strike of unskilled workers in Kharkov.[117]

At the start of September an estimated one hundred thousand Donbass miners and fifty thousand metal workers were unemployed.[118] In September it was calculated that the minimum coal supply needed to maintain the economy was 125 million puds per month, but that the Donbass could ship no more than 85 to 87 million puds. Metallurgy was receiving only 60 percent of its normal coal supply, and other industries only 20 percent.[119] By October, the flight of administrators and industrialists was general. Some were being arrested, and during a single week in October two hundred Donbass mines closed down.[120] Economic hardship and political tensions were feeding on each other. The breakdown of the economy heightened the suspicions between workers and employers, and the lack of mutual confidence frustrated any effort that might have been made to improve the conditions of the economy.[121]

There were numerous attempts throughout 1917 to alleviate the situation. The workers tried to improve their economic condition: unions and consumer cooperatives were established throughout the Donbass; food and supply committees were set up in individual enterprises, either independently or in conjunction with a local soviet, and, as in Iuzovka, with the

[115] Kuranov, "Sovety na Artemovshchine," p. 171.

[116] Vilisova et al., *Bor'ba za vlast' sovetov v Donbasse*, p. 88.

[117] Ibid., p. 93.

[118] Modestov, *Rabochee i professional'noe dvizhenie*, p. 115.

[119] *Tret'ia konferentsiia*, p. 10, report of engineer Priadkin. The estimate of minimum needs appears exaggerated, for it represents an annual total equal to the 1913 peak production of 1,500 million puds.

[120] Vilisova et al., *Bor'ba za vlast' sovetov v Donbasse*, p. 141; Gaponenko, *Rabochii klass Rossii v 1917 godu*, p. 69.

[121] Kuranov, "Sovety na Artemovshchine," p. 176, is explicit in linking the radicalization of the Donbass workers to the economic crisis and to the failure of the provisional government's industrial policies. He gives no credit to the activity of the Bolsheviks, for which the editors of *Letopis' revoliutsii* criticize him harshly. The article appeared in 1927.

factory administration. At the end of June, delegates from the Nikopol-Mariupol factory turned to the Iuzovka soviet for help in supplying them with sufficient coal to prevent a shutdown of their factory, and to build up a reserve for the winter. They noted with anxiety the growing number of lockouts in mines, the general neglect of maintenance, and the difficulty in obtaining coal cars for transport of fuel.[122] In another instance, the First Working Miners' Artel' of Russia took over the operation of a mine abandoned by its owners, organizing the hundred remaining miners into shareholders in a cooperative enterprise. The artel' advertised for another hundred members, fifty of whom were to be coal cutters. Members were required to purchase at least one share in the co-op, at a price of ten rubles.[123]

Yet all the efforts, large and small, were in vain. Russia's economy had neither the infrastructure nor the organization to sustain its production efforts. Transport of coal and iron declined at an increasing rate throughout 1917, and repeated efforts to revive the railways had no effect. In 1917, only 644 million puds of coal were hauled, compared with 875 million pud in the previous year, and 1,175 million puds in 1915. By December, monthly haulage had declined to 29 million puds, compared with 73 million puds in January.[124] The collapse of transport meant a shortage of food and raw materials for the enterprises of the Donbass, and a fuel and metal crisis for Russia's industry and urban populace. Despite growth in the labor force of the metallurgy factories, production fell off sharply during 1917, and by the end of the year twenty-three out of sixty-two blast furnaces in South Russia were shut down completely, while another eighteen were working at reduced capacity.[125] A survey of fifty-eight mines, employing an average of five hundred miners each in September 1917, showed that only twenty-one of them were working around the clock. Lack of transport and other technical equipment was the most frequent reason given for reduced production.[126]

Table 8.1 allows a comparison of the relatively successful striving for

[122] Vilisova et al., *Bor'ba za vlast' sovetov v Donbasse*, p. 65. See Kuranov, "Sovety na Artemovshchine," p. 172, for a similar appeal by the Konstantinovka workers at the end of July. "By working harder you save yourselves and us. Give coal!" See also *VOSR* (*dokumenty i materialy*), vol. 1, p. 146, for the Moscow soviet's resolution to send a delegation to the Donbass in October to prevent mine closures and assure supplies to the city.

[123] *Izvestiia Iuzovskogo soveta*, no. 43 (October 26, 1917).

[124] *Narodnoe khoziaistvo*, no. 1 (March 1918), p. 17.

[125] Ibid. p. 21.

[126] Lozinskii, "Vremennoe pravitel'stvo," pt. 1, p. 152.

TABLE 8.1

Donbass Coal and Pig Iron Production, 1916–1917 (Millions of Puds)

	Coal Production				Iron Production	
Month	1916	Pud/Miner	1917	Pud/Miner	1916	1917
January	118	721	123	535	13.9	12.9
February	117	660	114	492	13.4	9.8
March	131	746	116	536	14.9	10.1
April	76	737	94	424	12.0	12.5
May	110	636	100	472	14.0	13.7
June	116	663	97	469	14.5	11.7
July	114	620	90	437	15.4	11.3
August	108	566	86	422	15.7	11.7
September	116	602	82	423	16.2	11.0
October	121	602	86	442	16.4	9.6
November	134	n.a.	84	n.a.	n.a.	n.a.
December	112	n.a.	67	n.a.	n.a.	n.a.

Source: Production: *Narodnoe khoziaistvo,* no. 1, (1918), pp. 17, 19. Productivity: Lozinski, "Vremennoe pravitel'stvo," pt. 1, p. 150.

production in 1916 and the decline and collapse of iron and coal in 1917. The size of the labor force of the Donbass mines did not diminish during 1917. At the end of the summer it surpassed the numbers of miners working during all the summer months. Monthly productivity rose in October, when men had returned from the fields to the mines, supplementing the numbers of women, children, and war prisoners who were the mainstay of the labor force; nevertheless production was only 442 puds per worker, compared with 535 puds in January of 1917, and 721 puds in January 1916. Throughout 1917 productivity was falling, and the fall gained momentum with each passing month.

A conference of mine committees held in Debaltsevo at the beginning of October pointed out the deteriorated state of the mines, the erosion of real wages, and the semistarvation that were demoralizing and physically weakening the miners, but added three political factors as well: the continuation of the war, "which is killing everything"; the first signs of counterrevolution, as anti-Soviet cossack groups organized in the south following the failure of the Kornilov rebellion; and the indifference of the mine administrators to their duty, as evidenced by their abandonment of numerous mines.[127] The conference was not merely a forum for propaganda, but worked to produce a program to improve conditions. A four-point resolution was approved, calling for the setting of a minimum wage and the fixing of food prices; permission for workers' organizations to import food; legislation dealing with supervision of industrial operations, including local institutions of workers' control; and provision of adequate supplies of rails, horses, and other necessities. This was a radical program, calling, as it did, for workers' control, but it was by no means revolutionary. There was no talk of nationalization or of chasing out mine and factory owners. Rather, the tone was patriotic, and the owners and managers were condemned for abandoning their responsibilities. The resolutions reflected the growing frustration of the workers as negotiations with the employers proved fruitless. The workers were clearly determined to maintain their source of livelihood, despite the difficult conditions and the growing polarization between workers and employers.

A Iuzovka committee for the implementation of the Debaltsevo resolutions was set up almost immediately. The committee's composition illustrates the approach taken by the leaders of the Iuzovka workers to industrial and economic problems in the town at this time. It was to consist of five members of the soviet; four members of the committee of elders of the mines and factory; two representatives of the union of metal workers; two members of the coal union; two members of the engineering-technical staff; two representatives of the office workers; three representatives of the workers' cooperative; three representatives of the Iuzovka duma; and two members of the factory's management.[128] There was a clear majority of representatives of workers' institutions, but representatives of management and of the technical staff were accorded legitimacy and included in the committee. The polarization that was becoming more extreme in Russia in these months was much less evident here. Rather, there was a genuine effort to alleviate the hardships of society by guaranteeing a continuation of

[127] *Izvestiia Iuzovskogo soveta*, no. 39 (October 17, 1917), p. 3.

[128] The announcement of the committee's formation is in ibid., no. 40 (October 19, 1917), p. 1. No reports of meetings or activities of the committee appeared in subsequent issues of the newspaper available to me.

activity in the New Russia factory and mines, providing employment for the town's population.

The Food Crisis of 1917

This effort, however, was to be frustrated by the inreasing severity of the food shortage that had been growing since 1915. In early 1917 numerous local emergency measures were suggested. Awareness of the impending crisis brought the Kharkov Provincial Soviet of Soldiers' Deputies to suggest immediate release of 5 percent of the soldiers for the spring planting period. General Brusilov accepted this suggestion, and within his command deputies were chosen to organize this operation among the front-line units.[129] Only toward the end of June, when there was danger that even the diminished local harvest might not be gathered in time, was there an intensified effort to divert labor into agriculture. Field brigades made up of unemployed workers, war prisoners, and soldiers on leave were organized by the local Donbass supply boards, and sent to gather the harvest.[130] A meeting of representatives of the mines and factories of the Gorlovka-Shcherbinovka district soviets resolved to send 5 percent of the local workers for work in the fields and machine repair, and to support the request of the Donbass Central Food Commission that horses be released from mines and factories for the use of machinery-repair crews. A nine-person commission was set up to supervise the formation of the field crews, and to determine the wages and payment procedures for the worker-peasants.[131] Numerous soviets in the Donbass were setting up local workshops for the repair of agricultural implements, aiding the peasantry, and receiving payment in kind to alleviate local scarcities.[132]

Both the radicalization and the fragmentation of society were intensified by the inability of the central and local authorities to meet the needs of the populace. By October, "disorders and excesses" were breaking out because of food problems. Miners in the vicinity of Iuzovka were working only twelve shifts a month, instead of the eighteen shifts scheduled, because they

[129] *Birzhevye vedomosti* (March 23, 1917).

[130] Kuranov, "Sovety na Artemovshchine," pp. 174–75.

[131] Ostrogorskii, "Stranichki iz istorii," pp. 19–20.

[132] Kuranov, "Sovety na Artemovshchine," pp. 174–75.

were spending time searching the countryside for food.[133] Individual shop committees of the New Russia factory advertised their willingness to trade iron and other necessities to the peasants in return for grain.[134]

Iuzovka was in a better position than were most Donbass settlements. The Peski farm supplied approximately half the needs of the population of all New Russia Co. factory and mine settlements in and around Iuzovka.[135] In addition, the New Russia Co. owned large tracts of land on which Iuzovka district peasants were tenants. In September 1917, all the produce of these farms went to the workers of the New Russia Co. under the strict supervision of the Central Food Committee of the factory, in which both management and labor were active participants. Suglitskii describes the situation of the peasants as "relatively comfortable" at this time.[136] Additional testimony about the relatively privileged situation of Iuzovka comes from a discussion among the miners at the New Russia Co.'s Smolianin mines. They were concerned about repairs for children's shoes, and distressed that their payday had been postponed. The workers were anxious to be paid while the autumn fair was still in session, for there were goods to be bought there. The company, however, had no cash on hand, and neither did the Iuzovka banks. The workers had no alternative but to await the arrival of the payroll from Petrograd. Only in third place on the agenda did they include the question of the quality of the flour that they received. The mine's baker reported to the meeting that he had received 510 puds of rye flour from the mill at the New Russia Co.'s farm. The miners decided that the rye flour should be used to bake bread for the prisoners of war, and that the Central Food Committee of the New Russia Co. should be asked to allot

[133] *Izvestiia Iuzovskogo soveta*, no. 39 (October 17, 1917), p. 2. In the factory, management demanded a minimum of twenty-five days' work each month as a condition of eligibility for factory-subsidized food.

[134] Ibid., no. 41 (October 21, 1917), p. 3.

[135] The population of Iuzovka in mid-1917 was about fifty-five thousand. Of these, some twelve thousand were New Russia miners and factory workers. The total labor force of the company at this time was about twenty thousand, and the total population of all the company's settlements about eighty thousand. *Gorno-zavodskoe delo*, no. 3 (1917), p. 15096, gives the "standard calculation" of food needs as one *funt* (409.5 grams) of flour per day for city dwellers and one and a half funts for coal miners. *Vestnik truda*, nos. 7–8 (10–11) (July–August 1921), p. 3, sets a "minimum norm" of ten to eleven puds per year per "eater." In either case, the Peski harvest of approximately seventy-five hundred tons of grain amounted to over half the population's needs of thirteen thousand to fourteen thousand tons.

[136] See the report of Suglitskii to the Bolshevik secretariat in Petrograd, September 6, 1917, in Institut istorii, *Bol'shevistskie organizatsii Ukrainy*, pp. 607–8.

them 100 puds of white flour from Kogan's mill, and 150 puds from Fillipova's mill.[137] This is hardly the response of starving people. At the same time, the supply of white bread was limited, for a special decision of the food committee was required to allot white bread for the fifty typhus patients in the factory hospital, and the Iuzovka soviet had to approve the allocation of ten puds of sugar to the charitable organization "A Cup of Tea."

In addition, the soviet heard a report on food shortages, but the problem was diagnosed as disorganization in the food committee rather than objective circumstances.[138] The factory-mine joint food committee was, in fact, swiftly reorganized. A New Russia Co. memorandum noted management's readiness to give the new committee a trial period of one month's responsibility for the workers' food supply. The company would pay the salaries of the new committee, and would continue to subsidize the foodstuffs purchased by the committee at government prices and distributed by ration to the workers at lower prices.[139] The subsidies, which Kir'ianov noted as having cut food prices by 50 percent for the workers of the New Russia Co., amounted to sums ranging from 97 kopeks to 2 rubles 85 kopeks per shift worked at various mines around Iuzovka. Miners' wages at this time ranged anywhere from 3.85 to 12 rubles per shift.[140]

Food shortages played a large part in the disorganization of Donbass life in 1917, and in the dissatisfaction and consequent radicalization of the populace. Yet it would appear from the example of Iuzovka that where there had been some foresight, and where some degree of social coordination could be achieved, the food shortage in itself was not fatal. Hughes had considered the proper provisioning of his workers to be no less important than the control of raw materials. In 1917 this made all the difference between debilitating hunger and a minimal but adequate diet, which apparently allowed the miners to enjoy for a little longer their traditional indulgence in white bread.

In the autumn of 1917, when the polarization of social relations was tearing Russia apart, there was still sufficient cooperation in Iuzovka to maintain the joint efforts of management and the workers in the Central

[137] *Izvestiia Iuzovskogo soveta*, no. 28 (September 16, 1917), p. 4.

[138] Ibid., p. 3; no. 39 (October 17, 1917), protocol of the October 10 session of the Iuzovka soviet.

[139] DOGIA, F. 6, op. 1, d. 13, p. 5.

[140] TsGIAL, F. 37, op. 75, d. 199, p. 53. Report of the district engineer, September 9, 1917.

Food Committee. Even in mid-October, when Svitsyn was threatening to close the factory, and the workers were demanding that work carry on and that they be allowed to earn their living as before, cooperation on the food committee continued unquestioned. But this was a rare exception to the failure of the efforts to unite employers and workers.

Labor Relations: Attempts to Bridge the Social Gap

The most important effort in the direction of social integration was the attempt to create a joint conference of the government, the employers, and the representatives of the mine and factory workers of the Donbass to maintain the society and economy of the region. At the end of March 1917, a committee representing the Association of Southern Coal and Steel Producers met with representatives of twenty-one Donbass soviets, with the participation of Duma members Tuliakov, now the representative of the provisional government for Kharkov province, and Dobrovolskii.

Engineer Fenin, one of the more enlightened industrialists, gave clear expression to the ambiguous feelings of the employers. At the opening of the conference he spoke to the workers' representatives of the need to control their movement, to hold it back and not let it grow to a point at which it could no longer be restrained. Explaining his colleagues' participation in this new constellation of forces, he added: "We are looked upon with mistrust, and for us it is very difficult to speak to the masses of workers, and so we turn to you, remembering that we have a single common cause."[141] In the two days of the meeting, broad areas of agreement were mapped out. Both sides agreed to petition the government to consider Donbass mine and factory settlements on a par with the army at the front for priority of food supply. There was also a pious declaration that all efforts would be made to improve living conditions, sanitary and housing conditions, and cultural facilities for the workers. Though the employers objected to the participation of representatives of the factory and mine committees in administration of the eight-hour day, they agreed to workers' involvement in supervising mine safety measures. A network of conciliation chambers (*primiritel'nye kamery*) was set up, with equal representation of workers and employers, to resolve grievances regarding labor relations and individual workers' com-

[141] Chernomaz, *Bor'ba rabochego klassa Ukrainy*, pp. 30–31.

plaints. A central chamber was established in Kharkov to serve as a court of appeals.

But at the heart of the conference was the question of wages and hours. The workers made it clear that recognition of the eight-hour day was a symbolic demand and that they would work as many hours as the army and the country needed, provided they were paid properly for overtime work. The industrialists then gave their blessing to the eight-hour day.[142] In addition, a wage agreement was reached, granting an immediate increase of 50 percent in miners' pay, and setting a minimum per-norm wage of two and a half rubles. The employers' conditions for granting these concessions were that productivity per shift should not fall below the level of the second half of 1916, and that miners should be required to work no fewer than twenty-two full days per month. Fulfillment of these conditions would have already meant a new intensification of labor efforts in the declining coal industry. A commission of workers' representatives was set up to work out an overall set of wage norms for all classes of mine work. These norms were to be presented for ratification to a workers' conference scheduled for the end of April, and then negotiated with the industrialists.[143]

Since few representatives of the metallurgy industry attended the March conference, it was suggested that the steel producers hold a separate conference to work out similar agreements with their workers. The success of the coal producers and the miners in reaching agreements on wages and conditions appeared to augur well, and on April 11 a delegation of metallurgy employers, headed by A. A. Svitsyn, general manager of the New Russia Co., met with workers' delegates to consider a seven-point agenda covering the same points that had been discussed in the coal industry.

The first session managed to find common ground regarding food supply. Gurevich, representing the workers, gave details of places where the food shortage was causing workers to fall ill, lowering the productivity of industry. Given the importance of metallurgy, this affected the entire country. He

[142] *Birzhevye vedomosti* (April 6, 1917), noting the agreement to inaugurate the eight-hour day in the Donbass, expressed a fear of further reduction of coal production. The same issue also carried a report of a joint meeting of soviets of workers' and of soldiers' deputies that voted against the eight-hour day for the industrial and manufacturing enterprises of Ekaterinoslav. Although the newspaper gives no details of the reasons, it may be assumed that the workers feared a loss of wages if hours were limited. The agreement covering the coal mines provided for unlimited overtime at time and a half.

[143] Detailed reports of this and the two succeeding conferences are found in *Konferentsii*. The decisions of the first conference are given on p. 62. See also *Birzhevye vedomosti* (March 31, 1917).

also noted that there were cases in which employers refused to supply some product to the workers, claiming that it was unavailable due to supply shortages. Often it turned out that in fact the employers had the product in their storehouses, and "such unfounded declarations aroused a certain lack of confidence." The question of confidence may seem marginal in the context of the great changes that were taking place, but as Fenin's statement indicates, the social gaps that existed had been widened and reinforced over the years. The "cultured society" and the "benighted folk" had little or no understanding of each other. All attempts through the years to establish institutions that would bridge such gaps had been blocked by both the government and the employers, each for its own reasons. A time of crisis was not a propitious occasion for experiments in social cooperation, and without precedents of mutual trust and recognition on which to build, the crisis was to result in the destruction of Russia's society.

On the food question, Svitsyn found formulations that satisfied both sides. He presented the findings of the Ekaterinoslav commissar for food, G. V. de St. Laurent, who noted that the impassable state of many local roads and the devotion of all available rural labor to the planting of spring crops had caused a temporary halt in grain haulage, leading to shortages. Svitsyn suggested that the conference ask the government to decree a temporary ban on the export of grain from the province, as well as a release from the obligation to provide grain to the mines of the Don Cossack territory. The workers added three points of their own: the establishment of a joint worker-employer food purchasing commission, the "democratization" of the factory consumer cooperatives, and the lowering of prices of iron goods to the peasants to encourage them to sell grain and buy implements. The employers accepted all three points.[144]

When the question of wages and hours came up, the atmosphere changed. Sandomirskii, a Menshevik, who in August would chair the Ekaterinoslav Province Congress of Soviets, presented the issue for the workers. He explained that adoption of the eight-hour day was a matter of principle. Gototskii, manager of the Alexandrovsk factory, claimed that adoption of the eight-hour day meant, in fact, a wage increase of 32 percent, and that given the labor shortage it was impossible to implement. He claimed that time and a half for overtime would cost four million rubles a year, at a time when the entire dividend to the shareholders amounted to

[144] The discussion of the food problem is in *Konferentsii*, pp. 48–49. Pankratova, *Fabzavkomy*, p. 37, notes similar demands by workers' representatives in Petrograd.

four and a half million. Genak, speaking for the Petrovskii workers, stated that the Petrovskii factory had earned fifteen million in profits during the previous year, and could well afford to invest four million in additional pay for its workers. Sandomirskii, in his reply to the employers, pointed out the gains in productivity to be expected from an eight-hour day, and rejected the patriotic moralizing of the employers who called on the workers to sacrifice in support of the army. "What about the wife and child of the soldier? He is at the front, and they are hungry and cold working in the mines." He added a lesson of his own in moral economy. A hungry, ignorant worker works badly. Advanced technology demands developed, productive workers. Svitsyn countered with national economic calculations. What would this cost the country? How was Russia to compete after the war?

Though these exchanges illustrate the tension that lay just below the surface, there was no expression here of the outlook that class antagonisms were irreconcilable.[145] Rather, Fenin's view that there was a common interest appears to have been shared, perhaps more out of perceived necessity than choice on either side. On this basis, shaky though it may have been, the conference ended in a temporary compromise. The employers accepted the eight-hour day and the workers' demand for extra overtime pay. Minimum wages were kept in line with the employers' original offer of two and a half rubles per day, and the lowest-paid categories were to get immediate wage increases. The workers' delegates accepted this, explaining their concessions as a recognition of the current "threatening situation" in Russia, and calling on the workers to continue working without interruption. They also called for a general conference of employers and workers to be held in Kharkov at the beginning of May to settle all their remaining disputes with the employers.[146] The workers' representatives evidently felt that a general conference would enjoy the relatively benevolent influence of the coal producers, softening the hostility of the metallurgists. In this they failed to recognize the power of the latter, who represented large, heavily capitalized enterprises, as well as the strong personalities and uncompromising outlooks of such individuals as Svitsyn.

On May 2, a letter was sent to the delegates of the South Russian Conference of Soviets and Representatives of Factory Committees and Trade Unions, who were working out proposals of a general agreement on wages

[145] See Bonnell, *Roots of Rebellion*, p. 7, for a discussion of the origins and spread of the notion of irreconcilable class antagonisms among the Russian workers.

[146] The debate on wages and hours is in *Konferentsii*, pt. 2, pp. 48–49, 51–52, 63–64.

and working conditions, notifying them of the formation of a committee made up of representatives of all sections of the Association of Southern Coal and Steel Producers, and empowered to meet with the workers to examine the implications of all their demands, including the eight-hour day, on which there had been earlier agreement. The workers' conference had already drawn up a twenty-one-point proposal for wages and conditions, and sent it to the employers on May 3, requesting their answer by six o'clock that evening. In this letter the workers also inquired whether the signatories to the May 2 letter, von Ditmar, Sokolov, and Fomin, were authorized to make decisions in the name of the committee, and whether such decisions would obligate all the employers.

The workers' proposals included a minimum wage of four rubles for eight hours' work, with women and children getting equal pay when doing the same work as men. The minimum wage for women doing light work was to be three and a half rubles a day, and for fifteen- to seventeen-year olds two and a half rubles a day. Children under fifteen years old were not to be employed, and the employers were to remove them from the factories and mines within two months, meanwhile paying them a minimum of two rubles for a six-hour day. Basic consumer products were to be sold at July 1916 prices, and workers were to oversee their sale. A scale of wage increases was presented for all workers earning less than twelve rubles per day, to be retroactive to April 1. Employers who closed their plants or parts of them would still be responsible for payment of wages to their workers. The same was to apply to mines closed due to flooding, gas explosions, or collapse. A final point stipulated that workers occupied with the affairs of soviets, factory committees, or other public institutions were to be paid by their employers as before.

As might have been anticipated, the employers were unable to answer by the six o'clock deadline (they noted in their response that they had received the proposals only at three-thirty, and that the matters were "complex and responsible"). Von Ditmar, who signed the reply, pointed out gaps in the workers' proposals ("What are your decisions regarding conciliation chambers and trade unions?") and promised an answer to be delivered by an authorized team of negotiators. He proposed that the workers prepare a similarly empowered delegation.

When the industrialists' answer was ready on May 6, it was further than ever from satisfying the workers' demands. Although the principles of the eight-hour day and time and a half for overtime were accepted, they were to be based on a basic wage of two and a half rubles per day, including food, cost-of-living payments, and all other fringe benefits. The money wage for an eight-hour day was to be calculated at one and a half rubles, far below what had been the norm until that time. The principle of equal pay for equal work was rejected and women were to receive only 60 to 80 percent of a man's wage. Citing the war crisis, the employers refused to dispense with child labor. They contended that even this partial acceptance of the workers' demands would raise the wage bill by 65 million rubles a year, and that had they agreed to all the workers' demands the cost would have been 228 million rubles.

To no one's great surprise, the workers' conference summarily rejected the industrialists' counteroffer, while the industrialists covered themselves by sending telegrams to Prime Minister Lvov and five other ministers in his government pointing out the concessions they had offered, and complaining that the workers threatened industrial action if the employers did not capitulate to all their demands. The industrialists stated that meeting the workers' demands would have meant such a catastrophic rise in the prices of coal and metal that they were not only economically unable to pay the amounts involved, but also had no moral right to do so, and therefore were passing the decision on to the provisional government. Forty years of subservience to government rulings had conditioned the industrialists for this moment, and they acted true to historical form.[147]

Through the summer of 1917, conditions deteriorated steadily. Having failed to establish any solid understanding with the workers, the employers could only regroup. The workers did the same, and even the tentative efforts at a cooperative solution of the food crisis faltered. Nevertheless, there were almost no work stoppages initiated by the workers. There had been a strike in the Petrovskii works in February due to irregularities in the supply of food from the company store. It ended with the workers threatened with dismissal and mobilization. In mid-August, a two-week strike of the Union Co. factory and mines in Makeevka, demanding a six-hour workday, ended inconclusively.[148] Although labor relations were tense throughout the year

[147] The exchange of offers and counteroffers, and the industrialists' telegram to the government, are in *Konferentsii*, pt. 3. The workers' proposals were signed by Popov, Sandomirskii, and Zotov. The letter of May 6 with the employers' counteroffer was sent in the name of the metallurgy section of the association, even though von Ditmar had informed the workers of the formation of a joint commission. It would appear that the metallurgy section's intransigence was not to the liking of the coal producers.

[148] TsGIAL, F. 37, op. 58, ed. khr. 187, pp. 52–54, 82, 102.

as the workers gained in strength and organization, there does not appear to have been anything like the 1916 strike wave in which tens of thousands went on strike all over the Donbass.

In 1916 there had been a half-day strike of 164 women working in the New Russia Co. brickyards.[149] There was no other strike in Iuzovka until the beginning of October 1917, when the electrical workers disconnected Svitsyn's house and the Vetka mine and took over the company's telephone and telegraph services, demanding a review of pay rates and the institution of an eight-hour day. At the same time, the workers at the Marten ovens instituted their own eight-hour day, dividing their work into three shifts. The strike lasted only one day, with the management agreeing to the demands on the condition that production would be maintained and that no additional workers would be needed. A commission formed of representatives of the soviet, the factory committee, the metallurgy union, and management investigated and reported that complete conversion to an eight-hour day would create a need for an additional 1,005 workers. In the light of these findings, and despite the tentative agreement that had been reached, all the workers from the Marten shop were fired for insisting on their eight-hour shift. The electrical shop, with the exception of the maintenance section, returned to work.[150] Two weeks later, the hired barbers of the town went on strike against their employers, opening a temporary shop of their own in which the customers were invited to pay whatever sum they wished for a haircut, with the proceeds divided among the strikers. Unfortunately, a multitude of strikebreakers, including soldiers, was willing to replace them in the established shops, and the strike collapsed.[151]

As was the case in the October strike in the New Russia factory, the workers' institutions, factory committees, soviets, and unions frequently found ways of arbitrating differences between labor and capital over local, particular grievances that had in earlier days been the subject of strikes. Despite the increasing radicalization around them, and their own deteriorating conditions, the people of Iuzovka appear to have been far from revolutionary extremism. Zaitsev suggests that Svitsyn's policy of "bread-and-sausage wages," along with the Menshevik-inspired defensist mood in the town, kept the factory workers peaceful even while the mines all around them were striking.[152]

[149] DOGIA, F. 10, op. 1, d. 13, p. 11.

[150] TsGIAL, F. 37, d. 58, ed. khr. 870, p. 198.

[151] *Izvestiia Iuzovskogo soveta*, no. 39 (October 17, 1917), pp. 1, 4.

[152] Zaitsev, "Kak my tvorili oktiabr'," p. 133.

The working of the conciliation council in the New Russia factory is illustrative. Reports appearing in the *Izvestiia Iuzovskogo soveta* indicate that the conciliation council of the factory was active through October 1917, achieved success in its actions, and enjoyed the respect of both employers and workers. A session on October 13 acceded to the request of the blast-furnace workers to transfer the assistant foreman, N. L. Emelianov, to other work because of his rude attitude toward the workers. At the same session, the council settled a disagreement over pay rates in one of the shops, and set criteria for future adjustments. Both management and workers had agreed in advance to accept the conciliation council's ruling.[153] Earlier, the Council of Elders (*Sovet starost*) had received with satisfaction the report that bad feelings in the factory hospital over what was seen as unfair distribution of foodstuffs had been solved by the conciliation council's decision to remove the housekeeper, Kissileva, from her post.[154]

The deteriorating relations between labor and capital found sharper expression in the wave of lockouts (and, to a lesser extent, plant seizures by workers) that spread through the Donbass at the end of the summer. A British observer was sent by his embassy to evaluate the situation, and at the end of September filed two documents: an official report and a personal letter of observation. In the letter, he writes:

> My own impression is that the whole thing [seizure of factories by the workers] has been very greatly exaggerated and this is partly due to the English employers here, who are only all too ready to make the worst of any situation that arises between them and their work-people. The workmen have been rottenly treated in the past, paid starvation wages, and kept down in every possible way, while the mills made huge profits: now they are getting their own back and the wonder to me is that they have not gone further than they have.

In his report, Dickinson cites attacks on French subjects at the Providence factory and mines and writes that British subjects coming from Iuzovka stated that the workers were expelling the British from the New Russia plant.[155] He had evidently met Alexander Cameron, Sr., his son, Alex-

[153] DOGIA, F. 6, op. 1, d. 13, p. 4. See also the report in *Izvestiia Iuzovskogo soveta*, no. 39 (October 17, 1917), p. 3.

[154] See the reports in *Izvestiia Iuzovskogo soveta*, no. 28 (September 16, 1917), p. 2; no. 30 (September 21, 1917), p. 3; and no. 41 (October 21, 1917), p. 4.

[155] FO, 395/109–188, p. 528, report to the Anglo-Russian Commission in Petrograd by D. Dickinson, September 29, 1917.

ander James Cameron, and their families, who left Iuzovka at about this time. A brother-in-law, Frederick Loxley, who intended to stay on, had been unceremoniously "wheelbarrowed" out of the factory by workers, and had returned to England with the Camerons.[156] While the British contingent in Iuzovka had dwindled to 101 souls by July 1917, it should be remembered that senior executives such as Glass and Revilon remained active in management through the end of the civil war. During 1917 they were in constant negotiation with the workers, and there is no record of any objection to their presence. The time-honored custom of wheelbarrowing people out was usually reserved for those immediate supervisors whom the workers found personally unbearable.

The full crisis in the Donbass came in the wake of an attempt by the minister of labor, Skobelev, to resolve the growing conflicts by broadening the rights of the factory committees that had been established by law at the end of April. In response to the "Skobelev circular," the Association of Southern Coal and Steel Producers resolved not to accept the status of the factory committees.[157] In part, this was a refusal to pay the wages of the growing number of officials and delegates carrying on workers' business on company time. In the New Russia factory, Glass and Revilon signed an order that as of November 1, only the delegates of the company store and the chairman of each shop committee, as members of the main factory committee, would be financed by the company.[158]

The final split between employers and workers came at the Third Conference of Coal and Steel Producers of South Russia, held in Kharkov at the end of September, and attended by 460 mine owners and metal industrialists.[159] Here there was little or no attempt at conciliation, but a demonstration of hostility and of the threats of force that characterized the relations then existing between capital and labor in the Donbass. The atmosphere reflected the sense of crisis that pervaded Russia at the time. It was also an expression of a resurgence of confidence among the conservative elements that they could stand successfully against the socialist movement. Together

[156] Letter of Kathleen Kay, daughter of Alexander James Cameron, February 6, 1990. F. S. Loxley is identified among those working in the New Russia factory in 1914, in DOGIA, F. 6, op. 9, d. 241, p. 3.

[157] Pankratova, *Fabzavkomy*, pp. 67–68.

[158] *Izvestiia Iuzovskogo soveta*, no. 41 (October 21, 1917), p. 4.

[159] The following account is based mainly on *Tret'ia konferentsiia*. The number of those attending, and an account of von Ditmar's speech at the opening session, are in *Rabochii put'*, no. 17 (September 22, 1917) (facsimile edition, Moscow: Partizdat, 1932).

with this, there existed the fear of an ongoing radicalization that made them abandon the attempts at conciliation and social unity that had marked much of their activity during the spring and early summer.

The industrialists had organized, and their conference included representatives from all the extractive and refining industries of Kharkov, Rostov, and Ekaterinoslav provinces, as well as the anthracite producers of the Don Cossack territory. All of these interests were coordinating their policies much more closely than at the time of the March conference, which, as von Ditmar noted in his opening speech, had not been planned, but was rather a spontaneous reaction necessitated by the events themselves.

By the time of the third conference, the employers were boycotting any contact with the commissars of the Ministry of Labor, as well as with representatives of the soviets and trade unions.[160] Speaker after speaker gave details of the deteriorating conditions in the coal and iron mines and in the factories. The assembled industrialists told tales of factory directors arrested "not by hooligans coming from God knows where, but in the name of specific organizations and their leaders."[161] On the opening day of the conference a telegram was sent to the government telling of the threat of the United Revolutionary Committee of Kharkov to arrest the entire Association of Southern Coal and Steel Producers unless the wages of unskilled workers were raised within three days.[162]

In his opening speech to the conference, von Ditmar put the general view bluntly. The basic fact of Russian life, he said, was anarchy. "We have no government, no ruler, and it may yet come about that we will have no state."[163] In presenting the situation of the coal industry, Priadkin glossed over the shortages of technical supply and transport, and even of food supplies, referring to them as obstacles that could, with a little effort, be overcome. The basic factor in the poor situation of industry, as he saw it, was the low productivity of the mine workers; this, he claimed, was due to anarchy, lack of discipline, unwillingness to work, interference by the workers in organizational and technical matters, and violence against supervisory personnel. Wages had outrun the workers' needs, and the employees

[160] Report of Boiarkov in *Metallist*, no. 5 (1917), p. 10. At the industrialists' conference, N. I. Skorut complained that labor commissars were appointed in consultation with local workers' organizations and should thus be considered agents of the socialist parties rather than neutral government officials.

[161] *Tret'ia konferentsiia*, pp. 4–5.

[162] Ibid., p. 5.

[163] Ibid., p. 4.

therefore had no incentive to work. As a result, coal cutters were working only 80 to 90 hours per month, as compared with 120 to 130 in the previous year.[164] Not a word was said about hunger, poor mine maintenance, a deteriorating labor force, or substandard living conditions. Despite the tone of the various presentations, ranging from plaintive to aggressive, the draft political resolution presented to the conference would not have been out of place at an early session of the Petrograd soviet. It embodied a "decisive condemnation of the prerevolutionary political system, and a struggle against all attempts to return to prerevolutionary institutions," while at the same time calling for "a decisive struggle against all open or hidden attempts to lead us into a socialist system and economic relations inappropriate to Russia's present level of development and to the task of developing the productive forces of the country." The resolution referred to the necessity for a national coalition regime uniting all "the healthy forces of the country, and enjoying actual authority, the confidence of society, and the coercive power to implement its decisions." The only real dissonance was reflected in the final point, calling for "carrying on the war in full agreement with our allies, to a peace consistent with the honor and dignity of Russia."[165]

The debates at the conference reveal a strong determination to curb the workers' recently gained independence and restore the undivided authority of management, thus restoring, in their view, stability to the entire social structure. As one of the delegates phrased it, the industrialists and their industries were essential to the workers' well-being. A special delegation of employers, headed by N. N. Kutler, a former government minister, explained that every cloud had a silver lining; accession to the workers' extreme demands would force many industrialists to close their plants, but after that, the workers, deprived of their wages, would come to their senses and realize the error of their revolutionary ways.[166]

In Iuzovka there was growing tension between management and the workers in the autumn of 1917, yet the institutions that had been set up at the beginning of the revolution continued to function, lessening the friction to some extent. The various shop committees each sent a delegate to

[164] Ibid., pp. 10–12. This speech completes Priadkin's transition from young radical sympathizer to staunchly establishment conservative.

[165] Ibid., p. 19.

[166] See ibid., p. 17, and Lozinskii, "Vremennoe pravitel'stvo," pt. 1, p. 158. For a detailed analysis of the conference of industrialists, see Pliukhina and Shepelev, "Ob ekonomicheskoi polozhenii Rossii," pp. 167–68.

the main factory committee that elected the Council of Elders as its executive organ. The main committee, together with representatives of the miners' and the metal workers' unions that were formed in the early summer, negotiated with management on all matters of pay and working conditions. There is no sign that this committee attempted to oust management, or to share responsibility for the technical and financial aspects of factory operation, as was done in other parts of the Donbass.

This approach was supported by the Iuzovka soviet, moving the Iuzovka Bolsheviks to complain early on that the executive committee of the soviet was completely ineffective in its relations with the management of the New Russia Co.[167] What is reflected here is the difference of approach between the Bolsheviks and almost all the other workers' groups taking part in Iuzovka's public affairs at this time. The Bolsheviks strove to give a political character to all the institutions created. Although tactically the Bolsheviks understood the need for restraining the workers at certain times, their basic creed was that of class war. For them, trade unions and factory committees were instrumental to the gaining of state power. Essentially they were, at this point, future-oriented. The Mensheviks and Socialist-Revolutionaries, in contrast, were oriented toward making life livable in the present through improvement of wages, food supplies, and working conditions.[168] They were willing to restrain the workers from extreme actions and maintain cooperation with the New Russia Co. management.

Typical of such cooperation was the attempt to solve the payroll crisis in September.[169] When neither the banks nor the company had enough money to pay the workers on time, there was great discontent. The workers, as noted, were anxious to stock up for the winter with goods available at the autumn fair. Both the executive committee of the soviet and the Council of Elders of the workers' committee advised moderation, telling the factory workers that "any outburst will only reflect badly on themselves." Meanwhile a delegation composed of two representatives of management, two of the soviet, and two of the factory committee set out for Petrograd to get the necessary funds. The agreement of the workers to this

[167] Institut istorii, *Bol'shevistskie organizatsii Ukrainy*, p. 174, protocols of Iuzovka Bolsheviks' meeting, June 10, 1917.

[168] For a discussion of this point, see Chernomaz, *Bor'ba rabochego klassa Ukrainy*, p. 26.

[169] The details of this event are set out in *Izvestiia Iuzovskogo soveta*, no. 28 (September 16, 1917), p. 2; no. 30 (September 21, 1917), p. 2.

step is evidence of the authority of their factory committee and of the soviet, for at the start of the month, when it was first known that there would be difficulty in meeting the payroll, there had been open complaints.

After a conference between the factory elders and Revilon, at which it was explained that there was no way to meet the payroll, a compromise was reached. An advance of ten thousand rubles would be distributed to those workers and miners who were particularly in need. Even this was a complicated matter, for there was an acute shortage of small bills and change, and the factory committee had to arrange groups of workers, each to be paid a large sum, while one of the group was responsible for finding ways to break the large bills and give each worker the proper amount. The entire arrangement caused a furor in the factory committee. What good was an advance of ten thousand rubles to be divided among twenty thousand workers? There was a good deal of anger and shouting, with a group of miners threatening those who were against accepting the token advance. In the end, only eleven workers came to claim the advance, and a general meeting condemned the elders for the arrangement and demanded that they apologize to the workers. Only at the end of September was the full pay distributed.

Political Institutions in Iuzovka: The Soviet and the Duma

The activities of the Iuzovka soviet during the summer and autumn of 1917 reflect this same outlook. When the soviet was formed in early March it had declared itself the supreme power in the settlement, but it did little to impose its authority over other bodies, and acted primarily as a coordinator for the autonomous functioning of a myriad of social organizations that sprang up. When workers in several mines and shops of the factory complained about the low quality of bread the soviet debated the issue and issued a number of recommendations that were passed on to the mine and factory Central Food Committee, a separate body, for implementation.[170]

Throughout 1917, there were continual efforts at social organization. Each issue of Iuzovka's *Izvestiia* carried notices of the founding of a new health-insurance fund, trade union, cooperative, or workers' club. The

[170] Ibid., no. 39 (October 10, 1917), p. 2.

initiative for these organizations was generally taken within the shop committee of each unit in the factory. Later, as these institutions became organized and began to function, they formed district organizations that standardized the practices of each local group.[171] Little by little, a web of community was being spun by the workers.

In the New Russia Co. auditorium, in the People's Auditorium set up in the Larinskii Bazaar, and in the former English Social Club, a rich menu of adult education courses was offered. Lectures were given to inform the workers about proper working conditions, workers' insurance, and the development of production techniques. A second series of lectures explained the difference between socialism and communism, the concept of state socialism, and the social policies expected under municipal self-government. Courses were also offered in the history of the French Revolution (1789, 1848, 1870); in the history of the Russian revolutionary movement; and in the programs of the various parties. Those interested in improving their language skills could also study English, French, or German. Registration in the club cost fifty kopeks, and there was a fifty-kopek monthly charge as well.[172] In the New Russia Co. auditorium, the cultural-educational committee of the soviet organized a political evening at which representatives of the three main socialist parties could debate "the current situation," with the proceeds from ticket sales going to the kindergarten fund of the soviet.[173] While the soviet was the sponsor of the kindergarten, it was through the shop committees, as the basic cells of the workers' society, that children were registered for attendance, and their needs regarding clothing and footgear listed. The deputies of the local soviet acted as go-betweens, bringing the soviet's requests, suggestions, and decisions to the shops and mines they represented. Nevertheless, the soviet was the place to address the workers' demands and requests.

At the end of July the miners of shaft no. 19 outside Iuzovka drafted a petition to the Iuzovka soviet, asking for a school and a library. "We miners wish to learn, but there is no school, and we therefore remain in the same darkness in which for tens and hundreds of years Nicholas the Second held us."[174] In the open-hearth shop of the New Russia factory, the workers turned to the soviet, complaining that despite the foreman's promise of a

[171] See, for instance, the notice of elections for a unified district health fund in ibid., no. 28 (September 16, 1917), p. 3.

[172] Ibid., no. 42 (October 24, 1917), p. 3.

[173] Ibid., no. 28 (September 16, 1917), p. 4.

[174] Korolivskii, *Podgotovka*, vol. 1, p. 636.

raise of 15 percent, their pay had actually diminished in the last three months. They concluded: "We request that the executive committee of the soviet take the most serious steps to obtain a raise . . . and if the director refuses, then permit us to transfer to a different shop."[175] (Note that the tone is that of a traditional petition rather than of militant demand.)

As the new social institutions, unions, health-insurance funds, and particularly the municipal food committee, formed in the late summer, took on more and more of the burdens of managing society, the soviet found it possible to reduce its executive committee to eleven members, and to cut the size of the soviet in half, basing elections on one deputy for every two hundred workers.[176]

In the September reelection of the Iuzovka soviet, the Bolsheviks had improved their representation, taking a third of the places, gaining three representatives on the eleven-member executive committee and one in the three-member presidium of the soviet.[177] Though this was the best showing by the Bolsheviks in Iuzovka, far outstripping their performance in the late August elections for the Iuzovka duma, it was regarded as a disappointment. After the Kornilov rebellion, the Bolshevik movement had been growing rapidly, and by the beginning of October Kharechko had reported to a provincial party conference that the Iuzovka Bolshevik organization numbered two thousand members and that "our group of Bolsheviks in the [Iuzovka] duma has an influence greater than its numbers."[178] Zaitsev explained the disappointment of the September elections as due to a total lack of support for the Bolsheviks among all the artisans, salespeople, and service personnel, with the exception of the bakery workers. An additional factor was said to be the representation of parties and organizations in the soviets, in addition to the deputies elected at workplaces, giving the Bol-

[175] Vilisova et al., *Bor'ba za vlast' sovetov v Donbasse*, p. 81.

[176] *Izvestiia Iuzovskogo soveta*, no. 39 (October 17, 1917), p. 3; no. 42 (October 24, 1917), p. 1. The new executive committee, chaired by Myshkin, had in addition three Mensheviks, two S-Rs, two Bolsheviks (Zalmaev and Zaitsev), and one each from the Bund, the SERP, and Poalei Tsion.

[177] The elections for the officers of the soviet were held on October 17. In voting for the presidium, Myshkin was elected chairman with 121 votes, and Kornienko, a Bolshevik, associate chairman with 87 votes. Gorodetskii, an S-R, received 104 votes. These three also served on the executive committee, together with Zaitsev (Bolshevik) as secretary—100 votes, Manaenko (Menshevik) as secretary—89 votes, Surel (S-R) as treasurer—114 votes, and Molchan (Menshevik) without portfolio—108 votes. See ibid., no. 40 (October 19, 1917); no. 42 (October 24, 1917), notes the co-opting of four more members by the executive committee, including Zalmaev as Bolshevik representative.

[178] Vilisova et al., *Bor'ba za vlast' sovetov v Donbasse*, p. 133.

sheviks' opponents twenty extra seats.[179] Both the increase in Bolshevik representation and the Bolsheviks' disappointment point to the rapid radicalization that began to sweep the Donbass after the Kornilov uprising. This is borne out by results from some other Donbass centers. In Makeevka, the Bolsheviks took forty of the seventy seats in the soviet. In Gorlovka, they received forty-two out of fifty. In Lugansk they received 95 percent of the seats, and Voroshilov was elected chairman of the soviet. In the Lugansk duma as well, the Bolsheviks were the largest faction, though they did not hold an absolute majority. The results were somewhat different when it came to elections for the zemstvos, which reflected the mood of the rural population. Suglitskii reported from Vetka that in the county zemstvo in mid-September, the Bolsheviks took only six seats, as compared with forty-one for the Socialist-Revolutionaries, and three for the Mensheviks.[180]

There was an additional factor limiting the soviet's activity. At long last Iuzovka had been granted municipal status, and in the third week of August elections for a municipal duma had taken place. On November 1, 1913, the Russian government had recommended municipal status for five Donbass settlements, despite the opposition of the Council of the Association of Southern Coal and Steel Producers and of the various companies owning the land and buildings of each settlement.[181] The war had interrupted the deliberations of the commission set up to prepare the change, and only in mid-1917 was the process of municipalization resumed.

The Iuzovka Bolsheviks entered the election campaign for the municipal

[179] Zaitsev, "Kak my tvorili oktiabr'," p. 137. Avrich, *Anarchists in the Russian Revolution*, p. 12, notes that the syndicalist anarchists had particular influence in the bakers' unions in Russia, as well as among the miners and in a few other professions. Anarchist groups had been active in Iuzovka as early as 1905, and had some influence in the town in the period immediately following the October Revolution. Since there is no record of their having nominated their own candidates in the elections to the Iuzovka soviet, it is reasonable to think that they might well have supported the Bolsheviks, who opposed the provisional government, and actively supported the idea of workers' control over production—a central anarchist proposal.

[180] For Makeevka, see Modestov, *Rabochee i professional'noe dvizhenie*, p. 114. For the Gorlovka and Lugansk soviets, see Gaponenko, *Rabochii klass Rossii v 1917 godu*, p. 430. For the Lugansk duma and the county zemstvo, see Institut istorii, *Bol'shevistskie organizatsii Ukrainy*, pp. 571, 612–14. Election results from other parts of the Donbass show the same pattern of growth of Bolshevik representation in many mines and factories, but little success in the various zemstvo elections.

[181] *Trudy, XXXIX, 1914*, p. 68. The five settlements approved for municipal status were Iuzovka, Enakievo, Grishino, Kamenskoe, and Amur-Nizhnedneprovsk. The ataman of the Don Cossack territory petitioned to have Dimitrievka added to the list.

duma with considerable enthusiasm, but with few resources. They printed three hundred copies of their brochure "A Municipal Program," two hundred copies of a poster, and a thousand leaflets for general distribution. In addition they ordered 100 copies of *Sotsial demokrat* and 150 copies of the Kharkov *Proletarii* for distribution. According to Zaitsev, the Bolsheviks spent only seventy rubles on the election campaign, as compared with three thousand rubles spent by the Mensheviks.[182] The Socialist-Revolutionaries and Mensheviks had suggested a united front of the socialist parties, but this was rejected by the Bolsheviks, who named ten candidates for places in the duma.[183] The expectations of the Bolsheviks ran high, for during the campaign they had brought two speakers from the district buro of the party, S. Turlo and V. Garekol', and attracted a crowd of five thousand workers who enthusiastically adopted all the proposed resolutions calling for workers' control, an end to the coalition government, the abolition of the death penalty, and power to be taken by the people, creating a workers', soldiers', and peasants' regime.[184] In the final count, all six parties that ran received places in the new assembly. The Socialist-Revolutionaries won decisively, taking fifty of the seventy-three seats. The Mensheviks received ten, the Bolsheviks six, the Kadets five, and Poalei Tsion and the Independent Socialists one each.[185] For the Bolsheviks this represented a good showing, since the elections took place before the Kornilov uprising, during the period when they were still under a cloud for their party's role in the July Days riots in Petrograd.[186]

The Iuzovka soviet welcomed the election of the duma as embodying

[182] Zaitsev, "Kak my tvorili oktiabr'," p. 137.

[183] Institut istorii, *Bol'shevistskie organizatsii Ukrainy*, pp. 555–57. *VOSR (khronika sobytii)*, vol. 2, p. 534, notes that the meeting rejecting the united front proposal was held on July 8, and was attended by twenty members.

[184] *VOSR (khronika sobytii)*, vol. 3, p. 261. Gudzenko, *Robitnichii kontrol' i natsionalizatsiia*, doc. 59, p. 124, presents a detailed description of the meeting and the resolutions.

[185] The election results are given by Zaitsev, "Kak my tvorili oktiabr'," p. 137. In "Bolsheviki Iuzovki v 1917 godu," pp. 89–90, Zaitsov writes that the Bolsheviks had 12 percent of the seats in the municipal duma (i.e., 8–9 places) and that the S-Rs received 55 percent of the vote. *Izvestiia Iuzovskogo soveta*, no. 30 (September 21, 1917), p. 1, says that fifty-three of the seventy-three representatives in the duma were from the socialist parties, while part of the remaining twenty represented the revolutionary democracy.

[186] Hough and Fainsod, *How the Soviet Union is Governed*, p. 51, note that in the municipal elections held throughout Russia at this time the Bolsheviks received 7.5 percent of the vote in provincial cities, and only 2.2 percent in small towns. Taking Iuzovka as a provincial city, the Bolshevik showing in the elections was thus slightly above average. If we call it a small town, then the Iuzovka Bolsheviks should be considered extremely successful.

the realization of the population's long-expressed desire for local self-government, delayed for years by the narrow self-interest of "certain people."[187] In the course of this welcoming editorial, and a second, more detailed editorial appearing several days later, it becomes clear that the soviet looked to the duma as the legitimate instrument of state power in the new city, and in no way saw it as a competitive interloper.[188] The recommendation of the soviet to the duma that the latter establish a solid basis for municipal finance by instituting a graduated income tax makes clear that in the six months of its existence the soviet had been wholly dependent on workers' contributions, and levied no taxes on the citizens or the economy of the settlement. The short-lived Iuzovka soviet of 1905 had taxed the local merchants to provide funds for its operations, though it had not declared itself an organ of state power, as had the 1917 soviet in its earliest declaration.

The editorials in the local *Izvestiia* also contained a call to the citizens of Iuzovka to attend the meetings of the duma and to interest themselves in its activities so that the duma deputies "working in the spotlight of *glasnost'* should not be wrongfully criticized if they fail in their efforts to do battle with the difficult conditions of general ruin."[189] The Menshevik Gerbanenko, active in both the soviet and the duma, gave a rather different opinion of why the Iuzovka workers should oversee the work of their municipal duma. In his opinion it was the variety of views represented among the duma deputies that should make the proletariat eager to exercise scrupulous supervision over what was decided there.[190] In fact, except for the five Kadet delegates, all the duma deputies were from parties represented in the soviet.

The first meeting of the Iuzovka duma took place on September 15 in the hall usually used by the soviet. When the Socialist-Revolutionary, Weite rose to read his party's proposals for the municipality, the galleries, said to be generally filled for soviet meetings, were almost empty. The following meeting, held in the Brothers' School, attracted even less attention. Yet the Iuzovka duma continued to meet and function until the German occupation of the town at the end of April 1918. This was despite an early order of the

[187] *Izvestiia Iuzovskogo soveta*, no. 28 (September 16, 1917), p. 1.

[188] Ibid., no. 30 (September 21, 1917), p. 1.

[189] Ibid. The term *glasnost'* in the sense of "open to public scrutiny" was used not infrequently at this time, and can be found even earlier.

[190] Ibid.

Soviet regime disbanding all local governments except for the soviets.[191] The program presented at the first meeting differed little from the recommendations set forth in an editorial of the soviet's *Izvestiia*. It included better hospitals and sanitation ("in advanced countries the doctors have forgotten what smallpox is like"); improved educational facilities for both youth and adults ("illiteracy is the death of a free people"); and proposals for a free legal-aid system for the poor; welfare for demobilized war veterans and orphans; improved food supply; rehabilitation centers for released criminals; labor exchanges to help them find work; and the graduated income tax as a financial basis for the municipality. Weite added only two points not raised by the soviet: land rights for all those working the soil, and a guarantee of the rights of national minorities.[192] The Iuzovka duma also assumed responsibility for the town's militia, a force of two hundred to three hundred armed men, and appointed the Socialist-Revolutionary Kliuev as its commander, a post he was to hold until Iuzovka was captured by the Germans in late April 1918, despite all the political changes in the town.[193] At the same time it set up a public committee to investigate allegations of militia brutality, in particular the beating of those arrested, calling on citizens to testify and complain about every instance of lawless behavior.[194]

There were, nevertheless, clear differences of opinion about the duma. Dr. Kantorovich, leader of the Menshevik Internationalists in Iuzovka, condemned the Kadets for supporting the Kornilov uprising, noting that general state affairs should be given precedence over local questions of self-government. But even he, radical as he was, called for a town duma that would express the democratic, rather than the socialist, nature of the revolution.[195] Myshkin, chairman of the soviet and a supporter of the Men-

[191] Pavliuk et al., *Bol'shevistskie organizatsii Ukrainy*, pp. 122–24, presents the report of Ivan Kochubei to the Seventh Congress of Bolsheviks in March 1918. Kochubei notes that the Iuzovka duma continued to function "though it has been brought under the control of the soviet." For the order to disband all local governments outside the soviets, see Lesnoi, *Sotsialisticheskaia revoliutsiia i gosudarstvennyi apparat*, p. 19.

[192] Compare the editorial in *Izvestiia Iuzovskogo soveta*, no. 30 (September 21, 1917), p. 1, with the report of Weite's declaration in the same issue, p. 2.

[193] Gritsenko, *Robitnichii klas Ukraini*, p. 84.

[194] *Izvestiia Iuzovskogo soveta*, no. 39 (October 17, 1917), p. 1. What other actions the Iuzovka duma took remains unclear. The *Izvestiia* carries no other references, and the duma did not have its own newspaper. No documents of the duma were available in the Donetsk Oblast' State Historical Archive.

[195] *Izvestiia Iuzovskogo soveta*, no. 28 (September 16, 1917), p. 1.

shevik defensists, shared Kantorovich's approach, but differed with the duma's emphasis on minority rights. In Myshkin's opinion, the minorities, having gained recognition for their national-cultural autonomy, should now forget their particularism and work wholeheartedly with the workers to improve the economy of the country. The difference between the two institutions highlights the differences between the Mensheviks, who concentrated their activities among the Russian workers of the industrial enterprises of the Donbass, and the Socialist-Revolutionaries, who, as a party traditionally upholding peasant interests, were far more sensitive to the strong national feelings and frustrations of the Ukrainian people in the Donbass villages. Along with Kantorovoich, Myshkin pointed to the dangers facing the revolution as a whole: the Kornilov rebellion and the problem of achieving a democratic peace. In Myshkin's opinion, as in Kantorovich's, "there is nothing in the urgent tasks of the Iuzovka duma that differs from the task of the whole revolutionary democracy of Russia."[196]

The Iuzovka Bolshevik faction in the town duma was offered, and accepted, a place in the duma's executive committee. This caused something of a scandal in the local organization, for the duma faction members had acted without consulting their comrades. Sima Pevtsova, one of the longtime members of the Iuzovka Bolsheviks, raised this at the party's weekly meeting, criticizing the duma Bolsheviks sharply. In the discussion that followed, Zaitsev smoothed things over, defending the duma faction's action and recommending that it remain in the town's ruling coalition, but adding that if all its proposals were rejected, the faction should resign from the executive. This was adopted forty-nine to five, with four abstentions. Unmollified, Pevtsova proposed a motion censuring the Bolsheviks of the duma faction, but hers was the only hand raised in support.[197] For the Bolshevik organization to support the participation of their representatives in a coalition government outside the soviet, which included a Kadet, speaks volumes regarding the organization's membership at this time. It is significant that this was after the state conference in Moscow, and after the Kornilov rebellion.[198] It should also be remembered that the greatest

[196] Ibid., no. 30 (September 21, 1917), p. 2.

[197] Institut istorii, *Bol'shevistskie organizatsii Ukrainy*, p. 619, protocol of the meeting of September 30, 1917.

[198] Articles by two Donbass Bolshevik leaders, Sergeev and Voroshilov, published in the local Bolshevik press, had attacked the state conference in Moscow as a sign of rising counterrevolution and growing class conflict. See ibid., pp. 580–87.

moment of the Bolshevik campaign for the Iuzovka duma was the public meeting at which, "by an overwhelming majority," those present voted in favor of an end to the coalition government headed by Kerenskii.[199] Only at the end of January 1918 did Tolmachev report to the weekly Bolshevik meeting that the faction had decided to withdraw from the duma executive because of the "impossibility of working within the executive, partly thanks to the dictatorial methods of the town's heads, and in particular because of the policies adopted by the majority." The withdrawal was approved by the meeting.[200]

Despite the cooperation of the soviet, the Iuzovka Duma appears to have done little during its existence. No records of discussions of organizational questions, of the levying of taxes, or of other portions of the municipal platform have been found. Yet the duma retained control over appointment of the militia commander. It also proved useful in shielding the soviet from anti-Bolshevik forces, and was credited by Zaitsev with preventing the entry of a cossack force into Iuzovka in the late autumn of 1917.[201] The duma remained in existence until the German occupation of Iuzovka at the end of April 1918, with the Kadets still represented, and Bolshevik representatives participated in the presidium of a joint duma-soviet session that demanded the Bolsheviks' ouster from the leadership of the soviet in the wake of the Zalmaev scandal in March. This was not the only joint session of the two institutions; they had met early in 1918, this time as well with Bolshevik participation, to discuss the arming of the town militia in view of the breakdown of law and order.[202] The life of Iuzovka centered, however, as it always had, on the New Russia factory and mines, and the effective institutions—the town's Central Food Committee and the Mine and Factory Workers' Committee—guided whatever vital functions still remained.

The Donbass on the Eve of October

Two clouds hung over Iuzovka, and over all of the Donbass. Economic life was grinding to a halt, and even the great New Russia factory was threat-

[199] Vilisova et al., *Bor'ba za vlast' sovetov v Donbasse*, p. 92.

[200] Pavliuk et al., *Bol'shevistskie organizatsii Ukrainy*, p. 373.

[201] Zaitsev, "Kak my tvorili oktiabr'," p. 138.

[202] See Kharechko, "Bor'ba za oktiabr' v Donbasse," p. 152.

ened with closure by mid-October. In addition, as class polarization became sharper in the main centers of Russia, armed bands were organizing under the leadership of General Kaledin to fight the growing radicalization of the Donbass soviets. The threat of civil war was clear and present in the Donbass even before the Bolshevik seizure of power in Petrograd.

Much of the tension that existed was caused by the soviets' indifference to the Ukrainian national movement, and their ignoring of the central Rada, maintaining connections only with Petrograd. In the urban dumas, and even more so in all the levels of the zemstvo organization, the Ukrainian national movement had strong support, looking to the Rada as an authoritative institution. While the workers' Red Guard units were recently formed, poorly armed, and almost untrained, they faced a cossack population made up of professional soldiers, whose community leaders were more and more hostile to the movement of soviets.[203] An additional source of militance was the return to the villages of soldiers, particularly older ones, released from the army under Kerenskii's order to perform agricultural work to relieve the food crisis.[204]

The political polarization that was taking place against the background of spreading economic paralysis was much more real. Wherever authoritative institutions had been created, social tensions could be channeled through these institutions, and the potential for violence and instability lessened. The situation in the mines must have been worse, though less was written about it in contemporary sources. The phenomenon of miners trying to leave the pits and find employment in the factory was becoming common enough that it was blamed for contributing to the decline of coal production. The Central Council of Elders of the Mine and Factory Workers' Committee discussed the possibility of banning such transfers, but after a lengthy debate decided to refer the question to the soviet.[205]

The inability of the company to meet its payroll on time in mid-September, though resolved in a cooperative fashion, heightened the workers' frustration, created an aggressive mood among them, and undermined the authority of the shop representatives who attempted to calm the workers. Many representatives were recalled by their constituents during

[203] See the report of the Lugansk Bolsheviks to the Central Committee in Pavliuk et al., *Bol'shevistskie organizatsii Ukrainy*, p. 338. See also the report of the concentration of Kaledin units in Lugansk during October 1917, in Vilisova et al., *Bor'ba za vlast' sovetov v Donbasse*, pp. 147–49.

[204] Kuranov, "Sovety na Artemovshchine," p. 165.

[205] *Izvestiia Iuzovskogo soveta*, no. 30 (September 21, 1917), p. 3.

the month of October, and new, more radical representatives, among them a number of Bolsheviks, "whose representation in the soviet has grown considerably," were sent to the factory committee in their place.[206] This was one of the factors that brought on the abortive strike in mid-October, with the renewed attempt by the workers to introduce an eight-hour day in some of the shops.

The tensions existing in Iuzovka were magnified many times over in other parts of the Donbass. By mid-October four thousand miners were striking in Makeevka, urged on by anarchists, who were particularly active there.[207] The most radical center in the Donbass was the Gorlovka-Shcherbinovka district soviet. On August 30, when the first news of the Kornilov rebellion reached the district, the Shcherbinovka soviet immediately formed the Committee for the Salvation of the Revolution to supervise a proletarian dictatorship opposing the forces of the right. The same day, a full district conference of soviets announced the assumption of all power by the soviets and began issuing emergency decrees, including a ban on any executives leaving their factories or mines, or removing materials from the enterprises without the permission of the committee.[208] The Shcherbinovka committee telegraphed VTsIK (the All-Russian Central Executive Committee) in Petrograd that if the mine owners' provocations did not cease immediately (the provocations mentioned were the flooding of mines, closing of enterprises, cutting of wages, and refusal to pay full wages to workers occupied in public affairs such as workers' committees and soviets), the committee "will immediately establish dictatorial rule over the small mineowners of the Shcherbinovka district."[209] Nonsocialist newspapers were banned in the district, as were some Socialist-Revolutionary newspapers. Trains passing through the district were searched, and food, money, and weapons were expropriated for the use of the local authorities, as had been done during the seizure of the Ekaterinin railroad in December 1905.[210] These extreme actions, harbingers of the policies that the Bol-

[206] This phenomenon is noted in ibid., no. 39 (October 17, 1917), p. 3.

[207] *Perepiska sekretariata*, vol. 1, p. 355.

[208] Vilisova et al., *Bor'ba za vlast' sovetov v Donbasse*, p. 104. Only Gruzman's personal authority had prevented the more radical mine leaders from taking similar steps earlier. At the time the Committee for the Salvation of the Revolution was formed and issued its first decrees, Gruzman was in Moscow (where he had been nominated as a Bolshevik candidate for the municipal duma), returning to the Donbass only in mid-September. See Ostrogorskii, "Stranichki iz istorii," p. 17.

[209] Vilisova et al., *Bor'ba za vlast' sovetov v Donbasse*, p. 111.

[210] Kazimirchuk, "Revoliutsionnoe dvizhenie," pp. 55–60.

sheviks would institute throughout the country when they took power, were evidently popular with the local miners. By mid-October the Shcherbinovka Bolshevik organization numbered three thousand members, almost half the total number of miners working in the settlement.[211]

Other nearby soviets followed the Shcherbinovka example. On September 5, the Gukov soviet, headed by the Bolshevik Kovalev, who was later to be chairman of the executive of the Donbass–Krivoi Rog Autonomous Republic, declared a similar local revolutionary dictatorship.[212] Three days later, the Druzhkovka soviet set up its own Committee for the Salvation of the Revolution, calling for the trial of all those involved in the Kornilov affair, freedom for all those jailed after the July Days, formal dispersal of the state duma and state council, and a long list of other demands; it was, however, clearly less radical than the Bolshevik-controlled soviets with regard to local affairs.[213] At the same time, the organization of United Internationalists in the settlement, claiming 2,100 members, announced that henceforth they would recognize the Bolshevik Central Committee in Petrograd as their sole authority.[214] In various parts of the Donbass, the local soviets and workers' committees began to use the system noted by von Ditmar at the opening of the industrialists' conference: enforcing demands for wage increases by arresting those employers who refused them.[215]

The provisional government felt a natural anxiety at this deteriorating state of affairs, and as early as August, the Bakhmut district commissar had issued a circular to all local institutions noting that the resolutions of mass public meetings, no matter by whom they were convened, had no legal validity unless approved by the provisional government's representative. The district Congress of Peasant Soviets, in session when the circular was issued, replied that this was "an extreme reactionary measure, casting upon the peasant the familiar old chains of the land captains, and limiting the peasants' civil rights."[216] The bureaucratic rigidity and lack of resources

[211] Institut istorii, *Bol'shevistskie organizatsii Ukrainy*, p. 651.

[212] Modestov, *Rabochee i professional'noe dvizhenie*, p. 116.

[213] Kuranov, "Sovety na Artemovshchine," p. 186.

[214] Institut istorii, *Bol'shevistskie organizatsii Ukrainy*, p. 651.

[215] Modestov, *Rabochee i professional'noe dvizhenie*, p. 117.

[216] Kuranov, "Sovety na Artemovshchine," p. 181. Martynova, "Agrarnoe dvizhenie v 1917 g.," p. 184, working according to statistics of the provisional government's Central Land Commission, places Ekaterinoslav province in a middle position regarding frequency of peasant uprisings in Russia between March and August. Vilisova et al., *Bor'ba za vlast' sovetov v Donbasse*, pp. 138–39, report armed clashes over land seizure by peasants in Bakhmut district in early October.

that marked most of the provisional government's activities are evident here. The reaction of the peasant gathering was no doubt moderate in comparison to the feelings of the restless masses of miners, whose nature was more extreme, and whose frustration and deprivation were mounting daily in most parts of the region.

As tension spread through the Donbass, reflecting both the political polarization of Russia and the deteriorating economic situation, lockouts by employers proliferated. On the workers' side, a general strike was planned for October 26, to coincide with the opening of the Second All-Russian Congress of Soviets. Zalmaev had returned to Iuzovka and reported on September 30 to the Bolshevik meeting on the failure of the democratic conference in Petrograd. He had informed his audience of the opinion already prevalent among the Petrograd Bolshevik leadership that "the calling of the Second Congress of Soviets is our turning point."[217] But the plan for a general strike in the Donbass was not a Bolshevik initiative. It had been put forward by all the workers' organizations.[218] The reason for the strike was that the industrialists were thought to be intentionally causing economic chaos to disrupt the coming elections to the constituent assembly.[219] In Iuzovka, the strike committee in the New Russia factory was led by Mensheviks, largely because of the lack of organized activity among the local Bolsheviks, which both Magidov and Petrovskii, sent to Iuzovka to bolster the faltering Bolshevik organization, found intolerable.[220]

Conditions were ripening for radical action. On October 3, at the end of the industrialists' conference in Kharkov, Svitsyn had announced that the New Russia factory was losing a hundred thousand rubles a day, and was to be closed forthwith unless the workers accepted new working conditions.[221] The government, however, had already decided to dispatch A. S. Orlov, associate commissar for trade and industry, to the Donbass as a special plenipotentiary to arbitrate all aspects of wages and working condi-

[217] Institut istorii, *Bol'shevistskie organizatsii Ukrainy*, pp. 618–19. One hundred members attended this meeting, the largest recorded in all the protocols published. It should be noted that this was before the Bolshevik Central Committee had formally accepted Lenin's idea of insurrection

[218] See Kharechko, "Bor'ba za oktiabr' v Donbasse," p. 130.

[219] *Izvestiia Iuzovskogo soveta*, no. 41 (October 21, 1917), p. 3.

[220] See the lectures of Magidov and Petrovskii to the Iuzovka Bolshevik meeting on October 23, in which they urge the locals to reactivate their own internal committees, as well as working to have their representatives included in the various factory committees. Institut istorii, *Bol'shevistskie organizatsii Ukrainy*, p. 655.

[221] *Izvestiia Iuzovskogo soveta*, no. 40 (October 19, 1917), p. 3.

tions between the owners and the workers.[222] Svitsyn, notified that Orlov was on his way to the Donbass, agreed on October 7 to postpone the closing of the factory, but warned that if the workers did not accept the new conditions that the management was working out, the factory would close on October 14, and all the workers would be discharged.[223]

The representative of the Commissariat of Labor in Kharkov brought together Svitsyn and representatives of the New Russia workers on October 11. In a letter summing up management's position, Svitsyn complained that "regarding the conditions set by management that would have made it possible to run the factory without loss, and with benefit to the country, the workers' representatives had made no substantive response." Nevertheless the New Russia Co. would await Orlov's arrival and "not hasten yet to announce the dismissal of the workers and the closing of the factory." At the same time, Svitsyn warned, "the company will go forward without delay to create those conditions in which it will be possible to continue working, taking measures of a most decisive kind against those who do not want order, productive work, and obedience to law—up to, and including, discharging them."[224]

Svitsyn's threat, coming even before Orlov had arrived and consulted with the contending sides, was rejected by shop after shop of the New Russia workers, with most of their resolutions published alongside Svitsyn's ultimatum. In Vetka, where the Bolsheviks, led by Suglitskii, had particular strength, the workers expressed full support for the soviet ("We ask that the old past be forgotten"), rejected threats of closure of the plant, and declared that they would continue working whatever happened, and would take up arms against any counterrevolution.[225] The gist of most of the resolutions was that management threats to close the plant constituted treason. The closure of the New Russia factory and mines would doom all of Russia to cold and hunger, and therefore the workers would refuse to leave the plant; they would continue production under the leadership of their unions, the factory committee, and the soviet.

The resolutions were phrased in terms of patriotic anxiety for the future of Russia and its people, rather than as class antagonism. The closing appeal

[222] Korolivskii, *Pobeda velikoi oktiabr'skoi sotsialisticheskoi revoliutsii i ustanovlenie sovetskoi vlasti na Ukraine*, p. 451 n. 38.

[223] DOGIA, F. 10, op. 1, d. 13, p. 6.

[224] Svitsyn's letter appears in full in *Izvestiia Iuzovskogo soveta*, no. 40 (October 19, 1917), p. 3.

[225] Ibid., no. 39 (October 17, 1917), p. 4.

of the workers' declaration was that if management closed the factory, then the provisional government should assume ownership and operate it.[226] One week before the convocation of the Second All-Russian Congress of Soviets, it was to the provisional government, rather than to the VTsIK or to the Petrograd soviet, that the Iuzovka workers turned in their appeal to keep their factory open, producing, and paying wages. There was nothing here of the revolutionary extremism of Shcherbinovka or of the Leninist call for workers' control over production and distribution, though these latter slogans had been embodied in the resolutions of Bolshevik-convened mass public meetings of workers and miners in the Iuzovka area during the summer and autumn.[227]

The workers' approach to the problems was economic rather than political. They were deeply angered by management's ultimatum, and by the unilateral management decision, announced by Glass and Revilon, that delegates to workers' organizations other than the main factory committee and the cooperative store would no longer be paid by the company. Earlier there had been grumbling when the company balked at paying overtime to members of shop committees for meetings held outside working hours.[228] The managers also announced new rules cutting off workers' pay when smelting facilities were shut down by malfunction or shortage of materials.

In response, the workers of several shops declared a work stoppage to begin October 16 until they were granted an eight-hour day in place of the ten or twelve hours then in force, with no cut from the previous pay level. The new conditions announced by management had not allowed for wage increases, although they gave the workers the option of choosing either three eight-hour shifts or two twelve-hour shifts. Pay for work on holidays listed in the workers' pay books was to be at time and a half, while work beyond the hour fixed by law on the eve of a holiday would be paid at time and a quarter. The company undertook to maintain fixed prices for food sold to the workers, but this privilege would be extended only to those working

[226] Ibid., no. 40 (October 19, 1917), p. 4.

[227] The call for the provisional government to take over the factory, printed in the newspaper of the soviet, is omitted in such documentary collections as Chernomaz, *Bor'ba rabochego klassa Ukrainy*, p. 86; Vilisova et al., *Bor'ba za vlast' sovetov v Donbasse*, p. 151; and *VOSR (khronika sobytii)*, vol. 4, p. 448, although they all present the other parts of these resolutions as important evidence of the workers' radicalism.

[228] *Izvestiia Iuzovskogo soveta*, no. 30 (September 21, 1917), p. 3. There had been an agreement in effect since April that meetings of the shop committee could be held on work time, with the company paying the delegates' wages.

at least twenty-five days each month. Those working less would be charged the full market price. Given the unpredictability of raw material supplies, and the deterioration of maintenance, this meant a significant worsening of conditions for most of the labor force.[229]

At the same time, a telegram was received from Commissar of Labor Kolokolnikov, declaring: "The provisional government has appointed a special plenipotentiary with broad powers. Leaving soonest. He will personally settle dispute with New Russia as well as other factories. No ultimatum of management or workers until he comes. Work must go on. Stoppage from either side insupportable and will be opposed by full strength of government." A general meeting of the main factory committee, called to consider the government telegram, the management announcement, and the workers' angry response, decided to advise the workers to hold off their strike.[230] The soviet was painfully aware of the polarization that was tearing the Donbass asunder, and of the dangers of a mass strike. In an unsigned article under the heading "The Approaching Catastrophe," one of the leaders of the soviet wrote: "More than half a year has been wasted. We have yielded position after position. We have weakened our own prestige and undermined the prestige of our great revolution. It is not yet too late. But soon we will lose our last resources, our last prestige."[231]

Nevertheless, alongside an editorial setting forth their awareness of these conditions, the soviet's leaders published a proposal of cooperation and of reliance on the good offices of Orlov, the plenipotentiary, who had meanwhile finally arrived in the Donbass.[232] Although the workers of the rail-casting shop and of the Marten ovens had been fired for their unilateral

[229] The company's new regulations and offers appear in ibid., no. 41 (October 21, 1917), p. 4. The decisions of the workers are reported in TsGIAL, F. 37, op. 67, d. 808, p. 3, as well as in *Izvestiia Iuzovskogo soveta*, no. 43 (October 26, 1917), p. 4. At the conference between the coal producers and the workers in March, a minimum work month of only twenty-two days had been demanded by the employers.

[230] *Izvestiia Iuzovskogo soveta*, no. 43 (October 26, 1917), p. 4. The date when the telegram, in which it is announced that Orlov is "leaving soonest," was sent or received is unknown. It was, however, discussed at the factory committee meeting on October 16. The decision to send him was evidently made no later than October 7, the date on which Svitsyn agreed to postpone closure of the factory. Even in emergencies, the provisional government machinery showed little improvement over the dilatory habits that had characterized government attention to the 1892 cholera epidemic.

[231] Ibid., no. 39 (October 17, 1917). In this editorial, evidently written by a Menshevik Internationalist, the continuation of the war is seen as the root of all the evils afflicting Russia.

[232] Ibid., no. 44 (October 28, 1917), pp. 1–2.

institution of the eight-hour day, the chairman of the soviet, Myshkin, called on them to maintain order and quiet, and to continue working.[233] The chilling realities of Russia's polarized politics of class war went hand in hand with the persisting dream of a better world being born.

At this critical juncture, the Bolsheviks of Iuzovka, after appearing to have overcome their slow start (which was due, as Zaitsev claimed, to their lack of experience under open, legal conditions), were in a deep crisis.[234] Artem (F. A. Sergeev) had written to Petrograd that Bolshevik work throughout the Donbass area was chaotic and weak, lacking both people and funds.[235] Petrovskii, reporting from Iuzovka at the end of the summer, had noted the persistence of the filth, soot, and poverty in the workers' quarters, no different than it had been decades before, but he recognized the political potential that now existed among the workers, concluding: "If only there were comrades to organize and explain."[236] A session of the Donetsk–Krivoi Rog Oblast' Committee of Bolsheviks was informed that "large areas around Iuzovka are almost entirely neglected. Only one comrade is working there, and he devotes all his time to Iuzovka. Because of the lack of responsible party forces, we neither can exploit nor serve a single one of the general soviet organizations of the Donbass."[237] On October 21, Elena Stasova, in charge of the Bolshevik secretariat's contacts with the party's various branches throughout the Russian Empire, wrote from Petrograd to Shulem Gruzman in Shcherbinovka, asking that he send someone to the Iuzovka-Makeevka-Petrovskii district. "The district committee has disintegrated, and in general things are going badly there. It is necessary to go through the district, check up on everything, and get the work going again."[238] But Gruzman himself had only recently returned to the Donbass from Moscow, and he had his hands full rebuilding the Gorlovka-Shcherbinovka organization that had crumbled in his absence. In addition, as leader of one of the most radical areas in the Donbass, he was a central Bolshevik figure in the attempt to organize the Donbass general strike that was being prepared for October 26.

In the end it was Magidov who was sent to bolster the spirits of the

[233] Ibid., no. 42 (October 24, 1917).

[234] For Zaitsev's somewhat tortuous explanation, see "Bolsheviki Iuzovki v 1917 godu," p. 79.

[235] Vilisova et al., *Bor'ba za vlast' sovetov v Donbasse*, pp. 114–15.

[236] Institut istorii, *Bol'shevistskie organizatsii Ukrainy*, p. 653.

[237] *VOSR* (*dokumenty i materialy*), vol. 9, p. 37. The phrases "responsible party forces" and "one comrade" evidently refer to paid emissaries of the Central Committee.

[238] *Perepiska sekretariata*, vol. 2, p. 90.

Iuzovka Bolsheviks, while G. I. Petrovskii paid frequent visits to the town, contributed articles to the local *Izvestiia*, and even took part in a meeting of the local soviet, where, as a veteran Donbass revolutionary, and as a member of the Fourth Duma, he was granted recognition by being elected honorary chairman of the session.[239] Although the two visiting activists could not sway the political balance in the town, they did inject the militant tone of Bolshevism into its political discourse. Petrovskii attacked the Socialist-Revolutionaries for allegedly denigrating the masses' capability for political creation, calling on the workers to take up arms—and the sooner the better. Magidov's contribution was an article accusing the bourgeoisie—mine and factory engineers and technical personnel—of slandering the workers when they complained that "the miners have become wild beasts, they kill and rape peaceful citizens, plunder the goods of others, [and] devastate people."[240] At the same time, Magidov spoke to the Iuzovka soviet, urging unity of all "the vital forces" of the proletariat.[241] Magidov succeeded in rallying the Bolshevik forces to the extent of putting together a district conference, but it would appear indicative of what was going on in the main Donbass centers that the meeting was scheduled to be held in Bakhmut rather than in Iuzovka or Makeevka.[242]

The need for political reinforcement was evident. The Bolshevik organization in Iuzovka did not seem conscious of the fateful events that were looming on the horizon. The weekly meeting on October 7 consisted of a lengthy and acrimonious debate over the list of Bolshevik candidates for the elections to the constituent assembly, with the membership complaining that the Central Committee in Petrograd had nominated "strangers" in the Donbass electoral districts, leaving out local Bolsheviks.[243] The following week, the main item on the agenda was the report of comrade Ryzhkova on her course on Marxism in Bakhmut, accompanied by her lecture on the basic principles of the Marxist worldview. Comrade Ryzhkova was elected treasurer of the Iuzovka Bolsheviks and a member of the buro.[244]

[239] See the protocol of the session of the Iuzovka soviet in *Izvestiia Iuzovskogo soveta*, no. 40 (October 19, 1917).

[240] Both articles appear in ibid., no. 42 (October 24, 1917). Where Magidov found such sayings is unknown, but they probably reflect a growing anxiety over the breakdown of law and order resulting in such happenings as the Bakhmut vodka riot described in vol. 1, and the palpably increasing impatience of the workers.

[241] Ibid. Magidov's status in the soviet is unclear. Presumably as a party emissary he was granted representation.

[242] *Perepiska sekretariata*, vol. 1, p. 355.

[243] Institut istorii, *Bol'shevistskie organizatsii Ukrainy*, p. 639.

[244] Ibid., p. 647.

In the soviet, great attention was paid to the events that were shaping the course of revolution in the rest of Russia. On October 17, the Iuzovka soviet debated the question of the impending Second All-Russian Congress of Soviets, scheduled to meet near the end of October in Petrograd. The Socialist-Revolutionaries held forth against participating or sending delegates. The majority of the members of the soviet, however, voted for the congress to be convened as scheduled, and voted to send Zalmaev, a Bolshevik, and Troianskii, a Menshevik Internationalist, as delegates from the Iuzovka soviet.[245] The two hastened to Petrograd, not knowing that they would return with news of a far more serious crisis than any with which Iuzovka had contended until then. How Iuzovka reacted to the challenge of the October Revolution will be the focus of the next chapter.

[245] *Izvestiia Iuzovskogo soveta*, no. 40 (October 19, 1917).

CHAPTER 9

The October That Wasn't

Like the February Revolution, the Bolshevik coup of October came to Iuzovka by telegraph. On the night of October 25 the Iuzovka Executive Committee received the first accounts of the events in Petrograd. The immediate reaction was to put a reinforced militia guard on duty at the town's telegraph station and telephone exchange. In addition, the leaders of the soviet established a Military Revolutionary Committee (*revkom*), made up of three representatives of the soviet, two from the town duma, two from the local soldiers' committee, and one from each socialist political party and large trade union. Anatolyi Myshkin, the chairman of the soviet's executive committee, chaired the revkom. Myshkin also headed the six-member military staff elected on October 28, with Alferov as associate chairman and Lukianenko as commander of all military forces in Iuzovka. The revkom issued an appeal for calm and order, sent delegations to the nearby mines to prevent "excesses," and mounted armed patrols in Iuzovka. It was announced that the postal and telegraphic personnel were cooperating with the revkom.[1] The anxieties of the executive committee appear to have been caused by the possibility of a cossack-led counterrevolution rather than of a repetition of the Petrograd events in Iuzovka.

The Iuzovka Soviet and the October Revolution

It was only on October 31 that Zalmaev and Troianskii returned from Petrograd, and the Iuzovka soviet assembled to hear their respective accounts of what had taken place at the Second Congress of Soviets. Zalmaev was first to speak, accusing the VTsIK elected at the First All-Russian

[1] *Izvestiia Iuzovskogo soveta*, no. 45 (October 31, 1917), p. 1.

Congress of Soviets in June of trying to sabotage the convening of the second congress. He explained the Bolshevik seizure of power as an act of the Petrograd proletariat and the revolutionary soldiers, who, frustrated by the ineffectiveness of the Kerenskii government, decided, "with the active cooperation of the Second All-Russian Congress of Soviets," to assume all state power. In his explanation there was no hint of Bolshevik initiative in or leadership of the Petrograd events.

Following Zalmaev's speech, Troianskii, the Menshevik Internationalist, reported that his party comrades at the congress had urged the Bolsheviks not to take to the streets, but to resolve the political problems of Russia within the congress hall. But the Bolsheviks, he said, "would not listen, and shouted down all other factions." The discussion that followed was limited. Two representatives each of the Bolsheviks, the Socialist-Revolutionaries, and the Mensheviks (one defensist and one Internationalist), and a representative of the Jewish SERP presented their respective parties' positions. Then Zalmaev for the Bolsheviks and Troianskii for the Menshevik Internationalists each presented a draft resolution. The Bolshevik resolution pointed to the decrees already issued by the Sovnarkom (the Council of People's Commissars) in Petrograd, calling for an immediate end to the war, and a general peace conference; decreeing the distribution of the land to the peasants; and calling for elections to the constituent assembly no later than November 12. The Menshevik resolution condemned the Bolshevik coup as splitting the democratic camp and thus enabling the forces of counterrevolution to manipulate the "politically backward portion of the democracy" in order to crush the revolution. The Mensheviks called for an all-democratic government without participation of the propertied classes, immediate transfer of the land to local land committees, and control (whether state control or workers' control is left unspecified) over production. The Menshevik resolution was supported by seventy-one deputies, while eighteen voted against and eight abstained. The Bolshevik resolution received forty-one votes. There is no record of whether opposition and abstention were counted in that vote.[2]

[2] The main speeches, the draft resolutions, and the results of the voting are recorded in ibid., no. 47 (November 4, 1917). In two different places the numbers of those supporting the Menshevik resolution are recorded variously as seventy and seventy-one. Liubimov, *Revoliutsiia 1917 goda*, vol. 6, p. 43, records the vote as seventy to forty-one, thus softening the Bolshevik defeat by ignoring the small number of those opposing the Menshevik resolution, and notes that a considerable number of those who voted for the Bolshevik resolution had also apparently supported the Menshevik resolution. This phenomenon fit the

The outcome of the soviet's vote was scarcely a surprise. A week earlier the soviet had debated establishing a strike committee, and this had been approved with the support of sixty-nine deputies. When Petrovskii had attempted to interject the question of transfer of all power to the soviets, his resolution had been defeated, garnering only thirty-six votes. The principal difference between the two resolutions at that session was that the Menshevik-sponsored draft focused on the fight against the "clear intent of the industrialists to return the proletariat to the despotic conditions of prerevolutionary life," while Petrovskii's draft condemned the provisional government as being a partner of the industrialists, and proposed the seizure of state power by the soviets, and of industry by revolutionary workers' institutions.[3]

The town's leaders were deeply engrossed in the campaign for the constituent assembly, and for the development of effective local institutions. An editorial discussing the Iuzovka duma noted that the fate and future of Iuzovka, and indeed of all of Russia, rested on the exercise of free voting, and that the electoral institutions had to be defended and cherished above all else. To emphasize this, the soviet's executive announced that all Iuzovka residents who had not been on the electoral rolls for the duma elections in August, but who would be twenty years old by November 12, the day set for the constituent assembly elections, were invited to register with the electoral commission from the beginning of October.[4] At long last Iuzovka's population was asked to voice an opinion in both national and local affairs.

Political participation presented the citizens of Iuzovka with much that was new to consider. A long article in the local *Izvestiia* weighed the pros and cons of the presidential system as compared with the parliamentary cabinet system and the British constitutional monarchy. Fearful of the overconcentration of power, the author concluded that Russia would be better off without a president.[5] On the same day that the Bolsheviks were seizing power, the central article in the Iuzovka *Izvestiia* was about the land

political culture of Iuzovka at that time, expressing support for soviet power as an institution but not for any particular party. Zaitsev, "Kak my tvorili oktiabr'," p. 137, writes that, after listening to Zalmaev's report, a majority of the members of the Iuzovka soviet supported the Bolshevik resolution.

[3] Liubimov, *Revoliutsiia 1917 goda*, vol. 5, p. 174. For the texts of the resolutions and the results of the voting, see *Izvestiia Iuzovskogo soveta*, no. 44 (October 28, 1917).

[4] *Izvestiia Iuzovskogo soveta*, no. 30 (September 21, 1917), p. 1.

[5] Ibid., nos. 41–42 (October 21 and 24), 1917.

program that the Menshevik Social-Democrats proposed to present at the constituent assembly.[6] But both the tone and the style of these leading articles in the Iuzovka *Izvestiia* were divorced from the town's rough ambience. They did not speak to the unemployment and hunger that were the town's main problems. As the resolution of one of the New Russia factory shops later phrased it, the decisions of the Iuzovka soviet were "inappropriate to the mood and demands of the working masses."[7] The time frame for party policies had switched. The Bolsheviks were now dealing with the present, while the Mensheviks looked toward a more perfect future.

The mood of the Iuzovka soviet evidently reflected the majority opinion in the soviets of the Donbass, if not that of the workers, for the Donbass–Krivoi Rog Oblast' Committee of Soviets issued a call for a government of all the socialist parties: "All the parties must make compromises, and above all, Lenin, and those who think like him, must abandon the thought that we are undergoing a socialist revolution."[8] In the end, however, it was the Bolsheviks' power-oriented activism that was to win out against the intelligentsia's appeal to patience and self-restraint. An additional point worth noting is the Menshevik fear that the "politically backward" portions of "the democracy" (that is, the mine workers and peasants) could be manipulated by the right. Here we have a clear expression of the widespread fear of the "benighted masses," the *temnyi narod*, an attitude that was evidently felt and understandably resented by these "politically backward" elements of the population, newly permitted to taste the heady wine of political freedom.

At a second session of the Iuzovka soviet, the resolution condemning Lenin's seizure of power was reconfirmed, despite Bolshevik efforts. The Socialist-Revolutionaries, who had opposed participation in the Second All-Russian Congress of Soviets, then announced that they were leaving the soviet, and proposed that the town duma be recognized as the sole repository of state power. There they had a solid majority, and were free from the constant supervision of the shop meetings, with their threat to recall the elected deputies. The withdrawal only weakened them, however, for when they walked out, the Left Socialist-Revolutionaries remained, though they refrained from condemning their erstwhile colleagues' move.[9]

[6] Ibid., no. 43 (October 26, 1917).

[7] Ibid., no. 50 (November 11, 1917), p. 4.

[8] Ibid., no. 47 (November 4, 1917).

[9] Korolivskii, *Podgotovka*, vol. 3, p. 265.

Magidov had been in Petrograd for the meetings of the Congress of Soviets, and returned quickly to report to the Iuzovka Bolsheviks, even before the return of Zalmaev and Troianskii. In the expectation that the seizure of power in Petrograd would arouse armed opposition in the south, he urged the Iuzovka Bolsheviks to hasten the arming of workers to guard against Kaledin's gathering forces. At the same meeting the suggestion was made that the factory be asked to contribute to a defense fund.[10]

The Bolsheviks were indeed active among the workers, and on November 8, after the two meetings of the Iuzovka soviet, an assembly in the New Russia Co.'s blacksmith shop, attended by 450 workers, denounced the soviet's decision, voted support for the Bolshevik resolution, and recalled their deputy from the soviet, reversing an earlier vote of support for the soviet's anti-Bolshevik resolution.[11] This was evidently not the only such meeting, for Suglitskii later reported to the Central Committee that all the New Russia shops, "without exception," passed Bolshevik resolutions opposed to that of the soviet.[12] The reports in the Iuzovka *Izvestiia* are somewhat more reserved. They note the resolution passed in the New Russia factory's electrical shop, stating: "We foremen and workers of the electrical shop, considering the Petrograd proletariat the avant-garde of the revolution, and often doing its bidding, unite around the Petrograd soviet, supporting it with all our strength." The newspaper then added that all the shops in the factory were busy discussing the political events, and "in most of the shops, the resolution defeated by the soviet is getting the largest number of votes."[13] The workers' anger and frustration were finding political expression. On November 5, a Bolshevik election meeting for the constituent assembly elections, held in the Iuzovka People's Auditorium, also passed a resolution supporting the steps taken "by the Petrograd soviet and the Second All-Russian Congress of Soviets." The resolution avoided

[10] Institut istorii, *Bol'shevistskie organizatsii Ukrainy*, pp. 661–62, protocols of Bolshevik meeting, October 28, 1917.

[11] *Izvestiia Iuzovskogo soveta*, no. 51 (November 14, 1917), p. 4.

[12] Pavliuk et al., *Bol'shevistskie organizatsii Ukrainy*, p. 342. Korolivskii, *Podgotovka*, vol. 3, p. 265, citing *Donetskii proletarii*, names the blacksmith shop as one of two New Russia shops that did not vote in favor of the Bolshevik resolution. *Izvestiia Iuzovskogo soveta*, no. 48 (November 7, 1917), p. 4, writes of the blacksmith shop, the stables, and others supporting the Mensheviks, but the date of the report suggests that later meetings reversed the decision.

[13] *Izvestiia Iuzovskogo soveta*, no. 47 (November 4, 1917), p. 4. Reports of fifteen other shops and mines passing the Bolshevik resolution are in ibid., nos. 47–50 (November 5–11), 1917, while only two ignore the politics of Petrograd and discuss current questions of production and administration.

any mention of Lenin, or of the Sovnarkom, but called on the audience to support the proposition that "whoever is against our demands for peace, land, and the constituent assembly, is no friend, but an enemy."[14]

Meanwhile, the news published in Iuzovka of what was happening in Petrograd and Moscow was confused, to say the least. The list of members of the Sovnarkom, and the texts of the decrees on land and on peace, were published in the soviet's newspaper. The same issue carried a story, delivered by direct telegraph, relating the news of the coalition negotiations sponsored by Vikzhel, the Central Executive Committee of the Railway Workers' Union, and the consequent postponing of the scheduled general strike of the railways. Independently, the Coal Miners' Union was preparing a strike against the mine owners, on economic grounds.[15] The smoke of revolutionary battle only grew thicker as the days passed, and the Iuzovka *Izvestiia* lagged behind, publishing four days' reports in a single issue. Under the dateline November 2, Vikzhel member Stampo is quoted as reporting by telegraph that Kerenskii had fled, that nothing was known of Kornilov's whereabouts, and that an agreement in principle had been reached regarding formation of a socialist government to include all parties from the Bolsheviks to the Popular Socialists. He reported continuing clashes with 2,500 casualties in Petrograd, and 4,500 in Moscow, where the total destruction of St. Basil's Cathedral was also reported.[16] A report from a different member of Vikzhel in Moscow, dated November 3, reported continued shooting in Moscow despite reports of an agreement to end the incipient civil war, and complained that nothing had been heard from Petrograd regarding a new government. The next day, a report from Moscow told of Vikzhel commissars having supervised the dissolution of the Committee for Public Safety, with Junkers and White Guards surrendering

[14] Ibid., no. 49 (November 10, 1917), p. 3. Vilisova et al., *Bor'ba za vlast' sovetov v Donbasse*, p. 189, records the passing of a Bolshevik resolution at the meeting, but fails to note that it was a Bolshevik-sponsored meeting.

[15] *Izvestiia Iuzovskogo soveta*, no. 46 (November 2, 1917). The threatened coal strike is evidently the basis for Zaitsev's charge that the Mensheviks were using their influence in the unions as a threat to cut off the coal supply of Petrograd in protest against "the adventure of the Bolsheviks." See Zaitsev, "Kak my tvorili oktiabr'," p. 137.

[16] Chamberlin, *Russian Revolution*, pp. 313, 328, 341, writes that in both the February Revolution and the July Days there was greater loss of life than in October, and gives a figure of two hundred killed in the storming of the Vladimir Military School in Petrograd on October 30, the most serious clash in the city. Regarding Moscow, he writes of the mass burial of five hundred Bolsheviks, but gives no overall figures. Rumors of wanton destruction of historic buildings in Moscow were widespread at the time.

their arms. A last, undated report told of the Kremlin in ruins, St. Basil's and Uspenskii Cathedrals burned, as well as the whole of Nikitin Street, where the Moscow duma was located. Cossacks were reported approaching Moscow, and new bloodshed was feared, for though every effort was being made to forge a compromise agreement, the Bolsheviks were said to remain intransigent.[17] Clearly these calamitous reports, including the burning of two of Russia's most famous churches, and the destruction of the historic Kremlin, were calculated to arouse enmity toward the Bolsheviks. Nevertheless, it is during precisely this period that Zalmaev and his comrades succeeded in convincing shop after shop and mine after mine that the seizure of power in the name of the soviets was the only sure way to end the war, distribute the land, and convene the constituent assembly. The frustrations and anxieties of the workers' lives made them receptive to the immediacy of Bolshevik urgings. There was a growing dissonance between the mass of workers and their elected representatives and leaders, and this offered the Bolsheviks an opportunity for influence.

Throughout this period the Iuzovka *Izvestiia* yielded not an inch to the Bolsheviks. The crisis that struck the Bolsheviks in their internal debate over the formation of a coalition government, with the resignation of a number of people's commissars, along with several members of the Bolshevik Central Committee, was reported under the maliciously gleeful (but premature) headline "Collapse of the Soviet Government."[18] The entire front page of the November 16 issue was devoted to fiercely anti-Bolshevik articles.[19] As late as December 2, the newspaper carried a clearly tendentious account of a political evening at the workers' club that attracted several hundred persons. (The sale of tickets, priced between forty kopeks and one ruble, brought in 243.60 rubles.) The reporter described how Myshkin and Gerbanenko were greeted with great applause, while "Gorichev (Bolsh.), who was evidently unprepared, and limited himself mainly to justifying his party's actions, gave a brief and pale presentation that left little impression."[20] Nevertheless, the defection of the Right Socialist-Revolutionaries from the soviet, and the recall of some of the remaining deputies by the factory workers, tipped the balance of power, and on November 17, with the support of the Left Socialist-Revolutionary faction,

[17] *Izvestiia Iuzovskogo soveta*, no. 48 (November 7, 1917).

[18] Ibid., no. 50 (November 11, 1917).

[19] Ibid., no. 52 (November 16, 1917).

[20] Ibid., no. 59 (December 2, 1917).

and the large bloc of nonparty deputies, Zalmaev was elected chairman of the executive committee of the Iuzovka soviet, with Alferov and Zaitsev as additional Bolshevik representatives.[21]

The Mensheviks of Iuzovka were as split as were their colleagues all across Russia. A month after the Bolsheviks took control of the Iuzovka soviet, Skachko, Chikirisov, and Volin attempted to organize a new Menshevik group to regain some influence in the town. Dr. Kantorovich attacked them scathingly, daring them to define what kind of menshevism they represented: "Potresov? Plekhanov? Defensists? Internationalists?"[22] With the opposition thus divided, the Bolsheviks were able to take some first steps toward ruling Iuzovka. On December 5 a special session of the Iuzovka soviet adopted a resolution of no confidence in the central Rada of the Ukraine, demanding the convening of an All-Ukrainian Congress of Soviets to set up a new government, and demanding recognition of the VTsIK and the Sovnarkom in Petrograd as the sole and supreme power in the Soviet Republic.[23] No less important in the light of future developments, this resolution came out against any possible partitioning of the Donbass.[24] These two closely interlinked issues—the integrity of the Donbass, and its belonging to Russia rather than to an independent Ukraine—were to play a central role in Donbass politics.

The Iuzovka Bolsheviks, however, were painfully aware of the tenuous nature of their control, and of the need to work ceaselessly to broaden their influence. The day after their victory in the soviet, the weekly party meeting heard complaints that no Bolshevik literature had been arriving, and that there was scarcely enough reading material to keep party activists informed of developments, let alone to spread the Bolshevik message among the masses.[25] In December 1917, the Bolshevik delegates to the Third Regional Congress of Soviets of the Donbass and Krivoi Rog caucused to coordinate their efforts and learn about each other's achievements and problems. The report from Iuzovka was pessimistic indeed. Although they

[21] *Istoriia mist i sil*, p. 91. Zaitsev, "Kak my tvorili oktiabr'," p. 137, gives the members of the executive committee as Zalmaev (chairman), Alferov and an unnamed Menshevik (deputy chairmen), Zaitsev (secretary), and an additional Menshevik and an S-R (members). With the support of the S-R, the Bolsheviks enjoyed a four-to-two majority in the executive.

[22] *Izvestiia Iuzovskogo soveta*, no. 63 (December 16, 1917), p. 2.

[23] Liubimov, *Revoliutsiia 1917 goda*, vol. 6, p. 287.

[24] Vilisova et al., *Bor'ba za vlast' sovetov v Donbasse*, p. 236.

[25] Pavliuk et al., *Bol'shevistskie organizatsii Ukrainy*, p. 326, protocols of Iuzovka Bolsheviks, November 18, 1917.

held the chair in the local soviet, the executives of the trade unions were Menshevik, and the workers' committees of the factory, the mines, and other institutions were largely either nonparty or Socialist-Revolutionary. The rapporteur stated that the Bolsheviks were working badly for lack of experienced members.[26] This report brought down an official party rebuke on the Iuzovka delegation.[27] The resources of the central party authorities were stretched even thinner than before, as the groups attempted to lay the foundations of Bolshevik control across the entire empire.

The entire Donbass was split in similar fashion. Of thirty-one representatives of Donbass soviets at the Second All-Russian Congress of Soviets, twenty-one are said to have been given imperative mandates in favor of transferring political power to the soviets.[28] Lugansk, Shcherbinovka, and Gorlovka were all Bolshevik immediately, while Iuzovka, Bakhmut, Mariupol, Konstantinovka, Popasnaia, and Aleksandrovka remained outside Bolshevik control.[29] Zaitsev visited Bakhmut in November 1917, and at first could find neither the Bolshevik party headquarters nor the soviet. He finally found the latter quartered in semiunderground fashion in a billiard hall. There, the people with whom he spoke, including Kharechko, were worried about the garrison's mood and intentions. Zaitsev noticed that the local zemstvo appeared to enjoy greater influence than the soviet.[30] Some nuts were tougher to crack than others. Arriving in Kharkov shortly after the Bolsheviks took power, Petrovskii, long an authoritative figure among Donbass workers, was asked by Sergeev to sway opinions at a meeting of Donbass miners who had decided not to support the new Soviet regime. Petrovskii's message, as he later recounted it, was simple: "In the name of the Soviet regime I announced that one does not joke with revolution, and that if they did not support it, they would be arrested."[31]

The Iuzovka Mensheviks initiated the organization of a district soviet that included Makeevka, Enakievo, Konstantinovka, Kramatorsk, and

[26] Ibid., pp. 105–6.

[27] Ibid., p. 354, report of Bolotskii to the Iuzovka Bolshevik meeting December 16, 1917.

[28] Goncharenko, *Bor'ba za ukreplenie vlasti sovetov v Donbasse*, p. 15. As was later made clear, however, this did not mean that the workers envisioned or wanted a single-party government. *Istoriia mist i sil*, p. 30, records twenty-four Donbass delegates to the Second All-Russian Congress of Soviets, of whom nineteen were said to be Bolsheviks.

[29] Modestov, *Rabochee i professional'noe dvizhenie*, p. 124; Kuranov, "Sovety na Artemovshchine," p. 169.

[30] Zaitsev, "Pis'mo v redaktsiiu," p. 368.

[31] Petrovskii, "O revoliutsionnykh sobytiiakh 1917 g.," p. 257.

Zheleznaia. In this, the Bolsheviks were a minority, and they were unable to gain control until they imposed military rule with the beginning of the civil war.[32] The revolution made for some strange bedfellows. In Ekaterinoslav, when the news of the Bolshevik coup was received, an enlarged plenary session of the soviet with representatives of factory and military committees, plus an overflowing lay audience, heard a twelve-hour debate on the subject. In the end, the Ukrainian Social-Democrats and Anarchists proposed an amendment to the Bolshevik resolution supporting the transfer of state power to the soviets. The amendment called for all the soviets in the Ukraine to be subordinated to the Revolutionary Committee of the Central Rada. The Ekaterinoslav Bolsheviks accepted the amendment, and the resolution then carried.[33]

In Iuzovka, after the Bolsheviks took over the chair of the executive committee, it was the Mensheviks' turn to appeal to the broad public. On November 19, a conference of representatives of soviets, mine committees, and trade unions of the Iuzovka district, claiming to represent 160,000 workers, called for an all-party socialist government; an immediate end to the war and an honorable democratic peace with no annexations or indemnities; all monastery, estate, and large private landholdings to be turned over to revolutionary land committees; workers' control in the factories; an eight-hour workday; state control of banks; and fixed prices and government control of distribution for food and consumer goods.[34] Everything that the Bolsheviks had been preaching throughout the summer, while the other parties waited for the constituent assembly, was now accepted. The tide of revolution was coming to the flood, and it was too late for the moderates to dam or divert it. As Petrovskii found occasion to write even earlier: "Life forms consciousness. What has already taken place in Piter and in Moscow is slowly spreading to our area."[35]

First Flames of Civil War

The anxiety lest a seizure of power by the soviets galvanize the forces of counterrevolution against the workers had been basic to the thinking of all

[32] Ostrogorskii, "Stranichki iz istorii," p. 26.

[33] Bachinskii, Kviring, and Perel'man, *Kviring* p. 54.

[34] *Izvestiia Iuzovskago soveta*, no. 58 (November 30, 1917).

[35] Ibid., no. 42 (October 26, 1917), p. 2. Petrovskii is referring to the Bolshevik majorities in the soviets of the two capitals.

the socialist parties since February. In Iuzovka, the first reaction to the October Revolution had been the forming of the Military Revolutionary Committee to prepare for the anticipated attacks. In early October, a cossack unit returning to Makeevka had offered to preserve order and property in return for being quartered in the town. The offer had been politely refused by the chief engineer of the Makeevka factory, Putilin, on the grounds that the workers themselves were maintaining exemplary order.[36] Among the resolutions adopted by the Second Oblast' Congress of Soviets of the Donbass and Krivoi Rog when it opened on October 6 was the removal of cossack forces recently stationed in various parts of the Donbass.[37]

There were grounds for fears of civil war. The first move against a Donbass soviet was led by the cossack officer Chernetsov, in Makeevka. As noted above, Chernetsov had been active in the Makeevka Committee for Public Safety since February, but had been removed and arrested for expressing Kornilovist sympathies. He was later freed, at which time he attached himself to General Kaledin. Immediately after the Bolshevik uprising in Petrograd, Chernetsov led a squad of cossacks into the Makeevka soviet and declared it dissolved. Representatives of the Iuzovka soviet immediately protested to Chernetsov's superior, General Balaban, and with added pressures from the miners and factory workers of Makeevka, Chernetsov withdrew and the soviet was reinstated.[38] This first confrontation passed without violence.

The war broke out in earnest ten days later, when Kaledin seized Rostov, and then Taganrog, and sent his forces north toward the Donbass. The first soviet attacked was at Ilovaisk, twenty kilometers southeast of Iuzovka, where twenty workers and officials of the soviet were killed. On November 26, Chernetsov led a cossack force against Sulinsk and Makeevka, where the soviets were disbanded, their buildings destroyed, their executives arrested, their militias disarmed, and thirty to forty workers killed. His forces also made a sortie against the Rykovskii mines, only one kilometer from Iuzovka.[39] At the same time, a number of echelons of cossacks arrived at the Iuzovo station, sent by request of the Kharkov-based Mine Industry Committee. Their arrival provoked tension in Iuzovka; the executive of the

[36] Vishniakov, "K bor'be," p. 229.

[37] Chernomaz, *Bor'ba rabochego klassa Ukrainy* p. 93.

[38] Institut istorii, *Bol'shevistskie organizatsii Ukrainy*, pp. 662, 925, report of Alferov to the Iuzovka Bolshevik meeting, October 28, 1917.

[39] Modestov, *Rabochee i professional'noe dvizhenie*, p. 125; Zaitsev, "Kak my tvorili oktiabr'," p. 138.

soviet informed the factory management that the workers were agitated by the cossacks' arrival, and that this agitation "might affect the factory's production." The factory management prudently denied any connection to the cossacks. Neither the soviet nor the Iuzovka duma agreed to receive the cossacks formally, and the Revolutionary Committee suggested that they be requested to leave the station. Zalmaev then interviewed the cossacks' commander, who pledged himself never to turn them against the workers.[40] Rejected in Iuzovka, the cossack force turned to Vetka, where the factory manager and former factory inspector I. A. Neudachin had expressed readiness to quarter sixty cossacks and five hundred horses in his settlement to defend the workers. Neudachin was unsuccessful in this gambit, for the factory soviet countered with an offer to provide fifty armed Red Guards to safeguard the settlement. After some haggling, the director and the workers agreed on a paid force of thirty, recruited from workers who had previously served in the local militia.[41]

The workers' reaction to Kaledin's attack, and the advance of Chernetsov toward Makeevka and Iuzovka, intensified attempts to form a Red Guard capable of defending the region. With the defection of the Socialist-Revolutionaries from the soviet, and the defeat of the Mensheviks in the mid-November elections, the Iuzovka Revolutionary Committee had ceased functioning. A new, entirely Bolshevik committee was set up for the Iuzovka-Makeevka district, with Zalmaev at its head.[42] A Red Guard of between one and two thousand men was formed, recruited from miners and factory workers, a few returnees from the army, and a sprinkling of Austrian war prisoners. They were armed with weapons that began arriving from the north, together with a military instructor, Comrade Zhlob, who personally led a force of eight hundred men to Lozovo station to defend it against cossack attacks.[43]

[40] Pavliuk et al., *Bol'shevistskie organizatsii Ukrainy*, p. 345, Zalmaev's report to the Iuzovka Bolsheviks, December 2, 1917. Zaitsev, "Kak my tvorili oktiabr'," pp. 138–39, named General Balaban, whose headquarters were then in Makeevka, as pledging not to harm the workers "if the latter did not violate the law," but credited the Iuzovka duma with preventing the quartering of the cossacks in the town.

[41] *Perepiska sekretariata*, vol. 2, pp. 378–79, report of Suglitskii, dated January 11, 1918. Pavliuk et al., *Bol'shevistskie organizatsii Ukrainy*, p. 354, letter from Matusevich to the Central Committee.

[42] Zaitsev, "Pis'mo v redaktsiiu," p. 367. One Menshevik, Polunov, joined the committee, whereupon he was ejected from his party, and joined the Bolsheviks.

[43] Zaitsev, "Kak my tvorili oktiabr'," p. 138, writes of one thousand armed Red Guards deployed around Iuzovka following the Chernetsov raid. On p. 139 he mentions a Red

Recruitment and training of the Red Guard became urgent after Kaledin's forces massacred 117 coal miners at the Iasinovata mines, and killed and mutilated Pereverzev, the chairman of the Bogodukhov-Khrustal mine soviet, together with his two bodyguards.[44] The protocol of the Iuzovka soviet for December 15 reported that the people of the district were terrorized and the local soviets outside Iuzovka destroyed.[45] In the wave of refugees that fled the countryside to the relative security of Iuzovka were many trade-union and soviet officials from the outlying mine settlements. In addition to providing for the needs of the Red Guard, the need for augmented supplies to feed the influx of refugees was said to be one of the reasons that the Military Revolutionary Committee engaged in food requisitioning from local peasants.[46]

On December 23 and 24, the Red Guards cleared the Iuzovo station of cossacks and, with the help of additional forces from Kharkov, pushed Kaledin's men into retreating from the entire Iuzovka-Makeevka district south toward Taganrog. The first White attack had been repelled by the Donbass workers' forces, imbuing them with a measure of self-confidence, and earning a valuable breathing space for organization. Although Kaledin's forces were, at this time, still relatively small and overextended, they were well-trained professionals, and they inflicted casualties on the Red Guards, including on the Rutchenko mines battalion, led by I. Danilov and N. S. Khrushchev.[47]

Kaledin's offensive drew the attention of the British, who were deeply interested in finding some force that would keep Russia in the war and frustrate Lenin's plans for peace. A "most secret" telegram to Sir George Buchanan in Petrograd inquired about Kaledin's forces and plans, and requested information about the grain supply in the south and whether the

Guard with two thousand enlisted at the end of November. Vishniakov, "K bor'be," p. 230, writes of the weapons, the composition of the force, and the instructor. Kharechko, "Bor'ba za oktiabr' v Donbasse," p. 135, recounts Zhlob's leadership of the Lozovo expedition.

[44] Goncharenko, *Sovety Donbassa v 1917 g.*, p. 126.

[45] *Izvestiia Iuzovskogo soveta*, no. 1 (January 11, 1918).

[46] Zaitsev, "Kak my tvorili oktiabr'," p. 138.

[47] See Pavliuk et al., *Bol'shevistskie organizatsii Ukrainy*, p. 363. The mention of Khrushchev as one of the leaders of the Rutchenko battalion is in Goncharenko, *Sovety Donbassa v 1917 g.*, p. 102. The book was published in Stalino in 1957 during the same period as much of the other literature glorifying Khrushchev. He was, however, politically active at the Rutchenko mines, and it would have been natural for him to be involved in organization of the mines' Red Guard.

Germans were being given access to it.[48] The British consul at Jassy, Barclay, passed on a negative description of Kaledin as "cunning, silent, but not very clever, and probably unreliable unless his personal interests are involved." This report was circulated to the cabinet and bears a handwritten note signed H. (Arthur Henderson?) remarking that a French diplomat had offered a similar description of Kaledin, while another, signed R. C., states that the British author and journalist Arthur Ransome had described Kaledin as "energetic."[49] The British government's opinion was finally decided by a telegram from Buchanan stating that Kaledin was capable of controlling Russia by occupying the Donets Basin and stopping shipments of coal and oil to the rest of Russia.[50]

But the British were not the only ones who understood the importance of the Donbass to Russia's fate. The Bolshevik leaders, both in Petrograd and in the Donbass, were painfully aware that a quarter of a million Russian workers, and the raw materials that could determine the life or death of the Soviet Republic, hung in the balance. The threat of military suppression of the soviets had been clear since the summer. In the first month after they took control of Petrograd, the Bolsheviks sent twenty-four emissaries to bolster their political power in the Donbass and lay the foundations of military organization.[51]

The Bolsheviks had not waited for the threat of counterrevolution before arming themselves. They had adopted the idea of armed uprising as an integral part of their revolutionary theory in December 1905. The Lugansk Bolsheviks began arming themselves in April. The first Red Guard unit at the Iasinovata mine was formed in August 1917, its iron pikes and dynamite bombs supplemented by fifty rifles procured by Vishniakov from Petrograd.[52] Consciousness of the need for a defensive force to guard the

[48] FO, 371/3018, p. 114 (November 26, 1917).

[49] Ibid., pp. 122, 124.

[50] Ibid., p. 138A, telegram of November 28, 1917.

[51] Goncharenko, *Bor'ba za ukreplenie vlasti sovetov v Donbasse*, p. 17. Apparently a number of these were renewals of previous party assignments following the Second Congress of Soviets, for among the names of the emissaries are Petrovskii, Magidov, Gruzman, and Zalutskii, all of whom had been active in the Donbass during the autumn of 1917.

[52] Vishniakov, "K bor'be," pp. 227, 230. Vishniakov writes that he was sent by the Bolshevik party specifically to organize the Red Guard at the mine. The unit was commanded and trained by Vishniakov and Sokolov, but in December it retreated from Iasinovata without a fight, after an artillery bombardment by the White forces, leaving the miners to be slaughtered by Chernetsov.

mines, the factories, and the soviets against cossack attacks was supplemented by the Bolshevik search for an opportunity to seize power by armed uprising. As the autumn passed, with Bolshevik strength growing, the militant right wing organizing, and the Mensheviks and Socialist-Revolutionaries stymied, preparations for violent insurrection in the Donbass proceeded apace. On October 4, a plenum of the Donbass–Krivoi Rog Oblast' Committee of Bolsheviks had heard a report by Sergeev about the state of preparations.[53] But the rise of military tensions in the area, and the response of the soviets in creating military revolutionary committees and recruiting Red Guards, made any uprising superfluous.

It was not easy to organize an effective committee in Iuzovka. The first attempt to create a military revolutionary committee and draft a Red Guard had come at the time of the Kornilov uprising, at the end of August.[54] In Iuzovka, as in most of the Donbass settlements, these committees were large bodies representing trade unions, soviets, the socialist parties, and other public groups.[55] Although the Bolsheviks were a minority in the committee that was set up, only persons approved by the Iuzovka Bolshevik kollektiv were drafted by Zalmaev into the town's Red Guard.[56] The activity of the committee included the establishing of a central military staff (*tsentroshtab*) in Iuzovka to register Red Guards in all the mines and villages of the district.[57] It would appear that little or nothing came of this effort, for a new committee was set up when the Bolsheviks took power in Petrograd two months later. Only at the start of December, when Kaledin's men began their onslaught against the Donbass soviets, does there appear to have been any serious military organization, and even then a comprehensive organization and command structure were said to be lacking.[58]

[53] Chernomaz, *Bor'ba rabochego klassa Ukrainy*, p. 96.

[54] Institut istorii, *Bol'shevistskie organizatsii Ukrainy*, pp. 599, 607, gives the decision of the Iuzovka Bolsheviks to instruct Zalmaev to support the formation of a committee to combat counterrevolution. Suglitskii later reported that Zalmaev was in charge of recruiting the Iuzovka Red Guard.

[55] For a description of the representation, see Kharechko, "Bor'ba za oktiabr' v Donbasse," p. 131. Kharechko noted that the Bolsheviks controlled such committees in the Gorlovka-Shcherbinovka district, in Makeevka, and in Lugansk. In the other areas there were S-R and Menshevik coalitions.

[56] Zaitsev, "Bolsheviki Iuzovki v 1917 godu," p. 89. How exactly this was accomplished goes unexplained.

[57] Vilisova et al., *Bor'ba za vlast' sovetov v Donbasse*, p. 112. The date of the sending of these forms was September 6, 1917. This was two days *before* the Bolsheviks of Iuzovka instructed Zalmaev to support a Committee to combat counterrevolution.

[58] Zaitsev, "Kak my tvorili oktiabr'," p. 139.

The problem of arms was acute. Vishniakov had brought one shipment of rifles, and some additional arms had been taken from military units that were dispersing, with a few of their members enlisting as squad leaders in the newly formed Red Guards.[59] But the prospect was that of large-scale warfare, and great quantities of arms were needed. When the cossacks had first appeared in the Donbass, Matusevich had written from Vetka to the Bolshevik Central Committee saying that they had sufficient recruits, but lacked arms, asking that these be provided immediately.[60] At the same time, Alferov traveled to Petrograd, returning to the Donbass in early December with six hundred rifles, eight machine guns, thirty pistols, and other equipment.[61]

The repelling of Chernetsov near Iuzovka was achieved with these weapons. The shortage of weapons remained severe even after Antonov-Ovseenko was dispatched to the Donbass as military commander in January 1918, with Sergo Ordzhonikidze as his chief commissar. He too had only minimal supplies for his army, and was unable to satisfy the appeals of the Donbass Revolutionary Committee, preferring to funnel the arms and matériel that he acquired to his own units, deploying to attack Kaledin and preparing for armed conflict with the forces of the Ukrainian Rada.[62] The Sovnarkom had decided to give priority to the Donbass, but had trouble impressing this priority on its field commanders, each of whom developed his own goals and priorities. When Trotsky was sent to Kharkov to supervise the efforts of the Red Army, Lenin sent an urgent telegram protesting that Antonov-Ovseenko must be transferred, and that both Dybenko and Voroshilov "are making off with supplies. . . . There is complete chaos. No effective aid is being given to the Donbass."[63] Such competition remained the rule throughout the civil war, as will generally happen in a complex bureaucratic organization plagued with chronic shortages. Each higher echelon was besieged with requests from its subordinates for assistance, and had to dole out supplies as best it could. The local commanders, operating

[59] Kharechko, "Bor'ba za oktiabr' v Donbasse," p. 136, tells of agitators succeeding in bringing an entire division to the decision to disband and hand over its arms, supplies, and horses to the Red Guard tsentroshtab. This was evidently not the Iuzovka tsentroshtab, but a new body set up on December 23. See Modestov, *Rabochee i professional'noe dvizhenie*, p. 126.

[60] *Perepiska sekretariata*, vol. 2, p. 323.

[61] Zaitsev, "Kak my tvorili oktiabr'," p. 138. According to *Dokumenty iz istorii grazhdanskoi voiny v SSSR*, vol. 1, p. 38, Alferov appealed to Lenin himself for the arms.

[62] Kharechko, "Bor'ba za oktiabr' v Donbasse," p. 135.

[63] Meijer, *Trotsky Papers*, vol. 1, p. 515.

with little coordination or restraint from above, filled their urgent needs by plundering whatever sources fell under their control. In April 1918, when the Germans were advancing on the Donbass, the Bolsheviks of the Vetka executive committee of the soviet turned to the district party committee, complaining that they controlled only twenty rifles and twenty dynamite bombs. The district party committee was able to allot them only twenty additional weapons.[64]

Frustrated in their efforts to obtain support from Petrograd, and after delegations to Kharkov, Moscow, and Petrograd yielded only minimal results, the Donbass Revolutionary Committee organized its own economic base. Red Guard detachments were sent throughout the Donbass to collect contributions in both cash and kind from "landowners, kulaks, and merchants." Aided by "the support and sympathy of local peasants," they collected over two hundred thousand rubles and large quantities of food and other supplies. Other units were posted at railway stations throughout the Donbass, disarming military units that were heading home, and searching trains for arms and valuables. The result was the acquisition of several hundred additional rifles and revolvers.[65] Though every little bit was valuable, these quantities were still clearly insufficient to meet the defensive needs of the Donbass.

All sides were sharply conscious of the strategic value of the Donbass. For the Bolsheviks in Petrograd, control of Donbass coal and metal was seen as a matter of life and death, and the predominantly Russian Donbass proletariat was seen as Soviet Russia's best hope for displacing the Ukrainian Rada and retaining control of the Donbass industrial complex as well as the agricultural riches and strategic territories of the Ukraine. Faced with a politically weak position, with the countryside unsympathetic to bolshevism, and only patchy and slowly growing political support in the mine and factory settlements, the Bolsheviks adopted the tactic that had succeeded in Petrograd. They organized military control of the Donbass, preempting the open discussions of the soviets and factory committees. Cossack activities lent both urgency and legitimacy to the organization, and the Bolsheviks could build on the splintered nature of the opposition, the general "positive neutralism" of the mass of nonparty workers and miners, and the coopera-

[64] Pavliuk et al., *Bol'shevistskie organizatsii Ukrainy*, pp. 411–12.

[65] Kharechko, "Bor'ba za oktiabr' v Donbasse," p. 134.

tion of Left Socialist-Revolutionaries and of anarchists. The latter were particularly active in all phases of military organization.[66]

The first step at organizing a Bolshevik-controlled Donbass Revolutionary Committee was taken even before the beginning of active anti-Bolshevik activity. On November 3, Petrovskii, acting as delegate of the Sovnarkom, gathered a group of Bolsheviks at Nikitovka to discuss proposals for unification of control of the Donbass. Gruzman, Kazimirchuk, and Kharechko were designated as a preliminary buro to contact all the local Bolshevik organizations and assure the sending of Bolshevik-controlled delegations to choose an all-Bolshevik Donbass revkom at a conference to be held later that month.[67] On December 4, fifteen delegates from eleven different districts gathered in Nikitovka for this purpose. Nikitovka was chosen as the seat of the committee because it served as the administrative and political center of the Gorlovka-Shcherbinovka district, the stronghold of the Bolsheviks in the Donbass. Gruzman and Kharechko were both elected to the permanent buro to be the executive arm of the committee, along with E. Trifonov, a Red Guard commander newly arrived from Petrograd, and a large staff, each charged with a particular aspect of organization.[68]

The first act of the revkom was the imposition of a general mobilization throughout the Donbass. Military service in the Red Guard was declared a "sacred duty," and each mine and factory was obliged to draft 10 percent of its work force. The draftees were to be selected by the factory and mine committees from among those pledging revolutionary discipline and the readiness to obey all combat orders and undergo any hardship or danger. For those violating "fundamental proletarian discipline," revolutionary tribunals were established in each battalion.[69]

[66] Zaitsev, "Kak my tvorili oktiabr'," pp. 143–45, notes activity of the anarchists on the Iuzovka military staff, including one Shota, who was a deputy commander. Avrich, *Anarchists in the Russian Revolution*, pp. 21–22, describes South Russian anarchism as particularly violent, with the Bakuninists of Ekaterinoslav singing hymns to "a new era of dynamite," and the Kharkov anarcho-futurists proclaiming "Death to World Civilization."

[67] Kharechko, "Bor'ba za oktiabr' v Donbasse," pp. 132–33.

[68] Ostrogorskii, "Sh. A. Gruzman," p. 372; Kharechko, "Bor'ba za oktiabr' v Donbasse," pp. 133–34, contains an extensive, though not complete, list of the leaders and staff of the buro.

[69] The text of the buro's declaration is given in Kharechko, "Bor'ba za oktiabr' v Donbasse," pp. 134–35.

Party members were expected to be the first to volunteer for active duty, and this further weakened the party's already overburdened apparat. In a telegram dated January 31, 1918, Sergeev protested that the drafting of numerous veteran Donbass Bolsheviks into the Red Army had left the party's daily work in the hands of "new, untested, and unstable elements, who have no deep loyalties."[70] Though there was no disputing the need to recruit a strong military force, the mobilization of workers also impaired the production of coal and metal, equally vital priorities for the Bolsheviks. By March 1918, the Donbass Bolsheviks had recruited thirty thousand men for their army, and a commissar responsible for fuel production was soon to complain that "the best coal cutters joined the Red Guard, weakening the nucleus of the working class," and that subsequent White Guard attacks then completed the dislocation of production.[71] In addition, these Red Guard units were initially a stopgap—infantry units without significant cavalry or artillery support. Kharechko calls them little more than partisan groups, given two or three days' training, equipped with rifles and dynamite bombs or occasionally machine guns, and sent to the front. This included the later-legendary First Proletarian Regiment, in which both Klimentii Voroshilov and Nikita Khrushchev began their organized military careers.[72]

The principal importance of the Donbass Military Revolutionary Committee was political rather than military. Although the hastily assembled Red Guards could beat back the first foray of White Cossacks, they had no effect whatsoever in the face of the advancing German troops in the spring of 1918, and the later battles against the Whites were conducted by Trotsky's centrally organized Red Army.

On January 15, 1918, however, the buro of the Central Military Revolutionary Committee of the Donbass declared itself to be the organ of revolutionary political power in the region.[73] It thus arrogated to itself the powers that had previously belonged to the soviets. By assuring themselves control of the Donbass revkom and of its armed forces, the Bolsheviks had found the key to subduing the non-Bolshevik soviets of the region, a scattered and

[70] Pavliuk et al., *Bol'shevistskie organizatsii Ukrainy*, p. 112.

[71] Ossinskii-Obolenskii, "Polozhenie,"

[72] Kharechko, "Bor'ba za oktiabr' v Donbasse," p. 154. Pistrak, *Grand Tactician*, p. 13, has Voroshilov as one of the organizers of the regiment. It was at this time that Khrushchev joined the Bolshevik party and served as a political commissar in the First Proletarian Regiment.

[73] Ostrogorskii, "Stranichki iz istorii," p. 29.

virtually unarmed public. In later Soviet historiography this military coup was considered an embarrassment, and its existence was denied.[74]

THE IUZOVKA BOLSHEVIKS, NOVEMBER 1917–APRIL 1918

At the end of October 1917, there were reported to be two thousand members of the Bolshevik party in Iuzovka.[75] Nevertheless, Stasova, as secretary of the Central Committee, had reported that the organization was crumbling, and had recruited Magidov and Petrovskii to pull it together. A month later, another Bolshevik organizer, Sin'chenok, reported that there was nobody in Iuzovka capable of working to create a Bolshevik majority in the soviet[76]—this despite Zalmaev's election as chairman of the executive committee. What was happening in the Bolshevik organization in Iuzovka? What problems were discussed, and what solutions attempted? The protocols of the Bolshevik meetings of this period, when the whole of Russia was locked in mortal struggle, and a dozen potentially fatal conflicts were threatening Iuzovka, paint a picture of petty bumbling, disorganization, and obtuseness, all of which might have been comic had they not cost so many lives.

The Bolshevik movement was indeed growing, and at the end of November, Zalmaev suggested that new members should be confirmed weekly, rather than monthly.[77] It would appear, however, that the expansion of the party came at the expense of quality. These were not professional revolutionaries. At the beginning of December the party meeting was notified that members were laggard in the payment of dues. A special levy of one ruble per member had been announced in September, but only fifty persons had paid by this date. In mid-February the problem of dues was discussed again, and it was decided that all arrears must be paid by March 5, on pain

[74] Zaitsev, "Pis'mo v redaktsiiu," p. 367, denies the statements made by Kharechko in "Bor'ba za oktiabr' v Donbasse" regarding the seizure of political power by the Donbass revkom. There was an extensive polemic in *Letopis' revoliutsii* during late 1927 and the beginning of 1928. Its essence was that Kharechko, who during the preceding years had written a full history of the revolutionary movement and of the Social-Democrats of the Donbass in the journal, was identified with opposition groups that were being suppressed within the party as Stalin tightened his grip.

[75] Rodichev, *Rasskazy o velikikh dniakh*, p. 199.

[76] Korolivskii, *Podgotovka*, vol. 2, pp. 289–90.

[77] Pavliuk et al., *Bol'shevistskie organizatsii Ukrainy*, p. 330.

of expulsion from the party. On March 17 a long list of those in arrears was read out to the party meeting, and was also hung in the office for all to see. Seven days' grace were given to pay up.[78] But delinquency in the payment of dues, understandable in the economic environment of Iuzovka, was not the only shortcoming of the new Bolsheviks. Party meetings generally drew only a small audience. In March 1918 this became the central point on the agenda, with Tolmachev and Verbitskii haranguing those active members present on the iniquities of absenteeism and passivity. There was some debate about a total reorganization of the membership, but no decision was recorded.

It was not only the rank and file that had an unacceptable attitude to party responsibilities. Even those who undertook leadership assignments failed to measure up. Until mid-November the task of secretary of the kollektiv was filled on an unpaid basis. With the growth of the party, it was suggested that a full-time paid secretary be hired. Zalmaev, then chairman of the Bolshevik kollektiv, and newly elected as chairman of the soviet, used the occasion to explain to the meeting that the job of party secretary was not merely to sell Bolshevik publications, but also to be an active party worker who would build the party organization.[79] At Zalmaev's suggestion, Kornienko was elected secretary at a salary of three hundred rubles per month, half paid by the Iuzovka committee, and half by the oblast' committee.[80] A week later an argument flared up when Kornienko proposed new elections for the kollektiv because some of its members were not actively fulfilling their assigned tasks. The cultural-educational committee was subject to similar criticism ("committee members are not serious and don't attend meetings"), but reelection was postponed because there was not a full quorum attending the meeting.[81] More than once in these months, party

[78] Ibid., pp. 349–50, 375, 388. At this time, the ruling that a party member not paying dues for three months was considered to have resigned from the party was already in effect.

[79] Ibid., p. 325.

[80] Ibid. In February this arrangement was changed, with the local party committee paying only fifty rubles. This would indicate a concentration of resources and control in the higher-level committees.

[81] Ibid., pp. 326, 330. P. 345 records the addition of seven members to the original nine-member kollektiv on December 2. The protocol of the party meeting for March 23 records Tolmachev as reporting that the *nine* members of the kollektiv were overburdened, and proposing the election of a fifteen-member executive with four candidate members. See p. 395. Of the nineteen people elected in accordance with Tolmachev's proposal, only three were from the seven added to the kollektiv in December, and only six were figures familiar from records of Bolshevik activity before October.

discussions of current political events were cancelled because the comrade charged with being rapporteur did not show up.[82]

It is not clear how the lists of laggard dues-payers were drawn up, for in mid-November it was reported that the existing party records were in disorder, that a mass of documents had been destroyed, and that no clear audit report could be made. On December 9, the auditing commission reported itself reduced to three persons, and new members were added. In mid-February and again toward the end of March new elections were held for the auditing commission in the wake of complaints that it was not functioning.[83]

One can understand something of the apathy of a large part of the new rank and file. They were joining the party that held central control out of prudence as much as out of identification, and found themselves in an organization with well-entrenched power. For the mass of politically inexperienced miners and workers, there was little in the political culture of bolshevism to encourage civic responsibility. The kollektiv ruled; when a library for the exclusive use of party members was established, Korneev was given the job of librarian at the recommendation of the kollektiv, though the party meeting had elected Sapozhnikov to the job.[84]

With the proliferation of posts to be filled, the Bolsheviks' resources were stretched thinner and thinner, and they did not succeed in establishing a stable and growing pool of activists who could gather experience and learn their new jobs. The discussion of new appointments suggests nothing so much as a game of musical chairs with a small group shifting frenetically from post to post, while an ever-changing group on the periphery moved on and off the stage. A revolutionary tribunal was established in Iuzovka in January 1918 and the Bolsheviks sent Shmanev to be their representative. At the time of his election to the revolutionary tribunal he was also elected as a member of the Iuzovka Bolshevik kollektiv, and on April 20, he was co-opted to the military buro of Iuzovka, to help prepare the evacuation of the town. Whether he had by this time ceased to serve on the tribunal is not recorded, but in April, when the resignation of a different Bolshevik from the tribunal is recorded, the meeting of the Iuzovka Bolsheviks decided that if no fit candidate was to be found in their party organization, they would

[82] Ibid., p. 374, records this as happening on both January 27 and February 16, 1918.
[83] Ibid., pp. 326, 349, 375, 396.
[84] Ibid., p. 367.

support a Left Socialist-Revolutionary candidate.[85] Out of their membership of two thousand, they could not find one person qualified to sit on the local revolutionary tribunal!

There were internal frictions as well. Zalmaev commented on this in mid-November, observing "the bad attitude of comrades who are party members toward people of other nationalities, insulting them at every opportunity." By unanimous vote it was resolved that "any party member insulting a person on the basis of different nationality will be swiftly excluded from the party."[86]

National prejudice was not the only fault to be found among the Iuzovka Bolsheviks. It would have been strange indeed if the impoverished and poorly educated public attracted by Lenin's party did not have a taste for vodka. At the beginning of April, three party members, jailed for drunken hooliganism, were expelled from the Iuzovka Bolsheviks amidst denunciation of growing drunkenness in the party ranks, and a three-person commission was elected to explore the problem. At the same meeting Yarov, a Bolshevik member of the tsentroshtab, was relieved of his duties because of his weakness for strong drink. The problem of drunkenness in the party was sufficiently serious to be moved to the head of the agenda, taking precedence over reelection of the party committee. Two weeks later, Comrade Gordon, who had raised the issue at the earlier meeting, renewed the demand to expel from the party persons found to be drunk and disorderly. This time she added the suggestion that a ban be put on the sale of intoxicants in Iuzovka.[87]

As can be discerned from all the above, the Iuzovka Bolsheviks spent an inordinate amount of time and energy in fruitless and frustrating introspection, discussing and rediscussing organizational questions. Even when they raised some more substantive problem, no action ensued. In January the Iuzovka Bolsheviks suggested that since the local *Izvestiia* still reflected a Menshevik presence, a Iuzovka Bolshevik newspaper should be printed. Though a committee of four was appointed to look into the question, it was never followed up, and only in 1920, after the civil war, did the Bolshevik *Diktatura truda* appear in Iuzovka.[88]

[85] Ibid., pp. 371, 406, 413.

[86] Ibid., p. 325.

[87] Ibid., pp. 402, 413. I have found no reference to any formal ending of the prohibition that was instituted in 1914.

[88] Ibid., p. 367.

Perhaps more significant than the decisions that were not implemented are the discussions that never took place, or that took place only belatedly. Most surprising among these neglected questions was that of war and peace. This question aroused passions all through the Donbass, and indeed was the focus of debate at the Seventh Congress of the All-Russian Communist Party (Bolsheviks) (RKP[b]) in March 1918. Yet according to one Iuzovka Bolshevik delegate, Kochubei, who was upon his return to be chairman of the Iuzovka soviet and a member of the district tsentroshtab, the Iuzovka party organization had never discussed this question.[89] At the start of April, the Iuzovka Bolsheviks were busy trying to rid their ranks of drunkards, and elect committees that would function. They did find time for a lecture by Verbitskii: "The International Significance of the Russian Revolution." But by this same time, the Germans were advancing on the Donbass and had reached Lugansk. In other places the Bolsheviks were feverishly organizing and training for armed resistance.[90]

In Iuzovka, these questions were left to higher authorities, and the local party organization showed no interest in them until catastrophe arrived at their doorstep. Only in mid-April was there a discussion of local conditions, and it was rife with mutual recrimination among the representatives of the town executive committee, the district executive committee, and the local tsentroshtab, all of which were blamed for interference in one another's affairs, while evacuation was a shambles, and no competent military staff existed. Comrade Gordon, by now a member of the kollektiv (despite being a relative newcomer she received 153 votes, second only to the veteran activist Tolmachev, who received 171), and active in party discussions, complained that there was neither an authoritative nor a centralized regime in the town. She asked why the local Red Army staff should be subordinate to the district executive. Before this point could be resolved, Comrade Krusser, a member of the local tsentroshtab, invoked a point of personal privilege and asked the meeting to decide whether an order given by a party member who had more seniority than another member should be considered mandatory and be unconditionally obeyed by the junior member. After a long discussion, the Bolshevik meeting resolved that no decision be taken in this matter because of its lack of importance.[91] The only other item on

[89] Anikeev and Lavrov, "Bol'shevistskie organizatsii," p. 34.

[90] Pavliuk et al., *Bol'shevistskie organizatsii Ukrainy*, p. 402. For the activities of other Bolshevik groups, see Voroshilov's reports on pp. 397 and 401.

[91] Ibid., pp. 406–7. Krusser was later killed at the front during the civil war.

the Bolshevik agenda that day, three days before a decision was made to close the New Russia factory, and about a week before the Germans occupied Iuzovka, was Comrade Gordon's report on efforts to prepare a choir for May Day. Two days later the party members reconvened in a special session that attracted nearly two hundred members, to establish a twenty-person military buro composed of sections to deal with agitation, technical affairs, mobilization, sanitary problems, and evacuation. The last section was evidently treated most seriously, for its members were four of the town's ranking Bolshevik veterans: Alferov, Tolmachev, Verbitskii, and Zaitsev.[92] Throughout this period, the party organization appears to have added nothing to the strength of the movement and contributed nothing to carrying on the life of Iuzovka's society, or moving it toward socialist self-government.

In the soviet, now chaired by Zalmaev, things were little better. The Iuzovka soviet had, throughout 1917, been more of a forum for coordination of the various new social bodies that were springing up than an institution of state power. Most important, the town's food supply and the employment that was the oxygen of Iuzovka's economy were both centered in the New Russia factory and mines, and these were still operating much as before. The Main Factory Committee, composed of representatives of the shop committees, and its executive, the factory Council of Elders, were the primary bodies negotiating agreements on wages, work conditions, and food supplies with the factory management. The soviet served only in an advisory capacity regarding these central institutions of life in Iuzovka.

The difficulties faced by the Bolshevik-controlled Iuzovka soviet are reflected in the session of December 15. Samylin's report on the Ekaterinoslav Province Congress of Soviets, convened with a majority of Bolshevik delegates, was disputed by Abramzon of the SERP. Koval reported that the Bakhmut Congress of Soviets had broken up when a dispute arose between the Bolsheviks and representatives of the Ukrainian parties. Matters within Iuzovka were no better. Talks with the factory administration, aimed at maintaining employment in the factory, were deadlocked. The closure of additional shops appeared imminent because the army was no longer ordering ammunition and other goods. The best the soviet could do was to resolve that if the ammunition shops should close down, their workers should be taken into the remaining functioning shops of the factory. A

[92] Ibid., pp. 410–11.

second resolution recommended that instead of closing defense-related shops, the factory should reorient them to the needs of the civilian economy. At this time the New Russia factory was one of only four Donbass metallurgy enterprises remaining open. Fourteen other plants had closed, supposedly for lack of fuel. Despite the very real difficulties of obtaining coal and transporting it, the perception of the workers' representatives was that the employers were again using the lockout as a political and economic tactic.[93]

A no less serious crisis appeared to be brewing with regard to the town's militia. The rank and file, evidently radical in mood, was threatening to arrest the militia commanders. Zalmaev requested that the executive committee of the soviet intervene, and that body voted for election of a new militia commissar. How this official was to be elected then became the focus of a stormy debate. The soviet suggested that its executive committee, the municipal duma executive, and elected representatives of the militia convene to agree on a candidate. This proposal was rejected by the Iuzovka duma, which claimed exclusive jurisdiction over the post of militia commander. Apprised of this opposition, the executive committee of the soviet sent a compromise suggestion of a joint soviet-duma nomination to be confirmed by vote of the Iuzovka duma. Even when chaired by Zalmaev, the Iuzovka soviet was unwilling or unable to claim sole authority against the duma. Meanwhile, despite the turnover in control of the soviet, the militia continued to function under its former commanders.[94] This session took place in mid-December, when the first offensive of Kaledin's forces was at its crest. The Red Guard that was organized at the time was in desperate need of funds, and a proposal to levy a 2 percent tax on the wages of each worker had been referred by a district congress of military revolutionary committees to the executive committee of the Iuzovka soviet for implementation. It would seem that the soviet doubted its authority to impose such a tax, and the readiness of the workers to pay it, for the proposal was referred to the shop committees for discussion.[95]

[93] On this point, see the discussion in *Izvestiia Iuzovskogo soveta*, no. 62 (December 12, 1917), p. 2.

[94] Kharechko, "Bor'ba za oktiabr' v Donbasse," p. 152, specifies that the Menshevik Lekhko and the S-R Kliuev still commanded the Iuzovka militia in March 1918.

[95] *Izvestiia Iuzovskogo soveta*, no. 1 (January 11, 1918), protocol of the soviet session of December 15, 1917. The publication of the first *Izvestiia* for 1918 on January 11, with a delay of nearly four weeks in publishing the protocol of the soviet, is indicative of the political difficulties in the town.

Such a session was typical of the Iuzovka soviet throughout 1917 and the beginning of 1918. The soviet was not the sole, or even the dominant, institution of state power in the town. Even on such a sensitive matter as control of the militia, it had to negotiate with the duma. In every sense, the term "pluralism of authority" (*mnogovlastie*), later used by Zaitsev to describe Iuzovka in the spring of 1918, was applicable to the political structure of the town throughout 1917, and continued even after the Bolsheviks became the dominant faction in the soviet's executive committee.[96]

In using this term, however, Zaitsev was referring to a different situation. He used it in a pejorative sense, to refer to the lack of order that prevailed among the various authorities in the Iuzovka district in the spring of 1918. This tangled competition among various bodies evoked one of the few discussions devoted by the local party organization to local politics and administration. The example given by Zaitsev is the competition for resources between the soviet and the local tsentroshtab. In March 1918, the Iuzovka soviet decreed a compulsory loan of five million rubles from "the local bourgeoisie," to provide working capital for the factory. When the soviet succeeded in collecting a good part of this sum, the Iuzovka tsentroshtab, acting under the inspiration of the newly formed Donetsk–Krivoi Rog Autonomous Republic, adopted the idea and decreed a similar tax on the same public. Predictably, it had less success, but this did not deter the district tsentroshtab from also requisitioning resources along the same lines. As Zaitsev complained, "There was no order in this."[97]

At this point, in mid-March 1918, the local Bolsheviks lost the town's confidence, and had it not been for the intervention of the Donbass military revolutionary committees they would have lost control of the Iuzovka soviet. The incident that caused this turn of events was an armed robbery in which four militiamen were murdered, and the factory payroll, amounting to a million rubles or more, was stolen. Several suspects were arrested, among them a Bolshevik named Tulupov, who had been active in the Donbass throughout the autumn.[98] Zalmaev, as chairman of the soviet,

[96] For the term *mnogovlastie*, see Zaitsev, "Pis'mo v redaktsiiu," p. 371.

[97] Zaitsev, "Kak my tvorili oktiabr'," p. 140. Here Zaitsev writes that the soviet's assessment on the town was 2.5 million rubles and the tsentroshtab's tax was 5 million. In "Pis'mo v redaktsiiu," p. 371, he writes of the soviet's tax amounting to 5 million rubles, of which 2.5 million was actually collected.

[98] See *Izvestiia Iuzovskogo soveta*, no. 56 (November 21, 1917), p. 2, where Comrade Tulupov is named as Bolshevik representative of the Konstantinovka foundry workers at a conference in Iuzovka.

interceded with the militia for Tulupov's release, and provided security for his availability for questioning. There was a certain urgency to Zalmaev's actions, for when news of the robbery spread through the town, the workers demanded the lynching of the robbers. As soon as he was released, Tulupov disappeared.

When it became known that Zalmaev had interceded on behalf of Tulupov, the anger was focused at Zalmaev and the Bolsheviks. From the factory came a demand for Zalmaev's arrest. A mob, including the militia, and its commander, the Socialist-Revolutionary Kliuev, gathered in front of the offices of the Iuzovka Executive Committee, shouting for Zalmaev's immediate dismissal. At this point the tsentroshtab, sensing the broader political implications of the situation, intervened. Martial law was declared, and the mob was promptly dispersed. The militia was disarmed by the Red Guard and its commander was arrested. The tsentroshtab also proposed the arrest of all Menshevik and Socialist-Revolutionary leaders in Iuzovka. The Bolshevik leaders of the Iuzovka Executive Committee protested these steps, fearing that the tsentroshtab's actions could provoke a general anti-Bolshevik uprising among the Iuzovka workers.[99] In the meantime, Zalmaev, sensitive to public opinion, left town without informing any of his comrades in the party or in the executive of the soviet. This, of course, further inflamed the emotions of the town's workers, as rumors spread that Zalmaev had absconded with two million rubles.

The opposition members in the soviet demanded the immediate abolition of the martial law imposed by the tsentroshtab, but they were defeated by "a majority, though an insignificant majority," as Kharechko later wrote. Following this vote, Alferov, who as deputy chairman had taken over Zalamaev's position, resigned, pending an official investigation of Zalmaev's actions.

At this point the Socialist-Revolutionaries and Mensheviks convened a joint session of the Iuzovka duma and the Iuzovka soviet. The Kadets of the duma participated, and the Bolsheviks of the soviet accepted the places alloted to them in the presidium of the meeting, although by this time they were boycotting the executive of the Iuzovka duma. The demands placed

[99] Kharechko, "Bor'ba za oktiabr' v Donbasse," p. 152. Goncharenko, *Bor'ba za ukreplenie vlasti sovetov v Donbasse*, p. 186, writes of an unsuccessful anti-Bolshevik uprising in Iuzovka in April 1918. He is evidently referring to this incident, but no other source expresses more than a fear that the Tsentroshtab's actions might provoke such an uprising. The detailed accounts of the "Zalmaev-Tulupov affair" are in Zaitsev, "Kak my tvorili oktiabr'" and "Pis'mo v redaktsiiu," as well as Kharechko.

before this session went far beyond the immediate irritation of the Zalmaev affair, and struck at the foundations of Bolshevik influence in the Donbass. In addition to the arrest of Zalmaev, and the abolition of martial law in Iuzovka, the meeting's resolution proposed the closing of the *Donetsk pravda*; dispersal of the exclusively Bolshevik Red Army and Red Guards and their replacement by fighting units that would include members of all the socialist parties; and the dispersal of the tsentroshtab. This resolution was carried by sixty-six votes against the twenty-eight supporting an unspecified Bolshevik counterresolution.[100]

Here, the Central Military Committee of the Donbass and the Sovnarkom of the then-extant Donbass–Krivoi Rog Autonomous Republic intervened and dispersed the Iuzovka soviet, calling for new elections. They also created a new body, the Iuzovka-Makeevka District Executive Committee, almost totally Bolshevik in its composition, and exercising no authority over any soviets in the district except Iuzovka and Makeevka, the only two large local centers in which the Bolsheviks were then dominant.[101] This new creature ratified the revkom dissolution of the Iuzovka soviet and undertook hierarchical supervision of the future Iuzovka Executive Committee to prevent recurrence of the opposition uprising.

The new elections were scheduled for mid-April, and as Kharechko observed, the central revkom of the Donbass expended great efforts on these elections. The Iuzovka Bolsheviks also threw themselves energetically into the election campaign, designating fifteen agitators to cover the various shops of the factory.[102] The result of these efforts (and one may suspect that the revkom, with its armed Red Guards, had more effect than did the Iuzovka Bolsheviks) was that the new Iuzovka soviet had a huge Bolshevik majority. The executive committee was to be made up of eight or nine Bolsheviks and 4 or 5 Left Socialist-Revolutionaries, with the Mensheviks

[100] Kharechko, "Bor'ba za oktiabr' v Donbasse," pp. 152–53. Zaitsev, "Pis'mo v redaktsiiu," p. 369, points out that the Iuzovka soviet had about 250 deputies at that time, and that only 94 took part in the voting on this resolution. He says nothing of the participation of duma members.

[101] Zaitsev, "Kak my tvorili oktiabr'," p. 140 and "Pis'mo v redaktsiiu," p. 370, "credits" Verbitskii of the tsentroshtab for this maneuver, calling the district central executive committee "the abortive child of the tsentroshtab," a definition later disputed by Kharechko. There existed a Menshevik-controlled Iuzovka-Makeevka district soviet, drawing on all the mines and factories of the area.

[102] Pavliuk et al., *Bol'shevistskie organizatsii Ukrainy*, p. 388, Iuzovka Bolshevik meeting, March 17, 1918. Among those named, strangely enough, is Zalmaev, who by this time had fled the town.

totally excluded. The presidium of the executive committee would be three Bolsheviks: Alferov as chairman, Zaitsev as his deputy, and Tolmachev as secretary, along with two Left Socialist-Revolutionaries. At the same time, the Bolshevik group in the soviet discussed the question of whether parties that did not accept the platform of the soviets should be allowed representation.[103] The opposition leaders in Iuzovka understood the message, and in the wake of the elections, the leaders of the right-wing Mensheviks and Socialist-Revolutionaries,—Myshkin, Shub, Bartov, Galuzin, and others—left Iuzovka.[104] Six months after taking power in Petrograd, the Bolsheviks had gained control in Iuzovka.

Meanwhile, an investigatory commission had traced Zalmaev's steps. He had traveled to Mariupol, where, claiming he was penniless, he borrowed five hundred rubles from comrades, and set out on March 29 for the Caucasus. Hearing this report, the Iuzovka Bolsheviks expelled Zalmaev from the party for having abandoned his post.[105] Three weeks later the local party organization learned that he had been arrested, and resolved that he should be returned to Iuzovka for trial. But the trial never took place; the Germans were rapidly approaching Iuzovka, and as Kochubei, who had replaced Zalmaev as chairman of the soviet and in the Iuzovka Military Revolutionary Committee, noted, the military situation was threatening, and the Iuzovka Red Guard was as yet unready for battle.[106]

Elections to the Constituent Assembly

In the eight months of the February Revolution, the constituent assembly had become the symbol of the new order to come. For the public and for almost every party, including the Bolsheviks, the convening of the constituent assembly was regarded as sacred. In Iuzovka and in the entire Donbass, the necessity of conducting the assembly elections at the appointed time figured prominently in the resolutions of all the meetings, whether supporting or opposing the establishment of Bolshevik power. Even before the

[103] Ibid., pp. 404–6, meeting of Bolshevik faction of the Iuzovka soviet, April 12, 1918.

[104] Kharechko, "Bor'ba za oktiabr' v Donbasse," p. 153.

[105] Zaitsev, "Pis'mo v redaktsiiu," p. 370, editor's note.

[106] Pavliuk et al., *Bol'shevistskie organizatsii Ukrainy*, pp. 412–13, Bolshevik meeting, April 20, 1918. Zalmaev eventually was returned to the ranks of the Communist party and served for the remainder of his career as a minor diplomatic courier.

results of the Second Congress of Soviets were known, the campaign for these elections had been under way throughout the Donbass. On October 17, the Iuzovka Mensheviks had published their party program in the local *Izvestiia*, following a general discussion of the political principles that should guide the emergent Russian Republic.[107] The political tensions accompanying the Bolshevik coup in Petrograd raised the temperature of the campaign for the constituent assembly, and soon the editors of *Izvestiia*, speaking in the name of the leadership of the Iuzovka soviet, found it necessary to voice a protest, complaining: "In recent days impermissible phenomena have appeared. Posters are torn down, as well as placards and announcements of various parties and groups in connection with the constituent assembly. Such coarse violations of freedom of election are impermissible and will be strictly put down by all legal means."[108] In the rough atmosphere of life and politics in Iuzovka, this was a serious attempt at civilized civic behavior, consistent with the tone of the Menshevik leadership of the soviet. The interlude was all too brief, yet the pressures for a fair and open election campaign were not totally ineffective. In keeping with the pattern of behavior of the Petrograd Bolsheviks, the Ekaterinoslav province revkom had ordered the closing of the Kadet-leaning newspaper, *Pridneprovskii krai*. Permission to reopen the paper was announced by Kviring, chairman of the revkom, "in light of the preservation of public order, and the approaching elections".[109]

The Bolsheviks were to do well in the Donbass, garnering more than their countrywide proportion of votes. The beginnings, however, were difficult, and the atmosphere of the campaign tense. The Bolshevik list for the elections in Ekaterinoslav province was made up in consultation between the Central Committee in Petrograd and the province party committee, elected at the beginning of October. When Zalmaev reported the list to the Iuzovka Bolsheviks, something of a storm erupted, with members accusing the Central Committee of putting "strangers" high on the list, and neglecting local activists. The fear was that the workers and miners of Iuzovka would shun a list led by outsiders.[110] In fact, the twenty-five candidates, headed by Petrovskii, were almost all prominent Donbass activ-

[107] For the program, see *Izvestiia Iuzovskogo soveta*, no. 39 (October 17, 1917).

[108] Ibid., no. 49 (November 7, 1917), p. 4.

[109] Ibid., p. 2.

[110] Institut istorii, *Bol'shevistskie organizatsii Ukrainy*, p. 639.

ists. These included Gruzman, Voroshilov, and Iurii Lutovinov. Only V. P. Nogin of Moscow, in second place on the list, was a total outsider, while of the Bolshevik leaders of the Donbass, only Sergeev appears to be missing. Iuzovka received three places, with Kharechko, Zalmaev, and Alferov as nominees.[111]

The Iuzovka Bolsheviks mobilized for the elections, sending teams of observers to all six of the town's voting precincts as well as to the overall town election commission.[112] It may be assumed that the remaining parties did no less, for the elections that were held on November 12 in Iuzovka must have been regarded as an important test of strength, coming at a time when the town was turning more and more toward the Bolsheviks, but before they had achieved a predominant place in the soviet. It is therefore somewhat surprising that the turnout of voters appears to have been small—between eighteen thousand and twenty thousand votes were cast, although between thirty thousand and fifty thousand people were eligible to vote.[113] There are two conflicting sources for the results. Suglitskii reported to the Central Committee that the results in Iuzovka were: Bolsheviks—nine thousand votes; Kadets—three thousand votes; Socialist-Revolutionaries—two thousand votes; Mensheviks—one thousand votes.[114] An alternate source gives the results as: Bolsheviks—40 percent; Socialist-Revolutionaries—18 percent; Mensheviks—7 percent; Jewish National List—7 percent; others—"insignificant."[115] This count adds up

[111] The list of candidates appeared in *Izvestiia Iuzovskogo soveta*, no. 50 (November 11, 1917). Kharechko was nominated as chairman of the Congress of Peasant Deputies, and Alferov as chairman of the executive committee of the Rykovskii mine soviet.

[112] Pavliuk et al., *Bol'shevistskie organizatsii Ukrainy*, p. 322.

[113] The July 1917 census of Iuzovka showed that 54 percent of the town's population, 31,154 persons, were of voting age at that time. See table 8.7, p. 244, in vol. 1. On November 7, 1917, the management of the New Russia Co. wrote that 21,000 workers and 58,000 dependents were on the factory's food rolls. Using the same age structure, this would yield an electorate of 42,660, in addition to the nonfactory population, which would add at least 10,000 more to the electoral rolls. See *Izvestiia Iuzovskogo soveta*, no. 51 (November 14, 1917), p. 3, letter of Revilon. It is possible that the factory food rolls were misleading. Miners were leaving the Iuzovka area in increasing numbers as hunger, civil war, and turmoil threatened. Perhaps not all who left were deleted from the ration lists. However, the turnout of the electorate appears to have been somewhere between 35 percent and 65 percent. According to Pavliuk et al., *Bol'shevistskie organizatsii Ukrainy*, pp. 338–39, 70 percent of those eligible voted in Lugansk.

[114] Pavliuk et al., *Bol'shevistskie organizatsii Ukrainy*, p. 340.

[115] Korolivskii, *Podgotovka*, vol. 3, p. 266.

to 72 percent of the vote, and to it we may add 13 percent for the Kadets, leaving 15 percent for the remaining lists.[116] In the general Donbass region, the Bolsheviks received 32.3 percent, the Ukrainian parties 23 percent, the Socialist-Revolutionaries—18.7 percent, the Kadets—7.4 percent, and the Mensheviks—5.4 percent.[117]

These results must have been very encouraging for a party organization that a month earlier was supposed to have been on the verge of disintegration. There were, however, other places where the Bolsheviks did even better. At Nelepovka the Bolshevik list gathered 1,673 votes, as compared to 13 for the Socialist-Revolutionaries, and 6 for the Mensheviks. At Shcherbinovka the Bolsheviks received 3,175 votes, the Socialist-Revolutionaries 430, and the Mensheviks only 10.[118]

In light of the importance attached to the constituent assembly a strong reaction might have been expected when it was dispersed. The elections, however, were in November, when there was still a certain measure of continuity with the hopes of the February Revolution. By the following January the Bolsheviks had repelled the first challenges to their power, the first clashes of the civil war had taken place, and a totally different set of hopes and anxieties held the attention of the Donbass population. A debate was held between a Socialist-Revolutionary representative and a Bolshevik at the end of January at the Iuzovo railway station. The miners of the

[116] The assumption here is that the Bolsheviks did receive 9,000 votes and that this represented 40 percent of the total. The Kadets' 3,000 would then be 13.3 percent. However, the two reports are incompatible, for if the Bolsheviks' 9,000 votes are 40 percent of the total, then the Mensheviks' 7 percent should come to 1,575 votes, and not 1,000, as Suglitskii reports. If he reported the Menshevik vote accurately, and if the percentages given in the other report are correct, then Suglitskii exaggerated the Bolshevik vote. I have found no third source with which to compare these. Zaitsev, "Bolsheviki Iuzovki v 1917 godu," p. 90, writes that in the town the Bolsheviks received "about half" the vote. This account, however, must be treated with caution.

[117] Korolivskii, Rubach, and Suprunenko, *Pobeda Sovetskoi vlasti na Ukraine*, p. 334. This leaves 13.2 percent for other parties. A total of 577,010 votes was cast. The areas covered were Ekaterinoslav, Kharkov, Lugansk, Iuzovka, Bakhmut, and Slavianoserbsk districts. These areas were the central industrial areas of the Donbass and environs. Full coverage of both industrial and rural areas yields a somewhat different picture. Radkey, *Russia Goes to the Polls*, notes that in Ekaterinoslav province the Bolsheviks received 213,163 votes out of 1,193,049 (17.8 percent). In Kharkov province they received 110,844 out of 928,526 (11.9 percent). In the Ukraine as a whole, the Bolshevik vote was 859,330 out of 8,201,063, (10 percent).

[118] *Proletarskaia mysl'*, no. 19 (November 30, 1917), carries extensive results of the constituent assembly elections, both in the Donbass and elsewhere.

immediate district who attended approved the dispersal of the assembly with only a few abstentions.[119]

Conquest and Economic Collapse

At the beginning of April, the military situation became desperate, but this time the threat was the German army. With the entire Iuzovka-Makeevka district lying exposed to the Germans, the tsentroshtab, now under the command of Kharechko, was located in Iuzovka. Under the command of the "Extraordinary Staff of the Donbass Republic" it was assigned a sector in what was to be a fight to the last man. An elaborate plan of positional warfare was worked out, but "not the tenth part was fulfilled."[120]

The first orders for evacuation of Iuzovka had been given at the start of April by the tsentroshtab, over the signatures of Kharechko and Gruzman. Mining equipment, food, and particularly printing presses and paper were given priority in evacuation. "Not a letter of type, not a page of paper should be left."[121] Iuzovka's five banks were also evacuated at this time.[122] Late at night on April 17, the tsentroshtab supply train and forces left Iuzovka. They tried to set themselves up in Alexandrovsk-Grushevsk but were driven out by hostile cossacks and withdrew to Rostov, where they established themselves as the Military Commissariat of the Southern Republics.[123] On April 25 and 27, the Iuzovka Bolshevik party committee distributed money to those comrades who did not have the means to finance their own evacuation. At this point the town was without any ruling institutions. The only armed force remaining was that of a few anarchists commanded by Malov, and the former Bolshevik Biriukov. But theirs was only a flamboyant gesture, and other than challenging and briefly detaining Zaitsev and Alferov, who remained until the Germans were in sight, they accomplished nothing.[124]

[119] Vilisova et al., *Bor'ba za vlast' sovetov v Donbasse*, p. 302.

[120] Ibid., pp. 155–58. Korolivskii, *Grazhdanskaia voina na Ukraine*, vol. 1, bk. 1, pp. 110–12, gives the complete text of Antonov Ovseenko's elaborate defense plan, in which Iuzovka was to have been a second line, with all the surrounding railway stations defended by specially mobilized Red Guard units.

[121] Kharechko, "Bor'ba za oktiabr' v Donbasse," pp. 159–60. From today's perspective, the Bolshevik priorities appear somewhat strange.

[122] Zaitsev, "Kak my tvorili oktiabr'," p. 140.

[123] Korolivskii, *Grazhdanskaia voina na Ukraine*, vol. 1, bk. 1, pp. 160–61.

[124] Zaitsev, "Kak my tvorili oktiabr'," pp. 140–41.

The political uncertainties only exacerbated the economic ruin. Factories and mines were closing daily. The Bolshevik authorities and individual groups of workers made desperate efforts to maintain some level of employment and production. Under these conditions, direct barter between the factories and the population spread rapidly. The Makeevka factory contracted to supply 250,000 puds of iron to surrounding areas in return for grain, at the prewar ratio of one pud of iron to two puds of grain. The local soviet was then to distribute the grain.[125] The New Russia Factory Workers' Committee, together with the Workers' Control Committee, did the same. They rejected a management proposal to market a large quantity of iron in the Don areas (where Kaledin's forces were in control), and sold the iron to local cooperatives and peasant committees for cash, using the returns to pay the workers, who had not received the wages due them. Chernomaz comments: "Such distribution of metal totally disorganized the basis of any regulation, and increased economic chaos. Only very rarely did workers' organizations resort to such extreme steps."[126] Yet it would appear that both the predicament of a shortage of working capital and the solution of small-scale cash sales to local consumers were more often the rule in Iuzovka than the comment by Chernomaz would indicate. In the coming years, an economy of barter was to dominate, where sellers accepted almost anything and buyers offered almost anything to survive.[127]

In an effort to provide the working capital necessary for the Donbass economy, Ordzhonikidze had been delegated to supervise the allocation of funds from Petrograd, and he was said to have arranged the transfer of 860 million rubles to the state bank in Kharkov betwen October 1917 and April 1918.[128] Ordzhonikidze's financial aid to the Donbass was, however, not a one-sided affair. In return for the funds, Ordzhonikidze had taken all the grain stores and all the coal that could be shipped. In the first half of January two thousand carloads of coal and two hundred of grain were shipped from the Donbass to Petrograd and Moscow.[129] The formal bread ration of a coal miner at that time was three-quarters of a funt per day (a little over 300

[125] Ibid., p. 141.

[126] Chernomaz, *Bor'ba rabochego klassa Ukrainy*, p. 129.

[127] See the graphic discussion in Brower, "City in Danger," particularly pp. 72–73.

[128] Chernomaz, *Bor'ba rabochego klassa Ukrainy*, p. 127. Iuzovka is named as one of the localities benefiting from these funds.

[129] *Pravda* (January 21, 1918).

grams), though in the New Russia factory and mines the workers were allocated twice this amount.[130]

The harvests in Ekaterinoslav in the years 1917 to 1919 were relatively good, attracting the attention of those who required supplies for urban centers and the military.[131] By the start of 1918 the authorities in the province had set up a purchasing and dispatch center through which representatives of consuming areas were supposed to coordinate all purchases, paying either in cash or in consumer goods. "Nobody is permitted to purchase food independently in Ekaterinoslav province."[132] Anarchy, however, was stronger than Bolshevik centralization at this point. A legitimately procured food train carrying supplies from Ekaterinoslav had been sent without armed guards, and was "diverted" en route, provoking the chairman of the Extraordinary Commission for Food Supply, Trotsky, to order that no goods addressed to the Moscow City Food Commission were to be diverted to any other institution.[133] A. I. Rykov was sent to head the Moscow food purchasing mission in Ekaterinoslav, and together with Kviring he met with twelve hundred delegates of the local peasantry who agreed to send grain to the new capital, but asked Moscow for basic consumer necessities in return. This arrangement evidently broke down quickly, for only days later complaints were raised by the local soviets of the Donbass that the Muscovites, under Rykov's leadership, were persisting in organizing their own food-gathering efforts.[134] By the beginning of March, the food shortage was driving miners away in masses, and an emergency program was proposed. Not only was it necessary to bring food to the Donbass, but the "excess population, not contributing to the restoration of industry, must be mercilessly resettled out of the region." It was admitted that this might violate individual civil rights, but was justified as a "revolutionary

[130] Kondufor, *Istoriia rabochikh Donbassa*, vol. 1, p. 166. For the ration of the Iuzovka workers, see *Izvestiia Iuzovskogo soveta*, no. 59 (December 2, 1917), p. 2. As noted in vol. 1, the minimum diet proposed ten years previously had included 460 grams of bread, and the miners then actually consumed between 1,100 and 1,500 grams of bread daily.

[131] Gerasimovich, *Golod na Ukraini*, p. 15.

[132] *Biulleten' Moskovskogo gorodskogo prodovolstvennogo komiteta*, no. 18 (January 30, 1918), p. 3.

[133] Ibid., no. 21 (February 2, 1918), p. 12. The emphasis on the train having been sent unguarded suggests that Trotsky's decree was to be enforced by armed escorts for future trains.

[134] Ibid., no. 24 (February 7, 1918), p. 3, and no. 27 (February 10, 1918), p. 1.

necessity."[135] Mercifully for the many pensioners who had settled in Iuzovka, and for the Jewish community that was still largely uninvolved in the mines and factories, the Bolsheviks had neither the resources nor the time to implement this suggestion.

At the New Russia factory in Iuzovka, questions of production and of food supply were closely and explicitly interwoven. A tense and unstable symbiosis existed between the management, headed by the director, Svitsyn, who appears to have been in Rostov for most of this period; his deputy, Revilon, and the chief engineer, Glass, who were the actual directors of the factory; and the factory's workers, represented by the Central Council of Factory and Shop Committees. The struggle for control was constrained by the common interest of both sides in keeping the factory in production as long as possible. More than in most Donbass centers, this was possible in Iuzovka, for Hughes' foresight had made the plant relatively independent of the increasingly uncertain transport system. Iuzovka had been sited and developed so that the greater part of its production needs could be met by its own internal resources. Where other large producers needed to transport four to five puds of ore and flux for every pud of pig iron produced, and smaller smelters had to haul in as much as nine puds, the New Russia factory was dependent only on three puds of outside materials.[136]

By decree of the provisional government's Food Commissariat, a new Mine and Factory Food Committee had been established under the Iuzovka soviet in mid-October 1917. Its bylaws gave it the power to requisition and distribute supplies and to set prices. Its duties included the auditing of available supplies and the estimation of future needs. This committee replaced the food committee that had functioned since March. The company continued subsidizing food supplies to workers as it had done throughout the war, rationing the quantity of subsidized food each worker was eligible to receive.[137] The new committee was large, made up of management representatives, twenty delegates from the factory and central mines, five from the Vetka mine, and four workers each from the coke ovens and from the Novosmolianin mine.[138] The change in the food committee

[135] Boiarkov, "Reorganizatsiia Donetskoi industrii," p. 3.

[136] *Narodnoe khoziaistvo*, no. 1 (1918), p. 21.

[137] The bylaws of the new food committee appear in *Izvestiia Iuzovskogo soveta*, no. 39 (October 17, 1917), p. 3. The management response is in DOGIA, F. 6, op. 1, d. 13, p. 5, dated October 30, 1917.

[138] *Izvestiia Iuzovskogo soveta*, no. 49 (November 7, 1917), p. 3.

must have appeared to the managers to offer a propitious opportunity to restructure the whole web of relations between management and workers; on November 7, they addressed a long and detailed letter to the Council of Elders that acted as executive for the Main Factory Committee, setting forth the factory's situation and the new rules proposed by management.

The stated rationale for these new rules was to keep the factory running despite the worsening economic environment. Production was falling steadily, and those goods that were produced could not be marketed. The currency shortage meant that wages might not be paid on time, and the workers were to be informed that some shops within the factory might have to be closed, and their staffs laid off. Management would continue to supply subsidized food, but in limited amounts, for the growing numbers of Iuzovka residents drawing on these subsidized food supplies had become a financial drain on the company. To be eligible for subsidized food, workers in the factory and surface workers at the company's mines were to be obliged to work twenty-four days in a thirty-day month, and twenty-five days in a thirty-one-day month. Underground workers were required to put in the same number of days minus three. Those not working the required minimum would have the cost of food subsidies deducted from their wages. Surprisingly, the work regulations, the threat of partial closure, and the late payment of wages (which had begun several months earlier) aroused little debate. The question of food supply was something else. The Iuzovka soviet convened an extraordinary session at which it was proposed that the workers should take over complete control of the Iuzovka consumers' cooperative, with the soviet organizing the enrollment of new shareholders from among the workers to provide necessary capital. In the interim, the soviet resolved that any diminution of the supply of subsidized food should be regarded as a wage cut, and any failure to supply the customary amounts should be registered as a company debt to the factory and shop committees.[139]

The reaction of the soviet was evidently a reflection of the general mood in Iuzovka, for the same issue of the Iuzovka *Izvestiia* reporting the debate carried a supplementary letter from Revilon to the Council of Elders, greatly increasing the range and quantity of goods that the factory management undertook to supply. At the same time, Revilon proposed that as long as the currency shortage lasted, the workers should lend their savings to a special food-purchasing fund, with the company paying fifty kopeks in

[139] Ibid., no. 51 (November 14, 1917).

interest on each hundred rubles whenever the money was reimbursed. At the same time, the company announced that it would attempt to reduce the number of those eligible for subsidized food. According to Revilon, twenty-one thousand workers and fifty-eight thousand dependents were on the food rolls, and by careful screening this was to be reduced to twenty thousand workers and forty thousand family members, with all children under three years of age excluded.[140] A subsequent meeting of Glass and Revilon with representatives of the factory Council of Elders, representatives of the executive committee of the soviet, (Zaitsev and Pulai), and six members of the food committee carried on a businesslike discussion that settled the transfer to the new committee of food stocks previously managed by the company, with the management committing itself to pay six thousand rubles per month for salaries of the food committee officials, and to rent food storehouses to the committee. In addition, the factory shoe shop and tannery would be turned over to the food committee on the condition that they be kept fully operational.[141] Clearly the management and workers were finding common ground, and there was a give-and-take to the negotiations that made possible a consensual outcome. It should be noted that this was going on at the same time that the Bolsheviks were gaining predominance in the Iuzovka soviet, and that Zaitsev, one of the Bolshevik leaders, was involved in these negotiations.

Such cooperation was not always found at higher levels. The growing radicalization in Iuzovka found expression in two documents adopted by the Main Factory Committee. One was a resolution on workers' control, stating that "the only way out of the present situation . . . is workers' control over the production and distribution of products, which, if taken seriously, creates favorable conditions for the development of industry as well as for the workers' self-discipline."[142] Following up on the matter of discipline, the committee adopted the "Workers' Code of Self-Discipline," setting strict norms of labor performance and social behavior, with penalties ranging from a rebuke to dismissal, and enforcement resting on the shop and factory committees and on the Comradely Court that had been set up. Violations included calls to strike without authorization of the trade union,

[140] Ibid., p. 3. Bread supplies were to be increased from thirty thousand to sixty thousand puds per month, and meat from six thousand to eight thousand puds. In addition to the salt, sugar, and kerosene mentioned in the original proposal, barley, sunflower oil, laundry soap, and shoes from the factory shoe shop would be sold at cost plus operating expenses.

[141] Ibid., no. 53 (November 18, 1917).

[142] Chernomaz, *Bor'ba rabochego klassa Ukrainy*, p. 117.

denunciation of other workers to the factory management, and intentional spoiling of machines or products.[143]

Both the resolution on workers' control and the code of self-discipline were suggested as models for general adoption, and as such were presented by representatives of the workers for consideration to the Council of the Association of Southern Coal and Steel Producers. The answer came in the context of the ongoing negotiations between the workers' delegates and the representatives of the metallurgy industry, headed by Svitsyn. The employers responded:

> Their honors, having reviewed the documents presented by you on November 27, "Draft on Workers' Control and Self-Discipline," "Instruction for Shop Committees," and "Code of Self-Discipline," the Assembly of the Association of Metallurgical and Metal Working Industries deems all three documents unacceptable since they in essence suggest that the factory administrations give over direction of the factories to the workers, and this is totally impermissible, since in all conditions the material responsibility remains with the owners and they have not empowered the directors to take those steps demanded by the workers.[144]

Two points of interest emerge from this reply. The first is that a month after the Bolsheviks had taken power in Petrograd, negotiations between the employers and the workers were still continuing in the Donbass in much the same framework as they had since March. The second is that although Revilon and Glass, who must be assumed to have been acting under the supervision of Svitsyn, were willing to concede to the workers considerable authority in areas formerly controlled by the company, no such concessions were forthcoming in the high-level negotiations that were carried on with the direct participation of Svitsyn. Indeed, the tone of all the employers' presentations as recorded in the protocols of the meetings of the metallurgy industrialists and workers' representatives is one of truculent intransigance.

The growing privations and tensions left their mark on the workers, and the atmosphere in the New Russia factory grew strained despite all the efforts of the factory committee. A group of workers asked Revilon when they would be paid; dissatisfied with his reply, they shouted that he should be arrested. They were rebuked by the factory committee, which, while

[143] The full code is in ibid., p. 141.

[144] Gudzenko, *Robitnichii kontrol' i natsionalizatsiia*, p. 224.

emphasizing that the factory management bore a portion of the blame for the atmosphere, condemned the workers' action as undemocratic, stating that Revilon had the same right to personal security as anyone else in the factory. Zaitsev attacked the question from a different point of view. Speaking to a meeting of the Metal Workers' Union, he condemned the workers' lack of self-discipline, emphasizing that they should always act in organized fashion under the leadership of their own proletarian institutions. Comrade Popov replied bitterly that the workers had seen all their hopes dashed, and had lost faith in their institutions. The workers' impatience was growing, and such examples were infectious. The workers of the ammunition shop had a meeting with Glass and would not let him leave until he had promised them a pay raise of 25 percent. This act, too, was condemned by the workers' official institutions.[145]

When considering the overall behavior of the factory workers, it must be admitted that these acts are mild, and that on the whole, the Iuzovka workers acted in a restrained and remarkably disciplined fashion. By this time, Bakhmut had had its vodka riot, and the Bakhmut district commissar had notified Ekaterinoslav that communal peasants and individual farmers were involved in armed clashes with each other over "land allocation."[146]

In Iuzovka, public order was also breaking down. The local commissariat informed the weekly meeting of the Bolsheviks that "disorder has become greater, with all types of wild outbursts," and tried to enlist their aid in maintaining the peace.[147] When, in December, the Iasinovata Red Guard had retreated toward Gorlovka under the attacks of Krasnov's cossacks, their seizures of supplies and looting of a hospital train brought accusations from the Gorlovka Mensheviks that they were thieves and hoodlums. In rebuttal, Vishniakov blamed the incident on a group of anarchists active in the Red Guard.[148] Certainly the history of Russia in 1917 abounds in unrestrained physical violence. The violent activity of the anarchists in sup-

[145] *Izvestiia Iuzovskogo soveta*, no. 59 (December 2, 1917), p. 3; no. 62 (December 12, 1917); no. 63 (December 16, 1917), p. 4.

[146] Kondufor, *Istoriia rabochikh Donbassa*, vol. 1, p. 157. The clashes were not with the large landowners, but between individual farmers (who had presumably bought and consolidated their landholdings under the Stolypin reforms) and those who held land jointly within the village associations.

[147] Pavliuk et al., *Bol'shevistskie organizatsii Ukrainy*, p. 346, meeting of December 2, 1917. The meeting noted the request and adjourned without resolving any measures on the question.

[148] Vishniakov, "K bor'be," p. 231.

port of the revolution during this period attracted the attention of foreign observers, and the British ambassador reported that the "anarchist wing of Bolshevist party is coming more to the fore. It is being supported by Lenin as well as by reactionaries of whom there are many in ranks. Latter hope that short spell of anarchy will serve as a stepping stone to restoration of monarchy."[149]

The Gorlovka miners had forcibly "nationalized" small peasant mines as well as larger commercial mines; in many parts of the Donbass, owners and managers, along with technical personnel, had been physically expelled. Ossinskii-Obolenskii's observation was that nationalization of Donbass coal had proceeded from below, and that as many as one-third of the Donbass mines had been seized by the workers.[150] No such thing happened around Iuzovka. In addition to the large commercial mines of the New Russia Co., Rykovskii, and Rutchenko, all of which continued producing under their former owners through the winter of 1917–18, nine small privately owned mines near Iuzovka were listed as producing and freely selling a total of over one hundred thousand puds of coal daily in late November.[151]

Despite Popov's opinion that the workers had lost faith in their institutions, there is evidence that the factory's conciliation commission, set up on a parity basis between workers and management, was still receiving "a mass of workers' complaints" at this time.[152] In this it continued the level of effectiveness that had been established through 1917.

The behavior of the workers during this period indicates some measure of both political and social community. The aspirations and priorities of that community appear to be quite different than those that were guiding the destinies of the rest of the people of the Donbass and of Russia during this period. They focused on securing what they and their families needed right away, rather than on any grand universal scheme of government. They had, however, gone beyond fatalism and passive parochialism, and had become a

149 Buchanan to Foreign Office, FO, 371/3017, p. 286, telegram of December 18, 1917. Perhaps Buchanan was influenced by the then-popular jingle, "First came the Mensheviks, then came the Bolsheviks, next will come the Anarchists, and then will come the Monarchists."

150 Ossinskii-Obolenskii, "Polozhenie," p. 39.

151 The list appears in *Izvestiia Iuzovskogo soveta*, no. 53 (November 18, 1917). Modestov, *Rabochee i professional'noe dvizhenie*, p. 130, notes that the Rutchenko mines were formally nationalized at the same time as the New Russia Co., in January 1918.

152 Pavliuk et al., *Bol'shevistskie organizatsii Ukrainy*, p. 375, report of Efanov to Bolshevik meeting, February 16, 1918. Efanov claimed that the factory administration was obstructing submission and review of these complaints in every possible way.

modern community that could organize and act in an integrated fashion to shape their environment.

The factories and mines of the New Russia Co., along with all its other assets, were formally nationalized on January 24, 1918. A decree of the presidium of the All-Russian Supreme Economic Council (VSNKh) signed by Larin, Lomov, and Smirnov declared that in view of the importance of the company to the Soviet state, and the inability of the owners to maintain the operation of its enterprises, it would henceforth be owned and managed by the state. All personnel were obliged to remain at their posts.[153] The sovnarkom had discussed nationalization at its meeeting of November 18, 1917, and had ordered the Donbass–Krivoi Rog Oblast' Executive Committee to establish a fact-finding committee that would prepare the ground for actual seizure of the Donbass enterprises.[154] In December, Ossinskii-Obolenskii headed a VSNKh delegation to study the state of the Donbass coal and metallurgy industries, and early in 1918 he returned at the head of a joint Central Committee–VSNKh group charged with the preparation and implementation of nationalization in the Donbass and the revival of its productive capacities.[155] As Ossinskii-Obolenskii noted, there was more nationalization 'from below' than from the center, and in most cases this involved small enterprises whose owners had abandoned them or been forced out. Although Ossinskii-Obolenskii wrote that one-third of the mines were nationalized in this period, Chernomaz wrote that 230 mines had been nationalized by March 29, 1918.[156] There were, by this time, some twelve hundred coal mines in the Donbass.

Only the large commercial mines were formally taken over by the state and integrated into the burgeoning structure of enterprises operating under the aegis of the VSNKh. Smaller mines were put under workers' control, meaning that the former owners might retain nominal control, but a workers' committee was responsible for the actual operations as well as for the financial decisions. The smallest and most primitive mines, those needing no outlays for maintenance or working capital, and having no need for skilled labor, were simply put under the nominal supervision of one of

[153] Gudzenko, *Robitnichii kontrol' i natsionalizatsiia*, p. 337. At this time there were, all told, seventeen listed shareholders, of whom seven were in Russia. See Companies' House, 4467, list of July 1918.

[154] Korolivskii, *Podgotovka*, vol. 3, p. 261.

[155] Chernomaz, *Bor'ba rabochego klassa Ukrainy*, p. 147.

[156] Compare Ossinskii-Obolenskii, "Polozhenie," p. 39, with Chernomaz, *Bor'ba rabochego klassa Ukrainy*, p. 159.

the district economic councils that operated under each regional sovnarkhoz (economic council).[157] This arrangement was substantially different from that suggested by Ossinskii-Obolenskii after his first visits in the Donbass. He had proposed nationalizing all mines producing over five million puds of coal per year, with the management composed of one-third representatives of the local soviet, one-third workers' representatives, and one-third representatives of the technical staff, with an official of the local sovnarkhoz holding the right of veto over all decisions. Mines yielding one to five million puds were to be syndicated and provided with a central source of technical and financial support. Workers were to make up at least a third of the management of these mines, and the owners were to be paid a fixed percentage of the profits for their role in management. The small peasant mines were to be controlled by the local soviet.[158] In practice, the local soviets played no role whatsoever, while the centrally controlled economic councils took on a major role. A later, more detailed outline of a plan for the organization of Donbass industry also omitted any role for the local soviets.[159]

Ossinskii-Obolenskii related how the miners of seventy-two small mines in the Chistiakov district banded together to form a district economic council to manage their newly nationalized mines. As he described it, wherever the workers found themselves in possession of a mine, they would convene a general meeting and draw up a protocol, declaring the mine to be the property of the Soviet Republic. "This pleases the anarcho-syndicalists. They encourage this in every way, considering it socialization of the mining property. The miners, in fact, *nationalize*, by declaring the mine the property of the republic."[160] While direct seizure of an enterprise by the workers or by local authorities would certainly affect its operation, nationalization from Moscow, unsupported by local action, often remained on paper only. The central government was as yet insufficiently organized to take advantage of the distant and unfamiliar assets that it had so suddenly acquired. Indeed, in the confusion of setting up an administration, an enterprise might simply be forgotten. A list of nationalized enterprises published in June 1918, specifying date of nationalization and form of management of

157 Chernomaz, *Bor'ba rabochego klassa Ukrainy*, p. 157.

158 Ossinskii-Obolenskii, "Tezisy," p. 29.

159 See Ossinskii-Obolenskii's eleven-point presentation as reported in *Narodnoe khoziaistvo*, no. 2 (1918).

160 Ossinski-Obolenskii, "Polozhenie," p. 37 (emphasis in the original).

all nationalized enterprises in Soviet Russia, makes no mention of the New Russia factory and mines.[161]

Until late April, reduced though its operations were, the New Russia factory and mines had continued to function, furnishing the workers employment and livelihood. On April 23, 1918, a meeting of the factory management, together with the Main Factory Committee, the Workers' Control Committee, and the metal workers' and mine workers' unions, decided to close down the blast furnaces and suspend coking and all other subsidiary operations. Coal reserves were exhausted because mobilization, evacuation, and flight had depleted the mine labor force. Whatever coal was available was to be devoted to fueling the pumps that kept the mines from being flooded.[162] Through more than a year of political revolution and economic dislocation, the New Russia factory and mines had continued to function, though their operations had been curtailed to a point where the New Russia Co. was a mere shadow of the once-dominant metallurgy complex. The orderly way in which the plant was closed down and the mines were preserved was in sharp contrast to many Donbass closures caused by owners' flight, by workers' seizure and expulsion of management, or by migration of the mine labor force. Even in the face of foreign conquest, the workers of the New Russia Co. were first and foremost concerned with preserving their livelihood, and they cooperated with management to that end. John Hughes' efforts to create a local labor force of skilled and dedicated iron workers had indeed borne fruit.

However, had all gone smoothly this would not have been Iuzovka. The Iuzovka Bolshevik meeting had been in the midst of a stormy debate over the disorder of the evacuation when Krusser had interrupted with his personal point. They tried to organize, and Vishniakov, having come to Iuzovka when Iasinovata was again abandoned, had been put in charge of preparing the party offices for evacuation, packing those records that were to be taken and destroying the rest. He threw himself into the task vigorously and completed it in the allotted time, only to sense an oppressive silence. The soviet was gone; so was the duma, and all the other comrades.

[161] *Narodnoe khoziaistvo*, no. 4 (1918), p. 51. This may have been because Iuzovka was then held by the Germans and the New Russia factory was thus outside the control of the Soviet Republic. For a description of the confusion that reigned in the realm of statistics regarding the number of nationalized enterprises existing in this period, see Nove, *Economic History of the USSR*, pp. 68–70.

[162] Vilisova et al., *Bor'ba za vlast' sovetov v Donbasse*, p. 368.

Only several hours later did a cart and shamefaced driver appear and admit that in the haste to evacuate, Vishniakov and the party office had been forgotten.[163]

War, Peace, and Self-Determination in the Donbass

Even earlier, as the Iuzovka Bolsheviks and those of other Donbass localities came to grips with the complex problems of maintaining a living society and economy, two interconnected problems overshadowed all their activities. Above all was the question of defending the Donbass aginst any and all potential invasion forces: the Germans, the Rada, and the Whites. At the same time, they were forced by events to take a stand on the question of the political status of the Donbass within a future Soviet Republic. At the heart of this stood the problem of Russian-Ukrainian relations. The Donbass, with its coal and iron riches, was in the Ukraine geographically, but its population, particularly in the burgeoning industrial towns, was overwhelmingly Russian and Jewish. In July 1917, when the provisional government had decided in favor of federative autonomy for the Ukraine, emissaries of the Rada had gone to Lugansk to enlist the political support of the revolutionary parties in the town. As spokesperson for the Bolsheviks, Iurii Lutovinov opposed "Ukrainization" on the grounds that it would split the local proletariat.[164] Yet Lutovinov's view was not the only Bolshevik view. Zatonskii, who was to be among the organizers of the Communist Party of the Ukraine in 1918, and a member of its first Central Committee, recognized that even in the vicinity of Kharkov and Ekaterinoslav, the Ukrainian population was strongly in favor of its own national self-determination. This was not a one-sided discussion, for opinion among Ukrainians was divided as well. In 1905 the Revolutionary Ukrainian party had split over the question of future relations with Russia, with a portion of its members joining the Social-Democrats of Russia in supporting a federative structure, while others insisted on complete independence for the Ukraine.[165] The one point on which there was Ukrainian unanimity was

[163] Vishniakov, "K bor'be," p. 233.

[164] Nikolaenko, "Pamiati tovarishcha," p. 185. This memoir, published in 1925, when "Ukrainization" was in the mainstream of Soviet policy, evoked this editorial comment: "An underestimation of the national question was quite usual at this time among the Bolsheviks, particularly in the Left Bank Ukraine."

[165] Lawrynenko, *Revolutionary Ukrainian Party*, p. 19.

that the old policy of denying any Ukrainian national identity had to be changed.

The need to take a stand on matters of self-determination and the political fate of the Donbass became acute as soon as Lenin began pursuing seriously a policy of making peace with the Germans. This was not a popular stand in the Donbass. Zaitsev, returning from the Third Congress of Soviets, at which the Brest Litovsk peace negotiations had been discussed, reassured the Iuzovka Bolsheviks that the congress was against a "capitulatory" peace, or in fact any peace other than the democratic peace that had been proposed earlier by the Russian Republic.[166] This was the first time the Iuzovka Bolsheviks had given any attention to the question.[167]

Ivan Kochubei, the delegate representing Iuzovka at the Seventh Congress of the RKP(b), where ratification of the Brest Litovsk treaty was the central item on the agenda, declared himself a supporter of Bukharin's policy of revolutionary war, while explaining that this was a personal stand and that the Iuzovka Bolsheviks had not yet discussed the matter.[168]

In preparation for the party congress, the local Bolshevik organizations had been polled by the center. The consensus of the Bolshevik Central Committee was that the peasants and the large industrial centers were in favor of signing the peace, but the "small towns" wanted to continue the war.[169] The Donbass Bolsheviks were clearly for the continuation of the war. A district conference of the Gorlovka-Shcherbinovka Bolsheviks on February 24 voted in support of theses presented by Gruzman advocating revolutionary war against the Germans. The committee elected at the conference voted four to three to support Gruzman in opposing the Brest Litovsk peace at the party congress.[170] On March 1, two days before the peace treaty was signed, and a week before the party congress, a joint session of the Kharkov Bolsheviks and representatives of the Donbass soviets dis-

[166] Pavliuk et al., *Bol'shevistskie organizatsii Ukrainy*, p. 373, Bolshevik meeting of January 27, 1918.

[167] Goncharenko, *Bor'ba za ukreplenie vlasti sovetov v Donbasse*, pp. 116 n. 5, 166. Goncharenko writes that the first discussion of war and peace came on March 18, 1918, when the decisions of the Seventh Congress of the RKP(b) were approved. He adds that subsequently there were several discussions of the question, but that no clear stand was taken.

[168] Pavliuk et al., *Bol'shevistskie organizatsii Ukrainy*, pp. 122–24.

[169] *Perepiska sekretariata*, vol. 3, pp. 11–12.

[170] Ostrogorskii, "Stranichki iz istorii," pp. 30–31.

cussed the question. Ossinskii-Obolenskii, who was visiting the Donbass as a representative of the VSNKh, joined Mezhlauk in supporting the idea of revolutionary war; they were opposed by Voroshilov and others who supported Lenin's decision to sign the peace treaty at any cost. The meeting voted fifty-four to ten, with four abstentions, in support of revolutionary war.[171] The "Kiev Left," represented by Piatakov and Evgeniia Bosh, also opposed the signing of the peace. Even after the peace had been signed and ratified by both the party congress and the All-Russian Congress of Soviets, the opposition continued, and Bolotskii, reporting to the Iuzovka Bolsheviks, found it necessary to soften the blow by assuring the meeting that Lenin was intent on carrying on a partisan war even though the peace had been signed. Although the general tone of the meeting was supportive of the ratification of the peace, Gordon remarked that the result had been a split in the party.[172]

The British were naturally deeply interested in the outcome of the struggle for and against Brest Litovsk. A report from Stockholm outlined the Left opposition point of view that the signing of peace would weaken the European revolutionary movement, and that if no revolution broke out in Germany the Bolshevik regime was doomed.[173]

The question of Russia's relationship with the Ukraine antedated the question of peace with Germany, and was fraught with even sharper political thorns, threatening relations with the Ukrainian population and the Bolshevik central authorities, as well as splitting the party within the Ukraine. When the Bolsheviks had assumed power in Petrograd, the central Rada had declared itself the "unitary, revolutionary, and democratic government of the Ukraine."[174] With the infant Bolshevik regime still in confusion, the Rada's initiative threw the Donbass into a whirlpool of conflict. A two-day session of the Donbass–Krivoi Rog Oblast' Executive Committee, made up of thirteen Socialist-Revolutionaries and Mensheviks and seven Bolsheviks, produced a tangle of conflicting resolutions. A call was put out for a referendum on the political future of the entire Donbass–

[171] Pavliuk et al., *Bol'shevistskie organizatsii Ukrainy*, p. 113.

[172] Ibid., pp. 394–96, Iuzovka Bolshevik meeting, March 23, 1918.

[173] FO 371/3017–221855, telegram of Sir E. Howard to the foreign minister. There was nothing unique in this bit of intelligence, as Lenin and almost all the other Bolshevik leaders, held, and openly expressed, the same view. The belief that the Bolsheviks constituted a passing episode is probably the single most common recurring theme in the inflow of diplomatic evaluations reaching the British Foreign Office at this time.

[174] *Izvestiia Iuzovskogo soveta*, no. 50 (November 11, 1917).

Krivoi Rog territory. At the same time, a suggestion was floated that the entire area, together with the Kharkov district, be constituted as a special united administrative district within the Russian Republic. This was the first time that the question of separating the Donbass from the Ukraine had been raised publicly.[175] The meeting urged that all the soviets of the area take an active part in the elections to the constituent assembly of the Ukraine, agitating for protection of their interests "to prevent Ukrainian nationalism from capturing the Donbass and instituting national discrimination."[176] This dual line of thinking, combining the urge for separatism with an attempt to maintain political influence within the Ukraine, persisted throughout the period. Clearly the direction of political developments was as disturbing as it was surprising to all the political parties of the Donbass.

It turned out, however, that the executive committee was out of step with its membership, for the Third Congress of Soviets of the Donbass–Krivoi Rog Oblast', meeting in Kharkov on December 9, supported the Rada, voting for a totally independent Ukraine.[177] In this vote, the Bolsheviks themselves were at loggerheads. The long-simmering disagreements between "Left Bank" and "Right Bank" Bolsheviks found expression in disagreement over whether the Ukraine should be organized by national principle or by economic features. The Donbass Bolsheviks claimed that since Russia was now to build socialism, the national question was a thing of the past, establishing a theme that was to dominate their political thinking in the coming political debates over the future of the territory. They did, however, retain a modicum of sensitivity to the "special circumstances" of the Ukraine, and therefore "the Left Bank comrades recognized the right of the Ukrainian people to self-determination," but without the Donbass.[178]

[175] Myshkis, "K materialam," p. 246, states that the idea of separation of the Donbass from the Ukraine was first broached among the Donbass Bolsheviks in September 1917, and was "warmly supported by the broad masses of the workers." The Shcherbinovka miners had wanted to declare themselves an independent state power, but had been restrained by Gruzman. Myshkis cites memoirs by Magidov and Skrypnik to the effect that Lenin then supported the idea of separating the Donbass from the Ukraine, weakening the Rada and strengthening Russia. Bilinsky, "Communist Takeover of the Ukraine," p. 127, writes that Lenin had disregarded the suggestion that the Donbass be detached from the Ukraine.

[176] *Izvestiia Iuzovskogo soveta*, no. 55 (November 23, 1917), p. 3.

[177] See Bolotskii's report to the Iuzovka Bolsheviks in Pavliuk et al., *Bol'shevistskie organizatsii Ukrainy*, p. 354.

[178] Myshkis, "K materialam," p. 246.

The Iuzovka Bolsheviks, who by this time controlled the local soviet, saw things from this Donbass perspective. After hearing Dimitrenko, a representative of the Rada, set forth that body's claims to power, a special session of the Iuzovka soviet debated three resolutions. The first, offered by the Ukrainian Hromada representative, called for recognition of the local committees of the Rada as the revolutionary democratic regime of the Ukraine until the convening of a constituent assembly for the Ukraine. The Iuzovka Mensheviks proposed a plebiscite in the Ukraine, and negotiations with the All-Russian Constituent Assembly to assure the rights of minorities through institutions of political and cultural autonomy. The Bolshevik resolution denounced the Rada, declared the Sovnarkom and the VTsIK elected by the Second Congress of Soviets to be the only legitimate power, and ended by calling for what had by then become Bolshevik policy, the convening of the All-Ukraine Congress of Soviets to establish a Soviet (Bolshevik) government of the territory claimed by the Rada.[179] The Iuzovka soviet adopted the Bolshevik resolution.

Two weeks later the Iuzovka Bolsheviks heard a report on current events at their weekly meeting. Asking rhetorically why the Bolshevik party was opposed to the Ukrainian Rada's concept of self-determination, the lecturer explained that the Rada might declare itself a socialist institution, but that its policies were nevertheless bourgeois. In the same breath he offhandedly dismissed the Ukrainian question as a nonproblem, observing that in the not-too-distant future the self-determination of national groups in all states was bound to find a solution.[180]

Meanwhile two things had happened. The Donbass Bolshevik delegates at the Third Congress of Soviets of the Donbass–Krivoi Rog Oblast', acting under pressure from Petrograd, met with their comrades from the Kiev Oblast' Congress of Soviets, and declared their meeting to be the First All-Ukrainian Congress of Soviets, setting up a competitive government against the Rada. According to later recollections, the Donbass delegates, though they accepted places in the new central executive committee that was established, were inactive there, feeling it had little bearing on their region.[181]

[179] *Izvestiia Iuzovskogo soveta*, no. 63 (December 16, 1917), p. 2. This is the only mention I have found of a Ukrainian Hromada deputy in the Iuzovka soviet. It is likely that for this session, members of other neighboring soviets and zemstvos were invited.

[180] Pavliuk et al., *Bol'shevistskie organizatsii Ukrainy*, p. 357, Iuzovka Bolshevik meeting of December 19, 1917.

[181] Myshkis, "K materialam," p. 248.

After having repelled the first attacks by Kaledin's forces in the Donbass, the Red Army under Antonov-Ovseenko had turned its attention to ousting the Rada, and succeeded in capturing Kiev. On January 21, 1918, the Central Executive Committee of Soviets of the Ukraine moved from Kharkov to Kiev. The relocation of the Bolshevik center in the Ukraine was short-lived. The uprising against the Rada, and that government's lack of effective military power, brought the Central Powers into action; soon the Rada was replaced by Skoropadskii, the head of the Ukrainian Directorate, and German troops were advancing toward the Donbass on the heels of the retreating Bolsheviks.

The Donbass–Krivoi Rog Autonomous Republic

The internal frictions of the Bolsheviks and the worsening military situation, creating apprehension about the political future of the Ukraine, provided the background for the next turn of events in the Donbass. The Fourth Congress of Soviets of the Donbass–Krivoi Rog Oblast' met from January 27 to January 31, 1918. It ousted the Mensheviks and Socialist-Revolutionaries from their leadership in the executive institutions of the region's soviet and, under Bolshevik leadership, the meeting declared the creation of the Donbass–Krivoi Rog Republic as an autonomous political unit, federated with the Russian Soviet Republic. Its borders were set along the western edge of Kharkov and Ekaterinoslav provinces and along the railway to Krivoi Rog, and included the coal areas of the Don Cossack territory, the coast of the Sea of Azov to Taganrog, and a section of the Rostov-Voronezh railway north to Likhaia station.[182]

The decision to declare the autonomy of the Donbass was not easily pushed through. The dissenters included all the other parties participating in the congress, as well as part of the Bolshevik delegation. Although this option had been discussed sporadically among Bolsheviks in the Donbass for several months, the press of revolutionary developments had evidently prevented an orderly consideration of the matter, and it would appear that to some extent the operative resolution was the initiative of a small group of Donbass Bolshevik leaders. Ostrogorskii writes that Gruzman was surprised to hear of the step—but nevertheless supported it.[183] Two

[182] Pavliuk et al., *Bol'shevistskie organizatsii Ukrainy*, p. 138.

[183] Ostrogorskii, "Stranichki iz istorii," p. 24.

main lines of opposition were set forth. The delegation of Socialist-Revolutionaries disputed the legitimacy of such a fundamental change in the region's political structure when relatively few workers' soviets were represented at the congress, and no peasant soviets whatsoever were participating.[184]

The Menshevik approach was somewhat more subtle, evidently fishing for support from the minority group among the Bolsheviks. Sandomirskii, speaking for the Mensheviks, was in favor of recognizing both the self-determination of nations and the right of economic regions to autonomous administration, as part of an overall federated political structure to be set up. He suggested, however, that any such principles would have to be ratified in both the All-Russian Constituent Assembly (which by this time had already been dispersed by the Bolsheviks) and a Ukrainian constituent assembly to be convened as soon as possible.[185] He had evidently taken his cue from Skrypnik, who had argued that though organization on an economic basis was a correct principle, the realities of the world made such a leap into the future impracticable, and that the principle of national self-determination was still to be reckoned with. Skrypnik tried to point out that the Bolsheviks were fighting for implementation of the principle of national self-determination at Brest Litovsk. This reference to the sensitive question of the negotiations with Germany brought a storm of heckling, and cries of "Be done with that!" In the end, Skrypnik proposed that the Donbass be recognized as "an Autonomous Region of the South Russian Ukrainian Republic as part of an All-Russian Federation of Soviet Republics"—a composite formulation that satisfied neither the Russians nor the Ukrainians. Attacked from all sides, Skrypnik stated that he meant his resolution to have only declarative force, and since he had no intention of splitting the Bolshevik delegation, he would withdraw the proposal.[186]

Artem, slated to head the new Donbass Republic, set forth the Donbass Bolshevik response to all the critics, along with the Bolshevik interpretation of self-determination. "We do not recognize the right of the White Guards to self-determination, neither in the Ukraine, nor in Finland (where our soldiers have gone to the aid of the Finnish workers). National preju-

[184] Summaries of the debates and either full or summarized texts of the resolutions, as printed in the regional press (primarily *Donetskii proletarii*, *Izvestiia iuga*, and *Nash iug*) at the time, are presented in "Materiali ta dokumenti. The discussion here is drawn from this source. The S-R position is given on p. 260.

[185] "Materiali ta dokumenti," pp. 255–56.

[186] Ibid., pp. 254, 257–58.

dices have died out together with the central Rada."[187] The congress resolution on the subject reflected this view, declaring: "The Federation of Russian Socialist Republics will be formed on the basis of particularities of economic life and not on a national basis. The Donbass and Krivoi Rog Basins constitute such a self-contained economic unit. The Donetsk Republic can serve as a model of a socialist economy for other republics."[188]

The road to setting up the autonomous Donbass Republic was cleared when the congress voted to elect an oblast' committee of eleven members, rejecting proposed amendments of the Mensheviks and Socialist-Revolutionaries both to enlarge the obkom and to guarantee places in it for all the socialist parties of the region. Each of these amendments received only fourteen votes in support, while fifty votes were cast for the Bolshevik proposal, with the Mensheviks and the Socialist-Revolutionaries refusing to participate. The oblast' committee, serving as regional executive between congresses, had seven Bolsheviks, three Socialist-Revolutionaries, and one Menshevik.[189] The task of the obkom was to form the Council of People's Commissars, which would be responsible to the obkom, which itself would be responsible to the periodic congresses of soviets of the region.

A fifteen-member Council of People's Commissars was set up, chaired by F. A. Sergeev (Artem), who also headed the Commissariat of the Economy. The Bolsheviks named Vasil'chenko to head the Commissariat of Internal Affairs; Zhakov, Education; Mezhlauk, Finance; Magidov, Labor; Rukhimovich, Military Affairs; and Filov, Justice. Kaminskii was to be state comptroller. The Commissariat of Supply was left open for a Bolshevik, while Agriculture, Health, and State Properties were to be left open for Socialist-Revolutionaries, and the Commissariat of Railways and that of Posts and Telegraphs were to be offered to workers in those branches. It was explicitly assumed in the Bolshevik proposal that the Mensheviks would refuse to be part of such a council.[190] This proved correct; Rubinshtein, though present, was unwilling to participate in the discussions regarding formation of the Donbass Sovnarkom. Golubovskii, speaking for the Socialist-Revolutionaries, declared that both the question of participation in the Sovnarkom and the specific posts and candidacies would be discussed

[187] Ibid., p. 256.

[188] Ibid., p. 254.

[189] Ibid., pp. 259–61.

[190] Ibid., p. 262. The concession to syndicalism in this proposal is of some interest. By this time, the Bolsheviks in Petrograd had abandoned any such tendencies.

by the Socialist-Revolutionary regional committee. Without waiting for further answers, or attempting to convince the other parties, the Bolsheviks called the matter to a vote, and the obkom confirmed the proposal by six votes to none, with four abstentions and one member either not present or not voting.[191]

The inclusion of Vasil'chenko and Zhakov in both the obkom and the Donbass Sovnarkom caused a new controversy. Rubinshtein pointed out that if the Council of People's Commissars of the new republic was to be accountable to the oblast' committee, then joint tenure in the two bodies would create a conflict of interest, and therefore should be impermissible. Ignoring the administrative principle, the Bolsheviks replied with a torrent of oratory regarding the collective revolutionary responsibility of each member of the oblast' committee before all his committee colleagues whatever their party identification, and the accountability of each commissar to the Congress of Soviets, as well as to his own party. Rubinshtein's objections were voted down six to three.

The next challenge placed by the opposition was to define the relations of the Donbass–Krivoi Rog Republic Sovnarkom to the All-Russian Sovnarkom and to the TsIK (central executive committee) of the Ukraine that had been set up at the First All-Ukrainian Congress of Soviets. The first part was easy. Vasil'chenko introduced a resolution stating that the Donbass–Krivoi Rog Sovnarkom was responsible for implementation on its own territory of the decrees of the All-Russian Sovnarkom. The Donbass Bolsheviks had no problem accepting their subordination to Moscow. The convoluted phrasing of the second half of the resolution reveals the inner split that rent Bolshevik souls when they were instructed to see themselves as part of the Ukraine. They could not bring themselves to do this, so the resolution states that the TsIK of the Ukraine was considered to be *parallel* (and not superordinated) to the Donbass Sovnarkom. At the same time, these were Bolsheviks, accepting of their party's discipline, sensitive to its tenuous position of control, and challenged by envious opponents. The second half of their resolution defining the relationships between the competing revolutionary organs stated that the soviets of the Donbass should participate in the general structure of state life together with all the soviets of South Russia, including the Ukraine and the Don-Kuban-Tauride re-

[191] Ibid., pp. 262–63. The missing eleventh man was evidently a Bolshevik, and may have been Razin, who was a member of the obkom, and originally proposed as candidate for people's commissar for justice, but removed without explanation in favor of V. G. Filov.

gion.[192] It was simply beyond the capacity of the Donbass Bolsheviks to acknowledge the Ukraine as a national entity with sovereign political authority over the Donbass. Decades of migration to the Donbass, and concentration within industrial enclaves having minimal or strained relations with the Ukrainian peasants of the area, had left their mark.

But once again, it was the question of war and peace that made the Donbass Bolsheviks most aware of the painful duality of their position. Toward the end of February a joint session of the Executive Committee of Soviets of Kharkov Province and the Donbass–Krivoi Rog Committee of Soviets was convened to discuss the impending signing of the Brest Litovsk peace treaty. Vasil'chenko dismissed the treaty contemptuously as "a scrap of paper that binds nobody to anything." He explained the founding of the Donbass–Krivoi Rog Autonomous Republic as an appropriate response to the challenge posed by the treaty, since those articles of the peace agreement dealing with the Ukraine would no longer be valid regarding the Donbass and Kharkov provinces. The Bolshevik explanation was not well received, for it was their party leaders who were pressing for the acceptance of German conditions. The Mensheviks, represented by F. Kon, called the negotiations a shameful capitulation to German imperialism and a betrayal of all those in Poland, the Baltic territories and the Ukraine who had linked their fates with the Russian Revolution. He demanded an uncompromising rejection of the German ultimatum. The Left Socialist-Revolutionaries, erstwhile allies of the Bolsheviks, supported Kon in his attack, and the session grew stormy to the point that the presidium of the meeting was dismissed and re-formed, with the Bolshevik participants walking out in protest.[193]

The uproar caused by this meeting must have left an impression, for on February 28, a meeting of the Donbass–Krivoi Rog Oblast' Committee heard Vasil'chenko denounce the peace treaty. He called the signing of the treaty suicide, and stated that if it were signed, it should be repudiated and a partisan war started against the Germans. He called for merciless suppression of all counterrevolutionary activity, with martial law to be activated if needed. Having pressured the Donbass Bolsheviks into coming out publicly and unequivocally against the separate peace that Lenin was about to sign, the opposition pushed further. It called for a broad unity of all parties

[192] Ibid., p. 263.

[193] The meeting was reported in the Menshevik *Nash iug* of February 27, 1918, but no date is given. See "Materiali ta dokumenti," p. 264.

to rally the mass of workers behind the soviets. Both Rubinshtein and Golubovskii emphasized that this could only be achieved if there were a cessation of political terror (against non-Bolshevik socialists) and of the civil war that was weakening the revolutionary camp. The TsIK of the Ukraine had openly declared war and was trying to form a united military confederation of South Russian Soviet Republics. Rubinshtein and Golubovskii were pressing to have the Donbass Republic join this confederation, and work toward a united all-Russian position that would bring about the rejection of the peace in Moscow, allowing what they termed "an organized defense [or] an organized withdrawal from the war." In addition, the opposition resolution drawn up by Rubinshtein contained the statement, "The question of power on the territories of the Ukraine and the Russian Republic can be decided only by the Ukrainian Constituent Assembly, which must be convened without delay."[194]

But the Mensheviks had overplayed their hand. The Bolsheviks were unwilling to swallow these demands, and once more, a tortuously ambiguous Bolshevik resolution was rammed through in place of compromise. The Donbass–Krivoi Rog Autonomous Republic recognized that the military activities in the Ukraine constituted "an uprising of the oppressed against their oppressors." The obkom "will support the uprising with all its strength and means, and instructs the Sovnarkom of the Donetsk Republic to find concrete forms for uniting the uprising in all the republics of the south."[195] The Donbass Bolsheviks were thus able to claim that they were supporting the locally popular war against the Germans and the Ukrainian national government, while by not calling it a war, and emphasizing its class rather than its national aspects, they avoided any formal repudiation of Moscow's diplomacy.

Menshevik and Socialist-Revolutionary harassment of the Bolsheviks went on unmercifully. When Magidov presented a draft decree on social insurance for discussion in the Sovnarkom, Rubinshtein proposed a small amendment, the substitution of *oblast'* for *republic* throughout the document. The amendment was rejected.[196] When the TsIK of the Ukraine returned to Kharkov, Golubovskii pointed out that the existence of two sovereign governments in one territory was ridiculous, and called for the

[194] Ibid., pp. 264–65, 269. Golubovskii, the S-R representative, did not support the last point in Rubinshtein's proposal.

[195] Ibid., p. 269.

[196] Ibid., p. 267.

convening of a new All-Ukrainian Congress of Soviets to decide on the future political structure of the Ukraine, including the Donbass. Rubinshtein joined in this attack, pointing out the conflicting and uncoordinated nature of the decrees of the Ukrainian TsIK and the Donbass Sovnarkom, and condemning both of them for ignoring the representation of peasants.[197] As examples of governmental confusion he claimed to have learned from the press, rather than from obkom debates, of new taxes, political declarations, mobilization orders, and the creation of a totally new military command for the Ukraine with Antonov-Ovseenko at its head.[198]

Questions of war and peace were undoubtedly the central issue for the Donbass Republic—indeed, they were the raison d'être of the republic—but there were additional items on the agenda. In their revolutionary fervor the Donbass Bolsheviks were determined to build socialism in a single oblast', and to do so quickly. At the Fourth Congress of Soviets of the Donetsk and Krivoi Rog Basins, with the declaration of the autonomous republic, a resolution was passed blaming sabotage by the owners and by the "forces of counterrevolution" for the economic dislocation that was plaguing the region. Rejecting the Menshevik suggestion that the region's industry be under worker control, the meeting called for nationalization and for industrial production to be organized on a social basis as the foundation of socialist change in the Donbass. Transformation of underground minerals and mining-industry enterprises of the Donbass into property of the Russian Soviet Republic was declared to be one of the main tasks of the Donbass–Krivoi Rog Autonomous Republic.[199]

Iuzovka felt the authority of the Donbass Sovnarkom. When the soviet voted against the Bolsheviks after the Zalmaev affair, it was an order from Vasil'chenko as people's commissar for internal affairs that decreed the new elections.[200] When a request to St. Petersburg for a million rubles to finance the first actions of the new republic evidently went unheeded, the Donbass Sovnarkom drew up a comprehensive tax of forty-two million rubles, canceling all local levies. Iuzovka's share was to be two million, and the task of collecting the levy, to be completed by March 15, was assigned to the Donbass Military Revolutionary Committee.[201]

[197] Ibid., March 11, 1918, meeting of the Donbass–Krivoi Rog obkom.

[198] Ibid.

[199] Ibid., p. 270.

[200] Zaitsev, "Pis'mo v redaktsiiu," p. 369.

[201] Korolivskii, *Podgotovka*, vol. 3, p. 694. Ekaterinoslav was assessed three million; Bakhmut, Lugansk, and Mariupol, one million each. For the request to Petrograd, see

But influence in Iuzovka was an insufficient reason for the existence of an autonomous republic. Lenin's politics had broader goals, and the secession of the Donbass Bolsheviks from the Ukraine was harming the Bolshevik party in its attempts to maintain a measure of influence in the republic. On March 15, 1918, the Central Committee of the RKP(b) declared the Donbass part of the Ukraine and ordered the Donbass–Krivoi Rog Autonomous Republic to send its representatives to the Second All-Ukrainian Congress of Soviets.[202] This was essentially the death knell of the Donbass Republic. The Donbass Bolsheviks faithfully reported to Taganrog on March 17, where the Second All-Ukrainian Congress of Soviets was meeting. They were needed there, for even with them, there were only forty-seven Bolsheviks facing forty-nine Left Socialist-Revolutionaries and five Ukrainian Social-Democrats in the TsIK of Soviets of the UKraine that was elected.[203] The party whips, Leninists led by Kviring, Gamarnik, and Skrypnik, also gathered enough support to have the Congress approve the Brest Litovsk treaty, thus relieving Moscow of embarrassing pressures.[204]

But all of this was essentially symbolic politics, for the German and Austro-Hungarian armies were advancing steadily through the Ukraine. The Communist party of the Ukraine, which the Bolshevik caucus in Taganrog resolved to organize, was to have its founding congress in Moscow rather than Kharkov or Kiev. Meanwhile, Iuzovka awaited the German invaders, its factory silent, its mines barely alive. This was the beginning of three new years of political turmoil that was to see a series of governments attempting to reap some benefit from the riches of the New Russia properties. I will now turn to how Iuzovka weathered occupation and civil war.

"Materiali ta dokumenti," p. 259. The Iuzovka soviet had preempted the taxing function and the revkom had no success in further squeezing the population.

202 Reshetar, "Communist Party of the Ukraine," p. 175.

203 *Russkie vedomosti* (March 27, 1918).

204 Bachinskii, Kviring, and Perel'man, *Kviring*, pp. 169–70.

CHAPTER 10

Interlude of Occupations: Iuzovka in the Civil War

The German troops marching into Iuzovka in the last days of April 1918 were capturing a dead town. The miners had fled to their villages; the factory was cold and still. The soviet, the duma, and the activists of the revolutionary parties had left for safer places. A similar situation existed throughout the Donbass. Even after the German forces had completed their conquest and installed Skoropadskii's government, the Directorate, as the administrator of the conquered Donbass, only two blast furnaces were working in the entire region, and the ten thousand metallurgy workers who still remained—less than a tenth of the full complement—produced only the barest trickle of metal. By mid-1918 the Donbass was producing only 10 percent of the pig iron it had produced in mid-1916. Transport of iron ore from Krivoi Rog had been 5.23 million puds in January 1918, but dropped to only 1,000 puds (one single carload) in April 1918.[1] But the Central Powers' occupation was not intended as a permanent investment. It was, rather, an opportunity provided by conquest. In the seven months that the Germans had free run of the Ukraine and of the Donbass within it, they are said to have evacuated 32,488 carloads of food and 4,567 carloads of industrial raw materials from the region, making Ordzhonikidze's efforts look small indeed.[2] By July 1918 they were taking 2.44 million puds of iron ore monthly from Krivoi Rog.[3] As the food and raw materials were shipped to the south and west, much of the population moved in the opposite direction. As was always the case in the Donbass, natural or

[1] Krut, "Proletariat Ukrainy v bor'be," p. 108. See also Kondufor, *Istoriia rabochikh Donbassa*, vol. 1, p. 175, and Arskii, *Donetskii Bassein*, p. 20.

[2] Kondufor, *Istoriia rabochikh Donbassa*, vol. 1, p. 175.

[3] Krut, "Proletariat Ukrainy v bor'be," p. 108.

political calamity spurred emigration. Nevertheless, a considerable population remained. More important, the coal mines and steel mills that were the central reason for the German occupation of the Donbass remained. The people had to work and eat, and for this the mines and factories had to be brought back into production.

Living in Occupied Iuzovka

In Iuzovka, though the decision to close the factory had been made while the town was still under Russian rule, the discharge notices to all employees, posted as of May 1, were said to have been phrased to indicate that they were dismissed for "having been in the service of the Council of People's Commissars."[4] The industrialists were not disposed to forgive or forget when politics were the issue. Yet the relative stability brought by the occupation appears to have had an effect, and the profit imperative that was the foundation of Svitsyn's position made itself felt. Efforts were quickly made to get the factory into production once again. This was not easy, for despite the presence of an ostensibly strong political authority, the fundamental economic and organizational problems had not been solved. Rather, they had been further complicated by the presence of what was seen by the Russian workers of Iuzovka as an illegitimate regime propped up by a foreign invader. This element was prominent, for the Germans had decreed the mines to be under the direct administration of the Austrian military command, with both the industrialists and the workers subject to Austrian orders. Liberman makes this the center of his analysis, claiming that the workers did not want to give the Germans metal and coal, and therefore fled.[5] At the same time, much of the operative civil administration and police work had been turned over to the Ukrainian government headed by Hetman Skoropadskii. A report from a Krivoi Rog trade unionist characterized the Varta (Skoropadskii's police) as made up of military officers, former police officers, and all the castoffs of society.[6] In Iuzovka this was not much more popular than the Central Powers' occupation, though important

[4] Kondufor, *Istoriia rabochikh Donbassa*, vol. 1, p. 174, citing a source in the Donetsk Oblast' State Historical Archive.

[5] Liberman, *V ugol'nom tsarstve*, pp. 131–32.

[6] German and Lukomskaia, "Iz istorii," doc. 10, p. 138.

civil institutions functioned during this period, and some aspects of free life were maintained.

There were, however, harsh economic problems driving the workers away. When the factory rehired its staff, the management refused to pay back wages for the three previous months, claiming that the debt had been incurred in the period during which the company had been nationalized by the Bolshevik regime.[7] The New Russia management clung to this principle, even in individual cases. Ivan Bykaborov, who had worked in the New Russia factory in March and April 1918, found himself destitute in August 1919, and petitioned the New Russia management to pay him the wages still owing from that period. The petition was refused under the claim that the management accepted no responsibility for debts relating to the period of Bolshevik control.[8] This was not Svitsyn's personal whim, but was said to be a policy followed by all the Donbass industrialists during the periods of German and White occupation.[9]

The workers, however, showed little patience for such subtleties of commercial law, and held Svitsyn and Revilon responsible for living up to the previous wage agreement, which, after all, they had negotiated with the workers. The unions of the mine workers and metal workers were charged with choosing a strike committee and calling a strike. The Iuzovka soviet was called into special plenary session to debate the problem of nonpayment of the workers' wages. However, the Austrian garrison dispersed the session, and machine guns were set up in the factory. When a strike in the electrical shop caused a work stoppage in the mines, an order from the commandant was posted declaring that those forcibly preventing others from working would be shot immediately.[10] Not only was it forbidden to strike or prevent others from working, but any damaging of machines, or even simple failure to appear for work, was forbidden by the authorities. Nevertheless the unrest among the workers continued to grow.[11]

The ban on strikes was part of a general prophylactic campaign by the occupation authorities, aimed at pacifying the populace. When leaflets calling for "Death to the Bourgeoisie and the Germans" were found in a

[7] *Metallist*, nos. 3–4 (1918), p. 29. This would intimate that the formal nationalization decreed in January by the Sovnarkom took effect immediately.

[8] DOGIA, F. 6, op. 1, d. 34, p. 17.

[9] Krut, "Proletariat Ukrainy v bor'be," p. 106.

[10] *Izvestiia*, no. 122 (June 16, 1918).

[11] Liberman, *V ugol'nom tsarstve*, p. 131.

village near Iuzovka, the German command posted warnings that revolutionary agitation was punishable by death, agitators were to be turned over to the authorities, and in cases in which this order was not carried out the offending village would be razed to the ground.[12] This incident exposed the interparty conflicts over tactics that had begun before the occupation. Peasants in the Grishino district had sympathized with the Grishino miners when the latter had struck in July. A letter of appreciation was sent to one of the villages, purportedly from the district committee of Gornotrud (the union of the mine workers), and ending with an inflammatory slogan. The letter was turned over to the German authorities, who promptly arrested the signatories and threatened them with hanging. The Menshevik-controlled regional committee denounced the letter as a provocation and a forgery since it was said "to contradict the essence of a professional movement which does not tolerate violence against any class or nation." The committee then went on to warn all its locals and district committees not to fall victim to any "conscious or unconscious provocation."[13]

The Mensheviks continued their policy of union activity within the framework of whatever state and law existed at any given time. The Bolsheviks and anarchists of the Donbass were for class war and revolutionary war, regardless of the consequences. At the Kadievka and Maksimovka mines, "individuals" from the workers' fighting groups killed two of the technical staff, after which all the other technical and administrative staff members abandoned the mines, threatening them with closure and the miners with unemployment.[14] This was evidently an attempt at "revolutionary war" against those collaborating with the occupiers.

The Mensheviks sought to maintain their institutions and some framework of economic life for their members; this led them into a web of complex and often contradictory relations with the government, the occupation authorities, and the industrialists on the one hand, and with their members and their more radical socialist and anarchist opponents on the other. In Bolshevik-held regions this led to an attempt by the soviets and military revolutionary committees (in which the Bolsheviks had greater

[12] Korolivskii, *Grazhdanskaia voina na Ukraine*, vol. 1, bk. 1, p. 173. This source specifies leaflets, but as will be seen, other documents attribute the call to a single letter.

[13] German and Lukomskaia, "Iz istorii," doc. 54, protocol of Gornotrud obkom session, August 23, 1918, p. 181.

[14] Ibid., "Iz istorii," doc. 157, report of the Kadievka district committee of Gornotrud, January 1919, p. 187.

influence) to overpower the unions. Toward the end of 1918, Gornotrud tried to define its position, and particularly its relations with the soviets, in a circular sent to all the district committees.

> Soviets of workers' deputies are a purely political organization of the working class, carrying on the struggle for power or for influence over the regime. They educate the working class politically, but they do not lead the struggle of labor against capital. For the latter they command neither the time, the resources, the experience, nor the manpower. The struggle for improvement of the economic situation of the proletariat, and the winning of new positions from capital, can be carried on only by the trade unions, uniting the workers by profession, or by industrial branch, and well acquainted with the situation in any given branch of industrial production.[15]

Such a separation of economics and politics was not easily sustained in the revolutionary Russia of 1918 and 1919.

The union's outlook is reflected in an urgent telegram sent to the Ministry of Labor and to the All-Ukrainian Council of Trade Unions by the Oblast' Buro of the Mine and Metal Workers' Unions of the Donbass, protesting the position of the New Russia management regarding the payment of back wages. "By immense effort we have prevented the workers from spontaneous, unorganized response, noting that government will take immediate, firm measures against violation of agreement. Such things happening frequently all over Donbass. Factories are threatened with stoppage, and mines face ruin if industrialists' actions go unpunished, prompting workers to spontaneous action."[16] The First All-Ukrainian Conference of Trade Unions had assembled in Kiev in May 1918; permission was granted by the newly installed government of Skoropadskii. The Menshevik Social-Democrats dominated with 184 delegates, the Jewish Bund had 83, nonparty delegates numbered 66, and the Socialist-Revolutionaries and their sympathizers 40. The radical left was represented by 45 Communists and their sympathizers, 19 Left Socialist-Revolutionaries, and 11 Anarchists. An additional 92 delegates represented the Ukrainian Social-Democrats (19), the SERP (34), the Poalei Tsion (15), and others (24).[17] Though the Ukrainian Council of Trade Unions evidently responded to this

[15] Ibid., doc. 53, undated circular of the central council of Gornotrud, p. 180.

[16] *Metallist*, nos. 3–4, (1918), p. 29.

[17] Krut, "Proletariat Ukrainy v bor'be," p. 111.

call, as well as to other, similar appeals coming in from various quarters, its arguments with the Directorate resulted only in the authorities' arresting the council members.[18]

Repression of the Council of Trade Unions was no surprise. Somewhat earlier, the leadership of the unions had taken stock of their situation and expressed wonder that the expected repression by the German authorities had not occurred. The unions were in a shaky position. Flight and fear had cut into the ranks of the newly formed organizations of the Donbass workers. The membership of *Metallist* had risen to eighteen thousand in November 1917, but had dwindled back to two thousand by mid-1918. In Ekaterinoslav only eighty-seven of two thousand members remained loyal to the union.[19] In September, Gornotrud sent out questionnaires to all the anthracite and bituminous mines of the Donbass. Of 310 anthracite mines answering, only 2 had active union organizations. Of 55 bituminous mines answering, including all the largest mines of the Donbass, only 25 had active unions.[20] The German occupation, however, appears to have been an interlude of law compared to the violent chaos that characterized these years in the Donbass. The Directorate had its own interest in encouraging social organization. It was in an ambivalent position, having been the creature of foreign occupiers, and it sought to gain some legitimacy by benevolence toward as many sectors of the public as possible. The unions affiliated with the Bolshevik government also attempted to carry on in the face of the dismantling of industrial plants and the consequent growth of unemployment. A report from the Ukraine to Moscow outlined the problems. "With the disorganized state of power in the Ukraine, and lacking thus far any plan for fighting unemployment, our only means of aiding the unemployed is through the distribution of grants by the unions. We have insufficient means, since with the Germans' arrival, union funds were sent to Moscow. The executive requests that the Central Committee in one way or another return funds to Kharkov."[21]

With their enterprises partly under German occupation, and partly in territory controlled by White forces, the industrialists tried to reactivate the Association of Southern Coal and Steel Producers. A meeting was convened at the beginning of June 1918 in Rostov under the chairmanship

[18] Liberman, *V ugol'nom tsarstve*, p. 131, citing *Novaia zhizn'* (June 9, 1918).

[19] Krut, "Proletariat Ukrainy v bor'be," p. 113.

[20] Ibid.

[21] *Metallist*, no. 2 (1918), p. 23.

of von Ditmar, who chided Ataman Krasnov for neglecting the interests of the Donbass mining industry.[22] At this time, however, the Krasnov forces were not prepared to maintain a civilian economy or society, most of the Donbass was under German control, and efforts to organize the Donbass were still a year away; they would be undertaken after von Ditmar's death.[23]

The Council of the Association meanwhile met in Kiev at the end of June and called for abolition of all the laws passed by the provisional government that in the industrialists' view "hindered" the mining industry, such as the law granting official standing to the factory and mine committees, and the laws relating to collective bargaining and wage agreements.[24] A similar process of intensification of labor, though perhaps differently motivated, was taking place in Bolshevik-controlled areas. As the Bolsheviks found themselves under increasing pressure from both the Germans and the Whites, they stepped up their efforts to get that part of the economy still under their control into operation. First and foremost, this meant the mobilization of greater efforts on the part of the workers.[25] In mid-May the All-Ukrainian Central Council of Trade Unions had been informed by Moscow that the workday was to be lengthened, with only underground workers in the mines entitled to an eight-hour workday. This change was put into effect beginning in mid-July.[26]

Industrial unrest was not confined to Iuzovka or the Donbass, nor were the privations of the workers of the Ukraine limited to wages alone. The German occupation and the Skoropadskii government had reinstituted corporal punishment, and this had been applied in Iuzovka, Gorlovka, and Shcherbinovka.[27] In some places, the attempts of the new regime and the employers to roll back the workers' gains in autonomy destroyed the recovery of production. In Makeevka, the workers' management that had been instituted in November, and destroyed in Chernetsov's raids, had been reconstituted, and in the spring of 1918 it had been successful in stabilizing the work force and increasing production even after the German occupa-

[22] Liberman, *V ugol'nom tsarstve*, p. 130, citing *Novaia zhizn'*, no. 7 (June 6, 1918).

[23] *Iuzhnii krai* (November 5, 1919) mentions the suggestion to build a museum of the coal industry in memory of the recently deceased N. F. von Ditmar.

[24] Liberman, *V ugol'nom tsarstve*, p. 130.

[25] For the resolution on labor discipline adopted by the All-Russian Council of Trade Unions on April 3, 1918, see *Vestnik narodnogo komissariata truda*, nos. 4–5 (1918), pp. 351–52.

[26] Ibid., citing *Izvestiia VTsIK* (July 4, 1918).

[27] Krut, "Proletariat Ukrainy v bor'be," p. 114.

tion. In May 1918, the workers' management had been dismissed; by the end of June the work force had dropped from 6,014 miners to 2,800, and production had dwindled from a six-month high point of 2.3 million puds in April to 400,000 puds in June.[28] The Makeevka workers went on strike along with the railway workers of the Ukraine. Their strike dragged on through July and August. The coal miners' strike failed totally due to poor leadership and dissension between the miners and their leaders. The metal workers of Makeevka also struck, but were forced to settle for conditions somewhat inferior to those prevailing under the collective agreement in force in the previous year.[29] In June and July there had also been a long strike at the Gorlovka mines and at the factory in Shcherbinovka, taking advantage of the lack of police or militia in the area. Nonetheless, the strike leaders in Gorlovka had been arrested.[30]

Throughout the Donbass there were scattered strikes of miners, metallurgy workers, printers, and leather workers.[31] Between July and December 1918 there were seventeen strikes of the Metal Workers' Union involving ten localities, twenty factories, and 10,193 workers.[32] The strikes were not particularly large, involving an average of 600 workers each, but they were prolonged, with an average duration of twenty-nine days. It is worth noting that though threats abounded and the Gorlovka strike committee was arrested, there does not appear to have been any violence or loss of life connected with these strikes. This was clearly a victory for the leadership of the Menshevik-controlled unions of the time. In the wake of these strikes, and particularly of the railway workers' strike, the Skoropadskii government invoked the tsarist law promulgated in December 1905, setting harsh penalties for strikes in enterprises of public and state importance.[33] As is so often the case with governments today, this government reached back into the bag of tricks of a despised and oppressive predecessor to solve its own current security problems.

[28] Bazhanov, "Kamennougol'naia promyshlennost' Donetskogo Basseina," p. 26.

[29] Korolivskii, *Grazhdanskaia voina na Ukraine*, vol. 1, bk. 1, pp. 346–47.

[30] German and Lukomskaia, "Iz istorii," doc. 16, p. 145, letter of July 25, 1918, from the district committee of Gornotrud to the Central Council of Trade Unions, complaining that twenty-one men, eleven women, and fourteen children were being held in prison in Belgorod for their part in the Gorlovka strike. For a full account of the strike, see ibid., doc. 26–34, pp. 150–60.

[31] Korolivskii, *Grazhdanskaia voina v Ukraine*, vol. 2, pp. 172, 346–47, 362–63.

[32] Krut, "Proletariat Ukrainy v bor'be," p. 111.

[33] Korolivskii, *Grazhdanskaia voina v Ukraine* vol. 1, bk. 1, p. 230. The text of the decree, is given in Krut, "Proletariat Ukrainy v bor'be," p. 105.

Inflation, deficiencies of food supply, erratic transport, political hostility to the Directorate, and the underlying resentment of German occupation all played their part. An all-Ukrainian rail strike broke out in the southwest of the Right Bank Ukraine, and then spread eastward across the Dnepr, affecting the Ekaterinin and North Donetsk railroads, among others, and paralyzing Iuzovka, bringing the Iuzovka workers to strike. The strike was successful in gaining recognition of the collective-labor agreement and a reinstatement of the eight-hour day.[34] This was achieved, however, only by virtue of the longest strike in the history of the New Russia factory.

When it reopened soon after the German occupation, the factory had not been able to resume full operations, and it was employing only about three thousand of its skilled workers in maintenance and in the auxiliary shops. At the end of June there was an attempt to put the rail-casting shop into operation on the basis of a ten-hour workday. After three days it closed down, and the workers used the opportunity to voice their demands for an eight-hour day, a raise in pay, and recognition of the previous collective agreement.[35] This was the beginning of a two-month contest between workers and management. As the Metal Workers' Union saw it, the employers were attempting to roll back all the gains of the workers since March 1917. "They began in Iuzovka because the workers there had barely experienced the school of struggle; the trade union was new and untested, and the workers have lived and worked at the factory for thirty and forty years. They receive free living quarters and coal, and there is a large proportion of invalids and older people among them."[36] The union set up a strike fund, and the regional bureau of the Metal Workers' Union took over the direction of the strike from the local leaders. When the management of the company tried to gain sole control of food distribution, the food committee that had been working for over a year and a half was strong enough to insist on its rights and maintain its position. The union augmented the local supplies by setting up a union kitchen that provided low-cost meals and sold food to the workers at subsidized prices. In the near-starvation conditions of the Donbass, control of food was the most tangible sort of power. At Shcherbinovka and Gorlovka, both in the summer of 1918, and in subsequent outbreaks of tension, the employers also attempted to control food supplies,

[34] Kondufor, *Istoriia rabochikh Donbassa*, vol. 1, pp. 176–77.

[35] Korolivskii, *Grazhdanskaia voina na Ukraine*, vol. 1, bk. 1, p. 345.

[36] Ibid., pp. 345–46, extract from *Golos metallista*, no. 1 (September 23, 1918). The entire account of the strike is drawn from this source.

and the authorities prevented the miners from sending purchasing expeditions to the villages in search of food. There too, the union extended credit to the cooperatives, and actively assisted them in acquiring and distributing the necessary food supplies, knowing that this was a key to the miners' loyalty.[37] When economic pressures threatened the solidarity of the workers, strike pay was increased.

The crucial moment of the Iuzovka strike came on August 8, when the factory management gathered a crew of longtime workers and the unemployed, lit the casting furnaces, and tried to put the rail shop to work. At the same time, Ukrainian police and Austro-Hungarian soldiers were brought to threaten the strikers with eviction from company housing. The workers were wavering in the face of this threat to their families' well-being, but the union had prepared itself for this moment. It had turned earlier to legal counsel and with the help of the law prevented the evictions from taking place. With that threat removed, and their economic sustenance guaranteed, the workers remained steadfast.

Throughout the strike there had been attempts at negotiation. The first four meetings of union and management broke down over the employers' refusal to consider the central demands: an eight-hour day, a raise in pay, and a reinstatement of the collective agreement. Then the union negotiators began to concentrate on secondary issues, on which management was willing to work out a compromise. An atmosphere of confidence and agreement was created, and meanwhile the strike remained solid. On September 2, in the seventh meeting of the negotiating teams, the management representatives indicated their willingness to meet the workers' demands with a guaranteed minimum wage and the rates of the former collective agreement, rather than any pay raise. At three o'clock in the morning of September 3, 1918, the workers happily voted to return to work.

The entire course of the strike tactics and negotiations bespeaks the skill and maturity of the union leadership. There were, however, other factors influencing the outcome. The workers showed discipline and persistence. There was no violence and no drunkenness. This may have been because these were the most senior and experienced of the factory workers, persons well acquainted with each other, and well rooted in the traditions of factory labor. The virtual nonintervention of the authorities, despite their abun-

[37] German and Lukomskaia, "Iz istorii," doc. 39, report of Gorlovka committee of Gornotrud, July 17, 1918, p. 165; doc. 55, report of Shcherbinovka Congress of Delegates of the Mine Workers' Union, December 24, 1918.

dant threats, also played its part. Although soldiers and police were present at the eviction attempt it would appear that they were in no hurry to enforce the wishes of the management, or to implement literally the German ban on strikes. As outsiders they carried slight authority with either management or workers, leaving the two sides to work out their problems by direct negotiation. Skoropadskii had his hands full with other matters, and he had good reason to exercise restraint toward the citizens. The German authorities, for their part, had other priorities than enforcement of the will of the Russian managers on their workers. Some months later, with privations becoming even more severe, and robbery and violence more common throughout Bakhmut district, Svitsyn sent an angry telegram to the minister of the interior. "The work of the factory and mines of Iuzovka in which so much capital has been invested is disturbed by the flood of Bolsheviks in the settlements and villages of the vicinity, and by the intensified propaganda that they carry on, both directly and through their trade-union organizations. Their agitation succeeds due to the absence of a strong regime and the indifference of the military authorities here."[38]

Economic problems, particularly the problem of buying enough food to sustain life, were again foremost. The inflation that had plagued the workers continued and even intensified. Bazhanov, the Makeevka engineer who became the Bolsheviks' authority on the Donbass, reported that the price of a pud of flour in the Donbass rose during 1918 from 20 rubles to 120 rubles.[39] The tangle of currencies grew even more complex as German occupation scrip and Directorate bills were added to the tsarist and Kerenskii paper rubles, the Rada currency, and the newly printed "Novocherkassk rubles," issued by Krasnov's administration, none of which enjoyed any great measure of public confidence among the people of the Donbass.

The factory food committee continued much as before. The only visible change was that its letterhead now contained the inscription "U. D. [Ukrainian Directorate?] Ministry of Food" in addition to "New Russia Mining Industry Food Supply Committee." The impression is one of orderly management and a continuing, but restrained, contest for authority between management and workers at all levels, in an environment of severe scarcity.

[38] Korolivskii, *Grazhdanskaia voina na Ukraine*, vol. 1, bk. 1, p. 365, telegram of October 15, 1918. For a report on worsening living conditions, unemployment, and the rise in violent crime, see pp. 218–19.

[39] *Ekonomicheskaia zhizn'*, no. 57 (March 15, 1919), p. 3.

The tenor and substance of the negotiations reflect the Menshevik domination of the unions both locally and centrally.

The Bolsheviks were closely watching the political and economic affairs of the Donbass, and were anxious to maintain their contacts with the workers. During the strike, Zaitsev was sent back to Iuzovka, where his mother and wife still lived. Although he tried to hide under the name of Fiodor Ivanovich Kornev, he was immediately arrested, and he spent the next two months in jail in Iuzovka and Bakhmut.[40] While the trade-union movement was allowed to continue under the German occupation, the fate of the revolutionary movement was the same as it had been under the tsar.

In October 1918, with a German withdrawal becoming an ever-clearer prospect, the Bolsheviks began to take stock and organize for the future. Within Iuzovka there remained a few of the veteran comrades: the two Sonias, Okun and Godos; Andrei Koval (Kizliarskii), Aleksandr Boldyrev, Egor Zimin, and Lagutenko. An underground revolutionary committee was formed, directed by Zaitsev from outside Iuzovka. Two machine guns were said to be hidden in the town.[41] The committee called for a strike to mark the first anniversary of the Bolshevik seizure of power. In the mines of Iuzovka there was said to have been a full response, but in the factory only a partial strike.[42]

The Mensheviks were active as well, and in early November, evidently as the German forces prepared their withdrawal, the Ukrainian Council of Trade Unions called for a one-day political general strike to protest "Hetmanate repression."[43] The instructions for the strike included a warning that there was to be no violence against administrative and technical personnel in the mines. A clear chain of command was presented and a demand voiced for strict discipline, avoiding all possible provocations, individual excesses, and unauthorized initiatives. The plan presented for demonstrations during the strike included provision for union participation in maintaining order in the cities during these demonstrations.[44] The strike leaders were evidently well aware of the volatile nature of their constituents and of the tendencies of the Bolshevik and anarchist activists. To the Iuzovka

[40] Zaitsev, "Kak my tvorili oktiabr'," p. 142.

[41] "Iz deiatel'nosti," p. 159.

[42] Zaitsev, "Kak my tvorili oktiabr'," pp. 142–43.

[43] Ibid., p. 143.

[44] German and Lukomskaia, "Iz istorii," doc. 51, protocol of the special session of the Shcherbinovka Congress of Delegates of the Mine Workers' Union, November 8, 1918, p. 178.

Bolsheviks this seemed a pale half-measure. They issued a call for an armed uprising to reinstate Soviet rule. They even had an underground revolutionary staff. The Menshevik Internationalist army officer Khoroshko had worked out the military aspects, together with Koval-Kizliarskii and the anarchist Shota. The uprising was to include such important objects as the ammunition factory at Vetka.[45] A date was even set: the beginning of the fourth week in November.[46]

Iuzovka under the Whites

The plans for an uprising were never implemented in Iuzovka, for on November 10, 1918, a detachment of Krasnov's forces, commanded by Podesaul (junior officer) Abramov, took control of Iuzovka from the withdrawing German army. Abramov's first action was to post an order throughout the town announcing summary justice for all those suspected of revolutionary sympathies.

> The following telegram refers not only to the working population of the town of Iuzovka and its district, but to all areas under my orders. I declare that I have received the following telegram:
>
> 1. I forbid any detention of workers and order that they be summarily shot or hanged. Order 2428, November 10.
>
> 2. All arrested workers are to be hanged in the main streets and not removed for three days. Order 2431, November 10.
>
> (signed) Commandant Makeevka Mining District Esaul Zhirov. In accordance with order of 10.XI, no. 2431, the following were hanged as Bolsheviks: Nikolai Fedorovich Litvinenko, Vasilii Filipovich Krivitskii."[47]

[45] Korolivskii, *Grazhdanskaia voina na Ukraine*, vol. 1, bk. 1, p. 33. The Vetka uprising was scheduled for November 27, 1918.

[46] Zaitsev, "Kak my tvorili oktiabr'," p. 143.

[47] DOGIA, F. 6, op. 1, d. 27, p. 14. Kondufor, *Istoriia rabochikh Donbassa*, vol. 1, p. 181, gives the date of entry of the Krasnov troops as November 18. Zaitsev, "Kak my tvorili oktiabr'," p. 143, writes that Chernetsov, who had led the first raids against the Donbass soviets, was the Iuzovka commandant, and attributes the order to hang workers to the cossack General Denisov, as retribution for the killing of several of his men. Neither of the two men hanged was memorialized in Donetsk as a hero of revolutionary resistance.

Some two weeks later, with the aid of Makhno's forces, Zaitsev and Koval armed seventy-five men at the Vosnesenskii mine, joined a partisan group at Maxmilianovka, and held it for some time against the advancing White forces.[48] There were numerous armed bands and partisans fighting each other as well as fighting the Bolsheviks or the Whites. In the rapidly changing alliances that emerged, nobody was safe, and the anarchist Shota, who had been part of Zaitsev's revolutionary staff, eventually was killed by Makhno's men, who disarmed and dispersed the Iuzovka force.[49]

With the German withdrawal, Skoropadskii's regime swiftly fell. This was the beginning of a month of anarchy. Landlords, administrators, Varta (guards; these were police who had been subordinate to Hetman Skoropadskii)—all had fled.[50] The New Russia management also left town, though the factory continued to function at least in part, with the workers of the railway yard keeping the rolling stock in order under threat of being shot.[51]

The shooting of every tenth man for any violation of order was routinely practiced by the Denikin forces. In Konstantinovka thirteen men were shot this way, and at the Kramatorsk factory, fifty-four.[52] Bazhanov wrote that the White forces were massacring men and women indiscriminately in the Donbass, not because they were Bolsheviks, but simply because they were workers, under the slogan "Death to calloused hands!"[53] The harshness and ubiquitous nature of the White terror was blamed for a wave of suicides that swept the Donbass in that period.[54] The population that had stabilized during the later months of the German occupation now dwindled sharply once again as workers fled the severity of the regime, as well as a twelve-

[48] Zaitsev, "Kak my tvorili oktiabr'," p. 144.

[49] Ibid., p. 145. Khoroshko was saved by being absent when the clash took place. For another instance of a Red insurgent band disarmed by Makhno's men in January 1919, see Malet, *Nestor Makhno in the Russian Civil War*, p. 130

[50] Ibid., p. 20.

[51] DOGIA, F. 6, op. 1, d. 34, p. 15. For a good part of the German occupation, Svitsyn had been in Rostov.

[52] For a report of the shooting of the Kramatorsk workers for refusal to surrender the Bolsheviks among them, see Korolivskii, *Grazhdanskaia voina na Ukraine*, vol. 1, bk. 2, p. 69. The killing of fifty-two miners at the Kadievka mine in the context of clashes between cossacks and Petliura troops is reported by the district executive of Gornotrud on January 18, 1919. See German and Lukomskaia, "Iz istorii," doc. 57, p. 186.

[53] Cited in Gudzenko, *Robitnichii kontrol' i natsionalizatsiia*, p. 495.

[54] Kondufor, *Istoriia rabochikh Donbassa*, vol. 1, p. 183, and "1918–1919gg. v profdvizhenii Ukrainy," p. 9. On p. 12 of the same report, hunger is given as a contributing factor in the suicides.

hour workday that paid at most eight rubles.[55] Liberman, a mining technologist by profession and a Socialist-Revolutionary by conviction, wrote of this period: "That wild reaction that set out to replace Bolshevism in the Donbass, completed the destruction of everything that the Bolshevik regime had not managed to destroy during its notorious regime of 'workers' control,' and its bacchanal of dividing the workers and destroying all militant workers' organizations."[56]

When Denikin's Volunteer Army came to Iuzovka, its Samursk Regiment bivouacked at the New Russia's Peski farm. They not only denationalized the purebred Percherons and Brabants, but also forty sheep, with appropriate accompaniments of potatoes, lard, bread, and flour, as well as boots, overcoats, and other belongings of the farm's residents.[57] But this type of disorder was too dangerous to be allowed in such an important economic center as Iuzovka. The common denominator of all Iuzovka's occupiers was a recognition of the great potential for power that lay in the mines and factory of the town. General Mai-Maevskii, Denikin's representative for Ekaterinoslav province, who made Iuzovka his headquarters, tried to instill order and bring the town back to normality. His first decree, issued December 20, 1918, ordered all his units to pay cash for any goods or services taken from the local population. It would appear that he had some success in this, for two weeks later he was able to rescind the eleven o'clock curfew that had been declared in the town.[58]

In mid-February 1919, a two-day congress of delegates of consumer organizations was convened in Iuzovka, an act that implies stability and security.[59] The bringing of order was not, however, accompanied by any political liberalization, for when the Iuzovka Bolsheviks attempted to bring in revolutionary leaflets, Bogachev was shot, Kobzenko and Poddubnyi were hanged, and Koval-Kizliarskii, Boldyrev, and Lagutenko, leaders of the underground committee during the German occupation, fled

[55] See Bazhanov's report to the VSNKh, *Ekonomicheskaia zhizn'*, no. 57 (March 15, 1919), p. 3. As I will show, wages in Iuzovka were considerably higher during the summer of 1919.

[56] Liberman, *V ugol'nom tsarstve*, p. 127. For Liberman's profession, see Kondufor, *Istoriia rabochikh Donbassa*, vol. 1, p. 62. Here he is called a Social-Democrat. For his not being a Bolshevik, see Kir'ianov, *Rabochikh iuga Rossii*, p. 5. Before 1917 he published in the S-R press. It is significant that Liberman's book was published in Petrograd in 1918.

[57] DOGIA, F. 6, op. 1, d. 215, p. 121.

[58] Ibid., d. 27, pp. 121–22.

[59] Bazhanova, *Narodnoe khoziaistvo SSSR v 1917–1920*, p. 195.

Iuzovka.[60] Mai-Maevskii, in his capacity as governor-general of Ekaterinoslav province, also published a decree that for any damage to rail lines, the nearest population, and in the first instance, the village elders and the zemstvo officials, would be brought to account before a field court-martial.[61] Food supplies were also used as an incentive to keep order. Konstantinovka was excluded from distribution of foodstuffs by the Volunteer Army, "due to hostile actions by the workers' committee of the Konstantinovka bottle factory against a unit of the Volunteer Army stationed there." The railway workers at Avdeevka, on the other hand, were given preferential supplies of food at the personal order of General Mai-Maevskii, "for excellent and conscientious service."[62]

Food was an effective arbiter of politics, for the whole region was living from hand to mouth. A report of January 1919 declared:

> The food situation at all the mines is severe because of the events and the cessation of rail traffic. At some mines there has been no food for several days. At the Irmino mine there is a total lack of forage and as a result, most of the horses, both in the mines and aboveground, have died. . . . At Debaltsevo station there were numerous wagons with grain intended for our district. A few of these we managed to wheedle out of the cossacks and bring here, but in view of the Bolshevik advance they are sending all the rest to the Don region.[63]

The food inventory for mid-March 1919 shows the Vetka mine possessing no lard, twenty-three puds of onions, ninety-four puds of flour, no sugar, and eighteen puds of laundry soap. Nearly two-thirds of the total inventory was on the store shelves, with virtually nothing in reserve.[64] At the same time the New Russia Co. was petitioning Mai-Maevskii to authorize the transport of straw to Peski since the only fodder left there for the livestock was the thatch on the roofs of huts built only the year before.[65] Two months earlier, the company's management had ordered the immediate sale of fifty

[60] Zaitsev, "Kak my tvorili oktiabr'," p. 146.
[61] DOGIA, F. 6, op. 1, d. 27, p. 45.
[62] Ibid., d. 215, p. 201.
[63] German and Lukomskaia, "Iz istorii," doc. 57, p. 187.
[64] DOGIA, F. 6, op. 9, d. 302, pp. 66–67.
[65] Ibid., op. 1, d. 215, pp. 91–92.

horses because of the lack of fodder, though the shortage of horses was one of the factors affecting coal production. The Karpov estate had once provided forage, but the presence of Makhno's cavalry units in that area made the supply uncertain. Only a strong armed convoy could assure the safe delivery of foodstuffs and forage, and the fluidity of the fortunes of battle meant that Mai-Maevskii's troops were kept busy in combat and could not secure outlying areas against armed raiders.[66]

As much as any other factor, the instability of the front in the Donbass was responsible for the crisis of the first half of 1919. Mai-Maevskii favored the innovative tactic of holding a series of important rail junctions and sending his forces on sorties along the rail lines rather than maintaining a continuous front. This was the reason he had chosen Iuzovka, with its many-branched rail connections, as his headquarters. One of the results was, however, that in the first half of 1919, Konstantinovka changed hands twenty-seven times.[67] The wonder is not that famine eventually came to the Donbass, but that the various food committees and administrations were able to maintain a semiadequate level of supply through nearly four years of turmoil, until nature added her own cruel twist to the compounded follies of man.

Confusion and scarcity were not limited to the White side of the lines. I have already noted the disorganization that prevailed in the requisitioning of food from Ekaterinoslav province during the early days of Bolshevik rule. This evidently became only more severe with the return of Bolshevik forces in early 1919, and in April Kamenev was sent from Moscow to Kharkov as a plenipotentiary to untangle the question of food supply.[68] This followed the presentation of a report to the Sovnarkom on the state of the railways and coal mines as factors in the revival of Donbass metallurgy. In the report, it was pointed out that the miners were losing workdays because they were occupied in searching for food in the countryside—and that if the government could not organize a system of food supply, they would abandon the mines permanently, moving back to their villages. This would doom any hopes of strengthening the struggling Soviet economy. The report also commented on the persistence of tradition among the miners. In drawing up a forecast of coal production, the author noted that the production for

[66] Ibid., pp. 157, 168.

[67] Kondufor, *Istoriia rabochikh Donbassa*, vol. 1, p. 182.

[68] Malet, *Nestor Makhno in the Russian Civil War*, pp. 33–34.

April 1919 would be low because the miners would be taking their usual extended Easter holiday.[69]

But Soviet Russia was in dire need of coal, and coal was the special treasure of the Donbass. As the Red Army became organized and advanced into the northern Donbass at the beginning of 1919, it found huge stocks of coal piled up at railway junctions and mine heads. An estimated 31 million puds were already there, and the production for February would add another 8 million. By a supreme organizational effort perhaps 11.2 million puds could be hauled north to warm Moscow and Petrograd, and to provide steam and electricity for the factories. All passenger traffic on the southern railways was stopped and 3,857 freight cars were sent to the Donbass to load coal. But only 379 returned north. Locomotives were lacking, with a growing number falling out of service, and others had been requisitioned for military needs.[70]

There were also interdepartmental squabbles in the Bolshevik regime. At the outset, the Soviet regime had decreed the mobilization of workers. At that time, a differentiated approach had been taken to minimize the impact on vital production. In the metal-working industry, the workers had been divided into five categories, from the most professional to the unskilled. Only 20 percent of the most skilled workers were to be taken, while 80 percent of group five were to be mobilized. In each case the particular workers to be mobilized were to be determined by the factory management.[71] In May 1919 the civil war flared up and the Bolsheviks came under great pressure, with Ataman Grigor'ev's forces revolting against the Bolsheviks, and Makhno's anarchists regarded with increasing mistrust and suspicion. On May 7, the Council of Labor and Defense in Moscow ordered a full call-up of all Donbass miners born between 1891 and 1898. Glavugol', the Main Coal Administration, located in Kharkov, protested, as this would have removed the strongest young miners from the shafts. Lenin's reply was a compromise, exempting coal cutters, and thus protecting the industry's basic capability to produce, but affirming that "general cancellation of Donbass workers' mobilization is utterly imper-

[69] Report of engineer Takhtomyshev, March 1919, in Korolivskii, *Grazhdanskaia voina na Ukraine*, vol. 1, bk. 2, pp. 282–86.

[70] *Ekonomicheskaia zhizn'*, no. 41 (February 21, 1919), p. 2; no. 45 (February 27, 1919), p. 3.

[71] *Biulleten' vserossiiskogo soveta normirovaniia truda v metallicheskoi promyshlennosti*, nos. 2–3 (November 23, 1918), p. 4.

missible given the present situation at the front."[72] A similar telegram was sent to Kamenev, who was then on his Donbass mission, so that Lenin might be sure that his point of view carried the day with the local administration.[73]

Returning to the Donbass from Moscow in April 1919, Artem sent in an alarming report. Where previously the Mensheviks had been ignored by the workers, their speeches were now listened to and applauded. In Artem's opinion this was the fault of the Bolshevik apparat, "whose work is beneath criticism, particularly in matters of food supply, and in seeing that the workers are paid and supplied with goods. (They are literally going naked.)"[74]

Such bureaucratic bumbling at a time of near-total disaster drove Lenin to fury. An angry message sent at the beginning of June to the Donbass party leaders in Kharkov demanded an end to "speechifying" (*mitingovanie*), to false reports, and to petty political jockeying for position. Henceforth, wrote Lenin, strict military discipline should prevail among all party officials. He wanted to receive only factual reports on numbers of men actually mobilized and sent to the front, and arms already delivered to the Red Army.[75] Trotsky, for his part, agreed that the Donbass should be the Bolsheviks' first priority, but he concentrated more on factors outside the Communist party. He thought to use the Grigor'ev mutiny as an opportunity to eliminate all independent partisan groups—particularly those of Makhno. He urged a vigorous campaign for revolutionary order and discipline "so as to score a deep notch in the consciousness of the working masses of the Ukraine."[76] Lenin's anger was understandable, for the Bolsheviks had invested great energy in concentrating forces in the Donbass, and at this juncture enjoyed a considerable numerical advantage over the White armies. In a report to Denikin in January 1919, Ataman Zimov had estimated Bolshevik forces as growing rapidly toward an army of ninety thousand, with strong artillery, preparing for an attack to take the Donbass. His

[72] Meijer, *Trotsky Papers*, vol. 1, p. 437.

[73] For the telegram addressed to Kamenev, see Korolivskii, *Grazhdanskaia voina na Ukraine*, vol. 2, p. 55.

[74] Ibid., vol. 1, bk. 2, pp. 297–99. As noted above, affordable food and timely wage payments were sufficient to hold the workers' loyalty. Artem evidently understood and agreed with this analysis.

[75] Ibid., vol. 2, p. 110. The telegram is addressed to Artem, Voroshilov, Mezhlauk, Mel'nichanskii, and Kaminskii.

[76] Meijer, *Trotsky Papers*, vol. 1, p. 431.

own forces numbered an estimated seven thousand, in addition to Mai-Maevskii's division.[77]

The intractable nature of both military and civilian supply problems was exemplified by the situation of the Lugansk artillery factory, and in particular its ammunition shops. In response to Lenin's demand that the factory work to a production goal of 1.5 million cartridges daily, supplies and capital were provided from every possible source. Six weeks later, a secret order instructed all Red Army commanders to observe strict economy of ammunition due to short supply. A report dated at the end of May stated that although the Lugansk factory was now technically equipped to meet its production quota, Dybenko controlled both production and distribution of the ammunition produced, and that the preparations for full exploitation of the factory's capacities were bound up with "a whole set of conflicts."[78] Nevertheless there is a growing sense of organization and achievement in the Bolshevik supply reports. All types of equipment, from boots to heavy cannon, were coming into production and beginning to reach the front. The Bolshevik talent for mass organization and for campaigning began to yield results.

Food, military equipment, human resources, and all kinds of supplies were ferreted out with the aid of numerous social organizations. An all-Ukrainian congress of county executive committees, convened at the beginning of June 1919, decreed June as "Arms for the Red Army Month," and adopted a resolution for gathering weapons throughout the villages of the Ukraine. The resolution read in part: "4. Arms are to be given over voluntarily. 5. All citizens who do not hand over their weapons by June 1 of this year are declared to be enemies of the people and repressive measures are to be taken against them."[79] Even then, party workers were judged by the results achieved, and not by the external elegance or logic of their methods. The important point was to gather arms for the Red Army and take away as many weapons as possible from a potentially hostile village population.

Shortage was the one feature of life common to everyone. The New

[77] Krasnov, "Vsevelikoe voisko-Donskoe," p. 166. The ataman appears to have exaggerated the Bolshevik's strength and understated his own.

[78] Korolivskii, *Grazhdanskaia voina na Ukraine*, vol. 2, pp. 35, 100; secret order dated May 10, 1919, report to the people's commissar for war, Podvoiskii, dated May 29, 1919. The report surveys the entire effort to provide military supplies to the Ukraine. For reports on the supply and production effort, see ibid., vol. 1, bk. 2, pp. 146, 268–69.

[79] Ibid., vol. 2, p. 116. The June 1 date is presumably an error, since the resolution was adopted after that date.

Russia Co. archive contains numerous petitions from workers requesting advances on their wages to prepare for winter, to repair their houses, or to stockpile suddenly available provisions. Most of these were refused. All bear the handwritten approval or denial and signature of Svitsyn. The paternalistic tradition continued through these years unabated. The worker Gusarov, earning 968 rubles in September 1919, requested an advance of 500 rubles for winter preparations. It was denied. A worker wishing to buy an overcoat asked for a two thousand–ruble advance to be repaid over eight months. This was approved. Parents and spouses of workers serving in the ranks of Denikin's army turned to the factory management for help. The shortages were not only in market-purchased goods. Given the instability of the Donbass, torn by civil war, the right to company-distributed rations and the right to occupy company housing were still privileges to be cherished, and therefore an incentive to good behavior. When Nikolai Kozlovskii was fired from the New Russia machine shop for unjustified absence from work, an order was sent to the housing department to evict him from house no. 27 on the Fifteenth Line, and to put the house at the disposal of Semen Savenkov, another machine-shop worker.[80] A company circular set norms for coal distribution to workers in various types of housing. However, a note at the end of the circular stated that by order of the administration, only two-thirds of the norm was actually to be distributed.[81]

Politics found numerous and strange channels of expression. Registration of all medical personnel was carried out by Denikin's Volunteer Army, and the doctors were obliged to remain at their posts. New doctors were also hired. A. L. Belotserkovskii was taken on at the Vetka mine in March 1919. In April, when the Bolsheviks twice captured the area for brief periods, he remained at the mine hospital, tending his patients. This was reported to White headquarters, and he was included in the list of those who had served the Reds.[82]

Ideological matters were not neglected by Mai-Maevskii's staff. The head of the Propaganda Department of the Armed Forces Command of South Russia announced the formation of a "Culture and Enlightenment Society

[80] DOGIA, F. 6, op. 1, d. 27, p. 26. The order is dated July 1, 1919.

[81] For the workers' petitions, see ibid., d. 34, pp. 30–37, 60–63. For the circular on coal distribution, see p. 48.

[82] For the registration of medical personnel, see ibid., d. 27, p. 50. For the case of Dr. Belotserkovskii, see ibid., d. 215, p. 59.

of Iuzovka," inviting the town's intelligentsia to attend.[83] The propagandists also requisitioned the services of the New Russia Co. print shop to prepare supplies of their pamphlets "General Denikin's Declaration on the Labor Question" and "On the Land Question," claiming that "every day couriers come from the mines asking for agitational material for the workers, but have to return empty-handed."[84]

Iuzovka's sanitation problems had not been alleviated during the revolution and civil war. A sanitary review of the settlement in January 1919, drawn up by Dr. Moskat, the provincial zemstvo public health officer, together with his opposite number in the factory, Dr. Fonberg, and the veteran director of the factory hospital, Dr. Gedgovt, found garbage collection faulty and numerous outhouses in disrepair and overflowing. The only benefit that had emerged from the political tangle was that the crowding of housing had been alleviated. In some of the housing projects there was now a bed for each inhabitant, and the living quarters were clean and well aired.[85] Bazhanov, analyzing the flight of workers from the Donbass at this time, states that those with large families remained, while the single men and smaller families fled.[86] Clearly this indicates that the older, more-settled factory workers remained, along with the stable portion of the mine labor force, who had created better living conditions for themselves, and who cared more for the quality of life in their immediate environment.

The relations between the management of the New Russia Co. and the new masters of Iuzovka were cautious. The local soviet and duma having evacuated, General Mai-Maevskii's staff looked to the New Russia Co. to run the town. The management, unsure of the stability and longevity of the Whites, was reluctant to be identified with the new regime. The Bolsheviks did, on two occasions in April and May 1919, return to Iuzovka, though their conquest was short-lived: two days the first time and twenty days on the next attempt. During these interludes a Bolshevik Revolutionary Committee was activated, headed by Zaitsev, and taxes were levied from prop-

[83] Ibid., d. 27, p. 93.

[84] Ibid., pp. 83–85. Numerous leaflets and proclamations issued by Mai-Maevskii's headquarters bear the imprint of the New Russia print shop.

[85] Ibid., d. 215, p. 142. See also a slightly later letter by Dr. Korchinskii, identified as the Iuzovka district public health officer, calling on the New Russia Co. for paving of the areas around the water cisterns, better garbage removal, and installation of additional garbage receptacles.

[86] Bazhanov, "Kamennougol'naia promyshlennost' Donetskogo Basseina," p. 27.

erty owners, some of which were turned over to the factory management to meet wage payments and the needs of the hospital.[87] Each such overturn only added to the suffering of the townspeople. With the return of the Whites to Iuzovka on May 9, 1919, a telegram to Svitsyn at the Astoria Hotel in Rostov summarized the situation. "Mines not flooded, factory unharmed, food, forage, money lacking. Situation critical. We are all starving. For three weeks no delivery of food cargoes." A second telegram told of the looting of houses of company administrators, and informed Svitsyn that many workers left together with the Reds, while the rest refused to work unless food were provided.[88]

When the staff commander of the Volunteer Army somewhat peremptorily turned to the New Russia managers to organize refuse collection, the latter replied that this was a matter for the municipal administration.[89] Although the New Russia Co. had its own electric generating plant to meet the factory's requirements, the general needs of the settlement for electricity had been supplied since 1911 by a private firm, the Ivanov Electric Company. The winter of 1918–19 was particularly severe, with storms that damaged the wires and poles in Iuzovka. The Ivanov Electric Company no longer had enough workers to repair this damage. In addition, it had difficulty acquiring from the New Russia Co. the coal supplies necessary to fuel its generators. Mai-Maevskii's staff, stating that a prolonged cessation of electrical power to the town was unthinkable, turned to the New Russia Co. to assume administrative and technical responsibility for the electrical supply, including provision of fuel for the company's generators, until conditions were normalized.[90]

When Denikin's forces asked the New Russia Co. to repair their armored cars, the factory management answered that this would be difficult since the skilled mechanics had been sent over to the Russian Co. factory in Make-

[87] Zaitsev, "Kak my tvorili oktiabr'," p. 146. Zaitsev claims that when the Bolsheviks retreated from Iuzovka in mid-May, "thousands of workers" left the town with them.

[88] DOGIA, F. R-231, op. 1, d. 46, pp. 1–2. The telegrams were signed by Zaporozhets, Galitskii, and Andratskii, three senior engineers.

[89] Ibid., F. 6, op. 1, d. 27, pp. 25–26. Thus was the company's once jealously guarded monopoly over the life of Iuzovka discarded!

[90] Ibid., d. 215, pp. 75, 197, request of March 29, 1919. No answer is recorded, but supplies of coal from the New Russia mines to the electric company continued until May 1919. With the mines and the factory operating at a low level, the company probably had a considerable reserve of generating capacity, for *Novorossiiskoe obshchestvo* (1919) states that a new five thousand–kilowatt generator was being installed "at the present time." The tenor of the material in the brochure suggests that it was prepared in 1916 or 1917.

evka where they were working by special contract, and therefore there was no one in the Iuzovka factory to carry out the work.[91] In fact, the New Russia Co. had rented a building belonging to the Russian Co. in Makeevka and had established a shop for repairing railway freight wagons, handling three hundred cars each month.[92] The workers and the shop were thus under the control of the New Russia Co., and could presumably have accommodated the needs of the Whites had Svitsyn wished. Ultimately it would seem that the White commander had his way, for there are reports in the Donetsk Oblast' State Historical Archive of repairs to the armored train "General Kornilov," and the mounting of a machine-gun turret on the "St. George the Victorious."[93] Mai-Maevskii had issued an order for his wounded soldiers to be treated in the New Russia factory hospital. Svitsyn appealed for the order to be rescinded, since the typhus epidemic had already caused overcrowding, and the added burden of the needs of the Volunteer Army might hinder the recuperation of the company's workers, disrupting production.[94]

The New Russia management had no ideological antagonism to Denikin's regime. The Bolshevik side claimed that in June 1919, when Svitsyn was convinced that the Whites were about to be completely driven from the Donbass, he prepared the evacuation of all the factory's spare parts and supplies.[95] But it was, after all, a military regime in the midst of war, with its own well-defined priorities, needs, and methods of governance. The New Russia Co. remained a commercial enterprise, seeking to protect its capital and to work at a profit. It also had a historically formed expectation of state protection and support. This may be discerned in a tense negotiation between the White Army and what was termed the "Provisional Executive of the New Russia Co." A. V. Rutchenko and N. S. Gruzov, representing the company, met with Denikin's plenipotentiary for trade and commerce and undertook to produce six hundred thousand puds per month of metal and metal goods at the direction of the Volunteer Army, provided that Denikin's regime would guarantee ten million rubles per month in payment. If such funds were not forthcoming, it was stated that the factory would close completely. Denikin's representative refused the request for

[91] DOGIA, F. 6, op. 1, d. 27, pp. 29–30.

[92] *Novorossiskoe obshchestvo* (1919), p. 64.

[93] DOGIA, F. R-231, op. 1, d. 57, pp. 1–15.

[94] Ibid., F. 6, op. 1, d. 27, p. 40.

[95] Gudzenko, *Robitnichii kontrol' i natsionalizatsiia*, p. 495. This testimony is not particularly convincing, since Denikin's fortunes were at their peak in June 1919.

funds, but termed the closing of the factory "impermissible."[96] At this time typhus was rampant in Iuzovka, employment was limited, and those working were receiving only a partial advance against their wages. The White authorities sent an urgent telegram to Svitsyn in Rostov demanding that he send money for wages without delay.[97]

One of the fears of the company management was that the White armies might see the factory as a rich source of resources to meet their military needs. In mid-March, the commander of the detachment at the Novosmolianin mine addressed a "suggestion" to Svitsyn that he grant rewards amounting to 11,380 rubles to the thirty-three soldiers of the unit "who displayed courage and daring during the Reds' attack on Iuzovka." In a note sent from the Astoria Hotel in Rostov, Svitsyn authorized the payment of five thousand rubles, with the rest "perhaps to be given at some future date."[98] The company's anxieties and fears regarding the Whites sometimes erupted into open hostility. An unsigned letter from the New Russia management, addressed to the commandant of Bakhmut district, demanded the removal of G. F. Khlebin as commander of the detachment at the company's Peski farm. The accusation was dishonesty and cowardice. The letter set forth the claim that he took horses from the farm without authorization, and reported that they were killed in battle, though it later turned out that this was not so. When Makhno's forces, at that time cooperating with the Bolsheviks, approached Peski, Khlebin, "and in his wake, the entire guard of the estate, abandoned the farm and went in the opposite direction, toward the Vetka mine, leaving Peski unguarded for twelve hours. Only the arrival of a reconnaisance patrol of the Volunteer Army chased off Makhno's men, who, with the aid of a locksmith, were already opening the farm's strong room."[99]

When Denikin's army arrived in Iuzovka it immediately turned to the New Russia Co. to provide ten thousand puds of coal per month for military needs. Replying on behalf of the company, engineer Galitskii explained that typhus and food shortages had so reduced coal production that the company could spare no fuel. With some subtlety he appealed to the new military governor for assistance in acquiring sixty thousand puds of coal for Christmas distribution to the workers, either from the Briansk Co. mine,

[96] DOGIA, F. 6, op. 1, d. 215, p. 125, protocol of meeting of February 21, 1919.
[97] Ibid., pp. 80–81.
[98] Ibid., d. 27, p. 52.
[99] Ibid., p. 62, letter of February 10, 1919.

where a surplus of a million and a half puds was sitting, or from the Nikopol-Mariupol mine, where the New Russia Co. had purchased coal but was unable to effect delivery. As an incentive, Galitskii stated that once a proper operating reserve had been gathered, in approximately a year's time, the New Russia Co. would be able to reach a level of production of seventy thousand puds per day, sufficient to meet the needs of the Volunteer Army as well as those of the factory.[100]

Meanwhile the factory was slowly dying. At one time, orders for millions of puds of rails and pig iron or huge prefabricated bridge sections had been routine. Now the blast furnaces stood cold. One by one, the various metal-producing operations had shut down. During this period letters were exchanged with the pomp and formality that had earlier marked major negotiations, now working out the production of boots or harnesses in the factory's leather-working shop. If the customer would supply the materials (for the leather shop had no reserve of raw hides or leather), then high boots could be supplied for eighty-seven rubles a pair, and "Austrian boots" for ninety-two rubles.[101] Yet it took nearly nine months to put even these modest orders into production. Telegrams and requisitions flew back and forth regarding the ordering of a single carload of kerosene or two carloads of potatoes. The metallurgy complex that was once the wonder of Russia now strained to meet the most limited regional needs. How are the mighty fallen!

Buying coal from mines where a surplus was on hand involved one round of permissions. Moving that coal to Iuzovka involved additional forms, requests, and explanations. A stifling bureaucracy existed, making the acquisition of freight cars as problematic as it had been forty years earlier. Even cart haulage had returned, though it was slow, uncertain, and expensive. When a revival plan was drawn up by the New Russia management, the production of six hundred thousand puds of metal goods each month was predicated on the availability of the crucial mass of three million puds of coal monthly. Since there was not enough food to maintain the number of miners needed for such production, the suggestion included in the plan was that half the coal and a substantial amount of coke should be purchased from outside sources. This was a total abandonment of the principle of self-

[100] Ibid., d. 28, p. 1. The level of production suggested by Galitskii still leaves about a million puds a month to be purchased if a blast furnace were to be in operation.

[101] Ibid., d. 27, p. 86. The draft of the letter offered the boots at fifty-five and forty-five rubles a pair, respectively, but the prices were drastically revised in the final text.

sufficiency on which John James Hughes had founded Iuzovka, and in the existing circumstances of ruin of the transport system, it made the entire plan an exercise in futility.[102] A French report in mid-1919 notes Iuzovka as having been hit particularly hard by the regional instability, with the mines working at only 20 percent of capacity, and the factory even less.[103]

The improving fortunes of Denikin's army during the summer of 1919 gave him breathing space to organize the society and economy of South Russia. In mid-June the White commander approved a plan to establish a provisional committee for state financing of enterprises in the Donbass. The chairman was to be appointed by Denikin's director of finance, and the committee was to include representatives of all the offices dealing with finance, industry, transport, fuel, and supply, as well as two delegates from the Association of Southern Coal and Steel Producers, and two from other branches of industry. These would be invited by the director of financial administration. The aim of the committee was to repair the war damage to the economy, and secure the rapid restoration of the Donbass as a productive unit.[104] It is perhaps a measure of the limited capabilities of the Denikin regime that nothing appears to have come of this proposal. A little later there is record of a proposal to establish a "Committee for the Mining and Industrial District of South Russia," and in September 1919, a draft charter for a "Committee for the Restoration of Russia's Industrial Forces."[105] Another proposal, also dated September 1919, was an invitation to the New Russia Co. to join a "Committee of the Donbass for Cooperation with the Armed Forces of South Russia."[106] No decision was recorded as to whether the New Russia Co. would join this group.

Whatever plans and efforts were made to organize an economic revival, they appear to have had little efficacy. At the end of September the New Russia Co. was still barely alive. Instead of the minimum of three million puds of coal per month needed to fire one blast furnace, the company was receiving only six hundred thousand. The number of miners working had dropped from 12,000 in 1913 to 2,440. Productivity per worker per day

[102] For examples and references to all these sad phenomena, see ibid., d. 215, pp. 156–62.

[103] AN, 65 AQ K69, *Côte libre*, July 17, 1919.

[104] DOGIA, F. 6, op. 1, d. 215, p. 10.

[105] Ibid., d. 30, pp. 92, 139.

[106] Ibid., p. 118.

had dropped from forty-five puds to twenty puds.[107] Analysis of these figures reveals that the miners were working only a little more than ten days each month. When the authorities inquired about the production of roofing iron in July 1919, the figures given for the first three weeks of the month totaled 13,351 puds, a quantity that must be seen as minimal in the context of such an enterprise, though it must have been thought a considerable achievement under the conditions of 1919.[108] Nevertheless, the factory appears to have retained a larger proportion of its work force than did the mines, for on December 2, 1919, it was reportedly employing nearly nine thousand workers, almost double the number employed a year earlier.[109] Perhaps it was simply that the grass looked greener on the White side of the front, or perhaps there was a substantial difference between the areas held by the Whites and those held by the Reds, but in April, the metal department of the VSNKh, surveying the state of the White-held Donbass along with the areas under Bolshevik control, reported that those Donbass metallurgy plants working on their own coal (Iuzovka and Makeevka were cited specifically) were at work and in profitable condition. The report also stated that Krasnov had instituted martial law, tying workers to their jobs, and that the factories were busy producing military material.[110] This was not true in any substantive sense in the case of the New Russia factory. Nevertheless, the factory was still a center of employment sustaining thousands of families. Perhaps the principle of self-sufficiency had been abandoned in view of the exodus of coal miners, but Hughes' principle of retaining the skilled core of his metallurgy work force was maintained throughout the German and White occupations, and as long as the New Russia factory lived, Iuzovka lived, however poorly.

Wages remained fairly stable through the second half of 1919. An unskilled worker received 1 ruble 80 kopeks per hour (1.35 for women), while skilled workers made up to 3.40 per hour, amounting to 540 rubles for a month of twenty eight-hour days. This compared to 600 to 900 rubles for

[107] Ibid., p. 112. In contrast, in 1914 the New Russia Co. had mined eight million puds of coal each month, enabling it to pour seventeen million puds of pig iron during the year. See Korolivskii, Rubach, and Suprunenko, *Pobeda Sovetskoi vlasti na Ukraine*, p. 21.

[108] DOGIA, F. 6, op. 1, d. 27, p. 101.

[109] Ibid., d. 28, p. 11. The report gives a total employment of 11,222 workers. Subtracting an estimated 2,400 in the mines leaves 8,822, the bulk of whom may be assumed to have been in the factory.

[110] *Ekonomicheskaia zhizn'*, no. 72 (April 3, 1919), p. 3.

office workers, and 570 to 700 for fel'dshers. Only those engaged as machine repairmen (*montery*) received more, earning 800 to 1,200 rubles per month. Despite the existence of a coal miners' union and a metal workers' union, there was a return to the phenomenon of small groups of workers presenting their particular requests or grievances to management in the form of petitions.[111]

As the year 1919 proceeded, there was little prospect that the Bolsheviks could maintain an economy based on that part of the Donbass remaining under their control. A comprehensive memorandum presented by Bazhanov at the beginning of June set forth a gloomy picture. Coal production, which had averaged over 40 million puds per month in 1918, dropped to 5.5 million in Bolshevik-held territories.[112]

From the beginning, the war in the Donbass had been intense and difficult. The Bolshevik forces had battle thrust on them before they were organized, trained, and supplied. A report of January 26, 1919, notes the lack of almost all supplies—no boots, no overcoats, a random mixture of weapons of various types and calibers, only sixty-three thousand cartridges for the rifles in place of the million rounds planned for.[113] The difficulties were not only material, though the material side was prominent. The Eleventh Ukrainian Soviet Regiment was in constant battle at the front, even though it had no footgear and had not been paid. Both the soldiers and their commanders were drawn from various partisan groups or from deserters from Denikin's Volunteer Army. The command had been investigated and purged, and was considered reliable despite its origins. Political work in the regiment was weak. There was no regimental organization of the Communist party, but sympathizers were being organized in the various battalions. To complicate matters, the political commander, Comrade Shapiro, was "not fully experienced in battlefield conditions," and due to the highly developed anti-Semitism throughout the regiment, he was almost totally unable to work. There was no cultural or educational commit-

[111] For wages from May through July, see DOGIA, F. 6, op. 1, d. 30, pp. 51, 110. An example of a workers' petition is the request of thirty-five blast-furnace stokers to work an eight-hour day at pay equal to that of other stokers in the factory. See ibid., d. 34, p. 64. The petition is undated, but apparently is from the end of 1919. Other stokers then earned the relatively high wage of 2.45 rubles per hour.

[112] Bazhanov's report, dated Moscow, June 1, 1919, is from TsGAOR, F. 3984, op. 1, d. 418, pp. 1–3, reprinted in Gudzenko, *Robitnichii kontrol' i natsionalizatsiia*, doc. 450, pp. 493–96.

[113] Korolivskii, *Grazhdanskaia voina na Ukraine*, vol. 2, pp. 65–68.

tee, though two students had recently undertaken to organize such work. A few old newspapers sometimes reached the regiment, but clubs, lectures, and evening activities were impossible. The Eighth International Regiment was better organized, but the Twelfth Ukrainian Soviet Regiment was much the same as the Eleventh.[114] It would be nearly the end of 1920 before the Bolsheviks would have a system of mechanized transport and be able to field tanks and armored cars captured in battle and repaired in Donbass factories, as well as an air force equipped for both reconnaissance and combat.[115]

In two weeks of heavy fighting, a Bolshevik offensive had taken Iuzovka on April 3, 1919, only to have Shkuro and Mai-Maevskii recapture it three days later.[116] Throughout the month of April the front stood doubtfully across the Donbass. Heroic pathos diverted the troops from the slaughter that was taking place. Red Brigade Commander Basov took a red banner in his left hand and, brandishing a saber in his right, shouted to his commanders: "Tell the Red warriors that the capture of the Iuzovka district holds immense political and economic importance for the Soviet regime. The happiness of the Soviet Republic is, in my opinion, dearer than my life. Perhaps my death will awaken the heroic spirit of attack in my regiment." When he was promptly cut down in a storm of White bullets, his troops attacked wildly, driving out the Denikin forces.[117] At the same time, driven by Lenin's urgings from Moscow and a stream of high-ranking emissaries, the Donbass Bolsheviks were changing commanders and trying new organizational methods to maintain the cohesion and supply of their forces. But new officers like Voroshilov, who on April 15 accepted command of the Fifth Army in the Donbass, and the best organizational intentions, as already noted in the case of the Lugansk cartridge factory, need time to become effective. In the spring of 1919, the Soviet regime was anxious that time was running out. With a massive overall effort the Red Army pushed

[114] Ibid., vol. 1, bk. 2, p. 181. See p. 184 for an account of two battalions that mutinied, refusing to fight until they were paid and given better living conditions.

[115] See ibid., vol. 3, pp. 468–69, for a report of the repair and maintenance of tanks and armored trains; pp. 470–72 for the repair and distribution of 143 automobiles and trucks; p. 473 for the report of three aircraft factories in South Russia producing and repairing aircraft for the Red Army; and p. 733 for the report of sixty-two combat planes and thirty-eight reconnaissance aircraft in flying condition and an additional sixty-five under repair.

[116] Kondufor, *Istoriia rabochikh Donbassa*, vol. 1, p. 183.

[117] *Krasnaia zvezda* (April 30, 1919), cited in Korolivskii, *Grazhdanskaia voina na Ukraine*, vol. 1, bk. 2, p. 388.

Denikin's forces back at the end of April, capturing Iuzovka on the night of April 28, and holding it against repeated White counterattacks for twenty-two days until the exhausted Red Army broke and retreated northward under heavy pressure.

Brief though the Bolshevik control of Iuzovka was at this time, it was marked by considerable revolutionary energy. Under the leadership of Zaitsev, as chairman of the Military Revolutionary Committee, an attempt was made to reshape all facets of life, replacing the existing municipal administration with "all the castoffs of society, hooligans, people with a dark past, soldiers, sailors, and finally, large numbers of Jews."[118] Despite such an unprepossessing description of its personnel, the new Bolshevik regime apparently received some support from the population. The post and telegraph workers are said to have cooperated closely with them, and the union of metal workers, the typographers' union, the tailors' cooperative, and the flour mill workers sympathized and helped implement Bolshevik decrees "that were tantamount to nationalization." At the same time, the zemstvo hospital and the workers' cooperative store maintained considerable reserve toward the Bolsheviks, even speaking out against them at some public and professional meetings.[119] At times the attitude of the population to the Bolsheviks appears to have been determined by deep-rooted values. When rumors circulated that in Lugansk the Bolsheviks had turned their artillery on the church and had arrested and shot members of the clergy, a meeting of workers resolved that should the Bolsheviks show disrespect to the church and its people in Iuzovka, all the workers would rise up against them. Communication of this resolution to the Bolsheviks is credited with saving the Iuzovka churches and clergy from harm.[120]

The justice system, as part of the state apparatus, was an immediate object of Bolshevik attention. Justices of the peace and county court officials were dismissed, and replaced by revolutionary tribunals and a *cheka*, a special commission to fight sabotage, speculation, and counterrevolution.

[118] "Akt rassledovaniia zlodeanii bol'shevikov pri glavnokomanduiushchem vooruzhennymi silami na iuge Rossii, dela 59–64" (Ekaterinoslav, July 1919), Russkii zagranichnyi istoricheskii arkhiv, Slavonic Library, Prague, item 5269, p. 2. On p. 16, as part of the end of the document, it says: "The report is based on data gathered by the commission in accordance with the rules of a court of law." Nonetheless, the reader should keep in mind, as always, the origins of the report in evaluating its normative determinations and expressions.

[119] Ibid., pp. 2–3.

[120] Ibid., p. 8.

Alferov is said to have handed out "life and death mandates" for investigation of such activities, though the commission was formally headed by Samsukov, a shoemaker and former janitor, and Elfonov, "who had a record of six or seven armed robberies and murders, and had been under criminal investigation when the Bolsheviks took the town." These activities are said to have resulted in the execution of twenty peaceful citizens, including the aged, women, and children, but only two former members of the local militia are named. The only recorded act of the revolutionary tribunal was to hear the complaint of a woman whose neighbor's cow had eaten the laundry off her line. After lengthy debate over the "principled question" of whether the guilty party was the cow or its owner, the court dismissed the case without a decision.[121]

Reform of the educational system was particularly vigorous, under two unnamed commissars, one a former student and the other a worker who had completed a popular school. The former educational authorities were replaced by a pedagogical council with one-third of its members students of the senior grades, two representatives of the lower ranks of school employees, who were also to sit in the economic and technical committees, and several members of the local soviet. End-of-year and matriculation exams were abolished along with the marking system. In their place, the pupils were issued testimonials listing the courses they had attended. Homework was abolished, as was the compulsory study of Latin. Religious studies were forbidden, and all ikons and religious ceremonies were banned from the schools. In their place, a day of meetings, discussions, excursions, and musical or theatrical activity was instituted. The Iuzovka Boy Scout troop was disbanded and a Communist Youth League was organized.[122] All this was undertaken during less than a month of unrestrained Bolshevik revolutionary rule in Iuzovka. The extremism of policy in this period serves well to highlight the comparative moderation of the period from November 1917 to April 1918, when the Bolsheviks were restrained by existing opposition-controlled institutions.

By the start of June, Denikin's army had captured Grishino, Konstantinovka, Nikitovka, and Gosudarev-Bairak, pushing north and east as far as

[121] Ibid., p. 4. Whatever the prominence of Jews in the Bolshevik administration, it seems unlikely that any Jews sat on this tribunal, for the first lesson in Talmudic law studied by any child deals with just such a case of responsibility for damage caused by an animal.

[122] Ibid., p. 5.

Millerovo, and capturing a good deal of the Red Army's equipment, including an armored train trapped in Grishino station.[123] The Red Army would not return until the end of the year.

It is impossible to judge the accuracy of the intelligence available to the Bolshevik Council of Labor and Defense when it urged an all-out effort to conquer the Donbass, nor the quality of judgment of Antonov-Ovseenko, who pushed his troops to fulfill the commands from Moscow. The one recorded dissenting opinion, based on long-term strategic thinking, is that of the commander of the Second Ukrainian Army, A. Skachko. On the eve of the heroic but futile April offensive of the Bolsheviks, he wrote to Antonov-Ovseenko, warning him that even if the Bolsheviks should capture the Donbass, they did not have the strength to hold it. He pointed out to Antonov-Ovseenko that as a result of the Bolsheviks having captured and lost the Iuzovka area, forty thousand coal miners had abandoned their mines and fled, fearing White retribution. "The mines are abandoned, and a mine abandoned for a week is so destroyed that it takes months to restore it. One more week of delay and of fruitless and indecisive blows in the Iuzovka district and it will be irreversibly ruined so that even if we later succeed, it will not yield coal to us. And that will truly be the most bitter defeat of our army and our revolution."[124]

Although the Red Army had been pushed out of the Donbass, the Communist party maintained contact with the areas under White control. For this purpose a bureau for work behind the front (*zafrontburo*) was set up in Kremenchug. During the first week of July it sent sixty-two Communists to various Donbass localities, including seven to Iuzovka. Each was given money for travel and living expenses, since it would be difficult for them to support themselves in the harsh economic conditions that prevailed. A strict chain of command was established in an attempt to avoid the disorganization and lack of communication that had plagued the revo-

[123] On the second capture of Iuzovka in April 1919, and the subsequent fighting, see Korolivskii, *Grazhdanskaia voina na Ukraine*, vol. 1, bk. 2, pp. 387, 417; vol. 2, pp. 18–19, 82, 112. The full details of the Red Army attack that began on April 27, 1919, are set forth in the operational order to the Thirteenth Army in vol. 2, pp. 3–4.

[124] See Skachko's letter of April 18, 1919, to Antonov-Ovseenko in ibid., vol. 1, bk. 2, p. 355. Skachko's letter is a comprehensive critique of Bolshevik military strategy in South Russia, and begins thus: "Permit me to address you not as a front commander, but as a Communist and a revolutionary, presenting in comradely fashion some remarks that I cannot make in my capacity as an army commander without risk of committing insubordination." Antonov-Ovseenko's reply, dated April 20, is brief and biting, including the phrase "there have been no strategic errors whatsoever on our side." See ibid., p. 356.

lutionary movement in previous years. Each local committee was to report to the underground Donetsk province committee that had been formed, and the latter was to report to the central committee of the Communist Party (Bolshevik) of the Ukraine through the zafrontburo. A plan was set up to have underground committees in eight localities in Donetsk province, with a total of sixty "responsible" workers and ninety "technical" workers. Of this, Iuzovka was to have eight responsible and thirty technical workers.[125]

Soon reports from the underground committees and from traveling intelligence agents began to come in. These could add little to the spirit of the embattled Bolsheviks. Reporting after a tour of the Donbass in July and August, Naumenko reported that the underground organization of the Bolsheviks in Iuzovka was strong and active, but that Denikin's propaganda was broadcasting claims of huge successes so that none of the town's inhabitants really knew what was happening.[126] Reports of refugees who had arrived in Odessa stated that when the Whites recaptured Iuzovka in early May, they drafted all men up to the age of forty-five for military service, and that those refusing were being beaten with knouts and straps, and shot "by whole groups." Another report from an unidentified source claimed that the White commanders had permitted a three-day pogrom against the town's Jews, in addition to general looting. Those suspected of being Red Army soldiers were summarily executed, and when a suspect fled, the local policeman entrusted with guarding the suspect was shot in his place.[127] Reporting on his behind-the-lines reconnaissance in September 1919, Karlov wrote that the miners of the Iuzovka district were receiving no cash wages, but worked in return for a meatless ration. At some, but not all, of the mines, the families of those serving in the Red Army had been evicted from company housing. Peasants' grain and animals were being requisitioned by the Whites. The majority of the workers were said to be waiting impa-

125 See the report signed by Bubnov as a member of the zafrontburo, dated July 7, 1919, in ibid., vol. 2, pp. 214–16. Donetsk province had been formed from Bakhmut and Slavianoserbsk districts on February 5, 1919. Eventually it was to include some parts of Kharkov province and of the Don Cossack territory.

126 Ibid., p. 441.

127 Ibid., p. 239, dated July 16, 1919, and p. 326, dated August 1919. No other source supports the claim of pogrom and unbridled looting in May 1919. The Jewish community remained intact in Iuzovka, and there exists an explicit statement that none of the successive rulers of Iuzovka permitted any disorder or any attacks on the Jewish community during the revolution and civil war. The reports of the traveling intelligence agents appear to have no more accuracy and objectivity than did the White investigation of Bolshevik misdeeds.

tiently for the Red Army, while among the peasants Makhno was widely popular. Karlov added that he had been unable to ascertain the real extent of Makhno's military strength.[128]

As the autumn of 1919 wore on, the superior organization of the Bolshevik war effort turned the tide, and Denikin's forces were pressed back from the Donbass. On December 31, the Twelfth Sharpshooters' Division and units of Budenny's First Cavalry Army captured Iuzovka, taking two armored trains, a quantity of military equipment, and the entire First Markov Division of Denikin's army.[129] Soviet power had returned to Iuzovka. The military campaign had ended, but the fight for survival remained undecided. Iuzovka's population was less than half its 1917 peak of seventy thousand. The mines were in disrepair, the factory almost closed. The returning Bolsheviks were faced with the Herculean task of restoring Iuzovka's economic and social vigor. Their efforts and the measure of their success are the subject to which I turn next.

[128] Ibid., pp. 347–48.
[129] Ibid., pp. 620, 622.

CHAPTER 11

From Iuzovka to Stalino: The New Russia Reborn

Red Army troops entering Iuzovka in the first days of 1920 found a city even more impoverished and demoralized than that occupied by the Germans nearly two years before. The social crises that had thinned the town's population with each successive conquest had radically changed its structure. The Ukrainian population had dwindled as its members sought physical and economic security in their home villages. The relative newcomers among the Russian coal miners and factory workers had also fled Iuzovka, and the political core, whether Bolshevik or Menshevik, had marched off to the battle fronts, or to political tasks in the Soviet-held areas. Only the Jewish community, having no alternative refuge, remained relatively intact, and now made up close to half of Iuzovka's sharply diminished population.

As was proved later in the year, when Soviet rule in Iuzovka was again threatened, the Bolsheviks enjoyed little sympathy in the town, though they encountered no open resistance from its population, for the alternatives were no more popular. Unlike many other cities and towns in the Ukraine, Iuzovka had suffered comparatively little physical destruction during the years of revolution and civil war. A local observer, writing about the town in the autumn of 1923, commented: "It appears that all governments without any exceptions, aware of the town's economic importance, took measures against its destruction. It explains also why the town suffered but slightly from the 1921 famine, the state supplying it with plenty of grain. In consequence the town's population starved less than the rest."[1]

[1] JDC, 506, L. Kulkes, "Report on Uzovka" [*sic*], September 1923 (typescript), p. 1. It is on the basis of this statement, and because the number of Jews in Iuzovka remained stable

Though two-thirds of the miners and much of the industrial working class had fled, and many of those remaining were idled by the ravages of typhus, or engaged in "bagging" (scrounging, *meshochnichestvo*), petty trade, and barter to find food for their families, the coal mines and the shops of the New Russia factory remained, awaiting the return of stability.[2]

Iuzovka's situation was paradigmatic of the entire Donbass. Kalinin, visiting the area in April 1920, reported that in Gorlovka, where twenty thousand miners normally worked, only twenty-five hundred remained.[3] The region was valued as the key to restoring production and prosperity throughout the new Soviet Republic, yet the two years of civil war had only complicated the task facing the Bolsheviks. The ruin had spread, and social antagonisms had sharpened. The technical workers of the mines and industries, both Russian and foreign, had fled almost to a person, rendering the condition of the mines and factories even more desperate than they had been at the end of 1917.[4] It would take another year before the nucleus of a new technical staff could be assembled. It would also take another year before the civil war was fully ended, releasing energies for economic and social reconstruction.

In these affairs, as always, Iuzovka had its own peculiarities. When the old regime disappeared and the new authorities had not yet installed themselves, a meeting of sixty-eight New Russia Co. employees convened on the factory premises. Svitsyn and his senior assistants had left "unexpectedly," without appointing any replacements, so it was suggested at this meeting that a provisional collegium of three persons administer the plant. Mining engineer V. Zaporozhets was elected to represent the mines, engineer-technologist V. N. Galitskii was to represent the factory, and Pavel Cesarevich Bialokur was named representative for the commercial and maintenance areas of activity. Zaporozhets, who had been a senior executive of the Department of Mines of the New Russia Co. as far back as 1908, chaired the meeting and spoke of the unprecedentedly bad state of the factory, totally

from 1917 to 1923, that I cast doubt on the report of pogroms and looting discussed in the previous chapter. As will become apparent, the phrase "starved less than the rest" should be taken in a very relative sense.

[2] See the report of the Iuzovka sovnarkhoz in Gudzenko, *Robitnichii kontrol' i natsionalizatsiia*, doc. 491, p. 551.

[3] Ibid., doc. 492, pp. 550–52.

[4] Bazhanov, "Ekonomicheskaia politika sovetskoi vlasti," p. 4.

lacking coal supplies and at a complete standstill.[5] A resolution was adopted requesting the head of each shop and section to prevent looting or damage to the installations. All possible measures directed at the swift restoration of production were promised. Among the decisions published by the temporary committee was one resolving that as of January 1 the factory would go over to the "new style" of dates. In addition to the political symbolism (the Whites stuck adamantly to the old Julian calendar), this had some economic consequences. January 1 would become January 14, and at the end of the month the workers would receive pay for only eighteen days. It was important that they understand the reason for this. At the same time it was decreed that all those on the company payroll would receive holiday pay for both the Orthodox Christmas and New Year, days that would be skipped by the reform.[6] It was only on January 30 that M. G. Tolmachev, one of the veteran Iuzovka Bolsheviks, was appointed by the VSNKh to manage the renationalized New Russia factory. He managed the factory until his death from typhus in 1921, when he was succeeded by A. Frolov, who managed the factory for a year before being replaced by I. G. Makarov, who was to give the factory stability of management for a full decade.[7]

Meanwhile, a bitter struggle was taking place, and the new Soviet state was mobilizing every resource for survival under the system known as "war communism." These policies proved effective in the military sense, and at that time, the military aspect was crucial. Yet the battle that was taking place was much more complex, and in other spheres of life the draconian mobilization policies only delayed the day when the Soviet state could claim to be a legitimate ruler. Writing of this period, H. H. Fisher comments: "Struggles, imperialistic, nationalistic, racial, and social in origin, drenched the land in blood, ruined its farms and fields, closed its mines and factories, and brought on an era of barbarism. The attempt to force military communism on a stubborn and individualistic peasantry delayed recovery; it did not cause the ruin."[8]

[5] He appears in a photograph of the executives of the Department of Mines of the New Russia Co., 1908 (see fig. 6.1). Zaporozhets and Galitskii were in charge of the factory in April 1919, when Svitsyn had retreated to Rostov.

[6] DOGIA, F. R-231, op. 1, d. 39, p. 1.

[7] Volodin, *Po sledam istorii*, pp. 159, 173. Tolmachev was appointed under his real name, M. G. Titov.

[8] Fisher, *Famine in Soviet Russia*, p. 255.

The Bolsheviks were well aware of their tenuous situation and of the complexity of the problems they faced. A Bolshevik party conference of Ekaterinoslav province, convened in February 1920, had on its agenda the problem of worker-peasant relations, the problem of nationalism, and the fight against "banditry."[9] Before tackling these problems, however, the Bolsheviks had to gain final victory in the civil war, and this proved more difficult than had been anticipated.

Last Gasps of the Civil War in the Donbass

Stability did not come easily. The Bolshevik ranks in Iuzovka and throughout the Donbass had been thinned by the evacuation and by party assignment to the front. In mid-1919 the number of Communist party members in the Soviet-held areas of the Donbass was only 3,198, of whom 616 were said to be still in the underground, emphasizing the shakiness of the Bolsheviks' power, even in areas they claimed to control. These were reinforced by an additional 760 candidate members and 1,530 sympathizers.[10] Painfully aware of their numerical weakness and of the tenuous character of their hold on power, the Bolsheviks maintained a continuous attack on their rival socialists, whether led by Makhno or Menshevik, as well as against the White forces, now headed by Baron Wrangel. As the Whites began to press their attack on the Donbass in the late summer of 1920, an article appeared in Iuzovka's *Diktatura truda* linking an alleged Menshevik underground conference with the enemy activity. Twenty-six supposed conspirators had been arrested, including two Communists and seven members of the Iuzovka Mensheviks.[11] An angry letter of rebuttal by three other Iuzovka Mensheviks dismissed the charges as baseless. There had indeed been a Menshevik conference, but it had been held early in July, when there were as yet no signs of an imminent White offensive, and it had been open and public, not underground. Of the twenty-six originally arrested, only four had been held; all the others were released immediately. The letter also pointed out that numerous Menshevik Social-Democrats were serving in

[9] Bachinskii et al., *Promyshlennost' i rabochii klass*, p. 89.

[10] Kondufor, *Istoriia rabochikh Donbassa*, vol. 1, p. 185. At the end of 1917, Iuzovka alone had claimed two thousand Bolsheviks.

[11] *Diktatura truda* (July 22, 1920).

positions of command in the Red Army on the southern and southwestern fronts.[12] The Menshevik influence in Iuzovka remained, however, for another two years. Kondufor's *History of the Workers of the Donbass* says that in the 1921 and 1922 elections for town and settlement soviets around Iuzovka, Menshevik elements attempted disruption, but were "met with a stormy protest of the Iuzovka metallurgists."[13] Under the conditions of hunger and deprivation that prevailed in those years it is quite understandable that there was a continuing political opposition. As I shall discuss below, strikes and labor unrest were widespread in these years.

At the end of August, mobilization intensified in the face of the renewed White threat, but the Bolsheviks, sharply aware of the importance of Donbass industry to the entire Soviet Republic, granted exemptions to underground workers in the mines, to the workers of defense-related metal plants such as the Lugansk cartridge factory, and to the three operative metallurgy plants.[14] The trade unions were to mobilize a thousand recruits within one week, respecting these exemptions.[15] On February 28, the administration of the factory had published a notice that all males from eighteen to forty years of age would be registered and put at the disposal of the local Military Comissariat.[16] In mid-October, when Wrangel's forces were at the gates of Iuzovka, the military commissar requested that the factory prepare an updated list of all those aged twenty to thirty-one, with details of their military ranks and specialties.[17] Even before the crisis became intense, the Iuzovka Komsomol had organized a "Red Youth Volunteers' Week," registering 350 recruits, including 20 working women.[18] The staffs of the local soviets were to be cut by as much as 75 percent to free personnel for the front.[19] When Wrangel's forces began to press seriously on Iuzovka itself, the town's party group looked inward and sent two hundred party members to the front, along with an additional forty-seven Kom-

[12] Ibid. (August 8, 1920). The three signatures on the letter were illegible. The editorial comment of the Bolshevik editors was: "You sit in cushy jobs in the unions and health funds. You draw down good wages and rations, and laugh at the workers and Red Army men."

[13] Kondufor, *Istoriia rabochikh Donbassa*, vol. 1, p. 229.

[14] On the realization of the importance of the Donbass, see Arskii, *Donetskii Bassein*, p. 18. The exemptions from mobilization are specified in Korolivskii, *Grazhdanskaia voina na Ukraine*, vol. 3, pp. 420–21.

[15] *Diktatura truda* (September 2, 1920).

[16] DOGIA, F. R-231, op. 1, d. 101, p. 4.

[17] Ibid., F. R-1, op. 1, d. 101, p. 133.

[18] Korolivskii, *Grazhdanskaia voina na Ukraine*, vol. 3, p. 287.

[19] Ibid., p. 392.

somol youth.[20] Whatever the weaknesses of the Donbass Bolsheviks, they understood the art of social organization and knew how to mobilize themselves as well as the local population for whatever task was at the top of their agenda.

Yet even this skill at mobilization was insufficient. Wrangel's troops, four thousand strong, pushed steadily northward, aiming at Makeevka and threatening to envelop Iuzovka from the east. The combined infantry and cavalry of the Don Corps included the Markov Division, once again active in the White Army after having been captured in toto in January. Frunze, commanding the Red Army troops defending the Donbass, reported that he had been forced to withdraw the hastily mobilized "workers' battalions" from the front as completely unfit for battle. His remaining two divisions had only fifteen hundred fighting men, and were incapable of sustained resistance to Wrangel's superior forces.[21] At this point the Bolsheviks were much in need of allies, and once again they negotiated a military and political agreement with their erstwhile enemy, Makhno. Under this agreement all anarchists held in Bolshevik prisons were to be freed and were to enjoy unlimited rights of movement as well as of oral and written propaganda.[22]

The fighting came to the edges of Iuzovka itself, and continued until November 3, with losses on both sides described as enormous. When the White forces reached the Rutchenko mines, evacuation began in Iuzovka and looting broke out. Groups of people gathered in the town, awaiting the arrival of Wrangel's troops and telling anti-Soviet jokes. Even when a Red Army victory was announced, rumors of imminent White success persisted.[23] This was the last large-scale battle of the civil war, and though Iuzovka never fell, the town's economic and social revival was set back nearly a full year. The mobilization cut coke production in half, and when on November 15 Tolmachev's administration decided on the demonstrative lighting of a blast furnace, the attempt lasted only a month for lack of fuel.

[20] *Diktatura truda*, no. 83 (October 10, 1920); Donii and Fedorchenko, *Obrazovanie i deiatel'nost' komsomola Ukrainy*, doc. 505, p. 557.

[21] Bachinskii, Kviring, and Perel'man, *Kviring* p. 94; Korolivskii, *Grazhdanskaia voina na Ukraine*, vol. 3, pp. 543, 550.

[22] Korolivskii, *Grazhdanskaia voina na Ukraine*, vol. 3, p. 571. The agreement was signed by Frunze and Bela Kun in the name of the Red Army Command of the Southern Front.

[23] Ibid., pp. 623, 696; *Diktatura truda*, no. 83 (October 10, 1920).

A second attempt at the end of January 1921 was similarly unsuccessful.[24] In this "kingdom of coal," where workers had been used to receiving forty puds of coal a month free as part of their working contract, coal was now rationed by coupons at ten puds per month.[25] Bitter memories of the town's demonstrated contempt for the Bolsheviks were to remain for some time. The uncertainties of Iuzovka life affected the rank and file of the Bolsheviks as well. At the height of the mobilization for fighting, the Communist party organization's Comradely Court recommended the expulsion of a number of members for unspecified "breaches of discipline." In line with general party policy, a reregistration of members was being prepared in which the accent was supposedly to be on quality, not on numbers. A troika composed of Zaitsev, I. Notko, and V. Kalatukhin was to direct the party purge.[26]

The first expressions of Iuzovka's revival and the subsiding of public passions may be felt in the pages of *Diktatura truda* in December 1920 and January 1921. Schools were reopening and registering students. The local soap factories resumed operations. The Bakhmut paper mill and the great Hartmann locomotive plant in Lugansk went back into production in January 1921. Looking back six months later, Bazhanov saw 1920 as the worst year for the workers of the Donbass, a year during which it was not unusual for miners to be absent from work for lack of shoes and work clothing.[27] Little did he know that the lower depths of suffering still lay in Iuzovka's future. There was momentary quiet, but the Bolshevik culture was not one of reconciliation or relaxation. At the Sofievka mine, shortly after Wrangel's troops had been driven off, the Political Department of the Mobilized Industry and Labor Armies of the Donetsk Basin held a meeting to encourage restoration of production. The banners at the meeting read: "All Strength for Reconstruction!" "Death to Idlers and Parasites!" "Long Live World Soviet Power!"[28]

[24] Volodin, *Po sledam istorii*, p. 161. See also *Diktatura truda*, no. 96 (November 13, 1920), for a report on plans to activate the "State New Russia Factory," and no. 106 (December 11, 1920) for a report on progress toward relighting the first blast furnace.

[25] *Diktatura truda*, no. 85 (October 16, 1920).

[26] See ibid., no. 85 (October 16, 1920); no. 88 (October 23, 1920); and no. 108 (December 21, 1920).

[27] Bazhanov, "Donetskii Bassein v 1920 godu," nos. 8–9, p. 102.

[28] Korolivskii, *Grazhdanskaia voina na Ukraine*, vol. 3, p. 217.

Whatever stability had come to the towns of the Donbass, full peace did not arrive in Iuzovka with the end of the military campaign against the Whites. A new conflict was forming around the search for food, and guerrilla warfare continued well into 1922. In February 1921, F. Z. Chikirisov, head of the New Russia factory trade-union committee, and G. P. Kamenev from the New Russia factory were ambushed and killed on their way to a metal-workers' congress in Bakhmut.[29] In the park in the center of Donetsk, where the great cathedral once stood, visitors can still see the grave of the veteran Iuzovka Bolshevik Aaron Isakovich Slavin, "murdered by bandits" in May 1922. At the beginning of 1921, the requisitioning of food supplies had been declared the new campaign, and twenty-five Iuzovka party members were mobilized for this work.[30] Andrei Koval, one of the Iuzovka party veterans, was killed, along with another Bolshevik, in the village of Platonovka while on a food-requisitioning mission, and on March 19, twenty-one members of a Iuzovka food detachment were massacred in Novo-Beshevo.[31] So serious was the situation that on March 2, 1921, the food supply commissar of the Ukraine, Vladimirov, sent a report to Tsiurupa, with a copy to Lenin, noting that seventeen hundred food workers had been killed, mainly by Makhno's men, disrupting the dispatch and distribution of food throughout the Donbass.[32] On the night of September 21, 1921, Ivan P. Lagutenko, who was then one of the chief food-supply officials in Iuzovka, and head of the city's consumer cooperative, was ambushed and shot within the town, near his home on the Ninth Line.[33]

Even after New Economic Policy (NEP) was officially declared, the peasants remained reluctant to expose themselves to Bolshevik control, and a document concerning the depths of the famine period relates that from October 1921 to April 1922, a total of 242,230 desiatinas of land was discovered to be under "secret cultivation" in Donetsk province.[34] While the Bolsheviks had succeeded in maintaining military control of Iuzovka's wealth, the dissolution of the fragile society and the violence so prominent in life in those years meant that the struggle for legitimacy, and particularly

[29] Volodin, *Po sledam istorii*, pp. 164–67.

[30] *Diktatura truda*, no. 6 (115) (January 25, 1921).

[31] Volodin, *Po sledam istorii*, p. 169.

[32] Meijer, *Trotsky Papers* vol. 2, pp. 386–88.

[33] Notation at the Donetsk Oblast' Historical-Geographical Museum.

[34] League of Nations, "Report on Economic Conditions," p. 46. The "secrecy" was presumably for avoidance of requisitioning and taxes.

for acquiescence of the surrounding Ukrainian peasant population to a Bolshevik regime, was to be both prolonged and bloody.

In such a precarious situation, the Bolsheviks sought a promising loose end to grasp and unravel the tangled skein of social, political, and economic relations that faced them. Kviring was delegated to purge the trade unions and cooperatives of Socialist-Revolutionaries, anarchists, and Mensheviks, and by September 1921 could report to Moscow that in agriculture, industry, the trade unions, and the cooperative movement, the "commanding heights" were in Communist hands.[35] Despite this claim, the battle for control of the workers was far from over; in February 1922, with the Donbass sliding into famine, and the Soviet government speeding up production plans in an attempt to "force the rehabilitation process,"[36] the Central Committee of the Communist Party of the Ukraine found it necessary to ban the newspaper *Donetskii shakhter*, because of its "impermissible tone and character."[37] Two years later, a discussion of the earliest years of Bolshevik control of the trade-union movement included an appeal by a group identified in an editorial note as "Menshevik Union Bureaucrats" against "Red Terror, which is spilling the blood of innocent hostages."[38] Another problem of control in the trade unions arose during a discussion by union secretaries. It appeared that former police, former White officers, and religious cult officials, who had been expelled from trade unions, often joined another union, or a different local of the same union, since there was no overall list of those expelled. In response to the suggestion that a central list be established, one discussant pointed out that this meant reinstitution of the prerevolutionary blacklist system—a step explicitly contravening union bylaws.[39] Some roots of democratic behavior and individual rights still survived.

Control of the working class was difficult. The Bolsheviks had been a small minority throughout the development of the revolutionary movement, and this had only slightly changed. In December 1922, there were sixty-three hundred workers employed in the New Russia factory. Of these,

[35] Bachinskii, Kviring, and Perel'man, *Kviring*, p. 97.

[36] *Gornoe delo*, nos. 1–2 (7–8) (1921), p. 61, citing a resolution of the Eighth Congress of Soviets.

[37] Denisenko, "Iz istorii," p. 100.

[38] *Vestnik profdvizheniia Ukrainy*, no. 47 (September 30, 1924), supp.; "1918–1919 gg. v profdvizhenii Ukrainy," pp. 19–20.

[39] *Vestnik profdvizheniia Ukrainy*, no. 45 (August 30, 1924), p. 93.

only seventy were members or candidates of the Communist party. Of the seventy, only twenty-four worked in production. The remainder were administrative officials, and this gave the officials of the Communist regime the character of "bosses," answerable for whatever problems the workers faced.[40] The party had succeeded in gaining power and a measure of popular support by adopting the issues that moved the masses. However, when party interests and the workers' interests diverged, the workers had no hesitation about expressing their discontent in strikes and in antisocial behavior. The Bolsheviks now found that the considerations of a ruling party were not at all those of a revolutionary underground. The trade unions, and the demands put forth by the workers, looked quite different from the new heights to which the party had risen.

Labor and Strikes in the Donbass, 1921–1924

A combined policy of coercion, mobilization, and persuasion was undertaken to deal with the problems of working the mines and factories in the harsh conditions that prevailed at the time. This involved not only control of the trade unions, but enforcement of discipline through coercive police action on the one hand, and persuasive exhortation to create motivation on the other. In April 1921, in a preview of the Stakhanovite movement that was to be born in the Donbass fourteen years later, Ignatii Andreevich Shalupenko was declared a "hero of labor" for loading 150 wagons of 30 puds each in a single month. Heroic as this may have been in the conditions of 1921, it represented only fifteen days' average labor in prewar years.[41] At that time, the average number of norms mined by a Donbass miner was 15.7, but a selected group of coal cutters in the Tsentral'naia mine was averaging 43 to 52 norms per month, for other groups to emulate.[42] Much later, when conditions were improving, a decree of the Mines Administration stated that any worker producing twenty-five norms per month would be rewarded with a free set of work clothes. This was a tempting award, for protective clothing was scarce, and since the quality was low, it did not hold up for the time specified in the norms of operation; there was an incipient

[40] Kondufor, *Istoriia rabochikh Donbassa*, vol. 1, p. 210.
[41] Zaks, "Trud i byt' rabochikh Donbassa," pp. 85, 108.
[42] Kondufor, *Istoriia rabochikh Donbassa*, vol. 1, p. 211.

labor conflict over this point.[43] Nevertheless, in March 1923, there were only seventy award recipients among the thousands of miners employed in three of the largest of the Iuzovka mines.[44]

Discipline was harsh. In February 1920, the new regime dismissed and tried for sabotage ten workers who had not reported for work. Six others, who had either missed work or had been an hour late, were fined twenty-five rubles, to be used for the cultural and educational fund.[45] In April, on the eve of the Easter holiday, the factory administration announced that those not reporting for work during the next three days would be subject to disciplinary action before a comrades' court.[46] Getting a reasonable number of work days each month from the labor force was high on the regime's agenda. Absenteeism in the Iuzovka labor force ran at a rate of close to 30 percent at the beginning of 1921. Illness accounted for a third, arbitrary absences (*samovol'nyi progul*) for another third; "official business" and authorized vacations each played an equal role in the remaining third.[47] In the first four months of the year, 874 workers were discharged from their positions. Of these, 757 were fired for absenteeism, and another 108 because of a "negligent attitude to work," while only 1 was discharged for insubordination and 5 for political unsuitability.[48] It must be assumed that a large proportion of these arbitrary absences involved the search for food and other basic items mentioned above, for Volodin claims that up to two-thirds of the time of the 697 coal cutters employed in the New Russia mines in mid-1921 was spent searching for food in the nearby villages.[49]

The search for food and other basic necessities continued to occupy the workers' attention through the end of 1923. Two workers accused of speculation in matches were sentenced to five years' hard labor and confiscation of their property. The sentence was commuted to two years' imprisonment, and the confiscation of property was suspended due to an amnesty declared

[43] *Vestnik profdvizheniia Ukrainy*, no. 49 (October 30, 1924), p. 120. The journal reports that the norms had been sent to Moscow for revision, and there, since April, "they [had been] blundering about."

[44] The decree and its results are on display in the Donetsk Oblast' Historical-Geographical Museum.

[45] DOGIA, F. R-231, op. 1, d. 94, p. 5. Both the means and the end differ little from John Hughes' operational code.

[46] Ibid., F. R-1, op. 1, d. 101, p. 65.

[47] Prasolov and Gofman, "Tiazhelaia industriia Donbassa," p. 61.

[48] Ibid.

[49] Volodin, *Po sledam istorii*, p. 167.

by the Congress of Soviets, the workers' proletarian origins, and the time that had elapsed since the crime was committed.[50] These cases are representative of a basic alienation that appears to have grown up between the workers and the new management. Among the many and detailed recommendations of the extraordinary Donbass commission appointed by the Sovnarkom in November 1920 are eighteen paragraphs devoted to the struggle against theft of coal, ranging from orders to load and ship the coal in sealed freight cars, to recognition that the miners, loaders, and soldiers working at the mines were cold and received inadequate coal rations, and were therefore tempted by the huge piles of coal all around them.[51] A forty-three-page list in the Donetsk Oblast' State Historical Archive contains the names of those arrested for stealing materials from the factory during 1924, when pressures on the workers had already diminished perceptibly.[52]

The campaign for discipline does not appear to have evoked the organized resistance of the workers. Rather, an examination of the strikes that broke out during these years reveals the pattern of protest against breaches of the social contract noted above in connection with earlier strikes. The workers in the Donbass mines and factories appeared to accept the right of the new masters to rule and chastise them, but it was also the masters' obligation to provide food, shelter, clothing, and wages. The local managers understood this and did what they could to pry the necessary goods from the central authorities. The ubiquitous ruin scotched any orderly supply, and the promises remained on paper, provoking the miners and metallurgists to abandon work.

In the autumn of 1920, a report on the Donbass emphasized that for production to be raised there would have to be an improvement in the supply of fodder for draft animals, and of warm clothes, particularly boots, since the miners, when insufficiently unclothed, simply abandoned work.[53] In the New Russia factory in March 1922, the union had raised the problem of work clothing with the new director, Makarov, who promised that the twenty pairs of boots allocated to the firm would all be given to shaft workers in the mines.[54] Lack of clothing and late payment of wages were among the grievances put forward by the factory's blast-furnace crews as

[50] *Vserossiiskaia kochegarka* (August 15, 1920), p. 2.

[51] "Meropriiatiia," p. 88.

[52] DOGIA, F. R-231, op. 1, d. 531.

[53] "Otchet," p. 179.

[54] DOGIA, F. R-1, op. 1, d. 16, p. 80.

part of a strike in September 1923. The main grievance, however, was that the production norm had been raised to sixty-five hundred puds (85 percent of the 1913 level). After what are described as "lengthy negotiations," the norm was reduced to forty-five hundred puds and the crews returned to work.[55] Volodin characterized the dispute as between the administration's demand for strict discipline and the workers' determination that the rates and rules be set from below, not from above.[56] At Makeevka in July 1922, a three-day strike in the coal mines ended when management promised that back wages owed would be paid before September 1, and a union representative arrived to investigate the miners' complaints of poor food.[57]

Not all strikes were negotiated peacefully. At the Aleksandrovsk-Grushevsk mines the workers' grievances included demands for the dismissal of rude Communist party officials, as well as complaints regarding timely payment of wages and poor housing. The striking workers were cowed by knouts, shooting, and arrests. People's Commissar Krylenko came to warn and calm the miners, blaming "evil agitators" for the strike, and promising a fair trial for those arrested.[58] Coercion appears to have been used whenever the workers' discontent took political form. There were elections to the local soviet in Iuzovka in November 1923. In the sheet-rolling shop of the factory, only thirty-five to forty of the seven hundred workers voted. The list of candidates was nevertheless declared unanimously elected. Among the causes thought to contribute to the workers' apathy was the chronic late payment of wages. A week later, at a factory meeting celebrating the anniversary of the October Revolution, Petrov, a worker, called for solidarity in the workers' ranks; it was needed, in his words, "now more than ever to fight for their vital interests, and possibly to overthrow someone." Zaitsev, who was among the organizers of the meeting, angrily shouted that these words would be written in the protocol of the meeting. The report ends with the comment, "Petrov, they say, has been arrested."[59]

No systematic report of labor unrest in the Donbass during this period

[55] Ibid., pp. 17, 26. Minutes of the Iuzovka Subdistrict Committee of the Metal Workers' Union, September 26, 1922.

[56] Volodin, *Po sledam istorii*, p. 170.

[57] *Sotsialisticheskii vestnik*, no. 1 (47) (January 1, 1923), p. 23. The wages remained unpaid as of November 1. This source is rich in news of unrest and discontent. It should, however, be remembered that this was an émigré newspaper, controlled by the Mensheviks.

[58] Ibid., no. 1 (71) (January 10, 1924).

[59] Ibid., no. 2 (72), (January 17, 1924), p. 18.

has been found, but the proportion of strikes by miners and metal workers in the overall number of strikes in Soviet Russia during the years 1921–23 indicates a preponderance of labor unrest focused in the region. During the year from October 1, 1921, to September 30, 1922, 183,680 workers were on strike, involving the loss of over half a million worker-days of labor. Of these, 30.7 percent of the strikes and half the striking workers were in the mining industry, while close to a quarter of the strikes and 28.8 percent of the strikers were in the metal industry.[60] The same source notes that the mine strikes were chiefly in the Donbass, and between one-fifth and one-quarter of the coal miners then working were involved in strikes.[61]

The dynamics of the mine strikes for 1922–23 show the spring and summer of 1923 as the peak of the wave. Of the 155 strikes, involving 77,189 strikers in the industry in that year, 71 came between April and June, involving 36,775 miners, with 35 in the preceding quarter and 46 in the following quarter. In the autumn of 1922, the famine was still felt, and strikes were largely irrelevant in the face of that cataclysm. Moreover, what food there was available was distributed as wages for work, and to strike meant to lose even this small aid to survival. With the ebbing of the famine at the start of 1923, pent-up resentments boiled over, and the tide of strikes came to its flood. Toward the autumn of the year normality and reconstruction were evidently felt, and the discontent behind the strikes diminished. The strikes averaged about five hundred participants each, and the mine strikes only slightly more—517 strikers. This would indicate that for the most part individual shops and shafts of mines, rather than entire enterprises, struck. The strikes in the mines were generally brief, with 90 percent lasting one day or less, and strikes of more than ten days were virtually nonexistent. Yet at the peak of the wave there were strikes of five to seven days' duration, and one million puds of coal production were lost. Only "at the last minute" did the Glavugol' of the Donbass mines receive the funds for wages that headed off even greater unrest.[62] Among the metallurgists and metal workers the strikes were also brief, with three-quarters of them lasting less than three days, although three strikes dragged on for three weeks and one for more than a month.

[60] Stopani, "Eshche ob osobennostiakh nashikh zabastovok," pp. 38–39.

[61] Ibid., n. 1, and p. 40.

[62] Ibid., p. 40, and *Sotsialisticheskii vestnik*, no. 14 (60) (August 16, 1923), p. 16, citing *Trud* (July 26, 1923).

TABLE 11.1
Strike Grievances, January 1922–September 1923

Grievance	Jan.–Sept. 1922 (% strikes)	Oct. 1922–Sept. 1923 (% strikes)	Oct. 1922–Sept. 1923 (% strikers)
Late pay	47.9	50.1	65.7
Pay rates	38.8	22.0	22.0
Late pay and pay rates	7.5	3.4	2.6
Other monetary grievances	—	4.3	5.6
Collective agreements	1.7	13.7	1.7
Other	3.9	6.5	2.4
Total	99.8	100.0	100.0

Source: Derived from Stopani, "Eshche o osobennostiakh nashikh zabastovok," pp. 38–43.
Note: Percentage discrepancies are due to the rounding of decimals for 1922.

What emerges from this picture, both from the statistics and from the anecdotal evidence, is a serious effort on the part of the local authorities to respond to the workers' demands for timely wage payment and decent food, clothing, and housing. The local authorities, however, commanded little in the way of resources; even then, in the early stages of the centralization of the Bolshevik economy, they were largely dependent on a central authority that was overburdened with problems, and that was itself severely constrained by the economic ruin that was the central feature of Soviet life at this time. Tables 11.1 and 11.2 enumerate the causes and disposition of all strikes throughout Soviet Russia in the first nine months of 1922, and during the 1922–23 operations year.

The sharp financial crisis persisted into 1923 (see table 11.1). The greatest number of strikes and the largest strikes were due to the late payment of wages, much as had been the case under John Hughes, fifty years earlier. In the autumn of 1922, the twelve thousand workers of the New Russia factory and mines signed a collective agreement. However, when on November 10 neither the food nor the money components of the October wages had been paid, discontent broke out. I. G. Makarov, the factory director, declared that an advance on the October wages was to have been paid between November 1 and 6, that the flour for payment in kind was on hand, that he had no idea why it had not yet been distributed, and that as

TABLE 11.2
Strike Results, January 1922–September 1923

Demands	Jan.–Sept. 1922 (% strikes)	Oct. 1922–Sept. 1923 (% strikes)	Oct. 1922–Sept. 1923 (% strikers)
Fully satisfied	39.8	34.2	17.2
Partly satisfied	39.4	31.1	37.6
Unsatisfied	20.8	34.7	45.6
Total	100.0	100.0	100.4

Source: Derived from Stopani, "Eschche o osobennostiakh nashikh zabastovok, pp. 38–43.
Note: Percentage discrepancies are due to the rounding of decimals in the source.

soon as the plant received money it would be paid over to the workers—certainly no later than November 20. When the workers continued to protest, Makarov declared that whoever did not accept his decision could leave. The Makeevka and Petrovskii factories were soon to be closed, and as a result plenty of labor was available to him.[63] Late payment of wages was to remain a sore point in labor relations even after strikes ceased; in October 1924 the Stalino (formerly Iuzovka) subdistrict committee of the Metal Workers' Union complained that only half its twenty-two thousand members paid dues on time, but asserted that "it may be stated with confidence that if wages were paid on time, and in cash, rather than as orders on the workers' cooperative, the percentage of on-time dues-payers would rise to ninety."[64] There was good reason for the workers to be disturbed over late wage payment in the conditions of galloping inflation that prevailed during the NEP.

Although a considerable number of strikes erupted because of disputes over the collective work contract or other complaints, the small percentage of strikers involved indicates that they were either individual groups at mines, striving to improve the position of their particular occupation, or the work crews of very small mines—probably those leased out to private entrepreneurs.

With the passing of time there was a considerable drop in the percentage

[63] *Sotsialisticheskii vestnik*, no. 2 (48) (January 16, 1923), p. 17.
[64] *Vestnik profdvizheniia Ukrainy*, no. 49 (October 31, 1924), pp. 119–20.

of strikes in which the workers received either full or partial satisfaction of their demands (see table 11.2). Moreover, it would appear that it was in the smaller strikes that full satisfaction of the demands was achieved, while in the larger strikes, most likely those in the state-operated enterprises, the demands were either rejected or only partly satisfied. Success or failure, both in the political penetration of a recalcitrant society and in persuading the proletariat to produce the material wherewithal for social reconstruction, depended first and foremost on economic recovery, and this became the focus of Bolshevik efforts once physical and political survival had been assured.

Beginnings of Reconstruction

As early as the beginning of 1919, three clear tasks had been identified as crucial to the reconstruction of the Donbass coal and metallurgy industries. At the top of the list was a steady supply of food and consumer goods for the miners and factory workers. Next was the amassing of a wage fund of thirty-five million rubles per month to pay one hundred thousand miners fifteen to seventeen rubles per day for twenty to twenty-two days' work each month. Solving these two problems would greatly facilitate the achievement of a third goal, the recruitment of a labor force of 280,000 permanent mine workers, more than 50 percent greater than the 1913 mine labor force.[65] The problems were clear and persistent throughout the four years of reconstruction: lack of mechanical equipment, hindering pumping and coal raising; lagging maintenance work; a shortage of trained specialists; most basic of all, a desperate shortage of work boots and clothing; and no solution to the food question that more than anything else determined both the miners' willingness to work and their productivity.[66] The precarious hand-to-mouth existence of the Donbass coal industry, and indeed of the entire Soviet economy, was evident. A clear symptom of this frailty was that in 1919, wood made up 88 percent of Russia's fuel, as against only 45 percent in 1916.[67]

[65] *Ekonomicheskaia zhizn'*, no. 13 (January 19, 1919), p. 1. This turned out to be a long-term project. Carr, *Bolshevik Revolution*, vol. 2, pp. 315–16, cites the 1922 complaint of a VSNKh official against the Commissariat of Finance that Donbass miners were being laid off because of a shortage of cash for wage payments.

[66] See the list in the report published in *Gornoe delo*, no. 6 (1920), p. 86.

[67] Denisenko, "Iz istorii," p. 97.

The Donbass began its reconstruction in 1920 from almost nothing. The mines had no dynamite or fuses, only 15 percent of the machine oil needed, and even less of other lubricants and fuels—altogether enough for only a few weeks' operations.[68]

Yet persistent effort eventually bore fruit, at least for short periods. In July 1920, the Donbass produced 23 million puds of coal, and 17 million were actually transported from the mines.[69] Then came a sharp food crisis, increased "banditry," and Wrangel's near-capture of Iuzovka, frustrating expectations for the continued growth of production. The multiple pressures simply overloaded the capacities of the struggling Donbass Bolsheviks.

> A series of external political shocks has in large measure been responsible for a certain drop in coal extraction. On the other hand, the food crisis and the shortage of protective clothing and footgear over the past months have significantly worsened the situation. Often food is unavailable for several days, and it is even impossible to acquire it "on the side." There is a particularly severe situation in the supply of materials. Boiler repairs are insufficient and badly organized. As a result there have been cases of mine flooding.[70]

In response to the crisis, the STO (the Council of Labor and Defense) in Moscow decided in October 1920 to grant the Donbass the highest priority in assignment of protective clothing, boots, and other supplies, "taking steps" and "issuing instructions" to see that the miners' needs were met. Prodonbass, the region's food-requisitioning agency, was given an advance of twenty-six million rubles to supply food on credit to the nationalized mines.[71] But where was the food to be found?

By December only 50 percent of the immediate needs had been met, with only forty-five hundred pairs of boots in place of the thirty thousand pairs needed. Through January and February nothing additional was delivered, though requisitions had been put in for a million *arshin* of various textiles, and production and acquisition plans included enterprises in the

[68] See Arskii, *Donetskii Bassein*, p. 19, and Bazhanov, "Organizatsiia i deiatel'nost'," p. 28.

[69] *Diktatura truda* (August 8, 1920).

[70] See V. M. Bazhanov's report on Glavugol' in *Gornoe delo*, no. 6 (1920), p. 221. See also "Otchet," p. 177 (from which this quote is taken).

[71] Bazhanov, "Organizatsiia i deiatel'nost'," p. 29.

Kursk, Orel, and Chernigov regions as well as within the Donbass.[72] Investigating the miners' situation in mid-November 1920, Trotsky reported to Lenin and Krestinskii that "the workers are hungry and without clothing. Despite the revolutionary-Soviet mood of the masses, strikes break out in various places. The wonder is that the workers work at all." Trotsky appended a seven-point program to his report, covering political and administrative reforms as well as the obvious recommendations of more food, clothing, and footgear, and regular wage payment.[73] To give a scientific basis to their program, Trotsky's statisticians drew up a table showing a clear correlation between miners' productivity and the percentage of food supplies they usually received. In March 1920, when food supplies were 89 percent of normal, coal cutters produced 1,958 puds each. In July, when food supplies dropped to 30 percent of normal, productivity fell to 805 puds per cutter.[74] On the basis of his proposed program, Trotsky claimed that within two to three months coal production in the Donbass could be doubled to fifty million puds per month, with the entire additional quantity going to nourish Soviet Russia's struggling industrial base. In fact, this level of production was not to be reached until late in 1923.

An economic commission sent from Moscow near the end of 1920 had declared the possibility of getting the Krivoi Rog iron mines back in production quickly, and had set a target of fifty-seven million puds of ore for 1921. These mines, the main source for Donbass metallurgy, had totally ceased production in 1919, and in 1920 had only a thousand workers left out of a labor force that had numbered forty thousand at its wartime peak.[75] For the renewal of production, coal was needed to fire the boilers at the mines, and wood for necessary construction of housing and for underground propping. A whole array of institutions (local, in Kharkov, and in Moscow)

[72] One arshin equals 28 inches. See the decision of the STO in "Otchet," p. 177. Underfulfillment of this quota by the supply department of the Mines Administration was reported by B. Isaev in *Gornoe delo*, no. 6 (1920), p. 217. The gap between actual clothing supplied and the plan to provide clothing for 150,000 miners is discussed in "Meropriiatiia," pp. 89–90, and in Bazhanov, "Donetskii Bassein v 1920 godu," nos. 8–9, p. 102.

[73] Meijer, *Trotsky Papers*, vol. 2, p. 360. Krestinskii was at this time one of the heads of the party's secretarial apparatus and a supporter of Trotsky. For an additional source naming the food shortage as the chief factor in the low productivity of the mines at this time, see *Diktatura truda*, no. 69 (September 2, 1920), p. 3.

[74] The full table for January through September 1920 is reproduced and discussed in *Gornoe delo*, nos. 4–5 (1921), p. 205.

[75] For a description of the neglected state of the Krivoi Rog mines at this time, see Tomilin, "Obzor," pp. 168–74.

11.1 John Hughes, founder and manager of the New Russia Co., 1870–1889.

11.2 I. G. Makarov, general manager of the State New Russia Metallurgy Factory, 1922–1932.

had confirmed the urgent importance to the Soviet state of supplying Krivoi Rog with the necessary materials. Nevertheless, "to January 1, 1921, not one pud of coal nor one wagon load of wood had in fact reached Krivoi Rog. Moreover, the railroads and passing army units were stripping the remaining fences and wooden buildings to provide themselves with fuel. In those rare cases in which carloads of coal were sent from the Donetsk Basin, they were requisitioned en route by organizations having nothing whatsoever to do with mining."[76] When there was no other effective way to get fuel, the Hartmann locomotive factory sent a train of its own to a Donbass station; its workers loaded whatever coal they found there, and brought it back to keep the works going.[77] It was easier to remove the anarchists from the institutions of Soviet life than to eliminate the anarchy that characterized so much of the period.

Given the pressures generated by ruin and scarcity, historical experience, mass mobilization, and Bolshevik will served as the basis for industrial organization. All miners still serving in the Red Army were to be released. Miners for the Donbass were to be mobilized from the whole of Russia, "using the lists of names and professions listed in the democratic census." In addition, recruiters were sent out to the villages, under the supervision of local labor-supply committees, a trip Hughes and the other Donbass industrialists had made half a century earlier.[78] But mobilization could not substitute for investment, supply, and maintenance of the mines. Production fluctuated wildly, further disrupting economic planning. Faced with a broad political and economic crisis in the spring of 1921, the authorities made every effort to mobilize. The target of 450 million puds of Donbass coal for 1921 was declared a minimum, and a higher goal of 600 million puds was declared. All efforts were bent to recruiting labor and spurring productivity. Articles describing technological and organizational innovations to increase productivity appeared in the technical journals. By concentrating all drilling equipment in the most productive seams and instituting a scheme of "wage payments in kind" (that is, food), the Briansk factory mines had raised production from 158,000 puds in July to 671,000 in September.[79] A jubilant telegram was sent to all Donbass miners on January 1, 1922, congratulating them on "a new great victory on the coal front":

[76] *Gornoe delo*, nos. 1–2 (7–8) (1921), p. 37.

[77] *Ekonomicheskaia zhizn'* no. 82 (April 25, 1919), p. 1.

[78] "Meropriiatiia," pp. 90–91.

[79] *Gornoe delo*, nos. 4–5 (1921), p. 206.

overfulfillment of the 1921 production plan.[80] Only three months later the *gubkom* (provincial committeee of the Communist party) published a painful analysis of "the deep crisis caused by forced draught increase of production in the last quarter of 1921, without economic calculation."[81] None of these analyses acknowledges that just when production plans were being accelerated, the Donbass was dropping into a murderous famine. Mobilization was a short-term strategy leading to long-term disarray. Finance, transport, and food supply were inadequate, and the workers who had been gathered from all over Soviet Russia were now being laid off without pay. The call went out for a better-planned, more stable, and more rational system.

Yet it is typical of the period that even earlier, when Bolshevik military fortunes were low, and the Donbass largely still in enemy hands, a vision for the future was not lacking. In April 1919, an anonymous journalist published a note stating that much of the coal in the Donbass was produced in primitive conditions with a minimum of mechanical equipment. To overcome this backwardness he proposed the electrification of the Donbass through a combination of hydroelectric stations built on the rapids of the Dnepr, and thermal electric stations designed to use slate and the less-popular types of Donbass coal.[82] In October 1920, at the first Congress of Glavugol', managers, planners, and technical personnel met to make long-term plans for Donbass development, and six months later a permanent scientific planning commission was founded at the request of the Donbass Commission headed by Trotsky.[83]0

But actual production planning was arbitrary and chaotic, and had no relation to reality. The plan of the Central Administration of Heavy Industry for the first third of 1921 called for the New Russia plant to produce 1,000,000 puds of pig iron. The factory's own plan set a target of 475,000

[80] Bachinskii et al., *Promyshlennost' i rabochii klass*, doc. 32, p. 51.

[81] Ibid., doc. 39, p. 54.

[82] *Ekonomicheskaia zhizn'*, no. 76 (April 9, 1919), p. 3. This may well have been part of the early discussion of the plan of the State Commission for Electrification of Russia (Goelro) for modernization through electrification, adopted by the Ninth Congress of the Soviet Communist party in early 1920. The earliest suggestions for harnessing the Dnepr rapids came in the time of Peter the Great. It is perhaps ironic that when the great Dnepr hydroelectric dam was being built, one of its most vocal opponents was A. A. Svitsyn, then head of the Soviet Southern Steel Trust. See Rassweiler, *Generation of Power*, p. 47.

[83] Bazhanov, "Donetskii Bassein v 1920 godu," nos. 8–9, p. 108. Glavugol' had been founded in March 1918 to increase coal output, lower prices, administer and allot fuel stocks, and implement new technologies. See Meijer, *Trotsky Papers*, vol. 1, p. 436.

puds. Actual production was 46,604 puds.[84] In such conditions, production could not grow smoothly. The first blast furnace had been lit on December 4, 1920, but had been extinguished a month later. A second attempt was made at the end of January, and this time the furnace remained lit until March 9. A third attempt would not be made until June.[85] Though a new and never-used blast furnace, larger than any of the others, with a daily production capacity of 18,000 puds, was standing ready, it would be lit only in May 1923.[86]

Two months earlier, the Donbass Metal Workers' Union had sent the following telegram to Lenin. "In the name of the metal workers of the Donbass we greet you on the twenty-fifth jubilee of the Communist party. As a gift to the party the metallists of the Donbass have renewed the production of the rail-casting facilities in Iuzovka, idled for four years. The daily output at the start of production—twenty thousand puds of rails."[87] This spurt of energy was the result of a decision of the STO to concentrate southern metallurgy in the Iuzovka, Makeevka, and Petrovskii factories, combining them into the Southern Steel Trust, Iugostal', and putting an end to a period when the New Russia plant suffered for lack of funds for reconstruction, maintenance, and wages.[88] Between March 15 and June 20, 1921, three Marten furnaces and three metal-working aggregates were put into working condition. It is symptomatic of the fragility of the Soviet economy at the time that the latter machines, even after their repair, stood idle for lack of orders. During the 1922–23 operations year the reinvigorated New Russia factory produced 4.25 million puds of pig iron (27 percent of 1913 levels), 389,021 puds of sheet iron (117 percent), 1,556,000 puds of rails (36.6 percent), and 2,675,000 puds of Marten steel (19.1 percent).[89]

There were deeper political conflicts going on, some of them connected to policy matters in the economic sphere and intercommissariat rivalries;

[84] Prasolov and Gofman, "Tiazhelaia industriia Donbassa," p. 52.

[85] Volodin, *Po sledam istorii*, p. 163.

[86] Postriganov, *Metallurgicheskie zavody iuga Rossii*, p. 452, for the size of the furnace, and *Diktatura truda*, no. 5 (404) (January 15, 1924), for the date of ignition.

[87] Kabanov, *Partiia v bor'be*, pp. 339–40. Production figures for October 1923 given in *Diktatura truda*, no. 5 (404) (January 15, 1924), p. 2, show 280,000 puds of rails for the month—the equivalent of only fourteen days' full production. A three hundred–day production year at the rate of 20,000 puds daily would have brought the factory to the level of the New Russia factory's 1892 production of rails.

[88] *Sotsialisticheskii vestnik*, no. 1 (47) (January 1, 1923).

[89] *Diktatura truda*, no. 5 (404) (January 15, 1924), p. 2. (The prewar New Russia factory eschewed the production of roofing iron.)

others were concerned with the political struggles within the Bolshevik party that began to reach a crisis point during the last year of Lenin's life. The political department of the coal industry that Trotsky had criticized had been commented on earlier by Ossinskii-Obolenskii, who with a double-barreled blast had complained that "Comrade Stalin, whom I deeply respect, but with whom I don't go along on this question, has already surpassed Comrade Trotsky's ideas, and has established a political department for coal in the Donets coal industry."[90] The political department, established within the TsPKP (the Central Administration of the Coal Industry), was to have focused its activities on labor discipline, on raising the miners' political consciousness, and on the integration of labor army units in the work of the mines.[91] Trotsky complained that it did not perform these functions, and that it had no effect on productivity. In December 1921, Piatakov, a former Left Communist who had become one of Trotsky's close political allies, was dismissed as head of the TsPKP because of his "Trotskyist methods of brutal administration." He was replaced by Vlas Chubar, a recruit to Stalin's entourage.[92] Felix Dzerzhinskii, who headed the subcommittee on internal party affairs formed at the Twelfth Congress of the RKP(b), proved himself still to be the "Iron Felix" of old in hunting down all kinds of factionalists, deviationists, and saboteurs, while supplying the Politburo and Stalin with a steady stream of complaints. In these complaints, Smilga, head of the State Fuel Administration (GUT), was the person to blame for high coal prices, dictating to everyone and setting prices "around a coffee table" with no regard for the market, while maintaining needless intermediate layers of bureaucracy between producer and consumer. Altogether, claimed Dzerzhinskii, GUT was "a relic of War Communism and Glavkism, as a result of which we are brought to give the mines and the entire Donbass as concessions to our enemies." In addition, he complained that Professor Ramzin had attacked Vlas Chubar personally for a mistaken, *Communist*, antispecialist line, and had denounced recent wage increases for Donbass miners as unmerited.[93]

[90] Quoted in Daniels, *Documentary History*, vol. 1, p. 188.

[91] Denisenko, "Iz istorii," p. 98.

[92] Bachinskii et al., *Promyshlennost' i rabochii klass*, p. 97. See Lenin, *Sochineniia*, vol. 27, p. 133, for criticism of Piatakov's work in the Donbass, and p. 252 for criticism of "overadministration."

[93] Dzerzhinskii, "Dokumenty," letter no. 8, May 2, 1923, to Stalin, p. 63 (emphasis in the original); letter no. 10, September 28, 1923, to the Politburo, pp. 64–65. In 1925, Dzerzhinskii, addressing the Fourteenth Party Conference, urged a full acceptance of "former" technical personnel, so that they would work from conscience and not from fear.

The NEP in the Donbass

The New Economic Policy adopted in March 1921 at the Tenth Party Congress came slowly to the Donbass. Only at the end of December did Glavugol' publish the conditions under which rental of mines might take place. The Donetsk Province Economic Conference (Gubekonomsoveshchanie) was to act as the renting agency for all mines not exploited by the TsPKP and not included in the control figures for the Donbass five-year development program. Rental periods were to be kept "as short as possible, but in no case more than five years." The holder of a lease was to be responsible for maintaining all technical mining conditions, and was forbidden to carry on a "rapacious" (*khishchnicheskii*) policy that might harm the mine. Thirty percent of the coal produced was to be paid to Glavtop (the Main Fuel Administration) as rent, with a minimum production figure fixed in the contract. The rest of the coal could be sold at an unfixed price to consumers, primarily state enterprises and institutions, holding consignment orders from Glavtop. Leaseholders were also forbidden to hire workers from mines operated by the TsPKP on pain of immediate termination of their leases.[94]

Clearly, the history of Donbass development should have taught the bureaucrats of Glavtop that short-term leases and a demand for heavy investment were an unrealistic combination. It was, however, in this context that at the beginning of the NEP, the Russian and French consortium that had bought the New Russia Co. from the Hughes brothers attempted to regain control of the factory through a NEP concession. The attempt was frustrated by the determined opposition of Zaitsev, Lagutenko, and the factory's manager, Tolmachev, speaking in the name of the Iuzovka Military Revolutionary Committee.[95] While the forum to which this resistance was attributed was certainly one with authority in the Bolshevik context, it may be asked why the three veteran Bolsheviks could not base their opposition on a decision of the Iuzovka soviet, of the factory and mine trade unions, or

Otherwise, he claimed, it would be very difficult to develop the science and technology needed for victory over bourgeois Europe. See Kabanov, *Partiia v bor'be*, pp. 386–87. Professor Ramzin was the central figure accused in the trial of the "Industrial party" in 1930, though he served only a brief sentence and was returned to work and awarded honors in later years. See Conquest, *Great Terror*, p. 160. Chubar was then at the beginning of the prominence that was to bring him into Stalin's Politburo ten years later, and eventually to his death in the purges.

[94] Bachinskii et al., *Promyshlennost' i rabochii klass*, doc. 30, pp. 47–49.

of the New Russia workers. Evidently in early 1921 their prestige among the workers and institutions of Iuzovka was uncertain.

At the level of small-scale economic operation, the NEP meant a reinstitution of commercial relations that obliged the Iuzovka factory and mines to maintain cash relations with private contractors. Contracts both large and small were being signed by the Iuzovka factory and mines for services and supplies, and these had to be paid for. The Zelenchenok lumberyard was supplying wood for construction and maintenance; Iugilevich sold five thousand puds of baled hay to feed the mines' horses; R. Sh. Kogan contracted to clean a thousand meters of sewer pipe and to empty the cesspits at the Iuzovka mines. At the same time, NEP relations provided a small source of income. Unused land was rented out to local residents, and the factory's leather shop was leased to a cooperative through the intermediary of the Donetsk Province Leather Trust. In all, ninety-five contracts covering rentals, haulage, services, supply, and maintenance activities were concluded by the administration of the New Russia factory and mines in the first two years of the NEP.[96]

Short of cash, and with food the major issue in the workers' lives, the factory began paying the workers with coupons to be redeemed for supplies at the consumer cooperative, thus assuring that those who worked would have access to whatever supplies were available. However, the factory quickly fell into arrears in redeeming the coupons, causing a liquidity crisis in the cooperative, which soon was unable to buy the supplies needed for the workers. The cooperative then stocked only those goods that it could buy on credit. These were taken by the workers and sold to the peasants and merchants in the bazaar at a fraction of their worth, further worsening the workers' condition. Although both the STO and Narkomfin (the People's Commissariat of Finance) had at first forbidden payment in coupons, a "special dispensation" permitted up to 30 percent payment in scrip, and the employers were actually paying three-quarters in scrip.[97]

The late payment of wages, as noted, was a factor in the industrial unrest of the NEP years. The severity of this phenomenon was a function of the uncontrolled rise of prices throughout the first half of the 1920s, and in particular the rise of food prices in an attempt to overcome the "scissors crisis," the imbalance between prices of industrial and agricultural goods

[95] Volodin, *Po sledam istorii*, p. 163.
[96] DOGIA, F. R-231, op. 1, d. 33, pp. 20–24.
[97] *Sotsialisticheskii vestnik*, nos. 12–13 (82–83) (June 20, 1924), p. 18.

that threatened to drive the peasants out of the market. So sharp was the inflation that wages, calculated in the middle of the month that they were supposed to be paid, and then withheld for an extra three weeks because of the financial difficulties of the factories or mines, lost half their buying power. The workers were further squeezed because of the shortage of small-denomination notes. A single twenty-five *chervonets* note would be given jointly to two or three workers, who would then have to find someone in the bazaar who would change it for them—first deducting a fat comisssion.[98] During this period the workers were also given part of their wages in state bonds, which, because of economic hardship, they promptly cashed in the bazaar at a quarter to half their face value.[99] Late payment of wages went on throughout 1923, and even in August 1924 there was an appeal from the Donetsk provincial committee of the Communist Party of the Ukraine to the Central Committee in Moscow complaining that Donbass wage payments were three weeks and more in arrears.[100] This chronic fault not only caused tension between the workers and management but also weakened the authority of the trade unions in which the Bolsheviks were only now consolidating their control. In these basic conflicts over preservation of wages, the unions were all too frequently put in the position of convincing the workers not to strike or otherwise disrupt production.[101] All the old ways of squeezing the workers' wages reappeared in this period; even the employees' ostensible protectors and professional organizations worked against them.

Reconsideration of development plans in the coal industry went on continuously. In 1922, the Commission for Restoration of the Donbass had inspected 677 mines, finding 249 to be worth exploiting, and suggesting that the remainder be offered as private concessions or be closed. By concentrating resources in these large mines, the commission hoped to restore Donbass coal production to the 1913 level of 1,500,000,000 puds within five years. Because of the essentially large-scale nature of coal and metallurgy, the NEP was destined to remain marginal to the industrial economy of the Donbass.

The recovery in the coal and metallurgy industries was prolonged and painful (see tables 11.3 and 11.4). By October 1924 the Donbass was

[98] Ibid., nos. 23–24 (69–70) (December 17, 1923), pp. 16–17. The same phenomenon is common in post-*perestroika* Russia.

[99] Denisenko, "Iz istorii," p. 112.

[100] Ibid., p. 120.

[101] Ibid., p. 111.

TABLE 11.3
Donbass Production, 1920–1924 (Millions of Puds)

Year	Iron ore	Pig iron	Coal
1920	n.a.	0.90	272.8
1921	n.a.	0.11	355.7
1922	n.a.	4.78	390.3
1923[a]	11.8	6.87	583.0
1924[a]	24.6	23.65	739.4

Sources: Iron ore: 1920, M. Vindel'bot, "Metallopromyshlennost' v 1920 godu," p. 66. 1921, League of Nations, "Report on Economic Conditions," p. 116. 1922, *Khoziaistvennye itogi,* p. 90. 1923–1924, Bubleinikov, "Rudnaia promyshlennost' SSSR," p. 32. Pig iron: Sharyi, "Metallicheskaia promyshlennost'," p. 59. Coal: Denisenko, "Iz istorii," pp. 116–17, 121.

[a]The statistical year ran from October 1 of the previous year to September 30 of the cited year. Earlier years are on a calendar basis.

producing a little more than half its prewar total of coal, about as much as had been produced in 1903, but 80 percent of Soviet Russia's total coal production. Though the total was modest in comparison with the past, even this was an achievement, for in mid-1921 production had been set back to the level of 1890, and the Donbass had accounted for only 60 percent of it. Moreover, the proportion of the mines' own use of coal was dropping rapidly, from nearly half in 1920 to 17 percent in 1924, leaving a larger portion for the hungry market. Even this was, however, double the 8 percent of production that had been used to fuel the mines in 1913.

At this point new problems appeared for the Soviet economists. The improvement in the performance of the Donbass mines coincided with the industrial crisis at the end of 1923, and large reserves began piling up at the mines and railheads. This, however, was a happier problem, and the Central Committee of the Communist party issued an instruction that all local soviets and government departments should increase their use of Donbass coal, substituting it for other forms of fuel.[102] At the same time, this was one of the reasons for the swelling unemployment that began to replace the shortage of miners that had previously prevailed.

By October 1924 eight blast furnaces were back in operation in the

[102] Bachinskii et al., *Promyshlennost' i rabochii klass*, doc. 84, pp. 143–44.

TABLE 11.4.
Donbass Mine Labor and Productivity, 1920–1924

Year	No. of Workers (Thousands)	Percent Coal Cutters	Daily Output per Cutter (Puds)	Daily Output per Worker (Puds)
1920	115.8	15.9	57	8.3
1921	119.2	11.7	81	10.0
1922	98.6	10.8	127	13.3
1923	106.5	11.3	121	14.2
1924	133.2	13.4	140	18.9

Sources: 1920: No. of workers, *Ezhegodnik kominterna,* p. 469. Percentage of cutters, *Gornoe delo,* nos. 2–3 (1920), p. 85. Productivity, Denisenko, "Iz istorii," p. 116. 1921: No. of workers, *Ezhegodnik kominterna,* p. 469. Percentage of cutters, Denisenko, "Iz istorii," p. 111. Productivity, ibid., p. 116, table 3. 1922: No. of workers, League of Nations, "Report on Economic Conditions," p. 114, and *Khoziaistvennye itogi,* p. 89 (extrapolated from nine-month figures). Percentage of cutters, Denisenko, "Iz istorii," p. 111. Productivity, ibid., p. 116, table 3. 1923: No. of workers and productivity, ibid. Percentage of cutters, ibid., p. 121. 1924: All data, *Ekonomicheskoe obozrenie,* no. 2 (February 1925), p. 274.

Donbass, and pig-iron production that in 1919 had been less than 1 percent of the prewar level had climbed to 12.5 percent. Yet Soviet Russia still stood only on the threshold of the iron age, for annual per-capita iron consumption was less than half a pud, about 2 percent of that in the United States. The miners and workers of the Donbass could look back with satisfaction over the past five years. They had pulled themselves out of the lower depths of ruin and paralysis. Yet when they tried to focus on a vision of the radiant future, they found it only at the end of a no less painful road ahead.

Ordeal by Famine: The Southern Ukraine, 1921–1923

Before the populations of Iuzovka and of the Donbass could recover economically and begin their construction of socialism, they had to survive a famine that transcended anything the region had previously experienced. Hunger had been recurrent in tsarist Russia and chronic since the revolution, aggravated by government policy. Arskii had noted that the excellent transport facilities of the Donbass made it convenient to take its surplus production to satisfy the needs of Central Russia.[103] This had been going on even before the Bolsheviks had assumed power. It had, however, intensified during the civil war. In early 1919, two thousand special agents had been sent to the Ukraine to buy foodstuffs for the hungry Russian provinces—with half destined for the Red Army. This was evidently no organized campaign, but a catch-as-catch-can competition of various commissariats, administrations, institutions, and regions. Chubar protested against the disorganized way in which various official institutions of the Russian Soviet Federated Socialist Republic (RSFSR) or other republics were snapping up the resources of the Ukraine by making separate agreements with individual enterprises. Latvia was offering ten rubles per pud for Bakhmut salt, when the market price was two to three rubles. Intermediaries were taking payment for goods that later proved to be nonexistent, or that were already included in the supplies of the Ukraine's sovnarkhoz.[104]

As Trotsky's commission recorded, overall food supply in the first nine months of 1920 fluctuated irregularly between 30 percent and 89 percent of the norm, and with it the miners' productivity rose and fell. But the aggregate picture hides the true measure of deterioration of the workers' diet in this period, and the imbalance of deliveries. Between June and September 1920, when 65,500 people were listed as eligible for rations in the Iuzovka district, the deliveries to the New Russia Consumer cooperative were as follows: flour—96 percent of the ration, groats—23.5 percent, sunflower oil—6.9 percent, fat—0 percent, herring—0 percent, meat and fish—4.8 percent, tobacco—30.8 percent, matches (the ration was two small boxes per month)—49.2 percent, soap—29.5 percent, sugar—159 percent, salt—152 percent. A requisition for ten thousand puds of vegetables had been issued, "but for reasons of a military nature" no vegetables whatsoever could be delivered.[105] An article with details of day-by-day food deliveries to the Donbass at the end of 1920 was dominated by blank spaces, as even the feeble trickle of the middle of the year diminished.[106]

Even the former model farm established by Hughes at Peski was of little immediate help. It had been taken over as a state farm by the Soviet regime, had instituted production of agricultural equipment, and boasted a plant-

[103] Arskii, *Donetskii Bassein*, p. 3.

[104] See the announcement in *Ekonomicheskaia zhizn'*, no. 70 (April 1, 1919), p. 3, alongside Chubar's bitter protest against this indiscriminate stripping of the Ukraine.

[105] The statistics are given in *Diktatura truda*, no. 95 (November 10, 1920).

[106] *Ekonomicheskaia zhizn'*, no. 12 (January 19, 1921), p. 2.

disease station and a meteorological post. Its beehives, however, produced only twenty-eight puds of honey for the year, and the entire dairy herd of the district, including Peski, numbered only 138 cows.[107] The once proud horse-breeding farm stood empty, and in the summer of 1920 only 435 horses remained in the entire Iuzovka district, as opposed to 1,561 in prewar times, crippling the haulage of coal and mining materials.[108] Even the smaller, more primitive mines worked by horsepower were hard put to produce coal, particularly in summer when the few horses remaining were used for agricultural work. During the famine months between the autumn of 1921 and February 1922, 30 percent of the remaining cattle and horses in the Donbass were to die.[109]

One proposed solution was that workers be paid a quarter of their wages in industrial goods that could be traded to the peasants in exchange for food. This was said to be the origin of the *naturplata*, payment in kind, which became increasingly common in the Donbass during this period.[110] The transition from money wages to wages in food in the autumn of 1921 resulted in a stream of applicants for mining jobs and helped for a short time to raise production. These were, however, mainly new recruits to the mines, flooding in from other starving areas.[111] When the food supply faltered, they left as rapidly as they had come. As an incentive for raising productivity, and to fight featherbedding, a new system of supplying food was instituted. Each work collective received a ration in accordance with its production, and it divided that ration among its members, irrespective of their numbers.[112] At the end of 1920 and the beginning of 1921, when large numbers of workers were being recruited throughout Soviet Russia to service the Donbass industrial enterprises, food was understood as a principal limitation on that recruitment, and 650,000 puds of grain were delivered from the Russian Republic.[113]

[107] *Diktatura truda*, no. 85 (October 16, 1920). In 1910, Peski alone had maintained a dairy herd of 660 head.

[108] Gorno-tekhnicheskii otdel' TsPKP, "Pod"em," p. 110.

[109] League of Nations, "Report on Economic Conditions," p. 39.

[110] *Ekonomicheskaia zhizn'*, no. 44 (February 26, 1919), p. 4. In October 1921, when the famine was beginning, workers on the Donetsk railway received 60 percent of their pay in food. Even so, they were receiving only one-third of the planned ration. See *Dva goda deiatel'nosti*, p. 15.

[111] Bachinskii et al., *Promyshlennost' i rabochii klass*, doc. 25, p. 37.

[112] *Metallopromyshlennost' respubliki*, p. 66. See also Kondufor, *Istoriia rabochikh Donbassa*, vol. 1, p. 204. The same method, applied to wages, was hailed as a great innovation when introducced at the Shchekino chemical plant in the 1970s.

[113] Kondufor, *Istoriia rabochikh Donbassa*, vol. 1, p. 203.

In Iuzovka, following the two previous unsuccessful attempts to put a blast furnace into production, the New Russia workers resolved in June 1921 that the factory must resume operations so that there would be metal products that could be traded to the peasants for food. If their goals for production were similar to those of the authorities, their motivation was quite different. The workers' rations at this time were six hundred grams of bread per day, with wives and children allowed four hundred and three hundred grams respectively.[114] Even these meager rations were not always available. In an explanatory note to a table purportedly evidencing a high level of supply to workers in Iuzovka, Prasolov appends a note explaining that in early June, flour for twelve days of May was distributed, and at the end of June the workers received the balance of their May ration along with that for the first week of July. Distribution for June was left pending, while that for the last half of July was simply canceled.[115] A month later, the workers' rations were halved and dependents were excluded from any factory-purchased ration. As a result, nearly four thousand members of the factory and mine labor force abandoned the town. The blast furnace went on a reduced workday, and coking stopped altogether. Barter ruled, with coal and metal sold to purchase tobacco and industrial products that the peasants were willing to take in exchange for food.

As had been usual in Iuzovka's history, the apocalyptic horsemen were not to be separated. In 1919, war prisoners, returning ill from the front, had brought typhus to Iuzovka, overburdening the medical facilities and consequently incurring a high mortality rate. In March 1920 there were 30,600 registered cases of spotted typhus in the Donbass, and these were followed by an epidemic of intestinal typhus. Still later, hundreds of weakened residents fell ill with cholera, many of them being kept at home for treatment by their families, a tendency that the local newspaper termed "criminal"; the editors urged the town's citizens to bring their ill to the hospital.[116] Its laboriously woven institutional fabric worn to shreds, Iuzovka had regressed to the level of the debates of 1892. There was a brief

[114] Volodin, *Po sledam istorii*, p. 167. At the turn of the century, miners consumed from one to one and a half kilos of bread daily, as well as a quarter to a half kilo of beef. See vol. 1, pp. 118–22. The ration decreed for underground miners and similar occupations by the Sovnarkom in 1921 was 60 funt of bread per month—about eight hundred grams per day, along with 7.5 to 15 funt of meat monthly, according to work category. See *Dva goda deiatel'nosti*, p. 28.

[115] Prasolov and Gofman, "Tiazhelaia industriia Donbassa," p. 54.

[116] See *Donskaia rech'* (December 11, 1919); Kondufor, *Istoriia rabochikh Donbassa*, vol. 1, p. 194; *Diktatura truda*, no. 69 (178) (July 29, 1921).

upturn when the meager local harvest of 1921 was gathered, but this was merely the calm before the cataclysm. For the Soviet authorities, production was the central goal, and augmented food supplies were accompanied by a new draft of labor, which came willingly to wherever food was available. The result was that the subsistence level was barely maintained. By December reserves were exhausted, rations had been slashed once more, and a new exodus began.[117] Many of the workers, both skilled and unskilled, had been recruited elsewhere and brought to Iuzovka to get the factory back into production. In 1921 17 percent of the Donbass metallurgy workers were drafted from other regions.[118] In an effort to ease the famine that by then was in full swing, the New Russia's management signed an agreement to barter a thousand puds of coke to State Machine Building Factory No. 1, in return for a thousand puds of cleaned wheat.[119]

The beginning of the catastrophe came in the form of the crop failure that hit both the Ukraine and the Volga regions in 1921. By midsummer 1921, while Iuzovka was hungry, there was already starvation along the Volga. The Soviet government furnished grain to the starving areas from the Ukraine, as part of the *prodnalog* (the tax in kind), despite the difficult situation that prevailed in the Ukraine, particularly in the vital industrial areas. A half million tonnes out of the reported 5,700,000 tonnes harvested in 1921 from five distressed provinces of the Ukraine were sent to the Volga region.[120] In Donetsk province, the harvest in 1921 was said to have been 283,183 tonnes, as against 1,542,916 tonnes in 1916—18 percent of the last "normal" year, though the area planted had been 81 percent of that planted in 1916.[121]

Despite an expected food deficit, and even after that deficit had turned into the beginnings of starvation, the Soviet authorities persisted in sending help from the Donetsk workers to the starving of the Volga. In the same issue in which *Diktatura truda* ran an editorial regarding the "natural catastrophe" that had struck the poor peasants of the Donbass (with no

[117] Volodin, *Po sledam istorii*, pp. 167–74.

[118] *Metallopromyshlennost' respubliki*, p. 65.

[119] DOGIA, F. R-231, op. 1, d. 33, p. 20, dated December 24, 1921.

[120] JDC, 468, "Starvation and Epidemic Diseases in the Ukraine," pp. 2–3. The distressed provinces were Ekaterinoslav, Zaporozhe, Nikolaev, Odessa, and Donetsk.

[121] Gerasimovich, *Golod na Ukraini*, p. 68. For the area, see Quisling, "Famine Situation in Ukraina," p. 3. The figures are the same as those given by a representative of the Ukrainian Red Cross, Dr. Kholodny, in a letter of February 28, 1922. JDC, 468, "Starvation and Epidemic Diseases in the Ukraine," app., p. 2.

mention of any effect on the workers), the newspaper printed a satirical column excoriating those of the town's residents who were reluctant to contribute to Volga famine relief.[122] Only on January 11, 1922, when 10 percent of the province's population was already "without bread," was Donetsk freed of its centrally imposed obligation to feed the Volga. Even in the beginning of March there were still placards to be seen in Nikolaev province calling on the working masses to help the starving Volga.[123] Quisling, while acknowledging the agricultural disaster that struck the region, regards the drought as a principal, but not the sole, cause of the famine. He writes that the basic factors that turned the crop failure into massive tragedy were the instability of government that resulted from war, revolution, and civil war; the heavy requisitions imposed on the region under "war communism"; and the overlong continuation of the NEP tax in kind even after the onset of famine.[124] In short, policy failures transformed difficulty into disaster.

In an attempt to overcome the famine, the Soviet government allocated large quantities of winter and spring grain seed to the famine areas, but governmental ineffectiveness was once again apparent, and only about 15 percent of the allocation was actually delivered. This, together with the debilitation and demoralization of the peasantry, meant that in the affected regions only about 60 percent of the 1921 area was sown in the spring of the following year.[125] In addition, over 40 percent of Donetsk province lands suffered from crop failure in the autumn of 1922.[126] The result was that the 1922 crop was also totally inadequate, amounting to only twenty kilograms per person for the year. Donetsk province needed imports of an additional 1,306,666 tonnes of grain to maintain a miserly ration of four hundred grams of bread per day.[127]

Soviet efforts to overcome the shortage were spasmodic and inadequate. A special day of loading foodstuffs for the Donbass was declared, but had little effect. The prospect of growing grain in the Ukraine was small, for the

[122] See *Diktatura truda*, no. 90 (199) (October 20, 1921).

[123] Quisling, "Famine Situation in Ukraina," p. 1. Diptan, "Deti i golod," p. 109, writes that only in May 1922 was the Ukraine freed of the obligation to assist the starving of the Russian Republic.

[124] Quisling, "Famine Situation in Ukraina," pp. 2–3.

[125] League of Nations, "Report on Economic Conditions," p. 41.

[126] Diptan, "Deti i golod," pp. 109–110.

[127] JDC, 468, "Starvation and Epidemic Diseases in the Ukraine," p. 3, based on statistics of the Ukrainian Red Cross.

drought was widespread and the devastation of the civil war still fresh. An order for a million puds of foreign grain was approved, but its implementation was delayed by four months; even then, only part of the order was received, with all costs and charges taken by the central authorities in kind, further reducing the amount of grain delivered for distribution.[128] By the early spring of 1922, 400,000 children up to the age of fifteen were starving in Donetsk province. Forty thousand of these were receiving rations at various food-distribution points. An additional 26,000 were cared for in special children's homes and camps by the Commissariat of Health (Narkomzdrav) and the Commissariat of Education, where it was found that one-third were suffering from anemia and incipient tuberculosis. This left 334,000 starving children without any institutional assistance.[129]

The international community responded to the famine by sending two missions. One was the American Relief Administration (ARA), headed by Herbert Hoover; the second was the International Russian Relief Commission, sponsored by the International Red Cross and headed by the noted Norwegian explorer and scientist Fridtjof Nansen.[130] Nansen's representative for the Ukraine, a still unknown young army captain named Vidkun Quisling, set up his headquarters in Kharkov in February 1922, remaining in the region until the autumn of the following year.[131]

The beginnings were difficult. The Soviet authorities were suspicious of the ARA, and in particular of its insistence that American personnel control the distribution of the relief materials. Discussions over jurisdiction went on until April 1922, when the Donbass and Krivoi Rog were finally assigned to Nansen's group.[132] By this time famine was rampant. When registration of the starving in Donetsk province began in October 1921, there were only 2,299 persons listed. At the year's end the number was over a quarter million, having been reduced from 384,000 by the food shipments from the RSFSR to the Donbass workers in December.[133] But these

[128] See Chubar's report to the Third Congress of the Coal Industry in *Russkaia promyshlennost' v 1922 godu*, p. 18.

[129] Gerasimovich, *Golod na Ukraini*, p. 145. See also Diptan, "Deti i golod," p. 106.

[130] The American-Jewish Joint Distribution Committee (JDC) worked together with the ARA and under its aegis in the provision of famine relief.

[131] Hayes, *Quisling*, pp. 23, 27.

[132] Fisher, *Famine in Soviet Russia*, pp. 273–74.

[133] See the report by Vladimirov, commissar for food of the Ukrainian Republic, in Bachinskii et al., *Promyshlennost' i rabochii klass*, doc. 27, p. 40.

shipments were a onetime effort that the Soviet authorities were incapable of sustaining. The Soviet administrative system was simply not up to a prolonged and orderly reallocation of supply.

By March 1, 1922, 654,749 starving people were listed in the region.[134] The picture was similar throughout the Ukraine. According to the ARA-JDC projection, feeding in the Ukraine had been expected to peak by July 15, 1922, at 800,000 children and 400,000 adults. In fact, by that date 822,000 children and 600,000 adults were being sustained, and by August 1, the American relief effort alone was feeding over a million adults in the Ukraine.[135] In the first half of 1922, the Narkomzdrav reported 67,126 deaths from famine, and 741,532 famine-related deaths from disease in the republic. "Whole villages, swollen from hunger, lay down and were unable to apply for medical help."[136] Infant mortality, which in 1903 had been 18.6 percent in Ekaterinoslav province, averaged 31.4 precent during 1920–22.[137] By the end of 1922 the above-normal mortality, attributed almost entirely to the famine, totaled somewhere between the one and a quarter million officially estimated by the International Relief Commission, and the three million souls estimated privately by Nansen.[138] Ultimately, hunger was to affect nine and a half million of the Ukraine's population of twenty-six million, almost all of them in the south.[139]

The scope of this human tragedy, striking the peasantry perhaps even more harshly than the industrial workers, dragged humanity down. Professor Frank, head of the Department of Mental and Nervous Diseases at the University of Kharkov, established twenty-six cases of murder for cannibalism and seven more for commercial use in five southern provinces, and found the practice of necrophagia "very common in all districts." Quisling

[134] Quisling, "Famine Situation in Ukraina," p. 11. Although this constituted nearly one-quarter of the province's population, the situation was far better than in Zaporozhe, where 78 percent were already starving, or Nikolaev, with 50 percent famine. See League of Nations, "Report on Economic Conditions," p. 38. These differences may account for the remark cited at the beginning of this chapter that Iuzovka starved "less than the rest."

[135] Fisher, *Famine in Soviet Russia*, p. 270.

[136] League of Nations, "Report on Economic Conditions," p. 55. This was only a partial survey of the Ukraine.

[137] Tomiline, *L'hygiene publique*, p. 21.

[138] League of Nations, "Report on Economic Conditions," p. 1.

[139] Fisher, *Famine in Soviet Russia*, p. 246 n. 2. League of Nations, "Report on Economic Conditions," p. 1, estimates 20 to 24 million people affected by the famine—almost the entire population of the Ukraine.

appended to his report a gruesome annex of eyewitness testimony regarding a family eating its weakest members in order to survive.[140] By the end of March, Nansen had reported to the League of Nations:

> There is, therefore, the prospect that within a very few months, millions of people who have passed through a terrible winter under the perpetual menace of starvation, and who are threatened by a repetition of this experience next year, will migrate from their homes in search of countries where food may be obtained. These migrations will constitute in themselves a very grave problem for the governments of Europe, and particularly for the governments of the states that border on Russia.[141]

In Iuzovka district, eighteen of the twenty-six counties were declared famine areas, and by March 1, 1922, 48,000 children and 64,193 adults, 38 percent of the population, were starving.[142] At the New Russia factory, Ivan Gavrilovich Makarov, who served as director from 1921 to 1932, drew a dark picture for a session of the Metal Workers' Union. The factory had two days' bread supply, and though rumor had it that six carloads of grain were on their way, nobody knew exactly where they were and when they might arrive. Oil, sugar, and meat had not been seen for three months, and the workers, who had not yet been paid their January wages, could not afford the market prices for what few goods were available in the town. As a result, factory workers were dying daily at work, or at home, where their wives and children were also collapsing from hunger. Makarov's fear was a hunger riot (*golodnyi bunt*) that would close the factory entirely, paralyzing the metal-working industry of Soviet Russia, since the New Russia factory was a principal supplier of pig iron for all the factories of the north. The workers' only hope was a train, being prepared at the factory, that was to be sent to areas of food surplus to barter goods for food. The workers were giving their last belongings—sewing machines, household goods, even

[140] Fisher, *Famine in Soviet Russia*, p. 436 n. 9, and Quisling, "Famine Situation in Ukraina," annexes.

[141] League of Nations, doc. C. 173 M. 92 1922II [A]. Report of F. Nansen, March 29, 1922.

[142] Quisling, "Famine Situation in Ukraina," p. 13. One of those who died in this period was Nikita Khrushchev's first wife.

boots and clothing—in hope of their being bartered for a crust of bread.[143] Not even in the famine and the cholera epidemic of 1891–92 had Iuzovka been reduced to such straits.

The record of the Soviet government in the face of this crisis was dismal at best. Even taking into account the multitude of problems with which it was faced through the spring and summer of 1921, the continuation of grain requisitions for the Volga at the same time that a great effort was made to gather food for the Donbass must be accounted a bureaucratic tangle of the most incompetent sort. The highly advertised Save the Children Council (*Sovet zashchita detei*) managed to send only two medical-nutritional teams and equipment for one children's home to Donetsk province in the first half of 1922.[144] In addition, Soviet officials, high and low, both in contemporary comment and in retrospect, repeatedly ignored the crisis in the south. Chicherin, in a note of August 3, 1921, when the extent of the harvest failure was already known, did not list any of the provinces of the Ukraine as "distressed." Chubar's report quoted above made no mention of famine and death, or of Nansen's mission. His only concern was with the number of key workers abandoning the Donbass, and his concluding remarks were that toward the end of 1922 the food question lost some of its urgency, and reserves began to grow once more. A representative of the Ukrainian Red Cross, M. Ivanov, reporting to the League of Nations, declared that it was the Whites' shooting of "immense numbers of workmen in the south, particularly in the Donets Basin," that had caused an increase in the number of starving children. G. I. Petrovskii, recalling 1920–22, simply says: "The supply of material goods and food was below average."[145] In his report, Quisling comments: "On my way to Ukraina I sought in Moscow informations about the situation from presumptive well informed persons. They told me that in Ukraina the situation was very bad, about a half a million people starving. In reality the number was more than six times greater."[146] Whether ignorance, incompetence, sheer neglect, or malevolence was at the bottom of this behavior, the ignoring of millions of starving

[143] DOGIA, F. R-1, op. 1, d. 16, pp. 124–25. Report of I. G. Makarov, March 28, 1922. The report makes no mention of the Nansen relief effort.

[144] Diptan, "Deti i golod," p. 106.

[145] For Chicherin, see Fisher, *Famine in Soviet Russia*, p. 246 n. 2. For Chubar, see *Russkaia promyshlennost' v 1922 godu*, p. 18. Ivanov's explanation is in League of Nations, "Report on Economic Conditions," annex 5, p. 109. Petrovskii, "Oktiabr' v Donbasse," p. 9.

[146] Quisling, "Famine Situation in Ukraina," p. 1.

peasants and workers cannot reflect any credit on the Soviet regime. It was only in the spring of 1923 that a combination of a normal agricultural year, outside aid, and an improvement in the functioning of the Soviet administration put an end to the massive famine, restoring a viable level of supply.

Civic Reconstruction: Society and Politics in Iuzovka, 1920–1924

Although the central authorities saw Iuzovka chiefly as a source of highly important industrial production, the local Bolsheviks were faced with additional tasks of social, cultural, and civic reconstruction. The beginnings of this effort were carried out at a time when the town had shrunk to less than half its wartime peak population, and its demographic structure had changed. Russians and Jews now made up 90 percent of the 31,428 inhabitants who remained at the end of the famine. The number of Jews had grown by a third since 1917, as refugees from the civil war sought a safe place, and they now constituted over a third of the town's population. This was in stark contrast to many Jewish communities in the Ukraine that disappeared altogether in the fighting and pogroms, and even to major centers such as Ekaterinoslav, where only a third of the pre–World War I Jewish population remained.[147] Ukrainians and people of other nationalities, who, in mid-1917, had made up a quarter of Iuzovka's population, now made up only 8 percent.[148] One thing had not changed. In 1923, the Iuzovka district had a population of sixty thousand, double that of the town alone, and no less than twenty-five thousand of these were employed by the New Russia Co. factory and mines.[149] The success of Iuzovka's industry was the key to its people's welfare. The industrial settlements of New Russia had been the leading edge of development before the war, their growth rates far outstripping those of industry elsewhere in the empire. Their fall in the course of the civil war was likewise sharper than in Russia as a whole.[150]

[147] JDC, 460, "Ekaterinoslav *Guberniia*" (typescript).

[148] For the ethnic composition of Iuzovka from its founding to 1923, see vol. 1, table 8.1, p. 198.

[149] JDC, 506, Kulkes, "Report on Uzovka," p. 1.

[150] For a discussion of the nature of urban growth in the south see Thiede, "Industry and Urbanization," particularly pp. 135–37. Brower, "City in Danger," p. 61, notes that during the civil war, urban centers of over fifty thousand population lost an average of 25 percent of their people. Petrograd, however, lost two-thirds of its inhabitants.

It was not only in Iuzovka that Great Russians were predominant. As they had in the early years of the coal and metallurgy industries, Russians dominated the Donbass. Equally important from a social and political point of view, Great Russians made up 85 percent of the Red Army troops in the Ukraine, while Ukrainians constituted only 8 to 9 percent.[151]

The industrial centers were still very different in national composition from the countryside, in which the Ukrainian population was a large majority. A census in 1920 had shown a total population in Donetsk province of 3,111,700, of whom almost two-thirds were Ukrainian, while Russians numbered fewer than one million.[152] The birth rate in Donetsk province, which had been the highest in any region of the Ukraine in the years 1910–14, had fallen to last place in the republic.[153] Seven years of war, revolution, and civil war had turned the shortage of women recorded at the turn of the century to a surplus: 111.5 women for every hundred men in 1923, the beginnings of a social problem that plagues society in Russia to this day.[154]

Although Iuzovka's economic life, and in particular the supply of food, housing, and clothing, revolved around the factory and mines throughout the crisis years of 1918–22, a more mixed economy arose as normal conditions returned. The numerous leather-working shops that had flourished as artisan enterprises were merged into a single, state-owned trust, employing several hundred people in production of footgear and protective clothing for the factory and mines. Production was minimal for lack of raw materials. In January 1921 the leather works produced only 75 pairs of high boots and 250 pairs of work boots, but repaired 1,900 pairs of footgear for the Iuzovka population.[155] But a job in the leather trust guaranteed the right to at least a minimal ration, and was therefore a valuable acquisition, however low the wage earned. Alongside this trust, there were cooperatives of shoemakers, tinsmiths, and tailors, six hundred persons in all, producing for the hungry market. As Iuzovka revived, these artisans were said to have plenty of work, and unemployment among skilled workers of any sort was negligible.

[151] "Svod otchetov Sovet Narodnykh Komissarov Ukrainy za 1920 g.," p. 5. The explanation for the small number of Ukrainians serving is that only those Ukrainians born in the years 1896 to 1900 (that is, eighteen to twenty-two years of age in 1918) were mobilized, while Russians born between 1883 and 1900 were taken for service. The reasons for this difference in recruitment policy are not discussed.

[152] Gerasimovich, *Golod na Ukraini*, p. 12.

[153] Tomiline, *L'hygiene publique*, p. 17. The 1910–1914 rate was 52 live births per thousand population. The 1920–1922 rate was 21.5 per thousand.

[154] Ibid., p. 9.

[155] *Diktatura truda*, no. 11 (February 11, 1921).

As had been the case before the revolution, the artisan enterprises were almost all run by Jews. The town's commerce was, at this time still run largely by its Jewish population. The forty stores and three hundred bazaar stalls that were its first commercial system under the NEP were evidently only a part of the town's trade structure, for Kulkes writes of a thousand Jewish merchants "of every caliber," stating that 40 percent of the Jewish community was engaged in trading.[156] While a large number of these people must have been marginal peddlers, some evidently were highly successful, for 750 "well-to-do" donors supported a hundred indigent Jewish families, as well as the 150 Jewish widows, invalids, and aged aided by the Jewish community. In 1923, according to the report by Kulkes, the Jewish Religious Community still functioned as a legal entity, collecting the prerevolutionary tax on kosher slaughter of meat and on the sale of religious articles, and administering an orphanage with fifty children and a home for the aged with thirty residents, as well as various charities. The community budget amounted to thirty thousand rubles per month.[157]

While the Bolsheviks were still struggling to create new institutions and a new culture, the old structures continued to function, meeting some of the population's minimum needs on a familiar basis. This was perhaps the essence of the NEP period. This prosperity existed despite what was described as a "crushing burden" of taxes, which fell particularly harshly on the smaller merchants. The activity of the struggling smaller merchants was also hindered because the loan society, which had provided seed capital for refugees and small entrepreneurs during the war years, had ceased operation. The private banks that had grown up in Iuzovka before 1917 had been for several months in an anomalous situation before they were finally nationalized. When the Bolsheviks took Iuzovka in January 1920, no instructions were received from Moscow about what to do with these banks, so they were merely closed, with their assets frozen. Only in June did instructions for their nationalization arrive, and by September 1 they had ceased to exist.[158] Once the banks were closed there was no institutional source of credit available for nonstate enterprises.[159] In this sector, the NEP had no influence. The Soviet regime gave private entrepreneurs the right to

[156] JDC, 506, Kulkes, "Report on Uzovka," pp. 1–2.

[157] Ibid., pp. 3–4; JDC, 458, Bogen report, "Russia," for the year November 1, 1922 to October 31, 1923, pp. 20, 98.

[158] *Diktatura truda*, no. 88 (October 23, 1920).

[159] Ibid., pp. 2–3.

operate in the market, but the limited funds available to the state were all devoted to reviving the nationalized sectors of basic industry. Lenin's idea of an autonomous, state-funded cooperative sector, which would gradually introduce the artisan and the peasant to the advantages of collectivism through preferential credits and marketing conditions, never took root. Essentially, it was foreign to the culture of Bolshevism as well as to the structures of prerevolutionary Russian economic development. As Sidney Monas has pointed out, both the occupations of commerce and industry and their practitioners were looked down on, from both left and right.[160]

As Iuzovka grew, this largely impoverished trade system was seen to be both economically and ideologically inadequate. A united consumer cooperative association had been formed in Iuzovka in May 1920.[161] By the autumn of 1924, institutional development was proceeding and the Iuzovka cooperative was taking a larger part in the town's commercial life. The cooperative was then operating thirty-eight stores, seven bakeries, five restaurants, six meat stalls, and a sausage stand. In that year alone, its capital grew from 271,000 to 800,000 rubles, even though the metallurgy factory continued to lag in redeeming the food chits issued to the workers in lieu of money wages, and owed the cooperative close to 300,000 rubles.[162] Even this relatively broad activity was considered insufficient, and the trade unions were pressing particularly for credits to provide equipment and working capital for ten additional eating places for the workers and miners of the Iuzovka district.[163] A party commission that studied the Donbass in November 1923 recommended expanded activity for the trade-union cooperatives to provide a better assortment of food and goods, so that wage payments in cash might be made permanent and effective.[164] The return to a wage economy would be the acid test of normalization.

The same mixed economy that prevailed in production and in commerce can be discerned in the realm of social services as well. All residents of Iuzovka received health care from government clinics, but private charity helped subsidize the cost of medicines.[165] In health and social welfare, the situation of the Donbass improved rapidly. Amidst the ruin and disorgani-

160 Monas, "Twilit Middle Class," p. 29.

161 *Diktatura truda*, no. 89 (October 14, 1920).

162 *Vestnik profdvizheniia Ukrainy*, no. 49 (October 30, 1924), p. 121.

163 Ibid., no. 47 (September 30, 1924), p. 73.

164 Denisenko, "Iz istorii," pp. 109, 113.

165 JDC, 458, Bogen report, "Russia," pp. 45, 48. The amount contributed by the JDC in 1922–1923 was, however, less than a thousand dollars.

zation that prevailed at the mines and factories, and with homeless orphans abounding, a whole network of children's homes was established in the countryside around Iuzovka, sheltering 1,500 children toward the end of 1920.[166] There, despite shortages of clothing, equipment, and food, some semblance of normal life could be maintained, and the institutions could provide themselves with a minimum of nutrition. The children's homes were run as communes in which labor was an integral part of the experience. Even when normality had returned in mid-1924, some of these children's homes still operated, and one, ten verstas from Iuzovka, was said to be a model of cleanliness and order, with 250 healthy, well-fed youngsters.[167] For those remaining in Iuzovka through all its vicissitudes, the International Red Cross established a children's outpatient clinic that handled two hundred patients daily. After the famine it was turned over to the local health authorities.[168]

The famine left its mark deeply on those children who survived. A survey of 1,653 children in rural areas of Donetsk province in 1923 found that 16.1 percent were anemic and 1.8 percent were tubercular, as well as having other serious medical problems. However, 90.7 percent had been vaccinated, and half had had a second round of immunization.[169] Basic medical care was beginning to reach every part of the population once more. A visit to the Donbass by the Ukrainian Republic's people's commissar for health in the summer of 1924 reinforced this impression. He found that the basic hospital facilities of the region were in a satisfactory state as far as staff (whose wages were now generally being paid on time), linens, food, and medication. More sophisticated medical equipment was still scarce, and the surgical facilities in Gorlovka and Makeevka were rated "beneath all criticism." Outpatient care was generally of a simple dispensary nature, often taking on the character of fel'dsher care rather than full medical treatment. In this report, as in others of the period, the rapid growth in the number of visits to doctors was noted, with some doctors seeing a hundred patients daily. This tendency had increased with the establishment of a link between insurance payments and medical authorizations of disability and illness.

As was only natural, miners made up a substantial proportion of the

[166] *Diktatura truda*, no. 100 (November 25, 1920).

[167] V. M., "Mestnoe sotsial'noe strakhovanie v Donbasse," p. 57. As noted above, during the famine period the children's villages suffered widespread health problems.

[168] JDC, 506, Kulkes, "Report on Uzovka," p. 5.

[169] Tomiline, *L'hygiene publique*, p. 45.

patients cared for, and their medical problems had not changed. Rheumatic inflammations and work accidents were prominent among their complaints, but the anonymous author of this report included a high level of malingering, a phenomenon understandable given the pressures of the times.[170] There was also a rapidly growing demand for pharmacy services, with the numbers of prescriptions dispensed outstripping even the number of outpatient visits. The only truly dissonant note in the commissar's report was the comment on the parallel structure and duplication that existed between the trade-union medical facilities and those of the government. Commissar Gurevich would have liked them to be united, but the trade unions were unwilling to surrender this area of control.[171] Whatever the inadequacies of the medical system, it was clearly beginning to provide the basic institutions of preventive care to an increasingly responsive public. Here was one more of the points of contact that provided a basis of social interaction for the building of a community. Yet it should be remembered that this same process had been well advanced a generation earlier in old Iuzovka.

In addition to care of children and the ill, a broad social-service program was created for pensioners, work invalids, families of those killed or disabled at work, and the unemployed. By 1924, the Iuzovka district social-insurance fund covered a radius of seventy-five verstas, and included 50,533 workers, of whom 90 percent were employed by the coal and steel trusts.[172] Unemployment benefits were provided until work was found, even if this exceeded the six or nine months prescribed by regulations.[173] No hard data exists for the numbers of unemployed in Iuzovka in this period. Grigorenko describes the town in late 1923 as a magnet for the homeless, the hungry, and the unemployed because of its great industrial potential, but says it was undergoing fearful unemployment, just as it had in the 1892 famine.[174] In the Ukraine as a whole, unemployment climbed steadily from October

[170] V. M., "Mestnoe sotsial'noe strakhovanie v Donbasse," p. 56. The author is clearly giving an establishment account of the state of affairs, regarding both the level of services and the behavior of the public.

[171] *Vestnik profdvizheniia Ukrainy*, no. 45 (August 30, 1924), pp. 73–74. See also V. M., "Mestnoe sotsial'noe strakhovanie v Donbasse," p. 56. The dispute is strongly reminiscent of that between the mine doctors and the zemstvo health officials twenty years earlier, as well as of that between the trade unions and the government education authorities regarding control of literacy classes.

[172] Kaminskii, "Sotsial'noe strakhovanie na Ukraine," p. 48.

[173] V. M., "Mestnoe sotsial'noe strakhovanie v Donbasse," p. 57.

[174] Grigorenko, *V podpol'e mozhno vstretit' tol'ko krys*, p. 82.

1922 to July 1924, reaching a peak of 194,488 as the market economy of the NEP struggled to find its balance.[175] At the beginning of 1922, with growing famine paralyzing activity, there were 30,0000 unemployed in the Donbass. The Labor and Defense Council stopped recruitment and ordered those who had not found employment to be shipped home by rail, providing food for the journey. Twelve thousand rations were distributed for this.[176] In Donetsk province as a whole, in July 1924, 1,602 persons were receiving unemployment benefits, but they were said to make up only 13 percent of the total number of unemployed in the region.[177]

One of the privileges of the insured was the right to a vacation in a trade-union-supported rest home. During 1924, 1,234 persons enjoyed such vacations, while an additional 279 were approved, but for various reasons did not use the privilege.[178] Social-welfare benefits were not yet universal, as were medical benefits and primary education. Instead they were based on labor status and union membership. Here one can see the attempt to use persuasion rather than coercion in the attracting of social support for the new regime and its institutions.

The rebuilding of Iuzovka's educational system after the civil war had begun with the 1920–21 school year, but evidently it encountered difficulties, for only a little more than half the district's schools opened during that year, and these averaged only four teachers and fifty-five pupils each. The schools were handicapped by a shortage of textbooks. The thirst for education existed, however, for *Diktatura truda* noted that with the spread of the NEP, a number of private persons had suggested opening schools in the town.[179] The Jewish school, educating 150 pupils, one of six schools remaining in operation in Iuzovka apart from those attached to factories and mines, had come under the supervision of Narkompros (the People's Commissariat of Enlightenment) in September 1922, but the government paid

[175] Livshitz, "Letnaia bezrabotitsa i bor'ba s nei," pp. 35–36.

[176] Kondufor, *Istoriia rabochikh Donbassa*, vol. 1, p. 205.

[177] *Vestnik profdvizheniia Ukrainy*, no. 46 (September 15, 1924), p. 25. Kondufor, *Istoriia rabochikh Donbassa*, vol. 1, p. 206, gives the number of unemployed registered in Donbass labor exchanges in July 1924 as 28,700. The two figures are far apart, the *Vestnik* statistics yielding a total of only 13,000 unemployed.

[178] V. M., "Mestnoe sotsial'noe strakhovanie v Donbasse," pp. 56–57. Gorlovka sent 270 of its 12,405 insured miners to such rest homes. In the aftermath of the 1989 Donbass mine strike, miners' charges of corruption in distributing such privileges were the basis for dismissal of a local trade-union secretary.

[179] See *Diktatura truda*, no. 60 (August 15, 1920); no. 11 (120) (February 11, 1921); and no. 90 (199) (October 10, 1921).

only the teachers' salaries, leaving maintenance of the building to the community.[180] In addition to the Jewish religious community's support of its school, and government participation, the Iuzovka schools were subsidized by the trade unions. Of the twelve hundred pupils studying in them, 60 percent were said to be Jewish. The meeting of young people of differing backgrounds in the educational system that was one of the important social developments of prerevolutionary Iuzovka was thus maintained to some extent, though the factory and mine schools must be assumed to have had a population that reflected the continuing absence of Jews and of Ukrainians from the town's basic industries.

Although the factories and mines were training young people on the job in an attempt to increase production, the technical and vocational school that had served Iuzovka had closed down, and its lack was sorely felt. In fact, there had been plans to open a polytechnical school for people fifteen years of age and older, including mining, mechanical, electrotechnical, and other vocational courses, but the plans had evidently not been implemented, however badly such skills were needed.[181] Even in 1924, when the factory had its own vocational school with four hundred underage workers studying, these were less than half the underage workers in the town's mining and metallurgy enterprises. With the exception of the totally unskilled lamp boys, door tenders, and coal sorters, whose social and professional status remained much as it had been before the revolution, all 824 underage workers (706 boys and 118 girls) were theoretically obliged to study the labor codes and to pass technical qualification examinations before any promotion. In the 1923–24 school year, 70 percent of the factory workers under age eighteen were enrolled in factory study programs, while in the mines only 40 percent enrollment was reported, in part because in all of the Donbass mines, only nineteen schools were then in operation.[182] The cultural gap between factory worker and miner that was so apparent in the prerevolutionary period was being carried over into the Soviet period. In the evenings, the factory school offered technical courses for workers as well as providing evening study for workers preparing themselves for engineering examinations. The expansion of industry had already begun, creating a

[180] JDC, 506, Kulkes, "Report on Iuzovka," p. 4. Kulkes reported the school building as having a leaky roof, no window glass, and a damaged heating system. He estimated the amount needed for repair at between fifty and sixty thousand dollars.

[181] See the article in *Diktatura truda*, no. 108 (December 21, 1920), stating that the school was to open on January 1, 1921.

[182] Kondufor, *Istoriia rabochikh Donbassa*, vol. 1, p. 207.

shortage of skilled personnel, and the first tremblings of the upsurge of social mobility that was to be one of the central characteristics of Soviet society in the 1930s were beginning to be felt on the factory floor.[183]

Perhaps one of the reasons that the technical school for youth did not open earlier was the concentration on giving professional skills to a working class that had deteriorated seriously in skill through the eight years of troubles. The Iuzovka *rabfak* (workers' school) was organized in April 1921 to bolster the basic educational skills of workers who were candidates for higher technical study.[184] A higher technical institute was opened in May 1921, closed in August under the pressures of famine, and only reopened in March 1922. Its 208 students were almost all mine foremen and technologists with five years or more of work experience.[185] When the first students were graduated in 1924, they were not only a source of much-needed technical skills, but a cornerstone for the future growth of a workers' intelligentsia, the long-sought stratum that had been so woefully weak in prerevolutionary times. As such they were expected to share their newfound knowledge with their fellow workers, and there was a broad range of study groups at the factory and mine clubs led by workers who were now studying at the rabfak or at the technical institute.[186] At the beginning of 1924 the district educational authorities had finally, after a long delay, arranged special preparatory study courses for Communist youth, to prepare them for higher education. A call in *Diktatura truda*, "Communards! To Study!" (prefaced by a quotation from Trotsky), resulted in a long list of applicants.[187]

Education of all sorts was given high priority in Soviet Iuzovka, and it was pursued in many venues, not only in formally constituted schools. The anti-illiteracy movement, for instance, had value not only in raising the educational level, but as a tool for social mobilization. A meeting of non-party women at the Alexandrovsk mine in August 1920, called in connection with a general drive to mobilize women into social activism, resolved to eliminate illiteracy, joining in a drive to promote universal schooling.[188]

[183] *Vestnik profdvizheniia Ukrainy*, no. 49 (October 31, 1924).

[184] Ponomarenko, *Donetskii politekhnicheskii*, p. 9. The most eminent graduate of the Iuzovka rabfak was N. S. Khrushchev, who served as Communist party organizer of the school.

[185] Ibid., pp. 10–14.

[186] *Vestnik profdvizheniia Ukrainy*, no. 49 (October 30, 1924), p. 120.

[187] *Diktatura truda* (January 8, 1924).

[188] Ibid., no. 63 (August 21, 1920).

By December a school for illiterates and semiliterates had been opened.[189] In the autumn of 1924 this campaign had become institutionalized, and 112 women were to be found in the anti-illiteracy schools of the Metal Workers' Union in the town. Three classes, numbering 56 women, had completed their courses during the first eight months of the year. For some of these graduates, the anti-illiteracy course was the gateway to a professional life, for one graduate went on to the rabfak, and two others continued on in childcare courses, while nine underage working girls were able to attend the factory trade school at their place of work.[190] In a survey of members of trade unions in the Donbass and Krivoi Rog, it was found that there were over thirty thousand illiterate and semiliterate people. Seven thousand of these were enrolled in 158 anti-illiteracy courses, and four thousand had been graduated between October 1923 and April 1924.[191] Whatever the eduational efficacy of these courses, their widespread nature made a clear cultural point that illiteracy was intolerable and that education, however minimal, was the gateway to the brave new world.

Wherever these schools remained in the hands of the local trade-union activists they functioned relatively effectively, but when they were integrated into the general school system they nearly fell apart. The reason was the poor administration by the Narkompros bureaucracy. An example was the school at the Mariupol metallurgy factory, where the teachers had to make eleven trips totaling 154 verstas before they could collect the wages due them.[192] This complaint may be an exaggerated expression of the rivalry between the trade unions and the state administration, but it nevertheless reflects a reality in which an inefficient and overburdened apparatus was preferred by the regime because of the relative ease with which central control could be applied to ensure political orthodoxy and the maintenance of regime priorities.

Iuzovka, rough and dirty as it was, had a long tradition of culture, both from below, as sponsored by the revolutionary circles, and from above, as encouraged by the New Russia Co. management. Now these two streams merged in an attempt to acculturate the disparate sectors of the population to the new Bolshevik values. Only a month after the Bolshevik capture of the town, a public meeting was called at the *Narodnyi dom* (People's house)

[189] Ibid., no. 108 (December 21, 1920).
[190] *Vestnik profdvizheniia Ukrainy*, no. 49 (October 30, 1924), p. 122.
[191] Ibid., no. 44 (August 17, 1924), p. 87.
[192] Brodskii, "Itogi kul'traboty," p. 52.

to hear presentations on the theme of "Front Week." The resolution presented by the organizers and adopted by the audience promised support for both the military and the domestic fronts through honorable work for restoration of the economy, a contribution of one day's pay by all workers and employees of what was already termed the "former New Russia Co.," and donations of clothing, bedding, and footgear for the Red Army.[193] Iuzovka's citizens were already getting to know the military imagery of the Bolshevik rhetoric of mobilization, with its numerous struggles, fronts, and campaigns. Cultural institutions proliferated, but two were central, and their identities were to take on a peculiar significance. The meeting place of the Young Communists was called "The Club Named for Comrade Lenin," while the largest hall in town, the former New Russia Co. auditorium, where the Iuzovka soviet held its meetings, was renamed "The Club Named for Comrade Trotsky."[194] As head of the Donbass Commission set up by Sovnarkom and as one of the prominent leaders of the party, Trotsky enjoyed considerable prestige among the Bolsheviks of Iuzovka, and his personality and outlook were to contribute to the town's later political controversy.

The mines and factory of Iuzovka had ten such clubs altogether that carried on broad programs. In addition to the library that was basic to each club, there were evening technical and general courses for adults. By the mid-1920s the trade unions of what was by then Stalino district operated fifty libraries for their members.[195] In 1924, the Donbass was said to have only twenty-three libraries with a total of 27,644 books, which were used by less than 20 percent of the workers.[196] There were four classes for sewing and knitting, and an active sports program, including a summer olympiad in which two hundred persons competed. The prerevolutionary Sokoli (the Falcons, a gymnastics group) also continued its activities.[197]

Yet there were serious shortcomings felt in the cultural sphere. In particular, it was not reaching the core of the working class, at which such activity was particularly aimed. According to Kir'ianov, in 1922 51 percent of the Donbass miners declared themselves completely literate, and 24 percent

[193] Korolivskii, *Grazhdanskaia voina na Ukraine*, vol. 2, p. 732.

[194] See *Diktatura truda*, no. 91 (October 31, 1920), and no. 6 (115) (January 25, 1921).

[195] Krawchenko, "Impact of Industrialization," p. 354. Krawchenko notes that only 8 percent of the books were in the Ukrainian language.

[196] *Vestnik profdvizheniia Ukrainy*, no. 44 (August 17, 1924), p. 87.

[197] See ibid., no. 49 (October 30, 1924), p. 120, and *Diktatura truda*, no. 68 (August 31, 1920).

semiliterate, leaving the remaining quarter totally illiterate. Two-thirds of the miners declared that they never read a book or newspaper, and 60 percent stated that they never visited the workers' clubs.[198] According to a somewhat later trade-union survey, club work reached only 15 percent of the workers. Professional lectures in Kadievka were attended by 27 percent of women, but only 3 percent of men. Men also showed less readiness to overcome illiteracy. Classes were attended by 14 percent of illiterate women, but only 3 percent of illiterate men. Perhaps part of the problem was that the cultural fund, made up of a deduction of 1 percent monthly from each worker's wages, was used primarily for political enlightenment, with 70 percent of the expenditure going to pay staff wages rather than for educational facilities and materials.[199] Busy as they were at general and political education, the Bolsheviks were also concerned with building a professional political apparatus.

Aware of their narrow base, the Bolsheviks of Iuzovka invested considerable effort in reaching various groups outside the party. The aim of this effort was to mobilize nonparty women and nonparty working youth and young peasants to cooperate with the party in restoring the life of the district. The first nonparty women's conference of Iuzovka district was held at the end of August 1920. Following the conference, all the delegates, together with local party secretaries, were to explain the resolutions and program of action to all the women of the district. A similar conference for nonparty youth had been held two weeks earlier, developing a similar general program of consciousness of current events, working conditions, mass education, and restoration of the district's economic life.[200] Such programs seem to have had far more sophistication than was evident in the radical educational reforms implemented by the Bolsheviks during their brief rule in Iuzovka in mid-1919.

Public lectures and drama, two forms of public entertainment that had been popular in pre-1917 Iuzovka and throughout the Donbass, were somewhat more problematic than sports or knitting since they dealt with ideas rather than simple organized activity. Although lectures on current and cultural subjects were given beginning in early 1920, they were suspended without explanation in September, "until a new cycle is worked

[198] Kir'ianov, *Rabochie iuga Rossii*, p. 105.

[199] *Vestnik profdvizheniia Ukrainy*, no. 44 (August 17, 1924), pp. 86–87.

[200] See the reports of the two conferences in *Diktatura truda*, no. 61 (August 17, 1920), and no. 69 (September 2, 1920).

out."[201] Something of the approach of Iuzovka's new rulers may be discerned in the announcement of the Iuzovka "Jewish, proletarian, musical and dramatic circle 'Naie Kunst' [New Art]." The announcement leads off with the declaration that art should be a mighty tool of the revolution. In setting forth the principles of the new group, the organizers wrote:

> It will be Jewish theater developed on Soviet principles by means of an appropriate repertoire, performed artistically. In the past the Jewish theater repertoire was disorganized, backward, and also chauvinist. Twenty years ago steps were taken to remodel it. It was the Jewish bourgeoisie and their lackeys the Zionists who, wherever possible, organized music and drama groups such as Habima [The stage] and Hazamir [The nightingale]. Even Iuzovka had one such. Now a new proletarian theater has appeared, and from now on, all those former "nightingales" who stand aside and refuse to take part in it will be considered enemies.[202]

Even in the summer of 1917, one could note the peculiarly belligerent militance of Bolshevik tones, expressing the social antagonism that was the basis of the party's worldview.[203] As the passage above indicates, this tension was not eased in the years immediately following the revolution. This is evident in the pages of the local newspaper, *Diktatura truda*, whose very name ("The dictatorship of labor") reflects the Bolshevik approach. The first issue of the paper appeared on May 1, 1920, and featured details of the May Day celebrations planned for the town. The remainder of the issue was divided between communiqués from the war front (generally gloomy), and from the labor front (more optimistic). The newspaper was first edited by a collective, and later at various times by A. P. Zevaniagin, Kharechko, and Zaitsev before returning to a collective editor in October 1921. It suffered from the lack of paper, and various issues were printed on the reverse sides of paper intended as candy wrappings, and on mauve, blue, or

[201] Ibid., no. 69 (September 2, 1920).

[202] Ibid., no. 85 (October 16, 1920). Ibid., no. 95 (November 11, 1920), announces the presentation by Naie Kunst of a play, *Poslednye dni*, by the local playwright L. Shukhman, translated from the Yiddish into Russian. The Habima theater was organized in Moscow at the time of the revolution as a Hebrew-language avant-garde theater, under Vakhtangov's supervision. It later emigrated, and now is the national theater company of Israel. Hazamir choral groups still exist in numerous Jewish communities the world over.

[203] Haimson, "Problem of Social Stability," pt. 1, pp. 637–38, notes the strident bitterness of Bolshevik activists in the 1913–1914 strike wave.

pink cardboard.[204] This was most likely the reason that the print run was restricted to twenty-five hundred copies. Great emphasis was put on mobilizing youth, but frequently in a truculent, disparaging tone that could not have attracted many enthusiasts. The youth were criticized for inactivity. They did not turn out to meet with those who had their best interests at heart, and some obstinately "stick with old mama and papa who don't want to see their children modern." They would rather go to dances and flirt than work heroically loading coal at a *subbotnik* or *voskresnik*. (Subbotnik was the mobilization of workers and citizens for an extra, unpaid effort on their free day. A voskresnik was a subbotnik, using the word for Sunday [*voskresenie*] rather than sabbath [*subbota*], with its religious connotations.) Even Communist party and Communist Youth Organization members were apparently not immune to such slackness, for they too were harangued and reminded of their duty from the pages of *Diktatura truda*.[205] Rather more attractive was the announcement of a weekly page for Communist youth in the newspaper. "Comrades! Write for our page. Don't be embarrassed by your form of expression or your errors. It is enough if you will be simply sincere. The rest will be set right with a comradely hand."[206]

At first, the newspaper dealt little with the great events of the world, probably on the assumption that the central press covered these. It was, rather, a tool of mobilization of effort for the civil war, for local economic reconstruction, and for the revolutionizing of Iuzovka's society. Despite this local focus, articles by central party figures were sometimes reprinted as they had been in the Iuzovka *Izvestiia* during 1917. One such was a piece by Trotsky on the theme of the international Masonic conspiracy, accusing Petliura of having joined the Grand Masonic Lodge of the Ukraine in order to win the support of the French Freemasons in the fight against Soviet Russia.[207] Another piece, more understandable in the social and strategic context of Iuzovka, discussed the anti-Semitic nature of Wrangel's army,

[204] Nikol'skii, "Sto sem' nomerov 'Diktatury.'" The author writes that all 107 issues of *Diktatura truda* are preserved in the Central Archive of the October Revolution in Moscow. The bracketed numbers given in the editions that I saw of the newspaper go far beyond 107.

[205] *Diktatura truda*, no. 28 (June 20, 1920), reporting the expulsion of a Iuzovka Young Communist who did not take part in a subbotnik, and the slackness of the Novo-Smolianinov branch. See also ibid. (July 11, 1920).

[206] Ibid., no. 4 (May 9, 1920).

[207] Ibid. (October 19, 1920). This is of particular interest given the prominence with which the specter of an international "Jewish-Masonic plot" to dominate the world and destroy Russia has been raised by the Russian radical right throughout the years, and even today.

and of the Polish army and government.[208] An additional item for the morale of Iuzovka miners and steel workers was that 1,300,000 American workers had expressed a desire to resettle in Soviet Russia, but that the American government would not permit their emigration.[209]

By 1924, the newspaper's tone had softened and its focus broadened. The front page was devoted to subjects of national and international importance: construction and development throughout the USSR; Soviet-American relations and Senator Borah's call for recognition of the USSR; the fortunes of German Social Democracy; the Anglo-Afghan conflict; a strike in Bombay.[210] Civic pride was the theme of an article headlined "We Have Built and Are Building." "The familiar Iuzovka, little dirty Iuzovka, illiterate Iuzovka, still exists. It has known cold, hunger, and blockade. But now it has its own VUZ [institution of higher education]. The beginning was in technical courses, and the *rabfak*. Then came the secondary *tekhnikum*. Now we will produce the future Red Commanders of Labor."[211] An editorial dwelt on the theme of the professional culture of everyday work. "Every employee of the trade institutions should know that he is not simply doling out rations to the queue as was the case in 'the hungry years.' He must see himself as a public representative of the policies of the Soviet government and in his daily work must project the image of culture and sanitary enlightenment to the masses." There was a clear process of maturation and a gathering of self-confidence, along with a relaxation of the unrelenting pressures of the early years of Soviet Iuzovka. The NEP was fulfilling its assigned function.

One of the prominent subjects featured in the newspaper from its beginning was the subbotnik. The first Communist subbotnik in Iuzovka was held on January 26, 1920, almost immediately after the Bolsheviks' return.[212] What was started as an expression of revolutionary enthusiasm quickly found institutionalization, and the Donetsk province party committee soon had a Department of subbotniki, headed by one Comrade Ivachkin. In the beginning there were mobilizations for self-help. There was a subbotnik to mend the town's wells, and women mobilized to clean

[208] Ibid., no. 69 (September 2, 1920). This was at the time when Wrangel's forces were approaching Iuzovka, and the anti-Bolshevik elements in the population were awaiting his arrival.

[209] Ibid., no. 103 (December 4, 1920).

[210] See ibid. (January 1, 1924), p. 1.

[211] Ibid. (January 4, 1924), p. 2. The rhetoric, however, was still military.

[212] Belenko, *Vse o Donetske*, pp. 16–17.

the streets and alleys of garbage as a measure against cholera. This was probably the first time in Iuzovka's history that the citizens in general had been called upon to take active responsibility for the cleanliness of the town. In Bakhmut, the women mobilized to wash and mend underwear for the Red Army, an activity that marked many of the later subbotniki.[213] But the needs were so pressing, and the culture of mobilization so ubiquitous, that other, less local reasons came quickly into play. On July 24, 1920, in honor of the opening of the Second Congress of the Comintern, all Iuzovka's inhabitants were called on to give four hours of work for the oppressed proletariat of Western Europe, and of Hungary in particular.[214] It may be imagined that though they themselves had a limited coal ration at the time, the town's miners worked more willingly to produce the 139,500 puds of coal sent with the delegates to the All-Russian Miners' Congress in January 1921, for the benefit of the freezing children of Moscow.[215]

Where a new technique of mobilization succeeded in one locality, it was quickly copied by other enterprises. At the Voznesenskii mine "the workers decided" to work two extra hours daily for a week as well as preparing a "grandiose" subbotnik for the weekend, all for the benefit of wounded and ill Red Army soldiers.[216] Three months later all Donbass metallurgy workers were working two hours extra daily and Sunday as well, as part of a week of "aid to the front."[217] The mobilization techniques for subbotniki were not all stick. The carrot also served, and the Trotsky Commission ordered Narkomprod to provide the prizes of extra food won by outstanding participants in the "All-Donbass Voskresnik."[218] Neither were other techniques, familiar in the history of mobilization of Soviet workers, missing from this picture. In mid-April 1921, the Communist party issued a leaflet to the workers of Iuzovka. "The voskresnik of April 17 was the greatest in the entire era of Soviet rule in the Donbass. It yielded 205,000 puds of coal. The voskresnik of April 24 must be even bigger. It must yield 295,000 puds of coal. Iuzovka miner, prepare!"[219] In the event, the next week's voskresnik yielded 550,000 puds, "a head-spinning, colossal figure!"[220]

[213] See *Diktatura truda*, no. 63 (August 21, 1920), and Korolivskii, *Grazhdanskaia voina na Ukraine*, vol. 3, p. 357.

[214] *Diktatura truda*, no. 46 (July 22, 1920).

[215] Bachinskii et al., *Promyshlennost' i rabochii klass*, doc. 3, p. 6.

[216] Korolivskii, *Grazhdanskaia voina na Ukraine*, vol. 3, p. 324.

[217] Ibid., p. 728.

[218] "Meropriiatiia," p. 89.

[219] Kondufor, *Istoriia rabochikh Donbassa*, vol. 1, p. 199.

[220] *Diktatura truda*, no. 41 (150) (April 27, 1921).

The "ratchet principle," so hated by Soviet workers, by which today's record becomes tomorrow's obligatory norm, was in full use even then. In addition, one may infer from this leaflet that the voskresnik had been transformed from a special event to a weekly routine. Two months earlier, in February 1921, when the workers were already hovering on the brink of starvation, the Communist party secretary of Iuzovka district could report 480 subbotniki and 100 voskresniki in which 6,680 persons produced goods worth 450,000 rubles.[221] In effect, "voluntary" work in what was supposed to be free time had become a regular and universalized part of the Donbass production schedule, with its economic product factored into the district's plans.

Housing: A Chronic Sore Point

Housing had been one of the central problems of Donbass life throughout the region's development. At the same time, adequate housing was the key to gathering a stable, professional work force, and one of the reasons that miners had remained a semimigrant group was the poor housing accommodations at the Donbass mines. In 1914, L. G. Rabinovich had carried out a housing survey on behalf of the Association of Southern Coal and Steel Producers, and recorded 1,055 mine barracks and 21,080 apartments in family houses, with room for a total of 86,000 workers.[222] Housing was thus even then totally inadequate, since the number of Donbass miners rose as high as 200,000 in peak months. A survey of the Donbass in 1922 found that about a third of the existing housing stock was in ruins, with windows and doors missing, and stoves stolen from the houses and barracks. In some places the devastation reached as high as 75 percent of the total stock.[223] When the Donbass came under the control of the Red Army in 1920, the existing housing was found to be largely occupied by families of Red Army men, by invalids who had been unable to flee, and by various government

[221] Bachinskii et al., *Promyshlennost' i rabochii klass*, doc. 10, p. 9, figures for February 1921. See doc. 13, pp. 18–19, for even larger figures for the Iuzovka mining district for all of April 1921.

[222] Bazhanov, "Donetskii Bassein v 1920 godu," nos. 8–9, p. 98. It is likely that this housing stock was used by a rather larger number of miners, for Rabinovich has calculated only two workers per apartment.

[223] Postriganov, *Metallurgicheskie zavody iuga Rossii*, p. 412.

institutions and their staffs, who had commandeered space immediately upon their arrival. None of these contributed to the mines' production.[224]

The Trotsky Commission had recommended draconian steps to remedy this situation. All the nonworking population was to be removed from the mining settlements, though in the circumstances prevailing at the end of 1920 this would condemn many to near-starvation. Residents' rights were to be granted only to workers and employees of mines and their immediate families. New workers were to be brought without their families, even though it must have been clear that this would detract from the stability of the labor force. Finally, all social and political institutions were forbidden to occupy housing space in the mining settlements. As was the case with so many of the administrative decrees issued at the time, little resulted from these orders.[225] *Diktatura truda* complained that housing for Red Army men who had been sent to work in the mines of Iuzovka "does not meet the most elementary demands of hygiene, not only for people, but for livestock. Stench, damp, and filth are everywhere. These are the conditions offered to Communists mobilized under order no. 1 for underground mine work. Doesn't the factory administration know about the Soviet Republic's housing laws? They should live in these places!"[226] Certainly the executives knew of the living conditions of the workers, but they remained executives because they understood and applied the regime's priority of production over consumer welfare wherever a scarcity of resources prevented the satisfaction of both. All other legislation had to give way to this principle.

Trotsky's plenipotentiary commission to the Donbass in November 1920 gave housing, along with food, a special military-level top priority. Narkomtrud was ordered to assign fifteen hundred construction workers to the region immediately, and another five thousand in the spring of 1921. Neither men nor materials appeared, and only seven thousand apartments and three hundred barracks were made fit for habitation, with a plan for an additional twenty-one hundred apartments in all of 1921. "Use of existing housing had to be maximized, permitting deviation from the norms of space stipulated by Narkomtrud."[227] At that time it was estimated that to bring the largest Donbass mines up to the necessary level of production,

224 Bazhanov, "Donetskii Bassein v 1920 godu," nos. 8–9, p. 98.

225 Ibid., p. 99.

226 *Diktatura truda*, no. 28 (June 20, 1920).

227 Bazhanov, "Donetskii Bassein v 1920 godu," nos. 8–9, p. 98.

there would have to be housing for 35,000 additional workers and their families. Trade unions, factory directors, and government officials all recognized the urgency of the housing problem. The average living space was less than nine square arshin per worker—about half the minimum sanitary norm. It was generally recognized that out of hygienic, moral, and even simply productive considerations, workers' living conditions had to be improved.[228] With the caution appropriate to a powerless civil servant, Dr. Aronovich, the public health officer for Krivoi Rog, wrote of insufficient attention to workers' living conditions in the development of the district's enterprises, adding: "In any case, this question is not given a priority equal to that of production."[229] A less-inhibited source stated bluntly, "There is no mine at which air space in housing is more than one and a half cubic sazhen', most are in the vicinity of 0.65 cubic sazhen', and it goes as low as 0.28 cubic sazhen'."[230] For the 1924 building season in the Donbass, housing orders amounting to over 75,000 cubic sazhen' were placed, enough to house fifty thousand workers. However, as the plans were matched with financial resources, this was cut to 22,666, and later to 6,355, cubic sazhen', less than 9 percent of the original plan.[231] This was not during the pressure and ruin of civil war, as was Trotsky's abortive construction program, but nearly four years later, after war and famine had passed. In Krivoi Rog, only 30 percent of the workers had housing at the mines; the remainder lived up to six verstas from the mines, in villages where the sanitary standards were no better than in mine housing.

At the New Russia Co. factory (by this time Stalinskii Iugostal'), only a quarter of the workers had housing provided for them. In the mines, 70 percent lived in company accommodations, but the descriptions are horrifyingly reminiscent of the dugouts and barracks of fifty years earlier.

> Barracks for workers are three to four verstas from the mine. They have twenty-four apartments totaling three hundred square sazhen' in area,

[228] See, for instance, Kozhanyi, "Zhilishchnyi vopros," pp. 56–57, and M——v, "Zhilishchnyi vopros," p. 27, reporting discussions in the Iugostal' (the Southern Steel Trust) and Donugol' (the Donetsk Coal Trust); *Vestnik profdvizheniia Ukrainy*, no. 47 (September 30, 1924), p. 30, summing up the results of the Third Donetsk Province Conference on Wages and Economy; Bachinskii et al., *Promyshlennost' i rabochii klass* doc. 76, p. 130, November 1923 decision of the Politburo of the Communist Party of the Ukraine.

[229] M——v, "Zhilishchnyi vopros," p. 28.

[230] Vilents-Gorovits, "Zhilishchnye usloviia," p. 79. The minimum norm for air space established at the end of the nineteenth century was 1.5 cubic sazhen' per person.

[231] Ibid., p. 78.

> and accomodating 145 workers and 36 family members. Each apartment is a single room and washing room. The walls are plastered but dirty, the floors are wooden. Iron stands in two rows are covered with wooden planks. Beds are totally lacking. Everything is piled high with dirty bags and bedding infested by vermin. In each sleeping room is a stove on which the workers prepare their food. There is a dirty table for eating. The workers keep all their belongings here, along with remnants of food, bread, etc. Here, too, they change clothes and hang out their wet and dirty work garments. There is a keg of drinking water and a pile of wood to stoke the stove. In the absence of any designated person to maintain cleanliness, unbelievable filth abounds. Indeed, it would be difficult to attain cleanliness when one room serves for sleeping, eating, cooking, and laundry.[232]

If some areas of life, such as health and education, saw a continuation of prerevolutionary trends of improvement, housing must be accounted one in which there had been, from the beginning, a perpetuation by the Soviet regime of all the sins of omission and of commission of its predecessors.

Political and Social Transformation: The Donbass, 1923–1924

The industrial and agricultural recovery of the Ukraine after the famine was accompanied by the broadening of the Bolshevik base in the republic. Members and candidates of the Communist Party of the Ukraine numbered 71,387 at its seventh conference in April 1923, and 101,585 a year later.[233] Of the 31,544 persons joining the party in the Ukraine during the "Lenin enrollment" that followed the leader's death, more than half, overwhelmingly male industrial workers and coal miners, were from the Don-

[232] M——v, "Zhilishchnyi vopros," p. 28. The author is describing a particular barracks in Krivoi Rog, but maintains that this was typical of the great majority of miners' barracks. Kondufor, *Istoriia rabochikh Donbassa*, vol. 1, p. 208, writes that in the winter of 1924, 85 percent of the demand for housing in the Stalino metallurgy factory was met, and V. M., "Mestnoe sotsial'noe strakhovanie v Donbasse," p. 56, in an uncharacteristically upbeat assessment, writes that "housing conditions—an extraordinarily sharp question in the Donbass—are improving, for each year the Mining Administration extends the space available by building new, wonderfully equipped living quarters." The 1989 Donbass mine strikers had poor housing conditions as one of their sharpest complaints.

[233] Bachinskii et al., *Promyshlennost' i rabochii klass*, pp. 101, 109.

bass.[234] In mid-1924, a large group of former supporters of Ukrainian independence published a declaration hailing the policies of *korenizatsiia* (coopting native leadership, language, and folklore) that promised the use and development of indigenous culture in daily life as well as in the institutions of government, and sought to replace imported Muscovite rulers with locally raised Bolsheviks. The former oppositionists pledged their loyalty to the Soviet Ukraine.[235] Seemingly the revolution was over, and an era of social peace and perhaps even prosperity was at hand.

Certainly in comparison with the deprivation, uncertainty, and even horrors of war, revolution, and famine that had been the lot of the Donbass for nine years, it might already be claimed (as it would be in the midst of the purges in 1936) that "life had become better, life had become gayer." Grigorenko recalls that he now had steady work in the Donbass railway workshops and that his wages had risen to forty-five rubles a month hard cash—a sum he had never dreamed of earlier. For eighteen rubles a month each, he and two friends shared a room in a widow's home, including laundry and plenty of good food. On a Sunday stroll through the market in the summer of 1924, he reveled in the mountains of melons, watermelons, fruits, vegetables, sausage, bread, and cereals of all sorts—everything one might wish for, offered for sale by peasants and traders.[236] The NEP was at its zenith, and the social and economic organisms of the Donbass were beginning to gather strength.

Yet not everyone saw this as a favorable development. Looking askance at the bubbling enterprise around him, a factory worker named I. Pikarev wrote to *Diktatura truda* urging the Iuzovka soviet to imitate the actions of the Moscow political police in mounting a campaign against "speculators and socially harmful elements, currency dealers, and others who are subverting the workers' welfare." Many such were said to be active in Iuzovka, and the writer promised full support from the workers of any action taken by the local police.[237] There was also discontent with the lack of technical progress made by Soviet industry as compared with international standards. This was a fairly broadly held opinion, but of particular interest are the arguments of V. Sharyi in his survey of the Soviet metal industry, for he

[234] Bakumenko, *Ukrain'ska RSR*, p. 31

[235] *Visti* (May 18, 1924).

[236] Grigorenko, *V podpol'e mozhno vstretit' tol'ko krys*, p. 89.

[237] *Diktatura truda* (January 8, 1924).

bases them primarily on the arguments of engineer Svitsyn.[238] In four years, the bête noire of the workers had ensconced himself in Iugostal' and had become a technical authority on Bolshevik metallurgy.

There was still one more spasm of political conflict to be endured. Since 1917, the Donbass had been a center of political heterodoxy within the Bolshevik party. I have already noted the dominance of the Left Communists on the question of peace with Germany, as well as the attempt to set up the autonomous Donbass Republic. In addition, I have had occasion to remark on Trotsky's influence among the Communists of Iuzovka. Even before Lenin's death, Trotsky's policies had aroused division in the party. Now the ideological and administrative disagreements were intensified by the contest for power arising from Lenin's illness. The crisis, long in building, came to a head with the publication of the "Declaration of the Forty-Six," a comprehensive critique of the state of political and economic leadership of the Soviet Union, which included a demand for lifting the ban on intraparty factions that had been imposed in 1921.[239] A special session of the Politburo and the Party Control Commission met to condemn the declaration. This condemnation was then translated into a campaign in the provinces to isolate and oust from positions of influence all oppositionists associated with the declaration. Among the Bolshevik leaders of the Donbass who led this attack were Kviring, Petrovskii, and Chubar.[240] The Donbass, Kharkov, and Ekaterinoslav, the same industrial centers that had supported Lutovinov and Sapronov on the eve of the Tenth Party Congress in 1921, were now the focus of the fight against the Trotskyites and the Declaration of the Forty-Six.[241]

Grigorenko recalls being summoned by a Komsomol committee member to the trade employees' club in Iuzovka where there was to be a "discussion" with Trotsky's supporters. When the first of these rose to present his point of view he was drowned out by shouts, catcalls, whistling, and stamping that soon turned into a fistfight. Reproached for not having done his part in

[238] Sharyi, "Metallicheskaia promyshlennost'," pp. 60, 64. The article contains three separate references to Svitsyn's opinions.

[239] A detailed discussion of the politics of this period is provided in Schapiro, *Communist Party*, chap. 15. See also Deutscher, *Prophet Unarmed*, chap. 2. The text of the declaration in English is in Carr, *Interregnum*, pp. 374–80.

[240] Bachinskii et al., *Promyshlennost' i rabochii klass*, pp. 104–5.

[241] Ibid., p. 106.

the battle, Grigorenko replied: "For this you had to know how to be a hooligan, not how to fight. I do not know hooliganism."[242]

Though comparatively many of the signatories were from the Donbass, or had been recently associated with the region, Kharechko was the only prominent Iuzovka Bolshevik among the Forty-Six, signing with reservations. He apparently suffered little for this, except for literary polemics published in 1928, criticizing his account of the revolution. Pavel Alferov, though not a signatory, was accused of Trotskyism and sent to Vorkuta in 1928. He was released only in October 1942.[243] When, at the end of December 1923, there was finally a committee-by-committee vote on the censure of the Forty-Six, Iuzovka voted sixty-seven to twelve in favor of Moscow, with no abstentions. Of the votes recorded, Iuzovka's was the largest opposition group in the Donbass.[244]

The voting campaign at the end of 1923 put an end to opposition influence. Iuzovka, which for several months during 1923 had been called Trotsk, was now wholly in the hands of the Stalinists and their allies.[245] On April 24, 1924, a decree of the All-Ukrainian Executive changed the town's name from Iuzovka to Stalino, and the State New Russia Factory became the Stalinsk State Factory and Mines of the Southern Metallurgy Trust, Iugostal', with the new names to take effect one week later, on May Day.[246] The socialist transformation of Iuzovka was complete.

[242] Grigorenko, *V podpol'e mozhno vstretit' tol'ko krys*, p. 89.

[243] Donetsk Oblast' Historical-Geographical Museum, Alferov file.

[244] Bakumenko, *Ukrain'ska RSR*, p. 29. Lugansk is recorded as having eight against and nine abstentions, while Bakhmut is listed with none against and five abstentions.

[245] See *Komsomolskaia pravda* (May 19, 1989), p. 4. Gatchina, near Petrograd, was the only other place that bore Trotsky's name at the time. No archival documents, newspapers, memoirs, or other references confirming this renaming of Iuzovka were found.

[246] DOGIA, F. R-230, p. 1. The text of the decree is displayed in the Donetsk Oblast' Historical-Geographical Museum. Grigorenko, *V. podpol'e mozhno vstretit' tol'ko krys*, p. 86, writes that immediately after the capture of Iuzovka by the Bolsheviks the question of renaming the settlement was raised since it was "unthinkable that the proletarian center of the Donbass should bear the name of the exploiter, Hughes," and that at that time, Stalino was related only to "steel," and not to Stalin. While the suggestion may have been raised, the official decree renaming the town was issued only in 1924. When, in the summer of 1990, the question of renaming the central district of Donetsk arose, the name "Iuzovskii" was the second choice of the public, after "Tsentral'nyi."

CHAPTER 12

Conclusions: Modernization, Community, and Stability

In 1917, the people of Iuzovka hurried, ill-prepared, into an attempt at democratic society. Ultimately, the fate of this experiment was decided elsewhere, in the wave of military action that installed and removed regimes throughout the civil war. Yet even without this upheaval, it is doubtful that Donbass society was equipped to sustain an open, pluralist system of negotiation and compromise between contending values and interests.

This test was thrust on them by external circumstance: the collapse of the tsarist regime in the crisis of war. The Donbass workers had little experience to help them handle the new circumstances. Some of them were already the second generation in the factory, and they had been exposed to the urban style of living of Iuzovka, the interaction of its differing groups, the secularization, the broadening of experiential and cultural horizons—all the components of a society undergoing the industrial revolution. They lacked civic experience, however, having been consciously denied this both by the tsarist autocracy and by their employers.

The industrial revolution had introduced the Russian peasants to individualism. First, as workers whose place on the ladder of success was largely determined by the amount of money that they, as individuals could acquire, and then as actual or aspiring property owners, the Donbass workers found themselves assuming more individual responsibility for their and their families' welfare than had been the case in the village commune, or even in the early workers' artel'. The projected shadow of civic experience, a poor substitute for the thing itself, came, however, not from the industrial revolution, but from the political revolution. It was a vision conjured up by the intelligentsia as a reaction to exclusionary autocracy, and based on western European political values. As such, it could not be easily introduced to the workers for their consideration; in addition, it was illegal. Neither the environment nor the bearers of the new ideas facilitated acceptance of these ideas in the mine and factory barracks.

Blockage of Modernization

Foremost among the underlying reasons for this judgment is the consistent blockage of social and political modernization by the Russian autocracy at the same time that it had embarked on an ambitious and widespread campaign of industrialization, dictated by the military considerations of empire. This is essentially the same phenomenon that Tim McDaniel has called "Autocratic Capitalism."[1] But where McDaniel focuses on the phenomenon of capitalism in Russia, I have tried to broaden the focus to the entire gamut of social, political, and economic relations in the Donbass.

Blockage of modernization involved the regime in contradictory policies that, by their very contradiction, undermined their own effectiveness. Neither capital nor labor enjoyed the freedom of organization and action that would have maximized their development. In essence, the center of contention was the relative value given to state and individual, and whether the individual, as individual or aggregated into voluntary associations, was to be subject or citizen.

This involved, for instance, the persistent, overwhelming predominance of the state as both entrepreneur and consumer. Governmental ownership, state initiatives, and governmental concessions; state tariffs, subsidies, and regulation; government orders for the products of the Donbass—all these determined in large part the success or failure of industry. Autocratic considerations dictated the limitations on the industrialists' right to organize in pursuit of their particular interests. Whereas under a less rigid regime autonomous professional organizations and local institutions of government might have provided integration, reinforcing both the authority and the efficacy of central government, tsarist autocracy increased the distance between the state and the subject. It eliminated effective local administrative organs, and multiplied fragmentation in the society.[2] Within the Russian Empire there were innumerable cleavages of an ethnic,

[1] The concept is elaborated in McDaniel, *Autocracy*.

[2] On these phenomena, see Weissman, *Reform in Tsarist Russia*, p. 228.

social, and regional nature that made the formation of an integrated set of civic groups difficult. Autocratic politics strove to make such a structure impossible.[3]

The process of urbanization, which in Europe laid the foundations of individual property interest that underlay political democratization, was also late, weak, and impeded in Russia. In Iuzovka, this proved crucial. Autocracy combined there with capitalism to keep the settlement's workers from any civic or professional experience of legitimate collective organization. No less than the small middle class and intelligentsia, the growing mass of urban workers needed such experience to foster social integration and promote social stability. Much more than the middle class, the workers needed such institutionalization to compensate for the social frameworks they had lost when they left the village.

Russia began its social transformation in earnest after the Crimean War. By 1870, urban concentrations merited legislative recognition, giving legal status to them and their inhabitants. But this developmental process was not only halted, it was rolled back by the municipal counterreform of 1892. As a result, the urban franchise was held to only 1 percent of the population, and municipalities were sharply restricted in their governmental and financial competence. Only in 1913 were steps taken to provide a solid financial base for municipal government, and these were aborted by the war.[4] What should have been the cornerstone for a new and integrated social edifice was thus subject to what one observer has called "a virtually continuous administrative crisis."[5]

As part of the same trend, there was a consistent tendency to eliminate from the ranks of the autocracy's officeholders anyone endowed with "a civic sense."[6] The Donbass industrialists were products of a society hostile to innovation and to private enterprise, and one in which, as McDaniel points out, law and contract, as well as property rights, were regarded as inimical to autocratic prerogative, and were therefore kept as weak as possible by the regime.[7] The industrialists understood and largely accepted these parame-

[3] On this theme, see the discussion in Owen, "Impediments to a Bourgeois Consciousness," pp. 80–81.

[4] See Hamm, "Breakdown of Urban Modernization," pp. 186–87, 189–90.

[5] Rosenberg, "Conclusion," p. 134.

[6] Haimson, "Problem of Social Stability," pt. 2, pp. 10–11, quoting extensively from the comments of a contemporary observer, S. Elpatevskii, "Zhizn' idet," *Russkoe bogatstvo*, no. 1 (January 1914).

[7] See the discussion in McDaniel, *Autocracy*, p. 31.

ters. With few exceptions, it would seem that no less than their mercantile counterparts in Moscow and St. Petersburg, they were merchants rather than industrialists, and their aspirations focused on the financial rather than the technical side of enterprise. But it must be remembered that their entire history is brief, and as I noted at the outset, the pressures imposed by the late beginnings of modernization in Russia were an integral part of the environment. The blossoming of Russian industry occurred only in the 1890s, followed by a decade of economic and political crisis from which the industrialists showed admirable powers of recovery, against strong social and political opposition, only to have recovery cut short by the final crisis of World War I.

Throughout this history, the autocracy regarded the industrialists through the prism of *raison d'état*; the industrialists, however reluctantly, accepted this subordination, wrapping their abdication of autonomous status in patriotism. Their carefully phrased expressions of anxiety regarding Russia's entry into the war, and regarding government policy at this time, are examples of this phenomenon.

An important feature in this context was the reinforcement of regime attitudes by the industrialists in all that regarded the workers' professional autonomy. The refusal to grant legal recognition to the category of industrial worker, and the hindering of any institutionalization of the working class through trade unions or other workers' organizations, was enthusiastically supported by the industrialists for their own reasons. The price they paid was their reluctant acquiescence to regime *diktat* in matters of workers' welfare, for the government consistently pushed the employers to improve and regularize the workers' conditions of employment and labor. This was, however, considered by them a relatively modest price to pay. It was part of their continuing acceptance of the autocracy as an institution. Yes, the tsar autocrat was father of all his subjects, and theoretically cared for all equally. The industrial worker, a displaced member of the village commune, had full right to the strict, but just, care of the monarch.

The Russian Empire had labor laws that were as enlightened and advanced as they were unenforced. The application of laws on compensation and disability illustrates this graphically, as does the violation of laws on child labor in the mines. With no independent watchdog institution on the workers' side, the mutually reinforcing imperatives of economic need of individual workers and the employers' hunger for industrial profit generally won the acquiescent silence of the overworked factory and mine inspectors.

Where inspectors did not acquiesce to violation of the law, their reports were swallowed by seemingly endless bureaucratic negotiations that at best produced more unenforced laws. Where such injustices encountered workers' protests, as in the 1898 strikes in the Donbass, the autocracy's values, reinforced by the employers' fears, resulted in the restoration of quiet, under the threat of cossack whips, as a precondition for arbitration of grievances. Petition was acceptable, protest was not.

It must be remembered, too, that in the Donbass, just as there were no autonomous institutions of the working class, there was very little in the way of that liberal or enlightened interaction that in St. Petersburg or in Moscow was a force for humane society. The zemstvo, which in the villages played such a role, ignored or was hostile to the industrial developments of the Donbass, and began to establish a presence in the mine and factory settlements only late, and reluctantly. Liberal reformers, particularly within the zemstvo, saw institutions of self-government as instruments that would cause the bureaucracy to wither away, releasing the suppressed energies of society for social and political development.[8] Even in its limited presence in the Donbass the zemstvo could not be part of any such broad reform movement. The industrialists resented the zemstvo, feeling themselves underrepresented, and the workers had no legitimate point of contact whatsoever with the zemstvo and its institutions. The teachers, agronomists, doctors, and statisticians who played so remarkable a role in other parts of Russia operated under close company supervision throughout the Donbass, lacking the relative independence of zemstvo status.

It is no accident that the Russian autocracy succumbed to revolution in 1917. The regime consciously and consistently hindered social and political development, maintaining the power monopoly of a narrowly limited political class that had long since fallen into corrupt incompetence. New forces that might renew the energies of the regime were rejected. When the autocracy led the country into crisis in World War I, it was still unwilling to allow autonomous social forces to participate in their own way in extricating Russia from its troubles. The regime collapsed of its own dead weight, unsupported even by its sympathizers. The industrialists could have been a powerful body of support for the regime, and not simply for their own narrower interests. They were educated people, demonstratively patriotic, and with all their shortcomings, they were active supporters of the cause of

[8] This judgment is set out in detail in Weissman, *Reform in Tsarist Russia*, p. 32.

economic modernization. In the turmoil of the 1905 revolution they showed their eagerness to take part in politics, but this eagerness was repressed, if not destroyed, in the aftermath of revolution. As it was, this relatively limited group of people remained under the domination of commerce, and with a few notable exceptions it shared the narrow outlook and despotic pettiness of its provincial origins.[9]

Yet in the years before 1914, Russia, and with it the Donbass, was changing. Volume 1 was devoted to demonstrating the social and economic changes that were bringing about a crystallization of social identities and social expectations. But this process was still in its early stages. Economically as well, Russia was as yet unprepared for modernity. Its railways, for instance, were too few and too weak to bind the empire into a single, strong body. Its industries, impressive as their growth had been, were ill suited to meeting the needs of urban modernization of society. These were not after-the-fact diagnoses, but figured at the center of Durnovo's famous memorandum warning the tsar not to become embroiled in the coming European war.

On the basis of the strike wave of 1912–14, and the extremist nature of the strikers' political expressions, Leopold Haimson has suggested that the autocracy was very likely doomed to suffer revolution even without the war.[10] This is possible, but it ignores two factors. One is the ongoing social change and the spreading social support for liberalization of politics that had been coming more and more to the fore since 1905. Social stability had begun to be established. The second is the spasmodic nature of the strike movement. Whether in the form of a bunt or as organized workers' actions, the limited and incipient nature of trade unionism and of workers' political parties left the working class to its old pattern of flood and ebb, storm and calm, that is a familiar phenomenon in Russian history.[11] The integration of the workers' movement into the infant civic culture was still far off when the war reinforced all the retrograde features of the autocracy, and created in

[9] For a discussion of this analysis, see Shanin, *Russia as a Developing Society*, p. 119. Gerschenkron, "Problems and Patterns," p. 48, renders an even harsher judgment: "Its entrepreneurs were too few; their time horizon often limited, their commercial customs backward, and their standards of honesty none too high."

[10] Haimson, "Problem of Social Stability," pts. 1 and 2. See also the extensive discussion that follows in several issues of *Slavic Review*, with opinions both supporting and negating Professor Haimson's position.

[11] See McKean, *St. Petersburg between the Revolutions*, for a similar analysis of both these phenomena, emphasizing the fragmented nature of the working class and the revolutionary movement, as well as the prospect of avoiding violent revolutionary collapse.

addition the crises of national humiliation, economic collapse, and above all, hunger, that were the ultimate stimulus to revolution. The autocracy collapsed, and the population, generally far from aggrieved at this collapse, and used to receiving instructions from above, followed the directives of the new Petrograd authorities in reconstructing their government. But neither the Petrograd soviet nor the provisional government could cope with the legacy of political fragmentation, inexperience, and economic ruin that Nicholas left behind. The multiple crises were beyond their capacities, and Russia descended into a chaos that frustrated all local and central efforts to construct a civic society. The war had aggravated all the tensions and grievances that had riven Russia's society for over a decade, and the successive governments between February and October showed neither the will nor the capacity to end it and ease the crisis that was destroying the country.[12]

While many traditional frames of reference changed with the revolution of February 1917, October launched patterns of development in which the strands of continuity were strong indeed. The centralized, paternalistic state, the primacy of *raison d'état*, the mistrust of the masses' judgment, and the blaming of "evil agitators" for discontent all continued, prominently reinforced by the primacy of production that took precedence over the workers' welfare. Through the first seven years of Soviet power the problems of working conditions, housing, education, health, and food supply remained predictably the same as in prerevolutionary Russia. More surprising is the similarity of response between the old and new regimes to these problems. From Makarov as director of the factory, through Petrovskii, Artem, and Kviring, to Trotsky and Lenin, the treatment of the Donbass workers and their problems reflects the same precedence of the state over the citizen that tainted the autocracy. In particular, the incompetence and impotence of the authorities in the face of famine strains credulity.

The problem here is that the Bolshevik Revolution, initially a question of policy, ultimately centered on power. The Bolsheviks, willing to pay the price of civil war for withdrawal from World War I, had a coercion-oriented, class-conflict-based outlook from the beginning. This was one of the characteristics that made them a separate stream in Russian Social-Democracy, and until mid-1917, a small and unpopular group. Assuming power as a minority in an inchoate society made their reliance on coercion a

[12] For the opinion that the war was a catalyst for an existing malaise, see Elwood, *Russian Social Democracy*, p. 273.

self-fulfilling prophecy. Patterns of behavior relevant to a period of civil war were, in fact, basic personality traits.

The Bolsheviks, once their political power had been consolidated, found themselves out of phase with the exhausted society they led, and without the values and outlook that might have helped them bridge that gap. Faced with a civil discontent far more threatening than the White counterrevolution or foreign intervention, they could either adopt society's aims, deferring their own ideological tenets, or find a way to continue to impose the "dictatorship of the proletariat" on peasant Russia. In fact, as my survey of Donbass history in 1922–24 indicates, they did some of each. Society was given greater pluralist latitude under the NEP, while the Bolsheviks engaged in their internal battles. Society was opened, while the party system, and with it the state, was closing and becoming more exclusionary.[13]

Workers, the Working Class, and the Labor Movement

When examining the development of the working class, and indeed, of all the strata of Russia's society, one can see clearly the social and political consequences of the blockage of modernization. The seven years of troubles between 1914 and 1921 set the working class back decades in its development. A substantial number of skilled workers left the Donbass and were replaced by new migrants from the villages. Many more died in the civil war and the famine. Yet even without this breakup of the working class, the Donbass workers would have been ill prepared to run their own political lives in 1917. Lenin understood clearly the state of Russian society, though he skirted the issue of a working class unready for socialism. "From capitalism we inherited not only a ruined culture, not only wrecked factories, not only a despairing intelligentsia; we inherited a disunited and backward mass of individual proprietors; we inherited inexperience, an absence of the team spirit and of an understanding that the past must be buried."[14] Nevertheless, the Bolsheviks pushed on to build socialism.

In addition, the working class was split internally. The different patterns

[13] For a detailed discussion of the interplay and dissonance between state and society in this period, see Siegelbaum, *Soviet State and Society*, particularly his definition of the subject, pp. 3–4, chap. 4, "Living with NEP," and pp. 226–29.

[14] V. I. Lenin, speech of November 6, 1920, cited in ibid., p. 6.

of action engendered by the different conditions under which coal miners and factory workers lived reinforced the traditional parochial tendencies brought by each from the villages. The maintenance of these differences continued into the Soviet period.

The more stable factory workers gave their loyalty to the factory as the source of their well-being, and whether by choice or by necessity took part in its activities and defended it against outsiders.[15] This was a parochial, rather than a class-based, view of the world, and it changed only slowly. The workers were family people, and older, and as a consequence more conservative in their outlook, but with a sense that they were deserving of justice, and a readiness to demand this right as they were ready to defend their livelihood.

Their strikes and many of their political activities demonstrate this characteristic.[16] Even as they were coming more and more under the individualistic cultural influences of industrial capitalism, they maintained a sharp sense of society and of the social contract. In addition to these characteristics, they lived in a material and cultural environment that moderated their behavior. The factory workers as a group saw their standard of living rising steadily in the most tangible material ways. They had a realistic chance to become property owners, their diet was improving, their health services were lengthening both their working lives and their chances of living beyond working age, along with their children's prospects of survival and social advancement. The physical environment of Iuzovka was becoming more attractively urban, so that even a decade before the revolution, an observer could note that "the settlement gives the impression of a lively county town. . . . The three paved streets and the several electric lamps lighting the two central streets are the pride of the Iuzovtsi."[17] If this was still far from metropolitan European standards, it was at any rate unbelievably better than the narrowly circumscribed poverty of the village. It was the fact of progress and its direction that determined the factory workers' consciousness. No less important than the physical aspects were the cultural elements of modernization. The workers' children were receiving an education that enabled the parents to contemplate for them a future they could not have dreamed for themselves. In the course of this process they were

[15] For an early Soviet commentary on these differences, see Arskii, *Donetskii Bassein*, p. 29.

[16] For a generalization on industrial workers' tendencies toward conservatism rather than revolution, see Perlman, *Theory of the Labor Movement*, p. ix, cited in McDaniel, *Autocracy*, p. 37 n. 3.

[17] Stanislavskii, "K voprosu," p. 462.

mixing as a community with people from other backgrounds, to whom their parents had at best nodded coolly over a wall of prejudice. Here were seedlings of latent civic virtue that, if nurtured, could certainly have grown into sturdy qualities of citizenship. In the circumstances of autocratic Russia, they remained stunted.

The coal miners, while exposed to some of the same influences, were a somewhat different public. Even in the seventh year of Soviet power they retained in great measure all the characteristics that had made them a distinctive group for fifty years. Younger, more migrant, less educated, less professional, they tended to be more radical but less political in times of turmoil. Their propensity to strike was lower than that of metal workers in the years 1913–17, and their strikes were more likely to be for economic than for political demands.[18] As was evident in the 1898 strikes in Iuzovka, as well as in 1916, the Donbass miners showed less ability to achieve their goals, whether through strikes or political action, than did the factory workers.[19] The miners' ability to encompass a broad view of politics was hindered by geographic isolation, as well as isolation by generational experience, skill, and gender, a problem that plagued workers in other industries as well.[20]

In this situation, the revolutionary movement could have little effect. Denial of the legitimacy of their participation in regime affairs was sufficient to blunt the consciousness of many of the workers, keeping them from embarking on the spiral of political participation that could give rise to a demand for broader and more effective control.[21] As long as the regime was perceived as attentive and honest, its representatives were granted authority by the workers. In the course of this book I have had occasion to remark on a number of occasions in which a local police official was petitioned by the

[18] See the discussion in Koenker and Rosenberg, *Strikes and Revolution in Russia*, table 2.8, pp. 84–85.

[19] Questioned in 1989 about why the Donetsk miners' strike was not joined by the more than ten thousand workers of the city's steel mill, union and party officials couched their explanations in similar terms. They claimed that the steel workers were better organized, more sophisticated, and more educated, and that they knew how to bargain "through channels" to achieve their goals.

[20] Husband, "Local Industry in Upheaval," p. 453, discusses these factors in relation to textile workers. For a broad discussion of the entire spectrum of factors fragmenting the working class, see Koenker, "Moscow in 1917," p. 87.

[21] For a discussion of how participation stimulates a taste for enhancement of participation, see Nie, Powell, and Prewitt, "Social Structure and Political Participation," p. 372. For the blockage of participation stunting pressures for participation, see Gaventa, *Power and Powerlessness*, p. 18.

workers to present their case to higher authority. Moreover, until its collapse at its center, the regime's police authority was consistently effective in limiting the organizational efforts of the revolutionaries. Police surveillance, planted agents, and a multitude of informers kept the would-be revolutionaries on a treadmill of flight, hiding, and rebuilding of destroyed organizations that diverted the movement's energies from its principal social and political tasks.

In particular, the creation of an indigenous worker-intelligentsia did not take place. I have devoted considerable discussion to the absence of this stratum in the Donbass throughout its development. The consequence was that there was nobody to translate the ideas of the radical intelligentsia into a language understandable to the workers. This is not simply a matter of abstruse phrasing or complexity of concepts. Much more, it is a function of confidence in the source and receptivity to the voice as authentic, as emanating from "one of us." In a society still largely responsive to traditional mores, this is a crucial factor in the gaining of influence.[22] In addition, the paucity of representation of workers in the leadership of the revolutionary movement, whether in central bodies or on the local level, resulted in the movement having very different priorities than did the workers themselves. The revolutionaries, and particularly the Marxists, all too often leaped ahead into political extremism at a time when the workers were barely ready to challenge authority on basic questions of living and working conditions. Even during World War I, Haimson found a "wall of mutual incomprehension" that stood between the worker-intelligentsia and the rank and file workers.[23]

Nonetheless, the revolutionary movement did exist. Each time it was destroyed it arose again, phoenixlike and determinedly persistent, from the ruins of its most recent effort. It was able to do this because, despite all the efforts of the tsarist autocracy to discredit the revolutionaries, they enjoyed a grudging respect in society for their uncompromising opposition to the crude brutality and corrupt ostentation of a decadent power. In those circles

[22] Shipler, *Russia: Broken Idols, Solemn Dreams*, p. 73, describes vividly the gap in perceptions, and consequent lack of communication, between the late professor Andrei Sakharov and Vladimir Klebanov, a retired Donetsk miner who attempted to set up an independent trade union in the early 1970s.

[23] Haimson, "Problem of Social Stability," pt. 2, p. 19. Haimson is referring to the workers' representatives in the War Industries committees, but the same could be applied broadly even in such bodies as the New Russia factory Council of Elders in its attempts to coordinate management and workers.

of Russian society in which conscience was valued, the revolutionaries were honored as the conscience of society. On a more practical level, the revolutionaries also enjoyed foreign sanctuary in which institutions could organize, grow, and gain experience. Party bodies, a party press, training schools for revolutionaries—all enjoyed that continuity of consciousness and experience without which authoritative institutions cannot develop, a condition notably lacking for them within Russia. With all its weaknesses, the revolutionary movement provided the indispensable external source of ideas and stimulus necessary to bring the powerless to challenge the holders of power.[24] It was in the fleeting underground study circles of the revolutionary movements that the workers could first grapple with the abstraction and generalization of their immediate personal problems. This was the first step toward transformation of their innate sense of society into a reasoned understanding of social processes.

A mature revolutionary movement grows gradually; the creation of a workers' movement is far different. In the Russian context of determined control of both the workers and the revolutionaries by the autocracy, no mature workers' movement could develop. True, the workers did in time learn how to make the most of their local possibilities. By 1898, the workers of the New Russia factory were able to conduct an organized, disciplined strike to gain what they regarded as their due. In 1918, enjoying the nonintervention of outside authorities, as well as support and guidance from their newly founded union, they were able to negotiate skillfully for an advantageous settlement with their employers. Yet this was still far from a movement, and such manifestations were few. Many of the waves of working-class ferment in other parts of Russia passed by the Donbass, leaving it relatively quiet. In addition, years of organized action were often followed by a quiescent crumbling of workers' efforts at self-help. Even in 1916, the strike movement of the Donbass showed that a determined management, backed by the repressive organs of autocracy, could browbeat the workers into submission.

In my understanding, a movement is characterized by stable, autonomous institutions emanating from the mass of the workers themselves, and therefore enjoying authority over them. The function of these institutions is the development of a cultural, social, economic, and political framework of

[24] Gaventa, *Power and Powerlessness*, discusses this point extensively. Having a source in the intelligentsia introduce political consciousness to the working class was an integral part of Lenin's scheme of party structure.

activity for the movement's members. The workers must also be free to determine the agenda and priorities of the movement, rather than having these imposed from without. To achieve this, the institutions of the movement must be capable of aggregating and articulating the many particular interests they represent, maximizing the contacts that bind the various publics of workers together. Such a process, taking place continuously over a long period, creates the culture of community that cements the movement. Finally, a workers' movement must be headed by authoritative spokespeople for the interests of the class, representing the workers in their dealings with other groups and state institutions. A developed and united working-class movement must be based on far more than a common relation to means of production. Hence the importance of the missing stratum of worker-intelligent, the authentic representative who enjoys the confidence of his or her peers and has the capability to systematize, generalize, and abstract from the immediate to the long term, leading the entire class from within.

In Iuzovka gulfs of consciousness separated miners from factory workers, and Russian industrial workers from Jewish artisans or Ukrainian agricultural laborers. Class was only one of several characteristics that formed popular consciousness, and for the bulk of the Donbass workers it was not the most important element in their lives. Ethnic, regional, and occupational interests, all signs of a still largely parochial outlook, transcended any universal class motivations.[25] As parts of the working class stabilized and accumulated experience, they developed an increasing sense of class self. But as Charters Wynn so graphically demonstrates, this was a complex, fragmented, and nonlinear development.[26]

As long as their unions, health-insurance funds, and even dramatic and sports groups were restricted or suppressed, and their contacts with the authorities were restricted to those of individual supplicants, no true workers' movement could crystallize. During the brief interlude of 1917, there were ambitious beginnings of such institutionalization, much as existed during the "Days of Freedom" in 1905. Mine and metal unions, the soviet, the Iuzovka cooperative as a workers' institution, the factory food

[25] For a different view, see Haimson, "Problem of Social Stability," pt. 1, p. 635, who writes of the significance of the growth of an "instinctive class solidarity" against state oppression and the indifference of the privileged. See also Koenker, "Moscow in 1917," pp. 91–92, who writes that by October 1917 class had become the most important organizing principle for the way workers looked at the world.

[26] Wynn, *Workers, Strikes, and Pogroms.*

committee, the numerous shop committees, health funds, educational groups—all these began to interconnect in a comprehensive web of community, an inclusive democratic society, replacing the exclusionary caste system of autocracy. But 1917 was brief and crisis-ridden, and did not provide an encouraging ambience for such radical change. In the end, it was the lack of organization and experience in the working class that allowed the Bolsheviks to gain control of the workers, destroying in the process the few authentic, established working-class institutions that had existed, and replacing them with party-controlled substitutes.

This was a society built from above, not from below. The military revolutionary committees replaced the soviets or arbitrarily changed their composition and competence. Newly formed Bolshevik-controlled unions used regime authority to crowd out their less-compliant predecessors. All of this was backed by the coercive armed force of a regime avowing a dictatorship no less autocratic than its tsarist antecedent. When revolution came and the restrictions on participation were banished by the heady imperative of the revolutionary vox populi, there was no foundation of experience to support consistency of judgment. The ship of state was tossed by a maelstrom of contending public opinions. Every resolution offered by a revolutionary orator, however contradictory it might be to the one passed only minutes before, could be given enthusiastic approval by the crowd.

Thus the problem of introducing democracy into Russia was not only one of consciousness and of participation. It was also a problem of the absence of institutional frameworks in which the political process could be worked out in an orderly way. Political participation without institutions within which it can be channeled and regulated becomes a destabilizing factor. It is a flood overflowing weak riverbanks, washing away all that is in its path rather than providing a controlled flow for irrigation and turbines, or depth of water for navigation.[27] The New Russia Co. had fought long and successfully against the introduction of any municipal body that might limit absolute company control over Iuzovka. There was no thought that the workers, artisans, and merchants of Iuzovka should have some say in how their settlement was developed and managed. The townspeople, enjoying a steadily rising standard of living and of education, were left frustrated and inexperienced in the face of the all-powerful company-controlled "bazaar

[27] For a theoretical exposition of the relationships among social mobilization, participation, institutional development, and stability, see Huntington, *Political Order in Changing Societies*, p. 55.

office." The employers' adamant opposition to any autonomous organization of the workers' professional and personal lives was no less successful. Avdakov's battle cry of "Bez kontrolia nel'zia!" (There must be supervision!) was wholeheartedly supported by the autocracy, and accepted as axiomatic by the majority of his colleagues. In the Donbass, the few dissenters who were willing to see in the worker a legitimate partner in determining welfare and compensation, and even some aspects of working conditions, were lonely voices crying in a wilderness. In 1917 the employers' uncompromising attitudes, voiced most aggressively by the future Bolshevik official, Svitsyn, did much to bring on the October Revolution, blocking all proposals for the inclusion of workers' bodies in the management of industry. It was, in the final accounting, the autocracy, rather than the proletariat, that served as the gravedigger of capitalism.

To complete the circle of Iuzovka's tragedy one must return to the time factor. Revolution carries with it the connotation of extremely rapid change, a volcanic outburst of energy. Rapid change always suggests the possibility of crisis, and crisis is not conducive to long-term survival and development of innovations. The entire development that I have surveyed took place in fifty years—barely two generations. The political changes gathered strength and burst forth in little more than a decade. In the Donbass, 1905 was marked by even less institutional change than elsewhere in Russia, so political freedom came in one concentrated burst in 1917. In that year of multiple crisis there was no time to learn the lessons of "freedom broadening down from precedent to precedent" that the British had grappled with over seven centuries. The parochial peasants had already been torn up from their village soil, but had scarcely put down any new roots when they were challenged with the responsibility for transforming themselves and their entire social order. At the same time they were faced with war, famine, and a progressive breakdown of the economic structure that was the foundation of their world.

In trying to cope with these crises, the newly enfranchised Donbass workers were embroiled in partisan rivalries incomprehensible even to many who were far more experienced in revolutionary politics. Yet decisions were demanded, not only by the contending party leaders, but by the pressures of crises that threatened the workers' lives. In other parts of the Russian Empire, workers had sporadically enjoyed legal organization and had experienced political life in some form, but this was almost entirely missing in the history of the Donbass, and this inexperience had to be compensated for on the spot; thus the importance of the emissaries from the center who set up the organizational frameworks and set the agenda for the Donbass workers, and in large measure determined the outcome of the revolution. Rather than testing and developing its own representatives, the Donbass proletariat was led into revolution by the Gruzmans, Alferovs, and Sergeevs, themselves few and overburdened, and oriented to partisan rather than communal issues.

In early 1917, the provisional government attempted to create an all-inclusive basis of institutions for the regulation of society: soviets, municipal dumas, trade unions, joint mediation boards of industrialists and workers. In every direction, institutional bases were laid for a universal inclusion of interests within society, and ethnic, class, and regional barriers were dismantled. However promising many of these reforms were, they never had the opportunity to overcome the fragmentation, the mutual suspicion, and the growing polarization that set off the chain reaction of revolutions that marked 1917. The promise of a revolution that would sweep away all that was old and replace it with justice and plenty was more powerful than any admonitions of "little by little" and "line by line." Yet, while this storm raged, a longtime Iuzovka resident, then on his deathbed, could contemplate the lines he had written many years earlier, words that were not only appropriate for the settlement's problems then, but have a peculiar aptness even in today's Donetsk, in its struggles with the perils and problems of perestroika. Pondering the welfare of Russia's workers in the mid-nineteenth century, one of the first Russian sociologists, V. V. Bervi, wrote: "One must set up a corporation in which the workers would have the same influence as the capitalists. . . . Naturally, the social question would not be solved by this . . . , but at any rate the polarization between the proletarian and the capitalist would be brought to an end. For thousands of years . . . bricks, iron and wood have been bought at market prices . . . and for thousands of years, workers have bought bread, meat, and clothing at market prices, but never have buyers tried to bring these prices down by means of revolution, for revolution can only solve the question of power, and not the question of market prices."[28]

[28] Flerovskii (V. V. Bervi), *Polozhenie rabochego klassa v Rossii*, quoted in Pazhitnov, *Razvitiie sotsialisticheskikh idei v Rossii*, pp. 164–65. Released from years of exile toward the end of the nineteenth century, Bervi settled in Iuzovka, where he lived until his death in 1917.

GLOSSARY OF RUSSIAN TERMS AND ABBREVIATIONS

(Abbreviations of archive names will be found in the bibliography.)

Arshin—A measure of length equaling 71 centimeters or 28 inches.

Artel'—A group of workers organized cooperatively for work or for sharing living quarters and expenses.

Artel'shchik—The leader of an artel', usually elected by his fellows.

Bund—The Jewish Social-Democratic organization.

Bunt—A spontaneous riot, generally involving destruction of property.

Desiatina—A measure of area equaling 1.09 hectares or approximately 2.7 acres.

Desiatnik—A gang boss. The supervisor of a small work team in a mine.

Fel'dsher—A paramedic, generally male in the Donbass.

Funt—A measure of weight equaling 409.5 grams or 14.6 ounces.

Glavugol'—The Main Coal Administration of the VSNKh.

Gornotrud—The Mine Workers' Union.

Guberniia—Province or region. A large administrative unit responsible directly to the central government.

Gubkom—A provincial committee of the Communist party.

Iugostal'—The Southern Steel Trust.

Kollektiv—The body of workers staffing an enterprise or institution.

Korenizatsiia—A policy of coopting native leadership and using the native language and folklore in the national regions of the USSR.

Narodovol'tsy—Members of the populist-terrorist People's Will group, founded in 1879.

Naturplata—Payment of wages in kind rather than in cash.

Obkom—A regional committee of the Communist party.

Oblast'—Region or province.

Okhrana—The tsarist political security police.

Poalei Tsion—The organization of Socialist-Zionists.

Praktik—An active party worker in a locality, concerned with practice rather than theory.

Pud—A measure of weight equaling 16.38 kilograms or 36.06 pounds.

Rabfak—A study course preparing workers for higher technical education.

Rada—Council or soviet.

Revkom—A military revolutionary committee.

RKP(b)—The All-Russian Communist Party (Bolsheviks).

Rotmistr—A company commander of the police.

RSDRP—The Social-Democratic Workers' Party of Russia.

Sazhen'—A measure of length equaling 2.13 meters or 7 feet.

S-D—Social-Democrat.

SERP—The United Jewish Workers' party.

Sovnarkhoz—An economic council, usually regional.

Sovnarkom—The Council of People's Commissars. The Soviet government formed after the October Revolution.

S-R—Socialist-Revolutionary.

STO—The Council of Labor and Defense. Lenin's War Cabinet.

Subbotnik—Organized labor performed, supposedly voluntarily, on a rest day.

Tsentroshtab—A central military staff of a district or region.

TsIK—A central executive committee.

TsPKP—The Central Administration of the Coal Industry.

Uezd—District. An administrative-territorial unit subordinate to the guberniia.

Versta—A measure of length equaling 1.06 kilometers or 1,162 yards.

VSNKh—The Supreme Economic Council.

VTsIK—The All-Russian Central Executive Committee. The executive body of the Congress of Soviets.

Zemlianka—A long, low, earth-floored dugout that served as housing at the Donbass coal mines.

Zemstvo—An elected local council instituted in Russia in the mid-1860s. The zemstvo was particularly active in agriculture, health, and education.

Zubatovshchina—Police-sponsored trade unionism.

BIBLIOGRAPHY

Russian and Ukrainian Language Materials

Archives

(Initials in parentheses indicate the abbreviations used in the footnotes.)

Central State Archive of the October Revolution, Moscow. (TsGAOR)
Central State Historical Archive, Leningrad. (TsGIAL)
Donetsk Metallurgical Factory Museum.
Donetsk Oblast' Historical-Geographical Museum.
Donetsk Oblast' State Historical Archive, Donetsk. (DOGIA)
Russkii zagranichnyi istoricheskii arkhiv, Slavonic Library, Prague.

Documentary Collections, Reference Volumes, Newspapers, and Periodicals

Adres-kalendar i pamiatnaia knizhka Ekaterinoslavskoi gubernii na 1912 godu. Ekaterinoslav, 1912.

Akhankina, L. V., et al. "Pis'ma Artema (F. A. Sergeeva) iz Avstralii." *Istoricheskii arkhiv*, no. 1 (1960), pp. 55–75.

Bachinskii, P. P., et al., eds. *Promyshlennost' i rabochii klass Ukrainskoi SSR v period vosstanovleniia narodnogo khoziaistva (1921–1925 gody).* Sbornik dokumentov i materialov. Kiev: Politizdat Ukrainy, 1964.

Bakhmutskaia Narodnaia gazeta. Bakhmut.

Bazhanova, E. V. *Narodnoe khoziaistvo SSSR v 1917–1920.* Moscow: Nauka, 1967.

Birzhevye vedomosti. St. Petersburg, Petrograd.

Biulleten' Moskovskogo gorodskogo prodovolstvennogo komiteta. Moscow, daily.

Biulleten' narodnogo komissariata putei soobshcheniia. Moscow.

Biulleten' vserossiiskogo soveta normirovaniia truda v metallicheskoi promyshlennosti. Moscow, weekly.

Biulleten' vysshogo soveta narodnogo khoziaistva. Moscow.

Brockgauz-Efron. *Entsiklopedicheskii slovar'*. Vol. 81. St. Petersburg, 1904.

———. *Evreiskaia entsiklopediia*. Vol. 16. St. Petersburg, 1910.

Byloe. Monthly.

Chugaev, D., ed. *Vseobshchaia stachka v iuge Rossii v 1903 godu*. Sbornik dokumentov. Moscow: Gosudarstvennoe izdatel'stvo politicheskoi literatury, 1938.

Denisenko, P. I. "Iz istorii vosstanovleniia Donbassa (1922–1924 gg.)" *Istoricheskii arkhiv*, no. 3 (1957), pp. 97–122.

Diktatura truda. Iuzovka.

Dokumenty iz istorii grazhdanskoi voiny v SSSR. Moscow, 1941.

Donbass. Donetsk, bimonthly.

Donbass v revoliutsii 1905–1907 godov. Sbornik dokumentov. Stalino: Stalinskoe oblastnoe izdatel'stvo, 1957.

Donii, N. R., P. A. Lavrov, and P. M. Shmorgun. *Bolsheviki Ukrainy mezhdu pervoi i vtoroi burzhuazno-demokraticheskimi revoliutsiiami v Rossii*. Kiev: Politicheskaia literatura Ukrainy, 1960.

Donii, N. R., and V. S. Fedorchenko. *Obrazovanie i deiatel'nost' komsomola Ukrainy v gody grazhdanskoi voiny*. Dokumenty i materialy. Kiev: Gospolitizdat Ukrainy, 1959.

Donskaia rech'. Novocherkassk.

Dzerzhinskii, F. E. "Dokumenty F. E. Dzerzhinskogo po khoziaistvennym voprosam." *Istoricheskii arkhiv*, no. 2 (1960) pp. 60–70.

Ekonomicheskaia zhizn'. Moscow, daily organ of the VSNKh and the Narkomats of Finance, Supply, Trade, and Industry.

Ekonomicheskoe obozrenie.

Evreiskaia nedeliia. Petrograd.

Ezhegodnik kominterna. Spravochnaia kniga. Moscow and Petrograd: Izdatel'stvo kommunisticheskogo internatsionala, 1923.

German, Ek., foreword, and I. Lukomskaia, comp. "Iz istorii proletariata Donbassa v periode Germanskogo okkupatsii." *Istoriia proletariata SSSR*, no. 11 (1932), pp. 124–88.

Golos truda. Kharkov.

Gornoe delo. Moscow.

Gorno-zavodskii listok. Kharkov.

Gorno-zavodskoe delo. Kharkov.

Gudzenko, P. P., ed. *Robitnichii kontrol' i natsionalizatsiia promislovosti na Ukraini*. Kiiv: Akademiia nauk, 1957.

Institut istorii partii, tsentral'nogo komiteta Kommunisticheskoi Partii Ukrainy. *Bol'shevistskie organizatsii Ukrainy v periode podgotovki i provedeniia velikoi oktiabr'skoi sotsialisticheskoi revoliutsii (mart–noiabr' 1917)*. Kiev: Gosudarstvennoe izdatel'stvo politicheskoi literatury Ukrainskoi SSR, 1957.

Iskra.

Iskrovskie organizatsii na Ukraine. Kiev: Gosudarstvennoe izdatel'stvo politicheskoi literatury, 1950.

Istoriia mist i sil UkRSR. Vol. *Donetsk oblast'*. Kiev, 1970.

Istorik Marksist.

Istpart, otdel Ts. K. RKP(b) po izucheniiu istorii oktiabr'skoi revoliutsii i RKP(b-kov). *Revoliutsiia i RKP(b) v materialakh i dokumentakh*. Khrestomatiia. Vols. 1–7 (1870–1900). 2d ed. Moscow and Leningrad: Gosudarstvennoe izdatel'stvo, 1925.

Iuzhnaia zaria.

Iuzhno-Russkii listok. Kharkov, biweekly.

Iuzhnyi krai. Lugansk.

Iuzhnyi rabochii. Ekaterinoslav.

Ivanov, L. M., ed. *Rabochee dvizhenie v Rossii v 1901–1904 gg*. Sbornik dokumentov. Leningrad: Akademiia nauk, 1975.

"Iz deiatel'nosti Ts. K., K. P.(b) U. i Ts. Voenno-Revoliutsionnogo Komiteta v periode mezhdu 1 i 2 s"ezdom K. P.(b) U. (po materialam istparta)." *Letopis' revoliutsii*, no. 1 (22) (1927), pp. 120–73.

Izvestiia. Moscow, daily.

Izvestiia Iuzovskogo soveta rabochikh deputatov. Iuzovka, 1905. Facsimile edition appended to Kharechko, *1905 god v Donbasse*.

Izvestiia Iuzovskogo soveta rabochikh i soldatskikh deputatov. Iuzovka, 1917–1918.

Kabanov, M. V., comp. *Partiia v bor'be za vosstanovlenie narodnogo khoziaistva (1921–1925)*. Sbornik dokumentov i materialov. Moscow: Gospolitizdat, 1961.

"Kak do sikh por shakhtery i zavodskie borolis' khoziaevami i kak deistvovat' teper'?" *Letopis' revoliutsii*, no. 3 (12) (1925), pp. 203–7.

Khronika evreiskoi zhizni. St. Petersburg, weekly.

Komsomolskaia pravda.

Konferentsii rabochikh i promyshlennikov iuga Rossii. Materialy o zasedaniiakh. 1st ed. Kharkov, 1917.

Korol'chuk, Z. A. *Rabochee dvizhenie semidesiatykh godov*. Sbornik arkhivnikh dokumentov. Moscow: Izdatel'stvo politkatorzhan, 1934.

Korolivskii, S. M., ed. *Grazhdanskaia voina na Ukraine*. 4 vols. Kiiv: Naukova dumka, 1967.

———. *Pobeda velikoi oktiabr'skoi sotsialisticheskoi revoliutsii i ustanovlenie sovetskoi vlasti na Ukraine*. Kiev: Politicheskaia literatura Ukrainy, 1951.

———. *Podgotovka velikoi oktiabr'skoi sotsialisticheskoi revoliutsii na Ukraine (fevral'–oktiabr' 1917)*. 3 vols. Kiev: Politizdat Ukrainy, 1957.

Korolivskii, S. M., M. A. Rubach, and N. I. Suprunenko, eds., *Pobeda Sovetskoi vlasti na Ukraine*. Moscow: Nauka, 1967.

Krasnyi arkhiv. Moscow.

Kulibin, S., ed. *Sbornik statisticheskikh svedenii o gornozavodskoi promyshlennosti Rossii*. 15 vols. St. Petersburg: Gornyi uchennyi komitet, 1886–1901.

Liubimov, I. N. *Revoliutsiia 1917 goda: Khronika i sobytii*. 6 vols. Moscow and Leningrad: Gosizdat, 1930.

Masanov, I. F. *Slovar' psevdonimov*. 4 vols. Moscow, 1956.

Materialy dlia izucheniia narodonaseleniia Ukrainy. Kiev, n.d.

Materialy po voprosu o cherte evreiskoi osedlosti. Kiev: Trud, 1911.

"Materiali ta dokumenti pro Donetsko-Krivo'ryzku respubliku." *Letopis' revoliutsii*, no. 3 (30) (1928), pp. 250–71.

"Meropriiatiia polnomochnoi komissii soveta narodnykh komissarov po Donetskomu Basseinu." *Gornoe delo*, nos. 1–2 (1921), pp. 85–92.

Metallist. Moscow, monthly.

Narodnoe khoziaistvo. Petrograd, Moscow, semimonthly organ of the VSNKh.

Narodnoe khoziaistvo SSSR v 1978 g. Moscow: Statistika, 1979.

Nashe delo. St. Petersburg, Petrograd, monthly.

Nevskii, V. I. *Revoliutsiia 1905 goda*. Sbornik dokumentov i materialov. Kharkov: Proletarii, 1925.

Novoe vremia. St. Petersburg, daily.

Obshchestvennyi vrach'.

Pamiatnaia knizhka Ekaterinoslavskoi gubernii na 1875 g. Ekaterinoslav, 1875.

Pamiatnaia knizhka i adres-kalendar Ekaterinoslavskoi gubernii na 1894 g. Ekaterinoslav, 1894.

Pankratova, A. M., ed. *Rabochee dvizhenie v Rossii v XIX veke*. Moscow, 1952–1963.

Pavliuk, P. I., et al., eds. *Bol'shevistskie organizatsii Ukrainy v period ustanovleniia i ukrepleniia sovetskoi vlasti (noiabr' 1917–aprel' 1918)*. Kiev: Politizdat, 1962.

Peremoga velikoi zhovetnoi sotsialistichnoi revoliutsii na Ukraine. Kiiv: Naukova dumka, 1967.

Perepiska sekretariata Ts. K., RSDRP(b) s mestnymi partiinymi organizatsiiami (mart–oktiabr' 1917). Vols. 1–2. Moscow: Politizdat, 1957.

Pervaia vseobshchaia perepis naseleniia Rossiiskoi imperii 1897 g. Vol. 13, *Ekaterinoslavskaia guberniia*. St. Petersburg, 1904.

"Pokazately sostoianiia narodnogo khoziaistva." *Ekonomicheskoe obozrenie* (February 1925), pp. 272–77.

Poslednye izvestiia.

Pravda.

Pravo. St. Petersburg, weekly.

Proletarii.

Proletarskaia mysl'. Kharkov.

Protokoly sed'moi (aprel'skoi) konferentsii RSDRP(b). Moscow: Partiinoe izdatel'stvo, 1934.

Rabochaia gazeta.

Rabochee delo. Geneva, 1899–1902, monthly.

"Rabochie organizatsii iuga v 1914 g." *Letopis' revoliutsii*, no. 5 (1926), pp. 155–61.

Rabochii put.

Revoliutsionnaia Rossiia. Geneva, 1900–1905.

Rodzianko, M. V. "Ekonomicheskoe polozhenie Rossii pered revoliutsii." *Krasnyi arkhiv*, no. 10 (1925), pp. 70–79.

Rubach, M. A., ed. *Rabochee dvizhenie na Ukraine v gody novogo revoliutsionnogo pod"ema 1910–1915 gg*. Kiev: Gosudarstvennoe izdatel'stvo politicheskoi literatury, 1959.

Russkie vedomosti. St. Petersburg.

Russkii rabochii. Moscow and Petrograd, biweekly.

Russkoe slovo. St. Petersburg.

Shcherbina, I. T., ed. *Rabochee dvizhenie na Ukraine v period pervoi mirovoi imperialisticheskoi voiny*. Kiev: Naukova dumka, 1966.

Sotsialisticheskii Donbass. Donetsk, daily.

Sotsialisticheskii vestnik. Paris.

Strakhovanie rabochikh. St. Petersburg, semimonthly.

Svod otchetov fabrichnykh inspektorov za 1909 god. St. Petersburg, 1910.

"Svod otchetov Sovet Narodnykh Komissarov Ukrainy za 1920 g." Typescript. N.p., 1921.

Svod statisticheskikh dannykh po zhelezodelatel'noi promyshlennosti. St. Petersburg: Ministry of Finance, 1905–13.

Syn otechestva. St. Petersburg, daily.

Tret'ia konferentsiia promyshlennikov iuga Rossii (20–24 sentiabria, 1917). Kharkov: Soviet s"ezda gornopromyshlennikov iuga Rossii, 1917.

Tret'ia vserossiiskaia konferentsiia professional'nykh soiuzov, 20–28.6.1917. Petrograd, 1917.

Trudy s"ezda gornopromyshlennikov iuga Rossii. 39 vols. Kharkov: 1878–1917.

Ukazatel' pravitel'stvennykh rasporozhenii po ministerstvu finansov. Petrograd.

Ukrains'kaia radians'kaia entsiklopediia. Kiev, 1965.

Vechernii Donetsk. Donetsk, daily.

Velikaia oktiabr'skaia sotsialisticheskaia revoliutsiia. Dokumenty i materialy. 9 vols. Moscow: Akademiia nauk, 1957.

Velikaia oktiabr'skaia sotsialisticheskaia revoliutsiia. Khronika sobytii. 4 vols. Moscow: Akademiia nauk, 1957.

Vestnik Ekaterinoslavskogo zemstva. Ekaterinoslav, weekly.

Vestnik evreiskoi obshchiny. St. Petersburg, Petrograd, monthly.

Vestnik finansov, promyshlennosti i torgovli. St. Petersburg.

Vestnik narodnogo komissariata truda. Moscow, monthly.

Vestnik profdvizheniia Ukrainy. Kharkov, biweekly.

Vestnik truda. Moscow.

Vestnik trudovoi pomoshchi sredi evreev. Petrograd.

Vilisova, V. E., et al., comps., *Bor'ba za vlast' sovetov v Donbasse*. Stalino: Stalinskoe oblastnoe izdatel'stvo, 1957.

Visti.

Voprosy truda. Moscow: Narkomtrud, monthly.

Voskhod. St. Petersburg.

Vpered.

Vrachebno-sanitarnaia khronika Ekaterinoslavskoi gubernii. Ekaterinoslav.

Vserossiiskaia kochegarka.

Vtoroi vserossiiskoi s"ezd professionalnykh soiuzov, 16–25 ianvaria, 1919. Moscow, 1919.

Books and Articles

Aleksandrov, F. L., and L. M. Shalachinova. "Den' 9 ianvaria v Rossii v 1908–1919 gg." *Istoricheskii arkhiv*, no. 1 (1958), pp. 212–21.

Alekseenko, A. G. *Gorodskie sovety Ukrainskoi SSR (1917–1920)*. Kiev: Izdatel'stvo kievskogo universiteta, 1960.

Anatol'ev, P. "K istorii rabochego dvizheniia v Rossii 60-kh godakh XIX veka." *Istoriia proletariata SSSR*, no. 4 (20) (1934), pp. 27–48.

Anikeev, V. V. "Svedeniia o bol'shevistskikh organizatsiiakh s marta po dekabr' 1917 goda." *Voprosy istorii KPSS*, no. 2 (1958), pp. 126–93, no. 3 (1958), pp. 96–168.

Anikeev, V. V., and R. A. Lavrov. "Bol'shevistskie organizatsii nakanune VII s"ezda RKP(b)." *Istoricheskii arkhiv*, no. 4 (1957), pp. 18–37.

Anisimov, S. S. *Kak eto bylo*. Moscow: Izdatel'stvo politkatorzhan, 1931.

An——skii [Rappoport], S. A. "Ocherk kamenno-ugol'noi promyshlennosti." *Russkoe bogatstvo*, no. 1 (1892), pp. 1–18; no. 2 (1892), pp. 1–25.

Aptekman, O. V. *Vasilii Vasil'evich Bervi-Flerovskii*. Leningrad: Kolos, 1925.

Arskii, R. *Donetskii Bassein*. Moscow, 1919.

Astrakhan, I. D., ed. *Trudy vtorogo vserossiiskogo s"ezda fabrichnykh vrachei*. 4 vols. Moscow, 1911.

Atsarkin, A. N. *Zhizn' i bor'ba rabochei molodezhi v Rossii, 1900-okt. 1917*. Moscow: Mysl', 1976.

Auerbakh, A. A. "Vospominaniia o nachale razvitiia kamennougol'noi promyshlennosti v Rossii." *Russkaia starina*, nos. 138–40 (April–June 1909), pp. 451–72.

Babushkin, I. V. *Vospominaniia I. V. Babushkina*. Leningrad: Priboi, 1925.

Bachinskii, P. P., V. E. Kviring, and M. B. Perel'man. *Emmanuil Ionovich Kviring*. Moscow: Izdatel'stvo politicheskoi literatury, 1968.

Bakumenko, P. I. *Ukrains'ka RSR v period vidbudovi narodnogo gospodarstva, 1921–1925*. Kiiv: Vidanitstvo Kiivs'kogo universitetii, 1960.

Balabanov, M. *Istoriia rabochei kooperatsii v Rossii*. Kiev: Sorabkoop, 1923.

Batov, A., and M. Ostrogorskii. "Pis'mo v redaktsiiu zhurnala 'Letopis' revoliutsii.'" *Letopis' revoliutsii*, no. 1 (28) (1928), pp. 335–42.

Bazhanov, V. I. "Donetskii Bassein v ianvare–fevrale 1919 goda." *Narodnoe khoziaistvo*, no. 5 (1919), pp. 27–32.

———. "Donetskii Bassein v marte-aprele 1919 goda." *Narodnoe khoziaistvo*, no. 7 (1919), pp. 21–27.

———. "Donetskii Bassein v 1920 godu." *Narodnoe khoziaistvo*, nos. 1–2 (1921), pp. 115–26.

———. "Donetskii Bassein v 1920 godu." *Narodnoe khoziaistvo*, nos. 8–9 (1921), pp. 96–108.

———. "Ekonomicheskaia politika sovetskoi vlasti v Donetskom Basseine." *Narodnoe khoziaistvo*, nos. 1–2 (1920), pp. 2–7.

———. "Kamennougol'naia promyshlennost' Donetskogo Basseina v 1918 godu." *Narodnoe khoziaistvo*, no. 3 (1919), pp. 25–30.

———. "Organizatsiia i deiatel'nost' tsentral'nogo pravleniia kamennougol'noi promyshlennosti Donetskogo Basseina za ianvar' 1920g." *Narodnoe khoziaistvo*, nos. 5–6 (1920), pp. 26–30.

Belenko, A. I. *Vse o Donetske*. Donetsk: Izdatel'stvo Donbass, 1987.

Beligura, I. V. *Bol'shevistskaia gazeta "Donetskii kolokol."* Lugansk: Luganskoe oblastnoe izdatel'stvo, 1962.

Bender, I. "K stachechnomu dvizheniiu na iuge Rossii v 1903 g." *Arkhiv istorii truda v Rossii*, nos. 6–7, pp. 183–87.

Bogutskii, E. F. "Polozhenie gornorabochikh v Donetskom Basseine." *Iuridicheskii vestnik* (November 1890), pp. 442–61.

Boiarkov, Ia. [A. Goltsman]. "Reorganizatsiia Donetskoi industrii." *Metallist*, no. 3 (1918), pp. 2–3.

Borisov, K. "Zabastovka na Petrovskikh zavodakh." *Letopis' revoliutsii*, no. 5 (1926), pp. 175–82.

Borshchevskii, V. Ia. *Rabochii klass i sovety Donetskogo-Krivorozhskogo Basseina v oktiabr'skoi revoliutsii*. 2 vols. Dnepropetrovsk, 1962.

———. "Stachechnoe dvizhenie v Donbasse v period podgotovki oktiabria." In Ivanov, *Rabochii klass*.

Brandt, B. F. *Inostrannye kapitaly: Ikh vliianie na ekonomicheskoe razvitie strany*. Vol. 2. St. Petersburg, n.d.

Brodskii, A. "Itogi kul'traboty soiuzov v Ukraine." *Vestnik profdvizheniia Ukrainy*, no. 47 (September 30, 1924), pp. 48–53.

Bubleinikov, F. "Rudnaia promyshlennost' SSSR v 1923–1924 g. i vidy na 1924–1925 g." *Ekonomicheskoe obozrenie*, no. 21 (November 15, 1924), pp. 32–39.

Cherevanin, N. "Antialkogol'noe dvizhenie, ego prichiny i ego perspektivy." *Nashe delo*, no. 1 (1915), pp. 87–102.

Chernomaz, I. Sh. *Bor'ba rabochego klassa Ukrainy za kontrol' nad proizvodstvom, mart 1917–mart 1918*. Kharkov: Izdatel'stvo Kharkovskogo universiteta, 1958.

Demeshin, E. I. "O politike sindikata 'prodamet' nakanune i v gody pervoi mirovoi voiny." *Istoricheskii arkhiv*, no. 3 (1959), pp. 86–98.

Diptan, I. "Deti i golod na Ukraine v 1921–1922gg." *Filosofskaia i sotsiologicheskaia mysl'* (Kiev), no. 1 (1991), pp. 101–11.

Donii, N. R. "Obrazovanie Kommunisticheskoi Partii Ukrainy." *Voprosy istorii KPSS*, no. 3 (1958), pp. 33–49.

Dubrovskii, S. "Krestianskoe dvizhenie 1905ogo goda." *Krasnyi arkhiv*, no. 9 (1925), pp. 69–93.

Dva goda deiatel'nosti tsentral'noi komissii po snabzheniiu rabochikh i ee mestnykh organov (15.11.19–15.11.21). Moscow: Gosizdat, 1921.

Emets, V. A., and V. V. Lebedev. "O privlechenii Amerikanskogo kapitala v gornuiu promyshlennost' Rossii." *Istoricheskii arkhiv*, no. 3 (1957), pp. 154–59.

Ershov, K. G. "Dekabr'skoe vooruzhennoe vosstanie v Donbasse." *Katorga i ssylka*, nos. 8–9 (69–70) (1930), pp. 7–25; no. 10 (71) (1930), pp. 42–66.

Fenin, A. I. *Vospominaniia inzhenera: K istorii obshhchestvennogo i khoziaistvennogo razvitiia Rossii (1883–1906gg.)*. Prague: Russian Institute, 1938.

Fialkovskii, V. P. "Uchastie zemstva i promyshlennykh predpriiatii v bor'be s kholernoi epidemiei." *Vrachebno-sanitarnaia khronika Ekaterinoslavskoi gubernii*, no. 5 (May 1910), pp. 507–19.

Flerovskii, N. [V. V. Bervyi]. *Polozhenie rabochego klassa v Rossii*. Moscow: Gosudarstvennoe sotsial'noe-ekonomicheskoe izdatel'stvo, 1938.

Fomin, P. I. *Gornaia i gornozavodskaia promyshlennost' iuga Rossii*. 2 vols. Kharkov, 1915.

Gapeev, A. "K voprosu o roli Kuznetskogo Basseina v ekonomicheskoi zhizni Rossii." *Biulleten' vysshogo soveta narodnogo khoziaistva*, no. 2 (1918), pp. 49–56.

Gaponenko, L. S. "K voprosu o chislennosti promyshlennogo proletariata v Rossii nakanune oktiabria." *Istoricheskii arkhiv*, no. 5 (1961), pp. 158–65.

———. *Rabochii klass Rossii v 1917 godu*. Moscow: Nauka, 1970.

———, et al. "Chislennost' i sostav naseleniia Rossii nakanune velikoi oktiabr'skoi sotsialisticheskoi revoliutsii." *Istoricheskii arkhiv*, no. 5 (1962), pp. 57–81.

Gargaev, N. I. "V riadakh krasnoi gvardii." In Rodichev, *Rasskazy o velikikh dniakh*, pp. 96–103.

Garshin, E. M. "Poezdka na Iuzovskii zavod i poputnyia zametki o tekhnicheskom obrazovanii v Donetskom kamennougol'nom raione." In *Trudy komissii po tekhnicheskomu obrazovaniiu, 1890–1891*, pt. 3, pp. 1–49. St. Petersburg, 1891.

Gerasimovich, I. *Golod na Ukraini*. N.p.: Goverlia, 1973.

Gessen, Iu. *Istoriia evreiskogo naselenie v Rossii*. 2 vols. Leningrad, 1925–27.

Glivits, I. *Potreblenie zheleza v Rossii*. St. Petersburg, 1913.

———. *Zheleznaia promyshlennost' v Rossii*. St. Petersburg, 1911.

Golovanov, D. D., and V. P. Ivanov. "O voznikovenii i deiatel'nosti proizvodstvennykh iacheek v Donbasse i na Urale." *Istoricheskii arkhiv*, no. 6 (1961), pp. 118–28.

Goncharenko, N. *Bor'ba za ukreplenie vlasti sovetov v Donbasse*. Lugansk: Luganskoe oblastnoe izdatel'stvo, 1963.

———. *Sovety Donbassa v 1917 g*. Stalino: Stalinskoe oblastnoe izdatel'stvo, 1957.

Gonimov, I. A. *Staraia Iuzovka*. Moscow: Sovetskii pisatel', 1967.

Gor'kii, M. "O pisateliakh samouchkakh." *Sovremennyi mir* (February 1911), pp. 178–209.

Gorno-tekhnicheskii otdel' TsPKP. "Pod"em i podzemnaia otkatka v kamennougol'noi promyshlennosti Donbassa." *Narodnoe khoziaistvo* (October 10, 1921).

"Gornozavodskoe delo v minuvshem godu." *Gornyi zhurnal*, no. 1 (1875), pp. 1–38.

Grave, B. B. *Burzhuaziia nakanune fevral'skoi revoliutsii*. Moscow and Leningrad: Gosizdat, 1927.

———. *K istorii klassovoi bor'by v Rossii*. Moscow and Leningrad: Gosizdat, 1926.

Grigorenko, P. *V podpol'e mozhno vstretit' tol'ko krys*. New York: Detinets, 1981.

Gritsenko, A. P. *Robitnichii klas Ukraini i zhovtnevii revoliutsii*. Kiiv: Naukova dumka, 1975.

Gukovskii, A. "Frantsuzskaia interventsiia na iuge Rossii (1918–1919)." *Proletarskaia revoliutsiia*, no. 6 (53) (1926), pp. 60–92; no. 7 (54) (1926), pp. 90–121.

Iakovlev, N. N. *Vooruzhennye vosstaniia v dekabre 1905g*. Moscow: Politizdat, 1957.

Islavin, V. "Obzor kamennougol'noi i zhelezodelatel'noi promyshlennosti Donetskago kriazha." *Gornyi zhurnal*, no. 1 (1875), pp. 39–95.

Ivanov, L. M. "K voprosu o formirovanii proletariata Ukrainy." *Voprosy istorii*, no. 6 (1957), pp. 137–46.

———. "Pod"em massovogo dvizheniia gornozavodskikh rabochikh Donbassa, letom 1906." In *Iz istorii razvitiia rabochego klassa i revoliutsionnogo dvizheniia*, pp. 354–70. Moscow: Izdatel'stvo akademii nauk, 1958.

———. "Preemstvennost' fabrichno-zavodskogo truda i formirovanie proletariata v Rossii." In Ivanov, *Rabochii klass*.

———, ed. *Rabochii klass i rabochee dvizhenie v Rossii, 1861–1917*. Moscow: Nauka, 1966.

Ivanov, L. M., and M. S. Volin, eds. *Istoriia rabochego klassa Rossii, 1861–1900*. Moscow: Nauka, 1972.

Kaminskii, M. "Sotsial'noe strakhovanie na Ukraine (10.23–3.24)." *Vestnik profdvizheniia Ukrainy*, no. 46 (September 15, 1924), pp. 43–50.

Kavraiskii, N. "Rudnichnaia rel'sovaia otkatka liud'mi s tochki zreniia khoziaistvennoi, s prilozheniem tablitsy normal'nogo truda otkatchika." *Gornyi zhurnal*, no. 1 (1871), pp. 185–97.

Kazimirchuk, P. "Revoliutsionnoe dvizhenie v Gorlovo-Shcherbinovskom raione Donbassa." *Letopis' revoliutsii*, no. 3 (1923), pp. 41–69; no. 4 (1923), pp. 123–30.

Keppen, A. "Materialy dlia istorii gornogo dela na iuge Rossii." *Gornozavodskii listok*, no. 24 (1898). First part of a lengthy series that continued irregularly in this journal until 1902.

———. "Smertel'nye sluchai v kopiakh, rudnikakh, i kamennolomniakh raznykh stran." *Gorno-zavodskii listok*, no. 2 (1899), pp. 3643–46.

———, ed. *Istoriko-statisticheskii obzor promyshlennosti Rossii: Gruppa 4, Gornaia i solianaia promyshlennost'*. St. Petersburg, 1882.

Kharechko, Trofim. "Bor'ba za oktiabr' v Donbasse." *Letopis' revoliutsii*, nos. 5–6 (26–27) (1927), pp. 130–61.

———. "Nakanune fevral'skoi revoliutsii v Donbasse." *Letopis' revoliutsii*, no. 4 (25) (1927), pp. 164–85.

———. *1905 god v Donbasse*. Leningrad: Priboi, 1926.

———. "Otvet kritikam." *Letopis' revoliutsii*, no. 1 (28) (1928), pp. 342–48.

———. "Sotsial-demokraticheskii soiuz gornozavodskikh rabochikh." *Letopis' revoliutsii*, no. 3 (12) (1925), pp. 5–49.

Kharitonov, V. L. "Fevral'skaia revoliutsiia v Ukraine." *Voprosy istorii*, no. 3 (1987), pp. 70–77.

Khlystov, I. P. *Don v epokhu kapitalizma*. Rostov na Donu: Izdatel'stvo Rostovskogo universiteta, 1962.

Khoziaistvennye itogi 1923–1924 goda i perspektivy na 1924–1925 god. Leningrad: Gosizdat, 1925.

Kir'ianov, Iu. I. *Rabochie iuga Rossii (1914–fevral' 1917)*. Moscow: Nauka, 1971.

———. *Zhiznennyi uroven' rabochikh Rossii: Konets XIX nachalo XX v*. Moscow: Nauka, 1979.

Kogan, E. S. "K voprosu o formirovanii proletariata v Donbasse." In *Istoriko-bytovye ekspeditsii 1951–1953*, ed. A. M. Pankratova, pp. 68–80. Moscow: Kul'turno-prosvetitel'naia literatura, 1955.

Kolodub, E. *Trud i zhizn' gornorabochikh*. 2d ed. Moscow, 1907.

Kolpenskii, V. "Kholernyi bunt v 1892 godu." *Arkhiv istorii truda v Rossii*, no. 3 (1922), pp. 105–13.

Kondufor, Iu. Iu., ed. *Istoriia rabochikh Donbassa*. Vol. 1. Kiev: Naukova dumka, 1981.

Kontrakty zakliuchennye 27 iiulia 1892g. St. Peterburgskim komitetom s vremennym upravleniem kazennykh zheleznykh dorog. St. Petersburg, 1892.

Korbut, M. "Strakhovaia kampaniia 1912–1914 gg." *Proletarskaia revoliutsiia*, no. 2 (73) (1928), pp. 90–117.

Koshik, A. K. *Rabochee dvizhenie na Ukraine v gody pervoi mirovoi voiny i fevral'skoi revoliutsii*. Kiev, 1965.

Ko——v, A. "Ocherki Donetskogo Basseina." *Utro iuga* (June 21, 1915).

Kozhanyi, P. "Zhilishchnyi vopros." *Voprosy truda*, no. 10 (1924), pp. 56–60.

Krasnov, P. N. "Vsevelikoe voisko-Donskoe." *Arkhiv Russkoi revoliutsii* (Berlin) 5 (1922), pp. 191–231.

Krut, V. "Proletariat Ukrainy v bor'be s Germanskim imperializmom i getmanshchinoi." *Istoriia proletariata SSSR*, no. 3 (19) (1934), pp. 97–130.

Kulakov, A. A. "'Narodnaia volia' na iuge v polovine 80-kh gg." In *Narodovol'tsy*, vol. 1, pp. 140–44. Moscow: Katorga i ssylka, 1928.

Kuranov, G. "Sovety na Artemovshchine mezhdu fevralem i oktiabrem 1917 goda." *Letopis' revoliutsii*, nos. 5–6 (26–27) (1927), pp. 162–89.

Kurkin, L. I. *Zemskaia sanitarnaia statistika*. Moscow, 1904.

K——vich. "Zabastovochnoe dvizhenie rabochikh v Rossii v 1905 g." *Vestnik finansov, promyshlennosti i torgovli*, no. 35 (1905), pp. 336–39.

Larskii, I. "Protsent levy i protsent pravy." *Sovremennyi mir*, no. 7 (1908), pp. 81–95.

Lenin, V. I. *Sochineniia*. 4th ed. Moscow: Politizdat, 1951.

Leont'ev, V. V. *Ob izuchenii polozheniia rabochikh*. St. Petersburg, 1912.

Lesnoi, V. M. *Sotsialisticheskaia revoliutsiia i gosudarstvennyi apparat*. Moscow, 1968.

Levus [pseud.]. "Iz istorii revoliutsionnogo dvizheniia v Donetskom Basseine." In *Narodnoe delo*, vol. 3, pp. 43–84. Paris, 1909.

Liashchenko, I. I. "Usloviia truda na rudnikakh Donetskogo Basseina." *Obshchestvennyi vrach'*, no. 2 (1914), pp. 269–78; no. 3 (1914), pp. 422–38.

———. "Zhilishchnyi vopros na gorno-promyshlennykh predpriiatiiakh Donetskogo Basseina i dannie obsledovaniia zhilishch rabochikh Obshchestva iuzhno-Russkoi kamenno-ugol'noi promyshlennosti." In Astrakhan, *Trudy vtorogo vserossiiskogo s"ezda*, vol. 2, pp. 254–83.

Liberman, L. A. "Usloviia truda gornorabochikh v Donetskom Basseine." *Vestnik fabrichnogo zakonodatel'stva i professional'noi gigieny*, no. 1 (1905), pp. 1–28.

———. *V ugol'nom tsarstve*. Petrograd, 1918.

Livshitz, A. "Letnaia bezrabotitsa i bor'ba s nei." *Vestnik profdvizheniia Ukrainy*, no. 47 (September 30, 1924), pp. 35–37.

Livshitz, S. "Kazanskaia sotsial-demokraticheskaia organizatsiia v 1905 g." *Proletarskaia revoliutsiia*, no. 3 (15) (1923), pp. 92–178.

Los', F. E. "Dekabr'skoe vooruzhennoe vosstanie na Ukraine." *Istoricheskie zapiski*, no. 4 (49) (1954), pp. 53–85.

———. *Istoriia robitnichogo klasi ukrainskoi RsR*. 2 vols. Kiiv: Naukova dumka, 1967.

Lozinski, Z. "Vremennoe pravitel'stvo v 'bor'be' s promyshlennom razrukhoi." *Proletarskaia revoliutsiia*, no. 10 (69) (1927), pp. 138–65; no. 11 (70) (1927), pp. 103–39.

Lukomskaia, I. M. "Formirovanie promyshlennogo proletariata Donbassa 70-e, nachalo 80-kh godov XIX v." In *Iz istorii razvitiia rabochego klassa i revoliutsionnogo dvizheniia*, pp. 290–307. Moscow, Izdatel'stvo akademii nauk, 1958.

M., V. "Mestnoe sotsial'noe strakhovanie v Donbasse." *Vestnik profdvizheniia Ukrainy*, no. 46 (September 15, 1924), pp. 55–57.

Maksimov, A. "Revoliutsionnaia volna." *Donbass*, no. 1 (January–February 1962), pp. 135–39.

Martynova, M. "Agrarnoe dvizhenie v 1917g." *Krasnyi arkhiv*, no. 14 (1926), pp. 182–226.

Materialy k izucheniiu rabochego voprosa. St. Petersburg: Ministry of Finance, 1905.

"Mestnye organizatsii RSDRP(b) nakanune VI s"ezda partii." *Voprosy istorii KPSS*, no. 2 (1957), pp. 104–19.

Metallopromyshlennost' respubliki i ee nuzhdy. Moscow: VSNKh, 1921.

Mevius, A. F. "Obzor postepennogo razvitiia gornogo promysla na iuge Rossii." *Iuzhno-Russkii gornyi listok*, no. 2 (1880), pp. 17–20.

Mikhailik, I., and L. Vysotskaia. "Nerushimaia druzhba." *Donbass*, no. 1 (January–February 1962), pp. 128–34.

Mikhailov, I. "Nashy parovozy i vagony." *Narodnoe khoziaistvo*, nos. 5–6 (1920), pp. 2–7.

Mints, I. I. "Obrazovanie sovetov (fev.–mart 1917)." *Istoriia SSSR*, no. 1 (1967), pp. 3–17.

Modestov, V. *Rabochee i professional'noe dvizhenie v Donbasse do velikoi oktiabr'skoi sotsialisticheskoi revoliutsii*. Moscow: Profizdat, 1957.

Moiseenko, P. A. *Vospominaniia, 1873–1923*. Moscow: Krasnyi nov', 1924.

———. *Vospominaniia starogo revoliutsionera*. Moscow, 1966.

Morskoi, A. *Zubatovshchina*. Moscow, 1913.

Moshinskii, I. N. "K voprosu o S-D (Donetskom) soiuze gornozavodskikh rabochikh." *Proletarskaia revoliutsiia*, no. 5 (64) (1927), pp. 229–37.

M——v, I. "Zhilishchnyi vopros v rudnom i margantsevom raionakh Donbassa." *Vestnik profdvizheniia Ukrainy*, no. 46 (September 15, 1924), pp. 27–29.

Myshkis, Kh. "K materialam o Donetsko-Krivorozhskoi respublike." *Letopis' revoliutsii*, no. 3 (30) (1928), pp. 245–49.

Naperstock, V. "K perezakliucheniiu koldogovorov s Donuglem." *Vestnik profdvizheniia Ukrainy*, no. 47 (September 30, 1924), pp. 24–25.

Nesterov, D. "Rabochie organizatsii iuga v 1914 godu." *Letopis' revoliutsii*, no. 5 (1926), pp. 152–61.

Nikolaenko, I. "Pamiati tovarishcha (materialy k biografii Iuriia Lutovinova)." *Letopis' revoliutsii*, no. 3 (12) (1925), pp. 181–88.

Nikol'skii, V. "Sto sem' nomerov 'Diktatury'." *Vechernii Donetsk* (May 1, 1990), p. 2.

"1918–1919gg. v profdvizhenii Ukrainy: Doklad vseukrainskogo tsentral'nogo soveta profsoiuzov pervomu vseukrainskomu s"ezdu profsoiuzov." *Vestnik profdvizheniia Ukrainy*, no. 46 (September 15, 1924), supp.

Novopolin, G. "Iz istorii tsarskikh isprav." *Katorga i ssylka*, no. 5 (78) (1931), pp. 101–19.

———. "V mire predatel'stva." *Letopis' revoliutsii*, no. 4 (1923), pp. 23–40.

Novorossiiskoe obshchestvo, Iuzovka, Ekaterinoslavskoi gubernii. Ekaterinoslav, 1910.

Novorossiiskoe obshchestvo, Iuzovka, Ekaterinoslavskoi gubernii. Iuzovka: N.R.O. Typography, 1919.

Ol', P. V. *Inostrannye kapitaly v Rossii*. Petrograd, 1922.

Orlov, D. I., ed. *Trudy pervogo vserossiiskogo s"ezda fabrichnykh vrachei i predstavitelei fabrichno-zavodskoi promyshlennosti*. 2 vols. Moscow, 1910.

Ossinskii-Obolenskii, V. "Polozhenie Donetskoi kamennougol'noi promyshlennosti i nashi zadachi." *Biulleten' vysshogo soveta narodnogo khoziaistva*, no. 1 (1918), pp. 34–41.

——— "Tezisy ob organizatsii proizvodstva v Donbasse." *Narodnoe khoziaistvo*, no. 2 (1918), pp. 29–30.

Ostrogorskii, M. "Sh. A. Gruzman." *Letopis' revoliutsii*, 5–6 (26–27) (1927), pp. 371–73.

———. "Stranichki iz istorii bor'by za oktiabre v Donbasse (pamiati Sh. Gruzmana-Aleksandr)." *Katorga i ssylka*, no. 5 (90) (1932), pp. 7–37.

"Otchet o deiatel'nosti Glavuglia za avgust, sentiabr', oktiabr' 1920 goda." *Gornoe delo*, no. 5 (1920), pp. 177–82.

Pankratova, A. M. *Fabzavkomy i profsoiuzy v revoliutsii 1917 goda*. Moscow and Leningrad: Gosizdat, 1927.

Parasun'ko, Olga A. *Polozhenie i bor'ba rabochego klassa Ukrainy (60–90 g. XIX v)*. Kiev, 1963.

Pasiuk, A. N. "Rabochee dvizhenie na predpriiatiiakh Novorossiiskogo Obshchestva (1872–1905)," *Letopis' revoliutsii*, no. 3 (24) (1927), pp. 199–219.

Pavlov, M. A. *Vospominaniia metallurga*. Moscow: Gosudarstvennoe nauchno-tekhnicheskoe izdatel'stvo literatury po chernyi i tsvetnoi metallurgii, 1949.

Pazhitnov, K. A. "Ocherk razvitiia rabochei potrebitel'skoi kooperatsii." *Trud v Rossii*, no. 1 (1924), pp. 205–14.

———. *Polozhenie rabochego klassa v Rossii*. 2d ed., rev. and enl. St. Petersburg: Obshchestvennaia polza, 1908. Reprint, 2 vols. Leningrad, 1925. All cites are to the 1908 ed.

———. "Prodolzhitel'nost' rabochego dnia v razlichnykh otrasliakh russkoi promyshlennosti ran'she i teper'." *Vestnik finansov, promyshlennosti i torgovli*, no. 25 (1908), pp. 466–67.

———. "Rabochie arteli." *Arkhiv istorii truda v Rossii*, no. 10 (1923), pp. 54–74.

———. *Razvitiie sotsialisticheskikh idei v Rossii*. Petrograd: Byloe, 1922.

———. "Zarabotnaia plata v raznykh otriasliakh russkoi promyshlennosti." *Vestnik finansov, promyshlennosti i torgovli*, no. 32 (1908), pp. 192–95.

"Perepiska G. I. Petrovskogo s Donbasskimi i Ekaterinoslavskimi rabochami." *Letopis' revoliutsii*, no. 5 (1926), pp. 131–51.

Petrishchev, A. "Khroniki vnutrennoi zhizni." *Russkoe bogatstvo*, no. 8 (1910), pp. 69–94.

Petropavlovskii, N. E. [S. Karonin, pseud.]. *Ocherki Donetskogo Basseina*. Moscow: Khudozhestvennaia literatura, 1958.

Petrovskii, G. I. "Oktiabr' v Donbasse." In Rodichev, *Rasskazy o velikikh dniakh*, pp. 5–10.

———. "O revoliutsionnykh sobytiiakh 1917 g." In *Pobeda velikoi oktiabr'skoi sotsialisticheskoi revoliutsii*, pp. 245–59. Moscow: Politicheskaia literatura, 1958.

Pliukhina, M. A., and L. E. Shepelev. "Ob ekonomicheskoi polozhenii Rossii nakanune velikoi oktiabr'skoi sotsialisticheskoi revoliutsii." *Istoricheskii arkhiv*, no. 2 (1957), pp. 167–77.

Pokrovskii, P. "Kak zhivet Donetskii shakhter." *Russkoe bogatstvo*, no. 12 (1913), pp. 241–60.

Ponomarenko, G. Ia., ed. *Donetskii politekhnicheskii*. Donetsk: Izdatel'stvo Donbass, 1969.

Posse, V. A. *Rabochie stachki*. St. Petersburg: Biblioteka rabochego, 1906.

Postriganov, V. G., ed. *Metallurgicheskaia promyshlennost' iuga Rossii*. Kharkov, 1923.

———. *Metallurgicheskie zavody iuga Rossii*. Kharkov, 1923.

Potolov, S. I. "Iz istorii monopolizatsii ugol'noi promyshlennosti Donbassa v kontse XIX v." In *Iz istorii imperializma v Rossii*, ed. M. D. Viatkin, pp. 6–25. Leningrad: Akademiia nauk, 1959.

———. *Rabochie Donbassa v XIX veke*. Moscow and Leningrad: Izdatel'stvo akademii nauk, 1963.

———. *Rozhdenie velikana*. Donetsk: Izdatel'stvo Donbass, 1972.

Prasolov, A., and M. Gofman. "Tiazhelaia industriia Donbassa v 1-m polugodii 1921 g. " *Narodnoe khoziaistvo*, no. 10 (1921), pp. 51–71.

Promyshlennost' SSSR v 1924 g. Moscow: VSNKh, 1925.

Rabochee dvizhenie v Ekaterinoslave. Geneva: Izdanie soiuza Russkikh sotsial-demokratov, 1900.

Ragozin, E. I. *Zhelezo i ugol' na iuge Rossii*. St. Petersburg, 1895.

Rashin, A. G. *Formirovanie promyshlennogo proletariata v Rossii*. Moscow: Sotsekgiz, 1940.

———. *Formirovanie rabochego klassa v Rossii*. Moscow: Izdatel'stvo sotsial'no-ekonomicheskoi literatury, 1958.

———. *Naselenie Rossii za 100 let*. Moscow: Gosstatizdat, 1956.

———. "O chislennosti i territorial'nom razmeshchennii rabochikh Rossii v periode kapitalizma." *Istoricheskie zapiski*, no. 4 (44) (1954), pp. 126–81.

Razanov, E. "Takim bylo nachalo." *Vechernii Donetsk* (June 11, 1990).

Retivov, M. I. "Organizatsiia protivokholernykh meropriiatii i lechenie kholernykh bolnykh na ugol'nykh rudnikakh T——va dlia razrabotki kamennoi soli i uglia v iuzhnoi Rossii." In Orlov, *Trudy pervogo vserossiiskogo s"ezda*, vol. 1, pp. 68–87.

Rodichev, N., ed. *Rasskazy o velikikh dniakh*. Stalino: Stalinskoe Oblastnoe knizhnoe izdatel'stvo, 1957.

Russkaia promyshlennost' v 1922 godu. Petrograd: VSNKh, n.d.

Savel'ev, M. "Polozhenie metallurgicheskoi promyshlennosti." *Biulleten' vysshogo soveta narodnogo khoziaistva*, no. 1 (1918), pp. 41–46.

Semenov-Bulkin, F. "Ekonomicheskaia bor'ba rabochikh metallistov v 1905–1906 gg." *Trud v Rossii*, no. 1 (1925), pp. 3–17.

Sharyi, V. "Metallicheskaia promyshlennost'." *Ekonomicheskoe obozrenie* (February 1925), pp. 59–65.

Shekhter-Minor, A. "Iuzhno-Russkaia narodovolcheskaia organizatsiia." In *Narodovol'tsy*, vol. 1, pp. 131–39. Moscow: Katorga i ssylka, 1928.

Shestakov, A. V. "Na zare rabochego dvizheniia v Donbasse." *Proletarskaia revoliutsiia*, no. 1 (1921), pp. 156–64.

Shidlovskii, G. "Pamiati Semena Savel'evich Parizhera." *Katorga i ssylka*, no. 4 (89) (1932), pp. 113–15.

Shklovskii, G. "Perepiska Ekaterinoslavskoi i Luganskoi organizatsii s N. Leninom i N. K. Krupskoi." *Proletarskaia revoliutsiia*, no. 4 (51) (1926), pp. 5–45.

Shlosberg, D. "Iz istorii ekonomicheskoi bor'by rabochikh v Donbasse, fevral'–oktiabr' 1917 goda." *Letopis' revoliutsii*, no. 2 (23) (1927), pp. 189–203.

———. "Pervye shagi profstroitel'stva v Donbasse." *Letopis' revoliutsii*, no. 3 (24) (1927), pp. 227–39; no. 4 (25) (July–August 1927), pp. 207–34.

———. "Profsoiuzy v bor'be za Oktiabr'." *Letopis' revoliutsii*, nos. 5–6 (1927), pp. 317–30.

Shmidt, V. "Polozhenie del v Donetskom Basseine." *Vestnik narodnogo komissariata truda*, no. 1 (1918), pp. 145–50.

Shmorgun, P. M. "Sovety rabochikh deputatov na Ukraine v 1905 godu." *Istoricheskie zapiski*, no. 4 (49) (1954), pp. 21–52.

Shreider, Gr. "Ocherki kustarnoi gornoi promyshlennosti." *Russkaia mysl'*, no. 10 (October 1889), pp. 45–85.

Sidorov, A. L. *Ekonomicheskoe polozhenie Rossii v gody pervoi mirovoi voiny*. Moscow: Nauka, 1973.

Silenko, A. F. *V. V. Veresaev*. Tula: Tul'skoe knizhnoe izdatel'stvo, 1956.

Skarubskii, A. "Arteli kak forma bor'by s bezrabotitsei podrostkov." *Vestnik profdvizheniia Ukrainy*, no. 47 (September 30, 1924), pp. 66–69.

Sliozberg, G. B. *Dela minuvshikh dnei*. 3 vols. Paris, 1933–34.

———. *Dorevoliutsionnyi stroi Rossii*. Paris, 1933.

Smidovich, A. L. "K voprosu ob epidemiologii kholery." *Obshchestvennyi vrach'*, no. 1 (1911), pp. 7–18.

Smidovich, P. G. "Rabochie massy v 90-kh godakh." *Proletarskaia revoliutsiia*, no. 1 (36) (1925), pp. 161–66.

Smirnov, A. "O pervom kruzhke sotsial-demokraticheskoi rabochei partii goroda Ekaterinoslava v 1894 g." *Proletarskaia revoliutsiia*, no. 7 (1922), pp. 161–65.

Smirnov, P. "Pervaia zabastovka na Druzhkovskom zavode v Donbasse," *Katorga i ssylka*, no. 5 (78) (1931), pp. 89–100.

Stanislavskii, V. M. "K voprosu o sanitarnykh usloviiakh zhilishch gornorabochikh Donetskogo Basseina." *Vrachebno-sanitarnaia khronika Ekaterinoslavskoi gubernii*, no. 10 (1909).

Stepanov, N. "Pamiati A. L. Smidovicha." *Obshchestvennyi vrach'*, no. 2 (1916), pp. 121–26.

Stopani, A. "Eshche ob osobennostiakh nashikh zabastovok." *Voprosy truda*, nos. 7–8 (1924), pp. 38–43.

Sukenikov, M. "Evreiskaia samooborona." *Voskhod*, nos. 42–43 (October 27, 1905), pp. 57–58.

Surozhskii, P. "Krai uglia i zheleza." *Sovremennik*, no. 4 (1913), pp. 292–312.

Sviatlovskii, V. V. *Kharkovskii fabrichnyi okrug-otchet za 1885g*. St. Petersburg: Ministry of Finance, 1886.

———. *Professional'noe dvizhenie v Rossii*. St. Petersburg, 1907.

———. *Zhilishchnyi vopros*. 4 vols. St. Petersburg: Ministerstvo putei soobshchenii, 1902.

"Svod pokazanii dannykh nekotorymi iz arestovannykh po delam o gosudarstvennykh prestupleniiakh." *Byloe*, no. 8 (1909), pp. 89–123.

T., P. [P. Timofeev]. "Zavodnye budni." *Russkoe bogatstvo*, no. 8 (1903), pp. 30–53; no. 9 (1903), pp. 175–99.

Taskin, E. "K voprosu o privlechenii i uderzhanii rabochikh na kamennougol'nykh kopiakh Donetskogo Basseina." *Gorno-zavodskii listok*, no. 7 (1899), pp. 3729–32, no. 8 (1899), pp. 3753–55, no. 9 (1899), pp. 3776–78.

Terpigorev. "Rabota kamennougol'nykh basseinov obshchesoiuznogo znacheniia." *Ekonomicheskoe obozrenie*, no. 23 (December 20, 1924), pp. 38–52.

Tolstoi, L. N. "Tsarstvo bozh'e vnutri nas." In *Polnoe sobranie sochinenii*, vol. 28, pp. 250–51. Moscow: Khudozhestvennaia literatura, 1957.

Tomilin, V. N. "Obzor zhelezno-rudnogo raiona Krivogo Roga." *Gornoe delo*, no. 5 (1920), pp. 168–74.

Troshin, A. "Fevral' i oktiabr' v Makeevke." *Letopis' revoliutsii*, no. 4 (13) (1925), pp. 147–54.

Trudy pervogo s"ezda gornozavodskikh, fabrichnykh, i rudnichnykh vrachei Ekaterinoslavskoi gubernii. Ekaterinoslav, 1903.

Trudy vtorogo s"ezda gornozavodskikh, fabrichnykh, i rudnichnykh vrachei Ekaterinoslavskoi gubernii, 21–24.2.1908 g. Ekaterinoslav: Trud, 1908.

Tugan-Baranovskii, M. *Russkaia fabrika v proshlom i nastoiashchem*. 3d ed. St. Petersburg: Nasha zhizn', 1907.

U., V. "Bezhenskii vopros i obshchestvennye organizatsii v Rossii." *Obshchestvennyi vrach'*, no. 2 (1916), pp. 78–92.

Valuev, P. A. *Dnevnik, 1877–1884*. Petrograd: Byloe, 1919.

———. *Politicheskii dnevnik, 1861–1876*. 2 vols. Moscow: Akademiia nauk, 1961.

Vartminski, A. E. "K voprosu o zhilishchnykh usloviiakh gornorabochikh Donetskogo Basseina." *Vrachebno-sanitarnaia khronika Ekaterinoslavskoi gubernii*, nos. 7–9 (1910), pp. 501–14.

Varzar, V. E. *Statistika stachek rabochikh za 1905 god*. St. Petersburg, 1905.

Veresaev, V. V. *Povesti i rasskazy*. Moscow: Khudozhestvennaia literatura, 1956.

———. *Vospominaniia*. 3d rev. ed. Moscow and Leningrad: Gospolitizdat, 1946.

Vilents-Gorovits, E. "Zhilishchnye usloviia rabochikh i neobkhodimye meropriiatiia dlia ikh uluchsheniia." *Voprosy truda*, nos. 5–6 (1924), pp. 76–82.

Vindel'bot, M. "Metallopromyshlennost' v 1920 godu." *Narodnoe khoziaistvo*, no. 4 (1921), pp. 56–72.

Vinokurov, A. N. "Vtoroi s"ezd gornozavodskikh, fabrichnykh, i rudnichnykh vrachei Ekaterinoslavskoi gubernii, 21–24 fevralia 1908g." In Orlov, *Trudy pervogo vserossiiskogo s"ezda*, vol. 2, pp. 428–42.

Vishniakov, I. "K bor'be za diktaturu proletariata v Donbasse," *Letopis' revoliutsii*, no. 2 (29) (1928), pp. 220–33.

Vlasenko, T. S., A. B. Zaks, and E. I. Rozental'. "Formirovanie proletariata v Rossii v kontse XIX, nachale XX v." In *Iz istorii razvitiia rabochego klassa i revoliutsionnogo dvizheniia*, pp. 277–89. Moscow: Izdatel'stvo akademii nauk, 1958.

Volin', Iu. "V tsarstve chernoi zolota." *Birzhevye vedomosti* (January 31, 1917).

Volobuev, P. V., et al. "O periodizatsii rabochego dvizheniia v Rossii." In Ivanov, *Rabochii klass*, pp. 5–57.

Volodin, G. *Po sledam istorii*. Donetsk: Izdatel'stvo Donbass, 1967.

Volosti i vazhneishie seleniia evropeiskoi Rossii. Vol. 8. St. Petersburg, 1886.

Volskii, N. "Grigorii Fedorovich Tkachenko-Petrenko (opyt biografii)." *Letopis' revoliutsii*, no. 3 (24) (1927), pp. 167–224.

von Ditmar, N. F. "Neschastnye sluchai v iuzhnoi gornoi i gornozavodskoi promyshlennosti." In Orlov, *Trudy pervogo vserossiiskogo s"ezda*, vol. 2, pp. 497–526.

———, ed. *Kratkii ocherk istorii s"ezdov gornopromyshlennikov iuga Rossii*. Kharkov, 1908.

———. *Sbornik statisticheskikh svedenii o gornoi promyshlennosti iuzhnoi i iugo-vostochnoi gornykh oblastei Rossii v 1899g*. Kharkov: Statisticheskoe buro soveta s"ezda gornopromyshlennikov iuga Rossii, 1901.

———. *Statistika neschastnykh sluchaev v gornoi i gornozavodskoi promyshlennosti iuzhnoi Rossii za 1903 god i za 1-e polugodie 1904 goda*. Kharkov: Statisticheskoe buro soveta s"ezda gornopromyshlennikov iuga Rossii, 1905.

Voznesenskii, S. "Stachechnaia bor'ba rabochikh v 1870–1914 gg." *Arkhiv istorii truda v Rossii*, no. 8 (1923), pp. 148–74.

Zaitsev, F. I. "Bolsheviki Iuzovki v 1917 godu." In Rodichev, *Rasskazy o velikikh dniakh*, pp. 75–95.

———. "Kak my tvorili oktiabr' (1917–1918 v Iuzovke)." *Letopis' revoliutsii*, no. 4 (13) (1925), pp. 132–46.

———. "Pis'mo v redaktsiiu." *Letopis' revoliutsii*, no. 3 (30) (1928), pp. 367–72.

Zaks, A. B. "Trud i byt' rabochikh Donbassa." In *Istoriko bytovye ekspeditsii 1951–1953*, ed. A. M. Pankratova, pp. 80–108. Moscow: Kul'turno-prosvetitel'naia literatura, 1955.

Zavod Novorossiiskogo obshchestva. St. Petersburg, 1896.

Zemstvo i gornaia promyshlennost'. Kharkov: Sovet s"ezda gornopromyshlennikov iuga Rossii, 1908.

Ziv, V. S. *Inostrannye kapitaly v Russkoi gornozavodskoi promyshlennosti*. Petrograd, 1917.

Zotov, A. *Sposoby mirnogo razresheniia sporov mezhdu predprinimateliami i rabochami*. St. Petersburg, 1902.

Materials in Languages Other Than Russian or Ukrainian

Archives

(Initials in parentheses indicate the abbreviations used in the footnotes.)

American-Jewish Joint Distribution Committee Archive, New York. (JDC)

Archives Nationales, Paris. (AN)

Bakhmeteff Archive of Russian and East European History and Culture, Butler Library, Columbia University, New York.

Companies' House, London.

Credit Lyonnais, Paris. (CL)

Credit du Nord, Paris. (BUP)

Ecole Superieure des Mines, Paris.

Hoover Institution Archives, Stanford, California.
Hughesovka Research Archive, Glamorgan Record Office, Cardiff.
Khrushchev Archive, Harriman Institute, Columbia University.
Nansen Archive, Oslo University Library.
National Library of Wales.
Public Record Office, London.
Zionist Archives, Jerusalem. (ZA)

Documentary Collections, Reference Volumes, Newspapers, and Periodicals

Daniels, Robert V. *A Documentary History of Communism*. 2 vols. New York: Vintage, 1960.

Heilprin, I., comp. *Sefer Hagvura* (in Hebrew). 3 vols. Tel Aviv: Am Oved, 1950.

League of Nations, "Report on Economic Conditions in Russia with Special Reference to the Famine of 1921–1922 and the State of Agriculture." Doc. C. 705 M. 451 1922II [A].

Manchester Guardian.

Meijer, Jan M., ed. *The Trotsky Papers*. 2 vols. The Hague: Mouton, 1964–71.

New York Times.

The Times (London).

Books and Articles

Abramovitch, Raphael R. *The Soviet Revolution*. New York: International Universities Press, 1962.

Adams, Arthur E. *Bolsheviks in the Ukraine: The Second Campaign, 1918–1919*. New Haven: Yale University Press, 1963.

Alexinsky, G. *Modern Russia*. London: T. Fisher Unwin, 1913.

Anderson, Barbara A. *Internal Migration during Modernization in Late-Nineteenth-Century Russia*. Princeton, N.J.: Princeton University Press, 1980.

Anweiler, Oskar. *The Soviets*. New York: Pantheon, 1974.

Aronson, Grigorii, et al. *Die Geshichte fun Bund* (in Yiddish). 4 vols. New York: Undzer Tzeit, 1960.

Atkinson, Dorothy. "The Zemstvo and the Peasantry." In Emmons and Vucinich, *Zemstvo in Russia*, pp. 79–132.

Avrich, Paul, ed. *The Anarchists in the Russian Revolution*. Ithaca, N.Y.: Cornell University Press, 1973.

Baedeker, Karl. *Baedeker's Russia, 1914*. London: George Allen and Unwin, 1971.

Bailes, Kendall E. *Technology and Society under Lenin and Stalin*. Princeton, N.J.: Princeton University Press, 1978.

Baron, Salo W. *The Russian Jew under Tsars and Soviets*. 2d ed. New York: Schocken, 1987.

Bilinsky, Yaroslav. "The Communist Takeover of the Ukraine." In *The Ukraine, 1917–1921: A Study in Revolution*, ed. Taras Hunczak, pp. 104–27. Cambridge, Mass: Harvard University Press, 1977.

Black, Cyril E., ed. *The Transformation of Russian Society*. Cambridge, Mass.: Harvard University Press, 1967.

Bonnell, Victoria E. *Roots of Rebellion: Workers' Politics and Organizations in St. Petersburg and Moscow, 1900–1914*. Berkeley and Los Angeles: University of California Press, 1983.

Boris, Jurij. *The Sovietization of the Ukraine, 1917–1923*. Rev. ed. Edmonton, Alberta: Canadian Institute of Ukrainian Studies, 1980.

Bowen, Emrys G. *John Hughes (Yuzovka)*. Cardiff: University of Wales Press, 1978.

Bradley, Joseph. *Muzhik and Muscovite: Urbanization in Late Imperial Russia*. Berkeley and Los Angeles: University of California Press, 1985.

———. "Voluntary Associations, Civil Culture, and *Obshchestvennost'* in Moscow." In *Between Tsar and People: Educated Society and the Quest for Public Identity in Late Imperial Russia*, ed. Edith W. Clowes, Samuel D. Kassow, and James L. West, pp. 28–37. Princeton, N.J.: Princeton University Press, 1991.

Brooks, Jeffrey. *When Russia Learned to Read: Literacy and Popular Literature, 1861–1917*. Princeton, N.J.: Princeton University Press, 1985.

———. "The Zemstvo and the Education of the People." In Emmons and Vucinich, *Zemstvo in Russia*, pp. 242–78.

Brower, Daniel R. "The City in Danger: The Civil War and the Russian Urban Population." In *Party, State, and Society in the Russian Civil War: Explorations in Social History*, ed. Diane P. Koenker, William G. Rosenberg, and Ronald Grigor Suny, pp. 55–80. Bloomington, Indiana: Indiana University Press.

———. "Labor Violence in Russia in the Late Nineteenth Century." *Slavic Review* 41, no. 3 (Fall 1982), pp. 417–31.

———. "Urban Revolution in the Late Russian Empire." In *The City in Late Imperial Russia*, ed. Michael F. Hamm, pp. 319–53. Bloomington, Ind.: Indiana University Press, 1986.

Carr, Edward H. *The Bolshevik Revolution, 1917–1923*. Vol. 2. Harmondsworth: Penguin, 1966.

———. *The Interregnum, 1923–1924*. Harmondsworth: Pelican, 1969.

———. *Socialism in One Country*. Vol. 2. Baltimore: Penguin, 1979.

Carstensen, Fred V. "Foreign Participation in Russian Economic Life: Notes on British Enterprise 1865–1914," in *Entrepreneurship in Imperial Russia and the Soviet Union*, ed. Gregory Guroff and Fred V. Carstensen, pp. 140–58. Princeton, N.J.: Princeton University Press, 1983.

Chamberlin, William Henry. *The Russian Revolution, 1917–1921*. Vol. 1. New York: Grosset and Dunlap, 1965.

Chapuy, Paul J. "Journal de voyage en Styrie et dans le Bassin du Donetz." Ms. no. 798. Paris: Ecole Supérieure des Mines, 1887.

Conquest, Robert. *The Great Terror*. London: Macmillan, 1968.

Deutscher, Isaac. *The Prophet Unarmed: Trotsky, 1921–1929*. London: Oxford University Press, 1959.

Dobb, Maurice. *Soviet Economic Development since 1917*. Rev. enl. ed. New York: International, 1966.

Edelman, Robert. *Proletarian Peasants: the Revolution of 1905 in the Russian Southwest*. Ithaca, N.Y.: Cornell University Press, 1987.

Elwood, Ralph Carter. *Russian Social Democracy in the Underground*. Assen, the Netherlands: Van Gorcum, 1974.

Emmons, Terence, and Wayne S. Vucinich, eds. *The Zemstvo in Russia: An Experiment in Local Self-Government*. New York and London: Cambridge University Press, 1982.

The Famine in the Ukraine. Berlin: Dietz, 1923.

Fenin, Alexandr I. *Coal and Politics in Late Imperial Russia: Memoirs of a Russian Mining Engineer*. Ed. Susan P. McCaffray, trans. Alexandre Fedaievsky. De Kalb, Ill.: Northern Illinois University Press, 1990.

Fisher, H. H. *The Famine in Soviet Russia, 1919–1923*. New York: Macmillan, 1927.

Friedgut, Theodore H. "Labor Violence and Regime Brutality in Tsarist Russia: The Iuzovka Cholera Riots of 1892." *Slavic Review* 46, no. 2 (Summer 1987), pp. 245–65.

———. "Professional Revolutionaries in the Donbass: The Characteristics and Limitations of the *Apparat*." *Canadian Slavonic Papers* 27, no. 3 (September 1985), pp. 284–300.

Gaventa, John. *Power and Powerlessness*. Urbana, Ill.: University of Illinois Press, 1980.

Gerschenkron, Alexander. "Problems and Patterns of Russian Economic Development." in Black, *Transformation of Russian Society*, pp. 42–72.

Getzler, Israel. *Kronstadt, 1917–1921*. London: Cambridge University Press, 1983.

Gitelman, Zvi Y. *Jewish Nationality and Soviet Politics*. Princeton, N.J.: Princeton University Press, 1972.

Gliksman, Jerzy. "The Russian Urban Worker: From Serf to Proletarian." In Black, *The Transformation of Russian Society*, pp. 311–22.

Guthier, Steven L. "Ukrainian Cities during the Revolution and the Interwar Era." In Rudnitsky, *Rethinking Ukrainian History*, pp. 156–79.

Haimson, Leopold. "The Problem of Social Stability in Urban Russia, 1905–1917." *Slavic Review* 23, no. 4 (Winter 1964), pp. 619–42; 24, no. 1 (Spring 1965), pp. 1–22.

Hamm, Michael F. "The Breakdown of Urban Modernization: A Prelude to the Revolutions of 1917." In *The City in Russian History*, ed. Michael F. Hamm, pp. 182–200. Lexington, Ky.: University Press of Kentucky, 1976.

Hayes, Paul M. *Quisling*. Newton Abbot, England: David and Charles, 1971.

Herlihy, Patricia. "Ukrainian Cities in the Nineteenth Century." In Rudnitsky, *Rethinking Ukrainian History*, pp. 135–55.

Hough, Jerry F., and Merle Fainsod. *How the Soviet Union Is Governed*. Cambridge, Mass.: Harvard University Press, 1979.

Huntington, Samuel P. *Political Order in Changing Societies*. New Haven: Yale University Press, 1968.

Husband, William. "Local Industry in Upheaval: The Ivanovo-Kineshma Textile Strike of 1917." *Slavic Review* 47, no. 3 (Fall 1988), pp. 448–63.

Johnson, Robert E. "Liberal Professionals and Professional Liberals: The Zemstvo Statisticians and Their Work." In Emmons and Vucinich, *Zemstvo in Russia*, pp. 343–63.

———. *Peasant and Proletarian: The Working Class of Moscow in the Late*

Nineteenth Century. New Brunswick, N.J.: Rutgers University Press, 1979.

Kayden, Eugene M., and Alexis N. Antsiferov. *The Cooperative Movement in Russia during the War*. New Haven: Yale University Press, 1929.

Kazdan, Haim S. *Mein Dor* (in Yiddish). New York: Undzer Tzeit, 1977.

Keep, John L. H. *The Russian Revolution: A Study in Mass Mobilization*. New York: W. W. Norton, 1976.

Khrushchev, Nikita S. *Khrushchev Remembers*. Boston: Little, Brown, 1970.

Klausner, I. *Hatnuah Letzion Barussia* (in Hebrew). 3 vols. Jerusalem: Zionist Library, 1965.

Knight, Samuel. "John Hughes and Yuzovka." *Planet* 21 (1974), pp. 35–41.

Koenker, Diane. "Collective Action and Collective Violence in the Russian Labor Movement."*Slavic Review* 41, no. 3 (Fall 1982), pp. 443–48.

———. "Moscow in 1917: The View from Below." In *The Workers' Revolution in Russia, 1917: The View from Below*, ed. Daniel J. Kaiser, pp. 81–97. Cambridge and New York: Cambridge University Press, 1987.

———. *Moscow Workers and the 1917 Revolution*. Princeton, N.J.: Princeton University Press, 1981.

———. "Urbanization and Deurbanization in the Russian Revolution and Civil War." in *Party, State, and Society in the Russian Civil War: Explorations in Social History*, ed. Diane P. Koenker, William G. Rosenberg, and Ronald Grigor Suny. Bloomington, Ind.: Indiana University Press, 1989.

Koenker, Diane P. and William G. Rosenberg, *Strikes and Revolution in Russia, 1917*. Princeton, N.J.: Princeton University Press, 1989.

Krawchenko, Bohdan. "Aperçu de la structure sociale de l'Ukraine avant la revolution de 1917." *Revue des pays de l'est* 26, nos. 1–2 (1976), pp. 137–69.

———. "The Impact of Industrialization on the Social Structure of the Ukraine." *Canadian Slavonic Papers* 22, no. 3 (September 1980), pp. 338–57.

Lane, David. *The Roots of Russian Communism*. Assen, the Netherlands: Van Gorcum, 1969.

Laue, Theodore von. "Russian Peasants in the Factory, 1892–1904." *Journal of Economic History* 21 (1961), pp. 61–80.

Lawrynenko, Juriy. "The Revolutionary Ukrainian Party." Manuscript, Bakhmeteff Archive, Columbia University.

Linden, A., ed. *Die Judenpogrome in Russland.* 2 vols. Cologne and Leipzig, 1910.

McCaffray, Susan P. "The Association of Southern Coal and Steel Producers and the Problems of Industrial Progress in Tsarist Russia." *Slavic Review* 47, no. 2 (Fall 1988), pp. 464–82.

———. "The New Work and the Old Regime: Workers, Managers, and the State in the Coal and Steel Industry of Ekaterinoslav Province, 1905–1914." Ph.D. diss., Duke University, 1983.

———. "Origins of Labor Policy in the Russian Coal and Steel Industry, 1874–1900." *Journal of Economic History* 47 (1987), pp. 951–65.

McDaniel, Tim. *Autocracy, Capitalism, and Revolution in Russia.* Berkeley and Los Angeles: University of California Press, 1988.

McKay, John P. *Pioneers for Profit: Foreign Entrepreneurs and Russian Industrialization, 1885–1913.* Chicago and London: University of Chicago Press, 1970.

McKean, Robert B. *St. Petersburg between the Revolutions.* New Haven: Yale University Press, 1990.

Malet, Nicholas. *Nestor Makhno in the Russian Civil War.* London: Macmillan, 1982.

Mandel, David. *The Petrograd Workers and the Fall of the Old Regime.* London: Macmillan, 1983.

Manning, Roberta Thompson. *The Crisis of the Old Order in Russia: Gentry and Government.* Princeton, N.J.: Princeton University Press, 1982.

Mavor, James. *An Economic History of Russia.* 2 vols. London and Toronto: J. M. Dent and Sons, 1925.

Mendel, Arthur P. "Peasant and Worker on the Eve of the First World War." *Slavic Review* 24, no. 1 (Spring 1965), pp. 23–33.

Monas, Sidney. "The Twilit Middle Class of Nineteenth-Century Russia." in *Between Tsar and People: Educated Society and the Quest for Public Identity in Late Imperial Russia*, ed. Edith W. Clowes, Samuel D. Kassow, and James L. West, pp. 28–37. Princeton, N.J.: Princeton University Press, 1991.

Murphy, Paul J. *Brezhnev: Soviet Politician.* Jefferson, N.C.: McFarland, 1981.

Nie, Norman H., G. Bingham Powell, Jr., and Kenneth Prewitt. "Social Structure and Political Participation: Developmental Relationships." *American Political Science Review* 63, no. 2 (June 1969), pp. 361–78.

Nove, Alec. *An Economic History of the USSR*. Harmondsworth: Penguin, 1972.

Osherovich, Mendel. *Shtet un Shtetlekh in Ukraine* (in Yiddish). 2 vols. New York, 1948.

Owen, Thomas C. *Capitalism and Politics in Russia: A Social History of the Moscow Merchants 1855–1905*. New York: Cambridge University Press, 1981.

———. "Impediments to a Bourgeois Consciousness in Russia, 1880–1905: The Estate Structure, Ethnic Diversity, and Economic Regionalism." In *Between Tsar and People: Educated Society and The Quest for Public Identity in Late Imperial Russia*, ed. Edith W. Clowes, Samuel D. Kassow, and James L. West, pp. 75–89. Princeton, N.J.: Princeton University Press, 1991.

Paustovsky, Konstantin. *Slow Approach of Thunder*. London: Harvill, 1965.

Perlman, Selig. *A Theory of the Labor Movement*. New York: Augustus Kelley, 1949.

Pistrak, Lazar. *The Grand Tactician: Khrushchev's Rise to Power*. New York: Praeger, 1961.

Pourcel, Auguste. "Memoir sur les recents développements de l'industrie houillère au Donetz et la mine de Chtcherbinovka." Ms. no. 2041. Paris: Ecole Supérieure des Mines, 1897.

Quisling, Vidkun. "Famine Situation in Ukraina." Typescript, March 30, 1922. MS. fol. 1988: RU3 B, Nansen Archive, Oslo University Library.

Rabinowitch, Alexander. *Prelude to Revolution: The Petrograd Bolsheviks and the July 1917 Uprising*. Bloomington, Ind.: University of Indiana Press, 1968.

Radkey, Oliver H. *Russia Goes to the Polls: The Election to the All-Russian Constituent Assembly, 1917*. Ithaca, N.Y.: Cornell University Press, 1990.

Raleigh, Donald J. *Revolution on the Volga: 1917 in Saratov*. Ithaca, N.Y., and London: Cornell University Press, 1986.

Rassweiler, Anne D. *The Generation of Power: The History of Dneprostroi*. New York and Oxford: Oxford University Press, 1988.

Reshetar, John S., Jr. "The Communist Party of the Ukraine and Its Role in the Ukrainian Revolution." In *The Ukraine, 1917–1921: A Study in*

Revolution, ed. Taras Hunczak, pp. 159–85. Cambridge, Mass.: Harvard University Press, 1977.

———. *The Ukrainian Revolution, 1917–1920*. Princeton, N.J.: Princeton University Press, 1952.

Rieber, Alfred J. "Bureaucratic Politics in Imperial Russia." *Social Science History* 2, no. 4 (Summer 1978), pp. 399–413.

———. *Merchants and Entrepreneurs in Imperial Russia*. Chapel Hill, N.C.: University of North Carolina Press, 1982.

Rigby, T. H. *Communist Party Membership in the USSR, 1917–1967*. Princeton, N.J.: Princeton University Press, 1968.

Roosa, Ruth A. "Russian Industrialists during World War I: The Interaction of Economics and Politics." In *Entrepreneurship in Imperial Russia and the Soviet Union*, ed. Gregory Guroff and Fred V. Carstensen, pp. 159–87. Princeton, N.J.: Princeton University Press, 1983.

Rosenberg, William G. "Conclusion: Understanding the Russian Revolution." In *The Workers' Revolution in Russia, 1917: The View from Below*, ed. Daniel J. Kaiser, pp. 132–41. Cambridge and New York: Cambridge University Press, 1987.

Rosenboim, M. M. *Zikhronotav shel sotsialist-revoliutsioner* (in Hebrew). Tel Aviv: Omanuth, 1935.

Rudé, George. *The Crowd in History*. New York, London, and Sydney: John Wiley and Sons, 1964.

Rudnitsky, Ivan L., ed. *Rethinking Ukrainian History*. Edmonton, Alberta: Canadian Institute of Ukrainian Studies, 1981.

Sablinsky, Walter. *The Road to Bloody Sunday*. Princeton, N.J.: Princeton University Press, 1976.

Schapiro, Leonard B. *The Communist Party of the Soviet Union*. London: Methuen, 1963.

Shanin, Teodor. *Russia as a Developing Society*. Vol. 1. London: Macmillan, 1985.

Shipler, David K. *Russia: Broken Idols, Solemn Dreams*. New York: New York Times Books, 1983.

Siegelbaum, Lewis H. *Soviet State and Society between Revolutions, 1918–1929*. Cambridge: Cambridge University Press, 1992.

Sullivant, Robert S. *Soviet Politics and the Ukraine, 1917–1957*. New York: Columbia University Press, 1962.

Thiede, Roger L. "Industry and Urbanization in New Russia from 1860 to

1910." In *The City in Russian History*, ed. Michael F. Hamm, pp. 125–38. Lexington, Ky.: University Press of Kentucky, 1976.

Tomiline, S. A. *L'hygiène publique dans la population rurale de l'Ukraine*. Geneva: League of Nations, 1925.

Trotsky, L. D. *The History of the Russian Revolution*. London: Victor Gollancz, 1934.

Wallace, Anthony F. C. *The Social Context of Innovation*. Princeton, N.J.: Princeton University Press, 1982.

Weber, Eugen. *Peasants into Frenchmen*. London: Chatto and Windus, 1977.

Weissman, Neil B. *Reform in Tsarist Russia*. New Brunswick, N.J.: Rutgers University Press, 1981.

Westwood, J. N. "John Hughes and Russian Metallurgy." *Economic History Review*, 2d ser., 17 (1965), pp. 564–69.

Wildman, Allan K. *The Making of a Workers' Revolution*. Chicago and London: University of Chicago Press, 1967.

Wynn, Charters. *Workers, Strikes, and Pogroms: The Donbass-Dnepr Bend in Late Imperial Russia, 1870–1905*. Princeton, N.J.: Princeton University Press, 1992.

Zelnik, Reginald E. *Labor and Society in Tsarist Russia: The Factory Workers of St. Petersburg, 1855–1870*. Stanford: Stanford University Press, 1971.

INDEX

Studies of the Harriman Institute

Soviet National Income in 1937 by Abram Bergson, Columbia University Press, 1953.

Through the Glass of Soviet Literature: Views of Russian Society, Ernest Simmons Jr., ed., Columbia University Press, 1953.

Polish Postwar Economy by Thad Paul Alton, Columbia University Press, 1954.

Management of the Industrial Firm in the USSR: A Study in Soviet Economic Planning by David Granick, Columbia University Press, 1954.

Soviet Policies in China, 1917–1924 by Allen S. Whiting, Columbia University Press, 1954; paperback, Stanford University Press, 1968.

Literary Politics in the Soviet Ukraine, 1917–1934 by George S. N. Luckyj, Columbia University Press, 1956.

The Emergence of Russian Panslavism, 1856–1870 by Michael Boro Petrovich, Columbia University Press, 1956.

Lenin on Trade Unions and Revolution, 1893–1917 by Thomas Taylor Hammond, Columbia University Press, 1956.

The Last Years of the Georgian Monarchy, 1658–1832 by David Marshall Lang, Columbia University Press, 1957.

The Japanese Thrust into Siberia, 1918 by James William Morley, Columbia University Press, 1957.

Bolshevism in Turkestan, 1917–1927 by Alexander G. Park, Columbia University Press, 1957.

Soviet Marxism: A Critical Analysis by Herbert Marcuse, Columbia University Press, 1958; paperback, Columbia University Press, 1985.

Soviet Policy and the Chinese Communists, 1931–1946 by Charles B. McLane, Columbia University Press, 1958.

The Agrarian Foes of Bolshevism: Promise and Defeat of the Russian Socialist Revolutionaries, February to October, 1917 by Oliver H. Radkey, Columbia University Press, 1958.

Pattern for Soviet Youth: A Study of the Congresses of the Komsomol, 1918–1954 by Ralph Talcott Fisher, Jr., Columbia University Press, 1959.

The Emergence of Modern Lithuania by Alfred Erich Senn, Columbia University Press, 1959.

The Soviet Design for a World State by Elliott R. Goodman, Columbia University Press, 1960.

Settling Disputes in Soviet Society: The Formative Years of Legal Institutions by John N. Hazard, Columbia University Press, 1960.

Soviet Marxism and Natural Science, 1917–1932 by David Joravsky, Columbia University Press, 1961.

Russian Classics in Soviet Jackets by Maurice Freidberg, Columbia University Press, 1962.

Stalin and the French Communist Party, 1941–1947 by Alfred J. Rieber, Columbia University Press, 1962.

Sergei Witte and the Industrialization of Russia by Theodore K. Von Laue, Columbia University Press, 1962.

Ukranian Nationalism by John H. Armstrong, Columbia University Press, 1963.

The Sickle under the Hammer: The Russian Socialist Revolutionaries in the Early Months of Soviet Rule by Oliver H. Radkey, Columbia University Press, 1963.

Comintern and World Revolution, 1928–1943: The Shaping of Doctrine by Kermit E. McKenzie, Columbia University Press, 1964.

Weimer Germany and Soviet Russia, 1926–1933: A Study in Diplomatic Instability by Harvey L. Dyck, Columbia University Press, 1966.

Financing Soviet Schools by Harold J. Noah, Teachers College Press, 1966.

Russia, Bolshevism, and the Versailles Peace by John M. Thompson, Princeton University Press, 1966.

The Russian Anarchists by Paul Avrich, Princeton University Press, 1967.

The Soviet Academy of Sciences and the Communist Party, 1927–1932 by Loren R. Graham, Princeton University Press, 1967.

Red Virgin Soil: Soviet Literature in the 1920's by Robert A. Maguire, Princeton University Press, 1968; paperback, Cornell University Press, 1987.

Communist Party Membership in the U.S.S.R., 1917–1967 by T. H. Rigby, Princeton University Press, 1968.

Soviet Ethics and Morality by Richard T. De George, University of Michigan Press, 1969; paperback, Ann Arbor Paperbacks, 1969.

Vladimir Akimov on the Dilemmas of Russian Marxism, 1895–1903 by Jonathan Frankel, Cambridge University Press, 1969.

Soviet Perspectives on International Relations, 1956–1967 by William Zimmerman, Princeton University Press, 1969.

Krondstadt, 1921 by Paul Avrich, Princeton University Press, 1970.

Class Struggle in the Pale: The Formative Years of the Jewish Workers' Movement in Tsarist Russia by Ezra Mendelsohn, Cambridge University Press, 1970.

The Proletarian Episode in Russian Literature by Edward J. Brown, Columbia University Press, 1971.

Labor and Society in Tsarist Russia: The Factory Workers of St. Petersburg, 1855–1870 by Reginald E. Zelnik, Stanford University Press, 1971.

Archives and Manuscript Repositories in the U.S.S.R.: Moscow and Leningrad by Patricia K. Grimsted, Princeton University Press, 1972.

The Baku Commune, 1917–1918 by Ronald G. Suny, Princeton University Press, 1972.

Mayakovsky: A Poet in the Revolution by Edward J. Brown, Princeton University Press, 1973.

Oblomov and his Creator: The Life and Art of Ivan Goncharov by Milton Ehre, Princeton University Press, 1973.

German Politics Under Soviet Occupation by Henry Krisch, Columbia University Press, 1974.

Soviet Politics and Society in the 1970's, Henry W. Morton and Rudolph L. Tokes, eds., Free Press, 1974.

Liberals in the Russian Revolution by William G. Rosenberg, Princeton University Press, 1974.

Famine in Russia, 1891–1892 by Richard G. Robbins, Jr., Columbia University Press, 1975.

In Stalin's Time: Middleclass Values in Soviet Fiction by Vera Dunham, Cambridge University Press, 1976.

The Road to Bloody Sunday by Walter Sablinsky, Princeton University Press, 1976; paperback, Princeton University Press, 1986.

The Familiar Letter as a Literary Genre in the Age of Pushkin by William Mills Todd III, Princeton University Press, 1976.

Russian Realist Art. The State and Society: The Peredvizhniki and Their Tradition by Elizabeth Valkenier, Ardis Publishers, 1977; paperback, Columbia University Press, 1989.

The Soviet Agrarian Debate by Susan Solomon, Westview Press, 1978.

Cultural Revolution in Russia, 1928–1931, Sheila Fitzpatrick, ed., Indiana University Press, 1978; paperback, Midland Books, 1984.

Soviet Criminologists and Criminal Policy: Specialists in Policy-Making by Peter Solomon, Columbia University Press, 1978.

Technology and Society under Lenin and Stalin: Origins of the Soviet Technical Intelligentsia by Kendall E. Bailes, Princeton University Press, 1978.

The Politics of Rural Russia, 1905–1914, Leopold H. Haimson, ed., Indiana University Press, 1979.

Political Participation in the U.S.S.R. by Theodore H. Friedgut, Princeton University Press, 1979; paperback, Princeton University Press, 1982.

Education and Social Mobility in the Soviet Union, 1921–1934 by Sheila Fitzpatrick, Cambridge University Press, 1979.

The Soviet Marriage Market: Mate Selection in Russia and the USSR by Wesley Andrew Fisher, Praeger Publishers, 1980.

Prophecy and Politics: Socialism, Nationalism, and the Russian Jews, 1862–1917 by Jonathan Frankel, Cambridge University Press, 1981.

Dostoevsky and The Idiot: *Author, Narrator, and Reader* by Robin Feuer Miller, Harvard University Press, 1981.

Moscow Workers and the 1917 Revolution by Diane Koenker, Princeton University Press, 1981; paperback, Princeton University Press, 1986.

Archives and Manuscript Repositories in the USSR: Estonia, Latvia, Lithuania, and Belorussia by Patricia K. Grimsted, Princeton University Press, 1981.

Zionism in Poland: The Formative Years, 1915–1926 by Ezra Mendelsohn, Yale University Press, 1982.

Soviet Risk-Taking and Crisis Behavior by Hannes Adomeit, George Allen and Unwin Publishers, 1982.

Russia at the Crossroads: The 26th Congress of the CPSU, Seweryn Bialer and Thane Gustafson, eds., George Allen and Unwin Publishers, 1982.

The Crisis of the Old Order in Russia: Gentry and Government by Roberta Thompson Manning, Princeton University Press, 1983; paperback, Princeton University Press, 1986.

Sergei Aksakov and Russian Pastoral by Andrew A. Durkin, Rutgers University Press, 1983.

Politics and Technology in the Soviet Union by Bruce Parrott, MIT Press, 1983.

The Soviet Union and the Third World: An Economic Bind by Elizabeth Kridl Valkenier, Praeger Publishers, 1983.

Russian Metaphysical Romanticism: The Poetry of Tiutchev and Boratynskii by Sarah Pratt, Stanford University Press, 1984.

Ruling Russia: Politics and Administration in the Age of Absolutism, 1762–1796 by John LeDonne, Princeton University Press, 1984.

Insidious Intent: A Structural Analysis of Fedor Sologub's Petty Demon by Diana Greene, Slavica Publishers, 1986.

Leo Tolstoy: Resident and Stranger by Richard Gustafson, Princeton University Press, 1986.

Workers, Society, and the State: Labor and Life in Moscow, 1918–1929 by William Chase, University of Illinois Press, 1987.

Andrey Bely: Spirit of Symbolism, John Malmstad, ed., Cornell University Press, 1987.

Government and Peasant in Russia, 1861–1906: The Prehistory of the Stolypin Reforms by David A. J. Macey, Northern Illinois University Press, 1987.

The Making of Three Russian Revolutionaries: Voices from the Menshevik Past, edited by Leopold H. Haimson in collaboration with Ziva Galili y Garcia and Richard Wortman, Cambridge University Press, 1988.

Revolution and Culture: The Bogdanov-Lenin Controversy by Zenovia A. Sochor, Cornell University Press, 1988.

A Handbook of Russian Verbs by Frank Miller, Ardis Publishers, 1989.

1905 in St. Petersburg: Labor, Society, and Revolution by Gerald D. Surh, Stanford University Press, 1989.

Alien Tongues: Bilingual Russian Writers of the "First" Emigration by Elizabeth Klosty Beaujour, Cornell University Press, 1989.

Iuzovka and Revolution, Volume I: Life and Work in Russia's Donbass, 1869–1924 by Theodore H. Friedgut, Princeton University Press, 1989.

The Menshevik Leaders in the Russian Revolution: Social Realities and Political Strategies by Ziva Galili, Princeton University Press, 1989.

Russian Literary Politics and the Pushkin Celebration of 1880 by Marcus C. Levitt, Cornell University Press, 1989.

Russianness: In Honor of Rufus Mathewson, edited by Robert L. Belknap, Ardis Publishers, 1990.

Soldiers in the Proletarian Dictatorship: The Red Army and the Soviet Socialist State, 1917–1930 by Mark von Hagen, Cornell University Press, 1990.

Ilya Repin and the World of Russian Art by Elizabeth Valkenier, Columbia University Press, 1990.

The Genesis of "The Brothers Karamazov" by Robert L. Belknap, Northwestern University Press, 1990.

Autobiographical Statements in Twentieth-Century Russian Literature, edited by Jane Gary Harris, Princeton University Press, 1990.

Folklore for Stalin by Frank Miller, M. E. Sharpe, 1990.

Vasilii Trediakovsky: The Fool of the "New" Russian Literature by Irina Reyfman, Stanford University Press, 1990.

Russia, Germany and the West from Khrushchev to Gorbachev by Michael Sodaro, Cornell University Press, 1990.

Reforming Rural Russia: State, Local Society, and National Politics, 1855–1914 by Francis William Wcislo, Princeton University Press, 1990.

Remizov's Fictions, 1900–1921 by Greta N. Slobin, Northern Illinois University Press, 1991.

The Corporation under Russian Law, 1800–1917: A Study in Tsarist Economic Policy by Thomas C. Owen, Cambridge University Press, 1991.

Physics and Politics in Revolutionary Russia by Paul R. Josephson, University of California Press, 1991.

The Paradise Myth in Eighteenth-Century Russia. Utopian Patterns in Early Secular Russian Literature and Culture by Stephen Lessing Baehr, Stanford University Press, 1991.

Thinking Theoretically about Soviet Nationalities: Concepts, History and Comparision in the Study of the USSR, edited by Alexander J. Motyl, Columbia University Press, 1992.

The Post-Soviet Nations: Perspectives on the Demise of the USSR, edited by Alexander J. Motyl, Columbia University Press, 1992.